The Complete
Leafy
Greens
Cookbook

The Complete
Leafy Greens
Cookbook

67 Leafy Greens & 250 Recipes

Susan Sampson

Robert
ROSE

For complete cataloguing information, see page 461.

Disclaimer
The recipes in this book have been carefully tested by our kitchen and our tasters. To the best of our knowledge, they are safe and nutritious for ordinary use and users. For those people with food or other allergies, or who have special food requirements or health issues, please read the suggested contents of each recipe carefully and determine whether or not they may create a problem for you. All recipes are used at the risk of the consumer.

We cannot be responsible for any hazards, loss or damage that may occur as a result of any recipe use.

For those with special needs, allergies, requirements or health problems, in the event of any doubt, please contact your medical adviser prior to the use of any recipe.

Design and Production: Kevin Cockburn/PageWave Graphics Inc.
Editor: Judith Finlayson
Recipe Editor: Tracy Bordian
Copyeditor: Gillian Watts
Recipe Tester: Diana Lim-Colman
Proofreaders: Gillian Watts/Tracy Bordian
Indexer: Gillian Watts

Cover image: © iStockphoto.com/GomezDavid
Interior photographs: Photos on pages 58, 59, 150, 252, 253, 279, 280, 385, 386, 395, 396 by John Pucic. *Other photographs:* page 1: © shutterstock.com/optimarc; page 2: © istockphoto.com/lightfast; page 5: © istockphoto.com/xactive; page 6: © istockphoto.com/mschowe; page 9: © istockphoto.com/alexpacha; page 10: © istockphoto.com/GomezDavid; page 26: © istockphoto.com/MmeEmil; page 28: © shutterstock.com/Eldred Lim; page 29: © shutterstock.com/poganyen; page 33: © istockphoto.com/kcline; page 34: © shutterstock.com/Elena Schweitzer; page 35: © istockphoto.com/YinYang; page 36: © istockphoto.com/robynmac; page 46: © shutterstock.com/Wolna; page 47: © istockphoto.com/lensblur; page 48: © shutterstock.com/maribee; page 54: © istockphoto.com/Floortje; page 55: © shutterstock.com/studiogi; page 62: © istockphoto.com/Orchidpoet; page 65: © istockphoto.com/tzara; page 66: © shutterstock.com/jreika; page 71: © istockphoto.com/Elenathewise; page 72: © istockphoto.com/PicturePartners; page 73: © istockphoto.com/AlasdairJames; page 82: © shutterstock.com/Zaneta Baranowska; page 83: © shutterstock.com/Tish1; page 88: © shutterstock.com/ Madlen; page 89: © shutterstock.com/Shebeko; page 92: © shutterstock.com/Eldred Lim; page 93: © shutterstock.com/mikeledray; page 95: © shutterstock.com/bonchan; page 96: © shutterstock.com/PicturePartners; page 97: © istockphoto.com/AndreaAstes; page 100: © istockphoto.com/omersukrugoksu; page 101: © istockphoto.com/elzeva; page 104: © shutterstock.com/picturepartners; page 105: © istockphoto.com/nojustice; page 106: © shutterstock.com/picturepartners; page 114: © shutterstock.com/Ingrid Maasik; page 116: © istockphoto.com/bedo; page 117: © shutterstock.com/TZIDO SUN; page 121: © shutterstock.com/Le Do; page 122: © shutterstock.com/sunsetman; page 127: © istockphoto.com/ADole08; page 130: © istockphoto.com/Suzifoo; page 138: © shutterstock.com/nito; page 139: © shutterstock.com/nito; page 140: © shutterstock.com/Lidante; page 143: © istockphoto.com/Chushkin; page 144: © istockphoto.com/UroshPetrovic; page 145: © shutterstock.com/Dionisvera; page 154: © shutterstock.com/Elena Elisseeva; page 157: © istockphoto.com/Elenathewise; page 159: © istockphoto.com/YinYang; page 161: © istockphoto.com/jcarillet; page 164: © shutterstock.com/LU HUANFENG; page 167: © istockphoto.com/vladrakola; page 176: © shutterstock.com/wasanajai; page 177: © shutterstock.com/Hong Vo; page 179: © istockphoto.com/spaxiax; page 180: © istockphoto.com/HAVET; page 185: © veer.com/nowshika; page 187: © shutterstock.com/Peter Zijlstra; page 188: © shutterstock.com/Lyudmila Suvorova; page 190: © istockphoto.com/PoppyB; page 205:© shutterstock.com/Hong Vo; page 206: © istockphoto.com/PicturePartners; page 209: © istockphoto.com/PicturePartners; page 210: © istockphoto.com/PicturePartners; page 212: © shutterstock.com/picturepartners; page 213: © shutterstock.com/picturepartners; page 216: © istockphoto.com/Suzifoo; page 217: © istockphoto.com/Snatalie-claude; page 223: © istockphoto.com/gaffera; page 224: © istockphoto.com/YinYang; page 228: f© shutterstock.com/JIANG HONGYAN; page 229: © shutterstock.com/szefei; page 234: © istockphoto.com/nito100; page 235: © istockphoto.com/cynoclub; page 238: © istockphoto.com/PicturePartners; page 239: © shutterstock.com/Mukesh Kumar; page 241: © shutterstock.com/TRL; page 242: © istockphoto.com/Creativestock; page 248: © istockphoto.com/creacart; page 257: © istockphoto.com/Suzifoo; page 258: © shutterstock.com/Hong Vo; page 262: © istockphoto.com/egal; page 263: © shutterstock.com/BruceBlock; page 270: © istockphoto.com/small_frog; page 272: © istockphoto.com/Viorika; page 276: © istockphoto.com/witoldkr1; page 277: © istockphoto.com/lepas2004; page 284: © shutterstock.com/Le Do; page 285: © istockphoto.com/luamduan; page 287: © istockphoto.com/digitalr; page 289: © istockphoto.com/myibean; page 291: © shutterstock.com/eye-blink; page 292: © istockphoto.com/dangdumrong; page 295: © istockphoto.com/dirkr; page 296: © istockphoto.com/tpzijl; page 298: © istockphoto.com/salsachica; page 303: © shutterstock.com/melhi; page 310: © istockphoto.com/Suzifoo; page 311: © istockphoto.com/THEPALMER; page 316: © shutterstock.com/blowbackphoto; page 322: © istockphoto.com/Suzifoo; page 323: © istockphoto.com/salsachica; page 332: © istockphoto.com/YinYang; page 336: © istockphoto.com/AlasdairJames; page 337: © istockphoto.com/stuartbur; page 344: © istockphoto.com/keithferrisphoto; page 345: © istockphoto.com/keithferrisphoto; page 352: © shutterstock.com/small_frog; page 353: © shutterstock.com/Valentyn Volkov; page 359: © istockphoto.com/DNY59; page 361: © shutterstock.com/Dionisvera; page 363: © istockphoto.com/Kativ; page 381: © istockphoto.com/cosmonaut; page 382: © shutterstock.com/Le Do; page 389: © istockphoto.com/iaod; page 390: © istockphoto.com/ellefox; page 399: © istockphoto.com/Suzifoo; page 401: © istockphoto.com/anipecosa; page 405: © istockphoto.com/Suzifoo; page 406: © istockphoto.com/AlasdairJames; page 419: © istockphoto.com/PicturePartners; page 421: © shutterstock.com/JIANG HONGYAN; page 423: © istockphoto.com/Creativeye99; page 424: © istockphoto.com/AWEvans; page 426: © shutterstock.com/Quang Ho; page 427: © shutterstock.com/AN NGUYEN; page 428: © shutterstock.com/ChristineGonsalves; page 432: © istockphoto.com/ShaoWeiwei; page 446: © istockphoto.com/SensorSpot; page 457: © istockphoto.com/ninette_luz

We acknowledge the financial support of the Government of Canada through the Book Publishing Industry Development Program (BPIDP) for our publishing activities.

Published by Robert Rose Inc.
120 Eglinton Avenue East, Suite 800, Toronto, Ontario, Canada M4P 1E2
Tel: (416) 322-6552 Fax: (416) 322-6936
www.robertrose.ca

Printed and bound in Canada

1 2 3 4 5 6 7 8 9 TCP 21 20 19 18 17 16 15 14 13

This book is dedicated to my lovely daughter Eva Sampson,
a fan of fine food in general and fresh greens in particular.
Her exuberant reaction to the idea of a leafy greens cookbook
has been inspirational and, as always,
she is an enthusiastic and discerning taste-tester.

Contents

Introduction

Your mother was right. You should eat your greens.

They are good for you, body and soul. Usually colorful, always nutritious and often inexpensive, leafy greens are superfoods without the price tag to match. I have paid 60 cents a pound (500 g) for water spinach, $2.29 a pound for Malabar spinach and $1.69 a pound for amaranth leaves — each enough for four side servings. In Chinatown I bought a two-pound (1 kg) bag of garlic scapes for a buck and left the store laughing.

Going green makes sense. Now, if you only knew what to do with all those leaves, vines, shoots and stalks beckoning to you at farmers' markets and sharing supermarket real estate with that old standby lettuce. That's where this book comes in. It's your guide to the wide world of wonderful greens, from spinach to edible weeds. It will help you to embrace the unfamiliar as well as offer a new outlook on old favorites. This book takes you to kale and beyond — to African bitter leaf, Japanese mustard greens and Maritime fiddleheads.

Enjoying more leafy greens is a delicious way to expand your culinary horizons. It certainly expanded mine. Researching this book turned me into a culinary botanist. As I investigated, browsed and shopped, I discovered more and more leafy greens, to the point where I sometimes felt lost in a forest of foliage. I am amazed by the diversity of leafy greens consumed around the world. The list seems endless. Some are common and cultivated, but many are wild or obscure regional specialties. Some are more widely available to gardeners than to mainstream shoppers, or perhaps familiar mainly to foragers, world travelers, farmers' market habitués or culinary historians. A few are primarily medicinal greens, used as folk remedies for various ailments. Some were popular once upon a time but became mere footnotes in culinary annals as cooks moved on to more accessible modern cultivated greens. All are fascinating.

In this book I have limited my in-depth explorations to 67 leafy greens. To help you make the most of your greens, I offer instructions on purchasing, cleaning, storing and preparing them. Included are 250 food and fresh green drink recipes for vegetarians, flexitarians and anyone who wants to fill his or her body with leafy green nourishment.

Happy cooking!

— *Susan Sampson*

Acknowledgments

I owe many thanks to the industrious Robert Rose family, especially enterprising publisher Bob Dees and diligent editors Tracy Bordian, Judith Finlayson and Gillian Watts. Thanks also to Kevin Cockburn and the hard-working team at PageWave Graphics.

Home cooking is so vital that I also want to express my appreciation for all those food-lovers who keep the kitchen fires stoked. Chefs are dandy and cooking schools are handy, but over the years I have learned the most from fellow food writers and keen home cooks who kindly share their kitchen wisdom in person, via cookbooks and over the Internet. Thank you!

The Wide World of Greens

Humans have been consuming leafy greens since prehistoric times. If a plant was edible, our ancestors ate it. Creativity was an essential culinary ingredient. I wonder, for example, what brave soul first decided to toss stinging nettles into a soup pot? I am grateful, for today we can fearlessly indulge in delicious dishes such as Nettle Soup (page 274) and Pesto d'Urtica (page 275).

Leafy greens play important roles in cultures and cuisines across Europe, the Mediterranean, Africa, India and Asia. They have been a source of nutrition for locavores since the days when everyone was a locavore. Historically they played a particularly vital role in cuisines born of poverty or periods of famine. This is especially true in parts of Africa — the people of that continent are the world's largest consumers of leafy greens. In the American South, some leafy greens have been staples ever since slaves started gathering and cooking the discarded tops of turnips and beets. In developing countries it is still customary to forage for greens in forests and fields, while in prosperous regions it is becoming a trendy pastime.

In this new millennium, what's old is new again. We are undergoing a green revolution in more ways than one. Home cooks are rediscovering the world of leafy greens. They are good for the environment and for your health. They are the world's least expensive superfoods — low in calories and high in vitamins, minerals and antioxidants. And they are free of strange additives and (usually) excessive packaging. Leafy greens bring us a step closer to Mother Earth, especially when we "forage" for them at farmers' markets. Greens are honest, feel-good foods.

Frugal grandmas the world over didn't throw out perfectly good greens, foraged or cultivated. They used all the parts of a plant whenever possible: roots, stems, leaves, flowers and seeds. Consuming foliage that would normally feed only the compost bin is the vegetarian version of nose-to-tail cooking. It is still the practice in cultures where food is never taken for granted. Waste not, want not. If you are eating beets, use the greens. Don't throw out those radish tops. Pluck some pea vines or grape leaves. Even carrot tops are attracting attention nowadays — yes, they are edible. All are easily transformed into delicious dishes such as Dolmades (page 162), Thai-Style Pea Soup (page 282) or Carroty Couscous (page 91).

In North America, huge shifts in attitudes and demographics have combined to boost the popularity of leafy greens. One factor is the increasing number of shoppers with Hispanic, Asian, African and Indian backgrounds. These folks don't have a meat-and-potatoes mindset. They eat greens — and lots of

Frugal grandmas the world over didn't throw out perfectly good greens, foraged or cultivated. They used all parts of a plant whenever possible: roots, stems, leaves, flowers and seeds.

them — as part of their culinary heritage. Another factor is the growing number of vegetarians, vegans and flexitarians. As well as being health-conscious, they turn to greens for ethical and environmental reasons.

In the first wave of this green revolution, during the 1960s and early 1970s, vegetables gained respect in the counterculture thanks to publications such as *Diet for a Small Planet.* Over the following decades, the consumption of mild leafy vegetables (such as specialty lettuces) exploded off the charts. The current kale craze ushered in the second wave. Once considered too tough and assertive for mainstream tastes, kale is now the go-to ingredient for powerhouse salads, and baby kale has joined the ranks of specialty "gourmet" greens. Kale Chips (page 191) are today's trendiest snack, and Caldo Verde, a Portuguese classic (page 198), is appreciated far beyond its traditional community.

Meanwhile, greens once deemed "exotic" or "foreign" are becoming available in mainstream stores. In the past year I have been pleasantly surprised to find oversized bags of pea vines at a big-box store and Asian yu choy sum in a suburban supermarket, not to mention the ever-expanding array of microgreens for sale.

The Green Marketplace

Hundreds of species of leaves, vines, tops and weeds are consumed as vegetables around the globe. I am never likely to set my eyes upon, let alone cook, with the majority of leafy greens in this world. I couldn't possibly buy and try them all. That being said, I've purchased and prepared as many leafy greens as I could reasonably get my hands on. It's surprising to find what's available to fill your shopping basket, especially in a big city. Still, ticking off the greens on one's shopping list can involve expeditions into what is for many the uncharted territories of Asian, Indian, Filipino, Hispanic or Afrocentric grocery stores, where shopping can be complicated by differences in language and nomenclature.

Each green discussed in this book is accompanied by both the species and common names, which should help you to sort through this maze. Botany, however, is not a simple science. Botanists are still arguing about the scientific names of some species, and the common names can vary wildly. One green may have numerous names, or several different greens may share a name. *Callaloo*, for instance, refers to taro leaves or to braised amaranth greens, depending on where you are in the Caribbean, and both callaloo and amaranth have many alternative names. Also, it is not that unusual to see uncommon leafy greens mislabeled in stores. I've seen mibuna labeled "sour leaf," pennywort mixed up with laksa leaves, and catalogna tagged as "dandelion."

Don't worry — with the help of this book, you will be well on your way to solving the mysteries of shopping for greens.

Getting to Know Greens

What are leafy greens? That simple question did pose something of a challenge when I set out to write this book. I wanted to be comprehensive, to shed light on a subject that still puzzles many home cooks. However, greens don't fall into neat categories, and boundaries are hazy. Where do *vegetables* and *leafy greens* begin and end? Take these three close relatives, for example: a head of cabbage is more green than leafy, while savoy cabbage is looser and kale is mostly foliage. And what about the difference between *leafy greens* and *herbs*? Some herbs straddle the fence, doubling as salad or cooking greens (technically, basil could be a salad green). In this book I included only those herblike greens that commonly play a starring role as an ingredient. Sorrel, for instance, can command the culinary stage on its own, and methi leaves may be added in quantity to curries.

In the main section of the book, the greens are listed alphabetically. Here I've also categorized greens into four loose thematic groups: salad greens, cabbage relatives, leaves and vines, and wild greens and weeds. These are not scientific groups but rather culinary families that would make sense to a home cook.

The Salad Bowl and Beyond

North America's greatest love affair with vegetables takes place in the salad bowl.

Gone are the days when salad consisted of a few leaves of pale iceberg lettuce and a gloppy dressing, or even further back, when adding a few bits of chopped greenery to tuna or Jell-O made it a salad. Today's salads are more complex. When someone says "salad," the words *lettuce* and *raw* immediately come to mind. However, tender-crisp lettuce, the mildest of leafy greens, is just a start. Mesclun and baby greens are forging ahead in popularity. For more adventurous palates, there are the bitter endives and chicories, assertive leaves such as arugula, and cultivated "wild" greens such as mâche. You can garnish the lot with a mound of airy microgreens. In fact, you needn't stick to any traditional salad greens to make a salad. If nutrition is your main concern, the darker and bitterer the leaf, the better (see "The Bitter Truth," page 19). These days, raw kale is the star of trendsetting healthy salads.

There's no need to relegate so-called salad greens to the salad bowl. Stuffing burgers and sandwiches with lettuce is a familiar way to add crunch and substance. Interestingly, ages ago, lettuce was always cooked. However, most North Americans are still not comfortable with the idea of cooking lettuce or other traditional salad greens. Asian salads, however, are rarely eaten raw — the greens are blanched and dressed or they are brined or pickled. Taiwan lettuce, meanwhile, is treated like a vegetable and stir-fried. If you want to experiment, don't forget that you can braise endive, grill romaine lettuce, add escarole to soup and scatter radicchio on pizza, to give just a few examples.

Salad Greens

- Arugula (page 34)
- Belgian Endive (page 54)
- Butter Lettuce (page 82)
- Curly Endive and Frisée (page 138)
- Escarole (page 149)
- Iceberg Lettuce (page 179)
- Leaf Lettuce (page 216)
- Mâche (page 223)
- Mesclun (page 234)
- Microgreens (page 241)
- Mizuna and Mibuna (page 248)
- Radicchio (page 303)
- Romaine (page 332)
- Taiwan Lettuce (page 385)

Lettuce Count the Types

Lettuce is undoubtedly our most crowd-pleasing salad green. Native to the Mediterranean and eastern Asia, it has come a long way since it was first cultivated from a weed, probably by the ancient Egyptians. They depicted lettuce in tomb paintings, believed it boosted sexual prowess and considered it sacred to their reproduction god Min. Later the ancient Romans cooked and served their lettuce with oil and vinegar. They also started the tradition of eating dressed salad before the main course.

The first lettuces were likely stem lettuces. It wasn't until 50 CE that multiple varieties, ancestors of our modern lettuces, appeared in historic documents. According to culinary historians, our modern cultivars were bred between the 16th and 18th centuries. They were introduced to England in the 17th century and eventually grown in the gardens of colonial America. Although Columbus brought lettuce to the New World, it was not popular here until the 1900s.

The species name, *Lactuca sativa*, is derived from the Latin *lactus*, meaning "milk." Lettuce stems contain a bitter milky sap, also known as latex or lettuce opium, that is a soporific, particularly once the plant has matured and flowered. The ancient Greeks consumed lettuce as a sleep aid, and the Anglo-Saxons knew it as sleepwort.

Today there are hundreds of varieties of lettuce (*L. sativa*). They fall into the following groups:

- **butterhead lettuce** has a small, round, loosely formed head with buttery soft leaves that range from pale yellow to creamy green. It is also called butter lettuce or buttercrunch lettuce or is referred to by the names of its most famous varieties, Bibb and Boston lettuces. Historically, butterhead lettuces have been predominant in England and northern Europe.
- **crisphead lettuce** has a large, round, tightly packed head with crisp leaves. It is delightfully crunchy and wilt-resistant, but detractors dismiss it as the blandest of greens. It is commonly known as iceberg lettuce, but iceberg is just one variety of crisphead. Historically, crispheads, which are usually grown on corporate farms, have been predominant in North America.
- **loose-leaf lettuce** grows as a bouquet of delicate leaves that range from medium to dark green, sometimes tipped in red. It is best known simply as leaf lettuce but may also be called cutting or bunching lettuce.
- **romaine** has an elongated, tapered head of sturdy dark green to pastel leaves with frilly edges and firm ribs. It is also called cos lettuce. Historically, it has been predominant in Mediterranean countries.

Lettuces aren't allowed to mature before harvest because they turn bitter after flowering. However, they are available year-round. Cultivars are mainly green but may also be red, yellow, teal or variegated.

Hybrids include 'Sucrine' (also called 'Little Gem', sweet gem or sugar lettuce), a miniature cross between butterhead and romaine, and 'Batavia' (also called 'Summer Crisp'), a cross between crisphead and leaf lettuces.

Asian lettuces (*Lactuca sativa angustana*) are divided into stalk and leaf types, as follows:

- **celtuce** has a long, thick stem crowned by tapered leaves that resemble a duster. It is grown specifically for the stalk, which is peeled, cut and used in stir-fries and soups. The leaves can be cooked, but celtuce is often sold without foliage. It is also called stalk, stem, asparagus or celery lettuce, *laitue asperge, kakichisha, sutemuretasu* or *wosun*.
- **Taiwan lettuce** has a tall, slender, romaine-shaped head with spear-shaped leaves. Taiwan lettuce is not eaten raw but rather is stir-fried. It is also called Chinese lettuce or sword lettuce.

Wild about Lettuce

Modern lettuce's closest wild relative is thought to be prickly lettuce (*Lactuca serriola*), also called compass plant. A common edible weed in fields and along roadsides in Europe and North America, this lettuce can grow to five feet (1.5 meters), but it should be plucked when only a few inches tall. Other wild lettuces include Canadian lettuce (*L. canadensis*), wall lettuce (*L. muralis*), Indian lettuce (*L. indica*) and wild oak-leaved lettuce (*L. quercina*). Opium lettuce (*L. virosa*) was used by 19th-century doctors as an opiate; it was also called hemlock lettuce, poison lettuce, bitter lettuce or great lettuce.

The Cabbage Clan

East meets West in the cabbage patch, where choices range from trendy kale to traditional Brussels sprouts to the fusion favorite bok choy.

Botanically speaking, cabbages are members of the *Brassica* clan, a group so big and diverse it is hard to believe they are all relatives. *Brassica*s are known as cruciferous vegetables or cole crops. Cabbages (*B. oleracea*) are the most familiar, but the culinary category of inexpensive bittersweet winter vegetables also includes mustard plants (*B. juncea*) and turnips (*B. rapa*) bred for their stems and leaves. Western cabbages (traditionally eaten in North America and Europe) differ from the cabbages predominantly used in Asia. But members of the cabbage clan do have one thing in common: they offer plenty of low-calorie nutritional bang for your buck.

Western Cabbages

The word *cabbage* is derived from *caboche*, which is French slang for "head." However, cabbages come in hundreds of shapes, varieties and sizes.

Cabbages

Spindly wild cole (*B. oleracea*) is considered the mother of all *Brassica*s. Also known as field cabbage or colewort, it is native to the Atlantic and Mediterranean coasts of Europe.

Cabbage's history is murky. Leaf cabbages were probably cultivated at least 2,500 years ago, while head cabbages appeared in the Middle Ages. Cabbages spread from Europe to the Middle East, Asia and the Americas. The explorer Jacques Cartier is credited with bringing cabbage to North America, in 1541. By the 1600s cabbages were a welcome source of winter nutrition in both the Old and New Worlds. Modern varieties continue to evolve in response to consumer demand for milder, smaller, tenderer specimens.

Western-style cabbages fall into the following groups:

- **head cabbages** (*B. oleracea capitata*) have succulent leaves that may be smooth or crinkled and folded either tightly or loosely into heads. White cabbage (pastel green), red cabbage (bluish purple) and savoy cabbage belong to this group. Round cabbages are most familiar to shoppers, but head cabbages may also be conical, cylindrical, barrel-shaped or disc-shaped. Sizes range from one-pound (500 g) minis to hundred-pound (45 kg) Alaska kraut cabbages.
- **leaf cabbages** (*B. oleracea acephala*) are characterized by loose leaves in colors ranging from dark bluish green to purple, lavender or cream. Kale and collards are probably the most familiar examples. This group also includes ornamental cabbages.
- **bud cabbages** (*B. oleracea gemmifera*) are characterized by little heads (buds) that grow along a thick main stem. Bud cabbages are most familiar as Brussels sprouts.
- **stem cabbages** (*B. oleracea gongylodes*) grow as a rounded bulb, with foliage atop a long stem. The bulb is not a root but actually a swollen stem. The most familiar is kohlrabi, also called cabbage turnip. Although the bulb is the main attraction, the leaves are also edible.

Asian Cabbages

Like Western cabbages, Asian cabbages are slightly bitter and slightly sweet, but crisper, juicier, less fibrous, faster-cooking and not as odorous. They are more closely related to turnips. Although they have been cultivated in China since the fifth century, they were introduced to Europe only in the 18th century.

Asian cabbages are divided into two groups:

- **pe-tsai cabbages** (*B. rapa pekinensis*) are barrel- or romaine-shaped head cabbages with fleshy but delicate leaves. Napa is the best-known type. This variety is favored in northern China and Korea because it keeps well over the winter.
- **pak choi cabbages** (*B. rapa chinensis*) present as clusters of packed leaves on fleshy stems. The best known is bok choy. This type is favored in southern China.

Leaves and Vines

Although Asian cabbages are occupying more real estate on supermarket shelves than they did in the past, consumers still find the category confusing. "Chinese cabbage" and "Chinese leaves" are catchall terms for dozens of varieties of Asian cabbages that look totally different from each other. At the other extreme, a specific Chinese cabbage may have dozens of names, often reflecting differences between the Mandarin and Cantonese spellings and cultures. Napa may be called "napa bok choy" or "mock pak choi" while bok choy might be identified as "Chinese white cabbage" or even "white mustard cabbage." (Check the individual listings in this book to sort them out.)

Fresh Foliage

Around the world, people consume a lush cornucopia of foliage, from garden greens to supermarket staples to wild, weird plants eaten only in remote locations. Some are bitter, some mild. Some are tender enough to enjoy raw, while others require long cooking. They are all a welcome source of vitamins, minerals, fiber and sometimes protein. And they are the stuff of folk medicine too.

"Leaves and vines" is a catchall culinary category that reflects the wonderful diversity of greens. Vegetable tops, trees and shrubs, herbs, grasses, shoots, pseudo-spinaches, water plants, garden ornamentals — if it's leafy and green, people have tried eating and cultivating it.

Two for One

I like twofers — two vegetables for the price of one. That's what I call the greens tossed in free with your vegetables. While the beets, turnips, radishes and daikons, carrots, celeriac, parsley roots and the like may be the main attraction, it's a shame to let their lush foliage wither away and go to waste. Buying parsley root, for example, nets you a huge bunch of coarse but edible parsley (page 276).

I always try to buy vegetables with the greens attached. Some twofers, however, rarely appear in supermarkets, but you may find them at a farmers' market. Twofers are the freshest of vegetables. Because the greens wilt and discolor as the vegetables sit around, stores simply lop them off. Thus, leafy tops are evidence of freshness. Another reason the greens are cut off is that they leach moisture from the roots or bulbs. Thus twofers should be separated once you get them home. Leave the root or bulb with about $1/2$ inch (1 cm) of stem attached, to prevent dehydration and loss of nutrients.

Here's a tip: at farmers' markets or greengrocers, some savvy frugal shoppers ask for discarded foliage such as beet greens, and even get them for free.

Twofer greens may be enjoyed separately. I do, however, like the harmonious pairing of a vegetable with its greens. For instance, consider Roasted Beet Salad with Candied Walnuts (page 50), Carrot Parsnip Soup (page 90) or Roasted Radishes and Sesame Greens (page 314).

More Leafy Extras

Many kinds of produce have edible leaves. Here are a few examples of greens unfamiliar to most North Americans:

- **rutabaga leaves** (*Brassica napus napobrassica*) are said to taste like a cross between cabbage and turnip and are used in India and Nepal. They are usually ignored in North America, where supermarkets sell the root on its own.
- **asparagus leaves** (*Asparagus racemosus*), also known as *satavari, shatamull, vrishya* or *kurilo,* are plucked from a species common in India, Sri Lanka and the Himalayas. The small, spear-like leaves are used in Ayurvedic medicine.
- **katuk** (*Sauropus androgynous*), also known as sweet leaf, sweet bush, star gooseberry or *rau ngot,* is a tropical shrub grown as a leafy vegetable. It is a staple in Asia that grows from India to Vietnam. The leaves, shoots and flowers are eaten, raw or cooked; the leaves are said to taste like peanuts and snow peas. The shoots may be marketed as "tropical asparagus."
- **caper leaves** (*Capparis spinosa*) are used in Greece, in salads and fish dishes; in cheese production as a coagulant; or pickled or brined, like capers.

The Wild Ones

Foraging for edibles is as old as humanity. In far-flung locales around the globe, from ancient times to modern days, people have been heeding the call of the wild. At its most basic, they have succumbed to the thrill of finding free food.

In the contemporary Western world, gathering wild green edibles is a fringe pastime dominated by hard-core foodies, hippie types, survivalists and even professional foragers who supply restaurants with rare local plants. Like most urbanites, I do my foraging at grocery stores and farmers' markets. Foraging is dandy, but it requires knowledge. There are thousands of edible wild greens — and many are poisonous. Even botanists can get confused. If you think all plants look alike, purchase your wild greens from experts and save yourself a potentially toxic mistake.

Some "wild" greens are so popular they are cultivated — dandelion, watercress and chicory being prime examples. Actual wild greens — most notably fiddleheads and ramps — are highly seasonal. These popular greens appear in stores for a few short weeks, offering shoppers the gain without the pain. Some wild greens are better known as weeds — and the bias that goes along with that. In a conversation at a major food wholesale terminal, a farmer told me she had plenty of nettles and purslane in her fields. "I usually pull it all out," she said, laughing.

Weed is not a scientific term. It just refers to a plant that's growing where it's not wanted. Governments classify some weeds as noxious or invasive. However, weeds are in the eye of the beholder. If you are hungry to expand your repertoire of leafy greens, take note of this Ralph Waldo Emerson quote: "What is a weed? A plant whose virtues have not yet been discovered."

Wild Greens

- Catalogna (page 95)
- Chickweed (page 113)
- Dandelion Greens (page 143)
- Fiddleheads (page 154)
- Nettles (page 270)
- Purslane (page 295)
- Ramps (page 315)
- Sorrel (page 352)
- Watercress (page 405)
- Water Spinach (page 419)

The Bitter Truth

You may be slow to warm up to leafy greens. Some consumers avoid putting the bite on any greens more exotic than spinach because they can bite back. I could avoid the B-word and tactfully say that some greens are pungent or assertive. Or I could say straight out that they are bitter.

Admittedly, bitter greens are an acquired taste. However, with varying degrees of TLC, most can become deliciously palatable. And there are many good reasons to learn to love them. These dark greens are concentrated sources of nutrients yet low in calories. One reason they are packed so full of goodness is that they tend to cook down. Spinach is a classic example: that lush bunch of spinach you picked up at the supermarket will wilt down from 16 cups (3 L) of leaves to 2 cups (500 mL) or less.

Scientists are busy investigating various leafy greens because they are so-called functional foods. That means they provide benefits that extend beyond mere nutrition. In addition to vitamins and minerals, leafy greens provide antioxidants, fiber, chlorophyll and other phytonutrients (beneficial chemicals and enzymes). These compounds are being studied for their ability to reduce the risk of heart disease, cancer and chronic diseases such as diabetes. Ironically, some of the compounds that make greens such nutritional powerhouses also affect their flavor. The most potent plants seem to be the bitterest, the most peppery, astringent or aggressive — a catch-22 for consumers.

Bitterness is the major reason why consumers avoid vegetables in general. The tongue detects five basic tastes: sweet, sour, salty, bitter and umami (savory or aged). Because of genetic variations, some people, such as the finicky so-called supertasters, are more sensitive to bitterness. Humans evolved to instinctively reject bitter foods, it is theorized, because bitterness is a warning sign of poison or spoilage. (Interestingly, some bitterness in leafy greens is caused by common plant toxins. But despite the alarming term *toxin*, they are hazardous only in huge quantities or can be neutralized by cooking.)

Familiarity and proper preparation methods can mitigate the impact of bitterness in leafy greens. So don't be afraid. I recommend starting with a cup of leafy greens a day. You'll get used to it. The bottom line is that adding plenty of leafy greens to your diet is bound to make you look and feel better. There's a reason why Popeye is wiry but strong: he eats his greens.

Battling Bitterness

The fact that I enjoy bitter greens has been both a benefit and a handicap in writing this book because people's tastes are so different. Mitigating bitterness is a balancing act: Generally speaking, the longer leafy greens cook, the milder they become, but they can end up soggy or limp. On the other hand, shorter cooking times tend to result in greens that retain more bitterness but are pleasingly tender-crisp. You should cook leafy greens to

"What is a weed? A plant whose virtues have not yet been discovered."
— Ralph Waldo Emerson

suit your taste. Over time your preferences may change as you familiarize yourself with these delicious and diverse greens.

Here are some optional strategies to mask or mellow the bitter edge or peppery bite of leafy greens.

When shopping,

Admittedly, bitter greens are an acquired taste. However, with varying degrees of TLC, most can become palatable.

- Choose so-called spring greens over winter greens. Greens that are picked in the spring and summer (such as chickweed) tend to be milder and more delicate than greens harvested in the fall and winter (such as rapini).
- Choose young leaves rather than mature ones. For example, baby greens (such as baby kale) are milder than their full-grown counterparts (such as curly kale).
- Choose light over dark. The lighter green the leaf or stem, the less bitter. The cream and pastel green leaves found at the heart of some greens are less bitter than the darker exterior leaves.

When preparing,

- Add an acid, such as vinegar or lemon juice, during cooking.
- Sauté the greens in oil or butter, or add salad dressing to raw bitter greens. Coating greens with fat disguises bitterness.
- Add a small spoonful of sugar to your dish or cook the greens with sweet vegetables such as carrots, beets or peas.
- Add soy sauce to your dish or salt to the cooking water. Salt not only masks bitterness but helps greens stay tender-crisp.
- Blanch greens for a minute or two (or longer, to taste), rinse with cold water, chop, then carry on with your recipe. You can continue to cook them in a soup, stew or stir-fry.
- Use an abundance of water when cooking. The more water you use to blanch or simmer greens, they less bitter they will be.
- Discard the cooking water. Do not add any of it along with the greens when preparing soups or stews.
- Cook the greens longer. Sauté them slowly in oil for at least 10 minutes, or simmer or braise them for at least 30 minutes. The bitter compounds will disperse into the fat or water.
- Ferment or pickle greens.

Manhandling Greens

The "massage" method specifically applies to preparing raw kale for salads, but it can be used on other sturdy raw leaves. Massage mellows raw greens by breaking down cell walls and releasing enzymes that help disperse bitter-tasting compounds. Here's how: Trim tough stems and wash and dry the leaves, then massage them firmly with salad dressing or with lemon juice (or vinegar) and salt for two minutes, until the leaves darken, look shiny, feel softer and reduce in volume. A simpler but less effective method is to massage or toss the leaves with salt and let them sit in a colander to drain for a few minutes.

The Green Kitchen

Here are some general tips and tricks for handling and preparing leafy greens, including storing, cleaning and cooking them. For specifics, check the individual listings in the following section of this book.

Storing Greens

It is a challenge to keep leafy greens perky. They always need to be refrigerated. Most will start to wilt, turn brown or, worse still, rot within five days. Here are some tips to improve the longevity of your greens:

- Many greens are sold in bunches, tightly clustered with elastic bands or oversized twist ties. Rot starts in the center, where moisture accumulates. So, first things first: undo the bunch when you get it home and store the greens more loosely.
- Generally speaking, greens are usually stored unwashed, but some may be washed beforehand (check the individual listings for recommendations). Washing greens before storing them is a particularly good strategy for those that are difficult to wrap or are very dirty. Soil and grit are hard on foliage. Stem the greens, wash and dry them, then roll the leaves in paper towels and store in a plastic bag. If you are keeping the stems, store them in a separate bag. However, do not chop the leaves or stems before storing them.
- Paper towels are helpful for storing greens. Add a folded paper towel to a resealable bag to soak up the excess moisture that causes rot. Alternatively, to stave off wilting, lightly dampen a paper towel and wrap it around the bottoms of thin stems, or add it to a plastic bag with greens that tend to dry out quickly. Greens that are tightly packed or have a high moisture content are more likely to rot than to go limp.
- Some greens may be turned into a bouquet. Put the greens in a vase or glass filled with about an inch (2.5 cm) of water. Drape a plastic bag over the bunch and tie it loosely to secure. Refrigerate the vase, preferably out of the way, such as on a shelf in the door.
- A common way to store greens is to wrap them in plastic. Make sure the greens are dry. Depending on their shape, swathe them tightly in plastic wrap (cabbage and head lettuce are candidates for this) or store them in a resealable bag. If the greens are delicate (like watercress), leave air in the sealed bag to act as a cushion.
- Many greens can be blanched and frozen. This is particularly handy for greens that have a short season, such as fiddleheads. Trim and wash the greens, then blanch for one to two minutes in boiling salted water. Drain and rinse under cold running water to stop the cooking. Drain well and chop, if desired. Pack tightly in resealable bags with the air squeezed out and freeze. Use them thawed or frozen, but in cooked foods only — they will be soft.

It is a challenge to keep leafy greens perky. They always need to be refrigerated.

Preparing Greens

Preparing leafy greens needn't be onerous or time-consuming. Here are some preparation tips:

- A trip home in a hot car, neglect at room temperature or an unprotected sojourn in a cold, dry fridge can cause your greens to wilt. To revive and crisp greens, soak them in ice-cold water for 15 to 30 minutes before preparing them.
- Before using greens, peel off any outer leaves that are yellowed, browned or blackened. Tear off parts of leaves that are damaged. Beware of holes and insect eggs, which look like tiny lumps or bumps. If in doubt, throw out the leaf.
- Judging what part of a stem to keep and cook is tricky. With experience, you'll get the knack. Using the sharp edge of a chef's knife, I tap along the stem until I encounter a hint of resistance. (I picture a video clip of chef Gordon Ramsay working his knife along an asparagus spear, saying, "Good ... good ... good ... wood.") You can also use the thickness of the stem to help you assess what portion to discard (which I note in individual listings, where relevant).
- For even cooking, it's optimal to separate leaves from stems, then chop them separately. Stems take longer to cook, so they can go into the pan first. Alternatively, stems and leaves may be cooked as separate dishes.
- If you are trimming both stems and tough center ribs, fold the leaf in half and slice them out at an angle. Alternatively, use the slashing technique. This is the best way to trim large frilled leaves that feather along stems almost to the bottom, such as turnip or mustard greens. Holding the stalk at the bottom, slash upwards at the leaves with a sharp knife, scraping them off where they join the stem.
- Plucking wee leaves from watercress and the like is one kitchen task I dread: it's so fiddly. Don't be an overachiever and drive yourself crazy — it's usually okay to keep thin stemlets.
- To sliver or shred leaves, lay them in a stack, roll them up like a cigar and slice the roll crosswise. To chop them finely, slice lengthwise and carry on.
- To coarsely chop hardy greens such as stemmed kale, crumple a handful of leaves on the cutting board, cut the pile crosswise, and then chop lengthwise.
- If you are eating raw greens, note that tearing (rather than cutting) minimizes bruising and discolored edges.

Stems versus Stalks

In dictionaries, *stem* and *stalk* are basically the same. In this book, for more clarity, I refer to stalks when I mean full stems with leaves and other foliage attached. If the leaves are removed, I call them stems. As for stemlets, they are the tiny short stems that attach leaves to the main stem.

Leaves Only?

Should you use only the leaves, or the stems as well? Some cooks habitually toss out the stems of leafy greens, dismissing them as tough or stringy. Others bristle at the idea of feeding the compost bin with edible greens. I find that stems always have to be trimmed at least a little, but the tender portions are edible once cooked. At the very least, the stemlets are usually edible. (Check the listings for what to do with the stems of specific greens.) As an homage to society's growing "waste not" sensibility, I have included recipes to please both camps. If you don't like the stems, simply omit them.

Leafy greens are dirty. So it's important to wash greens very well — once, twice or even three times.

Cleaning Greens

Leafy greens are dirty. Grit and clay cling to the foliage, and insects, dead or alive, hide among the foliage. Ladybugs and other beetles particularly like to burrow between the clustered leaves of lettuces and cabbages. So it's important to wash greens very well — once, twice or even three times, until the water no longer looks murky. I wash greens even if they are in a package that says they have been prewashed. Here are some methods you may employ to ensure that your greens are clean:

- Wash greens whole or after they have been cut, whichever is more convenient or logical. Many people do not wash greens that grow in tight heads, such as cabbage, possibly because it seems inconvenient or awkward. However, the heads can be cut in half and soaked, or rinsed after chopping.
- Soak greens in salted water for 15 to 30 minutes. This drives out any live insects or worms and helps get rid of stubborn dirt. Some people use up to 1 teaspoon (5 mL) of salt per cup (250 mL) of water.
- Swish greens in a large bowl of cold water, allowing the dirt to sink to the bottom. Scoop out the leaves — do not defeat your purpose by pouring them into a colander with their wash water. Alternatively, wash them in a pasta pot or salad spinner, then pull out the insert with the greens in it. For safety reasons, don't use the sink to wash greens unless it has been sanitized. Otherwise, harmful bacteria may be transferred to your food.
- Some greens are tender, some tough. For the latter, rough treatment pays off. Africans, for example, may wash and wring bitter greens as vigorously as hand laundry. Sometimes salt or baking soda is rubbed on leaves to break them down.
- Dry sturdy leaves in a salad spinner or roll them in a clean kitchen towel. As for leaves that bruise easily, such as Malabar spinach, spin-dry only in small batches, or air-dry on paper towels or a clean kitchen cloth, or roll loosely in paper towels.
- If the greens in your salad bowl are too moist, absorb the excess by holding a piece of paper towel in each hand as you toss them.

Crisper Greens

Here are two ways to make lettuce or other succulent greens ultra-crisp or to redeem those that have gone limp:

- Soak greens in ice water for 10 minutes, then drain, spin-dry and refrigerate until very cold.
- Place in a bowl of ice water with a spoonful of lemon juice. Refrigerate the soaking greens for 30 minutes, then drain and spin-dry.

Staying Safe

Food safety rules apply to greens too. Despite several food-poisoning outbreaks that have been linked to greens, many people don't realize that they can be contaminated by toxins such as E. coli.

Certified North American growers and producers of bagged greens such as mesclun follow a number of safety protocols. These include testing water wells; installing tall netting to keep out animals; inspecting fields before harvest (for dead animals or feces); requiring sorters and packers to wear hairnets and gloves; filtering the air in plants; and disinfecting knives after use. The greens are refrigerated immediately after harvest and double- or triple-washed (first in water spiked with chlorine). There are separate areas for raw and bagged greens to prevent cross-contamination, and traceability codes are added to labels.

Still, a study done in 2010 found that prewashed greens in plastic clamshells and bags contained higher levels of bacteria than fresh greens, particularly E. coli. It made no difference whether they were organic or not.

Cooking Greens

Many greens can be used interchangeably in recipes, although cooking times vary. Check individual listings for specific cooking instructions and suggested substitutions. The following are a few general tips on cooking leafy greens:

- For voluminous greens that wilt down to small amounts, such as spinach and pea shoots, use a big pot and stir in the greens in batches, if necessary.
- Avoid adding long shreds or big pieces of leafy greens to soups and stews. They are prone to clumping and your dish will seem swampy. Also, when mixing greens with beans or other legumes, chop the greens finely so they will blend properly.
- Overcooking lessens the healthy impact of chlorophyll. Unless you are working especially hard at reducing bitterness, it's better to cook leaves to a vibrant green color, not a dull khaki.
- If you boil greens such as collards or nettles, the nourishing cooking liquid may be kept as a soup base, sipped like tea or added to blender drinks.
- If leaves are rough, tough, astringent or mature, tame them by adding a small spoonful of baking soda to the cooking water.

- Greens float, so when you blanch or simmer them, partially or completely cover the pan. This holds in the steam and helps them cook faster and more evenly.
- Steaming greens is generally better than boiling them, because fewer nutrients are lost. However, this doesn't work for all greens. Some remain unpleasantly tough or become bitterer when steamed (check the individual listings). An alternative to steaming is blanching the greens in plenty of water, followed by sautéing.
- Greens end up tenderer when they are steam-fried rather than stir-fried. Here's the technique: Heat the oil in a skillet over medium heat, add the greens and stir-fry to coat and wilt them slightly. Then add a bit of water or stock to the pan, cover, reduce the heat and simmer until the greens are fully cooked (check the individual listings and recipes for amounts). If necessary, increase the heat to high, uncover and cook to evaporate any excess liquid.

Using the Recipes

Here is some general information to help you successfully prepare the recipes in this book:

- All produce is presumed to be washed. In some recipes, where I note this, water should still cling lightly to the leaves. However, for stir-fries or when using very juicy greens such as bok choy, they should be dried well.
- The recipes have been tested using imperial (US) measurements.
- Quantities are given in both weight and volume. Going by weight is the most effective way to measure greens, but because many people don't own kitchen scales, I have included volume measures. That being said, it's tricky to measure greens by volume. Amounts can vary wildly depending on the size of the measuring cup and how the greens are packed into it. Don't be taken aback by the large volumes in some of the ingredient lists: all the greens are measured loosely packed. To do so, simply toss the greens into your measuring cup; do not shake or rap the cup to settle the contents or push down on the greens.
- The beverage recipes are geared to the average kitchen — no juicer is required. I used a standard household blender, but if you have a high-powered blender, by all means use it.
- The heat levels of stove elements, ovens and barbecues vary. Types and sizes of pans also affect cooking times and the end result. So pay attention to cooking cues, as well as the times noted in the recipes.

Many greens can be used interchangeably in recipes, although cooking times vary.

Greens A to Y

Amaranth

Amaranthus

> *Other names:* **callaloo, careless weed, Chinese spinach, Indian kale, Jamaican callaloo, leafy/vegetable/wild amaranth, pigweed, red spinach, tumbleweed, wild blite.**
>
> **Depending on where you are shopping, you may find amaranth identified as** *arowo jeja, bayam, biteku, chaulai sag, een choy, efo tete, hin tsoi, kulitis, lenga lenga, phak khom, quintoniles, rau den, santousai, tampala, vlita* **or** *xian cai.*

Amaranth is believed to have originated in South America before spreading across North America and being introduced into Europe and Asia. The plant was cultivated in Mexico thousands of years ago for both its grain seeds and its greens. Mayans and Aztecs ate amaranth, and it figured prominently in Aztec religious rituals. It has been used by both Native Americans and Africans in folk medicines as well as for food.

One of the world's most popular leafy greens, amaranth is commonly eaten in Malaysia, Indonesia, Vietnam, China, Japan, India, Africa, the Caribbean, Central and South America and parts of Europe. In North America it was often dismissed as an invasive weed, but it is now being acknowledged as a nourishing food.

Varieties

Dozens of species of leaf vegetables, cereal plants, weeds and flowering ornamentals are classified as amaranths. They are wild, cultivated and natural hybrids of the same plants that yield amaranth grain. Some cultivars are grown specifically for their edible leaves.

Colors include green (sometimes called white), variegated (green and purple), red (actually purple) and tricolor (green, red and yellow).

Well-known *Amaranthus* species include:

- **red spinach** (*A. dubius*), also known as caterpillar callaloo or spleen amaranth. It is valued as a vegetable in the Caribbean and Africa and across Asia and India.
- **Chinese amaranth** (*A. tricolor*), also known as Joseph's coat. Cultivars named 'Elephant Head' and 'Mangostanus' are grown in parts of North America.
- **green amaranth** (*A. viridis*), also known as slender amaranth. It is eaten in Jamaica as callaloo and in India as *kuppacheera*.

Tasting Notes

Amaranth is reminiscent of spinach but tastes less astringent and more delicate. It is nutty, with artichoke accents. When cooked, it is mellow and soft.

Equivalents

1 large bunch =
2¼ lbs (1.125 kg),
including 1 lb (500 g)
leaves and 1 lb (500 g)
trimmed stems

•

2 oz (60 g) coarsely
chopped leaves =
7 cups (1.75 L),
loosely packed

•

2 oz (60 g) stems
cut into 1-inch
(2.5 cm) pieces =
⅔ cup (150 mL),
loosely packed

- **purple amaranth** (*A. blitum*), native to the Mediterranean and grown in eastern North America. Both *A. viridis* (previous) and *A. blitum* are called *vlitat* in Greece, where they are eaten as wild greens.

- **blood amaranth** (*A. cruentus*) and **prince's feather amaranth** (*A. hypochondriachus*), prevalent mainly as Mexican grain amaranths. The greens are also eaten.
- **Thunberg's amaranth** (*A. thunbergii*), used mainly in Africa as a leafy vegetable and herb.
- **common amaranth** (*A. retroflexus*), which is coarser than other species when wild. It is foraged in the tropical Americas and India.
- **white pigweed** (*A. albus*), also known as prostrate pigweed. This is an edible weed native to the tropical Americas but also cultivated in England.
- **love-lies-bleeding** (*A. caudatus*), prevalent as a grain and leafy green in the Andes, where it is called *kiwicha*.

Health Notes

Amaranth provides vitamins A, B_6 and C, calcium, copper, folate, iron, magnesium, manganese, niacin, phosphorus, potassium, riboflavin and zinc. However, amaranth is high in oxalates (see page 355).

Amaranth has been used as a folk remedy to treat anemia, constipation, diarrhea, worms, diabetes, epilepsy and poor eyesight

Buy It

Mainstream supermarkets rarely carry amaranth. Look for it in Asian and Caribbean grocery stores. Red amaranth is a popular microgreen (page 241).

Amaranth is attractive looking, particularly the variegated green and purple kind and the green amaranth with red stems and veins. Vibrant colors indicate freshness. Avoid bunches with budding flowers; this means the plants are too mature.

Store It

Place amaranth in a glass or vase of water like a bouquet, with a plastic bag draped over the foliage; then refrigerate it. Or wrap a damp paper towel around the stems and store in a resealable bag.

Amaranth will keep in the refrigerator for up to four days.

Prep It

Do not wash amaranth greens until you are ready to use them. Then rinse them in cold water and drain.

There seems to be plenty of fussing over how to prepare amaranth. Popular suggestions include peeling larger stems, soaking the greens in cold salted water before cooking, and blanching before cooking (to reduce the oxalic acid content). The truth is that amaranth is very simple to work with.

You may separate the leaves and stems to help them cook evenly, but this is not essential. The stems, even thicker ones (more than $^1/_4$ inch/0.5 cm wide), cook to tenderness without peeling, and they require no more than 1 minute of extra cooking time than the leaves. In fact the stems often end up tenderer than larger leaves.

Trim no more than 1 inch (2.5 cm) from each stem to remove dry, withered or tough ends. Cut stems $^1/_2$ to 1 inch (1 to 2.5 cm) long.

Tear or coarsely chop the leaves. If you feel like sorting them, small leaves can be left intact. If you're in a hurry, chop or slice the leaves and stems together and toss them in a pan all at once — the result will be fine.

Consume It

Amaranth is usually cooked, although tiny leaves can be eaten raw in salads and sandwiches. Depending on the method and heat level, amaranth cooks in 5 to 10 minutes. Longer cooking brings out a slight bitter flavor.

Amaranth may be steamed or boiled. However, for the best flavor, sauté it: first the cut stems, then adding the chopped leaves a minute later. (Note that red amaranth will stain the juices of a dish pink.)

If you are using the leaves only, save the stems and cook them separately in another dish, if desired. To wilt the leaves, heat them briefly with just the wash water clinging to them.

SUBSTITUTES

spinach, Malabar spinach, beet greens, chard, sweet potato leaves

Callaloo Confusion

In the Caribbean, callaloo is in the eye of the beholder. It refers to several dishes and several types of leaf vegetables. But which is which?

Depending on the locale, the cook may be waving around a handful of amaranth or taro leaves (see page 389) or sometimes even mustard greens (see page 257) or Malabar spinach (see page 228). Greens are traditional ingredients in hearty Sunday lunches, the biggest meal of the week in the Islands.

The word *callaloo* turns up in Jamaican records as early as 1696, according to culinary historians. When Jamaicans say *callaloo*, they are referring either to amaranth or their signature dish of spicy braised amaranth leaves. This dish may be served for breakfast, lunch or dinner with starchy vegetables (yam, taro or cassava), which are known as "ground provisions."

In Trinidad and Tobago, amaranth is known as *chorai bhaji* or spinach and is cooked in a similar fashion to the Jamaican dish. Trini callaloo, however, is a rich, spicy soup packed with young taro leaves (dasheen bush), coconut and an assortment of whatever the cook has on hand. Callalloo soup is a national dish of Trinidad.

Jamaican Callaloo

This riff on Jamaica's signature greens dish is humble but nutritionally powerful and tasty. Jamaicans refer to both this dish and leafy amaranth as **callaloo** *(see "Callaloo Confusion," page 30).*

(see "Callaloo Confusion," page 30).

Makes 2 to 4 servings

Vegan Friendly

Side dish

Tips

Scotch bonnet and habañero chile peppers are scorching hot. For a less spicy dish, devein the pepper or reduce the quantity.

I prefer kosher salt because it tastes better than iodized table salt and (ideally) contains no additives. Table salts and some sea salts contain additives such as iodine compounds (iodides), anti-clumping agents and even sugar (in the form of dextrose, which is used to stabilize iodine). Although the North American Salt Institute states that kosher salt "contains no additives," some kosher salt brands do contain additives such as anti-clumping agents. If you have concerns, check the label.

1 lb	amaranth, trimmed, leaves and stems separated	500 g
1 tbsp	extra virgin olive oil	15 mL
1	onion, diced	1
½	Scotch bonnet or habañero chile pepper, seeded and thinly sliced (see Tips, left)	½
1	clove garlic, chopped	1
1½ tsp	kosher or coarse sea salt (see Tips, left)	7 mL
1 tsp	fresh thyme leaves	5 mL
½ tsp	freshly ground black pepper	2 mL
4	green onions (white and light green parts), thinly sliced	4
1	tomato, diced	1
1 tbsp	butter or non-dairy alternative	15 mL

1. Using a sharp knife, cut amaranth stems into ½-inch (1 cm) pieces. Stack leaves on top of each other and slice into ½-inch (1 cm) strips. Set aside in separate piles.

2. In a large saucepan over medium heat, heat oil until shimmery. Add onion and chile pepper. Cook, stirring often, for about 3 minutes, until softened and starting to turn golden. Stir in garlic for 20 seconds. Add amaranth stems, salt, thyme and black pepper and cook, stirring, for about 1 minute, until tender-crisp. Stir in amaranth leaves. Reduce heat to medium-low, cover and cook, stirring once, for about 5 minutes, until leaves are wilted and stems are tender. Stir in green onions and tomato for 1 minute.

3. Remove from heat. Stir in butter and season with salt to taste. Serve immediately.

Amaranth with Pepper Vinegar

Piquant greens doused with sweet-and-sour vinegar are bound to wake up your taste buds. Serve this versatile dish warm or at room temperature, alongside creamy mashed potatoes or parsnips. You can also spoon it onto crostini or use it as a relish.

Makes 4 to 8 servings

Vegan Friendly

Side dish

Tips

Cane sugar is likely to be filtered through bone char, while beet sugar is not. Most labels don't indicate the source of the sugar. If you are following a vegan diet, use unbleached organic sugar that has not been filtered through bone char, or a sweetener such as agave syrup.

For the finest minced garlic, push it through a press.

I prefer kosher salt because it tastes better than iodized table salt and (ideally) contains no additives. Table salts and some sea salts contain additives such as iodine compounds (iodides), anti-clumping agents and even sugar (in the form of dextrose, which is used to stabilize iodine). Although the North American Salt Institute states that kosher salt "contains no additives," some kosher salt brands do contain additives such as anti-clumping agents. If you have concerns, check the label.

1 lb	amaranth, trimmed, leaves and stems separated	500 g
1/4 cup	cider vinegar	60 mL
2 tbsp	finely chopped red bell pepper	30 mL
2 tbsp	granulated sugar (see Tips, left)	30 mL
1 tsp	freshly ground black pepper	5 mL
3 tbsp	extra virgin olive oil, divided	45 mL
1	large onion, halved and thinly sliced	1
2	large cloves garlic, minced (see Tips, left)	2
2 tsp	kosher or coarse sea salt (see Tips, left)	10 mL

1. Using a sharp knife, cut amaranth stems into 1-inch (2.5 cm) pieces. Coarsely chop leaves. Set aside leaves and stems in separate piles.

2. In a small saucepan over medium heat, combine vinegar, bell pepper, sugar and black pepper and bring to a boil. Boil for 1 minute. Set aside.

3. In a large saucepan over medium heat, heat 2 tbsp (30 mL) oil until shimmery. Add onion and cook, stirring often, for about 5 minutes, until soft and golden. Stir in garlic for 20 seconds. Add amaranth stems and salt and cook, stirring often, for about 1 minute, until tender-crisp. Stir in amaranth leaves. Reduce heat to low, cover and cook, stirring once, for 6 to 8 minutes, until stems are tender and leaves are wilted.

4. Using a slotted spoon, transfer mixture to a shallow serving bowl. Drizzle with pepper vinegar and remaining oil. Serve warm or at room temperature.

Arugula

Eruca sativa

Other names: Italian cress, Mediterranean rocket, rocket, salad rocket.

Depending on where you are shopping, you may find arugula identified as *ghargir, roquette, rucola, rughetta* or *tira.*

Arugula is widely cultivated. It is native to the Mediterranean basin, where it has been harvested since Roman times. Prior to the 1980s, arugula was considered too bitter for North American tastes and thus was little known outside immigrant communities. Its complex flavor eventually won over consumers. Chic and trendy in the 1980s, arugula has now become a staple for lovers of salads, leafy greens and Italian cuisine.

Varieties

Garden rocket (*Eruca sativa*) and wild rocket (*Eruca vesicaria*) are true arugulas. Various common weeds and wild or cultivated plants are also called rocket. Arugula is just one, but its complex flavor puts it ahead of the pack.

Do not confuse wild rocket (*E. vesicaria)* with the wild arugula sold in many stores. **Wild arugula** (*Diplotaxis tenuifolia*) belongs to the plant family known as wall rockets. It is also called sylvetta, selvatica, rustic Italian arugula, sand rocket and Lincoln's weed. Small but mighty, wild arugula is zestier and more succulent than true arugula. Like many heirloom plants that once were foraged, although it is called "wild," it is now a garden species. Two of sylvetta's close relatives are sometimes also marketed as wild arugula: wall mustard (*D. muralis*) and white rocket (*D. erucoides*).

Other rockets include Turkish rocket (*Bunias orientalis*), also known as hill mustard, and corn rocket (*B. erucago*). Both have been given the unflattering moniker "warty cabbage," even though neither looks like a cabbage. Turkish rocket is native to Russia and imported to North America. A weed with edible leaves, it's described as hairy, with a cabbage or mustard flavor.

London rocket (*Sisymbrium irio*), is better known as a medicinal herb; it got its name because it grew prolifically after the Great Fire of London in 1666. A related species, hedge mustard (*S. officinale*), is widely cultivated across Europe, particularly in Scandinavia and Germany. The leaves are said to be bitter, with a cabbage flavor. Despite its name, it is not related to mustard.

Equivalents

1 bunch = 6 to 8 oz (175 to 250 g), including 4 to 6 oz (125 to 175 g) leaves

•

2 oz (60 g) torn or coarsely chopped leaves = 3 cups (750 mL), loosely packed

•

2 oz (60 g) chopped leaves = 2 cups (500 mL), loosely packed

•

2 oz (60 g) baby arugula or wild arugula = 5 cups (1.25 L), loosely packed

Buy It

Arugula is a staple in supermarkets. Mature arugula is usually sold in bunches. When the leaves are smaller, arugula is sometimes displayed loose. Pale green baby arugula is sold in clamshells or bags or as part of salad blends.

Arugula grows in small clusters of long, frilly leaves. In general, the larger the leaves, the more pungent the flavor and the tougher the green. Look for bright leaves that are not yellowed, spotted, damaged, wilted or wet looking.

Because it is smaller than true arugula and also sold in clamshells, wild arugula (sylvetta) may be mistaken for baby arugula. Wild arugula leaves are a vibrant green and deeply notched, as well as spicier tasting.

Tasting Notes

True arugula is peppery, very nutty, bitter, aromatic and moist. The flavor varies from mild to spicy, depending on the cultivar and season.

Arugula harvested in the summer is stronger tasting than spring or autumn arugula. Arugula sweetens when cooked.

Wild arugula is juicier and tenderer but also more pungent and peppery, with a sharp mustard finish.

Store It

Arugula wilts easily and turns bitter as it ages, so it's important to refrigerate it as soon as you get it home.

Sometimes arugula is sold with the roots attached. If so, place it in a glass or vase of water like a bouquet, with a plastic bag draped over the foliage; then refrigerate it. Or trim the stems and wash the leaves, wrap in paper towels and store in a resealable bag.

Health Notes

Arugula provides vitamins A, C and K, calcium, copper, folate, iron, magnesium, manganese, niacin, pantothenic acid, phosphorus, potassium, riboflavin, thiamin and zinc.

In folk medicine, arugula has been used as a diuretic and a stimulant for the gallbladder, liver and stomach. Historically, it was noted as an aphrodisiac, which may be the reason it was banned from monastery gardens in the Middle Ages and why it was traditionally tossed with lettuce, which is considered a calming green.

SUBSTITUTES
dandelion greens, watercress, escarole, mizuna

Store baby arugula or wild arugula in its clamshell package or in a resealable bag with some air left in it to act as a cushion.

Arugula will keep in the refrigerator for up to three days.

Prep It

Arugula stems are edible but fibrous, so they are usually discarded. However, if you are cooking arugula, it's okay to pinch off the root ends and keep the tender parts of the stems.

Arugula is very gritty, so swish it in several changes of cold water, then drain and spin-dry before use.

Consume It

Because arugula can vary from mild to spicy, taste it before using.

Arugula is famous as a salad ingredient but it is also wonderful stuffed into panini, tossed with pasta, stirred into soup, briefly sautéed, or puréed as pesto. Because wild arugula is tender but tastes fiercer, it is best used as a garnish or as part of a mixed salad.

Although arugula is coarser than spinach, it's easy to overcook it. Heat arugula just until it wilts; in fact, the heat of a dish is often enough to "cook" this green. If you find it too bitter, note that longer cooking reduces bitterness; however, blandness quickly sets in.

Green Goodness Dressing

Nourish your inner goddess with this creamy but good-for-you dressing — my leafy green variation on a classic. It's easy to experiment with. Try it on tender lettuce, tofu, hard-cooked eggs or steamed veggies, or drizzle it over soup. Just resist the temptation to drink it straight!

Makes 1¼ cups (300 mL)

Vegan Friendly

Dressing

Tips

Bottled reconstituted lemon and lime juices usually contain additives. To avoid them, use freshly squeezed juice. Squeeze a whole lemon or lime and store the leftover juice in a small container in the fridge, or freeze it in 1 tbsp (15 mL) portions in an ice-cube tray.

Be careful not to overprocess extra virgin olive oil when using a food processor or blender. The forceful mixing action of these machines can release bitter compounds in the oil and thus affect the taste of your dish.

- Blender

¼ cup	chopped arugula leaves	60 mL
¼ cup	chopped spinach leaves	60 mL
¼ cup	watercress leaves	60 mL
1	large green onion (white and green parts), sliced	1
¼ cup	freshly squeezed lime juice (see Tips, left)	60 mL
1 tbsp	liquid honey or vegan alternative	15 mL
½ tsp	Dijon mustard	2 mL
½ tsp	kosher or coarse sea salt	2 mL
¼ tsp	freshly ground black pepper	1 mL
¾ cup	extra virgin olive oil (see Tips, left)	175 mL

1. Using blender, purée arugula, spinach, watercress, onion, lime juice, honey, mustard, salt and pepper. Add oil and pulse a few times, just until combined. Serve immediately or transfer to an airtight container and refrigerate for up to 1 week.

Variations

This is a freeform recipe as far as leafy greens go. Substitute equal quantities of your favorite tender greens for any of the greens in this dressing.

Arugula, Roasted Pear and Stilton Salad

Pears and blue cheese are salad soulmates nestled on a bed of nutty arugula — isn't that sensuous and sophisticated? Serve this salad with warm pears and warm dressing or, conveniently, at room temperature.

Makes 4 servings

Salad

Tips

You can use Bartlett pears instead of Anjous, but avoid Boscs — they are too coarse in texture when roasted.

To peel pears with ease, use a serrated peeler.

You may roast the pears 2 hours ahead of serving time, but do not refrigerate them or they will become unpleasantly firm.

To toast pecans, cook them in a dry skillet over medium heat, stirring often, for about 3 minutes, until golden and aromatic.

Most Stilton is made with non-animal rennet, so it is suitable for vegetarians. If desired, substitute other blue cheeses for the Stilton, checking the labels.

- Preheat oven to 400°F (200°C)
- 8-inch (20 cm) square baking dish

2	ripe but firm Anjou pears, peeled, cored and cut into 8 wedges (see Tips, left)	2
1 tbsp	Marsala or port	15 mL
1 tbsp	unsalted butter or non-dairy alternative, melted	15 mL
½ tsp	granulated sugar	2 mL
	Kosher or coarse sea salt	
2 tbsp	extra virgin olive oil	30 mL
1 tbsp	sherry vinegar	15 mL
1 tsp	liquid honey or vegan alternative	5 mL
	Freshly ground black pepper	
4 oz	baby arugula (about 10 cups/2.5 L, loosely packed)	125 g
½ cup	pecan halves, toasted and chopped (see Tips, left)	125 mL
4 oz	Stilton cheese, sliced into 4 wedges (see Tips, left)	125 g

1. In baking dish, arrange pears in a single layer. Drizzle with Marsala, then melted butter. Sprinkle with sugar and season with salt to taste. Roast in preheated oven for about 30 minutes, stirring midway through cooking time, until tender but firm. Using a slotted spoon, transfer pears to a plate.

2. To juices in baking dish, add oil, vinegar, honey and salt and pepper to taste. Whisk to combine.

3. In a large bowl, drizzle arugula with oil-and-vinegar mixture to taste (you may have some left over) and toss to coat. Transfer to a serving platter or individual plates. Arrange pears overtop. Scatter with pecans. Add cheese and serve.

Crete Salad

The people of Crete attribute their famous longevity to liberal consumption of extra virgin olive oil and **horta,** *their name for wild bitter greens (page 99). This effortless salad was inspired by a wonderful dish I ate in an ancient restaurant in Crete. Arugula stands in for the wild greens and, since this is a vegetarian version, smoked tofu replaces the tidbits of pork crackling in the original.*

Makes 4 servings

Vegan Friendly

Salad

Tips

This recipe makes about ¼ cup (60 mL) dressing. Use any leftover portions on other salads.

In keeping with the spirit of the recipe, try this using Cretan balsamic vinegar and fabulous Cretan honey from a Greek grocer.

Dressing

1 tbsp	balsamic vinegar (see Tips, left)	15 mL
1 tsp	liquid honey or vegan alternative (see Tips, left)	5 mL
	Kosher or coarse sea salt	
	Freshly ground black pepper	
3 tbsp	extra virgin olive oil	45 mL

Salad

4 oz	baby or wild arugula (about 10 cups/2.5 L, loosely packed)	125 g
4 oz	smoked tofu, cut into ½-inch (1 cm) dice	125 g
6	small figs (4 oz/125 g total), quartered	6

1. *Dressing:* In a small bowl, whisk together vinegar, honey and salt and pepper to taste. Whisk in oil.
2. *Salad:* In a bowl, drizzle arugula with prepared dressing to taste (you may have some left over) and toss to coat. Transfer to a platter or individual serving bowls. Top with tofu and figs and serve immediately.

Portobello and Arugula Burgers

I love mushroom burgers. These feature big, meaty portobellos, assertive arugula and lip-smacking lemon-sesame mayonnaise — ingredients that deserve crusty rolls, not soft, bland hamburger buns.

Makes 4 servings

Vegan Friendly

Main course

Tips

Toasted sesame seeds are available in most supermarkets. To toast your own, cook in a dry skillet over medium heat for about 2 minutes, stirring occasionally, until seeds start to clump and turn golden and aromatic. For an attractive presentation, use a mixture of white and black toasted sesame seeds.

Bottled reconstituted lemon and lime juices usually contain additives. To avoid them, use freshly squeezed juice. Squeeze a whole lemon or lime and store the leftover juice in a small container in the fridge, or freeze it in 1 tbsp (15 mL) portions in an ice-cube tray.

To prepare the portobellos: Pull off the stems and set aside for other uses (you can sauté them or add them to soups or pasta sauce). Using your fingers or a small spoon, gently scrape out the loose black gills. Using a paring knife, peel the skin off the caps. Briefly rinse under cold water and pat dry with paper towel.

Sesame Mayo

1 cup	mayonnaise or vegan alternative	250 mL
2 tsp	toasted sesame oil (see Tips, page 68)	10 mL
2 tsp	finely grated lemon zest	10 mL
2 tbsp	sesame seeds, toasted (see Tips, left)	30 mL
	Kosher or coarse sea salt	

Burgers

2 tbsp	extra virgin olive oil	30 mL
1 tbsp	freshly squeezed lemon juice (see Tips, left)	15 mL
2	cloves garlic, minced (see Tips, page 41)	2
½ tsp	kosher or coarse sea salt	2 mL
⅛ tsp	freshly ground black pepper	0.5 mL
4	large portobello mushrooms (6 to 8 oz/175 to 250 g each), skin, stems and gills removed (see Tips, left)	4
3 oz	arugula (about ½ small bunch), trimmed	90 g
8	thinly sliced rounds red onion	8
	Kosher or coarse sea salt	
4	crusty buns, split	4

1. *Sesame Mayo:* In a medium measuring cup, combine mayonnaise, sesame oil, lemon zest and sesame seeds. Season with salt to taste. Set aside.

2. *Burgers:* In a small bowl, combine olive oil, lemon juice, garlic, salt and pepper. Brush mushrooms with mixture until completely coated. Transfer mushrooms to a resealable bag and set aside for 1 to 2 hours at room temperature.

3. Preheat barbecue to High. Place mushrooms, cap side down, on grate and reduce heat to Medium. Cover and grill for 4 to 5 minutes per side, until char marks appear and mushrooms are warm and juicy.

4. Meanwhile, generously slather cut sides of buns with sesame mayo (you may have some left over). On bottom halves of buns, pile equal quantities of arugula. Top with onion, then mushrooms. Season with salt to taste. Replace tops of buns and serve immediately.

Winter Tomato Sauce with Arugula and Olives

Crave homemade tomato sauce? You could start with fresh tomatoes and simmer them for hours. In winter, however, canned tomatoes do the job better — and faster. Fortified with arugula and olives, this sauce is robust. Keep it handy to toss with pasta, or drizzle it over rice or steamed veggies.

Makes about 9 cups (2.25 L)		
Vegan Friendly		
Sauce		

Tips

For the finest minced garlic, push it through a press.

For the best tomato sauce, you need the best canned tomatoes. If you like, splurge on San Marzanos. These premium plum tomatoes from Italy are sold in well-stocked supermarkets.

Cane sugar is likely to be filtered through bone char, while beet sugar is not. Most labels don't indicate the source of the sugar. If you are following a vegan diet, use unbleached organic sugar that has not been filtered through bone char, or a sweetener such as agave syrup.

• Food processor or immersion blender

½ cup	extra virgin olive oil	125 mL
2	large onions, diced	2
2	carrots, diced	2
4	cloves garlic, minced, divided (see Tips, left)	4
2	cans (28 oz/796 mL each) plum tomatoes (see Tips, left)	2
½ cup	dry red wine	125 mL
1 tbsp	dried basil	15 mL
1 tsp	dried thyme	5 mL
1 tsp	granulated sugar (see Tips, left)	5 mL
1 tsp	kosher or coarse sea salt (see Tips, page 42)	5 mL
¼ tsp	hot pepper flakes	1 mL
1	bay leaf	1
1	bunch arugula (6 to 8 oz/175 to 250 g), trimmed and finely chopped	1
1 cup	oil-cured black olives, pitted and coarsely chopped	250 mL
1 tbsp	balsamic vinegar, optional	15 mL

1. In a large saucepan over medium heat, heat oil until shimmery. Add onions, carrots and 1 clove garlic. Reduce heat to medium-low, cover and cook, stirring occasionally, for about 15 minutes, until vegetables are softened and golden brown.

2. Add tomatoes and their juices, wine, basil, thyme, sugar, salt, hot pepper flakes and bay leaf. Increase heat to medium and bring to a simmer. Cover, reduce heat to low and simmer for 30 minutes or until thickened and vegetables are very soft. Remove from heat. Discard bay leaf.

3. In food processor fitted with the metal blade or using immersion blender, purée mixture. Return to pan, if necessary, and stir in arugula, olives and remaining garlic. Simmer over medium heat for 1 minute or until arugula wilts. Stir in vinegar, if using. Season with salt to taste. Refrigerate for up to 4 days or store in portions in the freezer.

Spaghetti with Arugula and Lemon Sauce

My peppery lemon sauce is luscious over pasta. It's even better with arugula, which adds a pop of color and good nutrients to this dish.

Tips

For the finest minced garlic, push it through a press.

I prefer kosher salt because it tastes better than iodized table salt and (ideally) contains no additives. Table salts and some sea salts contain additives such as iodine compounds (iodides), anti-clumping agents and even sugar (in the form of dextrose, which is used to stabilize iodine). Although the North American Salt Institute states that kosher salt "contains no additives," some kosher salt brands do contain additives such as anti-clumping agents. If you have concerns, check the label.

If substituting soy milk for the cream, use full-fat unflavored soy milk for best results. The sauce, however, will be thinner.

12 oz	spaghetti	375 g
1 tbsp	unsalted butter or non-dairy alternative	15 mL
2 tbsp	extra virgin olive oil	30 mL
6	slender green onions (white and green parts), cut diagonally into 1-inch (2.5 cm) pieces	6
1	large clove garlic, minced (see Tips, left)	1
2 tsp	finely grated lemon zest	10 mL
3 to 4 tbsp	freshly squeezed lemon juice	45 to 60 mL
1 tsp	kosher or coarse sea salt (see Tips, left)	5 mL
1/4 tsp	freshly ground white pepper	1 mL
1/3 cup	heavy or whipping (35%) cream or soy milk (see Tips, left)	75 mL
1	bunch arugula (6 to 8 oz/175 to 250 g), trimmed and finely chopped	1
1/4 cup	chopped fresh parsley leaves	60 mL

1. In a large pot of boiling salted water over medium heat, cook spaghetti for 15 minutes or until al dente. Drain, reserving 1/2 cup (125 mL) cooking water.

2. In a large skillet over medium heat, melt butter with oil. Add onions and cook, stirring, for about 1 minute, until softened. Stir in garlic for about 20 seconds. Stir in lemon zest, 2 tbsp (30 mL) lemon juice, salt and pepper. Stir in cream and simmer for about 1 minute, until slightly thickened. Add remaining lemon juice to taste.

3. Add arugula, then cooked spaghetti. Using tongs, toss until arugula wilts and spaghetti is well coated. If pasta seems dry or difficult to toss evenly with the sauce, loosen the mixture with some or all of the reserved cooking water. Season with salt to taste. Transfer to serving bowls and sprinkle with parsley. Serve immediately.

Pasta with Sun-Dried Tomato Pesto and Arugula

Red pesto and greens make this pasta vibrant. The pesto bursts with flavor. As a bonus, you can double the pesto recipe and slather the extra amount on crostini, dollop it in a creamy soup, or mix it with sour cream or cream cheese to create a tasty dip or spread.

Makes 4 servings
Vegan Friendly
Main course

Tips

To toast pine nuts, cook them in a dry skillet over medium heat, stirring often, for about 3 minutes, until golden and aromatic. Transfer to a bowl to cool.

Be careful not to overprocess the pesto into a paste. Traditionally the ingredients for pesto are ground together, so some texture is desired.

This recipe works well with mafalda corta, a type of ribbon pasta that resembles short, miniature lasagna noodles — complete with frilled edges. Because of its shape, the pasta will be evenly coated with pesto.

For the finest minced garlic, push it through a press.

If desired, sprinkle your favorite shredded cheese over the pasta. Also, you can add 2 to 4 tbsp (30 to 60 mL) freshly grated Parmesan-style cheese to the pesto.

- Mini food processor

Sun-Dried Tomato Pesto

2	cloves garlic	2
1/2 cup	oil-packed sun-dried tomatoes, drained, oil reserved	125 mL
3/4 cup	loosely packed fresh basil leaves (1/4 oz/7 g)	175 mL
1/4 cup	pine nuts, toasted (see Tips, left)	60 mL
1/4 tsp	hot pepper flakes	1 mL
3 tbsp	extra virgin olive oil (approx.)	45 mL
	Kosher or coarse sea salt	

Pasta

12 oz	small whole wheat pasta (see Tips, left)	375 g
1 tbsp	extra virgin olive oil	15 mL
1	onion, halved and thinly sliced	1
1	clove garlic, minced (see Tips, left)	1
1	bunch arugula (6 to 8 oz/175 to 250 g), trimmed and coarsely chopped	1
1 tsp	kosher or coarse sea salt	5 mL
1/8 tsp	freshly ground black pepper	0.5 mL
2 tbsp	chopped fresh parsley leaves	30 mL

1. *Sun-Dried Tomato Pesto:* In food processor fitted with the metal blade, chop garlic. Add sun-dried tomatoes, basil, pine nuts and hot pepper flakes. Pulse a few times, just until roughly chopped.

2. Measure reserved sun-dried tomato oil and transfer to a small bowl. Add enough olive oil to measure 6 tbsp (90 mL) combined. With food processor motor running, add oil mixture through feed tube and process until pesto mixture is puréed but retains some texture (see Tips, left). Set aside.

3. *Pasta:* In a pot of boiling salted water over medium heat, cook pasta for 15 minutes or until al dente. Drain, reserving 1/2 cup (125 mL) cooking water.

4. In a large skillet over medium heat, heat oil until shimmery. Add onion and cook, stirring often, for about 3 minutes, until softened. Reduce heat to low and cook for about 10 minutes more, until tender and golden brown. Stir in garlic for about 30 seconds. Stir in prepared pesto, then arugula. Add cooked pasta, reserved cooking water, salt and pepper. Remove from heat and toss until well coated. Transfer to serving bowls and garnish with parsley. Serve immediately.

Pizza Bianca e Verde

Nutty arugula makes a simple but alluring green topping for this classic white pizza. The blend of four cheeses used here is particularly tasty.

Tips

For the finest minced garlic, push it through a press.

If you are a vegetarian, check cheese labels. Traditional cheeses, especially artisanal types such as Parmesan, are made with animal-based rennet. However, many cheese companies now use vegetarian rennet instead. Note that fresh cheeses such as ricotta aren't usually made with rennet, but they may contain traces of it.

Baking the pizza near the bottom of the oven allows the crust to turn golden before the toppings can overcook.

- Preheat oven to 500°F (260°C), with rack in lowest position (see Tips, left)
- Preheated pizza stone or inverted baking sheet

2 tbsp	extra virgin olive oil	30 mL
2	cloves garlic, minced (see Tips, left)	2
¼ tsp	dried oregano	1 mL
¾ tsp	kosher or coarse sea salt	3 mL
⅛ tsp	freshly ground black pepper	0.5 mL
1 cup	shredded mozzarella cheese (3 oz/90 g; see Tips, left)	250 mL
¾ cup	shredded Asiago cheese (2 oz/60 g)	175 mL
½ cup	ricotta cheese	125 mL
	Flour for dusting	
1 lb	pizza dough, at room temperature	500 g
2 oz	baby arugula (about 5 cups/1.25 L, loosely packed)	60 g
1 tbsp	freshly grated Parmesan-style cheese (see Tips, left)	15 mL

1. In a small bowl, combine oil, garlic, oregano, salt and pepper.
2. In another bowl, place mozzarella, Asiago and ricotta. Using a fork, stir lightly to combine.
3. Lightly flour a piece of parchment paper. On parchment, stretch or roll dough into a 12-inch (30 cm) circle. Brush garlic oil evenly overtop, right to the edges. Spread with cheese mixture, leaving a ½-inch (1 cm) border.
4. Transfer pizza, still on parchment, to preheated pizza stone or baking sheet. Bake in preheated oven for 12 to 15 minutes, until bottom is golden brown and cheese is bubbly and golden. Remove from oven.
5. Immediately scatter arugula over hot pizza. Sprinkle with Parmesan-style cheese. Return to oven for 1 minute, just until arugula wilts slightly. Serve hot.

Orange-Glazed Tofu Triangles with Arugula

I love the fragrance of this nourishing meal. Sweet, spiced orange sauce makes a nice contrast to the arugula. Serve this dish warm, on a bed of quinoa or brown rice.

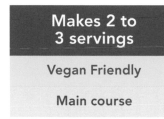

Makes 2 to 3 servings

Vegan Friendly

Main course

Tip

For easy tofu triangles, use a sharp knife to cut the block of tofu horizontally through the center into 3 slices, each about ½ inch (1 cm) thick. Cut each slice into 4 triangles.

- Preheat oven to 400°F (200°C)
- Large baking pan, greased

12 oz	medium or firm block tofu, patted dry and cut into triangles (see Tip, left)	375 g
1 tbsp	extra virgin olive oil	15 mL
1	large red bell pepper, cut into ½-inch (1 cm) strips	1
	Kosher or coarse sea salt	
	Freshly ground black pepper	
½ cup	freshly squeezed orange juice	125 mL
2 tsp	liquid honey or vegan alternative	10 mL
¼ tsp	hot pepper flakes	1 mL
3 oz	arugula (about ½ small bunch), trimmed and coarsely chopped	90 g

1. On one side of prepared baking pan, arrange tofu triangles in a single layer. Brush tops with oil. In other side of pan, place red pepper strips, drizzle with remaining oil and toss to coat. Season tofu and red pepper with salt and pepper to taste. Roast in preheated oven for about 20 minutes, until tofu is golden. Transfer tofu to a plate, cover with foil to keep warm, and set aside. Return pan to oven and roast pepper strips for about 10 minutes more, until tender; set aside.

2. In a small pan over medium-high heat, boil orange juice, honey and hot pepper flakes for about 5 minutes, until reduced to about ⅓ cup (75 mL). Remove from heat and season with salt and pepper to taste.

3. Arrange arugula on a serving platter or individual plates. Overlap tofu triangles on top of arugula and arrange roasted pepper strips around perimeter. Pour hot orange sauce over tofu. Serve immediately.

Beet Greens

Beta vulgaris

> *Other names:* **beetroot leaves, blood turnip greens. Depending on where you are shopping, you might find beet greens identified as** *biete d'aorta* **or** *hojas de betabeles.*

Beets have been consumed since prehistoric times in the Mediterranean, and traces of beetroots were found in a pyramid in Thebes, Egypt. Although beet greens are an afterthought nowadays, these plants were originally grown for their leaves, not their bulbous roots. In Roman times people began to eat the roots as well. The popularity of beet greens waned after the widespread introduction of spinach to Europe during the Renaissance. Today, beets and their greens are much more popular in Europe than in North America.

Varieties

Numerous cultivated species are classified as either tuberous or leaf beets. As their name implies, leaf beets are leafy greens, of which the best known is chard (leaf beets are discussed in the Chard section, page 104).

Tuberous beets have swollen roots, which we know best as simply beets or beetroot. They are divided into garden beets (*B. vulgaris*), for eating; sugar beets (*B. vulgaris altissima*), for processing into sugar; and mangold or mangel-wurzel beets (*Beta vulgaris crassa*), for fodder. Although tuberous beets are grown mainly for their roots, their greens are edible. Garden beets are the type the average consumer is likely to find in the supermarket.

Beet greens are pretty. Their stems and veins come in the same colors as their roots (the leaves of a yellow beet, for instance, will have yellow veins and stems). Beets range from white to yellow to garnet, the most common color. Chioggia (also known as candy cane beets) have red and white rings, and their stems are pink and white. Most beet greens are found attached to the roots, but some are grown specifically for their foliage. One such type has burgundy leaves.

Supermarket beets are cultivated descendants of wild beets. The sea beet (*B. vulgaris maritima*), for example, is a wild ancestor of beets and chard. It is native to some European seacoasts as well as the shores of North Africa and southern Asia. It is sometimes called wild spinach because its leaves are considered mild enough to be served raw as well as cooked.

Equivalents

1 bunch beets = 1¾ to 2 lbs (825 g to 1 kg), including 3 to 5 beets and 12 to 16 oz (375 to 500 g) greens

•

1 lb (500 g) beet greens = 6 oz (175 g) leaves and 10 oz (300 g) stems

•

2 oz (60 g) coarsely chopped or shredded leaves = 3 cups (750 mL), loosely packed

•

2 oz (60 mL) finely chopped leaves = 1 cup (250 mL), loosely packed

•

2 oz (60 g) stems, cut into 1-inch (2.5 cm) pieces or coarsely chopped = ½ cup (125 mL), loosely packed

Buy It

Beets are sold in supermarkets. If the tops are intact, they are called "bunching beets," with three, four or five beets (large to small) bundled with lush greens. Look for younger, smaller beets, as their greens are tenderer. Trimmed beets (without greens) are also sold to consumers, as well as to the food-processing industry for use in packaged goods or animal feed. Some supermarkets occasionally sell beet greens on their own.

Beet greens are attractive, with crisp leaves and colorful, shiny stems and veins. In the case of red beets, the stems and veins should be purplish, not faded pink or yellowish. It's hard to find a perfect set of greens, as they deteriorate quickly. Avoid leaves with brown edges, yellow mottling or insect holes.

Tasting Notes

Raw beet leaves are nutty, peppery, slightly bitter and astringent. They are moist but unpleasantly grainy, even the small, tender ones. The raw stalks are crisp, juicy and briny. Cooked beet greens are milder, earthy, somewhat sweet-and-sour. The leaves are nutty, with a slight beet flavor, but not sweet. Stems are crisp, slightly sweet, briny and astringent.

Store It

Greens leach moisture from the roots, so separate beets from their foliage before storing. Leave about $1/2$ inch (1 cm) of stem attached to each beet.

Beet greens fade and wither quickly. To store, cut the leaves from the stems before refrigerating them. Wrap leaves in paper towels and place them in a resealable bag. Store stems in a separate resealable bag.

Beet leaves and stems will keep in the refrigerator for up to two days.

Prep It

Beet juice stains, so wear gloves when handling or cutting beets and stems. To remove stains, rub your hands with a paste made from salt or baking soda mixed with lemon juice or vinegar, then wash with soapy water.

Beet greens tend to be very dirty. Swish them in several changes of cold water, then spin-dry before using.

Many recipes call for the leaves only, because the stems can be tricky. When cooked, they remain nice and crisp, but some may be stringy. Peeling them is an impractical solution. To use as much of the stems as possible, trim and discard any that are wider than $1/4$ inch (0.5 cm), which are likely to be the most stringy. Chopping the stems instead of cutting them into pieces also helps to reduce stringiness.

Consume It

Although beet greens may be eaten raw, they are best when cooked. They are sturdy, so the leaves hold up well and the stems retain their crunch. Depending on the cooking method, the thickness of the stems and ribs, and how they are cut, leaves will be cooked in 3 to 5 minutes and stems in 5 to 10 minutes.

Use steam to tenderize beet greens. Sauté stems until they soften, stir in the leaves, reduce the heat, cover and steam for 5 minutes.

Avoid red beet greens in soups or stews, because they will tint the food pink.

If using beet greens raw, add only the smallest leaves to a mixed salad. Don't serve them on their own, as they are grainy. Immature leaves are tender and are included in some commercial salad mixes.

Health Notes

Beet greens contain vitamins A, B_6, C, E and K, calcium, copper, folate, iron, magnesium, manganese, niacin, pantothenic acid, phosphorus, potassium, riboflavin, thiamin and zinc. Beets are particularly high in fiber and have strong anti-inflammatory properties. However, they are high in sodium and oxalic acid (see page 355).

In folk remedies, beetroots and leaves have been used to alleviate fever, constipation, wounds, indigestion and bad breath; they were also taken as a blood tonic. The ancient Romans believed that beet greens were an aphrodisiac.

SUBSTITUTES

chard, amaranth, spinach

Pickled Lime Beets and Greens

Quick-pickled beets are delightfully sweet-and-sour. They make a colorful addition to a buffet table or served simply as a side salad.

Makes about 1¾ cups (425 mL)

Vegan Friendly

Side dish

Tips

Choose smaller beets whenever possible. They are less fibrous and take less time to cook.

To avoid staining your hands, use gloves when handling beets.

When roasting or boiling beets, it's simplest to leave the skin on and just give them a good scrub before cooking. After cooking, the skins should slip right off.

When cooking beets whole, leave the rat-tail root (tap root) and about ½ inch (1 cm) of stem attached. This reduces loss of nutrients and leakage of color.

- Preheat oven to 400°F (200°C)
- Small baking dish with lid, greased

2 or 3	small to medium beets (8 oz/250 g total), scrubbed (see Tips, left)	2 or 3
1 cup	finely chopped beet leaves and stems (2 oz/60 g)	250 mL
¼ cup	freshly squeezed lime juice	60 mL
1 tbsp	granulated sugar	15 mL
½ tsp	kosher or coarse sea salt (see Tips, page 57)	2 mL
⅛ tsp	freshly ground black pepper	0.5 mL

1. Place beets in prepared dish, cover and roast in preheated oven for 45 to 60 minutes, until tender but firm. Set aside until cool enough to handle.

2. Using a chef's knife, trim, peel and cut beets into ½-inch (1 cm) cubes. Transfer to a heatproof bowl. Scatter beet leaves and stems overtop.

3. In a small saucepan over medium heat, combine lime juice, sugar, salt and pepper. Bring to a full boil, stirring occasionally. Immediately pour mixture over beets and greens; stir to coat evenly.

4. Transfer to an airtight container, cover and refrigerate overnight to allow beets to pickle before serving.

Roasted Beet Salad with Candied Walnuts

If you are not a beet lover, this refined and aromatic salad should turn you into one. The prep work can get a little messy but the result is good-looking. As a bonus, this recipe gives you a shortcut for candied walnuts.

Makes 4 servings

Vegan Friendly

Salad

Tips

When preparing candied walnuts, do not let the sugar brown too much. It will continue to darken after removing from the heat, and it will taste bitter if too dark.

This recipe uses every part of the beet. To prepare the beets, separate the greens from the beets at the base of the stalks. Using a vegetable peeler, peel the beets; set aside beets and discard peels. Trim the beet greens, separating leaves from stems. Discard parts of stems that are wider than 1/4 inch (0.5 cm). Cut tender stems into 1-inch (2.5 cm) pieces and set aside. Shred leaves.

Large beets may require a longer roasting time. To test roasted beets for doneness, gently poke them with a metal skewer; it should slide in with only a bit of resistance.

Unrefined walnut oil and other nut oils are sold in gourmet food shops and well-stocked supermarkets.

- Preheat oven to 375°F (190°C)
- Small baking dish with lid

Candied Walnuts

1 cup	walnut halves	250 mL
2 tbsp	granulated sugar	30 mL
	Kosher or coarse sea salt	
	Freshly ground black pepper	

Salad

1	bunch beets (about 2 lbs/1 kg), beets peeled and greens chopped (see Tips, left)	1
2 tbsp	extra virgin olive oil, divided	30 mL
1 tsp	kosher or coarse sea salt	5 mL
1 tbsp	walnut oil (see Tips, left)	15 mL
1 tbsp	sherry vinegar	15 mL

1. *Candied Walnuts:* In a dry skillet over medium heat, toast walnuts, stirring occasionally, for about 3 minutes, until golden and aromatic. Sprinkle with sugar. Cook, stirring constantly, for 30 to 60 seconds, until sugar melts and turns honey-colored and walnuts are lightly browned (see Tips, left). Transfer walnuts to a sheet of waxed or parchment paper and spread in a single layer. Season with salt and pepper to taste. Set aside to cool.

2. *Salad:* Place prepared beets in baking dish and drizzle with 1 tbsp (15 mL) olive oil. Cover and roast in preheated oven for about 45 minutes, until tender (see Tips, left). Set aside until cool enough to handle. Reserve juices in baking dish.

3. In a large skillet over medium heat, heat remaining olive oil until shimmery. Add beet stems and salt. Cook, stirring often, for about 2 minutes, until softened. Add leaves and stir to coat. Cover, reduce heat to low and cook for about 7 minutes, until tender.

4. Spread out greens on a serving platter. Using a mandoline or sharp knife, slice beets about 1/8 inch (3 mm) thick. Arrange beet slices over greens in overlapping rows or circles.

5. Add walnut oil and vinegar to baking dish and mix with reserved juices. Drizzle over beets. Season beets with salt and pepper to taste. Scatter candied walnuts overtop. Serve at room temperature.

Beet Relish with Orange Nut Oil Vinaigrette

Yes, you can eat beets raw. The leaves, however, taste better with a quick blanching. Enjoy this dish as a hearty relish or a side salad and serve it with your favorite grains dish.

Makes about 4 servings (1¾ cups/425 mL)

Vegan Friendly

Salad

Tips

Choose smaller beets whenever possible. They are less fibrous and take less time to cook.

To avoid staining your hands, use gloves when handling beets.

2 oz	beet leaves, coarsely chopped (3 cups/750 mL, loosely packed)	60 g
3	small beets (8 oz/250 g total), peeled and shredded (see Tips, left)	3
½ cup	Orange Nut Oil Vinaigrette (page 451)	125 mL
2 tbsp	chopped fresh chives	30 mL
1 tbsp	chopped fresh parsley leaves	15 mL

1. In a pot of boiling salted water over medium heat, blanch leaves for 1 minute. Using a colander, drain leaves, then immediately rinse with cold water until cool enough to handle. Drain again and then, using your hands, squeeze handfuls of leaves to remove excess liquid.

2. Using a chef's knife, finely chop leaves. Transfer to a serving bowl. Add shredded beets and vinaigrette and toss to coat evenly. Add chives and parsley; stir to combine. Serve at room temperature.

Simple Sautéed Beet Greens

Don't toss out extra beet greens — sautéing is a simple way to prepare them. Pile these greens over brown rice or quinoa, toss them with pasta or spoon them onto toast.

Makes 2 servings (about 2 cups/500 mL)

Vegan Friendly

Side dish

Tip

For the finest minced garlic, push it through a press.

1	bunch beet greens (about 1 lb/500 g)	1
2 tbsp	extra virgin olive oil	30 mL
½ tsp	kosher or coarse sea salt (see Tips, page 57)	2 mL
2	large cloves garlic, minced (see Tip, left)	2

1. Trim greens, separating leaves from stems. Discard parts of stems wider than ¼ inch (0.5 cm). Finely chop tender stems; you should have about 1¼ cups (300 mL). Chop leaves. Set aside.

2. In a large skillet over medium heat, heat oil until shimmery. Add stems and salt. Sauté for about 1 minute, until softened. Add garlic and stir constantly for 1 minute. Add leaves and stir to coat. Reduce heat to low, cover and cook for about 5 minutes, until very tender. Serve warm.

Beet Bunch Borscht

It's waste not, want not with this vegan-friendly borscht, a wholesome twist on the classic Eastern European soup. Both the beets and their greens are cooked, then puréed. This velvety garnet soup looks gorgeous. For an easy crowd-pleaser, double the recipe.

Makes 4 to 6 servings (about 4 cups/1 L)

Vegan Friendly

Soup

Tips

This recipe uses every part of the beet. To prepare the beets, separate the greens from the beets at the base of the stems; set aside in two piles. Using a vegetable peeler, peel the beets. Discard peels and cut beets into ½-inch (1 cm) chunks. Trim the beet greens, separating leaves from stems. Discard parts of stems that are wider than ¼ inch (0.5 cm). Coarsely chop tender stems. Stack the leaves, setting aside the tiniest ones for garnish. Coarsely chop the remaining leaves.

To avoid staining your hands, wear gloves when cutting beets.

- Blender

1 tbsp	extra virgin olive oil	15 mL
½	Spanish onion, diced	½
1	bunch beets (about 2 lbs/1 kg), beets peeled and greens chopped (see Tips, left)	1
½ tsp	kosher or coarse sea salt	2 mL
1 cup	vegetable stock	250 mL
1 cup	water	250 mL
2 tbsp	freshly squeezed lemon juice	30 mL
	Freshly ground black pepper	
	Sour cream or non-dairy alternative	
1 tbsp	chopped fresh chives	15 mL

1. In a saucepan over medium heat, heat oil until shimmery. Add onion, beet stems and salt. Cook, stirring often, for about 5 minutes, until softened. Add greens and cook, stirring occasionally, for about 5 minutes, until wilted. Add beets, then stock and water. When mixture comes to a simmer, cover, reduce heat to low and cook for about 2 hours, until beets are very tender.

2. Using blender, purée beet mixture in batches. Return to pan and stir in lemon juice. Season with salt and pepper to taste.

3. Ladle into serving bowls. Top with a dollop of sour cream, sprinkle with chives and garnish with tiny beet leaves. Serve warm.

Open-Faced Beet Sandwiches

Remember the serious sandwich craze a few years ago? That's when I first prepared beet sandwiches — and they were a revelation. These are not the type of sandwiches you just toss together. Rather, they are a meal, and worth the work. In fact, you can serve them with a knife and fork. This recipe is easily halved or doubled.

Makes 2 servings

Vegan Friendly

Sandwich

Tips

Choose small beets if possible. They are less fibrous and cook faster.

To prepare the beet greens for this recipe: use a sharp knife to trim them, separating leaves from stems. Coarsely chop the leaves and set aside. Trim stems, discarding any wider than $1/4$ inch (0.5 cm). Cut tender stems into 1-inch (2.5 cm) pieces. Set aside.

When roasting or boiling beets, leave the skin on and give them a good scrub before cooking; the skins will loosen during cooking and slip off easily afterward. Leave the rat-tail root (tap root) and about $1/2$ inch (1 cm) of stem attached to the beet. This reduces loss of nutrients and leakage of color.

To toast walnuts, cook them in a dry skillet over medium heat for about 3 minutes, stirring occasionally, until golden and aromatic.

Sourdough loaves are usually rounded. To get the large slices you need for this recipe, cut them from the center of the loaf.

- Preheat oven to 400°F (200°C)
- Small baking dish with lid, greased

2	small beets (6 to 8 oz/175 to 250 g total), scrubbed (see Tips, left)	2
2 tbsp	extra virgin olive oil, divided	30 mL
4 oz	beet greens (see Tips, left)	125 g
1	shallot, diced	1
$1/2$ tsp	kosher or coarse sea salt, divided	2 ml
$1/8$ tsp	freshly ground black pepper	0.5 mL
$1/2$ cup	cream cheese or non-dairy alternative	125 mL
$1/4$ cup	walnut halves, toasted and chopped (see Tips, left)	60 mL
2	large slices (1 inch/2.5 cm thick) sourdough bread (see Tips, left)	2
1 tsp	fresh thyme leaves	5 mL

1. Place beets in prepared baking dish, cover and roast in preheated oven for 45 to 60 minutes, until tender but firm. Set aside until cool enough to handle. Remove skins, trim and slice beets very thinly (a mandoline works well for slicing very thinly).

2. In a skillet over medium heat, heat 1 tbsp (15 mL) oil until shimmery. Add beet stems, shallot, $1/4$ tsp (1 mL) salt and pepper. Sauté for about 1 minute, until softened. Add beet leaves and stir to coat. Cover, reduce heat to low and cook for about 7 minutes, stirring once or twice, until stems are tender and leaves are wilted. Increase heat to medium-high and sauté for 1 minute to dry greens.

3. In a medium measuring cup, combine cream cheese, remaining oil (if desired) and remaining salt. Mix in chopped walnuts. Set aside.

4. Toast bread until golden but not too crisp. Slather each slice with equal amounts of cream cheese mixture. Top with equal amounts of greens. Overlap beet slices over greens. Sprinkle with thyme, cut each slice in half and serve.

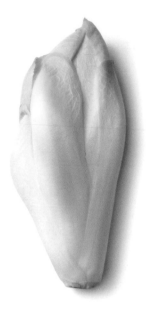

Belgian Endive

Cichorium intybus witlof

> *Other names:* **Belgium/Dutch chicory, blanching chicory, chicon, French endive, green-leaved blanching chicory.**
>
> **Depending on where you are shopping, you may find Belgian endive identified as *cicoria di Bruxelles, cikoriesalat, endive à feuilles blanches* or *witloof*.**

Belgian endive is a relatively new cultivar from the diverse chicory plant family. Its origins are a little hazy. According to some stories, a Belgian farmer accidentally developed the variety in the 19th century. Others attribute its creation to a Belgian botanist.

A farming method called blanching produces the white color of Belgian endive. Chicory is pulled from the ground and its green top is lopped off. The base is then replanted or hydroponically grown in darkness to stop the development of chlorophyll. Blanched leaves lack the extreme bitterness of the mother plant. Shoots sprouted from blanched endive are called chicons.

Varieties

White Belgian endive (*Cichorium intybus witlof*) is a standardized cultivar that varies very little. In Dutch, *witloof* means "white leaf."

Endigia, also known as red endive or carmine, is a new French cross between Belgian endive and radicchio. It is being marketed by California growers and is eaten raw, as it loses its distinctive color when cooked.

Buy It

Belgian endives are supermarket staples. The small, football-shaped heads of packed pastel greens are about 6 inches (15 cm) long, with leaves that are crisp and cream colored with yellow-green tips. Pick Belgian endives that feel heavy for their size, with closely packed leaves. Specimens that have the least green are preferable; the whiter the leaf and the yellower the tip, the less bitter the vegetable. Check the feathery edges of leaves for discoloration or wilting. Avoid browned or blemished leaves or heads that are reddish brown at the base.

Tasting Notes

Belgian endive has crunchy, slightly bitter, juicy leaves with a sweet finish and satiny texture.

Health Notes

Belgian endive contains vitamin B_6, calcium, copper, folate, iron, magnesium, manganese, potassium and thiamin.

In herbal medicine, endive has been used as a diuretic, a gallbladder and liver stimulant, and a sleep aid. Intybin is a sedative and analgesic found in the *C. intybus* species, to which Belgian endive belongs.

Store It

Store Belgian endive whole. Swathe the head in paper towels, place in a resealable bag and refrigerate it. Exposure to light can turn it bitter.

Belgian endive will keep in the refrigerator for up to one week.

Prep It

Before using Belgian endive, peel off and discard any outer leaves that have browned. To separate the leaves, cut a thin slice from the base of the endive and pluck off as many leaves as you can easily release. Repeat to release more leaves. The bitter core may be eaten or discarded. To lay leaves flat, cut off the stiff base of each. The leaves may then be arranged overlapping on a serving platter.

Cut Belgian endive just before using, as cut edges will brown when they come in contact with air. Halve lengthwise, then slice crosswise into shreds or larger pieces.

I prefer to wash Belgian endive, but many people don't (if anything, they just wipe the outer leaves). To wash it, briefly rinse whole leaves or the cut endive, then drain and pat dry or spin-dry. Do not soak.

Consume It

Belgian endive is tender, mild and crisp enough to eat raw in salads but sturdy enough to braise, roast or grill briefly. It is great for finger foods. The concave leaves are called spears or boats, and they make fine vessels for dips or cooked fillings. Use endive spears as healthy dippers instead of crackers or chips.

Belgian endive can be cooked tender-crisp in 5 to 10 minutes, although in some recipes it is braised over low heat for up to 30 minutes.

Equivalents

1 endive = 3 to 5 oz (90 to 150 g), comprising 12 spears/boats plus a tiny core

•

1 endive boat holds 1½ to 2 tbsp (22 to 30 mL) filling

•

2 oz (60 g) sliced endive = ¾ cup (175 mL), loosely packed

SUBSTITUTES

escarole, radicchio, romaine lettuce

Hands-On Endive Salad with Lemon Garlic Cream

Luscious and delightfully messy, this salad makes me want to lick my fingers and my plate. The endive spears are finished with a sprinkling of chopped green olives and toasted walnuts. This salad reminds me of the original Caesar, because the whole leaves are dressed and then eaten by hand. Distribute warm moist towels afterward.

	Makes 2 to 4 servings
	Vegan Friendly
	Salad

Tips

You can substitute black pepper for white pepper. White pepper is used mainly for aesthetic reasons, to avoid black specks in finished dishes. It is ground from white peppercorns, which are riper than black peppercorns and have had the skins stripped off. Also, unlike black peppercorns, they have not been dried and left to darken and shrivel.

To toast walnuts, cook in a dry skillet over medium heat for about 3 minutes, stirring often, until golden and aromatic.

Lemon Garlic Cream

2 tbsp	extra virgin olive oil	30 mL
1	small shallot, diced	1
¼ cup	heavy or whipping (35%) cream or vegan alternative	60 mL
4	cloves roasted garlic, mashed (see page 454)	4
½ tsp	finely grated lemon zest	2 mL
½ tsp	kosher or coarse sea salt (see Tips, page 57)	2 mL
⅛ tsp	freshly ground white pepper (see Tips, left)	0.5 mL
1 tbsp	freshly squeezed lemon juice	15 mL

Salad

2	large Belgian endives, trimmed, leaves separated	2
4	large green olives, pitted and chopped	4
2 tbsp	diced red onion	30 mL
¼ cup	walnut pieces, toasted and coarsely chopped (see Tips, left)	60 mL
1 tbsp	chopped fresh parsley leaves	15 mL

1. *Lemon Garlic Cream:* In a small saucepan over medium heat, heat oil until shimmery. Add shallot and cook, stirring often, for about 2 minutes, until softened and golden. Stir in cream, roasted garlic, lemon zest, salt and pepper. Simmer for 1 to 2 minutes, until thickened. Stir in lemon juice. Set aside for 5 minutes to cool.

2. *Salad:* In a large bowl, toss endive with lemon garlic cream to coat.

3. Arrange endive leaves on serving plates. Scatter olives, onion, walnuts and parsley overtop. Serve immediately.

Grilled Endives with Pears, Roquefort and Hazelnut Oil

Three fabulous flavors come together in this warm composed salad. Serve it with baguette as a starter or luncheon dish.

Makes 4 appetizer servings

Appetizer

Tips

You can barbecue the endives and pear instead of using a grill pan.

Unrefined hazelnut oil is sold in gourmet food shops and well-stocked supermarkets. It is aromatic, with a distinct hazelnut flavor.

I prefer kosher salt because it tastes better than iodized table salt and (ideally) contains no additives. Table salts and some sea salts contain additives such as iodine compounds (iodides), anti-clumping agents and even sugar (in the form of dextrose, which is used to stabilize iodine). Although the North American Salt Institute states that kosher salt "contains no additives," some kosher salt brands do contain additives such as anti-clumping agents. If you have concerns, check the label.

- Grill pan (see Tips, left)

2 tbsp	hazelnut oil, divided (see Tips, left)	30 mL
1 tbsp	water	15 mL
½ tsp	kosher or coarse sea salt (see Tips, left)	2 mL
4	Belgian endives, trimmed and halved lengthwise	4
1	large ripe Anjou pear, peeled, cored and halved	1
4 oz	Roquefort-style cheese, cut into 4 pieces	125 g
4	small lemon wedges	4

1. In a large bowl, combine 1 tbsp (15 mL) oil, water and salt. Add endive and pear halves; toss gently to coat. Set aside for about 10 minutes, until endives soften.

2. Heat grill pan over medium-high heat for 3 to 5 minutes. Add endive and pear halves, cut side down. Grill for 5 to 10 minutes, until warmed through and softened, with char marks on the bottom.

3. Divide endive halves among serving plates, cut side up. Thinly slice pear halves and place equal quantities on each plate, fanning out the slices. Drizzle endives and pear with remaining oil. Season endives with salt to taste. Place a piece of cheese on each plate. Serve with lemon wedges alongside to squeeze overtop.

Bitter Leaf

Vernonia amygdalina

Other names: **African leaf, goat killer, vernonie.**
**Depending on where you are shopping, you may
find bitter leaf identified as** *awonoo, buzut, etidod,
ewuro, ibicha, grawa, jankpantire, kossa fina, libo
que, mujonso, mtugutu, ndoki, n'dolé, onugbu,
oriwo, shiwaka* **or** *umubilizi.*

Tasting Notes

Bitter leaf lives up to its name. In
my experience, it is the bitterest
and most nuanced of all the leafy
greens. Its compelling smokiness
is its most appealing quality. The
raw leaves are inedible: they are
tough and severely bitter, with
an acidic, spicy, tannic finish. The
cooked leaves are peppery and
slightly tannic.

Equivalents

6 oz (175 g) package =
40 to 45 leaves

•

2 oz (60 g)
cooked, coarsely
chopped leaves =
⅔ cup (150 mL),
loosely packed

Bitter leaf is a shrub or small tree native to the tropics, including
regions in Africa, Asia and Central and South
America. It is found wild as well as cultivated.

A daily green in parts of Africa, bitter leaf is eaten
for its health benefits as well as for sustenance. It is
one of the most widely consumed leaf vegetables in
West and Central Africa. The huge number of African
languages means a huge number of alternatives to its
unappealing name (see "Other names," above).

Varieties

Bitter leaf (*Vernonia amygdalina*) is the most famous
of the hundreds of *Vernonia* species consumed as leaf
vegetables or medicinal herbs in Africa. Some are
cultivated but most are foraged. In North America,
more than a dozen relatives of this species are
edible, but they are ignored except for being cited occasionally
as folk medicines.

Buy It

Bitter leaf is sold in Africentric and Asian grocery stores. The
fresh leaves are sold in stacks, without their inedible stems.
Frozen or dried bitter leaf is also available. However, fresh leaves
are superior and seem to be easier to obtain.

Bitter leaf has attractive-looking, firm but thin dark green
leaves with teardrop points. The leaves are 6 to 7 inches (15 to
18 cm) long. Avoid any leaves with insect damage, withering or
discoloration at the edges.

Store It

Bitter leaf is more apt to dehydrate than to rot. Transfer it to a
resealable bag, or stack and wrap leaves tightly in plastic wrap,
then refrigerate.

Bitter leaf will keep in the refrigerator for up to one week.

Prep It

Before cooking bitter leaf, cut off any stubs of stems, which are tough. To soften them, the leaves are soaked, steeped or precooked and may be pounded.

To help decrease bitterness and neutralize plant toxins and irritants, bitter leaf must be thoroughly cleaned and preboiled.

African cooks use many different techniques to prepare bitter leaf; these may involve soaking or blanching and the use of baking soda, salt or a meat tenderizer. I tested several methods and favor the following process, which tempers the leaves yet retains their delicious smokiness:

- Swish, massage and squeeze the leaves in a large bowl of water, changing the water often, until the leaves lose some of their bitterness (taste a piece) and the water squeezed from them is no longer dark.
- Add a small spoonful of baking soda to a large pot of water. Simmer the leaves, covered, over medium-low heat for 15 to 20 minutes.
- Rinse with cold water twice, or until the water runs clear. Drain and squeeze excess liquid from the leaves. To avoid a swampy effect (unappealing clumps of greens) in a soup or stew, chop the leaves into small pieces.

Health Notes

Although no official government analysis is available, bitter leaf is thought to contain vitamin C, calcium, iron, phosphorus, selenium and zinc. Bitter leaf is high in tannins.

Bitter leaf is a prominent medicinal plant, not just in the realm of folk medicine but also as the subject of scientific studies. Seeing sick chimpanzees consuming bitter leaf, which is not part of their normal diets, captured the imagination of some researchers. Laboratory studies suggest that it is plentiful in antioxidants and may have a positive effect on blood cholesterol levels.

In herbal medicine, bitter leaf has been used to treat malaria (it contains the antimalarial compound quinine) as well as fevers, pneumonia, respiratory infections and coughs; diabetes and high blood sugar; high cholesterol and hardened arteries; constipation, diarrhea, stomachaches and intestinal parasites such as tapeworms; liver ailments; headaches, toothaches, gingivitis and tonsillitis; arthritis; skin infections, rashes, eczema and ringworm; snakebites; and insomnia.

SUBSTITUTES

collards, taro leaves, turnip greens, cassava leaves, bitter melon vines

Consume It

Bitter leaf is never eaten raw. It is added to soups and stews or sometimes used as an herb. Africans say that if bitter leaf is prepared properly, dishes containing it shouldn't be bitter. However, everything is relative — cooked bitter leaf will retain some of its pungency and bitter edge.

The cooking time varies. Bitter leaf is tender enough to eat in 20 to 30 minutes. However, the total cooking time may be much longer, since it is usually precooked, then added to a dish and simmered.

Green Africa

Africans are the world's largest consumers of leafy greens. Soups, stews and side dishes made with greens are a signature of African cuisine, particularly in the sub-Saharan part of the continent. These culinary traditions were also exported to the Caribbean and parts of the Americas.

Leafy greens have been used for food and as medicine in Africa since prehistoric times. They remain an inexpensive source of vitamins, minerals, protein, fiber and healthful antioxidants, particularly during periods of famine. In fact, they are often free for the picking.

Africans consume an amazing variety of greens, numbering in the hundreds. The greens may be cultivated but are often wild — and unusual. It is estimated that more than 40 indigenous non-starchy, leafy vegetables are consumed in Nigeria alone. Because there are so many African languages, these greens have a mind-boggling array of names. A particular name may refer to several plants, and several plants may share the same name. A generic term for greens in West Africa is *efo*, while in French-speaking African countries they are often called *feuilles*, meaning "leaves" (as in *feuilles de manioc*, or cassava leaves).

Africans are not gentle with their greens. In an ongoing quest to tenderize, tame bitterness and neutralize the herbaceous taste derived from chlorophyll, they vigorously wash, squeeze and even wring greens like laundry. Rubbing greens with baking soda or salt helps them to fall apart and cook easily, as does pounding them with a mortar and pestle before cooking.

The following are popular African leafy greens that are not specifically covered in this book:

- njamma-jamma (*Solanum scabrum*), also known as huckleberry leaf or country vegetable. Both the plant and the dish made with it are called *njamma-jamma*. The spicy sautéed greens, also known as Cameroonian green vegetables, are served with pounded corn.
- igbo (*Gnetum africanum*), also known as *fumbwa, afang, koko* and *ukazi*. This leaf vegetable and herbal medicine is collected in rainforests.
- Hausa potato (*Plectranthus rotundifolius*), also known as Chinese potato, Madagascar potato or coleus potato. This traditional food plant is found wild in Africa, as well as being cultivated there. It is valued mainly for its edible tubers, but the leaves are also eaten.

Bitter Leaf Soup

In Africa, cooks are judged by their bitter leaf soup. As they say, the leaves may be bitter but the soup shouldn't be. Everything but the kitchen sink seems to be included in this staple, with options that include smoked or dried salted fish, crayfish, beef, goat, chicken and various kinds of offal. In this relatively sedate (and less time-consuming) recipe, I stick to bitter leaf, okra and tomatoes in a traditional spicy peanut-coconut base. Bitter leaf soup is often served with fufu (pounded cassava, yam or plantain), but I prefer to add rice.

**Makes about
9 cups (2.25 L)**

Vegan Friendly

Soup

Tips

To prepare the bitter leaf for this recipe: Wash and massage the leaves in several changes of cold water until water runs clear. Add 1 tsp (5 mL) baking soda to a large saucepan of boiling water. Transfer leaves to pan and simmer over medium heat, covered, for about 15 minutes or until leaves have softened and taste assertive but not unpleasantly bitter. Drain, then rinse leaves in several changes of cold water until water runs clear. Drain, squeeze gently to extract excess liquid, and transfer to a cutting board. Chop into small pieces.

Scotch bonnet and habañero chile peppers are scorching hot. For a less spicy dish, devein the pepper or reduce the quantity.

2 tbsp	oil	30 mL
1	onion, diced	1
1	green bell pepper, diced	1
1	Scotch bonnet or habañero chile pepper, seeded and minced (see Tips, left)	1
2	cloves garlic, chopped	2
1 tbsp	finely chopped gingerroot	15 mL
4	tomatoes (1½ lbs/750 g total), peeled and chopped	4
2 cups	vegetable stock	500 mL
2 cups	water	500 mL
6 oz	bitter leaf leaves (40 to 45), precooked and chopped (see Tips, left)	175 g
1	bay leaf	1
1 tsp	kosher or coarse sea salt	5 mL
¼ tsp	freshly ground black pepper	1 mL
6 oz	okra, cut into ½-inch (1 cm) pieces (about 1½ cups/375 mL, loosely packed)	175 g
¼ cup	peanut butter	60 mL
¼ cup	coconut milk	60 mL
1 cup	cooked white or brown rice	250 mL

1. In a saucepan over medium heat, heat oil until shimmery. Add onion, green pepper, chile pepper, garlic and ginger. Cook, stirring often, for about 5 minutes, until softened and turning golden. Add tomatoes and stir for 1 minute. Add stock, water, bitter leaf, bay leaf, salt and pepper. When mixture comes to a simmer, reduce heat to low, cover and cook for about 30 minutes, until bitter leaf is very tender. Add okra, cover and simmer for 5 to 10 minutes, until okra is tender-crisp. Discard bay leaf.

2. In a small measuring cup, combine peanut butter and coconut milk; stir into soup. Add rice to soup and mix well. Serve warm.

Bitter Melon Vines

Momordica charantia

Other names: **African cucumber leaves, alligator pear leaves, balsam pear leaves, bitter cucumber leaves, gourd leaves, karella leaves, ugly grape leaves.**

Depending on where you are shopping, you may find bitter melon vines identified as *dahon ng ampalaya, daun peria, feuilles d'amer, foo gwa yip, goya, kaveli* or *la khoqua*.

Bitter melon vines are tropical and subtropical plants that probably originated in India and were transported to China in the 14th century. They are widely cultivated throughout Asia, Africa and the Caribbean.

The vines are famous for their fruit, which look like warty cucumbers. However, the leaves and shoots are also eaten as vegetables.

So far bitter melon is merely a curiosity in North American cuisine. However, the National Bitter Melon Council (www.bittermelon.org) was founded in 2005 to promote the vegetable. Its motto is "Better living through bitter melon."

Varieties

The vines may be plucked from bitter melon (*Momordica charantia*) cultivars ranging from the cucumber-shaped Chinese variety to the smaller, darker green Indian variety with pointed ends.

Buy It

Bitter melon vines are sold in Asian or Indian grocery stores in some regions. The fresh leaves are attractive and deeply lobed. However, frozen packaged leaves are much more common.

Although the greens are labeled "bitter melon leaves," they are more accurately described as vines. Frozen packages include leaves, thin stem segments, curly tendrils, a few baby gourds and, occasionally, small yellow flowers.

Tasting Notes

Not surprisingly, bitter melon vines are bitter! They are an acquired taste, beyond the pale even for many people who grew up with familiar bitter melon dishes. Besides being bitter, the thawed frozen leaves taste nutty, grassy and slightly sweet; they have a spinachy scent.

Health Notes

Bitter melon contains vitamins A and C and calcium. It is considered to be a potent herbal medicine. Steeped leaves have been used to lower blood sugar in diabetics; treat malaria and alcoholism; fight dysentery, colic, gastrointestinal problems and parasites; and alleviate hypertension and asthma.

Bitter melon is believed to impair fertility. It is also suspected of aggravating stomach ulcers when consumed in large quantities.

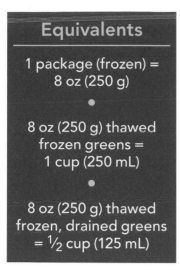

Equivalents

1 package (frozen) =
8 oz (250 g)

•

8 oz (250 g) thawed
frozen greens =
1 cup (250 mL)

•

8 oz (250 g) thawed
frozen, drained greens
= 1/2 cup (125 mL)

SUBSTITUTES

collards, turnip greens,
cassava leaves, bitter
leaf

Store It

If you can find fresh bitter melon vines, store them in a perforated resealable bag. They will keep in the refrigerator for up to three days.

Keep frozen bitter melon leaves in the freezer until you are ready to use them. Thaw them in the refrigerator overnight before using.

Prep It

Before consuming fresh bitter melon, wash the vines in cold water and spin-dry.

A package of frozen bitter melon vines contains up to 50 percent water. After thawing, the water may be used as cooking liquid or consumed as a tonic, but it tastes so bitter that draining is the best option. After draining, pull out any tough stems and wiry tendrils, then chop the greens.

Consume It

Bitter melon vines are not eaten raw. They are best added to soups, stews and stir-fries. Thawed frozen leaves are tender in 15 to 20 minutes.

Green Gourds

The foliage from many summer and winter squashes, pumpkins and gourds is edible and highly nutritious, including the following:

- In the West, the leaves of **pumpkins** (*Cucurbita maxima*) are left to wither away, coarsen and endure insect attacks on the ground while the gourds grow to massive sizes. However, these greens are popular in Africa and Asia, where they are added to salads, soups, stir-fries and wraps. The leaves, stemlets and tendrils are best plucked when pumpkins are tiny.
- The leaves, flowers, shoots and seeds of **Siam pumpkin** (*Cucurbita ficifolia*), also known as Malabar gourd or chilacayote, are used in Mexico and other countries. Mexicans also enjoy the leaves and stems of **chayote** (*Sechium edule*) and **zucchini** (*Cucurbita pepo*), also known as *guias*. *Sopa de guias* is squash vine soup, an Oaxacan dish.
- **Fluted pumpkin** (*Telfairia occidentalis*), also known as *iroko* or *ugu*, is a commercial crop in West Africa. This tropical vine is grown primarily for its edible leaves and seeds. Young shoots and leaves are added to soup. The leaves must be well washed and well cooked because they contain plant toxins.
- The leaves of **ivy gourds** (*Coccinia grandis* and *C. indica*) — also known as *tindola*, Indian perennial cucumber, miniature cucumber, scarlet gourd or *rau manh bat* — are cooked in Indian and Thai soups. In Burma the young leaves of the **bottle gourd** (*Lagenaria siceraria*) are boiled and eaten with a spicy sauce.
- The **luffa gourd** (*Luffa aegyptiaca, L. acutangula*) — also known as sponge cucumber, vegetable sponge, dishcloth gourd or Chinese okra — is a fascinating and versatile plant. The fruit and greens are edible. Matured, dried and processed, the fruit becomes a loofah sponge. Luffa gourds come in both smooth and ridged types (also known as *turi*).

Mongo

Here's a classic from the Philippines starring mung beans (mongo) and bitter melon vines, which Filipinos call dahon ng ampalaya. *This dish does have a bitter edge, but it's mitigated by the creamy beans, spicy chile and tart tomatoes and lime. Serve it with rice.*

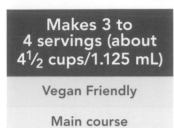

Makes 3 to 4 servings (about 4½ cups/1.125 mL)		
Vegan Friendly		
Main course		

Tips

Use whole green mung beans in this recipe, not the split mung beans that Indians call dal.

Bird's-eye chile peppers are also known as bird or Thai chiles. They are tiny, hot peppers about 1 to 1½ inches (2.5 to 3 cm) long. Handle hot chiles carefully and wear gloves when cutting them. Before chopping, slice the chile lengthwise and scrape out the seeds. If you wish to temper its heat, devein and rinse it. You can substitute any chile pepper you prefer for the bird's-eye chile in this recipe.

For the finest minced garlic, push it through a press.

After draining the bitter melon, discard any tough stems and wiry tendrils.

1 cup	mung beans (see Tips, left)	250 mL
1½ tsp	kosher or coarse sea salt, divided	7 mL
¼ cup	extra virgin olive oil	60 mL
1	onion, diced	1
1	red bird's-eye chile pepper, chopped (see Tips, left)	1
2	large cloves garlic, minced (see Tips, left)	2
3	small tomatoes (12 oz/375 g total), chopped	3
2	packages (8 oz/250 g each) frozen bitter melon vines, thawed, drained and chopped (see Tips, left)	2
1 cup	vegetable stock	250 mL
	Lime wedges	

1. In a pot of cold water, soak mung beans overnight. Drain, return to pot, cover generously with water and bring to a boil over medium-high heat. Reduce heat to medium-low and simmer for about 20 minutes, until barely tender. Add 1 tsp (5 mL) salt. Simmer for 10 to 20 minutes, until tender. Drain and set aside.

2. In a large skillet over medium heat, heat oil until shimmery. Add onion and chile pepper. Cook, stirring often, for about 5 minutes, until softened and golden. Add garlic and stir for 20 seconds. Add tomatoes and remaining salt. Cook, stirring often, for 1 minute. Stir in bitter melon vines and stock. When mixture comes to a simmer, reduce heat to medium-low and cook for about 15 minutes, until greens are tender. Add beans and stir gently to combine. Season with salt to taste.

3. Ladle into serving bowls. Serve with lime wedges alongside to squeeze overtop.

Bok Choy

Brassica rapa chinensis

Other names: **Chinese cabbage/chard/mustard, Chinese celery cabbage, Chinese chard cabbage, Chinese white cabbage, loose-headed Chinese cabbage, snow/spoon cabbage, white mustard cabbage.**

Depending on where you are shopping, you may find bok choy identified as *bai cai, cai thuong hai, cavolo cinese, chongee, joi choi, pak choi, pechay, phakkat farang, samho, sesawi putih, shakushina* **or** *taisui.*

Bok choy is native to central Asia. Although cultivated in China since the fifth century, it was introduced to Europe only in the 1800s. It is now commonly grown in North America.

Widely used in the cuisines of China, Thailand, Laos, the Philippines, Vietnam, Korea, Singapore and Malaysia, bok choy was introduced to the West wherever Asians settled. It has gone from being an exotic ingredient to a supermarket staple. It is now the most popular Asian vegetable in North America.

Varieties

There are dozens of varieties of bok choy (*Brassica rapa chinensis*) that North Americans rarely encounter. Although the name is translated as "white vegetable," not all varieties are white. Cultivars include tall and dwarf types, sweet hybrids and thick- or thin-stalked vegetables.

Mature bok choy may be up to 20 inches (50 cm) long. In comparison to standard bok choy, oversized varieties such as a Taiwan cultivar are bigger and heavier, while long bok choy is slenderer and taller, with stalks that are not as coarse.

Baby bok choy is no more than 6 inches (15 cm) long and is valued for its tenderness. The designation "baby" refers to either immature plants or dwarf and extra-dwarf cultivars. Dwarf bok choy, sometimes called Canton bok choy or *miu bok choy*, is short and squat, with plump white stems. It is succulent but is described as mild or bland, depending on one's taste. Extremely small baby or dwarf bok choy may be labeled "bok choy sprouts," although they are not actually sprouted greens.

Tasting Notes

Bok choy has distinct cabbage and mustard flavors. The stalks are crunchy, succulent and slightly sweet and briny. The leaves are peppery.

Health Notes

Bok choy contains vitamins A, B$_6$, C and K, calcium, folate, iron, magnesium, manganese, niacin, phosphorus, potassium, riboflavin and thiamin.

Bok choy has been used in traditional Chinese medicine to boost metabolism, treat diabetes, promote digestion, combat constipation, strengthen bones and relieve fever, sore throat and sinusitis.

Equivalents

1 head bok choy =
1¼ to 1½ lbs
(625 to 750 g)

•

1 Shanghai bok choy =
7 to 8 oz (210 to 250 g)

•

1 baby bok choy or bok
choy sum = 2 to 3 oz
(60 to 90 g)

•

1 dwarf bok choy =
¼ to ½ oz (7 to 15 g)

•

2 oz (60 g) whole
dwarf bok choy =
1¾ cups (425 mL)

•

2 oz (60 g) chopped
bok choy =
⅔ cup (150 mL),
loosely packed

•

2 oz (60 g) bok choy
cut into 1-inch (2.5 cm)
pieces or slices =
¾ cup (175 mL),
loosely packed

•

2 oz (60 g) bok
choy sum cut into
½-inch (1 cm) slices
= 1⅓ cups (325 mL),
loosely packed

Even smaller are bok choy shoots, which have just a few leaflets per cluster, but these are larger than microgreens (see page 241).

Shanghai bok choy (*Brassica rapa chinensis utilis*) is a small, green-stemmed type (see "The Green White Vegetable," page 67). Other non-white varieties include new hybrids with red or purple leaves or crimson veins.

Japanese white celery mustard is a bok choy of Japanese origin.

Bok choy sum refers to bok choy hearts. Like romaine hearts, they have been stripped down to the tender inner core. Bok choy sum comes in clusters of four or five stalks. Do not confuse it with yu choy sum (see "What Is Choy Sum, Anyway?" on page 428).

Buy It

Bok choy is sold in supermarkets year-round but is thought to be at its best in winter.

The stalks of standard bok choy are thick and creamy white, with firm crinkled, frilled dark green leaves. Choose bok choy that feels heavy for its size. Avoid cracked or limp stalks and wilted or yellowed leaves. Rusty discoloration on the stalks is undesirable; however, dark speckles on some specimens are naturally occurring (like freckles), not necessarily a sign of rot.

Store It

Swathe bok choy tightly in plastic wrap or wrap in lightly dampened paper towels, place in a resealable bag and refrigerate.

Bok choy will keep in the refrigerator for up to five days.

Prep It

Before cooking bok choy, peel off any damaged or discolored outer leaves. Cut a thin slice off the base to get rid of discolored or dry ends.

Slice or chop bok choy. To avoid long, swampy strands (unappealing clumps of greens) in soups, cut in quarters lengthwise, then slice crosswise. Baby bok choy may be halved lengthwise through the core and stir-fried as is.

Wash bok choy after cutting it, then spin-dry. Baby bok choy may also be patted dry. If you are not chopping or slicing bok choy, halve it through the core, then soak and swish the halves in a large bowl of cold water. Place the halves on a rack to dry. Bok choy may also be separated into stalks and washed.

Consume It

Despite its popularity in the West, bok choy remains firmly associated with Chinese cuisine. It can be stir-fried, steamed, braised or grilled. Baby bok choy is tender enough to enjoy raw in mixed salads or with dips. Use larger bok choy in cooked dishes.

Do not overcook bok choy; it should end up tender-crisp. Halved baby bok choy may be steamed for 5 minutes or seared in a grill pan for 8 to 10 minutes. Add chopped bok choy to cooked dishes during the last few minutes.

Serve stir-fried, braised or grilled bok choy immediately. It is so juicy that it weeps while cooking and continues to seep as it stands. (Serving bok choy over rice to soak up the juices is an excellent solution.) You may wish to increase the heat to high in the last minute to evaporate excess liquid. Also note that bok choy will dilute sauces, so make sauces thick to begin with.

SUBSTITUTES

tatsoi, Chinese broccoli, yu choy sum, napa cabbage, Swiss chard, komatsuna

The Green White Vegetable

Nowadays in the supermarket, there's sibling rivalry in the bok choy family. Common bok choy is jostling for shelf space with Shanghai bok choy. *Bok choy* translates as "white vegetable" but Shanghai bok choy is olive green, so it may be more accurate to call it by its other, lesser-known names: Shanghai cabbage, Shanghai choy sum, green baby bok choy, *ching cai* ("green vegetable") or *chingensai* ("green stemmed vegetable").

This small cultivar is lauded as the most popular vegetable in Shanghai. Devotees swear that it tastes better than common bok choy. Its leaves are lighter green and smoother and its pastel green stalks more flexible. It is not as succulent, so it doesn't release as much water when cooked. Shanghai bok choy also comes in a dwarf or tiny *miu* version.

Bok Choy, Tofu and Shiitake Stir-Fry

This classic combo of Asian greens, meaty mushrooms and saucy tofu adds up to a vegetarian delight. Serve it over rice or Asian noodles.

Makes 4 servings

Vegan Friendly

Main course

Tips

To prepare the bok choy for this recipe: Trim the base, then slice the head lengthwise into quarters. Slice each quarter crosswise into 1-inch (2.5 cm) pieces.

To maintain more control over the saltiness of dishes, use reduced-sodium soy sauce. Depending on the type, 1 tbsp (15 mL) regular soy sauce can contain 1,000 mg sodium or more. Reduced-sodium soy sauce contains about half that amount.

Toasted sesame oil, also known as Asian sesame oil, is made from toasted or roasted sesame seeds. Dark and aromatic, it is sold in small bottles as a flavoring agent. Do not confuse toasted sesame oil with yellow sesame oil, which is pressed from raw seeds.

For the finest minced garlic, push it through a press.

To grate or purée gingerroot, use a kitchen rasp such as the type made by Microplane.

- Wok

¼ cup	vegetable stock	60 mL
1 tbsp	soy sauce (see Tips, left)	15 mL
1 tsp	toasted sesame oil (see Tips, left)	5 mL
1 tsp	granulated sugar	5 mL
½ tsp	hot pepper flakes	2 mL
2 tbsp	oil, divided	30 mL
1	head bok choy (1¼ lbs/625 g), sliced into 1-inch (2.5 cm) pieces (see Tips, left)	1
1 tsp	kosher or coarse sea salt, divided	5 mL
4 oz	shiitake mushrooms, stemmed and thickly sliced	125 g
2	cloves garlic, minced (see Tips, left)	2
1 tsp	puréed gingerroot (see Tips, left)	5 mL
8 oz	medium-firm tofu, drained and cut into ½-inch (1 cm) cubes	250 g

1. In a small bowl, combine stock, soy sauce, sesame oil, sugar and hot pepper flakes. Set aside.

2. Heat a wok over medium-high heat for 1 minute. Swirl in 1 tbsp (15 mL) oil. Add bok choy and ½ tsp (2 mL) salt. Stir quickly to coat, then cook without disturbing for about 2 minutes, until tender-crisp. Transfer to a bowl and set aside.

3. Swirl remaining oil in wok. Add mushrooms and remaining salt. Stir-fry for 3 to 4 minutes, until they are softened, start to turn golden and sound squeaky. Push mushrooms to one side of wok. To center of wok, add garlic and ginger; stir-fry for 20 seconds. Add tofu and shake wok to combine. Add bok choy and prepared stock mixture. Stir-fry for about 1 minute, until sauce bubbles and thickens. Serve immediately.

Baby Bok Choy with Soy Glaze

A delicious soy glaze is the only finishing touch needed for crunchy baby bok choy. Grilling sweetens the juices of bok choy, and the smoky charred edges of the leaves taste like kale chips. Warning: this glaze is addictive. You can also brush it over tofu or steamed vegetables, or drizzle it over eggs.

Makes 4 to 6 servings
Vegan Friendly
Side dish

Tips

Instead of using a grill pan, barbecue the bok choy.

To maintain more control over the saltiness of dishes, use reduced-sodium soy sauce. Depending on the type, 1 tbsp (15 mL) regular soy sauce can contain 1,000 mg sodium or more. Reduced-sodium soy sauce contains about half that amount.

Any type of chile paste works well in this dish. Sambal oelek is one of my favorites.

For the finest minced garlic, push it through a press.

Shaoxing wine is a Chinese rice wine traditionally used for cooking. You can find it in Asian supermarkets. If you don't have any, substitute dry sherry.

- Grill pan

Bok Choy

1 lb	baby bok choy, trimmed, halved lengthwise and patted dry	500 g
2 tbsp	oil	30 mL
	Kosher or coarse sea salt	
	Freshly ground black pepper	

Soy Glaze

1 tbsp	water	15 mL
1 tsp	cornstarch	5 mL
¼ cup	vegetable stock	60 mL
2 tbsp	soy sauce (see Tips, left)	30 mL
1 tbsp	liquid honey or vegan alternative	15 mL
¼ tsp	chile paste (see Tips, left)	1 mL
1 tbsp	oil	15 mL
1	small shallot, finely chopped	1
1	clove garlic, minced (see Tips, left)	1
¼ cup	Shaoxing cooking wine (see Tips, left)	60 mL

1. *Bok Choy:* In a bowl, combine bok choy and oil. Season with salt and pepper to taste. Using your hands, toss gently to coat.

2. Heat grill pan over medium heat for 3 to 5 minutes. Working in batches, grill bok choy in a single layer, cut side down, for 8 to 10 minutes, turning once and pressing down occasionally, until lightly charred (stalks should be tender-crisp and leaves should be crispy at the edges). Transfer to a serving platter as completed.

3. *Soy Glaze:* Meanwhile, in a small bowl, combine water and cornstarch; set aside. In a small measuring cup, combine stock, soy sauce, honey and chile paste; set aside.

4. In a small saucepan over medium heat, heat oil until shimmery. Add shallot and garlic. Cook, stirring constantly, for about 1 minute, until softened. Stir in wine and simmer for 1 minute. Add stock mixture and simmer for about 2 minutes, until slightly syrupy. Stir cornstarch slurry and drizzle into pan. Cook for 30 to 60 seconds, until glaze bubbles and thickens. Remove from heat (do not cover).

5. Brush or drizzle bok choy halves with glaze. Serve immediately.

Sea Salt and Chile Shanghai Bok Choy

When you are short on time but long for flavor, this superfast and simple stir-fry hits the spot. Serve the crunchy bok choy over rice to capture its tasty juices.

Makes 4 servings

Vegan Friendly

Side dish

Tips

For the finest minced garlic, push it through a press.

Finger chiles are also known as cayenne peppers. They are slender, with pointed tips. You can substitute any kind of red chile you prefer.

Sea salt is light and flaky, and different types vary in saltiness. Adjust the amount according to your taste.

I use Shanghai bok choy in this recipe because it doesn't release as much water as white bok choy. To evaporate as much excess liquid as possible, cook this bok choy over high heat.

To sliver green onions, use a sharp knife to cut thin slices on an extreme diagonal from the root end to the stalk.

- Wok

2	large cloves garlic, minced (see Tips, left)	2
1	large red finger chile, seeded and chopped (see Tips, left)	1
2 tsp	coarse sea salt (see Tips, left)	10 mL
1 tsp	granulated sugar (see Tips, page 132)	5 mL
2 tbsp	oil	30 mL
2	large Shanghai bok choy (1 lb/500 g total), trimmed, halved lengthwise and cut crosswise into 1-inch (2.5 cm) pieces	2
2	green onions (white and green parts), slivered (see Tips, left)	2

1. In a small bowl, combine garlic, chile, salt and sugar. Set aside.
2. Heat wok on high heat for 1 minute. Swirl in oil. Add bok choy and stir-fry for about 1 minute, until softened. Add garlic mixture and stir-fry for about 1 minute, until tender-crisp. Remove from heat and stir in onions. Serve immediately.

Brussels Sprouts

Brassica oleracea gemmifera

Other names: **Brussels cabbage.**
Depending on where you are shopping, you may find Brussels sprouts identified as *briseles kaposit, brukselka, cai brussel, cavolo di Bruxelles, choux de Bruxelles, cols de brussel, prokulica, rosenkohl* or *spruitjes.*

Brussels sprouts look like tiny cabbages, because that's what they are. According to culinary historians, the first written reference to Brussels sprouts dates back to 1587 in Belgium, where they were by then an important crop — hence the name. By the late 18th century they were being grown in France and England. Former US president Thomas Jefferson is credited with introducing Brussels sprouts to North America in 1812.

Brussels sprouts have landed on several "most hated vegetable" lists, possibly because they are sulfurous when overcooked. Nevertheless, in many homes in North America they are still a must for holiday dinners.

Tasting Notes

Brussels sprouts have an assertive, nutty, slightly sweet yet slightly bitter flavor.

Health Notes

Brussels sprouts contain vitamins A, B_6, C and K, copper, folate, iron, magnesium, manganese, phosphorus, potassium, riboflavin and thiamin.

In herbal medicine, Brussels sprouts are believed to promote a healthy colon, improve vision and skin, and combat thinning hair.

Varieties

Brussels sprouts (*Brassica oleracea gemmifera*) cultivars range from early- to late-season varieties but are otherwise fairly standardized.

Red Brussels sprouts are an heirloom variety rarely seen by mainstream shoppers. This cultivar, known as 'Rubine', is actually purple.

A new hybrid called 'Flower Sprouts' is a cross between Brussels sprouts and kale. Like Brussels sprouts, its rosettes grow on stalks, but the leaves are looser.

Buy It

Brussels sprouts are usually sold loose in supermarkets. You might be surprised to see how they look *au naturel*: as buds growing on long, thick, fibrous stalks. Some supermarkets have started to sell Brussels sprouts on the stalk as a curiosity, or perhaps to rev up enthusiasm for this familiar vegetable.

The outer leaves are dark green, the inner leaves pastel green or yellow. Brussels sprouts should be packed into tight heads. Check for bright leaves with no blemishes, yellowing or browning at the edges and no tiny insect holes.

Sprouts vary in size. Smaller sprouts, 1 to $1^1/_2$ inches (2.5 to 4 cm) in diameter, are tenderer.

Store It

Place Brussels sprouts in a perforated resealable bag, add a paper towel to absorb any excess moisture and refrigerate.

Although Brussels sprouts will keep in the refrigerator for several weeks, they are best consumed within three days. They become stronger tasting the longer you store them.

Prep It

Before cooking Brussels sprouts, peel off any damaged, darkened or discolored outer leaves. Trim a thin slice off the base to remove any dry, discolored parts.

If you wish to mellow Brussels sprouts and temper any bitterness, soak them in cold salted water for 15 minutes before cooking.

To cook Brussels sprouts whole, cut an X in the base. This channels more heat to the core and promotes even cooking. Save any leaves that fall off and cook them separately or for a shorter time.

Brussels sprouts may also be halved, quartered, sliced, shredded or deconstructed into leaves and cores before cooking.

SUBSTITUTES

savoy cabbage, green
cabbage

To shred, halve each Brussels sprout lengthwise through the core, then cut it crosswise. To chop finely, halve each Brussels sprout lengthwise through the core, make cuts lengthwise through each half, and slice crosswise.

Sprouts have multiple personalities — the core is tough but the leaves are tender — so cooking them evenly can pose a conundrum. One solution is to deconstruct them. Slice off the base and pluck all the loose leaves, then slice off more of the base to get more loose leaves. Keep going until you reach the tight, light green core. Cook the cores and leaves separately. The core may be steamed and the leaves sautéed (see Two-Way Brussels Sprouts, page 76).

Consume It

You can eat the cores raw in salad, as you would cabbage. However, Brussels sprouts are generally boiled, steamed, sautéed or roasted.

For even cooking, choose Brussels sprouts of a similar size. They are ready in about 10 minutes if boiled, 12 minutes if steamed. They float, so cover the pan partially when boiling, to keep in the steam.

Overcooked Brussels sprouts are mushy and smell sulfurous. A sign of overcooking: the color transitions from vibrant green to a dull khaki

Although tradition tells you the opposite, Brussels sprouts are best when prepared with higher heat and the use of fat. The goal is to cook them as fast as possible to bring out their slightly sweet, nutty flavor. Thus they should be halved or quartered or, better still, shredded before sautéing.

Sautéed Brussels sprouts can end up rubbery unless they are steam-fried. To steam-fry, place the sprouts in a pan with oil and sauté over medium heat to soften and coat them. Add a bit of stock or water, reduce the heat to medium-low, cover and cook for 8 to 10 minutes, until tender. Then uncover the pan and sauté briefly over high heat to evaporate any excess liquid.

Brussels Sprouts with Almond Thyme Butter

Almond thyme butter transforms simple steamed Brussels sprouts from ordinary to extraordinary. Use the luscious leftover butter to add excitement to other steamed vegetables.

Makes 4 servings

Vegan Friendly

Side dish

Tips

To prepare Brussels sprouts for this recipe: Trim and cut a shallow X in the base of each sprout. Reserve any leaves that fall off in a separate pile.

To toast almonds, cook them in a dry skillet over medium heat, stirring often, for about 3 minutes or until golden and aromatic.

- Food processor

1 lb	Brussels sprouts, trimmed (see Tips, left)	500 g
1/3 cup	slivered almonds, toasted, divided (see Tips, left)	75 mL
1/4 cup	unsalted butter or non-dairy alternative, softened	60 mL
2 tsp	finely grated lemon zest	10 mL
1/2 tsp	fresh thyme leaves	2 mL
1 tsp	liquid honey or vegan alternative	5 mL
1/2 tsp	kosher or coarse sea salt	2 mL

1. In a covered steamer basket over boiling water 1 inch (2.5 cm) deep, cook Brussels sprouts for 10 to 12 minutes, until tender but firm, adding loose leaves midway through the cooking time.

2. Meanwhile, in bowl of food processor fitted with the metal blade, process all but 1 tbsp (15 mL) almonds until finely ground but not pasty. Add butter, lemon zest, thyme, honey and salt. Pulse a few times, just until combined; you should end up with 1/2 cup (125 mL).

3. Remove steamer basket from heat and set aside for 1 minute to allow Brussels sprouts to drain and release steam. Transfer sprouts to a serving dish and add almond butter to taste (you will have some left over); toss to coat evenly. Scatter reserved almonds overtop. Serve immediately.

Variation

Pecan Thyme Butter: Substitute an equal amount of coarsely chopped toasted pecans for the almonds.

Braised and Glazed Brussels Sprouts with Crumb Topping

Crunchy, garlicky, herbed crumb topping is the perfect finishing touch for these humble but fabulous Brussels sprouts. The braise cooks down to a glaze, concentrating the flavors. Serve this dish over pasta, rice or quinoa.

2 tbsp	extra virgin olive oil	30 mL
1 lb	Brussels sprouts, trimmed (see Tips, left)	500 g
½ cup	vegetable stock (see Tips, left)	125 mL
½ tsp	kosher or coarse sea salt	2 mL
	Freshly ground black pepper	
¾ cup	Garlic Herb Crumb Topping (page 456)	175 mL

Makes 4 servings

Vegan Friendly

Side dish

Tips

To prepare Brussels sprouts for this recipe: Trim and cut a shallow X in the base of each sprout. Reserve any leaves that fall off in a separate pile.

For best results, use a 10-inch (25 cm) sauté pan or saucepan, which will reduce crowding in the pan and promote even cooking.

Whenever possible, use reduced-sodium vegetable stock. Not only is it healthier, it also allows you to better control the saltiness of a dish.

1. In a wide saucepan (see Tips, left) over medium heat, heat oil until shimmery. Add Brussels sprouts and cook, shaking pan occasionally, for about 3 minutes, until browned and shiny. Add stock and salt. Cover, reduce heat to medium-low and cook for 10 to 15 minutes, until sprouts are tender but firm and glazed, with most of the liquid evaporated. Add loose leaves midway through the cooking time. If necessary, uncover, increase heat to high and cook for 1 minute to evaporate excess liquid.

2. Transfer to a serving dish. Season with pepper to taste. Scatter crumbs overtop, to taste (you may have some left over). Serve immediately.

Two-Way Brussels Sprouts

Julia Child, whom I met at a **Toronto Star** *cooking demo in the 1980s, taught me this valuable lesson: some foods should be deconstructed to bring out the best in them. Deconstructing Brussels sprouts involves extra prep work, but the effort is worthwhile. The buttery boiled cores contrast nicely with their bed of peppery sautéed leaves.*

Makes 4 servings

Vegan Friendly

Side dish

Tips

To prepare Brussels sprouts for this recipe: Use a paring knife to cut the base off each sprout, then pluck all the loose leaves. Trim more off base as necessary to loosen more leaves. Keep going until you reach the tight pastel yellow-green core. Reserve leaves and cores in separate piles.

The quantity of leaves and cores you end up with depends on the Brussels sprouts. Premium light green sprouts from a specialty greengrocer yield twice as many leaves as the dark green specimens from the supermarket.

1 lb	Brussels sprouts, trimmed and deconstructed (see Tips, left)	500 g
1 tbsp	extra virgin olive oil	15 mL
½ tsp	kosher or coarse sea salt	2 mL
¼ tsp	freshly ground black pepper	1 mL
½ cup	vegetable stock or water	125 mL
1 tbsp	unsalted butter or non-dairy alternative, cubed and softened	15 mL
¼ cup	hazelnuts, toasted and finely chopped (see Tips, page 194)	60 mL

1. In a pot of boiling salted water over medium heat, cook Brussels sprouts cores for about 10 minutes, until tender but firm. Drain.

2. Meanwhile, in a large skillet over medium heat, heat oil until shimmery. Add Brussels sprouts leaves, salt and pepper. Sauté for 3 to 4 minutes, until softened and lightly charred. Add stock, cover, reduce heat to low and cook for about 5 minutes, until leaves are tender-crisp and glazed but not wet. If necessary, uncover, increase heat to medium-high and cook for 1 minute to evaporate excess liquid.

3. Transfer leaves to a serving platter and arrange cores on top. Top hot cores with butter and allow to melt. Scatter hazelnuts overtop. Serve immediately.

Scratch Bubble and Squeak

The British recycle leftovers from Sunday dinner into a tasty mishmash called "bubble and squeak." The dish traditionally includes mashed potatoes and cabbage or Brussels sprouts. Bubble and squeak is too tasty to leave to chance, so I make it from scratch, starting with roasted vegetables. I use a cast-iron pan to develop a golden brown crust on the potatoes. It's wonderful with poached eggs or a big green salad.

Makes 6 to 8 servings
Vegan Friendly
Main course

Tips

To prepare the carrots for this recipe: Use a sharp paring knife to trim the carrots, separating the roots from the greens. Dice roots and set aside. Strip leaves from stems, discarding stems, and finely chop the leaves.

For best results, use russet potatoes, which are fluffy when mashed. Waxy red or white potatoes tend to become gluey when mashed.

- Preheat oven to 400°F (200°C)
- Rimmed baking sheet

8 oz	Brussels sprouts, trimmed and quartered	250 g
4	carrots with greens (8 oz/250 g total), trimmed, roots diced and leaves finely chopped (see Tips, left)	4
1	large turnip (6 oz/175 g), cut into ¼-inch (0.5 cm) dice	1
1	onion, cut into ½-inch (1 cm) pieces	1
¼ cup	extra virgin olive oil, divided	60 mL
1½ tsp	kosher or coarse sea salt, divided (see Tips, page 81)	7 mL
3	potatoes (2 lbs/1 kg total), peeled and cut into 1-inch (2.5 cm) chunks (see Tips, left)	3
½ cup	sour cream (14%) or non-dairy alternative	125 mL
	Freshly ground white pepper	
2 tbsp	unsalted butter or non-dairy alternative	30 mL
2 tbsp	chopped fresh chives	30 mL

1. On baking sheet, combine Brussels sprouts, carrot roots, turnip and onion with 2 tbsp (30 mL) oil and ½ tsp (2 mL) salt. Cover tightly with foil. Roast in preheated oven for 10 minutes. Uncover, stir and roast for about 15 minutes, until tender.

2. Meanwhile, in a pot of boiling salted water, cook potatoes over medium heat, until tender. Drain, then return to pan, reduce heat to low and cook for 1 minute, shaking once or twice to release steam. Remove from heat. Add sour cream and season with remaining salt and pepper to taste. Using a potato masher, mash until fairly smooth. Add roasted vegetables and carrot leaves and stir to combine. Season with salt to taste.

3. In a large skillet (preferably cast iron) over medium-high heat, melt butter with remaining oil. Add potato mixture. Using a spatula, even out and gently pat down mixture. Cook for about 5 minutes, until bottom is browned. Flip sections with a spatula, then even out and gently pat down. Cook for about 5 minutes, until bottom is browned. Transfer to a serving platter or individual plates. Sprinkle with chives. Serve hot.

Variation

Substitute coarsely chopped cabbage for the Brussels sprouts.

Festive Brussels Sprouts

This hearty, healthy dish dolls up Brussels sprouts with pearl onions, walnuts and cranberries. It is right at home on a festive holiday table, but you can treat yourself and prepare it for a family meal anytime.

Makes 2 to 4 servings

Vegan Friendly

Side dish

Tips

To peel pearl onions, blanch them for 30 seconds in boiling water, then shock them with cold water until they are cool enough to handle. Using a paring knife, trim the root and pull off the skin.

Whenever possible, use reduced-sodium vegetable stock. Not only is it healthier, it also allows you to better control the saltiness of a dish.

To toast walnuts, cook them in a dry skillet over medium heat, stirring often, for about 3 minutes, until golden and aromatic.

2 tbsp	unsalted butter or non-dairy alternative, divided	30 mL
2 tbsp	extra virgin olive oil, divided	30 mL
1 cup	red pearl onions, halved lengthwise (see Tips, left)	250 mL
1 lb	Brussels sprouts, trimmed and halved lengthwise, loose leaves reserved	500 g
⅓ cup	dried cranberries	75 mL
½ tsp	kosher or coarse sea salt	2 mL
½ cup	vegetable stock (see Tips, left)	125 mL
	Freshly ground black pepper	
½ cup	walnut halves, toasted and coarsely chopped (see Tips, left)	125 mL

1. In a large skillet over medium heat, melt 1 tbsp (15 mL) butter with 1 tbsp (15 mL) oil. Add onions, cut side down, and cook undisturbed for 2 to 3 minutes, until cut sides are golden brown. Transfer to a bowl and set aside.

2. In same skillet over medium heat, melt remaining butter with remaining oil. Add sprouts, cut side down, and cook undisturbed for 3 to 4 minutes, until cut sides are golden brown. Add loose leaves, onions and their oil, cranberries, salt and stock and stir to combine. When mixture comes to a simmer, cover, reduce heat to low and cook for 10 to 12 minutes, until Brussels sprouts are tender-crisp and glazed but not wet. If necessary, uncover, increase heat to high and shake pan to evaporate excess liquid.

3. Transfer mixture to a serving dish. Season with pepper to taste. Scatter walnuts overtop. Serve warm.

The Brussels Caper

People don't often use the words "yummy" and "Brussels sprouts" in the same sentence, but they do apply to this dish. Serve these over rice or your favorite cooked grain.

Makes 4 servings

Vegan Friendly

Side dish

Tip

Stand back when you add the capers to the hot oil — they will spatter. If you have a spatter screen, now is the time to use it.

- Preheat oven to 400°F (200°C)

¼ cup	extra virgin olive oil	60 mL
¼ cup	capers, drained and patted dry	60 mL
1 lb	Brussels sprouts, trimmed and quartered lengthwise	500 g
1 tsp	kosher or coarse sea salt	5 mL
⅓ cup	vegetable stock (see Tips, page 78)	75 mL
½ cup	hazelnuts, toasted and chopped (see Tips, page 194)	125 mL
	Freshly ground black pepper	

1. In a skillet over medium heat, heat oil until shimmery. Add capers and fry for about 1 minute, until they pop open. Add Brussels sprouts and salt and stir for about 1 minute, until coated. Add stock. Cover, reduce heat to medium-low and cook, stirring once, for 8 to 10 minutes, until sprouts are tender but firm and liquid has evaporated. If necessary, uncover, increase heat to high and shake pan for about 1 minute to evaporate excess liquid. Add hazelnuts and stir for about 1 minute. Season with pepper to taste and serve immediately.

Maple Walnut Brussels Sprouts

Maple walnut is not just an ice-cream flavor. In this recipe caramelized sprouts get the sweet-and-sour treatment, thanks to maple syrup and balsamic vinegar.

Makes 4 servings

Vegan Friendly

Side dish

Tip

The heady fragrance and distinctive taste of unrefined walnut oil is irresistible. You can find it in gourmet food shops and well-stocked supermarkets.

- Preheat oven to 400°F (200°C)
- Rimmed baking sheet

1 lb	Brussels sprouts, trimmed and halved lengthwise	500 g
1 tbsp	walnut oil (see Tips, left)	15 mL
½ tsp	kosher or coarse sea salt	2 mL
	Freshly ground black pepper	
2 tsp	maple syrup	10 mL
2 tsp	balsamic vinegar	10 mL
¼ cup	walnut pieces, toasted and coarsely chopped (see Tips, page 78)	60 mL

1. In a bowl, combine sprouts, oil, and salt and pepper to taste; toss to coat evenly. Transfer to baking sheet and arrange cut side down. Cover pan tightly with foil and roast for 15 minutes in preheated oven. Uncover and roast for about 10 minutes longer, until browned and tender.

2. Transfer to a serving bowl. Toss with maple syrup, then vinegar. Scatter with walnuts and serve immediately.

Curried Brussels Sprouts

It may seem strange to curry such a quintessentially North American vegetable, but this fusion works. With the addition of chunks of paneer (Indian fresh cheese) and tomato sauce enlivened by the pop of whole cumin seeds, these Brussels sprouts make a hearty meal. Serve with warm flatbread or basmati rice.

Makes 2 to 4 servings

Vegan Friendly

Main course

Tips

To peel tomatoes easily, use a serrated peeler.

To purée tomatoes, use a food processor or the large holes of a box grater. Do not substitute canned tomatoes in this recipe — the sauce will become pasty rather than loose.

Garam masala is a traditional spice blend sold in Indian grocery stores, specialty shops and well-stocked supermarkets.

Some supermarkets now sell paneer, which is a fresh, mild Indian cheese. If yours doesn't have it, look for it in an Indian grocery store. There is no good vegan cheese equivalent of paneer, but tofu may be substituted.

2 tbsp	unsalted butter or non-dairy alternative	30 mL
2 tbsp	oil	30 mL
1	large shallot, diced	1
1 tsp	cumin seeds	5 mL
4	tomatoes (1½ lbs/750 g total), peeled and puréed (see Tips, left)	4
1 tsp	kosher or coarse sea salt	5 mL
1 tsp	garam masala (see Tips, left)	5 mL
½ tsp	ground cayenne pepper	2 mL
¼ tsp	ground turmeric	1 mL
1 lb	Brussels sprouts, trimmed and quartered lengthwise	500 g
½ cup	water	125 mL
8 oz	paneer or firm tofu, cut into ½-inch (1 cm) cubes (see Tips, left)	250 g

1. In a large saucepan over medium heat, melt butter with oil. Add shallot and cumin and cook, stirring occasionally, for about 1 minute, until shallot is softened and fragrant. Stir in tomatoes, salt, garam masala, cayenne and turmeric. Cook, stirring occasionally, for about 5 minutes, until thickened and oil starts to separate.

2. Add Brussels sprouts and water and stir to combine. When mixture comes to a simmer, reduce heat to low, cover and cook for 20 to 30 minutes, until sprouts are tender-crisp. Increase heat to medium-low, stir in paneer and simmer for about 5 minutes, until heated through. Season with salt to taste. Serve immediately.

Brussels and Yukon Hash

This hash, which combines Brussels sprouts and Yukon Gold potatoes, is good for breakfast, lunch or dinner. Top it with a poached egg or serve a tomato salad alongside.

Makes 2 to 4 servings

Vegan Friendly

Main course

Tips

Yellow-fleshed potatoes are best for this recipe. Neither waxy nor dry, they are good all-purpose potatoes. The best-known yellow-fleshed potatoes are Yukon Golds.

I prefer kosher salt because it tastes better than iodized table salt and (ideally) contains no additives. Table salts and some sea salts contain additives such as iodine compounds (iodides), anti-clumping agents and even sugar (in the form of dextrose, which is used to stabilize iodine). Although the North American Salt Institute states that kosher salt "contains no additives," some kosher salt brands do contain additives such as anti-clumping agents. If you have concerns, check the label.

For the finest minced garlic, push it through a press.

It's best to cook hash in a cast-iron skillet. Hash prepared in a stainless steel skillet is likely to scorch.

2 tbsp	extra virgin olive oil	30 mL
12 oz	Brussels sprouts, trimmed, halved lengthwise and sliced crosswise into thick shreds	375 g
2	large Yukon Gold potatoes (1 lb/500 g total), cut into ½-inch (1 cm) cubes (see Tips, left)	2
1 tsp	kosher or coarse sea salt (see Tips, left)	5 mL
1 cup	diced red onion	250 mL
4	cloves garlic, minced (see Tips, left)	4
1 tbsp	fresh thyme leaves	15 mL
1 tsp	finely grated lemon zest	5 mL
2 tbsp	unsalted butter or non-dairy alternative, melted	30 mL
	Freshly ground black pepper	

1. In a large skillet (preferably cast iron; see Tips, left) over medium heat, heat oil until shimmery. Add Brussels sprouts, potatoes and salt and stir for 30 to 60 seconds, until coated. Reduce heat to medium-low, cover and cook for about 10 minutes, until potatoes soften and start to turn golden brown, stopping twice to scrape up brown bits from bottom of pan with a spatula.

2. Add onion, garlic, thyme and lemon zest. Drizzle with butter and stir to coat evenly. Cover and cook for 10 to 15 minutes, until onions are browned and tender, stopping twice to scrape up brown bits from bottom of pan. Remove from heat. Season with salt and pepper to taste. Serve immediately.

Butter Lettuce

Lactuca sativa capitata

> *Other names:* **buttercrunch/butterhead lettuce, limestone lettuce.**
>
> **Depending on where you are shopping, you may find butter lettuce identified as** *buttersalat, laitue beurre, gotte* **or** *salat kochanyi.*

Although the history of lettuce dates back to the ancient Egyptians, modern cultivars weren't bred until between the 16th and 18th centuries. Lettuce as we know it was introduced to England in the 17th century and eventually transported to colonial America, where it was grown in home gardens. Lettuce fans continued to develop new cultivars. For instance, John (Jack) Bibb, a military man and amateur horticulturist in Kentucky, developed Bibb lettuce in the 1850s as a hybrid of Boston lettuce.

Tasting Notes

Butter lettuce is sweet and juicy, with soft, tender leaves.

Health Notes

Butter lettuce contains vitamins A, B$_6$, C and K, calcium, folate, iron, magnesium, manganese, phosphorus, potassium, riboflavin and thiamin.

In herbal medicine, lettuces have been used to relieve stress and insomnia, maintain healthy vision, cleanse the liver, prevent osteoporosis and treat indigestion, colitis, constipation and gout. The ancient Egyptians believed lettuce increased sexual prowess.

Varieties

Butter lettuces come in green and red cultivars as well as baby versions. Boston and Bibb lettuce are the familiar varieties.

Buy It

Supermarkets sell butter lettuces as loose heads or in clamshells, as well as in salad mixes. Hydroponically grown Boston lettuce is widely available too; it comes with the root ball attached.

Boston lettuce is more common than Bibb. Boston lettuce has wider, lighter green leaves in a looser head. Bibb lettuce is smaller and costs more.

Heads of butter lettuce are small and rounded but not compact, with buttery soft but crisp leaves shaped in a rosette. The outer leaves are green; the inner leaves range from pale yellow to creamy green. Avoid leaves that are flaccid, broken or brown at the edges or along the ribs.

Store It

Refrigerate butter lettuce as soon as possible. It is so delicate that it quickly wilts at room temperature.

Store the whole head in a resealable bag in the crisper. If sold with roots, the head may be placed in a bowl with the roots in water; cover the bowl loosely with plastic. Alternatively, separate the head into leaves, wrap them loosely in paper towels and place them in a resealable bag with some air left in it to act as a cushion.

Butter lettuce will keep in the refrigerator for up to three days.

Prep It

Handle butter lettuce gently, as the leaves are easily bruised. Pull off and discard any wilted or damaged outer leaves. To remove the core, grab the stem end, pull and twist.

If lettuce leaves look flaccid or dry, rinse and refresh them in a bowl of cold water. Use them whole or tear into pieces.

To wash, rinse intact leaves (for wraps or for a bed of lettuce) under cold running water, then spin-dry. Swish torn leaves gently in a bowl of cold water, then drain, spin-dry or blot with paper towels or a clean kitchen towel. Allow washed lettuce to dry completely; otherwise, salad dressing won't cling properly.

To clean a whole head of butter lettuce, soak it in cold salted water for 15 minutes. Alternatively, hold the stem end and dunk the head up and down in cold water. Drain, then turn it upside down on a plate, cover with a kitchen towel and refrigerate for several hours.

Tearing the leaves is preferable to cutting, as cut edges tend to brown quickly. However, if you use it promptly, lettuce may be chopped or shredded.

Consume It

Butter lettuce is commonly eaten raw. It is best in salads and sandwiches. A crispy bed of lettuce is an attractive base for salads and other dishes. Pliable butter lettuce leaves also make good low-calorie wraps.

Butter lettuce may be cooked, however. When cooking lettuce, be brief — it softens quickly.

Equivalents

1 small head = 2 oz (60 g); 1 medium head = 4 oz (125 g); 1 large head = 6 oz (175 g)

•

2 oz (60 g) torn leaves = 2½ cups (625 mL), loosely packed

SUBSTITUTES

leaf lettuce, mâche, romaine hearts, chickweed

Garden Pea, Butter Lettuce and Radish Salad

Shaved radishes and their greens add a bit of bite and a dash of color to this refined salad with a citrusy herb dressing.

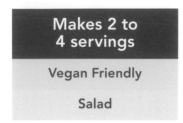

Makes 2 to 4 servings

Vegan Friendly

Salad

Tips

If the peas are not young and tender, cook them in a saucepan of boiling salted water for 3 to 4 minutes. Drain well and cool to room temperature before using. Fresh peas are seasonal, but you can turn this into a year-round salad by substituting thawed frozen peas. In a large, microwave-safe bowl, heat peas on High for about 1 minute, until warm and tender, then drain and cool to room temperature.

If you have one, use a mandoline to shave the radishes very thinly.

1	medium-large head butter lettuce, cored and torn into bite-size pieces (about 6 cups/1.5 L, loosely packed)	1
½ cup	Lime Herb Dressing (page 452)	125 mL
1 cup	shelled tender green peas (6 oz/175 g; see Tips, left)	250 mL
4	green onions (white and light green parts), cut diagonally into ½-inch (1 cm) pieces	4
2	red radishes, thinly sliced (see Tips, left)	2
¼ cup	loosely packed chopped radish greens	60 mL

1. In a bowl, toss lettuce with dressing to taste (you will have some left over).

2. Transfer prepared lettuce to a serving platter. Scatter peas, green onions, radishes and radish greens overtop. Serve immediately.

Boston Bloom

This may be the lightest salad you've ever eaten. The butter lettuce leaves are arranged in a floral formation but you don't need to be crafty to construct it.

	Makes 2 servings	
	Vegan Friendly	
	Salad	

Tips

Cocktail tomatoes are sold in supermarkets. They are also known as Camparis.

To toast almonds, cook in a dry skillet over medium heat for 2 to 3 minutes, stirring often, until golden and aromatic.

2	large cocktail tomatoes, quartered (see Tips, left)	2
⅓ cup	Simple Dijon Vinaigrette (page 448)	75 mL
1	head Boston lettuce	1
2	pitted green olives	2
1	large green onion (white and light green parts), chopped	1
1 tbsp	finely chopped parsley leaves	15 mL
1 tbsp	slivered almonds, toasted (see Tips, left)	15 mL

1. In a bowl, combine tomatoes with vinaigrette. Set aside for 15 minutes.
2. Meanwhile, core lettuce (see page 83) and separate leaves. On each of two serving plates, arrange leaves in a tight rosette shape, stacking from largest to smallest. Place an olive on top of each rosette. Using a slotted spoon, place tomatoes beside lettuce. Drizzle vinaigrette over lettuce, then scatter green onion, parsley and almonds overtop. Serve immediately.

Sunny Lettuce and Avocado Salad

Butter lettuce is paired with avocado and a sun-dried tomato dressing in this pretty salad. Add crusty bread and you have a light meal.

	Makes 2 to 4 servings	
	Vegan Friendly	
	Salad	

Tip

To dice avocados: Slice each avocado in half lengthwise and discard pit. Using a paring knife, cut a crosshatch pattern in each half, all the way to the skin, then scoop out the pieces with a spoon.

1	large head butter lettuce (6 oz/175 g), cored and leaves separated (see page 83)	1
2	small avocados, diced (see Tips, left)	2
½ cup	Sun-Dried Tomato Vinaigrette (page 450)	125 mL
2 tbsp	pepitas, toasted (see Tips, page 195)	30 mL
4	small red radishes, sliced	4

1. Line serving plates with lettuce leaves. Set aside.
2. In a bowl, gently toss avocado with vinaigrette to taste (you will have some left over). Spoon avocado onto lettuce, dividing equally. Scatter with pepitas. Arrange radishes in overlapping slices alongside avocado. Serve immediately.

Variation

Don't waste the radish leaves. If desired, sprinkle some finely chopped leaves over the lettuce at the end of Step 2.

Butter Lettuce with Grilled Apricots, Chèvre and Almonds

Fruit can be savory as well as sweet. No ordinary salad, this pretty dish features apricots served warm over tender lettuce, enhanced by goat's-milk cheese rounds and toasted almonds.

Makes 4 servings		
Salad		

Tips

You can barbecue the apricots instead of using a grill pan.

To toast almonds, cook in a dry skillet over medium heat for 2 to 3 minutes, stirring often, until golden and aromatic.

• Grill pan

3 tbsp	extra virgin olive oil	45 mL
1 tbsp	sherry vinegar	15 mL
1 tsp	liquid honey	5 mL
¼ tsp	kosher or coarse sea salt	1 mL
4	apricots, halved and pitted	4
1	head butter lettuce (4 oz/125 g), cored and leaves separated (see Variations, below)	1
2 oz	chèvre, cut into 4 rounds	60 g
	Freshly ground black pepper	
¼ cup	sliced almonds, toasted (see Tips, left)	60 mL

1. In a bowl, whisk together oil, vinegar, honey and salt. Set aside.
2. Heat grill pan over medium heat for 3 to 5 minutes. Brush apricots lightly on both sides with some oil mixture. Place, cut side down, in pan and grill for 4 to 5 minutes, until char marks appear. Turn and grill for 2 to 3 minutes more, until warmed through and lightly charred.
3. Line serving plates with lettuce leaves. Arrange warm apricots over lettuce. Drizzle with remaining oil mixture to taste. Place a chèvre round on each plate and season with pepper to taste. Scatter almonds overtop.

Variations

Instead of butter lettuce, try this salad with leaf lettuce, romaine, mâche, baby spinach, purslane, chickweed or watercress.

Lettuce Sauce

Surprise! You can make delicious sauces with lettuce. I love this one because it's piquant, with a pleasing, somewhat crunchy texture. You could create a reverse salad (for April Fool's Day, maybe?) by spooning it over sliced tomatoes and hard-cooked eggs.

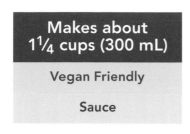

Makes about 1¼ cups (300 mL)

Vegan Friendly

Sauce

Tips

You can substitute black pepper for white pepper. White pepper is used mainly for aesthetic reasons, to avoid black specks in finished dishes. It is ground from white peppercorns, which are riper than black peppercorns and have had the skins stripped off. Also, unlike black peppercorns, they have not been dried and left to darken and shrivel.

If using non-dairy sour cream, which is thicker than regular sour cream, loosen it with a bit of vegetable stock to obtain the right consistency.

- Food processor

2 tbsp	unsalted butter or non-dairy alternative	30 mL
6	green onions (white and green parts), sliced	6
1	head butter lettuce (4 oz/125 g), cored and coarsely chopped	1
1 tbsp	chopped fresh tarragon leaves	15 mL
1 tsp	kosher or coarse sea salt	5 mL
⅛ tsp	freshly ground white pepper (see Tips, left)	0.5 mL
¼ cup	dry white wine	60 mL
½ cup	sour cream or non-dairy alternative (see Tips, left)	125 mL

1. In a saucepan over medium heat, melt butter. Add green onions and cook, stirring occasionally, for about 2 minutes, until softened and golden. Add lettuce, tarragon, salt and pepper. Cook, stirring occasionally, for about 1 minute, until wilted. Stir in wine. Cover, reduce heat to low and cook for 5 to 8 minutes, until very soft.

2. Transfer to bowl of food processor fitted with the metal blade and purée until sauce-like but not quite smooth. Add sour cream and pulse a few times to combine (be careful not to overprocess). Serve immediately or transfer to an airtight container and refrigerate for up to 5 days.

Carrot Tops

Daucus carota sativus

Other names: **carrot greens**

Wild carrots were eaten in prehistoric times. Babylonians cultivated them as aromatic herbs rather than edible roots. Carrot tops may have been among the bitter greens served at the first Passover in Egypt. Arabs brought carrots to Europe, and explorers and settlers took them to the New World in the 1500s.

During Second World War rationing in Britain, officials tempted the populace to eat carrot greens by disseminating recipes such as carrot top and potato soup. However, carrot greens have generally been ignored in times of plenty, except in France.

Carrot tops are the most underutilized supermarket vegetable green. With the growing consumer appreciation for leafy greens, more has been written about making use of carrot tops instead of tossing them in the compost bin. They are not worth pursuing on their own, but as long as they come attached to carrots, why waste them?

Varieties

While orange carrots are by far the most common, white, gold, purple and black cultivars, in tapered or round shapes, are becoming more widely available as interest in heritage vegetables grows.

Wild carrot (*Daucus carota*), the ancestor of cultivated carrots (*D. carota sativus*), is better known as Queen Anne's lace. The root is edible when young, as are the leaves, although those are rarely eaten. Today wild carrot is best known as a prolific weed as well as a garden ornamental.

Buy It

Carrots are supermarket staples. They come in bunches with their tops or loose or bagged without greens. If you are buying a bunch of carrots and want to use the greens as well, look for foliage that is moist and bright green, with no signs of rot in the center. The lacy foliage of carrots can vary from lush to scraggly, depending on the time of year, the store and the size of the carrots.

Baby carrots — immature carrots, not to be confused with mini carrots, which are mechanically whittled-down regular carrots — have the tenderest leaves. However, they seem more likely to be sold without their tops than mature carrots, possibly for aesthetic reasons.

Tasting Notes

Carrot greens are bitter, herbaceous and astringent, with a hint of sweetness in the finish. They are coarse and grainy when raw. The stems taste like celery but are too stringy to use.

Equivalents

1 bunch carrots = 1¼ to 1½ lbs (625 to 750 g), comprising 4 to 6 carrots (1 lb/500 g) and 4 to 6 oz (125 to 175 g) greens

•

4 to 6 oz (125 to 175 g) carrot tops, stemmed = 1 to 1½ oz (30 to 45 g) leaves and tender stemlets

•

1 oz (30 g) leaves and tender stemlets = 3 cups (750 mL), loosely packed

Health Notes

Although no official government analysis is available, carrot tops probably have a nutritional profile similar to their roots. This would suggest that carrot tops provide vitamins A, B_6, C and K, folate, manganese, niacin, potassium and thiamin.

The myth that carrot greens are toxic contributes to their lack of popularity. This misconception may have developed because carrot plants are related to hemlock and because some people with allergies can get dermatitis from touching the leaves, particularly if they are wet. Food scientists, including Harold McGee, say there's no evidence that carrot tops are otherwise unsafe. However, if you are in doubt, don't eat them — just toss them out.

In folk medicine, carrot greens have been used as an antiseptic. People chewed the greens to treat mouth ulcers, bleeding gums and bad breath. In medieval times they were boiled with honey and used as a poultice. Tea steeped from carrot greens was used to kill intestinal parasites.

Store It

Carrots are awkward to store in bunches, and the attached greens rob the roots of moisture and nutrients. As soon as you arrive home, remove the greens, leaving $\frac{1}{2}$ inch (1 cm) of stem on the carrots. Carrot tops dry out rapidly, so place them in a glass or vase of water like a bouquet, with a plastic bag draped over the foliage; then refrigerate. Or strip and discard the stems, wash and dry the leaves and tender stemlets, wrap them loosely in a paper towel, and place them in a resealable bag with some air left in it to act like a cushion.

Carrot greens will keep in the refrigerator for up to three days.

Prep It

To strip carrot stalks, pinch off the lacy leaves and tender stemlets at their base. Discard the tough stems.

Wash carrot greens well, as they are very gritty. Swish them in several changes of cold water, then spin-dry.

You can reduce (but not eliminate) the bitterness of carrot greens by using the following methods:

- Sprinkle the greens with vinegar or lemon juice and perhaps some salt and chop them finely before using.
- Toss wet leaves in a sieve with a spoonful of salt and let them drain for 30 minutes before squeezing and chopping.
- Blanch the leaves in boiling water, then drain and set aside to cool before chopping.

Consume It

Carrot leaves can be chopped and added raw to salads, but only in small quantities — a handful or less. They are best cooked.

Carrot leaves and tender stemlets may be sautéed, added to soups, stews or casseroles, or transformed into pesto. Some chefs use them in small quantities as aromatic bitter herbs.

SUBSTITUTES

parsley root tops,
celeriac tops

Carrot Parsnip Soup

Herbaceous carrot greens add depth to this naturally sweet, creamy soup with its hint of curry and coconut. You can serve it hot or cold.

Makes 4 to 6 servings (about 7 cups/1.75 L)

Vegan Friendly

Soup

Tips

Whenever possible, use reduced-sodium vegetable stock. Not only is it healthier, it also allows you to better control the saltiness of a dish.

Coconut milk beverage is sold in cartons and found in the supermarket dairy case. Do not confuse it with canned coconut milk.

You can substitute unflavored soy milk or 5% cream for the coconut milk beverage.

• Stand or immersion blender

1 oz	carrot leaves and tender stemlets (about 3 cups/750 mL, loosely packed)	30 g
1 tsp	kosher or coarse sea salt	5 mL
2 tbsp	unsalted butter or non-dairy alternative	30 mL
6	carrots (1 lb/500 g), diced	6
1	parsnip (8 oz/250 g), diced	1
2	onions, diced	2
2	cloves garlic, chopped	2
4 cups	vegetable stock (see Tips, left)	1 L
½ tsp	curry powder	2 mL
1 cup	coconut milk beverage (see Tips, left)	250 mL
	Sour cream or non-dairy alternative	
4 to 6	tiny carrot leaves	4 to 6

1. In a fine-mesh sieve, toss rinsed carrot greens (with wash water still clinging to them) with salt. Set aside for 30 minutes.

2. Meanwhile, in a large saucepan over medium heat, melt butter. Add carrots, parsnip, onions and garlic. Cook, stirring often, for about 10 minutes, until softened. Stir in stock and curry powder. Squeeze carrot greens to extract excess moisture and transfer to saucepan. When mixture comes to a simmer, cover, reduce heat to low and cook for about 20 minutes, until vegetables are very tender.

3. Using blender, purée carrot mixture. Return to pan if necessary. Stir in coconut beverage. Season with salt to taste. Serve warm, garnishing each bowl with a dollop of sour cream to taste and a tiny carrot leaf. Or transfer to an airtight container and refrigerate for several hours, until chilled, before garnishing and serving.

Carroty Couscous

This Moroccan-style dish tastes good, looks good and is good for you. Enjoy it warm or at room temperature. Carrot greens are used in place of herbs instead of going to waste.

**Makes
4 servings (about
5 cups/1.25 L)**

Vegan Friendly

Side dish

Tips

Bottled reconstituted lemon and lime juices usually contain additives. To avoid them, use freshly squeezed juice. Squeeze a whole lemon or lime and store the leftover juice in a small container in the fridge, or freeze it in 1 tbsp (15 mL) portions in an ice-cube tray.

For the finest minced garlic, push it through a press.

Made from granular semolina, couscous is akin to pasta but used like a grain. North American supermarkets sell instant couscous. Authentic Moroccan couscous (not instant) is steamed and dried several times; it is cooked in a double pot called a *couscoussière* over a simmering stew or salted water.

To toast pistachios, cook them in a dry skillet over medium heat for 2 to 3 minutes, stirring often, until golden and aromatic.

1 oz	carrot leaves and tender stemlets (about 3 cups/750 mL, loosely packed)	30 g
2 tbsp	freshly squeezed lemon juice (see Tips, left)	30 mL
1 tsp	kosher or coarse sea salt	5 mL
1	clove garlic, minced (see Tips, left)	1
1/8 tsp	freshly ground black pepper	0.5 mL
1 1/4 cups	vegetable stock	300 mL
1 cup	instant couscous (see Tips, left)	250 mL
1/4 cup	extra virgin olive oil	60 mL
2	carrots (4 oz/125 g total), shredded	2
1/2 cup	dried currants	125 mL
1/2 cup	pistachios, toasted and coarsely chopped (see Tips, left)	125 mL
1 tbsp	chopped fresh mint leaves	15 mL

1. On a large cutting board, combine carrot leaves with lemon juice and salt. Using a sharp knife, chop them finely. Transfer greens and juices to a serving bowl. Stir in garlic and pepper. Set aside.

2. In a saucepan over medium-high heat, bring stock to a boil. Add couscous in a steady stream, stirring constantly. When mixture returns to a simmer, cover and remove from heat. Set aside for about 5 minutes, until liquid is completely absorbed.

3. Add couscous to carrot leaves and mix with a fork. Let stand for 5 minutes, until slightly cooled. Add oil, carrots, currants and pistachios and mix gently with a fork. Scatter mint overtop. Serve warm or at room temperature.

Variations

Substitute chopped arugula, dandelion greens, microgreens, parsley root tops, celeriac tops, purslane or watercress for the carrot tops.

Substitute raisins, dried cranberries or chopped dried apricots for the currants.

Cassava Leaves

Manihot esculenta, M. dulcis

> *Other names:* **Brazilian arrowroot, bread of the tropics,** *casabe, mandioca,* **manioc greens, tapioca leaves, yuca leaf.**
>
> Depending on where you are shopping, you may find cassava leaves identified as *boodin, feuilles de manioc, guacamote, kamoteng, kahoy, kelala, maravalli, mogo, mpondu, mun sumpalung, saka-saka, singkong, tubero per tapioca* or *ubi kayu.*

Cassava is a tropical shrub native to the Amazon region, where it was first domesticated 10,000 years ago. The majority of the world's cassava now comes from Africa. It was transplanted there in the 1500s by Portuguese slavers and subsequently spread to Asia. Despite its potential toxicity (it must never be eaten raw), cassava is a major crop in the developing world.

Cassava leaves are a significant component of people's diets in some African countries; however, they may be regarded as "poor man's food." The leaves are also a staple vegetable in remote areas of Indonesia.

Tasting Notes

Cassava leaves should never be eaten raw (see "Consume It," page 93). Thawed frozen leaves taste grassy, slightly smoky and tannic, with a coarse texture.

Varieties

Cassava is cultivated primarily for its roots, which are eaten like potatoes or processed into tapioca pearls or flour. However, the leaves are also eaten as a vegetable. Do not fear cassava leaves. Like many plants, they contain toxins and thus require cooking, but poisonous varieties are not grown or marketed in North America.

There are three types of cassava:

- **bitter cassava** (*Manihot esculenta*), the starchy source of tapioca. It is poisonous unless cooked.
- **sweet cassava** (sometimes differentiated as *M. dulcis*), also known as *macaxeira*. It is less toxic and milder than bitter cassava.
- **wild cassava** (*M. esculenta flabellifolia*), the ancestor of cultivated cassavas.

Equivalents

1 lb (500 g) thawed frozen ground cassava leaves = 2 cups (500 mL)

•

1 lb (500 g) thawed frozen ground cassava leaves, drained = 1¼ cups (300 mL)

Buy It

Fresh cassava leaves are usually found only in the tropics. Small or young leaves, once cooked, are the tenderest.

Packages of frozen ground cassava leaves are readily available in Asian supermarkets.

Even in Africa people often opt to purchase frozen ground leaves, which save the cook from sweating over a mortar and pestle. Fresh leaves are described as fibrous, dense and grassy, and they must be broken down before they can be cooked and consumed.

Store It

Store fresh cassava leaves in a resealable bag in the refrigerator. They deteriorate within two days.

Keep frozen cassava leaves in the freezer until you are ready to use them.

Prep It

Frozen cassava leaves are ground or chopped. Toss them into boiling water while still frozen or thaw them in the fridge overnight before using them. If desired, drain the water after thawing. A frozen package contains up to 40 percent water. Fresh cassava leaves are traditionally pounded using a mortar and pestle, but may be minced instead.

Consume It

Never eat raw cassava leaves — the plant toxins must be neutralized, the bitterness must be eliminated and the greens must be tenderized. A two-step cooking process is recommended for fresh leaves. They are dried or pounded, then boiled, drained and simmered until tender, on their own or as part of a prepared dish.

Here is one technique: Remove stems, rinse leaves under cold running water and drain. Stack, then roll leaves into a cigar shape and slice crosswise. Place them in a saucepan, cover generously with water and boil for 10 minutes. Drain, discarding cooking water. Return leaves to the saucepan and cover with fresh water. If desired, add baking soda to soften the leaves and give them a salty flavor (traditionally done in regions with few sources of salt). Return water to a boil, cover and simmer over medium-low or low heat for up to 1 hour, until tender. Alternatively, after boiling for 10 minutes, drain, discard cooking water, add leaves to a spicy soup or stew and simmer until tender.

In most recipes that use frozen ground leaves, they are cooked until most of the liquid evaporates. African cooks often add a nut butter to dishes containing cassava leaves, while Indonesians flavor them with coconut. Dishes containing cassava leaves are often served over steamed rice. The leaves are also used in cooked salads and pilafs in Indonesia.

Health Notes

Although no official government analysis is available, product labels indicate that cassava leaves contain vitamins A and C, calcium, iron, manganese and phosphorus. It is important to note that cassava leaves are high in tannins and plant cyanides that must be neutralized by cooking.

In folk medicine, cassava has been used to fight anemia, increase production of breast milk, relieve headaches and pain, reduce blood pressure and kill intestinal worms.

SUBSTITUTES

collards, kale, turnip greens, bitter leaf, kohlrabi tops, sweet potato leaves, spinach, chard

Plassas

This vegetarian version of a Sierra Leone cassava leaf stew is like a robust, fragrant sauce. It's delicious over rice.

**Makes
2 servings (about
2 cups/500 mL)**

Main course

Tips

African cooks use red palm fruit oil, which gives the stew a pleasing color. However, grapeseed or extra virgin olive oil are more readily available, and I add color with turmeric.

Maggi is a liquid seasoning that African cooks often add to stews. It is available in most supermarkets.

African recipes may call for a cayenne spice paste blend, which in Africa is sold in huge jars. I make do with garlic chile paste, which is sold in Asian grocery stores and well-stocked supermarkets, and I add a bit of ginger to the stew.

1 lb	frozen ground cassava leaves	500 g
4 cups	water, divided	1 L
2 tbsp	oil (see Tips, left)	30 mL
1	onion, diced	1
1	small red bell pepper, cut into ½-inch (1 cm) dice	1
1 tsp	puréed gingerroot	5 mL
½ tsp	kosher or coarse sea salt	2 mL
½ tsp	Maggi seasoning (see Tips, left)	2 mL
¼ tsp	ground turmeric	1 mL
2 tbsp	peanut butter	30 mL
2 tbsp	garlic chile paste (see Tips, left)	30 mL

1. In a saucepan over medium heat, boil cassava in 2 cups (500 mL) water for 15 minutes, breaking it up with a wooden spoon to hasten thawing, then stirring occasionally.

2. In another saucepan over medium heat, heat oil until shimmery. Add onion and red pepper. Cook, stirring often, for about 3 minutes, until softened. Stir in ginger, then cassava with cooking liquid, salt, Maggi, turmeric and remaining water. When mixture comes to a boil, reduce heat to medium-low and simmer for about 1 hour, until leaves are tender and most of the liquid has evaporated.

3. Stir in peanut butter and garlic chile paste. Reduce heat to low and simmer for 5 minutes. Season with salt to taste.

Catalogna
Cichorium intybus catalogna

Other names: **cutting chicory, Catalonia/Catalan chicory, dandelion-leaf chicory, Italian dandelion, long-stemmed Italian chicory.**

Depending on where you are shopping, you may find catalogna identified as *cicoria de catalogna*.

Chicory plants are native to western Asia, North Africa and Europe. Noted in records dating back to antiquity, they have a long history as foraged and cultivated edibles. The Roman poet Horace mentions chicory as an essential part of his diet.

Catalogna is one type of cultivated chicory that has been eaten for centuries in southern Europe. Catalogna in particular and chicories in general are closely associated with Italy, but they are popular throughout the Mediterranean region, particularly in Greece (where people consume bitter greens for both health and pleasure), as well as in Spain and Turkey.

The alternative name "Catalonia chicory" suggests that this leafy green may have originated in the Catalan region of Spain, but the Italians also lay claim to it. Italian immigrants brought catalogna to North America.

Varieties

There are numerous chicories, wild and cultivated, and catalogna (*Cichorium intybus catalogna*) is one of them. It is a loose-leaf, dandelion-like chicory, usually green. It also comes in an attractive red cultivar with green leaves, red veins and red stems, as well as a white cultivar with red streaks.

Catalogna cultivars have tongue-twisting names such as 'Foglia Frastagliata', also known as tall indented-leaved Italian chicory or Italian dandelion chicory; 'Gigante de Chioggia', also known as chioggia giant; 'Italiko Russo', also known as red-stemmed asparagus chicory; 'Brindisina'; 'Pugliese'; 'Dentarella' and 'Foglia Liscia'.

Tasting Notes

Catalogna is crisp, with leaves that taste bitter, briny, astringent and slightly nutty. The stems are juicy and bittersweet. Red catalogna is less coarse, with thinner, slightly briny stems.

Health Notes

Although no official government analysis is available, catalogna is thought to contain vitamins A, B_6, C, E and K, calcium, copper, folate, iron, manganese, magnesium, niacin, pantothenic acid, phosphorus, potassium, riboflavin, thiamin and zinc. Catalogna also contains inulin, a beneficial insoluble fiber, and intybin, a sedative and painkiller found in all *C. intybus* species.

In herbal medicine, chicories are considered a potent treatment for internal parasites. They have also been used to treat gallstones, gastroenteritis and sinus problems and are applied as poultices to cuts and bruises.

Equivalents

1 bunch catalogna =
1 lb (500 g)

•

1 bunch stemmed
red catalogna =
8 oz (250 g)

•

2 oz (60 g) stems
cut into 1-inch
(2.5 cm) pieces =
$\frac{2}{3}$ cup (150 mL),
loosely packed

•

2 oz (60 g) coarsely
chopped stalks (leaves
and tender stems)
= $1\frac{1}{2}$ cups (375 mL),
loosely packed

•

2 oz (60 g) coarsely
chopped leaves =
3 cups (750 mL),
loosely packed

•

2 oz (60 g) stems
cut into 1-inch
(2.5 cm) lengths
= 1 cup (250 mL),
loosely packed

Buy It

Catalogna is familiar to some supermarket shoppers, but they may not know it. In my region at least, green and red types are often labeled simply "dandelion" because catalogna is also known as Italian dandelion. Green catalogna is often sold instead of true dandelion or is displayed alongside it.

How can you tell dandelion and catalogna apart? The leaves of catalogna are darker green, coarser, sparser and very deeply notched. The semi-rounded stems are whiter, longer and spindlier, and the leaves grow along them in patches. Catalogna is 15 to 20 inches (40 to 50 cm) tall. It grows in clusters and is sometimes sold with roots attached. Red catalogna is usually sold with trimmed stems, as is dandelion.

Look for glossy specimens. Avoid catalogna with dry-looking leaves or stems that are marred by rusty discolorations.

Store It

Swathe catalogna loosely in paper towels and place it in a plastic bag; then store it in the refrigerator.

Red catalogna will keep in the refrigerator for up to two days. Green catalogna will keep for up to three days.

Prep It

Before cooking catalogna, separate clusters and get rid of any tough parts of stems by cutting 1 to 2 inches (2.5 to 5 cm) off the base. Run your fingers from the bottom of the stalk upward to pull off leafy frills growing along the stem.

After cutting or chopping the greens, swish them in cold water and spin-dry.

Puntarelle

Catalogna

Consume It

The leaves and tender stems of catalogna may be eaten raw in salads. However, this green is usually cooked. Red catalogna is better suited for use in salads, as its color fades during cooking.

In Italy, Greece and other Mediterranean countries, cooks tame bitter chicory by blanching it, then sautéing it in olive oil. Another common technique is to add baking soda to the water when blanching, which softens it.

With simmering, catalogna is tender in 10 to 15 minutes. Longer simmering reduces bitterness but makes the greens mushy.

SUBSTITUTES
dandelion, curly endive, escarole

P Is for Puntarelle

Puntarelle is a seasonal Roman delicacy used to create a signature salad of the same name.

It is a variety of catalogna with a tasty secret: the long, dandelion-like stalks surround a hidden heart of tightly clustered crisp, succulent shoots with asparagus-like tips. Hence puntarelle is also known as asparagus chicory, as well as Roman chicory, *catalogna de galatina* or little tips.

To make puntarelle salad, the shoots must be thinly slivered, soaked in ice water for at least an hour (until they curl), dried, then marinated briefly with a pungent dressing. (The surrounding stalks are saved for other uses.)

In Rome, markets sell pre-slivered shoots, scooped from vats of water, to satisfy mass cravings for puntarelle salad. Here, however, puntarelle chicory is a rare treat. It makes its brief late-winter appearance in some supermarkets and at specialty greengrocers.

Hortapita

Most of us are familiar with spanakopita, the Greek spinach and feta pie. Hortapita is similar but more intense. It is traditionally prepared with bitter wild greens known collectively as **horta** *(page 99). I use catalogna, arugula and kale.*

Makes 12 servings

Appetizer

Tips

Feta is made from sheep's, goat's or cow's milk and comes in textures ranging from dry and crumbly to creamy. Use any type you like, but creamy sheep's-milk feta binds the filling nicely. If you are a vegetarian, check the label. Some brands are prepared with traditional (animal) rennet and others with vegetarian rennet.

Scoring the phyllo makes it easier to cut after baking. Use a light touch: do not cut deeply through the top layer of pastry or it will become too dry.

If you can't find catalogna, use dandelion greens.

- Preheat oven to 375°F (190°C)
- 13- by 9-inch (33 by 23 cm) baking dish, lightly greased

½ cup	extra virgin olive oil, divided	125 mL
1	bunch green onions (white and green parts), sliced	1
1 cup	diced red onion	250 mL
1 lb	catalogna (about 1 bunch), chopped	500 g
12 oz	arugula, chopped (about 12 cups/3 L)	375 g
4 oz	baby kale leaves (about 10 cups/2.5 L)	125 g
1 tsp	kosher or coarse sea salt	5 mL
½ cup	water	125 mL
½ cup	chopped fresh dill fronds	125 mL
½ cup	chopped fresh parsley leaves	125 mL
1 tbsp	chopped fresh oregano leaves	15 mL
¼ tsp	freshly ground black pepper	1 mL
8 oz	feta cheese, crumbled (see Tips, left)	250 g
2	large eggs, whisked	2
3 tbsp	unsalted butter, melted	45 mL
8	sheets frozen phyllo pastry, thawed	8

1. In a large saucepan over medium heat, heat 1 tbsp (15 mL) oil until shimmery. Add green and red onions. Cook, stirring often, for 3 to 4 minutes, until softened. Transfer to a large bowl. Set aside.

2. In the same pan, heat ¼ cup (60 mL) oil until shimmery. Add catalogna, arugula, kale and salt. Cook, stirring often, for about 5 minutes, until slightly wilted and coated. Add water, cover, reduce heat to medium-low and simmer for about 10 minutes, until very tender.

3. Using a fine-mesh sieve, drain greens and set aside to cool for 15 minutes. Once cooled, press with the back of a spoon to extract excess liquid. Transfer to a cutting board and chop. Add to onions. Using a fork, stir in (don't mash) dill, parsley, oregano, pepper and feta. Add eggs and stir to combine. Set aside.

4. In a small bowl, mix together thoroughly remaining oil and melted butter. Using a sharp knife, cut phyllo sheets in half to obtain 16 sheets (they will fit prepared baking dish almost exactly). Place 1 sheet in pan and brush lightly with oil mixture. Repeat with 7 more sheets. Spread greens mixture evenly over phyllo. Top with 1 sheet phyllo. Brush lightly with oil mixture. Repeat with remaining 7 sheets.

5. Using a sharp knife, lightly score top of phyllo to mark out 12 squares (see Tips, page 98). Cover baking dish with foil. Bake in preheated oven for 15 minutes. Remove foil and bake for 15 to 20 minutes longer, until phyllo is golden brown.

H Is for Horta

Horta is a catchall name for the wild bitter greens used in Greek cuisine. Horta comes in seemingly endless varieties that are used interchangeably in side dishes and salads.

Locals gather horta from hillsides and meadows as well as purchasing them from greengrocers and eating them in restaurants. These greens are often simply boiled or steamed, then tossed with extra-virgin olive oil and lemon juice or fragrant aged vinegar.

Greeks swear that horta helps keeps them fit. Scientists on the island of Crete credit both horta and extra virgin olive oil with making heart disease surprisingly rare there.

Greek Chicory

This old-school cooked salad is enjoyed in the Greek islands — and at my house. Bitter greens have been an essential part of Greek cuisine for millennia.

	Makes 2 small servings	
	Vegan Friendly	
	Salad	

Tips

To prepare the catalogna in this recipe: Trim 1 to 2 inches (2.5 to 5 cm) off the ends of the stalks, then cut the stalks with leaves into quarters.

There are many kinds of feta — made with sheep's, goat's or cow's milk — and they range in texture from creamy to crumbly. For this recipe I like to use a fairly dry imported Greek sheep's-milk feta.

Turn this salad into sandwiches by stuffing it into pita halves.

¼ tsp	baking soda	1 mL
½	bunch catalogna (8 oz/250 g), trimmed and quartered (see Tips, left)	½
2 tbsp	extra virgin olive oil	30 mL
1	large onion, halved and sliced	1
½ tsp	kosher or coarse sea salt	2 mL
	Freshly ground black pepper	
1 tsp	freshly squeezed lemon juice	5 mL
½ cup	crumbled feta cheese (1 oz/30 g), optional (see Tips, left)	125 mL
1	tomato, cut into small wedges	1

1. To a large saucepan of boiling water, add baking soda, then catalogna. Simmer over medium-low heat for 10 to 15 minutes, until tender. Drain, rinse with cold water and set aside.

2. In same saucepan over medium heat, heat oil until shimmery. Add onion and salt. Cook, stirring often, for 6 to 8 minutes, until golden brown. Remove pan from heat and set aside for 15 minutes to cool.

3. Squeeze handfuls of greens to extract excess liquid and transfer to pan with onion. Using a fork, stir to loosen clumps and combine. Season with salt and pepper to taste.

4. Transfer to a serving plate. Drizzle with lemon juice. Crumble feta overtop, if using. Arrange tomato wedges around perimeter and season with salt to taste. Serve at room temperature.

Celeriac Greens

Apium graveolens rapaceum

Other names: **celery root, knob celery, turnip-rooted celery**

Celeriac is a type of celery cultivated for its ugly, knobby, but delicious root. It has a full head of foliage, unlike the sparse leaves on common celery.

The celery family is likely native to the Mediterranean. Cultivated celery is derived from a type of celery known as "smallage," which was consumed by the ancient Greeks and Romans but associated with funerals and bad luck. Homer's works mention wild celery. Cultivated celery appeared many centuries later, in the 1600s, and became popular once the bitterness had been bred out of it.

Tasting Notes

Celeriac leaves taste like common celery leaves and parsley, but are tougher and have hints of cress and a bitter finish. The stems are aggressively celery-flavored but somewhat stringy.

Varieties

Celeriac (*Apium graveolens rapaceum*) is a sibling to common celery (*A. graveolens dulce*). Both are grown as vegetables but have tasty edible leaves. Their ancestor, pungent wild celery (*A. graveolens*), is not to be confused with various unrelated species also known as wild celery (page 126).

Buy It

Celeriac greens, like carrot tops, are twofers (see page 17) — when you can get them. The root is generally (but not always) sold in supermarkets without the foliage. You may also find celeriac with the greens intact at farmers' markets. The oversized serrated, celery-like, dark green leaves grow on thin stems. Look for moist leaves with no discoloration, and check the foliage in the center for signs of rot.

Health Notes

Although no official government analysis is available, celeriac greens are likely to have a nutritional profile similar to their roots. This suggests that celeriac greens may provide vitamins B_6, C and K, magnesium, manganese, phosphorus and potassium.

In herbal medicine, celery has been used as a diuretic, an appetite stimulant and a kidney and nerve tonic, and topically to relieve venereal itching. Celery tea, made from seeds and leaves, has been used as an antiseptic mouthwash and also consumed to alleviate gout, hives, hysteria, insomnia, kidney stones, lung congestion and rheumatism.

Store It

Cut off the foliage as soon as you get home, as it draws moisture and nutrients from the root. The leaves dry out quickly, so place the stalks in a glass or vase of water like a bouquet, with a plastic bag draped over them; then refrigerate. Or trim and wash the greens, spin them dry, then roll them in paper towels and store in a resealable bag.

Celeriac greens will keep in the refrigerator for up to three days.

SUBSTITUTES

Chinese celery, parsley
root tops

Prep It

Before cooking celeriac greens, separate the leaves from the stems. The thicker parts of the stems remain stringy even after cooking, so it's best to discard the parts that are more than ½ inch (1 cm) wide. If desired, use only the leaves.

Celeriac greens tend to be very dirty. Swish them in several changes of cold water until the water runs clear, then spin-dry.

Consume It

I'm a fan of delicate and delicious celery leaves. Celeriac leaves are their big brothers. They are bigger, darker, coarser and more potent but may be used in the same way. Add them to soups and stews, or match them with celery or celeriac in dishes to add another layer of celery flavor.

Celeriac leaves and tender stems are best cooked. However, finely chopped leaves may be used sparingly as you would use herbs, or for garnishing.

The tough stalks may be bundled like a bouquet garni and simmered in dishes to flavor them, then discarded.

Celeriac leaves may be dried in the oven, then blended with salt to create celery salt, which is used as a seasoning.

Harvest Risotto with Celeriac and Greens

Fall veggies and greens make this risotto a rib-sticking meal. Serve it with salad for an extra boost of greens.

Makes 4 to 6 servings (about 7 cups/1.75 L)		
Vegan Friendly		
Main course		

Tips

Whenever possible, use reduced-sodium vegetable stock. Not only is it healthier, it allows you to better control the saltiness of a dish.

To peel pearl onions: Blanch them in a small pan of boiling water for 30 seconds, drain and shock them with cold water. Using a paring knife, trim the root ends and pull off the skins.

Risotto rice is short-grained, creamy and starchy. Arborio is the most popular type, while Carnaroli and Vialone Nano are pricier.

Risotto is traditionally made with hot stock. However, you don't have to keep the stock simmering. It will work even at room temperature.

The speed at which risotto cooks depends on the width of the pan, the level of heat and the temperature of the stock. I use a 10-inch (25 cm) saucepan to cook risotto at a lively pace.

1 cup	diced (¼ inch/0.5 cm) celeriac	250 mL
1 cup	diced (¼ inch/0.5 cm) butternut squash	250 mL
5 cups	vegetable stock (see Tips, left)	1.25 L
1 cup	water	250 mL
2 tbsp	extra virgin olive oil	30 mL
12	small red pearl onions (about 1 cup/ 250 mL), peeled (see Tips, left)	12
1½ cups	Arborio rice (see Tips, left)	375 mL
⅓ cup + 1 tsp	finely chopped celeriac leaves	80 mL
1	clove garlic, chopped	1
1 tsp	kosher or coarse sea salt	5 mL
1 tbsp	unsalted butter or non-dairy alternative Freshly ground black pepper	15 mL

1. In a small saucepan of boiling salted water, cook celeriac over medium heat for about 2 minutes, until softened. Add squash and cook for about 5 minutes, until vegetables are just tender. Drain, place in a bowl, cover and set aside.

2. In same saucepan over medium-high heat, bring stock and water to a boil. Remove from heat and place on back burner (see Tips, left).

3. In a wide saucepan (see Tips, left) over medium heat, heat oil until shimmery. Stir in onions and cook for about 5 minutes, until softened and turning golden. Using a slotted spoon, transfer to a small bowl. Cover and set aside.

4. Add rice to same saucepan and cook, stirring often, for about 3 minutes, until coated and turning golden. Add ⅓ cup (75 mL) celeriac leaves, garlic and salt; stir for 30 seconds. Reduce heat to medium-low. Add stock about 1 cup (250 mL) at a time, stirring often — do not add more liquid until previous addition is almost absorbed. Repeat until all liquid has been used and rice is creamy and tender but firm; this should take 20 to 30 minutes (see Tips, left). Remove from heat. Stir in butter and pepper, then reserved onions, celeriac and squash. Season with salt to taste. Serve garnished with remaining celeriac greens.

Celeriac Mash with Caramelized Onions and Greens

Sweet browned onions with bitter greens create a taste sensation atop mashed celeriac. Serve this dish as an alternative to plain mashed potatoes.

Tips

Yellow-fleshed potatoes are best for this recipe; neither waxy nor dry, they are good all-purpose potatoes. The best-known yellow-fleshed potatoes are Yukon Golds.

You can substitute black pepper for white pepper. White pepper is mainly used for aesthetic reasons, to avoid black specks in finished dishes. It is ground from white peppercorns, which are riper than black peppercorns and have had the skins stripped off. Also unlike black peppercorns, they have not been dried and left to darken and shrivel.

For a rustic effect, I like to mash this dish by hand, leaving some small chunks for texture.

Onions and Greens

¼ cup	extra virgin olive oil	60 mL
4	onions (1 to 1¼ lbs/2 kg total), halved and thinly sliced	4
½ tsp	kosher or coarse sea salt	2 mL
⅛ tsp	freshly ground black pepper	0.5 mL
2 cups	coarsely chopped celeriac leaves and tender stems (3 oz/90 g)	500 mL
1 tsp	granulated sugar	5 mL
1 tbsp	cider vinegar	15 mL

Mash

1	large knob celeriac (1½ lbs/750 g), cut into 1-inch (2.5 cm) chunks	1
1	potato (6 oz/175 g), cut into 1-inch (2.5 cm) chunks (see Tips, left)	1
1 tbsp	extra virgin olive oil	15 mL
1 tsp	kosher or coarse sea salt	5 mL
⅛ tsp	freshly ground white pepper	0.5 mL

1. *Onions and Greens:* In a large skillet over medium heat, heat oil until shimmery. Stir in onions, salt and pepper. Cook, stirring often, for about 10 minutes, until starting to brown. Stir in celeriac greens for about 1 minute, until wilted. Reduce heat to low, cover and cook, stirring occasionally, for about 20 minutes, until onions are golden brown and very tender. Uncover, add sugar and cook, stirring occasionally, for 15 to 20 minutes, until color deepens. Stir in vinegar, reduce heat to medium-low and cook, stirring often, for 2 minutes. Set aside.

2. *Mash:* In a saucepan of boiling salted water, cook celeriac and potato over medium heat for about 20 minutes, until very tender. Drain and return vegetables to pan over low heat for 1 minute, shaking pan a couple of times to evaporate excess moisture.

3. Using a potato masher, mash vegetables (see Tips, left). Add oil, salt and pepper, then mash to combine. Transfer to a serving bowl. Top with caramelized onion, and greens and serve warm.

Chard

Beta vulgaris cicla, B. vulgaris flavescens

Other names: crab/leaf/seakale/spinach beet, perpetual spinach, roman kale, Swiss cardoon, Swiss chard.

Depending on where you are shopping, you may find chard identified as *acelgas, al-silq, biete de costa* or *bettes*.

Both chard and beets are descendants of the wild sea beet *(Beta vulgaris maritima)*.

Tasting Notes

Chard is similar to spinach but is stronger tasting and coarser. It tastes fairly mild, beet-like, earthy and astringent and is slightly bitter and briny. When cooked, a mineral, spinach-like flavor develops.

White chard has nutty-tasting leaves and the most succulent stems — sweet and juicy. Yellow chard stems are saltier and not as sweet and the leaves are more mineral tasting. Red chard stems are nuttier and not as sweet, and the leaves are bitterer and more minerally.

Health Notes

Chard contains vitamins A, B$_6$, C, E and K, calcium, copper, folate, iron, magnesium, manganese, phosphorus, potassium, riboflavin, thiamin and zinc. Chard is particularly high in fiber. However, it is very high in sodium and high in oxalates (page 355).

In herbal medicine, chard has been used as a laxative, a diuretic and a bladder tonic. It has also been used to treat anemia, skin diseases and acne, to relieve nervousness and migraines, to reduce blood sugar, to strengthen bones and to lower blood pressure.

Leaf beets have a long history, dating back to the second millennium BCE; the first varieties have been traced to Sicily. Beets were first cultivated as a leaf vegetable in ancient Greece. They were used medicinally in both Greece and medieval Europe. The popularity of leaf beets declined after the introduction of spinach.

Theories differ on how Swiss chard got its name. Some historians say the French confused chard and cardoon and called them both *carde*, which led to the misnomer "Swiss carde (or cardoon)." Others say that chard was widely cultivated in Switzerland and that a Swiss botanist gave chard its scientific name in the 19th century, to distinguish it from spinach.

Varieties

Although it is stacked on supermarket shelves alongside kales and collards, chard is a member of the beet family, not the cabbage clan. Chard is a leaf beet (in contrast to tuberous beets, page 46). Botanically, leaf beets are divided into two groups: chard (*Beta vulgaris flavescens*) and spinach beets (*B. vulgaris cicla*). Both are beet varieties cultivated around the world for their leaves rather than for their roots. Chard's thick, fleshy ribs are thought to be the result of a mutation from the spinach beet.

Chard comes in several colors, all of which are formally known as Swiss chard. However, the name *Swiss chard* may refer specifically to white chard, to distinguish it from colored types.

Chard is classified in the following groups:

- **white chard:** also known as green chard, white beet and silver beet. It has pastel stems and green leaves.
- **red chard:** cultivars such as rhubarb chard (reddish stems and green leaves) and ruby chard (red stems and reddish leaves). Ruby chard may go by the dramatic name 'Bull's Blood'.
- **rainbow chard:** not a type of chard but rather an attractive bundle of chards with white, red and gold stems and green leaves with veins matching the stems. Rainbow chard may be called 'Bright Lights'. Baby leaf rainbow chard is also available.

Buy It

Chard is sold year-round in supermarkets but is at its best during the summer.

Chard is attractive, with huge, crinkly, bright green leaves and crunchy celery-like stalks in white, red or yellow, with ribs and veins that match the color of the stalk. White chard has thicker stems.

Avoid purchasing chard that has wilted or yellowed leaves and cracked or discolored stems.

Store It

If you have room in the refrigerator, store chard in a vase of water like a bouquet, with a plastic bag draped over the foliage. Otherwise, wrap it loosely in paper towels and place in a plastic bag. Or separate stems from leaves, wrap them loosely in paper towels and place in resealable bags; then refrigerate.

Chard will keep in the refrigerator for up to three days.

Prep It

Before cooking chard, cut off $1/2$ inch (1 cm) at the base of the stem or any part of the stem that is dry or discolored. Pull off any obviously stringy fibers.

For even cooking, separate stems and leaves. Fold each leaf in half and cut out the thick center rib and stem at an angle.

Chop or slice the stems into similar-sized pieces. Stems vary a lot in width, so cut thicker stems lengthwise before slicing crosswise. Slice or chop the leaves.

Wash chard after cutting it: swish in cold water and spin-dry.

Consume It

Tender young leaves may be eaten raw in salads. However, chard is usually cooked. It is ready in 5 to 8 minutes if boiled, 10 minutes if sautéed. To prevent the vibrant colors of red and gold chard from fading, add a spoonful of lemon juice or vinegar when cooking. Note that red chard will stain cooked food.

Some cooks discard the stems, but that's a waste. Chard has perhaps the tastiest stems of all the leafy greens, and they cook up tender-crisp. If a recipe calls for leaves only, save the stems; they can be chopped and sautéed as a vegetable or used like celery in soups and stews. Chopped chard stems may also be used raw, to add crunch to dishes such as tuna salad.

SUBSTITUTES

beet greens, spinach, Malabar spinach

Chard and Harissa Relish

This braised chard spiced with cumin chile paste can be used as a sauce or a unique relish. It is so good you are sure to think of many ways to serve it. I have used it successfully as a topping for grilled eggplant and tossed with linguine to make a luscious vegetarian pasta. You may also be tempted to try it with rice or baked tofu.

Makes 4 to 8 servings (about 2 cups/500 mL)

Vegan Friendly

Sauce

Tips

To peel tomatoes easily, use a serrated peeler.

Harissa is a cumin-spiced Tunisian chile paste that is hot but not fiery. You can find it in specialty shops and well stocked supermarkets.

Bottled reconstituted lemon and lime juices usually contain additives. To avoid them, use freshly squeezed juice. Squeeze a whole lemon or lime and store the leftover juice in a small container in the fridge, or freeze it in 1 tbsp (15 mL) portions in an ice-cube tray.

You can make this relish ahead of time. Transfer it to an airtight container and refrigerate overnight. When ready to serve, heat it in the microwave on High, stirring often, for 1 to 2 minutes or until it reaches room temperature.

2 tbsp	extra virgin olive oil	30 mL
1	shallot, diced	1
4	cloves garlic, slivered	4
3	small tomatoes (about 1 lb/500 g total), peeled and diced (see Tips, left)	3
4 cups	loosely packed finely chopped chard leaves (6 oz/175 g)	1 L
1 tsp	kosher or coarse sea salt	5 mL
1 tbsp	harissa (see Tips, left)	15 mL
1 tbsp	freshly squeezed lime juice (see Tips, left)	15 mL

1. In a saucepan over medium heat, heat oil until shimmery. Stir in shallot and garlic for 30 seconds. Add tomatoes and their juices, chard and salt. Cook, stirring often, for about 3 minutes, until tomatoes soften and release liquid. Stir in harissa. Cover, reduce heat to medium-low and cook for about 10 minutes, until vegetables are very tender and mixture is slightly saucy and reduced to 2 cups (500 mL).

2. Remove from heat, stir in lime juice and set aside for 5 minutes, to release steam. Season with salt to taste. Serve warm or at room temperature.

Rustic Soup with Cheddar Toasts

Soup with chard and veggies is topped here with giant cheesy croutons — make a hearty meal of it. The fried bread is an old-school indulgence.

Makes 6 to 8 servings (about 11 cups/2.75 L)

Soup

Tips

The tender inner stalks of a bunch of celery are called the celery heart.

For best results, use creamy yellow-fleshed potatoes or waxy red or white potatoes in this recipe.

Use a full-sized baguette (about 16 inches/40 cm long), not a thin French stick. Cut off the rounded ends and set them aside for other uses.

• Baking sheet lined with paper towels

Soup

1	small bunch Swiss chard (12 oz/375 g)	1
2	carrots, with greens (about 6 oz/175 g total)	2
2 tbsp	extra virgin olive oil	30 mL
1	stalk celery heart with leaves, cut into 1/2-inch (1 cm) dice (see Tips, left)	1
4	shallots, thinly sliced	4
2	cloves garlic, chopped	2
6 cups	vegetable stock	1.5 L
2 cups	water	500 mL
2	large potatoes (about 1 lb/500 g total), cut into 1/2-inch (1 cm) dice (see Tips, left)	2
1 tsp	dried marjoram	5 mL
1 tsp	kosher or coarse sea salt	5 mL
	Freshly ground black pepper	

Toasts

1/2 cup	extra virgin olive oil	125 mL
1	baguette, cut diagonally into 1-inch (2.5 cm) slices (about 16 pieces; see Tips, left)	1
1 1/2 cups	shredded Cheddar cheese (6 oz/175 g)	375 mL
1/3 cup	chopped fresh parsley leaves	75 mL

1. *Soup:* Trim chard, cutting stems and center ribs from leaves. Place stems and leaves in separate piles. Chop stems and ribs and finely chop leaves. Set aside. Trim carrots. Peel and cut roots into 1/2-inch (1 cm) pieces. Strip leaves from stems, discarding stems. Chop leaves. Set aside.

2. In a large saucepan over medium heat, heat oil until shimmery. Add chard stems and ribs, carrots and leaves, celery, shallots and garlic. Cook, stirring often, for 5 minutes, until softened. Add stock, water, potatoes, chard leaves, marjoram and salt. When mixture comes to a simmer, cover, reduce heat to low and cook for 20 minutes, until vegetables are tender. Season with pepper to taste.

3. *Toasts:* Meanwhile, in a large skillet over medium heat, heat oil until shimmery. In two batches, fry bread slices for 1 to 2 minutes per side, until golden brown. Drain on prepared baking sheet.

4. Preheat oven to 400°F (200°F). Remove paper towels and arrange bread in a single layer on baking sheet. Mound equal quantities of Cheddar on top of each slice. Bake for about 5 minutes, until cheese is molten. Remove from oven and immediately sprinkle with parsley so that it sticks.

5. Ladle soup into wide, shallow bowls. Float 1 or 2 Cheddar toasts in each bowl. Serve immediately, with any remaining toasts alongside.

Cappelletti with Chard and Blue Cheese

Preparing this assertive pasta is a pleasure for lovers of blue cheese and greens. The dish was inspired by a freeform, toss-in-this-and-that recipe passed on by Toronto gardening columnist Sonia Day and demonstrated at a college cooking contest I was judging.

Makes 2 to 4 servings

Main course

Tips

Cappelletti look like little caps. You can substitute any small pasta, but avoid tube shapes — the chard and cheese won't coat them evenly.

To prepare the chard for this recipe: Trim, separating stems and thick center ribs from the leaves. Slice stems thinly and chop the leaves. Set aside in separate piles.

Gorgonzola is a traditional designation-of-origin cheese prepared with animal rennet. However, some companies make Gorgonzola-style cheese with vegetarian rennet. If you are a vegetarian, check the label.

8 oz	cappelletti pasta (see Tips, left)	250 g
2 tbsp	extra virgin olive oil	30 mL
1	bunch Swiss chard, trimmed, stems thinly sliced and leaves chopped (see Tips, left)	1
4	cloves garlic, minced (see Tips, page 118)	4
1 tsp	kosher or coarse sea salt	5 mL
1 cup	grape tomatoes, halved	250 mL
6 oz	Gorgonzola-style cheese, diced (see Tips, left)	175 g
	Freshly ground black pepper	

1. In a large pot of boiling salted water over medium heat, cook pasta for about 15 minutes, until tender to the bite (al dente). Drain.

2. Meanwhile, in a large skillet over medium heat, heat oil until shimmery. Add chard stems and cook, stirring often, for about 3 minutes, until softened. Stir in garlic for 20 seconds. Add chard leaves and salt and stir for about 1 minute, until coated. Cover and cook for 5 minutes, stirring occasionally, until stems are tender-crisp and leaves are wilted and tender. Stir in tomatoes. Remove from heat.

3. Add pasta and stir to coat. Scatter cheese overtop and toss quickly to mix evenly. Season with salt to taste.

4. Transfer to a serving platter or individual dishes. Season with pepper to taste and serve immediately.

Sautéed Red Chard with Lemon and Pine Nuts

This colorful and easy addition to the dinner table makes eating your greens a pleasure, not a chore. Serve it over brown rice or whole grains.

Makes 2 servings

Vegan Friendly

Side dish

Tips

To prepare the chard for this recipe: Trim, separating stems and thick center ribs from the leaves. Using a sharp knife, cut stems and ribs into ½-inch (1 cm) pieces. Chop the leaves coarsely. Set aside in separate piles.

Bottled reconstituted lemon and lime juices usually contain additives. To avoid them, use freshly squeezed juice. Squeeze a whole lemon or lime and store the leftover juice in a small container in the fridge or freeze it in 1 tbsp (15 mL) portions in an ice-cube tray.

2 tbsp	extra virgin olive oil	30 mL
2 tbsp	pine nuts	30 mL
1	small bunch red chard (12 oz/375 g), trimmed, leaves chopped and stems cut into ½-inch (1 cm) pieces (see Tips, left)	1
2	large cloves garlic, chopped	2
½ tsp	kosher or coarse sea salt	2 mL
⅛ tsp	freshly ground black pepper	0.5 mL
2 tsp	freshly squeezed lemon juice (see Tips, left)	10 mL
½ cup	shredded smoked Gouda (2 oz/60 g), optional	125 mL

1. In a large skillet over medium heat, heat oil until shimmery. Fry pine nuts, stirring often, for about 2 minutes, until golden. Using a slotted spoon, transfer nuts to a small bowl.

2. Add chard stems to same skillet and cook over medium heat, stirring often, for about 5 minutes, until softened. Stir in garlic for 20 seconds. Add chard leaves, salt and pepper and cook, stirring often, for about 5 minutes, until leaves are wilted and tender and stems are tender-crisp. Stir in lemon juice and remove from heat. Stir in pine nuts.

3. Transfer to a microwave-safe serving bowl or individual plates. Sprinkle with cheese (if using). Heat in microwave on High for 1 minute or until cheese is molten.

Fettuccine with Chard and Citrus Cream Sauce

Here's a multicolored, multiflavored pasta for dinner. The orange-lime sauce is a luscious coating for the fettuccine and greens.

	Makes 4 servings	

	Vegan Friendly	

	Main course	

Tips

Don't use red chard in this dish, as it will color your sauce hot pink.

To prepare the chard for this recipe: Trim, separating stems and thick center ribs from leaves. Chop stems coarsely. Chop leaves. Set aside in separate piles.

Celery hearts are the tender inner stalks in a bunch of celery.

If substituting soy milk for the cream, use full-fat unflavored soy milk for best results. The sauce, however, will be thinner.

12 oz	fettuccine	375 g
2 tbsp	unsalted butter or non-dairy alternative	30 mL
1	bunch chard, trimmed, stems and leaves chopped (see Tips, left)	1
1	leek, thinly sliced	1
1	stalk celery heart with leaves, diced (see Tips, left)	1
½	red bell pepper, diced	½
1	clove garlic, chopped	1
1 tsp	kosher or coarse sea salt	5 mL
¼ tsp	hot pepper flakes	1 mL
¼ cup	dry white wine	60 mL
¼ cup	vegetable stock	60 mL
1 tbsp	finely grated lime zest	15 mL
½ cup	freshly squeezed orange juice	125 mL
½ cup	heavy or whipping (35%) cream or soy milk (see Tips, left)	125 mL

1. In a pot of boiling salted water over medium heat, cook fettuccine for about 15 minutes, until tender to the bite (al dente). Drain.

2. Meanwhile, in a large skillet over medium heat, melt butter. Add chard stems, leek, celery, red pepper, garlic, salt and hot pepper flakes. Cook, stirring often, for about 5 minutes, until vegetables are softened and turning golden. Add wine and stir, scraping up brown bits from bottom of pan. Cook for about 1 minute, until almost evaporated. Stir in chard leaves and stock. Cover, reduce heat to medium-low and simmer for about 5 minutes, until chard is tender. Add lime zest, orange juice and cream. Reduce heat to medium and simmer for about 5 minutes, until thickened. Remove from heat.

3. Add pasta and toss with tongs until well coated. Season with salt and pepper to taste. Serve immediately.

Chard, Bean and Caramelized Pepper Ragout on Garlic Toast

This rib-sticking stew of beans, greens and veggies piled on thick multigrain toast makes a healthy meatless family meal.

Makes 6 servings		
Vegan Friendly		
Main course		

Tips

To prepare the chard for this recipe: Trim, separating stems and thick center ribs from leaves. Slice stems into 1-inch (2.5 cm) pieces. Chop leaves finely (if you don't chop them into small pieces, they will clump). Set aside in separate piles.

Romano beans are also known as cranberry or borlotti beans.

Choose bread with a dense, chewy crumb, such as a hearty artisan multigrain loaf with a crisp crust, baked in a wood-fired oven. Slices from a sandwich-type loaf are apt to quickly get soggy from the ragout.

7 tbsp	extra virgin olive oil, divided	105 mL
1	bunch chard, trimmed, stems cut into 1-inch (2.5 cm) pieces and leaves finely chopped (see Tips, left)	1
1	green bell pepper, cut into 1/4-inch (0.5 cm) strips	1
1	red bell pepper, cut into 1/4-inch (0.5 cm) strips	1
1	yellow bell pepper, cut into 1/4-inch (0.5 cm) strips	1
1	small red onion, sliced into 1/2-inch (1 cm) rounds	1
1 tsp	granulated sugar (see Tips, page 132)	5 mL
4	large plum tomatoes, peeled and diced	4
1 tsp	fresh thyme leaves	5 mL
1 tsp	kosher or coarse sea salt	5 mL
1/8 tsp	freshly ground black pepper	0.5 mL
1	can (19 oz/540mL) romano beans, rinsed and drained (see Tips, left)	1
1 tbsp	balsamic vinegar	15 mL
6	slices (1 inch/2.5 cm thick) rustic multigrain bread (see Tips, left)	6
1	large clove garlic, halved	1

1. In a large saucepan over medium heat, heat 1/4 cup (60 mL) oil until shimmery. Add chard stems, bell peppers, onion and sugar. Cook, stirring occasionally, for about 20 minutes, until softened and browned.

2. Stir in chard leaves, tomatoes, thyme, salt and pepper. Cover, reduce heat to medium-low and cook, stirring occasionally, for 5 minutes. Stir in beans. Cover and cook for about 5 minutes, until chard and vegetables are tender. Remove from heat. Stir in vinegar and season with salt to taste.

3. Meanwhile, preheat broiler. Arrange bread in a single layer on a large baking sheet and toast under preheated broiler for 3 to 4 minutes, turning once, until both sides are golden brown. Lightly rub tops of toasts with cut side of garlic, then brush with remaining oil (discard garlic or reserve for other uses).

4. Place one slice of toast on each serving plate. Spoon an equal quantity of ragout over each slice, about 1 cup (250 mL) each. Serve immediately.

Chickweed

Stellaria media

Tasting Notes

The raw leaves are soft and delicate. They taste herbaceous, slightly spinachy and astringent. The flowers and stems are nutty, with a slightly bitter finish. When cooked, chickweed leaves are milder and taste faintly like spinach, with a nutty finish and hints of tea.

Equivalents

1 bag trimmed chickweed = 2 to 3 oz (60 to 90 g)

•

2 oz (60 g) leaves and stemlets = 8 cups (2 L), loosely packed

•

2 oz (60 g) stemmed chickweed = 4 cups (1 L), loosely packed

This plant is botanically named *Stellaria* for its star-shaped white flowers and commonly named "chickweed" for its appeal to chickens and other birds.

Native to Europe, chickweed has spread worldwide, even to the Arctic. It is found in urban, suburban and rural areas throughout North America. Delicate yet hardy, it grows in mats and spreads, aggravating gardeners and perfectionists who fuss over their lawns.

In Japan, chickweed is one of the seven greens added to a rice porridge eaten every January 7 during the Festival of Seven Herbs. The porridge ritual is supposed to bring good luck and longevity.

Varieties

Common chickweed (*Stellaria media*) lives up to its name — it is one of the most common weeds found around the world.

Common chickweed may be confused with two almost identical relatives: greater chickweed (*S. neglecta*), which prefers damp and shade, and lesser chickweed (*S. pallida*), found in sandy soil or along coastlines.

A number of unrelated plants are also called chickweed, including mouse-eared chickweed (*Cerastium fontanum*). It is said to resemble common chickweed but is hairier; it is cooked before being eaten.

Buy It

As well as being foraged, chickweed is occasionally sold in farmers' markets. It is trimmed and bagged as a tangle of leaves, flowers, buds and small stems.

Small, pointed, smooth-edged green leaves grow in pairs along thin stems, topped with tiny white flowers as well as unopened buds. Common chickweed can be distinguished by a single line of fine hairs along the stems and leaf edges.

SUBSTITUTES

baby spinach, mâche, purslane, nettles, microgreens, jute leaf, Malabar spinach

Store It

When storing chickweed, be careful not to crush the delicate greens. Place in a resealable bag with some air left in to act as a cushion, then refrigerate.

Chickweed will keep in the refrigerator for up to two days.

Prep It

Chickweed leaves, flowers and stems are edible. However, even thin stems are stringy. If you are preparing chickweed salad, pluck only the buds and leaves, removing all but the tiniest stemlets. If you are cooking chickweed, it's fine to include stemlets.

To wash, swish chickweed gently in cold water. Drain the greens and lay them on paper towels to air-dry. Do not dry chickweed in a salad spinner, as that can bruise the leaves.

Consume It

Chickweed is best eaten raw in salads, but it may be used to prepare soups, pastas or pestos.

Toss chickweed salads with dressing at the last minute, because the soft leaves wilt quickly.

When cooked with the wash water clinging to its leaves, chickweed is ready in 1 to 2 minutes. When steamed, it takes up to 5 minutes to cook.

Be brief with the application of heat. When adding chickweed to pasta, rice or hot grains, simply stir it in at the end — the residual heat of the dish will cook the greens.

Like Malabar spinach (see page 228), jute leaf (see page 184) and purslane (see page 295), chickweed contains some mucilage, so it has thickening power when added to dishes.

Chickweed Salad with Tangerine Vinaigrette

*Don't say the word **weed** when serving this genteel salad. Delicate chickweed tossed with pecans and dried cherries makes a starter worth serving to guests. However, you needn't save it for special occasions.*

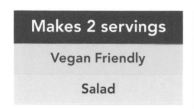

Makes 2 servings

Vegan Friendly

Salad

Tips

To toast pecans, cook them in a dry skillet over medium heat for 2 to 3 minutes, stirring often, until golden and aromatic.

You can purchase dried cherries at bulk food stores and gourmet food shops.

2 oz	stemmed chickweed (4 cups/1 L, loosely packed)	60 g
½ cup	Tangerine Vinaigrette (page 451)	125 mL
½ cup	pecans, toasted and coarsely chopped (see Tips, left)	125 mL
¼ cup	dried cherries (see Tips, left)	60 mL

1. In a bowl, toss chickweed with vinaigrette to taste (you will have some left over). Add pecans and dried cherries and toss lightly to combine. Serve immediately.

Variations

Substitute dried cranberries or raisins for the cherries, and walnuts, almonds or cashews for the pecans.

Chinese Broccoli

Brassica oleracea alboglabra

> ***Other names:*** **Chinese kale, flowering kale, mustard orchid, white flowering broccoli, white flowering Chinese cabbage.**
>
> **Depending on where you are shopping, you may find Chinese broccoli identified as** *cai ro, gai lan, gai lum, gelancai, jie lan, kairan, kan lan tsoi* **or** *phakkhana.*

Culinary historians believe Chinese broccoli to be a descendant of cabbage seeds taken to China by Portuguese traders in the 16th century. The cabbage was bred into Chinese broccoli through many generations. It is theorized that Chinese broccoli looks like the broccoli prevalent during the Roman Empire.

Varieties

Chinese broccoli comes in mature and baby versions. The latter may be labeled "gai lan junior."

Buy It

Chinese broccoli is sold in Asian supermarkets, usually labeled "gai lan." It looks more like rapini (page 322) or yu choy sum (page 426) than it does broccoli.

You can recognize Chinese broccoli by its clusters of fleshy light green stems topped by large green leaves, small, dark bluish green florets and a few tiny white flowers and buds.

Look for firm stalks and perky leaves. Avoid stems that are flaccid or dry and discolored at the base. The flowers should be mainly buds; open flowers are a sign that the vegetable is past its prime.

Store It

Swathe Chinese broccoli tightly in plastic wrap, then refrigerate it. Or separate the stems and leaves and store in resealable bags.

Chinese broccoli will keep in the refrigerator for up to three days. The stems will last twice as long but get bitter as they age.

Prep It

Before cooking Chinese broccoli, cut a thin slice off the base of each stem cluster to remove dry ends. Separate stems and leaves. If desired, use a vegetable peeler to peel the thickest parts of

Tasting Notes

Chinese broccoli stems are succulent, broccoli-flavored and slightly salty, with a faint mustard finish. The leaves are grassy and astringent, with a mustardy edge. The cooked stems taste like broccoli and the leaves taste like spinach.

Health Notes

Chinese broccoli contains vitamins A, B_6, C, E and K, calcium, copper, folate, iron, magnesium, manganese, potassium, phosphorus, riboflavin, thiamin and zinc.

In traditional Chinese medicine, Chinese broccoli has been used as a treatment for anemia.

Equivalents

1 bunch = 1½ to 2 lbs (750 g to 1 kg)

•

1 lb (500 g) bunch = 8 oz (250 g) stems and 8 oz (250 g) leaves and florets

•

2 oz (60 g) stems cut into 1-inch (2.5 cm) pieces = ½ cup (125 mL), loosely packed

•

2 oz (60 g) coarsely chopped or shredded leaves = 4 cups (1 L), loosely packed

SUBSTITUTES

rapini, yu choy sum, komatsuna

the stems to remove stringy bits. To promote even cooking, cut thicker parts of the stem in half lengthwise.

To wash, rinse stems in cold running water. Swish leaves in a bowl of cold water and spin-dry. Or wash both stems and leaves after cutting, then spin-dry.

Consume It

Chinese broccoli is a popular ingredient in Asian cuisine. In North America, however, Chinatown restaurants often substitute the milder, more recognizable Western broccoli for iconic dishes such as beef and broccoli.

Chinese broccoli is eaten as a cooked vegetable. It may be stir-fried, steamed or boiled. The stems, leaves, florets and flowers are all used.

In some recipes the stems are given a head start; then the leaves are added 2 to 3 minutes before the end of cooking time. Cook stems until they are fork-tender (easily pierced with a fork).

Chinese broccoli benefits from steam-frying. To steam-fry, stir-fry broccoli pieces over high heat for about 2 minutes. Add stock — about ⅓ cup (75 mL) per 1 lb (500 g) — cover, reduce the heat to medium and steam for 3 to 4 minutes. Uncover, increase the heat to high and stir-fry for about 1 minute to evaporate excess liquid.

The stems may be prepared separately and served like asparagus, for example, while the tops may be reserved for stir-fries and soups. When boiled, stems are ready in about 10 minutes.

To decrease bitterness, the Chinese may blanch these vegetables for up to 2 minutes, drain and refresh them under cold water, pat them dry and then stir-fry. If you are sensitive to bitterness, you could blanch Chinese broccoli even longer, to taste; however, the texture may become soggy. For an attractive presentation, whole stalks may be steamed, laid on a serving platter and drizzled with sauce.

Prepare Chinese broccoli just before you are ready to serve, because it releases liquid as it stands. If necessary, drain before adding sauce.

My Ponzu Scheme

Chinese broccoli is lip-smacking good with ponzu, a citrusy soy sauce. This dish is one of my favorite veggie stir-fries, and it's super easy.

Tips

To prepare Chinese broccoli for this recipe: Trim, separating stems from leaves and florets. Cut stems into 1-inch (2.5 cm) pieces, cutting the thickest pieces in half lengthwise. Coarsely chop the leaves. Set aside in separate piles.

After washing Chinese broccoli, pat it dry before stir-frying. Otherwise, water droplets will cause the hot oil to spatter and could burn you as well as make a mess on the stove.

For the finest minced garlic, push it through a press.

Ponzu, a blend of soy sauce and Asian citrus fruit, can be found in the Asian food section of well-stocked supermarkets.

Toasted sesame oil, also known as Asian sesame oil, is made from toasted or roasted sesame seeds. Dark and aromatic, it is sold in small bottles as a flavoring agent. Do not confuse toasted sesame oil with yellow sesame oil, which is pressed from raw seeds.

- Wok

2 tbsp	oil	30 mL
1 lb	Chinese broccoli, stems, leaves and florets trimmed, separated and chopped (see Tips, left)	500 g
1	large clove garlic, minced (see Tips, left)	1
½ tsp	kosher or coarse sea salt	2 mL
⅓ cup	vegetable stock	75 mL
1 tbsp	ponzu (see Tips, left)	15 mL
1 tbsp	toasted sesame oil (see Tips, left)	15 mL
1 tbsp	sesame seeds, toasted (see Tips, page 129)	15 mL

1. Heat wok over medium-high heat for 1 minute. Add oil and swirl to coat bottom of pan. Add Chinese broccoli stems (step back, as they will spatter) and cook, shaking pan often, for about 1 minute, until vibrant green. Stir in garlic, then immediately add leaves and salt. Stir-fry for 1 minute, until slightly wilted and coated with oil. Add stock, cover, reduce heat to medium and cook for 3 to 4 minutes, until stems are tender-crisp. Uncover, increase heat to high and cook, shaking pan, for about 1 minute, until most of the liquid has evaporated.

2. Remove from heat. Stir in ponzu, then sesame oil. Transfer to a serving platter and sprinkle sesame seeds overtop. Serve immediately.

Smoky Chinese Broccoli

Tossed with smoky salt and a touch of oil, Chinese broccoli is irresistible yet oh so simple to prepare. I got the idea for tea-smoked salt from a San Francisco restaurant.

Makes 4 servings

Vegan Friendly

Side dish

Tip

To prepare Chinese broccoli for this recipe: Trim, separating stems from leaves and florets. Cut the leaves crosswise into 2-inch (5 cm) pieces. Peel the stems. Halve the thickest stems lengthwise. Cut stems into 1-inch (2.5 cm) pieces.

- Spice grinder

1 tsp	lapsang souchong (smoked) tea leaves	5 mL
1 tsp	coarse sea salt	5 mL
1 lb	Chinese broccoli, stems, leaves and florets separated and cut (see Tip, left)	500 g
2 tsp	unrefined sesame oil (see Tips, page 123)	10 mL

1. Using spice grinder, grind tea leaves and salt to a powder. Set aside.
2. In a covered steamer basket above 1 inch (2.5 cm) of boiling water, steam Chinese broccoli over medium-low heat for about 10 minutes, until tender-crisp. Transfer broccoli onto paper towels and gently pat dry.
3. In a large serving bowl, toss broccoli with oil, then with smoked salt to taste (you will have some left over). Serve warm or at room temperature.

Chinese Broccoli with Nori Mayonnaise

This Pan-Asian dish stars Chinese broccoli stems, served at room temperature with a dip I'd love to see on a sushi train. Reserve the leaves for other dishes.

Makes 2 servings

Vegan Friendly

Side dish

Tips

To promote even cooking, cut thick stems of Chinese broccoli in half lengthwise.

Look for toasted nori and pickled ginger in well-stocked supermarkets. To chop nori, fold it along the serrations, then use kitchen scissors to cut it into tiny pieces.

8 oz	Chinese broccoli stems, trimmed and peeled (see Tips, left)	250 g
½ cup	mayonnaise or vegan alternative	125 mL
1	sheet toasted nori, chopped	1
1 tbsp	finely chopped pickled ginger, drained or ½ tsp (2 mL) puréed gingerroot	15 mL
1 tsp	rice vinegar	5 mL
¼ tsp	freshly squeezed lemon juice	1 mL
¼ tsp	kosher or coarse sea salt	1 mL

1. In a covered steamer basket above 1 inch (2.5 cm) of boiling water, steam stems over medium-low heat for about 10 minutes, until tender-crisp. Immediately rinse with cold water to stop the cooking, drain and set aside to cool to room temperature. Pat dry.
2. Meanwhile, in a medium measuring cup, combine mayonnaise, nori, ginger, rice vinegar, lemon juice and salt.
3. Serve stems with nori mayonnaise alongside for dipping.

Green Pad See Ew

In this leafy green vegetarian version of a signature Thai dish, slippery rice noodles are bathed in a simple soy-lime sauce, while tofu and egg provide additional protein. Make sure you have all the ingredients prepped and ready, or what should be a simple job will become massively confusing.

Makes 4 to 6 servings

Vegan Friendly

Main course

Tips

To maintain more control over the saltiness of dishes, use reduced-sodium soy sauce. Depending on the type, 1 tbsp (15 mL) regular soy sauce can contain 1,000 mg or more of sodium. Reduced-sodium soy sauce contains about half that amount.

To prepare Chinese broccoli for this recipe: Trim, separating stems from leaves and florets. Using a vegetable peeler, peel the thickest stems and cut in half lengthwise. Cut stems crosswise into ½-inch (1 cm) pieces. Coarsely chop leaves and florets.

---

* Wok

¼ cup	soy sauce (see Tips, left)	60 mL
1 tbsp	freshly squeezed lime juice	15 mL
1 tbsp	granulated sugar (see Tips, page 132)	15 mL
2	large eggs, optional	2
	Kosher or coarse sea salt	
8 oz	dried rice noodles, ½ inch (1 cm) wide	250 g
¼ cup	oil	60 mL
12 oz	medium tofu, drained and cut into ½-inch (1 cm) cubes	375 g
6	cloves garlic, slivered	6
1 lb	Chinese broccoli, stems, leaves and florets, separated and cut (see Tips, left)	500 g
2 tbsp	vegetable stock or water	30 mL
2 tbsp	slivered basil leaves	30 mL

1. In a small measuring cup, combine soy sauce, lime juice and sugar.

2. In a small bowl, lightly whisk eggs (if using) with salt to taste.

3. In a large pan of boiling salted water over medium heat, cook noodles for 5 to 8 minutes, until tender but firm. Drain.

4. Meanwhile, heat wok over high heat for 1 minute. Add oil and swirl to coat bottom of pan. Add eggs (if using) and fry undisturbed for about 1 minute, until very puffy. Flip over and then, using a slotted spoon, transfer to a large plate, leaving oil in wok. Using a spoon, break egg into large chunks.

5. In wok over high heat, add tofu (be careful, as it will spatter) and cook, shaking pan often, for 3 to 5 minutes, until golden. Using a slotted spoon, transfer tofu to a plate, leaving oil in wok.

6. Add garlic to wok and stir-fry for 20 seconds. Add Chinese broccoli, salt lightly to taste, and stir-fry for about 1 minute, until leaves are slightly wilted. Add stock, cover and cook for 3 to 4 minutes, until stems are tender-crisp. Add noodles and soy sauce mixture and, using tongs, toss gently to combine. Add eggs and toss briefly. Remove from heat. Season with salt to taste. Transfer to a serving platter or individual bowls. Top with tofu and sprinkle with basil. Serve immediately.

Chinese Celery

Apium graveolens secalinum

Other names: **Chinese small celery, cutting/leaf celery, French celery.**

Depending on where you are shopping, you may find Chinese celery identified as *aipo, ajmond, blegsselleri, can tau, céleri à côtes, gin cai, kan tsoi, karafs, khuen chai, kinchay, qin cai, saderi, sedano, seri-na* or *ten chai*.

Chinese celery is a slender, leafier sibling of common celery. Its delicate appearance is deceptive — the thin, rounded stalks can grow to more than a foot (30 cm) tall. Although it may be native to the Mediterranean basin, Chinese celery is considered to be more closely related to the wild celery that grows in Asia than to common celery. Celery is one of the ingredients in recipes written on bamboo slips dating from the Han Dynasty (206 BCE to 220 CE) in China.

Varieties

There are two types: white Chinese celery, which has yellowish white stalks and green leaves, and green Chinese celery, which is taller and more aromatic, with stems that may have a hollow or solid core.

Chinese celery (*Apium graveolens secalinum*) is related to common celery (*A. graveolens dulce*) and celeriac (*A. graveolens rapaceum*).

Cultivated celeries are descendants of pungent wild celery (*A. graveolens*), which Greeks may cook with and know as *selino* or mountain celery. A related wild celery is sea parsley (*A. prostratum*), also known as Maori or Australia celery.

Buy It

You can find Chinese celery in Asian supermarkets.

Tall Chinese celery stalks grow in a cluster, with a full head of green leaves ranging in color from pastel to dark green. Look for crisp stalks and vibrant leaves. Browning or dryness at the root ends, discolored stems and yellowed leaves are signs that the celery is past its prime.

Tasting Notes

Chinese celery has a familiar celery flavor but is more potent than common celery. The raw stems are juicy, slightly sweet and salty, and somewhat stringy. The leaves are coarse, slightly bitter and astringent.

Health Notes

Although no official government analysis is available, Chinese celery is likely to have a nutritional profile similar to common celery's, but higher in nutrients because it is leafier. This would suggest that Chinese celery contains vitamins A, B_6, C and K, calcium, folate, iron, manganese, magnesium, potassium, phosphorus, riboflavin and thiamin. It is also high in sodium.

In herbal medicine, celery has been used as a diuretic. It has also been used to stimulate appetite and digestion, alleviate rheumatism and lower stress.

SUBSTITUTES

celeriac greens

Store It

If you have room in the refrigerator, place Chinese celery in a vase of water like a bouquet, with a plastic bag draped over the foliage. Or swathe the stalks in damp paper towels and store them in resealable perforated bags in the refrigerator. Or cut the celery into pieces and place in a resealable bag.

Chinese celery will keep in the refrigerator for up to one week if intact or up to three days if cut.

Prep It

Before cooking Chinese celery, trim the base of the clusters to release the stalks. Discard the thicker parts of the stems that look fibrous. Slice or chop tender stems and leaves.

Washing whole stalks is difficult. Cut the celery into pieces, then swish in cold water, drain and spin-dry.

If Chinese celery is flaccid, immerse it in a bowl of ice water for 5 minutes.

Consume It

Unlike common celery, raw Chinese celery is unpleasant to munch on. It is best cooked, particularly in stir-fries, soups and rice dishes. Cook it the same way as for common celery. When stir-fried, it is tender-crisp in 5 minutes. When simmered, it is tender in 15 to 20 minutes.

Green Soup

Pleasantly slippery tofu floats in a green broth infused with aromatic Chinese celery and cilantro. Low in fat and high in flavor, this is a simple, healthful soup.

Tips

Finger chiles are also known as cayenne peppers. They are slender, with pointed tips. You can substitute any kind of chile you prefer.

To prepare the Chinese celery for this recipe: Trim the base to release the stems; discard tough parts of stems. Using a sharp knife, slice tender stems and leaves into small pieces.

Unrefined sesame oil has a pronounced nutty flavor. This golden oil is sold in gourmet food stores and well-stocked markets. Do not mistake it for toasted sesame oil, a dark, fragrant seasoning oil, also known as Asian sesame oil. If you can't find cold-pressed sesame oil, substitute extra virgin olive oil.

2 tbsp	unrefined sesame oil (see Tips, left)	30 mL
1	green finger chile, seeded and chopped (see Tips, left)	1
1	large clove garlic, minced (see Tips, page 118)	1
1 tsp	puréed gingerroot (see Tips, page 137)	5 mL
1	bunch Chinese celery (1 lb/500 g), trimmed and sliced (see Tips, left)	1
12	green onions (white and green parts), thinly sliced, divided	12
1 tsp	kosher or coarse sea salt	5 mL
3 cups	vegetable stock	750 mL
2 cups	water	500 mL
1 lb	medium-firm tofu, drained and cut into ½-inch (1 cm) cubes	500 g
¼ cup	finely chopped fresh cilantro leaves	60 mL
1 tsp	soy sauce (see Tips, page 120)	5 mL

1. In a large saucepan over medium heat, heat oil until shimmery. Add chile, garlic and ginger and stir for 20 seconds. Add Chinese celery, all but 1 cup (250 mL) of the onions, and salt. Cook, stirring occasionally, for about 5 minutes, until softened. Add stock and water. When mixture comes to a simmer, cover, reduce heat to low and cook for about 20 minutes, until celery is very tender.

2. Stir in tofu, cilantro and reserved onions. Simmer for 1 minute, until heated through. Stir in soy sauce and serve warm.

Chinatown Takeout Curry

Chinese curry bears only a passing resemblance to Indian curries. In Chinatown, assorted ingredients are tossed in a relatively mild, thick, glossy gravy seasoned with curry powder. Restaurants make their curry sauce separately or buy it ready-made, then pour it over stir-fried ingredients. This vegetarian recipe is but an introduction to the wide world of Chinese curries. It tastes of nostalgia. As Chinatown restaurants do, I've included Chinese celery, carrot slices, onion and green pepper chunks. The British use the sauce on its own as well, as a dip for french fries.

Makes 4 to 6 servings

Vegan Friendly

Main course

Tips

For the finest minced garlic, push it through a press.

I use Madras curry powder, which is a good all-purpose curry spice blend. For the liveliest flavor, make sure your curry powder is fresh. The aroma should be pleasantly pungent, not faded. Its shelf life is 2 to 4 months; check the label for a best-before date.

To maintain more control over the saltiness of dishes, use reduced-sodium soy sauce. Depending on the type, 1 tbsp (15 mL) regular soy sauce can contain 1,000 mg or more of sodium. Reduced-sodium soy sauce contains about half that amount.

Cayenne gives the sauce a bit of a kick. If you prefer a mild sauce, reduce the amount called for or omit.

- Wok

Sauce

4	large cloves garlic, minced (see Tips, left)	4
2 tbsp	curry powder (see Tips, left)	30 mL
2 tbsp	soy sauce (see Tips, left)	30 mL
2 tsp	tomato paste	10 mL
2 tsp	puréed gingerroot (see Tips, page 137)	10 mL
2 tsp	granulated sugar (see Tips, page 132)	10 mL
1 tsp	five-spice powder (see Tips, page 125)	5 mL
1/2 tsp	cayenne pepper (see Tips, left)	2 mL
1/4 cup	cornstarch	60 mL
4 1/4 cups	vegetable stock, divided	1.125 L
1/4 cup	oil	60 mL
1	large shallot, finely chopped	1
	Kosher or coarse sea salt	

Curry

1 tbsp	oil	15 mL
3 1/2 cups	trimmed and chopped Chinese celery (4 oz/125 g)	875 mL
1	onion, cut into 1-inch (2.5 cm) chunks	1
1	green bell pepper, cut into 1-inch (2.5 cm) chunks	1
2	carrots (4 oz/125 g total), sliced diagonally 1/4 inch (0.5 cm) thick and blanched (see Tips, page 125)	2
1/2 tsp	kosher or coarse sea salt	2 mL
1	can (14 oz/398 mL) baby corn, drained, rinsed and cut into 1-inch (2.5 cm) pieces	1

1. *Sauce:* In a small bowl, combine garlic, curry powder, soy sauce, tomato paste, ginger, sugar, five-spice powder and cayenne. Set aside.

2. In another small bowl, combine cornstarch and 1/4 cup (60 mL) stock. Set aside.

Tips

Five-spice powder is a blend sold at Asian grocery stores and spice shops. Blends vary by brand, but five-spice typically includes ground star anise, fennel, Chinese cinnamon (cassia), cloves and Szechuan peppercorns, plus spices such as ginger and black pepper. The name *five-spice* refers not to the number of spices but to what the Chinese consider to be the five principal tastes.

To blanch carrot slices, cook them in a pot of boiling water for 1 minute, then drain and immediately rinse with cold water to stop the cooking.

Make the sauce just before you plan to use it, and do not cover it once it is done. It will thin as it sits. To rethicken leftover sauce, combine equal amounts of cornstarch and water (about 1 tsp/5 mL each) and stir into the sauce while warming it over medium heat. Bring it to a boil to activate the thickening power of the cornstarch.

3. In a medium saucepan over medium heat, heat oil until shimmery. Add shallot and cook, stirring often, for 1 to 2 minutes, until softened. Add prepared spice paste and stir in for 30 to 60 seconds. Add remaining stock and stir, scraping up brown bits from bottom of pan. When mixture comes to a simmer, reduce heat to medium-low and cook for about 15 minutes, until shallot is very tender. Stir cornstarch mixture to loosen, then gradually add to the pan, stirring well to combine. Simmer for about 2 minutes, until sauce is thick and bubbly. Remove pan from heat but do not cover it (see Tips, left). Season with salt to taste. Set aside.

4. *Curry:* Heat wok over medium-high heat for 1 minute. Add oil, swirling to coat bottom of pan. Add Chinese celery, onion, green pepper, carrots and salt. Stir-fry for about 5 minutes, until vegetables are tender-crisp. Stir in baby corn for 1 minute, until heated through. Remove from heat and pour sauce, to taste, over vegetables (you may have some left over). Serve immediately.

Variations

This recipe makes about 4 cups (1 L) curry sauce. That's enough to accommodate the addition of 1 lb (500 g) of protein, such as cubed tofu. Alternatively, you can pour any leftovers over sautéed vegetables or use the sauce as you would a gravy.

Try adding about 1 cup (250 mL) mushrooms or snowpeas — or any other vegetable you fancy — to the curry in Step 4.

Green Rice with Pistachios

Green is the tasty color theme in this pretty rice dish packed with herbal flavors.

Makes 4 to 6 servings (about 6 cups/1.5 L)

Vegan Friendly

Side dish

Tips

To prepare the Chinese celery for this recipe: Using a sharp knife, trim the base to separate the stalks. Discard tough ends of stems and finely chop tender stems and leaves.

To toast pistachios, cook them in a dry skillet over medium heat for 2 to 3 minutes, stirring often, until golden and aromatic.

2 tbsp	extra virgin olive oil	30 mL
1½ cups	trimmed and chopped Chinese celery (4 oz/125 g; see Tips, left)	375 mL
1	leek (white and light green parts), thinly sliced	1
1 tsp	kosher or coarse sea salt	5 mL
1 cup	basmati rice, rinsed	250 mL
2 cups	water	500 mL
1 tsp	finely grated lime zest	5 mL
1 tbsp	freshly squeezed lime juice	15 mL
½ cup	finely chopped fresh parsley leaves	125 mL
½ cup	finely chopped fresh cilantro leaves	125 mL
1 cup	shelled unsalted pistachios, toasted (see Tips, left)	250 mL

1. In a saucepan over medium heat, heat oil until shimmery. Add Chinese celery, leek and salt. Cook, stirring often, for about 5 minutes, until softened. Stir in rice for 1 minute, until combined. Add water and lime zest. Bring to a boil, cover, reduce heat to low and simmer for about 18 minutes, until water is absorbed and rice is tender. Remove from heat, uncover and set aside for 5 minutes.

2. Add lime juice, parsley, cilantro and pistachios. Using a fork, gently fluff and mix the rice. Season with salt to taste.

Tastes Like Celery?

Celery-like greens are popular around the world. They include:

- **water celery** (*Oenanthe javanica*), also known as Korean watercress, Indian pennywort, Japanese/water parsley, water dropwort, *minari, brunnenkresse* or *seri*. It is enjoyed from Italy to India to Japan but is rarely seen in North American shops. Water celery is described as crunchy and vegetal, with assertive celery, watercress and parsley flavors. Koreans add it to kimchi and fish soup and they drink the juice as a liver tonic. One of the few greens indigenous to Japan, it is added to a rice porridge eaten every January 7 during the Festival of Seven Herbs. Do not confuse it with *mitsuba* (*Cryptotaenia japonica*), which is also called Japanese parsley, trefoil or honewort.
- **lovage** (*Levisticum officinale*), also known as *lovstikke, livèche, céleri de montagne, levistico* and *Maggikraut*. Famous for its celery flavor, lovage is a popular cultivated plant in Europe. The leaves and roots are used in salads and soups.
- **Asian wild celery** (*Trachyspermum roxburghianum*), also known as India wild celery, *radhuni* or *ajmud*. It is grown mainly for its seeds, as a spice, especially in South and Southeast Asia. However, its fresh leaves may be eaten as an herb (in place of parsley or cilantro) or as salad greens.

Chrysanthemum Greens

Chrysanthemum coronarium

Other names: chop suey greens, cooking/edible/garland chrysanthemum, crown daisy, margherita, *shungiku*, small leaves.

Depending on where you are shopping, you may find chrysanthemum greens identified as *antimonio, cai cui, chong ho, kek wah, guladaudi, kikuna, mantilda, mirabeles, moya, pak thang-o, ssukgat* or *tong ho.*

Tasting Notes

Chrysanthemum leaves are mildly grassy, with a bitter aftertaste if used raw. The stems are crunchy and slightly sweet. The greens have a hint of celery flavor.

Health Notes

Chrysanthemum leaves contain vitamins A, B_6, C, E and K, calcium, copper, folate, iron, magnesium, manganese, niacin, phosphorus, potassium and riboflavin. However, the greens are high in sodium.

In herbal medicine, chrysanthemum greens have been used to regulate blood sugar and alleviate liver conditions. A tea is brewed from the leaves to quell coughs and flu.

Chrysanthemum greens resemble herbs but they are used mainly as leaf vegetables, especially in Chinese, Korean and Japanese cuisine.

The plants are native to the Mediterranean and Asia. In China, chrysanthemums were first cultivated as medicinal herbs circa 1500 BCE. Japan imported the leafy greens from China and has cultivated them for centuries. They are revered as a type of *kaga yasai*, or traditional vegetable.

Varieties

Chrysanthemum greens come from a specific species of chrysanthemum grown for its leaves. Known as garland chrysanthemum (*Chrysanthemum coronarium*), it is botanically different from ornamental mums, so don't go rooting around in your flowerbeds for dinner ingredients.

There are two types of chrysanthemum greens: big-leaf, favored in China for stir-fries, and fine-leaf, favored in Japan and Korea for salads.

Buy It

You can find chrysanthemum greens in Asian supermarkets. They are seasonal from spring to autumn and turn bitter once they flower. When shopping, you are more likely to find mature greens.

Chrysanthemum greens have flat, serrated leaves on clusters of thin stems. Look for greens that are lush and feathery. Check the center of clusters and edges of leaves for moist, dark clumps, which are signs of rot.

SUBSTITUTES

spinach

Store It

Chrysanthemum greens don't keep well. Place them in a glass or vase of water like a bouquet, with a plastic bag draped over the foliage; then refrigerate. Or loosen the clusters, wrap the greens in paper towels and place them in perforated resealable bags.

Chrysanthemum greens will keep in the refrigerator for up to two days.

Prep It

Before cooking chrysanthemum greens, trim about ½ inch (1 cm) off the base of the stalks to remove dry or discolored bits. If desired, discard portions of stems wider than ⅛ inch (3 mm), as they tend to be bitter.

To wash them, swish the greens in a bowl of cold water, drain and spin-dry.

Consume It

Very young, fresh leaves and tender stalks may be added raw to mixed salads. However, chrysanthemum greens are usually cooked.

To eliminate bitterness, the greens are often blanched before use. Blanch whole or coarsely chopped greens in boiling water for 20 to 30 seconds (no longer, as they cook quickly). Drain and rinse immediately under cold running water. Using your hands, squeeze chopped greens to remove excess moisture, but be gentle or you will mangle them. Use as is or add them to prepared dishes at the end of the cooking time.

Chrysanthemum greens may be blanched, steamed or used in stir-fries, tempura, hot pots, soups and omelets. For a Japanese-style salad, toss blanched, cooled greens with sesame dressing.

Do not overcook chrysanthemum greens, or they will turn bitter and mushy. Stick to preparations that take less than a minute.

Sorting Out Asian Greens

Mild, bitter and in-between, from diverse species with enough names to give you a headache, and spellings all over the map — no wonder people find Asian greens confusing.

To sort them out, it's helpful to think of Asian greens as leaf types, stem types or flowerbud types.

Leaf types are the most diverse. They include chrysanthemum greens but are dominated by the mustard family, from red giants to delicate mizuna.

Stem types include the Chinese cabbages, napa cabbage and bok choy.

Flowerbud types are harvested with their stems, leaves, florets and flowers — all are meant to be eaten. Most noteworthy are Chinese broccoli and yu choy sum.

Sesame Shungiku Salad

In Japan they call chrysanthemum greens **shungiku** *and use them in soups, one-pot dishes and salads. This recipe is not a salad as North Americans know it, although it does have dressing and is eaten at room temperature. Whatever you want to call it, this dish is visually pretty and addictively delicious with its sesame dressing. In looks and texture, the greens remind me of seaweed salad, but they are not as strong-tasting.*

Makes 4 servings

Vegan Friendly

Salad

Tips

Shiitake stems are tough. Pull them out and discard them.

Supermarkets sell mini cucumbers, which are dwarf cucumbers related to seedless English cucumbers. You can eat them with or without the peel. In this recipe I leave the peel on because it looks more attractive.

Toasted sesame seeds are available in well-stocked supermarkets. To toast your own, cook sesame seeds in a dry skillet over medium heat for about 2 minutes, stirring occasionally, until seeds start to clump and turn golden and aromatic. For an attractive presentation, use toasted mixed white and black sesame seeds.

12 oz	chrysanthemum stalks (stems and leaves), trimmed	375 g
8 oz	firm block tofu, drained	250 g
2 tbsp	oil	30 mL
4	large, flat shiitake mushroom caps (see Tips, left)	4
	Kosher or coarse sea salt	
1/3 cup	Sesame Dressing (page 453)	75 mL
2	mini cucumbers, trimmed and halved lengthwise (see Tips, left)	2
2 tsp	toasted sesame seeds (see Tips, left)	10 mL

1. In a large saucepan of boiling salted water, blanch whole chrysanthemum stalks over medium heat for 20 to 30 seconds. Using a colander, drain and immediately rinse in cold running water until cooled to room temperature. Drain and set aside.

2. Pat dry tofu. Using a sharp knife, cut block in half horizontally through the center, then cut each half into two triangles.

3. In a nonstick skillet over medium heat, heat oil until shimmery. Add tofu and cook for about 5 minutes, turning with tongs, until golden brown on all sides and heated through. Transfer to a plate lined with paper towels.

4. Lightly wipe the skillet with a paper towel, leaving a thin sheen of oil. Return skillet to medium heat and add mushrooms, gill sides up. Sprinkle with salt to taste. Cook for about 1 minute, until softened. Turn and cook on gill sides for about 1 minute, until mushrooms are softened and turning golden. Remove from heat.

5. Coarsely chop chrysanthemum greens. Gently squeeze handfuls to extract excess liquid; transfer to a medium bowl. Add 3 to 4 tbsp (45 to 60 mL) dressing and toss to coat lightly.

6. Divide greens among 4 serving plates. Top each with a tofu triangle. Drizzle dressing over each triangle (you may have some left over). Arrange 1 mushroom and 1 cucumber half on each plate. Crumble salt, to taste, over cucumbers. Garnish with sesame seeds.

Variation

If desired, cook an entire medium bunch of chrysanthemum greens (about 1 lb/500 g) for this recipe. In Step 5, increase the dressing to 1/4 cup (60 mL).

Collards

Brassica oleracea acephala, B. oleracea viridis

> *Other names:* **borecole, couve, cut-and-come-again, rosette colewort, pamphrey.**
>
> **Depending on where you are shopping, you may find collards identified as *berza, chou précoce, col verde nueva, haak, kovi* or *rastika*.**

The name *collard* evolved from *colewort*, referring to a cabbage plant. Collards are popular in the American South, Brazil and Portugal. They are also grown in Africa, Slavic European nations, Spain and India.

Leafy cabbages originated in the Mediterranean basin. The ancient Greeks and Romans grew them and the Romans carried them as far north as Scotland. Centuries later, Scots carried collards to the American South, where they became an essential ingredient in the African-American cuisine known as soul food. Slaves used collards as a substitute for the African greens they had been accustomed to eating. Meanwhile, Portuguese colonists transplanted collards to Brazil.

Tasting Notes

When raw, collards are lemony and astringent, with a slightly bitter finish. When cooked, they taste deeply nutty and slightly smoky, with a faint lemony finish.

Health Notes

Collards contain vitamins A, B$_6$, C, E and K, calcium, folate, iron, magnesium, manganese, niacin, phosphorus, potassium, riboflavin and thiamin. Collard greens are particularly high in fiber and are considered strongly anti-inflammatory (inflammation can damage the body's cells and lead to chronic illnesses).

In herbal medicine, collards have been used to boost the function of the gallbladder, liver and immune system, increase bone mass, lower cholesterol and treat anemia and poor vision.

Varieties

Common collards come in several cultivars, but for cooks the differences are minimal.

Yellow cabbage collards are an heirloom variety rarely seen outside North Carolina. They are considered tenderer than common collards.

Buy It

You can find collards in supermarkets year-round, but they are at their peak in winter. Like Brussels sprouts and other cabbages, they are considered tastier after the first frost.

Clustered light green stems are topped by large dark green leaves with pastel green veins. The stalks grow up to 2 feet (60 cm) tall. Choose bunches with smaller leaves; they are more tender. Leaves should be stiff and crisp, with no yellowing, wilting or insect damage.

In some regions baby collards are available as salad greens.

SUBSTITUTES

kale, kohlrabi tops,
turnip greens,
mustard greens

Store It

To store whole collards, swathe with damp paper towels and place in a plastic bag, then refrigerate. Better still, separate leaves from stems, wrap loosely in damp paper towels and store in resealable bags.

Collards will keep in the refrigerator for up to five days.

Prep It

Both stems and the thick center ribs may be used or discarded. Either way, they should be separated from the leaves before cooking. Using a sharp knife, cut off and discard dry ends.

To trim collards, separate clusters by cutting off the base. Holding the end of each stalk, use a sharp knife to carefully cut upward along the stem and rib in stages to release the leaves. Alternatively, fold each leaf in half and cut out the stem and rib at an angle.

To prevent your dish from becoming swampy (with unappealing clumps of greens), cut collard leaves into small pieces. Stack the leaves, roll them into a cigar shape and then, using a sharp knife, slice into shreds or ribbons. Cut the pile of shreds to shorten them as desired.

Collards can be very dirty. Cut them into pieces before swishing them in several changes of cold water, then drain and spin-dry.

Consume It

Mature collards are never eaten raw. They are tough and indigestible.

To cook, simmer collards slowly for maximum tenderness or sauté them quickly to bring out their nutty flavor.

Collards are traditionally associated with long, slow cooking. The deeper you travel into the American South, the longer the cooking time is likely to be. Collards may be simmered or braised anywhere from 30 minutes to 2 hours, and correspondingly they end up anywhere from chewy to silky soft.

For quick results, collards may be chopped or finely sliced, then sautéed. Curiously, they toughen when sautéed for longer than 5 minutes.

The debate about whether the stems are edible is ongoing. I fall on the side of "it depends." When cut into small pieces and simmered or braised for a long time, they become tender enough to enjoy.

If the stems and thick center ribs are removed, the simmered leaves can be tender in 15 minutes.

The simmering liquid, colorfully known as "pot likker," is surprisingly tasty as well as nutritious. Don't pour it out — you can drink it like tea or add it to soup. In the American South, diners dunk cornbread or corn pones in it.

Old-School Collard Greens

A dish of long-simmered collards is a culinary classic from the American South. Serve these greens over grits for a Southern dining experience, or simply over brown rice.

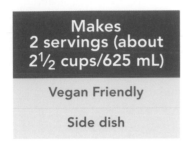

**Makes
2 servings (about
2½ cups/625 mL)**

Vegan Friendly

Side dish

Tips

To prepare the collards for this recipe: Using a sharp knife, trim leaves from stems, discarding stems and thick center ribs. Coarsely chop leaves.

Braise collards for 30 to 60 minutes or longer, depending on how soft and satiny you like them.

Whenever possible, use reduced-sodium vegetable stock. Not only is it healthier, it allows you to better control the saltiness of a dish.

Cane sugar is likely to be filtered through bone char, while beet sugar is not. Most labels don't indicate the source of the sugar. If you are following a vegan diet, use unbleached organic sugar that has not been filtered through bone char, or a sweetener such as agave syrup.

2 tbsp	extra virgin olive oil	30 mL
1	onion, diced	1
2	large cloves garlic, chopped	2
1	bunch collard greens (10 to 12 oz/300 to 375 g), trimmed and coarsely chopped (see Tips, left)	1
1 cup	vegetable stock (see Tips, left)	250 mL
1 cup	water	250 mL
½ tsp	kosher or coarse sea salt	2 mL
¼ tsp	granulated sugar (see Tips, left)	1 mL
⅛ tsp	freshly ground black pepper	0.5 mL
1 tbsp	white wine vinegar	15 mL
1 to 2 tbsp	unsalted butter or non-dairy alternative	15 to 30 mL
Dash	hot sauce, optional	Dash

1. In a large saucepan over medium heat, heat oil until shimmery. Add onion and cook, stirring often, for about 5 minutes, until softened and turning golden. Stir in garlic for 20 seconds. Stir in collards for 1 minute, until combined and slightly wilted. Stir in stock, water, salt, sugar and pepper. Cover, reduce heat to low and simmer for about 45 minutes, until very tender (see Tips, left).

2. Stir in vinegar and butter. Season with salt to taste. Serve with a slotted spoon and drizzle with cooking liquid to taste. If desired, add a dash of hot sauce to taste.

Couve Plus

In the United States, collards are synonymous with long, slow simmering. Travel further south to Brazil, however, and you'll find couve, a national dish of quickly sautéed collards. Slicing the leaves as thinly as possible dramatically reduces the cooking time. Couve is sautéed with garlic and onion, but I couldn't resist the temptation to embellish with red pepper for color and celery for crunch.

**Makes
2 servings (about
3 cups/750 mL)**

Vegan Friendly

Side dish

Tips

To prepare the collards for this recipe: Using a sharp knife, trim leaves from stems, discarding stems and thick center ribs. In batches, stack leaves, roll them into a cigar shape and slice into fine shreds. Cut shreds in half crosswise to shorten them.

Do not sauté collards for longer than 5 minutes or they will become tough.

2 tbsp	extra virgin olive oil	30 mL
1	onion, diced	1
1	small red bell pepper, cut into tiny dice	1
1	stalk celery, cut into tiny dice	1
4	cloves garlic, chopped	4
1 tsp	kosher or coarse sea salt	5 mL
¼ tsp	freshly ground black pepper	1 mL
1	bunch collards (10 to 12 oz/300 to 375 g), trimmed and cut into fine shreds (see Tips, left)	1

1. In a large skillet over medium heat, heat oil until shimmery. Add onion, red pepper, celery, garlic, salt and pepper. Cook, stirring often, for about 5 minutes, until tender-crisp. Add collards and stir for 1 minute, until slightly wilted. Increase heat to medium-high and cook, tossing often with tongs, for 3 to 5 minutes, until collards are just tender and still juicy. Remove from heat. Season with salt to taste and serve immediately.

Cajun Collards

Here braised collards get the Cajun treatment, sautéed with the "holy trinity" of onion, celery and bell pepper and simmered with tomatoes. In this recipe the collards are boiled until they are as soft as spinach. I've included the stems, just to say "I told you so." Serve these greens over creamy grits or polenta.

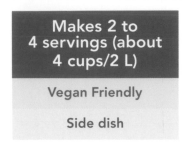

Makes 2 to 4 servings (about 4 cups/2 L)

Vegan Friendly

Side dish

Tips

To prepare the collards for this recipe: Using a sharp knife, trim dry ends of stems and separate the stems and thick center ribs from the leaves. Slice stems and ribs. Coarsely chop leaves.

For the finest minced garlic, push it through a press.

Cajun seasoning is a blend of spices, such as paprika, cayenne, oregano and pepper, and dried vegetables, such as onion, garlic, red or green bell pepper and celery. If you are a vegan, check the labels, as commercial blends may include traces of sugar. You can find Cajun seasoning in well-stocked supermarkets.

1	bunch collards (10 to 12 oz/300 to 375 g), trimmed and cut (see Tips, left)	1
2 tbsp	extra virgin olive oil	30 mL
1	onion, diced	1
1	stalk celery, diced	1
1	green bell pepper, diced	1
4	cloves garlic, minced (see Tips, left)	4
2 cups	canned tomatoes, with juices, chopped	500 mL
1 tbsp	Cajun seasoning (see Tips, left)	15 mL
½ tsp	kosher or coarse sea salt	2 mL
	Hot sauce	

1. In a large saucepan of boiling salted water with the lid ajar, simmer greens over medium-low heat for about 15 minutes, until tender. Drain, reserving liquid for other uses if desired.

2. In the same saucepan, heat oil over medium-low heat until shimmery. Add onion, celery and green pepper. Cook, stirring often, for about 10 minutes, until softened and golden. Stir in garlic for 20 seconds. Stir in tomatoes, Cajun seasoning and salt. Stir in collards and simmer for 5 minutes, until mixture is slightly thickened. Season with salt to taste. Add hot sauce to taste. Serve hot.

Gumbo Z'Herbes

Louisiana green gumbo is traditionally prepared on Holy Thursday for Good Friday, but it makes a hearty, healthy meal any time of the year. Mixed greens, the more kinds the better, are the hallmarks of this gumbo. They say that good luck and a new friend will come your way for every type of green you add. Serve the gumbo ladled over hot rice.

Makes 8 to 16 servings (about 16 cups/4 L)

Vegan Friendly

Main course

Tips

Gumbo z'herbes will taste deliciously different each time you prepare it, depending on the greens you use. In this version, I added arugula, chard, spinach, watercress, dandelion, catalogna, kale, collards and beet greens. Discard the stems and tough center ribs of the greens, and chop the leaves into small pieces to avoid a swampy gumbo.

Gumbos always start with a roux, made by browning flour in oil. Be very careful not to burn it. Once the roux turns a light caramel color, use a whisk to stir it often and watch it closely until it turns the color of milk chocolate.

Cajun seasoning is a spice and vegetable blend sold in many supermarkets.

Filé powder is powdered sassafras leaves used as a thickening and seasoning agent. It will become stringy if overcooked, so stir it in after the gumbo is done.

½ cup	oil	125 mL
½ cup	all-purpose flour	125 mL
1	Spanish onion, chopped	1
2	stalks celery, chopped	2
1	green bell pepper, chopped	1
4	large cloves garlic, chopped	4
10 cups	water	2.5 L
2 lbs	assorted trimmed greens, chopped (see Tips, left)	1 kg
1 tbsp	Cajun seasoning (see Tips, left)	15 mL
1 tbsp	kosher or coarse sea salt	15 mL
2	bay leaves	2
½ tsp	dried thyme	2 mL
2 to 4 tbsp	freshly squeezed lemon juice	30 to 60 mL
1 tbsp	filé powder (see Tips, left)	15 mL
	Hot sauce	
6	green onions (white and light green parts), sliced	6

1. In a large pot over medium-low heat, heat oil until shimmery. Add flour and cook, stirring often, for about 10 minutes, until nutty and milk chocolate–colored (see Tips, left). Add onion, celery and green pepper. Cook over medium heat, stirring often, for about 3 minutes, until softened. Add garlic and stir for about 30 seconds. Slowly add water, stirring constantly, until a smooth sauce forms. Add greens, in batches, stirring often until slightly wilted. Stir in Cajun seasoning, salt, bay leaves and thyme. When mixture comes to a simmer, cover, reduce heat to low and cook, stirring occasionally, for about 1 hour, until greens are very soft. Remove from heat. Discard bay leaves. Stir in lemon juice to taste. Season with additional salt to taste.

2. Just before serving, stir in filé powder. Dash in hot sauce to taste. Scatter green onions overtop and serve warm.

Hoppin' Green John

In the American South, hoppin' John is traditionally eaten on New Year's Day, anytime after midnight. This humble black-eyed pea dish makes a good hangover antidote, as well as helping diners satisfy the old saying that if you eat poor on New Year's, you'll eat rich the rest of the year. However, hoppin' John makes a fine meal any time of the year. This quick version is made with braised collards and canned beans.

Makes 4 servings

Vegan Friendly

Main course

Tips

Whenever possible, use reduced-sodium vegetable stock. Not only is it healthier, it allows you to better control the saltiness of a dish.

To prepare the collards for this recipe: Using a sharp knife, trim the leaves, discarding stems and thick center ribs. Chop leaves into large pieces.

Black-eyed peas are actually beans. They are sold in most supermarkets.

For best results, dash on a generous quantity of hot sauce.

2 cups	vegetable stock (see Tips, left)	500 mL
1	bunch collards (10 to 12 oz/300 to 375 g), trimmed and chopped (see Tips, left)	1
¾ cup	long-grain white rice	175 mL
1½ cups	water	375 mL
1 tsp	kosher or coarse sea salt, divided	5 mL
2 tbsp	extra virgin olive oil	30 mL
1	onion, diced	1
1	can (14 oz/398 mL) black-eyed peas, rinsed and drained (see Tips, left)	1
	Hot sauce (see Tips, left)	
	Shredded Cheddar cheese, optional	

1. In a large saucepan over medium-high heat, bring stock to a boil. Add collards and stir for 1 minute, until slightly wilted. When stock returns to a simmer, cover, reduce heat to low and cook for about 20 minutes, until collards are tender. Drain, reserving liquid for other uses if desired. Reserve pan. Cool collards briefly, then chop. Set aside.

2. Meanwhile, in a saucepan over medium heat, bring rice, water and ½ tsp (2 mL) salt to a boil. Cover, reduce heat to low and simmer for about 18 minutes, until rice is tender and water is absorbed. Uncover, set aside for 5 minutes and fluff with a fork.

3. In reserved saucepan over medium heat, heat oil until shimmery. Add onion and cook, stirring often, for about 5 minutes, until softened and golden. Add collards and remaining salt and stir for 1 minute, until combined. Remove from heat. Add beans and rice and, using a fork, stir to combine. Add hot sauce and salt to taste. Sprinkle with Cheddar, if using. Serve warm.

Ethiopian Collard Stew

Africans know the value of leafy greens and eat them every which way. Ethiopians serve stewed greens (and most everything else) on top of their signature flatbread, injera (see Tips, below). If you don't have any injera, rice is also nice.

Makes 4 servings

Vegan Friendly

Main course

Tips

Injera is a big, round, spongy sourdough flatbread made with teff flour. It is available in Ethiopian grocery stores, and some Ethiopian restaurants sell it for takeout. It traditionally takes the place of a plate and serving utensils, but I use it to line my plates. To serve, heat injera in a microwave on High for about 1 minute, until warm. Spoon the stew overtop. Diners tear off pieces of injera to scoop up the stew.

In this recipe I use yellow-fleshed potatoes, which are creamy but hold their shape. You could also use waxy red or white potatoes instead, but avoid russets.

To prepare the collards for this recipe: Using a sharp knife, trim the leaves, separating stems and thick center ribs from leaves. Trim dry ends of stems. Cut stems and ribs into ½-inch (1 cm) pieces. Chop leaves into 2-inch (5 cm) pieces.

To grate or purée gingerroot, use a kitchen rasp such as the kind made by Microplane.

2 cups	vegetable stock	500 mL
1 tsp	kosher or coarse sea salt	5 mL
1	potato, cut into ½-inch (1 cm) chunks (see Tips, left)	1
1	bunch collards (10 to 12 oz/300 to 375 g), trimmed and cut (see Tips, left)	1
2 tbsp	unsalted butter or non-dairy alternative	30 mL
1	small green bell pepper, cut in to thin strips	1
1	small red onion, diced	1
4	cloves garlic, minced (see Tips, page 142)	4
2 tsp	puréed gingerroot (see Tips, left)	10 mL
1 tbsp	berbere spice blend (see Tips, page 173)	15 mL

1. In a large saucepan over medium-high heat, bring stock and salt to a boil. Add potato and collards and stir for 1 minute, until greens are wilted. When stock returns to a simmer, cover, reduce heat to low and cook for about 15 minutes, until potato and collards are just tender. Set aside.

2. In a large skillet over medium heat, melt butter. Add green pepper and onion. Cook, stirring often, for about 5 minutes, until softened and golden. Stir in garlic and ginger for 20 seconds. Add reserved collards, potato and their cooking liquid; add berbere and stir to combine. Increase heat to medium-high and cook for 5 to 10 minutes, until most of the liquid evaporates. Season with salt to taste. Serve warm.

Curly Endive and Frisée

Cichorium endivia crispum

Other names: chicory, chicory endive, curly chicory, curly escarole, cut-leaf endive, loose-leaf chicory.

Depending on where you are shopping, you may find curly endive or frisée identified as *chicorée frisée*.

The origins of curly endives are still debated, with theories that the plant originated in India, Egypt or China. Endives were cultivated by the ancient Greeks and Romans.

In French, *frisée* means "curly," and this green is a mainstay of salads in France. The elegant-looking green became trendy among North American chefs in the 1990s. Frisée is pale because the plants are blanched, or shielded from the sun while growing, so chlorophyll fails to develop and bitterness is reduced.

Varieties

There is considerable confusion over whether curly endive and frisée are two separate greens. Mild, delicate frisée looks like a baby version of bitter mature curly endive. Although both belong to the same species, frisée is a miniature variety of curly endive, with leaves that are small and frizzy, pastel yellow rather than green. It may be called "French curly chicory." There are many cultivars of these endives, so they come in a range of sizes.

Buy It

You can find curly endive in most supermarkets. Frisée is slightly more difficult to find and may require a trip to a specialty greengrocer.

Not all curly endives are created equal. When it comes to mild flavor, small and yellow varieties trump those that are large and green. When it comes to nutrients, the opposite is true.

Both curly endive and frisée are distinguished by their loose heads of frilly, spiky leaves.

Tasting Notes

Curly endive: The stems are juicy and briny and the leaves are coarse, mineral tasting, slightly bitter and grassy, with a nutty finish.

Frisée: The smallest, palest frisée is moist and mild. Larger frisée is pleasantly juicy, slightly nutty and briny. It has a slightly bitter finish that is surprising, considering its lacy appearance.

Health Notes

Curly endive contains vitamins A, B$_6$, C, E and K, calcium, copper, folate, iron, pantothenic acid, magnesium, manganese, niacin, phosphorus, potassium, riboflavin, thiamin and zinc.

In folk medicine, endives have been used to treat gallstones, sinus and respiratory problems, to stimulate digestion, to banish internal parasites and to clear the skin.

1 bunch curly endive = 12 to 14 oz (375 to 400 g), including 8 oz (250 g) leaves and tender stems

•

2 oz (60 g) torn or coarsely chopped curly endive = 3 cups (750 mL), loosely packed

•

1 small bunch frisée = 2 oz (60 g); 1 large bunch = 10 oz (300 g)

•

2 oz (60 g) small frisée tendrils = 4 cups (1 L), loosely packed

Curly endive has deep green outer leaves and a heart that is white to pale yellow. Frisée comes in airy, tangled clusters of crunchy stems and slender, feathery leaves that are creamy yellow or pastel green.

Choose curly endive and frisée that look crisp and bright, with no signs of wilting or moist, blackened tips. When the greens are past their prime, the root ends at the base turn reddish or even slimy.

Frisée varies quite a bit in size. A bunch may weigh anywhere from 2 to 10 ounces (60 to 300 g).

Store It

To store curly endive, swathe it in plastic wrap or wrap it in paper towels and place in a resealable bag, then refrigerate it. Store frisée in an airtight container or a resealable bag with some air left in to act as a cushion.

Both curly endive and frisée keep in the refrigerator for up to three days.

Prep It

To prepare curly endive, cut off about 1 inch (2.5 cm) of the discolored or dried base and separate the stalks. Discard larger, fibrous stems. Use the frilly leaves and tender stems. The tender yellow core is edible too.

Wash curly endive (either whole or cut) in a bowl of cold water, then spin-dry.

For frisée, slice just enough off the base of the cluster to release the tendrils. If the frisée is large, pull it into pieces.

Frisée may be swished whole in cold water and air-dried on paper towels or a clean kitchen towel.

Consume It

Curly endive is used in salads or as a cooking green. It is really two greens: the outer leaves are green, bitter and coarse, while the creamy yellow inner leaves are milder and tenderer. For salads, use the latter.

Curly endive stands up well to dressings, but some salad lovers dismiss it as too bitter. Using it in a mixed salad with tender greens can mask the bitterness. It can also be added to hot dishes such as soups or pastas. You can temper curly endive beforehand by blanching it for 2 minutes, then draining it. If the bitterness still bothers you, increase the blanching time, but note that the texture will become soggy. Curly endive may also be blanched and briefly sautéed as a side dish.

Frisée is eaten raw. In France, however, warm dressings are often used to slightly wilt this salad green.

If you don't have salad-worthy young frisée, substitute the palest inner leaves and stems of curly endive.

SUBSTITUTES

catalogna, escarole, radicchio, Belgian endive, dandelion greens

Frisée with Grape Tomatoes, Mozzarella and Chapons

Chapons are oversized garlicky croutons. They complete this satisfying combination of delicate but assertive frisée, basil dressing, tomatoes and cheese.

Makes 2 to 4 servings

Vegan Friendly

Salad

Tip

If you are a vegetarian, check the label to make sure your mozzarella cheese is produced with vegetarian rennet. Vegans should substitute smoked tofu, not soy "cheese."

6 cups	loosely packed torn frisée (3 oz/90 g)	1.5 L
1/3 cup	Garlic Basil Vinaigrette (Variation, page 449)	75 mL
1 cup	grape tomatoes, halved	250 mL
1/2 cup	cubed mozzarella or non-dairy alternative (see Tip, left)	125 mL
1/2	recipe Chapons (page 456)	1/2

1. In a bowl, toss frisée with vinaigrette to taste (you will have some dressing left over).
2. Transfer frisée to a serving platter or individual plates. Scatter tomatoes and mozzarella overtop. Top with chapons. Serve immediately.

Frisée with Warm Chanterelles

Frisée holds up well to warm toppings. This simple salad is elegant, a delicious contrast between crunchy greens and satiny mushrooms. Serve it as a salad or arrange it over a bowl of your favorite cooked grain, such as quinoa.

Makes 2 servings

Vegan Friendly

Salad

Tip

Trumpet-shaped yellow chanterelles are an expensive treat. If you can't find any, use hedgehog mushrooms. For a more economical option, substitute oyster mushrooms or use mixed mushrooms.

4 cups	loosely packed torn frisée (2 oz/60 g)	1 L
1/3 cup	Garlic Herb Vinaigrette (page 449)	75 mL
1 tbsp	extra virgin olive oil	15 mL
3 cups	sliced chanterelle mushrooms (6 oz/175 g; see Tip, left)	750 mL
1 tsp	kosher or coarse sea salt	5 mL
2	green onions (white and light green parts), sliced	2

1. In a bowl, toss frisée with vinaigrette to taste (you will have some dressing left over). Transfer to a serving platter or individual plates.
2. In a skillet over medium-high heat, heat oil until shimmery. Add mushrooms and salt. Cook, stirring often, for 2 to 3 minutes, until moisture released by mushrooms evaporates and mushrooms sound squeaky.
3. Spoon warm mushrooms over frisée. Scatter green onions overtop. Serve immediately.

Curly Endive and Fingerling Salad

I like to experiment with potato salads. This one is sophisticated, unusual and tasty. The warm cider honey dressing tempers the bitterness of curly endive.

Makes 4 servings		
Vegan Friendly		
Salad		

8 oz	fingerling potatoes, scrubbed (see Tips, left)	250 g
6 oz	curly endive	175 g
¼ cup	extra virgin olive oil	60 mL
1 tbsp	cider vinegar	15 mL
1 tbsp	liquid honey or vegan alternative	15 mL
¼ tsp	Dijon mustard	1 mL
1 tsp	kosher or coarse sea salt	5 mL
⅛ tsp	freshly ground black pepper	0.5 mL
1	clove garlic, minced (see Tips, left)	1
4 oz	log goat cheese (chèvre), cut into 8 rounds, optional (see Tips, left)	125 g

Tips

If you can't find fingerling potatoes, use mini potatoes.

To cut chèvre neatly, make sure it is very cold and use a small, sharp, oiled knife.

For the finest minced garlic, push it through a press.

You can omit the cheese or replace it with smoked tofu pieces.

1. In a saucepan of boiling salted water, cook potatoes over medium heat for about 15 minutes, until tender. Drain and set aside to cool for 10 to 15 minutes.

2. Meanwhile, trim and coarsely chop curly endive — you should have about 9 cups (2.25 L), loosely packed. Transfer to a large bowl and set aside.

3. In a small saucepan over medium heat, heat oil until shimmery. Remove pan from heat. Whisk in vinegar, honey, mustard, salt and pepper. Whisk in garlic for 20 seconds. Immediately pour over endive and toss. Using tongs, divide endive among four wide, shallow serving bowls, pushing it to one side.

4. Transfer potatoes to bowl that held the endive and stir gently to coat with leftover dressing. Spoon potatoes beside endive in each serving bowl, dividing equally. Arrange two rounds of chèvre on top of greens, if using. Season fingerlings with salt to taste. Serve immediately.

Dandelion Greens

Taraxacum officinale

> *Other names:* **blowball, cankerwort, doon-head clock, face clock, rough dandelion, Irish daisy, milk witch, monk's head, swine's snout, pee-a-bed, priest's crown, puffball, telltime, witch's gowan.**
>
> **Depending on where you are shopping, you may find dandelion greens identified as *dent-de-lion, kanphool, khas berry, laitue de chien, lovetaan, pappous, pissenlit, pu gong ying, pusteblume, salade de taupe, soffione* or *tarassaco*.**

Tasting Notes

Dandelion is notoriously bitter. Wild dandelion is even bitterer than the cultivated kind. Dandelion leaves are nutty, astringent, mineral tasting, grassy and briny; the stems are slightly sweet.

Native to Eurasia, dandelion has been eaten since ancient times. The plant's jagged leaves inspired the name *dandelion*, derived from the French *dent de lion*, meaning "lion's tooth."

Cultivated in Europe, dandelion was a fashionable salad green in the latter half of the 1800s. Dandelions were brought to North America by early settlers, then largely forgotten. Now this pesky perennial grows wild almost everywhere, brightening up the urban landscape while taking over lawns and driving gardeners crazy.

Although reviled as a weed, dandelion is a nose-to-tail plant: everything from root to stem to leaf to flower is edible. The milky sap, known as latex, is not harmful. The roots have been used (like chicory) to make a coffee substitute, the flowers can be transformed into dandelion wine, and the leaves are added to salads and cooked as vegetables.

Varieties

Common dandelion (*Taraxacum officinale*) has several subspecies with names such as fleshy dandelion, horned dandelion and wandering dandelion. They are part of a complicated botanical family.

Heirloom varieties in North America include French dandelion (*T. officinale sativum*). Its larger, fleshier leaves are considered an improvement over garden-variety dandelion.

Wild or cultivated dandelion relatives include white-flowering Japanese dandelion (*T. albidum*) and yellow Japanese dandelion (*T. japonicum*), the endangered California dandelion (*T. californicum*), red-seeded dandelion (*T. laevigatum, T. erythrospermum*) and Cretan pentaramia (*T. megalorhizon*). Russian dandelion (*T. kok-saghyz*) is best known for its use in rubber production.

Health Notes

Dandelion contains vitamins A, B$_6$, C, E and K, calcium, folate, iron, manganese, magnesium, niacin, phosphorus, potassium, riboflavin and thiamin.

Dandelion ranks high among greens that are valued in herbal medicine. It has been used in Asian, Middle Eastern, Celtic, European and Native American folk medicine for a slew of ailments. Chinese medical texts that date from the 7th century mention dandelion. Arab physicians in the 10th and 11th centuries and Welsh ones in the 13th century also used it. In Celtic countries dandelion was considered a cure for diseases caused by fairies. It was cultivated in India for liver complaints such as jaundice. For centuries the greens have been used to treat kidney stones, stimulate appetite and bile production, improve skin and treat eczema. The milky sap was applied to corns and warts. Dandelion is most famous as a diuretic and is thus thought to cause bedwetting — hence the monikers "pee-a-bed" and *"pissenlit"* (which means "wet the bed" in French). Some allergies are linked to dandelion sap, which may cause contact dermatitis.

Hawkbits are an unrelated group of dandelion-like plants with edible species such as Cretan glykoradica (*Leontodon tuberosus*). Cat's ear (*Hypochaeris radicata*) and spotted cat's-ear (*H. maculate*) are also similar to dandelion, but they are not considered as tasty and are too fibrous unless very young.

Buy It

You can find dandelion greens in supermarkets, and they are also foraged wild. The bitterness of dandelion varies a lot. The greens are best in spring, when they are young and tender. They become inedible after the plant flowers and goes to seed. Cultivated dandelion is bred to be milder than its wild cousins.

Obtaining dandelion greens doesn't require much cleverness on the part of foragers. But beware! Urban dandelions absorb pesticides and chemicals from car exhaust and are watered by passing dogs. Areas alongside roadways, railway tracks and utility poles, as well as the lawns of perfectionists, have most likely been sprayed with weedkillers (in areas where they are legal). It's a better idea to forage at the supermarket.

Dandelions' perky, vibrant green leaves with notched frills grow along pastel green stems. They are likely to be confused with catalogna (page 95), or Italian dandelion, a type of chicory that is often simply labeled "dandelion" and displayed next to dandelions or sold in place of them. In fact, red dandelion sold in supermarkets is likely to be a chicory called red-ribbed catalogna.

Dandelion greens are lusher and lighter green than catalogna. Their stems are greener and usually trimmed rather than being attached in clusters. Look for tender-crisp leaves with no yellowing edges or wilted tips. Small leaves are desirable, as are lighter green ones. The leaves darken as they mature, from lime to dark green, and become bitterer.

Store It

To store dandelion, swathe the greens in paper towels, place them in a perforated resealable bag and refrigerate.

Dandelion can be refrigerated for up to three days.

Prep It

Before consuming dandelion, cut off and discard tough stems. Tear or coarsely chop the greens.

Dandelion greens tend to be dirty. Swish them in several changes of cold water, drain and spin-dry.

Consume It

Young leaves, ideally less than 4 inches (10 cm) long, are best for salads. More mature leaves are best cooked or added to soup; they are particularly good with lemony or creamy ingredients.

Dandelion leaves stand up well to warm salad dressings. They are also good in sandwiches. The French have been known to consume dandelion greens with bread and butter. This never caught on in North America, but it should — it's a simple, tasty combination.

To lessen dandelion's bite, simmer or braise it. However, do not sauté dandelion for longer than 5 minutes or it will begin to bite back. To reduce bitterness, blanch greens for 1 minute and drain before using in cooked dishes. If you still find dandelion greens too bitter, increase the blanching time; their texture, however, will suffer.

Equivalents

1 bunch = 10 to 12 oz (300 to 375 g), including 4 to 5 oz (125 to 150 g) leaves and tender stems

•

2 oz (60 g) torn or coarsely chopped leaves = 2½ cups (625 mL), loosely packed

•

2 oz (60 g) sliced or coarsely chopped leaves and stems = 2 cups (500 mL), loosely packed

SUBSTITUTES

escarole, arugula, curly endive, catalogna, watercress, mustard greens

Dandelion Salad with Balsamic Pepper Strawberries

If you haven't tried strawberries with balsamic vinegar and pepper, now's the time. Check out the amazing combination in this simply dressed, bitter/sweet dandelion salad.

Makes 2 to 4 servings

Vegan Friendly

Salad

Tips

Sweet onions are mild. The best-known variety is Vidalia. If desired, substitute red onion.

Cane sugar is likely to be filtered through bone char, while beet sugar is not. Most labels don't indicate the source of the sugar. If you are following a vegan diet, use unbleached organic sugar that has not been filtered through bone char, or a sweetener such as agave syrup.

To toast almonds, cook them in a dry skillet over medium heat, stirring often, for 2 to 3 minutes, until golden and aromatic.

1	bunch dandelion greens (10 to 12 oz/ 300 to 375 g), trimmed and coarsely chopped (about 5 cups/1.25 L)	1
1 cup	thinly sliced sweet onion (see Tips, left)	250 mL
2 tsp	freshly squeezed lemon juice	10 mL
2 tbsp	extra virgin olive oil	30 mL
½ tsp	kosher or coarse sea salt	2 mL
	Freshly ground black pepper	
1 lb	ripe strawberries, quartered	500 g
1 tbsp	balsamic vinegar	15 mL
1 tsp	granulated sugar (see Tips, left)	5 mL
¼ cup	slivered almonds, toasted (see Tips, left)	60 mL

1. In a large bowl, toss dandelion leaves and onion with lemon juice. Add oil and toss again to coat. Add salt and pepper to taste. Divide greens equally among serving dishes.

2. In a small bowl, toss strawberries with vinegar, sugar and additional salt and pepper to taste. Spoon over greens. Scatter almonds overtop and serve immediately.

Variation

Dandelion Salad with Roasted Strawberries: Replace the fresh berries with roasted berries, which have a concentrated flavor and creamy texture. To roast them, halve the berries and transfer to a baking sheet. Add 2 tsp (10 mL) extra virgin olive oil, 1 tsp (5 mL) granulated sugar and salt and pepper to taste. Combine with a spatula. Arrange berries cut side down. Roast in a preheated 400°F (200°C) oven for 5 to 8 minutes, until caramelized but still holding their shape. Spoon over greens in Step 2.

Dandelion Linguine with Chèvre and Garlic

Greens are darned good in pasta. This garlicky one is prepared with braised dandelion greens. The bitter greens and creamy cheese balance out each other nicely.

Makes 4 servings

Main course

Tips

Some types of sun-dried tomatoes are sold packed in oil. Don't throw it out — this recipe is but one of many good uses for it. If you don't have any sun-dried tomato oil on hand, substitute extra virgin olive oil.

For more control over the saltiness of dishes, I buy low-sodium or no-salt-added stock.

For the finest minced garlic, push it through a press.

12 oz	linguine	375 g
2 tbsp	sun-dried tomato oil (see Tips, left)	30 mL
1	bunch dandelion greens (10 to 12 oz/ 300 to 375 g), trimmed and coarsely chopped (about 5 cups/1.25 L)	1
1 tsp	kosher or coarse sea salt	5 mL
1 cup	vegetable stock (see Tips, left)	250 mL
4	large cloves garlic, minced (see Tips, left)	4
6 oz	chèvre (goat cheese), broken into chunks	175 g
	Freshly ground black pepper	

1. In a pot of boiling salted water, cook linguine over medium heat for about 15 minutes, until al dente. Drain.

2. Meanwhile, in a large skillet over medium heat, heat oil until shimmery. Add dandelion greens and salt and stir for 1 to 2 minutes, until slightly wilted. Add stock. Cover, reduce heat to medium-low and simmer for about 10 minutes, until tender.

3. Remove from heat and stir in garlic. Add chèvre and hot linguine. Toss with tongs to combine. Season with pepper to taste. Serve immediately.

Penne Boscaiola

In Italian cuisine, **boscaiola** *means "forester style." The name brought to mind foraged greens and wild mushrooms, and this is the result: hearty whole wheat pasta loaded with woodsy mushrooms and dandelion greens, their bitterness counteracted by glossy grape tomatoes bursting with sweetness.*

Makes 4 to 6 servings

Main course

Tips

For the finest minced garlic, push it through a press.

A mixture of cremini, portobello, shiitake and oyster mushrooms works well in this recipe. However, you can use any combination you prefer.

Be careful when biting into the cooked tomatoes — they retain heat and can burn your tongue.

1	package (¾ oz/20 g) dried porcini mushrooms	1
½ cup	boiling water	125 mL
12 oz	whole wheat penne	375 g
2 tbsp	extra virgin olive oil	30 mL
2 cups	thinly sliced red onion	500 mL
2	large cloves garlic, minced (see Tips, left)	2
1 lb	mixed mushrooms, sliced (see Tips, left)	500 g
2 tsp	kosher or coarse sea salt	10 mL
⅛ tsp	freshly ground black pepper	0.5 mL
1	bunch dandelion greens (12 oz/375 g), trimmed and chopped	1
12 oz	grape tomatoes	375 g
½ cup	heavy or whipping (35%) cream	125 mL

1. In a bowl, cover porcinis with boiling water and set aside for at least 15 minutes to soften. Drain, reserving liquid. Using a sharp knife, chop porcinis. Set aside.

2. In a large saucepan of boiling salted water, cook penne over medium heat for about 15 minutes, until al dente. Drain.

3. Meanwhile, in a sauté pan over medium heat, heat oil until shimmery. Add onion and cook, stirring often, for about 3 minutes, until softened and turning golden. Stir in garlic for 20 seconds. Stir in porcinis, mixed mushrooms, salt and pepper. Cook for 5 to 7 minutes, until liquid released from mushrooms evaporates. Stir in dandelion greens and tomatoes for 1 minute. Pour in reserved porcini soaking liquid and cream. Simmer for about 5 minutes, until cream thickens, dandelions are wilted and tomatoes are hot but still intact (not bursting).

4. Add cooked penne and toss to coat. Remove from heat. Set aside for 5 minutes to soak up sauce before serving.

Escarole

Cichorium endivia latifolia

Other names: **Batavia, Batavian endive, broad chicory, broad-leaved endive.**

Depending on where you are shopping, you may find escarole identified as *grumolo* **or** *scarola*.

Tasting Notes

Escarole is succulent, nutty, astringent and briny, with a slightly bitter finish. The leaves are sturdy.

Equivalents

1 small head = 12 oz (375 g); 1 medium head = 1 lb (500 g); 1 large head = 1¼ lbs (625 g)

•

2 oz (60 g) torn or coarsely chopped leaves = 3 cups (750 mL), loosely packed

Escarole belongs to the endive family. The ancestors of this endive originated in Sicily. The ancient Greeks and Romans ate endives as vegetables; they were grown in England in the 1500s. The first mention of cultivated escarole in the United States appeared in the early 1800s.

Escarole is most popular in Italian cuisine, where it may be sautéed as a side dish or used in soup or pasta dishes along with beans.

Varieties

Escarole is a standardized leafy endive cultivar, closely related to Belgian endive (see page 54) but nothing like it. Escarole looks like a head of lettuce, with pliable rather than stiff leaves.

Buy It

You can find escarole in supermarkets. It may be labeled "endive."

Escarole resembles leaf lettuce but is coarser. The base is pastel green and the broad, ruffled, succulent green leaves form a loose cluster. Inner leaves are creamy yellow, while the outer leaves are darker in color. Spring escarole is considered sweeter. Choose smaller heads with lighter green leaves that are crisp and perky at the tips. Avoid any with cracked leaves and red discoloration at the stem end — these are signs of spoilage.

Store It

To store whole escarole, swathe it tightly in plastic wrap or roll slightly damp paper towels around it, place in a plastic bag and refrigerate it. Or trim the base, separate the leaves, wash, spin-dry and roll in paper towels, then transfer to resealable bags.

Escarole keeps in the refrigerator for up to four days.

Prep It

To prepare escarole, pull off discolored or wilted outer leaves. Cut off the browned base. Tear or chop the leaves just before using; otherwise the cut edges will brown quickly.

To wash, rinse escarole well in cold water, drain and spin-dry.

To reduce bitterness, soak escarole in ice water for 30 minutes, drain and spin-dry. Alternatively, it may be blanched (see page 150).

Health Notes

Escarole contains vitamins A, C, E and K, calcium, copper, folate, iron, magnesium, manganese, pantothenic acid, phosphorus, potassium, riboflavin, thiamin and zinc.

In herbal medicine, endives have been used as diuretics and gallbladder and liver stimulants.

SUBSTITUTES

Belgian endive, curly endive, catalogna, radicchio

Consume It

Escarole is commonly cooked but may also be added to mixed salads. North Americans are more likely to eat it raw than are Europeans.

To make the most of a head of escarole, deconstruct it. The pale inner leaves have had less exposure to sunlight and are milder and more delicate. Darker green outer leaves are tougher, coarser and bitter because they contain more chlorophyll.

Use the inner leaves for salad. Escarole holds up well to warm or heavy dressings.

The sturdy darker green leaves are best when briefly cooked as a vegetable or sautéed "salad," or when added to soup, stew or pasta. These greens go particularly well with beans.

For best results, tenderize or temper escarole's bitterness with wet heat. Blanch escarole in boiling salted water, drain well, then sauté or add to other dishes. Blanch for no longer than 1 to 2 minutes, just until the greens are vibrant and tender-crisp. (If the bitterness still bothers you, blanch the escarole longer, to taste, but be aware that the texture will suffer.)

Another option is to sauté escarole until wilted, add some stock or water, cover, reduce the heat and braise until tender-crisp. If necessary, uncover the pan and increase the heat briefly to evaporate any excess liquid. Avoid simply boiling escarole to cook it; the result will be soggy and dull.

Be careful not to overcook escarole. Many recipes call for unnecessarily long blanching or cooking times. Braised escarole is tender in 5 minutes, blanched and sautéed escarole in less than 10 minutes.

Endive Family Salad

There's not much of a family resemblance among the endives. In this salad, a toss-up of escarole, frisée and Belgian endive is mellowed with milder leaf lettuce, dried cherries, toasted pecans and orange pecan vinaigrette. The result is fragrant and delicious.

Makes 2 to 4 servings

Vegan Friendly

Salad

Tips

To toast pecans, cook them in a dry skillet over medium heat, stirring often, for about 3 minutes or until golden brown and aromatic.

Dried cherries are sold in bulk food stores. If you don't have any, substitute dried cranberries or raisins.

1	Belgian endive, trimmed, halved and sliced	1
2 oz	coarsely chopped escarole (about 3 cups/750 mL, loosely packed)	60 g
2 oz	torn red leaf lettuce (about 3 cups/750 mL, loosely packed)	60 g
1 oz	frisée (about 2 cups/500 mL, loosely packed)	30 g
½ cup	Orange Pecan Oil Vinaigrette (Variation, page 451)	125 mL
½ cup	pecan halves, toasted and coarsely chopped (see Tips, left)	125 mL
¼ cup	dried cherries (see Tips, left)	60 mL

1. In a large serving bowl, combine endive, escarole, lettuce and frisée. Add dressing to taste (you will have some left over) and toss to coat evenly. Top with pecans and cherries. Serve immediately.

Sicilian Escarole Salad

Here is a delicious oddity for North America: a cooked salad. The escarole is blanched, then sautéed with signature Sicilian ingredients. The technique reminds me of blanched Asian salads. Serve rustic crusty bread with this dish.

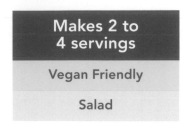

Makes 2 to 4 servings

Vegan Friendly

Salad

Tips

You can blanch the escarole up to an hour ahead and set it aside to drain.

The hot oil will spatter when the moist escarole is added to it. Use a splatter guard if you have one.

1	head escarole (1 lb/500 g), trimmed and chopped	1
¼ cup	extra virgin olive oil	60 mL
2 tbsp	pine nuts	30 mL
2 tbsp	raisins	30 mL
2	large cloves garlic, chopped	2
1 tsp	kosher or coarse sea salt	5 mL
¼ tsp	hot pepper flakes	1 mL
1 tbsp	freshly squeezed lemon juice	15 mL
1 tbsp	capers, drained, rinsed and chopped	15 mL
10	oil-cured black olives, pitted and halved	10

1. In a large saucepan of boiling salted water, blanch escarole over medium heat for 1 to 2 minutes, until wilted but still crisp. Drain and immediately rinse with cold water to stop the cooking. Set aside to drain completely (see Tips, left).

2. In a large skillet over medium heat, heat oil until shimmery. Add pine nuts and raisins and cook, stirring, for about 2 minutes, until nuts are golden. Using a slotted spoon, transfer nuts and raisins to a small bowl. Set aside.

3. In same skillet over medium heat, stir in garlic for 20 seconds. Add blanched escarole (see Tips, left), salt and hot pepper flakes. Cook, stirring occasionally, for 3 to 5 minutes, until tender and most of the liquid released evaporates. Remove from heat and set aside to cool to room temperature.

4. Stir in lemon juice. Season with salt to taste. Stir in pine nuts, raisins and capers. Transfer to a serving dish or individual plates. Scatter olives overtop and serve immediately.

Utica Greens

Escarole is the star of this signature dish from Utica, in upstate New York, where it is sautéed with garlic and chile, then finished with breadcrumbs and cheese in the oven. The crumbs absorb the delicious stock. The end result is a small, simple casserole that's totally addictive. This is a vegetarian version.

Makes 2 to 4 servings
Vegan Friendly
Side dish

Tips

To make fresh bread crumbs, use a food processor fitted with the metal blade to chop torn day-old bread into coarse crumbs. Crusty rustic white bread works best for this dish — you'll need two slices.

If you are a vegetarian, check cheese labels. Traditional cheeses are made with animal-based rennet. However, many cheese companies now use vegetarian rennet instead.

This dish is best when made nice and spicy. For a tamer version, reduce the amount of hot pepper flakes to taste.

- Preheat oven to 400°F (200°C), placing oven rack one level down from top

Topping

1½ cups	fresh bread crumbs (see Tips, left)	375 mL
¾ cup	grated Romano cheese (1 oz/30 g), optional (see Tips, left)	175 mL
1 tbsp	chopped fresh parsley leaves	15 mL
1 tbsp	extra virgin olive oil	15 mL

Greens

¼ cup	extra virgin olive oil	60 mL
4	large cloves garlic, slivered	4
1	head escarole (1 lb/500 g), trimmed and coarsely chopped	1
1 tsp	kosher or coarse sea salt	5 mL
1 tsp	hot pepper flakes (see Tips, left)	5 mL
1 cup	vegetable stock	250 mL
	Freshly ground black pepper	

1. *Topping:* In a medium bowl, using a fork, combine bread crumbs, cheese (if using) and parsley. Gently stir in oil.

2. *Greens:* In a large, ovenproof skillet over medium-low heat, warm oil. Add garlic and cook, stirring, for 1 to 2 minutes, until faintly golden and sticky (do not allow to brown). Add escarole, salt and hot pepper flakes. Cook, stirring often, for about 1 minute, until slightly wilted. Stir in stock, cover and cook for about 3 minutes, until tender-crisp. Remove from heat. Sprinkle topping over escarole.

3. Transfer skillet to preheated oven and bake for about 10 minutes, until topping is golden brown and escarole is tender. Serve immediately.

Fiddleheads

Matteuccia struthiopteris

Other names: **crozier, fiddlehead/ostrich/ shuttlecock fern.**

Depending on where you are shopping, you may find fiddleheads identified as *ogomi, lingri, pohole* or *têtes de violon*.

Tasting Notes

Fiddleheads are earthy, forest-scented and slightly tannic, with asparagus, spinach, okra and broccoli accents. They have a springy, meaty texture. They may be mild or slightly bitter, depending on the cooking method and timing.

Ferns emerge from the soil with their fronds tightly coiled. The coiled fronds look like the scrolled neck on a violin, hence the name fiddlehead.

Fiddleheads grow in northern regions, including northeast North America and parts of Europe and Asia. They appear on the banks of rivers, streams and brooks, on floodplains and in areas that are damp with spring runoff.

Aboriginal peoples harvested these greens long before white settlers discovered their deliciousness. In northern France they have been eaten since the Middle Ages. In North America they have become a harbinger of spring for gourmands. Although fiddleheads grow in other regions of Canada and the United States, they are particularly abundant in New England and the Maritimes. The village of Tide Head, New Brunswick, bills itself as the "fiddlehead capital of the world" because masses of these ferns appear in spring on the banks of the nearby Restigouche River and its islands. In Canada, fiddleheads were relatively unknown outside the maritime provinces until recently, but they are now an essential element of Canadian cuisine.

Varieties

Nearly all ferns have coiled fronds, but fiddleheads (*Matteuccia struthiopteris*) are specifically ostrich ferns. Similar "fiddleheads" of the less common wood ferns are also considered edible, but inferior in taste and texture.

Beware of coiled fronds from bracken ferns (*Pteridium aquilinum*), also known as *warabi*. They slightly resemble ostrich ferns but contain carcinogens. Bracken ferns have small fiddleheads in clusters on long stems. Despite health warnings, they are boiled or pickled in Japan, Korea and other Asian nations. A related species called *aruhe* (*P. esculentum*) is a traditional staple food for the Maoris of New Zealand.

Other foraged ferns include:

- **vegetable fern** (*Diplazium esculentum*)
- **lady fern** (*Athyrium filix-femina*)
- **sensitive fern** (*Onoclea sensibilis*), used as a vegetable by the Iroquois
- **cinnamon fern** (*Osmundastratum cinnamomeum*), also known as buckhorn fern
- **interrupted fern** (*Osmunda claytoniana*), **Old World royal fern** (*O. regalis*) and **Japanese flowering fern** (*O. japonica*), also known as Japanese royal fern or *zenmai*.

Buy It

Fiddleheads are not farmed but rather classified as harvested wild produce, as they grow on undeveloped land without intervention. Thus they are naturally (but not officially) organic. Fiddleheads are foraged mainly on the east coast of North America, from Canada to Virginia. The window of opportunity is short. The shoots remain coiled for about three days in early spring. Once they unfurl, they develop plant toxins that upset the stomach. Two weeks is considered the optimum harvesting period in any area.

The plants grow in clusters of three to a dozen shoots. They are picked when the coils are about $3/4$ to $1^1/2$ inches (2 to 4 cm) in diameter. Crisp shoots are snapped off by hand. Addicts require self-control: fiddleheads recur annually, but to ensure that they repopulate, no more than one-third of the shoots in any specific patch should be picked.

It's easy to confuse wild fiddleheads with inedible ferns, so I don't recommend foraging them. Buying fiddleheads from a trusted purveyor is your best bet. Supermarkets, specialty greengrocers and gourmet food shops sell them seasonally. Because they have a brief season and are in short supply, they are expensive.

Fiddleheads are dark green and 1 to 3 inches (2.5 to 8 cm) tall. Each coiled frond sits atop a smooth stem with a U-shaped groove. The shoots are covered with a papery brown scale called the chafe.

Look for small fiddleheads with tight coils. The stems should not be yellowed or soft. However, some browning is inevitable: the cut end of the stem quickly dehydrates and darkens from oxidation.

Store It

To store fiddleheads, wrap them in damp paper towels, place in a resealable bag and refrigerate.

Fiddleheads can be refrigerated for up to two days. The sooner they are eaten, the better: their flavor is more delicate when fresh.

Health Notes

Fiddleheads contain vitamins A and C, copper, iron, magnesium, manganese, niacin, phosphorus, potassium, riboflavin and zinc.

In folk medicine, fiddleheads have been used to treat high blood pressure and scurvy. Pioneers consumed fiddlehead tea as a remedy for constipation. Native Americans ate fiddleheads for a spring detox.

Prep It

To trim fiddleheads, pinch or slice off the dried, browned ends of the stems.

Fiddleheads are covered by papery brown husks that can taint them with a woody, bitter flavor. The husks are removed by the time fiddleheads reach the stores, but remnants remain. To get rid of intact husks, shake fiddleheads in a bag and/or rinse them using a faucet sprayer or even an outdoor hose. To get rid of remnants, rub them off with your fingers and pluck out wisps under cold running water.

Dirt also hides in the coils of fiddleheads. Swish them in several changes of cold water until the water looks clear.

Consume It

Never eat raw fiddleheads (see below). They may be steamed, sautéed, roasted, simmered in soup, cooked in omelets, marinated or pickled.

Some folks like to boil fiddleheads until they are soft and khaki green, but modern tastes generally run to cooking them only until al dente.

Cooking times remain a matter of debate because fiddleheads are believed to contain unidentified plant toxins. Government officials recommend boiling fiddleheads for 15 minutes or steaming them for 10 to 12 minutes, but that is overkill. Some chefs balk at the cooking guidelines, believing 5 minutes is enough. I fall somewhere in between.

This two-step cooking process is common: Blanch fiddleheads in plenty of lightly salted water for 3 minutes to neutralize potential toxins, temper their slight natural bitterness and tenderize them. Drain, discarding the cooking liquid, and rinse with cold water (if necessary for the recipe). Continue cooking or use the fiddleheads in a recipe. Alternatively, fiddleheads may be steam-blanched for 6 to 7 minutes.

After blanching, fiddleheads boiled in fresh water or sautéed are usually tender but firm in 5 to 7 minutes. Note, however, that cooking times vary by batch — some fiddleheads are meatier.

Fiddleheads may taste mild or somewhat bitter, depending on the cooking method:

- For mild fiddleheads, boil them. Cover the pan to keep in the steam and make sure the fiddleheads are immersed during the first minute of cooking (any exposed parts may discolor and darken). Use plenty of fresh water, as it turns a rusty color from the high iron content of fiddleheads.
- For a more assertive taste, steam fiddleheads. Steamed fiddleheads are somewhat bitter but taste nuttier and have a better texture than boiled ones.

Balsamic Roasted Fiddleheads

I still laugh when I think about my husband's first impression of fiddleheads many years ago. He complained that they tasted like ferns. I said, "That's because they are ferns." This recipe provides an easy two-step roasting technique.

Makes 2 servings

Vegan Friendly

Side dish

Tip

Like many cheeses, Parmesan is made with animal-based rennet and is unsuitable for vegetarians. However, some brands offer Parmesan-style hard cheese made with vegetarian rennet as a suitable substitute. Check the label to be sure.

- Preheat oven to 400°F (200°C)
- Rimmed baking sheet

8 oz	fiddleheads, trimmed	250 g
1 tbsp	extra virgin olive oil	15 mL
½ tsp	kosher or coarse sea salt	2 mL
	Freshly ground black pepper	
¼ cup	freshly grated Parmesan-style cheese, optional (see Tip, left)	60 mL
2 tsp	balsamic vinegar	10 mL

1. In a saucepan of boiling salted water over medium heat, blanch fiddleheads, covered, for about 5 minutes, until tender-crisp and lighter green. Drain, then immediately rinse with cold water to stop the cooking. Drain and pat dry.
2. Transfer fiddleheads to baking sheet and, using a spatula, toss with oil, salt and pepper to taste. Arrange in a single layer and sprinkle cheese (if using) overtop.
3. Roast in preheated oven for about 10 minutes, until fiddleheads are tender but firm and cheese is browned. Drizzle with vinegar and toss with spatula, scraping browned bits from bottom of pan. Serve immediately.

Fiddleheads with Garlic Crisps

Sautéing greens with garlic and chiles is arguably the easiest, most delicious way to prepare them. Here fiddleheads benefit from this tried-and-true combination.

Makes 2 servings

Vegan Friendly

Side dish

Tip

Be careful not to brown the garlic or it will taste bitter. Reduce the heat if necessary.

8 oz	fiddleheads, trimmed	250 g
2 tbsp	extra virgin olive oil	30 mL
2	large cloves garlic, thinly sliced	2
½ tsp	hot pepper flakes	2 mL
½ tsp	kosher or coarse sea salt	2 mL

1. In a pot of boiling salted water, blanch fiddleheads over medium heat, for about 3 minutes. Drain; immediately rinse with cold water. Drain and set aside.
2. Meanwhile, in a large skillet over medium-low heat, warm oil. Add garlic and cook, stirring often, for about 1 minute, until golden and crisp (see Tip, left). Using a slotted spoon, transfer to a bowl and set aside.
3. Return skillet to medium heat. Add fiddleheads, hot pepper flakes and salt. Cook, stirring often, for about 5 minutes, until tender-crisp. Transfer to a serving dish and sprinkle garlic overtop. Serve immediately.

Grape Leaves

Vitis vinifera

> *Other names:* grapevine/vine leaves.
> Depending on where you are shopping, you may find grape leaves identified as *dolma, feuilles de vigne, uva foglia, uzum yapragi* or *wara'inab*.

Most grape species are native to the northern hemisphere. *Vitis vinifera* is native to the Mediterranean basin, southwestern Asia and central Europe. Its wild ancestor is *Vitis vinifera sylvestris*. Other species are found in the Americas and Asia.

Grapevines were foraged and eventually cultivated in prehistoric times, mainly as a source of wine but also for their fruit and leaves. The earliest written references to wine are found in Sumerian texts.

Culinary historians theorize that grape leaves were first used as wrappers when Thebes was besieged by Alexander the Great in 335 BCE. Meat became so scarce that the Thebans cut it into bits and wrapped it in grape leaves.

Grape leaves are now used in diverse cuisines, including Greek, Bulgarian, Turkish, Arab, Romanian, Spanish and Vietnamese. They are a staple edible in Mediterranean and Middle Eastern countries.

Tasting Notes

Bottled leaves are salty, lemony and grainy, with a faint grape scent. Fresh leaves are described as milder, with lemon accents.

Varieties

There are many grape species, most of which are cultivars of *Vitis vinifera*. Leaves may be used from any type of grapevine that produces red or white grapes. Other species include *V. labrusca*, *V. riparia* and *V. rotundifolia*, as well as crossbred grapevines.

Buy It

Fresh grape leaves are rarely sold commercially in North America. They are usually grown and picked by gardeners, viticulturists and foragers. However, it's worth checking ethnic grocery stores or farmers' markets seasonally.

Grape leaves are picked from the vines in spring and early summer, when they are untouched by pests or pesticides. They are best before the grapes start growing. They should be big enough to stuff easily but still small enough to be digestible rather than fibrous. Wild grape leaves are considered the ideal kind. As for cultivated grapevines, some aficionados say that leaves from sultanas (white grapes) are the best. Grape leaves are light green, supple and deeply lobed, with prominent veins. Avoid any with black speckles, yellowing or insect damage, or leaves that seem thick or fuzzy rather than smooth.

Fresh grape leaves contain vitamins A, B_6, C, E and K, calcium, copper, folate, iron, magnesium, manganese, niacin and riboflavin. They are high in omega-3 fatty acids.

Bottled preserved leaves contain vitamins A and C, calcium, copper, folate, iron, manganese, niacin, pantothenic acid and riboflavin. However, they are high in sodium.

Grape leaves, particularly from vines with red grapes, were used for centuries as folk remedies for edema, varicose veins, hemorrhoids, heavy menstrual flow, canker sores, throat infections, fevers and headaches. Native North Americans drank grape-leaf tea to quell diarrhea and stomachaches.

Bottled preserved leaves are widely available in supermarkets, specialty shops and Greek grocery stores. They are usually packed in water with salt, ascorbic or citric acid and preservatives. The leaves are stuffed into jars in bundles by weight, so the number varies from jar to jar. Leaves are usually medium-sized and sometimes bottled with stem stubs attached. Quality can vary a great deal, so check different brands. The leaves in a recent bottle from one prominent brand, for example, were too coarse and had wiry veins. Occasionally grape leaves are sold in pouches, vacuum-packed in brine, or frozen in packages.

Medium-sized leaves — about the length of your hand and 4 to 5 inches (10 to 12.5 cm) wide — are the best bet for stuffing. Larger leaves are too mature and coarse. Leaves smaller than your palm require too much fussing to stuff and may be too thin and easy to tear.

Store It

To store fresh leaves, stack them, wrap them in paper towels, place in a resealable bag and refrigerate.

Fresh grape leaves will keep in the refrigerator for one day.

Keep unopened jars of grape leaves in a cool, dark place or, better still, in the refrigerator. After opening, refrigeration is a must.

Opened jars of grape leaves will keep in the refrigerator for up to three days.

Prep It

It is difficult to pull bundles of preserved leaves out of their jars. To prevent damage, be patient; tug and tease the bundle out slowly. Leaves packed flat in vacuum pouches are easier to extract and separate.

Some cooks rinse preserved grape leaves, then use them as is. However, the leaves are unpleasantly acidic and salty. I recommend blanching; it makes a big difference.

To blanch preserved leaves and prepare them for stuffing, unfold the grape-leaf bundles and stack the leaves in a large fine-mesh sieve. Place the sieve in a large bowl. Cover the leaves in boiling water, pushing them down gently with a wooden spoon to ensure that they are submerged. Set aside for 5 minutes. Drain, then rinse under cold water until cooled to room temperature. Return the sieve to the bowl, cover the leaves in cold water and set aside for 1 minute. Drain again. Working with one leaf at a time, peel the leaves off the stack, snip off the stem stubs (if necessary) and arrange in a single layer, face down, on paper towels or a clean kitchen towel. Pat the wet surfaces dry. The leaves are now ready to fill.

SUBSTITUTES

la lot leaf, perilla
(sesame leaf),
savoy cabbage

Fresh leaves may be blanched using the same technique; however, increase the soaking time in boiled water to 10 to 15 minutes.

Consume It

Fresh and preserved leaves are used chiefly as wraps, most famously in the Greek dish dolmades (page 162). However, the youngest, tiniest fresh grape leaves may be added to salads, and large mature leaves can be used decoratively (for example, serve a wedge of cheese on a clean fresh grape leaf). Large, tough leaves may also be used to line pans of dolmades and the like, to prevent burning or sticking.

Preserved leaves are surprisingly sturdy to work with. However, depending on the brand and processing, up to a quarter of the leaves in a jar may have tears or holes, and some will be too damaged to use at all for wraps. Waste not, however: cover holes or tears with small pieces ripped from other damaged leaves, then fill and roll. Use some of the remaining damaged leaves to line your pan.

Roll leaves over fillings snugly but not too tightly. The filling, particularly partially cooked rice, is apt to expand and the leaf may split.

Bottled grape leaves are acidic, so use less lemon in your recipe than you would with fresh leaves. You may have to reduce the amount by half.

Dolmades

Stuffed grape leaves are a Greek classic. Don't be afraid to make these tasty tidbits at home. The leaves are fiddly to work with but you'll go at a decent clip once you get the hang of it. Serve dolmades with tzatziki, the Greek yogurt-cucumber sauce.

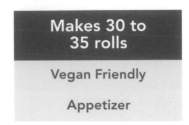

Makes 30 to 35 rolls

Vegan Friendly

Appetizer

Tips

For the finest minced garlic, push it through a press.

Rinse the rice briefly to clean it, but do not soak it. The rice is parboiled prior to stuffing to ensure that it is tender when the dolmades are ready. If you start with raw rice, the grape leaves overcook and the expanding rice will burst the rolls.

To toast pine nuts, cook them in a dry skillet over medium heat, stirring often, for about 3 minutes, until golden and aromatic. Transfer to a bowl to cool.

This recipe makes 3 cups (750 mL) filling, which is enough to fill 30 to 35 medium leaves.

To prepare jarred grape leaves for this recipe, see "Prep It" on page 160.

6 tbsp	extra virgin olive oil, divided	90 mL
1	large onion, chopped	1
1 tsp	kosher or coarse sea salt	5 mL
1	large clove garlic, minced (see Tips, left)	1
1 tsp	finely grated lemon zest	5 mL
1 cup	long-grain white rice, rinsed (see Tips, left)	250 mL
2¼ cups	vegetable stock, divided	550 mL
½ cup	pine nuts, toasted (see Tips, left)	125 mL
¼ cup	chopped fresh parsley leaves	60 mL
2 tbsp	chopped fresh dill fronds	30 mL
	Freshly ground black pepper	
1	jar (8 oz/250 mL) grape leaves, blanched, dried and trimmed (see Tips, left)	1
¼ cup	freshly squeezed lemon juice	60 mL

1. In a saucepan over medium heat, heat ¼ cup (60 mL) oil until shimmery. Add onion and salt. Cook, stirring often, for 5 to 8 minutes, until softened and golden. Stir in garlic and lemon zest for 30 seconds. Add rice and stir for about 1 minute, until well coated. Add 1 cup (250 mL) stock. When mixture comes to a boil, cover, reduce heat to low and simmer for about 12 minutes, until stock is absorbed. Remove from heat. Stir in pine nuts, parsley and dill; season with pepper to taste. Set aside to cool to room temperature.

2. Working in batches, lay prepared grape leaves on work surface, facing down (see Tips, page 163); set aside badly damaged leaves to patch holes and line pan. Place about 1½ tbsp (22 mL) filling near stem end of leaf (amount will depend on the size of each leaf). Fold stem end over filling, pat roughly to even it out, and roll leaf away from you for one half-turn. Fold both sides of leaf over filled section and finish rolling into a cylinder. Set roll aside, seam side down. If necessary, use pieces of reserved damaged leaves to patch over holes or tears before filling. You should end up with 30 to 35 rolls, each about 3 inches (7.5 cm) long.

Tips

Place the filling on the underside of the leaf, which is dull (not shiny) and has raised veins. Another clue: the stem curls toward the underside.

Be miserly when lining the skillet with damaged leaves, as they can absorb and steal liquid from the rolls.

The rolls are covered with a plate or the like when cooking to keep them snugly in place and thus prevent them from unrolling or becoming damaged.

3. Line a 12-inch (30 cm) skillet scantily with some of the remaining damaged leaves and arrange rolls in a single layer (they should just fit). In a medium measuring cup, stir together remaining stock, remaining oil and lemon juice; pour over rolls. Bring to a simmer over medium heat. Invert a heatproof plate or place a smaller lid over rolls (see Tips, left), then cover the skillet, reduce heat to low and simmer for about 45 minutes, until rice is cooked, leaves are tender and darkened, and most of the liquid has evaporated. Do not allow the dolmades to boil, or the leaves will start to fall apart.

4. Remove from heat, uncover and set aside to cool to room temperature and absorb remaining liquid. Serve at room temperature or transfer to an airtight container and store in the refrigerator for up to 1 week.

Green Cabbage

Brassica oleracea capitata

Other names: **white/sauerkraut cabbage, cole, colewort, Dutch cabbage.**

Depending on where you are shopping, you may find green cabbage identified as *cavolo cappuccio, kubis, weisskohl* **or** *yeah choy.*

Green cabbage is the Western world's standard cabbage. It has a long history of cultivation. In Greek mythology, cabbage sprang from the tears of a Thracian king about to be killed by Dionysos because the monarch had uprooted some of the deity's favorite grapevines. In Roman times, cabbage was a relatively expensive vegetable. It was widely used in a dish that evolved into corned beef and cabbage, long before the Irish had their way with it.

Cabbage was extensively cultivated in 15th-century Europe and early settlers brought it to North America. It is a source and symbol of humble sustenance. For example, "Cabbagetown" became the slang name for rundown urban areas where the residents were so poor they supposedly ate nothing but cabbage.

Tasting Notes

Green cabbage is succulent and firm. Its flavor is nutty and slightly sweet, but it becomes sulfurous if overcooked.

Varieties

Tight-head cabbages come in white (*Brassica oleracea capitata alba*) and red (*B. oleracea capitata rubra*) types. White cabbage actually ranges from ivory to pastel green and may be blanched, that is, shielded from the sun to inhibit chlorophyll production. Green cabbage is a subclass of white cabbage.

Green/white cabbages come in many sizes and varieties. Giant Alaska kraut cabbage is famous for setting Guinness world records. Flathead cabbage is sold in Asian supermarkets and may be labeled "Korean cabbage" or "Taiwan cabbage"; it looks like a squashed green cabbage. "Personal" heads of cabbage are showing up in supermarkets in response to consumer demand for smaller specimens. Baby green or red cabbages weighing about a pound (500 g) are either immature cabbages or mini cultivars.

Red cabbage is white's sibling. Its color is due to anthocyanin pigments that range from red to blue, depending on soil acidity. These pigments are the same kind of powerful antioxidants as those found in red wine.

Buy It

Cabbages are supermarket staples.

The very big, loose outer leaves of cabbage are removed at the farm and semi-loose ones at the store so shoppers end up with a compact head. Look for green cabbage that's heavy for its size, with slightly glossy, waxy, firmly packed tight, crisp leaves. Avoid any with leaves that are cracked, discolored or starting to separate from the base — the cabbage is past its prime.

Buy whole cabbage. When cut or shredded, it rapidly loses its vitamin C and other nutrients.

Heads range in size from softballs to basketballs. Commonly sold heads weigh 1 to 5 pounds (500 g to 2.25 kg). The smallest heads (less than 2 lbs/1 kg) are choice; their leaves are tenderer and taste sweeter.

Store It

To store a head or a leftover cut chunk of cabbage, swathe it tightly in plastic wrap.

Whole cabbage will keep in the refrigerator for up to one week or longer. Red cabbage has more antioxidants than green cabbage, so it keeps longer.

To preserve the vitamin C content, don't cut or wash cabbage until you are ready to use it.

Cooking a whole cabbage at once is too much of a good thing for modern diners. Leftover cut cabbage is best used within two days, as the edges will turn gray and dry and the nutrients dwindle. All is not lost, though; if necessary, gray edges may be sliced off before using the cabbage.

Green cabbage is traditionally fermented into sauerkraut to hold it over the winter (see Sauerkraut, page 168).

Prep It

Before consuming cabbage, pull off and discard wilted or tough exterior leaves. Pulling off outer leaves helps salvage older cabbage, but it does become less sweet as time passes.

Cabbage is not normally washed once the outer leaves are pulled off. However, I prefer to swish cut cabbage in cold water to clean it.

Carbon steel knives are rare, but if you have one, don't use it on cabbage. The metal can react with chemical compounds in the leaves to cause dark stains. Instead, use a stainless steel knife to cut cabbage.

If you need to keep the core in cabbage wedges to hold them together, turn the cabbage upside-down before cutting it. That way you can see the core and eliminate guesswork.

To core a whole cabbage, use a sharp knife to cut it into quarters through the center; then lay each quarter on its side and cut at an angle to remove the core. Don't forget that the core is tasty and sweet; you can munch it raw.

To shred cabbage by hand, core it, lay each quarter on its side, then use a sharp knife to slice the cabbage crosswise into shreds or ribbons. You can also shred it in a food processor.

SUBSTITUTES

savoy cabbage, napa
cabbage, Brussels
sprouts, kale

Cabbages are very watery. To extract moisture, toss cut cabbage with salt and let it stand in a sieve for 30 to 45 minutes. Use about 1 tsp (5 mL) salt per 3 to 4 cups (750 mL to 1 L) shredded cabbage.

To make cabbage crisper for salad, soak chunks in ice water for 15 to 30 minutes before chopping or slicing.

Here are some ways to tame cabbage:

- Soak shredded cabbage for an hour before cooking to make it sweeter and milder. (But I prefer unsoaked cabbage; it's firmer and nuttier and has more character.)
- Simmer shredded cabbage in nonfat (skim) milk for 5 minutes to make it sweeter and nuttier.
- Add $1/4$ tsp (1 mL) baking soda per 4 cups (1 L) cooking water to tenderize cabbage and make it greener.

For cabbage rolls, make the rolling easier by removing the thick center rib, cutting it out in a triangle shape. Or cut the leaf straight across the bottom and use only the tender portion. While rolling, trim any excess flaps and thick ribs.

To loosen and soften leaves for cabbage rolls (making them easier to roll), blanch separated leaves in small batches for 2 to 3 minutes in boiling water. However, pulling off intact raw leaves is difficult. A more awkward but effective technique is to dunk a cored head, facing up, into a large pot of boiling water. Cover and boil for 2 minutes, then rinse under cold running water. Pull off as many leaves as you can, then repeat. Steaming the head and pulling off leaves is a third option, but also awkward. Savoy cabbage (page 336), which has more pliable leaves, is a better choice for cabbage rolls.

Consume It

Green cabbage is the workhorse of the cole clan, a solid performer in salads, slaws, stir-fries, sautés and braises. You can boil or steam it in chunks, pickle or ferment it, or use the leaves as wrappers for iconic cabbage rolls.

Many of the healthful antioxidants in cabbage are derived from sulfur compounds, the source of smelly cooking odors. The odors worsen if cabbage is improperly cooked or overcooked (see "Cutting Cabbage Odors," page 167).

When steaming or grilling cabbage wedges, prevent collapse by leaving the core intact and/or shoving a metal skewer lengthwise through each wedge. Avoid using bamboo skewers for this task, as they are likely to snap.

Red cabbage is actually purple, and it turns bluish when cooked. Don't substitute it for green cabbage in soups and stews — the results look unappetizing. Adding an acid such as lemon juice, vinegar, wine or even apple juice helps set the purple color and lessens the bluish effect. Add about 1 tsp (5 mL) vinegar per 1 cup (250 mL) shredded red cabbage.

Cutting Cabbage Odors

There are several ways to lessen (but not eliminate) cabbage cooking odors:

- Soak cabbage in cold water to leach some of the smelly compounds.
- Don't overcook. Slow-braised cabbage is wonderful, but be aware that it will be smellier. Longer cooking also cuts down the nutrient content.
- Stir-fry or sauté. Hot oil coats the cabbage and helps seal in odors.
- Cook cabbage in large sections or wedges. Chopping releases pungent compounds.
- Chinese cooks may add bread to steamed cabbage to soak up sulfur compounds.
- Pickling or fermentation (think sauerkraut) reduces the pungency and sweetens the aroma.

Sauerkraut

You don't need much to make sauerkraut — just green cabbage and salt plus a sharp nose and a sharp blade. I like to prepare my own because it tastes crisp and lively.

Makes about 10 cups (2.5 L)

Vegan Friendly

Side dish

Tips

Shred cabbage using a food processor fitted with either the slicing disk, or large shredding disk. Finer pieces ferment faster and become more tender than coarser hand-sliced ones.

Make sure your container is roomy, as the cabbage will expand and bubble as it ferments. Place your container on a tray with a rim to catch any drips.

You can use a jar filled with water as a weight. Don't use a metal can; the salt will eat away at it.

To help prevent contamination with unwanted bacteria, sterilize your container, utensils, plate and weight with boiling water before beginning. Also, when taste-testing, be careful not to introduce bacteria from your mouth into the sauerkraut — use a sterilized fork and don't double-dip.

If desired, process sauerkraut in a hot water canner according to the manufacturer's instructions.

* Crock or large non-metallic container

Extra Brine

8 cups	water	2 L
3 tbsp	pickling salt	45 mL

Sauerkraut

1	green cabbage (5 lb/2.5 kg), shredded (see Tips, left)	1
3 tbsp	pickling salt	45 mL

1. *Extra Brine:* In a large, microwave-safe measuring cup, heat water and salt on High for about 5 minutes, until boiling. Stir to dissolve salt. Set aside to cool to room temperature.

2. *Sauerkraut:* In a very large pot or bowl, toss cabbage with salt. Set aside for 2 hours to draw out liquid. Using a heavy potato masher, pound and turn cabbage for 5 to 10 minutes, until it releases enough liquid to cover itself when pressed down.

3. Transfer cabbage and its liquid to a crock or non-metallic container large enough to hold cabbage with 2 inches (5 cm) headspace (see Tips, left). To keep cabbage submerged, cover it with an inverted plate and top with a weight (see Tips, left). Add enough extra brine to cover the plate by 1 inch (2.5 cm). Place cheesecloth over the container and secure by tying it around the rim with kitchen twine. Pour remaining brine into an airtight container, cover and set aside.

4. Store cabbage in a cool, dark place, preferably where the temperature remains between 60°F and 70°F (15°C and 20°C) without fluctuating. (If too warm, it will over-ferment, becoming mushy and unpleasant tasting. If too cool, it may not ferment at all, allowing bad bacteria to take over.) As the cabbage ferments, you should see little bubbles rising to the surface of the brine. Make sure the cabbage is covered by brine at all times. If any scum appears at the top of the brine, skim it off with a sterilized spoon. Start checking the brine level at day 7, adding reserved brine as needed. Start sniffing and tasting at day 14. If the cabbage starts to taste or smell fetid or looks pink or slimy, throw it out. Sauerkraut is ready when the taste and aroma transition from sharp horseradish to mellow sauerkraut, the cabbage is bleached and tender-crisp, and bubbles stop rising. Depending on the temperature, sauerkraut should be fully fermented in 2 to 6 weeks.

5. As soon as it finishes fermenting, transfer sauerkraut and its brine to airtight containers and refrigerate for several months.

F Is for Fermentation

Fermentation is one of mankind's oldest food preservation techniques. The science behind it is this: In the absence of air, benign microbes, including bacteria and yeast, thrive and suppress bad microbes that cause spoilage.

Fermented sauerkraut tastes pickled, but how so? After all, the cabbage is submerged in brine, not vinegary liquid. Well, during fermentation, good bacteria eat sugars in the cabbage and convert them to lactic acid. You could call this "salt-pickling."

There's a wide world of fermented foods. They are a staple in traditional cuisines, particularly in cold climates. Examples include sourdough bread, brine pickles, Korean kimchi (fermented spicy cabbage or other vegetables; see page 267), Japanese miso (soybean paste), kombucha (fizzy tea), cheese and yogurt.

Fermented foods offer a number of health benefits. Most prominently, they replenish and promote the growth of friendly intestinal bacteria, which in turn fortifies the immune system. Fermentation boosts the B-vitamin content of foods. This preserving process also makes food more digestible and thus helps the body absorb more vitamins and minerals.

Braised Ginger Pepper Cabbage

This dish is all that braised cabbage should be: tender but firm, silky and moist. Serve it over brown rice or grains to soak up the fragrant juices.

Makes 2 to 4 servings (about 6 cups/1.5 L)

Vegan Friendly

Side dish

Tips

To grate or purée gingerroot, use a kitchen rasp such as the kind made by Microplane.

For the finest minced garlic, push it through a press.

1 tbsp	unsalted butter or non-dairy alternative	15 mL
1 tbsp	extra virgin olive oil	15 mL
1	onion, diced	1
1	green bell pepper, diced	1
1 tsp	kosher or coarse sea salt	5 mL
1/2 tsp	freshly ground black pepper	2 mL
1 tbsp	puréed gingerroot (see Tips, left)	15 mL
1	clove garlic, minced (see Tips, left)	1
1 1/2 lbs	green cabbage, cut into 1-inch (2.5 cm) pieces (about 9 cups/2.25 L)	750 g
1 cup	vegetable stock	250 mL
1 tbsp	chopped fresh parsley leaves	15 mL

1. In a large skillet over medium heat, melt butter with oil. Add onion, green pepper, salt and pepper. Cook, stirring often, for about 3 minutes, until softened. Stir in ginger and garlic for 20 seconds. Add cabbage and stir for about 1 minute, until well coated. Add stock. Reduce heat to medium-low and cook, stirring occasionally, for 20 minutes, until tender and silky. Season with salt to taste.

2. Transfer to serving plates and sprinkle with parsley. Serve immediately.

Baja Coleslaw

I get a spicy kick out of this creamy coleslaw with Mexican flair. Although it is vegetarian, I got the idea for the recipe while preparing Baja fish tacos, which include shredded cabbage and spicy mayonnaise.

Makes 6 to 8 servings (about 7 cups/1.75 L)

Vegan Friendly

Salad

Tips

Use a sharp knife or a food processor to slice the cabbage. If using a food processor, insert the thin slicing disk to obtain the proper texture, not the shredding disk (the large shredder gives the cabbage a clumpy texture, while the fine shredder minces it).

The best-known variety of sweet onion is Vidalia, which is large and mild. Walla Walla is another popular type. If desired, substitute red onion for the sweet onion.

Dressing

½ cup	mayonnaise or vegan alternative	125 mL
3 tbsp	sour cream or non-dairy alternative	45 mL
3 tbsp	chopped fresh cilantro leaves	45 mL
2 tsp	minced chipotle chile in adobo sauce	10 mL
½ tsp	kosher or coarse sea salt	2 mL
	Freshly ground black pepper	

Coleslaw

1 lb	green cabbage, shredded (about 6 cups/1.5 L, loosely packed; see Tips, left)	500 g
2	carrots (4 oz/125 g total), shredded	2
1 cup	diced sweet onion (see Tips, left)	250 mL
	Kosher or coarse sea salt	

1. *Dressing:* In a measuring cup, combine mayonnaise, sour cream, cilantro, chipotle, and salt and pepper to taste.
2. *Coleslaw:* In a large serving bowl, combine cabbage, carrots and onion. Add dressing and toss to coat. Season with salt to taste. Serve immediately or transfer to an airtight container and refrigerate for up to 2 days.

Roasted Green Cabbage with Roasted Garlic Dressing

People don't generally think of roasting cruciferous vegetables, but it's a great idea. Cabbage caramelizes and develops a deep, satisfying nutty flavor. A drizzle of dressing is the finishing touch.

Makes 6 to 8 servings

Vegan Friendly

Side dish

Tips

There's no need to turn the cabbage during roasting. Disturbing it will increase the chances of its falling apart and leaving little bits on the baking sheet that will burn

Cane sugar is likely to be filtered through bone char, while beet sugar is not. Most labels don't indicate the source of the sugar. If you are following a vegan diet, use unbleached organic sugar that has not been filtered through bone char, or a sweetener such as agave syrup.

- Preheat oven to 400°F (200°C)
- Mini food processor
- Rimmed baking sheet, greased

1	small head green cabbage (3 lbs/1.5 kg)	1
2 tbsp	extra virgin olive oil	30 mL
1/2 tsp	granulated sugar (see Tips, left)	2 mL
	Kosher or coarse sea salt	
	Freshly ground black pepper	
1/2 cup	Roasted Garlic Dressing (page 454)	125 mL
1 tbsp	chopped fresh parsley leaves	15 mL

1. Using a sharp knife, cut cabbage in half lengthwise. Slice each half lengthwise into 1-inch (2.5 cm) slabs; you will have 10 to 12 slabs and end pieces. Cut out core sections.

2. Arrange cabbage on prepared baking sheet in a single layer. Brush top and sides of each piece with oil. Sprinkle with sugar and salt and pepper to taste. Roast in preheated oven for about 1 hour, until tender but firm and browned.

3. Chop coarsely, discarding any overly charred pieces. Place on a serving platter and drizzle with dressing. Sprinkle parsley overtop. Serve warm.

Variations

You can substitute your favorite dressing for the Roasted Garlic Dressing.

Omit the dressing and splash some white wine or cider vinegar over the roasted cabbage.

Cabbage Latkes

I like the bold taste of peppery cabbage latkes. Slightly sweet and nutty, they are a change from the same old same old.

Makes 15 latkes		
Side dish		

Tips

For best results, the cabbage should be shredded finely. To obtain the right consistency, use your food processor's shredding disk with the smallest holes. If you don't have a food processor, try a box grater.

For this recipe, a russet potato is required to give the latkes the proper texture. Russets are dry, starchy, oblong potatoes with brown skins.

Use the large holes of a box grater to shred the potato.

The frying oil in the skillet should be about 1/4 to 1/2 inch (0.5 to 1 cm) deep.

12 oz	green cabbage, finely shredded (about 3 cups/750 mL; see Tips, left)	375 g
2	green onions (white and green parts), chopped	2
4	large eggs	4
1 tsp	kosher or coarse sea salt	5 mL
1/4 tsp	freshly ground white pepper	1 mL
1	small russet potato, peeled and shredded (see Tips, left)	1
1/4 cup	all-purpose flour	60 mL
	Oil for frying (see Tips, left)	

1. In a large bowl, combine cabbage, onions, eggs, salt and pepper. Using your hands, squeeze liquid from shredded potato and add potato to cabbage mixture; mix well. Add flour and combine.

2. In a large skillet (preferably cast iron) over medium heat, heat oil until shimmery. For each latke, scoop about 1/4 cup (60 mL) batter into the skillet, then gently flatten with a spatula. Fry in batches, turning once, for 7 to 8 minutes, until cabbage is tender-crisp and latkes are browned. Transfer to a platter lined with paper towels to drain. Serve hot.

Variation

Lower-Fat Cabbage Latkes: In Step 2, heat a large griddle or nonstick skillet over medium heat. Brush the skillet lightly with oil before adding each batch of latkes. Cook for 8 to 10 minutes, turning once. These latkes will be firmer.

Ethiopian Cabbage Stew

Stew with cabbage, carrots, potatoes and other vegetables is a traditional Ethiopian Lenten dish. But you can happily mop this up any time of year with the Ethiopian flatbread called injera (see Tips, page 137), or serve it with rice or other grains. Like many stews, it tastes better the next day.

> ## Makes 4 to 6 servings
>
> ### Vegan Friendly
>
> ### Main course

Tips

To grate or purée gingerroot, use a kitchen rasp such as the kind made by Microplane.

Berbere, also called *awaze*, is the signature spice blend of Ethiopia. It may include ground red chile, garlic, ginger, ajwain and fenugreek, and it comes in the form of either a paste or a dry seasoning. In this recipe I use the latter. You can find berbere blends in spice shops and African grocery stores. When a stew is made with berbere, it is called a *wat*. When made with a mixture of warm spices, such as nutmeg and cardamom, it is called an *alecha*.

In this recipe use yellow-fleshed or waxy potatoes, which hold their shape well in stews, rather than russets, which are dry and tend to fall apart.

¼ cup	unsalted butter or non-dairy alternative	60 mL
2 tbsp	extra virgin olive oil	30 mL
2	onions, diced	2
2 tsp	kosher or coarse sea salt	10 mL
4	cloves garlic, chopped	4
2 tbsp	puréed gingerroot (see Tips, left)	30 mL
2 tbsp	berbere spice blend (see Tips, left)	30 mL
2 lbs	green cabbage, cut into 1-inch (2.5 cm) pieces	1 kg
4	large carrots (1 lb/500 g total), cut into 1-inch (2.5 cm) pieces	4
4	potatoes (1 lb/500 g total), cut into 1-inch (2.5 cm) pieces (see Tips, left)	4
1½ cups	water	375 mL
1 cup	chopped fresh parsley leaves	250 mL

1. In a large saucepan over medium heat, melt butter with oil until shimmery. Add onions and salt. Cook, stirring often, for about 3 minutes, until softened. Stir in garlic, ginger and berbere for 30 seconds. Add cabbage, carrots and potatoes and stir to combine. Add water. When mixture comes to a simmer, cover, reduce heat to low and cook for about 20 minutes, until vegetables are tender.

2. Remove from heat. Uncover and set aside for 10 minutes to thicken slightly. Stir in parsley and season with salt to taste. Serve warm.

Variations

You can add other vegetables, such as cauliflower, green bell peppers or green beans.

Mock Risotto with Cabbage

There's nothing like the real thing, but when you crave a relatively quick, fuss-free risotto, take this microwave shortcut. For a satisfying vegetarian meal, serve this risotto with a big, hearty salad.

Makes 4 to 6 servings (about 6 cups/1.5 L)

Vegan Friendly

Side dish

Tips

Arborio is the best-known type of risotto rice. It is sold in supermarkets.

For best results, shred the cabbage in a food processor using the medium holes of the shredding disk. Larger chunks will take too long to cook.

Like many cheeses, Parmesan is made with animal-based rennet and is unsuitable for vegetarians. However, some brands offer Parmesan-style hard cheese made with vegetarian rennet as a suitable substitute. Check labels to be sure.

This dish remains uncovered during all the stages of microwave cooking.

2 tbsp	extra virgin olive oil	30 mL
2 tbsp	unsalted butter or non-dairy alternative	30 mL
1	small onion, diced	1
1½ cups	Arborio rice (see Tips, left)	375 mL
3 cups	vegetable stock	750 mL
1 cup	water	250 mL
½ tsp	kosher or coarse sea salt	2 mL
⅛ tsp	freshly ground black pepper	0.5 mL
6 oz	green cabbage, finely shredded (about 1½ cups/375 mL; see Tips, left)	175 g
1	small carrot, shredded	1
¼ cup	chopped fresh parsley leaves	60 mL
	Freshly grated Parmesan-style cheese, optional (see Tips, left)	

1. In a large, microwave-safe dish, heat oil and butter on High for 1 minute (see Tips, left). Stir in onion. Microwave on High for 2 minutes. Add rice and stir to coat well. Microwave on High for 2 minutes. Stir in stock, water, salt and pepper. Microwave on High for 10 minutes. Stir in cabbage, carrot and parsley. Microwave on High for 10 minutes, until rice is tender.

2. Set aside for 5 minutes. Fluff with a fork and season with salt to taste. Sprinkle cheese (if using) overtop. Serve warm.

Hungarian Caramelized Cabbage and Noodles

One of the standbys of the Hungarian table is dark, sweet cabbage with a peppery bite tossed with egg noodles to make a meal. Hungarians are not known for their diet foods. As a compromise between calories and authenticity, I more than halved the amount of oil from my mom's recipe and switched to extra virgin olive oil, but it is what it is — greasy comfort food. Serve this with lots of steamed green vegetables to make up for the indulgence.

Makes 4 servings

Vegan Friendly

Main course

Tips

I use a 10-inch (25 cm) saucepan to obtain the right texture for the caramelized cabbage.

For best results, use a food processor fitted with the shredding disk to shred the cabbage. Use the medium holes on the disk.

Cane sugar is likely to be filtered through bone char, while beet sugar is not. Most labels don't indicate the source of the sugar. If you are following a vegan diet, use unbleached organic sugar that has not been filtered through bone char. Some brands specify this on the label.

For a vegan version, use wide, flat wheat noodles such as pappardelle instead of egg noodles.

2½ lbs	green cabbage, finely shredded (about 10 cups/2.5 L, loosely packed; see Tips, left)	1.25 kg
1 tbsp	kosher or coarse sea salt	15 mL
½ cup	extra virgin olive oil	125 mL
1 tbsp	granulated sugar (see Tips, left)	15 mL
1 to 1½ tsp	freshly ground black pepper	5 to 7 mL
8 oz	broad egg noodles or vegan alternative (see Tips, left)	250 g

1. In a large fine-mesh sieve, toss cabbage with salt. Set aside for 30 to 45 minutes. Using your hands, squeeze excess liquid from cabbage and transfer to a bowl.

2. In a wide saucepan (see Tips, left) over medium heat, heat oil until shimmery. Add cabbage and stir to coat. Cook, stirring occasionally, for about 5 minutes, until wilted. Cover, reduce heat to low and cook, stirring occasionally, for about 1 hour, until tender and golden. Stir in sugar. Increase heat to medium and cook, uncovered, stirring often and scraping up browned bits from bottom of pan, for 15 to 20 minutes, until cabbage is brown and very soft. Stir in 1 tsp (5 mL) pepper.

3. Meanwhile, in a large saucepan of boiling salted water, cook noodles for 10 to 12 minutes, until tender but firm. Drain.

4. Add noodles to cabbage. Using a fork or tongs, toss to mix evenly. Season with salt to taste. If desired, add remaining pepper.

Houttuynia

Houttuynia cordata

Other names: **bishop's weed, fish mint, fishwort, folded ears, heartleaf, lizard tail, saururis, white chaplu.**

Depending on where you are shopping, you may find houttuynia identified as *doku-dami, diep ca, ja mardoh, pak kao tong, rau dap ca* or *yu xing cao.*

This flowering plant is native to Southeast Asia and the Himalayas. It is cultivated in Vietnam, China, Japan and Korea as a leaf vegetable, root vegetable, herb and medicinal plant.

Houttuynia is used mainly in the south of Vietnam. Even there they are ambivalent about it, and some people can't stand to eat it. Highly invasive, the plant is the stuff of gardening horror stories. It has spread to North America and Australia.

Varieties

Cultivated houttuynia is either culinary or ornamental. Culinary houttuynia comes in Chinese and Japanese subspecies, both with green leaves. Ornamental houttuynia (also known as chameleon plant) has variegated red, yellow and green leaves.

Buy It

You can find houttuynia in Asian grocery stores, particularly those that sell Vietnamese specialty foods. The packaging may be labeled "heartleaf"— confusingly, as several plants go by that name. (If it were labeled "fishwort" it would likely have even fewer takers.)

Houttuynia leaves are heart-shaped and the tender stems are notched, with sections that transition from green to red. Avoid wilted or discolored leaves. Look for small leaves, which are considered superior. The older the plant, the fishier it tastes. The flavor is considered to be strongest in autumn.

Store It

Place houttuynia in a glass or vase of water like a bouquet, with a plastic bag draped over the foliage; then refrigerate it. Or wrap a damp paper towel around the stems and store in a resealable bag.

Houttuynia will keep in the refrigerator for up to three days.

Tasting Notes

Houttuynia is an acquired taste, with common reactions ranging from dislike to disgust.

The leaves are tender and demure, but don't be fooled — the flavor and aroma give taste buds a one-two punch. This green lives up to the name "fishwort." It has a raw fish flavor, more than hints of briny sea, and is extremely metallic. The Chinese/Vietnamese variety is differentiated by its citrus accents, while the Japanese variety has cilantro accents.

Equivalents

1 bunch = 3 oz (90 g), including 1 oz (30 g) leaves or 1¼ oz (37 g) leaves and tender stemlets

•

2 oz (60 g) leaves = 3 cups (750 mL), loosely packed

•

2 oz (60 g) shredded or chopped leaves = 2 cups (500 mL), loosely packed

SUBSTITUTES
Nothing comes close.

Health Notes

No official government analysis is available, but houttunyia is thought to contain vitamins A and C, copper, manganese and phosphorus. It is relatively high in fiber.

Houttuynia has been the subject of several scientific studies and is ranked high in herbal medicine. It is considered a diuretic and a laxative and is used to produce an antimicrobial extract. It has been used to treat hypertension, inflammation, pneumonia and lung conditions ranging from asthma to tuberculosis; to lower blood sugar; to relieve stomach ulcers; and to stimulate bone growth. It may be applied topically for snakebites, skin disorders and abscesses.

Prep It

Before using houttunyia, pluck the leaves off the main stem, along with the light green stemlets, if desired. Rinse the greens lightly in cold water and place them on paper towels to air-dry.

Consume It

Houttuynia is eaten raw as a salad green or in noodle salads, brewed into a tea or tonic, used as an herb and cooked as a leaf vegetable or added to stir-fries.

Cook houttuynia just until it wilts. In cooked dishes, leaves are ready in 1 minute; leaves with tender stemlets are ready in 2 minutes.

Houttuynia Lemon Vermicelli

This twist on a classic Vietnamese dish is appealing, despite the impossible-to-ignore metallic tang of the houttuynia. I wouldn't fault you if you decided to replace it with a more palatable tender green, such as baby spinach, watercress or mizuna.

Makes 4 servings
Vegan Friendly
Main course

Tips

To cut the tofu block, slice it in half through the center, then cut each slab crosswise into ½-inch (1 cm) slices.

To shred the houttuynia and mint, stack leaves, then roll into a cigar shape. Using a sharp knife, slice roll crosswise into thin strips. You should have about 1 cup (250 mL), loosely packed.

Instead of preparing Crispy Shallots, you can buy packaged fried onions in Asian grocery stores.

Don't worry about keeping the tofu and Crispy Shallots hot. Just add the toppings as soon as the noodles are done.

Unlike meat marinades, tofu marinade is not considered a source of cross-contamination. It could be used as is but I boil it anyway, both to be obsessively safe and to warm it up.

- Grilling tray
- Barbecue

Tofu

1 lb	firm tofu, patted dry and cut into ½-inch (1 cm) slices (see Tips, left)	500 g
¼ cup	freshly squeezed lemon juice	60 mL
2 tbsp	oil	30 mL
4	small cloves garlic, minced	4
¼ cup	finely chopped lemongrass	60 mL
¼ cup	granulated sugar	60 mL
1 tbsp	sea salt	15 mL

Noodles

8 oz	rice stick noodles (⅛ inch/3 mm wide)	250 g
1	bunch houttuynia (3 oz/90 g), trimmed and shredded (see Tips, left)	1
2 tbsp	shredded fresh mint leaves	30 mL
	Kosher or coarse sea salt	
¼ cup	roasted peanuts, chopped	60 mL
½	English cucumber, peeled and cut into thin 2-inch (5 cm) batons	½
⅓ cup	Crispy Shallots (page 455; see Tips, left)	75 mL

1. *Tofu:* In a shallow dish just big enough to hold them, arrange tofu slices close together in a single layer. Set aside.

2. In a measuring cup, combine lemon juice, oil, garlic, lemongrass, sugar and salt. Pour over tofu, shaking dish to evenly distribute marinade. Cover and refrigerate for 1 hour.

3. Place grilling tray on grate and preheat barbecue to medium. Arrange tofu on tray, letting excess marinade run back into dish; reserve marinade. Cover and grill for 3 to 5 minutes per side, until golden brown with grill marks. Set aside.

4. Pour reserved marinade through a fine-mesh sieve set over a small saucepan, discarding solids. Bring to a full boil over medium-high heat, then set aside (see Tips, left).

5. *Noodles:* In a large saucepan of boiling salted water, cook noodles over medium heat for 4 to 5 minutes, until tender but firm. Drain and rinse with cold water. Drain well and transfer to a large bowl. Pour boiled marinade over noodles. Add houttuynia and mint. Toss gently and season with salt to taste.

6. Divide noodles among serving bowls. Scatter peanuts overtop. Arrange grilled tofu and cucumber on top. Scatter shallots over tofu. Serve immediately or at room temperature.

Iceberg Lettuce

Lactuca sativa capitata

Other names: **cabbage lettuce, crisphead lettuce, head lettuce.**

Depending on where you are shopping, you may find iceberg lettuce identified as *bataviasalat, eissalat, fejes salata, jie qiu wo ju, kropsla, laitue pommée, latuga cappuccio, marouli* or *tama chisa*.

Tasting Notes

Iceberg lettuce is mild and succulent, with a cool crunch. It's the blandest leafy green.

Health Notes

Iceberg lettuce contains vitamins A, B$_6$, C and K, folate, iron, manganese, potassium and thiamin.

Historically, lettuce was considered a soporific and was used to calm nerves and combat insomnia. However, this doesn't jibe with the ancient Egyptians' belief that lettuce increased sexual prowess and was sacred to the fertility god Min.

In herbal medicine, lettuce has been considered useful in maintaining good vision and healthy skin; preventing osteoporosis and anemia; and relieving acid indigestion, colitis, constipation and gout.

Iceberg lettuce was originally grown in California's Salinas Valley, where it was packed in ice and shipped north year-round — hence the name *iceberg*. Food producers, restaurants and fast-food eateries liked iceberg because it was easy to handle, easy to transport and easy to shred. It stayed crisp for hours after cutting and could be used to bulk up salads containing more expensive greens.

Long before the appearance of the variety we know today, a lettuce named "iceberg" was developed in the 1890s from a French crisphead called Batavia lettuce. However, the name was adopted for another cultivar developed about 60 years later — the modern iceberg we are familiar with. It dominated produce shelves in North America until the 1970s, when nine out of every ten heads of lettuce sold was iceberg. The advent of trendy mesclun mixes and darker, more nutritious greens tipped the scales, and iceberg was dismissed as cheap, bland and boring. Still, even James Beard praised iceberg's cool crunchiness. The idea that no one uses iceberg lettuce anymore is a myth. Informal, semi-serious iceberg lettuce appreciation societies sprang up in the 1990s to help restore its reputation.

Varieties

"Iceberg" has become the generic name for crisphead lettuce. To be accurate, however, *iceberg* refers to several specific cultivars in the crisphead family. Crispheads are the only lettuces that do not have red-leaf versions.

Buy It

Iceberg lettuce is a supermarket staple.

Pastel green leaves form a compact round head. Choose heads that are heavy for their size and look crisp and moist. Avoid iceberg with blemished or spotted leaves, browned

edges or "rusty" ribs. Cracking and discoloration at the stem end are signs of age.

Store It

To store iceberg lettuce, swathe it tightly in plastic wrap, then refrigerate it.

Iceberg lettuce will keep in the refrigerator for up to five days.

Prep It

To prepare a whole head of lettuce quickly, tear off damaged or wilted outer leaves. Dislodge the core by either rapping the stem end against the counter or punching it. Grab and twist the stem end to pull out the core. Insert your fingers into the hole and break the lettuce into chunks. Tear the leaves into bite-size pieces or cut them into shreds. Rinse in cold water and spin-dry.

Iceberg lettuce remains crisp for several hours, but cut edges turn brown. For this reason, tearing the leaves is better than cutting. However, you may chop or shred iceberg lettuce just before using it.

To wash cut lettuce, swish it in cold water. Drain and spin-dry, then blot with paper towels, if necessary. Dressing won't adhere properly to damp lettuce.

To clean a whole head of lettuce, cut a wedge into the base to expose the layers of leaves. Run cold water vigorously through the wedge and place the lettuce in a colander to drain.

There are several ways to super-crisp lettuce or to redeem limp lettuce:

- Soak lettuce in cold water for 15 minutes, drain and spin-dry. Place in a resealable bag and refrigerate until very cold.
- Put a whole washed, drained head of lettuce on a plate, cover with a clean kitchen towel and refrigerate for several hours.
- Place lettuce in a bowl of water with ice cubes and a bit of lemon juice. Refrigerate for 1 hour.

Consume It

Iceberg lettuce is used raw in salads and sandwiches and as lettuce cups to hold fillings. It's difficult to peel firm leaves off the head without breaking them, so some supermarkets sell leaves specifically for lettuce cups.

If you are dressing lettuce with oil and vinegar, add the latter first. Vinegar won't adhere properly to oiled leaves.

Iceberg looks its best in wedge salads. Core the head, cut it into wedges, plate it and drizzle it with dressing.

Lettuce may be added to cooked dishes to supply crunch or moisture. Be brief, though: about 5 minutes of cooking time should do it.

Equivalents

1 small head = 1 lb (500 g); 1 medium head = 1½ lbs (750 g)

•

2 oz (60 g) coarsely chopped or torn leaves = 1½ cups (375 mL), loosely packed

SUBSTITUTES

Romaine, leaf lettuce, napa cabbage

Vegetarian Cobb Salad

Stripping Cobb salad of its standard roast chicken and bacon improves its nutritional status without marring its deliciousness. In this recipe, smoked tofu stands in for the meat. The Cobb was invented at the Brown Derby restaurant in Hollywood, probably in the 1930s. It is a composed salad, presented in layers rather than tossed, so show it off in a clear glass bowl. I use a retro French dressing that's light, not gloppy like the bottled kind.

Makes 4 to 6 servings

Salad

Tips

This recipe makes about 1 cup (250 mL) dressing. Use any leftover portions on other salads.

Vegetarian Worcestershire sauce is sold in some supermarkets and health food stores.

For a retro taste, use a neutral oil, such as canola or grapeseed oil, in the dressing.

I prefer to use a Roquefort-style cheese in Cobb salad. If you are a vegetarian, check cheese labels. Cheeses are traditionally made with animal-based rennet, but some brands substitute vegetarian rennet.

Dressing

¼ to ⅓ cup	white wine vinegar	60 to 75 mL
1	clove garlic, minced	1
2 tsp	granulated sugar	10 mL
½ tsp	vegetarian Worcestershire sauce (see Tips, left)	2 mL
½ tsp	Dijon mustard	2 mL
½ tsp	kosher or coarse sea salt	2 mL
½ tsp	paprika	2 mL
¼ tsp	freshly ground black pepper	1 mL
¾ cup	oil (see Tips, left)	175 mL

Salad

4 oz	iceberg lettuce, chopped (about 3 cups/750 mL, loosely packed)	125 g
4 oz	romaine lettuce, chopped (about 3½ cups/875 mL, loosely packed)	125 g
1 oz	watercress leaves (about 1¼ cups/300 mL, loosely packed)	30 g
1	small Belgian endive, thinly sliced	1
1	tomato, diced	1
4 oz	smoked tofu, cut into ¼-inch (0.5 cm) cubes	125 g
1	ripe but firm avocado, cut into ½-inch (1 cm) cubes	1
2	hard-cooked eggs, coarsely chopped	2
2 tbsp	chopped fresh chives	30 mL
1 oz	blue cheese, crumbled (about ¼ cup/60 mL; see Tips, left)	30 g

1. *Dressing:* In a medium bowl, whisk together ¼ cup (60 mL) vinegar, garlic, sugar, Worcestershire, mustard, salt, paprika and pepper. Whisk in oil. Whisk in some or all of the remaining vinegar, if desired. Set aside.

2. *Salad:* In a medium glass serving bowl, combine iceberg lettuce, romaine, watercress and endive. Place tomato in center. Arrange tofu and avocado around tomato. Top with eggs, then scatter chives in center. Top with cheese.

3. Just before serving, drizzle dressing, to taste, over salad (you will have some left over) or serve the dressing on the side.

Iceberg Wedges with Thousand Island Dressing

I look forward to digging into a crisp iceberg wedge with creamy dressing. So retro! Simple wedge salads, eaten with knife and fork, were all the rage in the 1950s, '60s and '70s, but their popularity has undeservedly waned. As for the dressing in this recipe, I wasn't a big fan of Thousand Island until I made my own. The bottled kind tastes like a chemical spill, but the real thing — homemade — is creamy and tangy without being overpowering. You can double the recipe and keep extra on hand.

Makes 4 servings

Vegan Friendly

Salad

Tips

This recipe makes about 1 cup (250 mL) dressing. Use any leftover portion on other salads.

Tomato chili sauce is spiced but not spicy hot. Look for it in grocery stores near the ketchup.

Cocktail tomatoes are sold in supermarkets; they are also known as Camparis.

Dressing

¾ cup	mayonnaise or vegan alternative	175 mL
1½ tbsp	tomato chili sauce (see Tips, left)	22 mL
1 tbsp	finely chopped sweet onion	15 mL
1 tbsp	drained, finely chopped sweet pickles	15 mL
2 tsp	drained, chopped pimientos	10 mL
1 tsp	kosher or coarse sea salt	5 mL
⅛ tsp	freshly ground black pepper	0.5 mL

Salad

1	head iceberg lettuce, cored and quartered	1
8	thin asparagus spears, steamed and cooled	8
4	cocktail tomatoes, quartered (see Tips, left) Freshly ground black pepper	4

1. *Dressing:* In a bowl, combine mayonnaise, chili sauce, onion, pickles, pimientos, salt and pepper.
2. *Salad:* Place each wedge of lettuce on a serving plate. Spoon about ¼ cup (60 mL) dressing over each wedge. Lean 2 asparagus spears in an X against each wedge. Place tomatoes alongside. Season with pepper to taste and serve immediately.

A Dressing Success

Thousand Island salad dressing was invented in the early 1900s by Sophia LaLonde in Clayton, New York. She was the wife of a fishing guide and served her dressing at shore dinners in the Thousand Islands resort town. A visiting actress was so taken with it that she told the owner of the posh Waldorf Astoria Hotel about the dressing, and it landed on the menu there.

Iceberg, Olive and Herb Salsa

This unusual crunchy, piquant salsa adds pizzazz to sandwiches and wraps. It also serves as a delicious side salad.

Makes 1¼ cups (300 mL)

Vegan Friendly

Side dish

1 cup	chopped iceberg lettuce	250 mL
½ cup	green olives, pitted and chopped	125 mL
2 tbsp	chopped fresh flat-leaf (Italian) parsley	30 mL
1 tbsp	capers, drained and chopped	15 mL
1 tbsp	chopped fresh basil leaves	15 mL
1 tbsp	chopped fresh chives	15 mL
2 tsp	white wine vinegar	10 mL
¼ tsp	kosher or coarse sea salt	1 mL
	Freshly ground black pepper	
1 tbsp	extra virgin olive oil	15 mL

1. In a medium bowl, toss together lettuce, olives, parsley, capers, basil, chives, vinegar and salt. Season with pepper to taste. Add oil and toss.

French Peas and Lettuce

In this French country recipe, the iceberg lettuce exudes moisture to help cook the peas, as well as adding a pleasant contrasting crunch.

Makes about 4 cups (1 L)

Vegan Friendly

Side dish

Tips

Avoid cutting the lettuce into strips or big pieces, which can create unappealing clumps.

To substitute frozen peas: Rinse off any ice crystals and break up clumps. Do not add with lettuce (Step 2). Stir the lettuce until coated with oil, cover and cook, stirring once, until wilted. Stir in peas, salt and sugar and cook just until peas are tender, 2 to 3 minutes.

2 tbsp	extra virgin olive oil	30 mL
3	cloves garlic, minced	3
⅛ tsp	hot pepper flakes	0.5 mL
1	small head iceberg lettuce (1 lb/500 g), cored and coarsely chopped (see Tips, left)	1
3 cups	fresh green peas (1 lb/500 g; see Tips, left)	750 mL
¾ tsp	kosher or coarse sea salt	3 mL
¼ tsp	granulated sugar	1 mL
	Freshly ground black pepper	

1. In a wide saucepan over medium heat, heat oil until hot. Remove from heat and stir in garlic and hot pepper flakes for about 20 seconds, until barely golden (do not brown garlic).
2. Return saucepan to heat. Add lettuce and peas and stir to coat. Cover and cook for about 1 minute, stirring once, until lettuce starts to wilt. Sprinkle in salt and sugar. Cook, uncovered, shaking pan occasionally, for about 5 minutes, until most of the liquid has evaporated, lettuce is wilted and peas are tender. Season with additional salt to taste. Serve warm.

Variations

If desired, add 1 tsp (5 mL) finely chopped tarragon or mint along with the salt.

Jute Leaf

Corchorus olitorius

Other names: **bush okra, edible/Jew's/jute mallow, Egyptian spinach, mallow, okra leaf, tossa jute, West Africa sorrel.**

Depending on where you are shopping, you may find jute leaf identified as *bai po, eeyo, ewedu, fakohoy, khudra, krain-krain, meloukhia, molokhia, mrenda, nalta sag, rama, rau day* or *saluyot*.

Although it is sometimes called "okra leaf," jute leaf is not related to the vegetable okra. It probably got the name because it is mucilaginous like okra.

Jute is thought to be native to India. It has been grown for food since 6000 BCE. The Middle Eastern name for jute, *molokhia*, is derived from an Arabic word meaning "kingly." The name refers to jute's history as a staple dish for pharaohs and noblemen in ancient Egypt. Jute is also mentioned in the book of Job as "Jew's mallow."

Jute is favored as a leafy vegetable in the Middle East and Africa. It is also used in the Philippines, Thailand, Vietnam and Central America. Bangladesh and India are the world's largest producers, but in those countries jute is cultivated mainly as a textile plant.

Tasting Notes

Fresh leaves are described as bitter.

Thawed frozen jute tastes spinachy and grassy but mild. It is mucilaginous (similar to Malabar spinach) and has an extremely slippery texture. It is disparaged as "slimy" by those who don't like it.

Varieties

Jute is more famously known as a natural fiber for coarse textiles and twine. Tossa jute (*Corchorus olitorius*) is cultivated for both fiber and food; it is found mainly in southern Asia, the Middle East and North Africa. White jute (*C. capsularis*) is grown mainly for fiber and is more prevalent in China and Japan. The plant is generally differentiated as *jute* when used for fiber and as *mallow leaves* when used as edible greens.

Do not confuse jute with other edibles also dubbed "mallow," such as the following:

- Egyptian mallow leaf (*Malva parviflora*), also known as cheeseweed and *kobbeizeh*. It grows wild in the Middle East. *Kobbeizeh* also refers to a soup of the same name.
- common marsh mallow (*Althaea officinalis*), considered a delicacy by the ancient Egyptians and Romans. They consumed the young leaves and flowers but mainly the roots, which are considered to be the predecessor of modern marshmallows.
- China jute (*Abutilon theophrasti*) leaves are reputed to suffer from a cloth-like texture.

Health Notes

Jute leaf contains vitamins A, B$_6$ and C, calcium, copper, folate, iron, manganese, magnesium, niacin, potassium, thiamin and zinc.

Jute contains mucilage, considered a detoxifying agent as well as a rich source of soluble fiber.

In folk medicine, jute has been reputed to aid digestion and kill worms; inhibit blood clotting; relieve headaches, stomachaches and fever; and treat hemorrhoids, ulcers, bladder inflammations and dysentery. Some historians say Cleopatra consumed it as part of her beauty and anti-wrinkle regimen.

Equivalents

1 lb (500 g) thawed frozen whole jute leaf = 2½ cups (625 mL)

•

1 lb (500 g) thawed frozen whole jute leaf, drained = ¾ to 1 cup (175 to 250 mL)

•

1 lb (500 g) thawed frozen jute leaf, drained and chopped = 1 cup (250 mL)

SUBSTITUTES

spinach, Malabar spinach

Buy It

Fresh jute leaves wilt quickly, so they are rarely found in North America.

Frozen jute leaves are available in ethnic supermarkets. Even in Africa recipes may call for frozen leaves — they are easier to prepare. Check labels: frozen leaves are commonly packaged whole, but some brands offer chopped leaves. Avoid the latter, as they tend to be gloppy when thawed.

Store It

If you can find fresh jute leaves, store them in a resealable bag in the refrigerator for up to two days.

Keep frozen jute leaves in the freezer until you are ready to use them. Thaw them in the refrigerator overnight.

Prep It

Before cooking fresh jute, the leaves are traditionally plucked from their stems, washed with cold water and air-dried on paper towels or a clean kitchen towel, then cut. In Egypt the leaves are minced with a double-bladed mezzaluna knife or put through an electric grinder. In Africa they are pounded. To draw out mucilage, fresh leaves may be salted and left to stand. To reduce bitterness, leaves may be blanched in boiling water, rinsed and then cooked.

Frozen packages usually contain whole small jute leaves with some stemlets attached, and sometimes a few flowerbuds. Once thawed, the greens are very tender. It isn't always necessary to chop them. A bag of frozen jute may contain more than 50 percent liquid, but the amount varies by brand and type; chopped jute leaf is packed with less liquid. Either drain the liquid or add it to a dish. The liquid can act as a thickener; its consistency resembles loose egg whites because it contains mucilage from the jute. However, I prefer to drain the liquid, since it can add a slimy texture to dishes.

Consume It

Jute leaf is not eaten raw. It is used as a cooking green in simple soups, stews and curries. The longer the cooking time, the slipperier (or slimier) the jute leaves become.

Molokhia (Egyptian Jute Soup)

Egyptians say that if you haven't tried molokhia, you haven't really been to Egypt. It is considered Egypt's national soup and is also popular in Jordan, Syria, Lebanon and Tunisia. How it is cooked and presented varies a great deal from family to family, but molokhia is always spiced and garlicky. Serve this vegetarian version with toasted pitas or a bowl of hot rice — the soup may be spooned over the rice or the rice added to the soup.

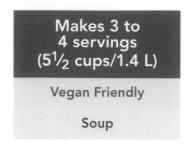

Makes 3 to 4 servings (5½ cups/1.4 L)

Vegan Friendly

Soup

Tips

For the finest minced garlic, push it through a press.

Whenever possible, use reduced-sodium vegetable stock. Not only is it healthier, it allows you to better control the saltiness of a dish.

Egyptians seem to worry a lot about this soup separating. They have devised various rules to prevent that occurrence: never allow the soup to boil, never overcook it and never leave a spoon or ladle in it. I found that the soup cooperated very well.

Tomato Drizzle

3 tbsp	hot water	45 mL
2 tbsp	tomato paste	30 mL
1 tbsp	extra virgin olive oil	15 mL
1	clove garlic, minced (see Tips, left)	1
1 tsp	hot pepper sauce	5 mL
1 tsp	kosher or coarse sea salt	5 mL
	Freshly ground black pepper	

Soup

1 lb	thawed frozen whole jute leaves, drained and chopped	500 g
4 cups	vegetable stock (see Tips, left)	1 L
2 tbsp	extra virgin olive oil	30 mL
3	cloves garlic, minced	3
½ tsp	ground coriander	2 mL
½ tsp	ground cardamom	2 mL
½ tsp	kosher or coarse sea salt	2 mL
1 tbsp	freshly squeezed lemon juice	15 mL

1. *Tomato Drizzle:* In a small bowl, combine hot water, tomato paste, oil, garlic, hot pepper sauce, salt and pepper to taste. Set aside.

2. *Soup:* In a saucepan over medium heat, bring jute leaf and stock to a simmer, stirring occasionally (do not allow it to boil; see Tips, left).

3. Meanwhile, in a small saucepan over medium-low heat, combine oil, garlic, coriander, cardamom and salt. Cook, stirring often, for 2 to 3 minutes, until golden (do not allow garlic to brown). Stir into simmering soup. Remove from heat and stir in lemon juice.

4. Ladle into individual bowls and top with tomato drizzle. Serve immediately.

Kale

Brassica oleracea acephala, B. oleracea viridis

Other names: **borecole, cow cabbage, farmer's cabbage, kail, colewort.**

Depending on where you are shopping, you may find kale identified as *boerenkool, cavolo de foraggio, chou cavalier, grünkohl, keeru* or *wo tu gan lan.*

Nowadays kale is the trendiest green in town. A mainstay in the produce section, it has been rediscovered as a super-hip superfood.

Culinary historians say leafy kale is the closest relation to wild cabbage and was probably the first type of cultivated cabbage. Modern specimens are descendants of Sabellian kale, a variety that the ancient Greeks and Romans ate. Kale was the dominant cabbage throughout Europe until the Renaissance. Russian traders introduced red kale to North America in the 19th century.

A true winter vegetable, kale grows best in colder climates and is considered sweetest after the first frost. It is extremely popular with northern Europeans. In Germany, kale clubs hold festivals and conduct tours to country inns where revelers consume kale and sausages. In the Scottish vernacular, the word *kale* or *kail* is synonymous with *food.*

Varieties

Kale is divided into four types:

- **curly kale**, also known as Scots/Scotch kale. This is common green kale.
- **black kale**, also known as dinosaur kale, black cabbage, *cavolo nero*, *lacinato*, Tuscan kale or dragon's tongue.
- **red kale**, also known as red Russian kale or ragged jack kale.
- **ornamental kale**, also known as flowering kale or cabbage. It is edible but mainly decorative.

Young kale leaves, attractively called "baby kale," are also sold on their own or added to bagged salad mixes. Baby kale may be a specific type of kale or a mixture of types.

Branching bush kale (*B. oleracea ramosa*), also known as perpetual kale or thousand-head kale, is an heirloom variety that was widely grown in medieval times. Today it is most likely to be found as a garden plant.

Health Notes

Kale contains vitamins A, B_6, C, E and K, calcium, copper, folate, iron, magnesium, manganese, potassium, riboflavin and thiamin. Nutrient-dense kale is touted as the vegetable that offers the biggest nutritional bang per calorie. Kale is strongly anti-inflammatory.

In herbal medicine, kale has been used as a gallbladder, liver and immune system stimulant; a tonic for the skin, hair, fingernails and bones; and a remedy for stomach ulcers, constipation and irritable bowel syndrome.

Tasting Notes

Curly kale is bitter, juicy and nutty tasting. The leaves are slightly lemony and slightly sweet.

Black kale is nutty, with lemony, peppery leaves. The stems and leaves are tenderer and juicier than curly kale.

Red kale is juicy and briny, with somewhat bitter leaves. When cooked, it is earthy and nutty, with a substantial tender-crisp texture.

In comparison to curly kale, red kale is saltier and black kale is sweeter.

The flavor of ornamental kale depends on the variety. Some lovely ornamental kales have crossed the line and are sold for consumption. One example is mini mauve-flowering kale, a briny, slightly nutty type. Ornamental potted green kale, commonly sold in the fall, is best admired rather than eaten. It is slightly bitter and semi-crisp; the outer leaves are tough and grainy, but the heart may be boiled.

Other kale-like plants include:

- **Hanover salad** (*Brassica napus pabularia*), also known as Siberian kale, asparagus/spring kale or hungry gap kale. Despite the names, this frilly-leafed plant is not a salad green and it is more closely related to rapeseed than to kale. To confuse matters, curly kale, turnip greens and rapini are all sometimes called Hanover salad.
- **sea kale** (*Crambe maritima*), also known as Portuguese kale. This plant has large, fleshy, kale-like leaves. It grows wild on pebbly beaches as well as being cultivated as an ornamental plant and vegetable. It was popular as a blanched vegetable in the early 19th century, but its use declined, perhaps because it spoiled easily during transport.
- **Ethiopian kale** (*Brassica carinata*), also known as Abyssinian mustard or *yabesha gomen*. The plant is thought to be a natural kale hybrid. Although it is mainly cultivated for the oil from its seeds, it is also used as a leaf vegetable.

Buy It

Kale is a supermarket staple. It is cultivated in shades ranging from mauve to bluish green, but types with green leaves are the most familiar. The leaves may be smooth, frilled or curly.

Curly kale is the most common type sold in North American supermarkets. It is green, with very frilly leaves. Black kale, the tenderest variety, is very dark green rather than black, with slightly thicker, crinkled leaves with straighter edges. Red kale has the largest and thinnest leaves; they are flat with ruffled edges and a reddish-purple blush.

Kale leaves grow in bouquet-like clusters. Look for richly colored leaves; avoid any with wilted or yellow edges.

In general terms, the larger the leaf, the tougher the kale. Younger curly kale comes in smaller bunches, as does black kale, which is considered choice and is thus more expensive than other varieties. If you can't find black kale, check the organic section, where it is often found.

1 large bunch curly kale = 1¼ to 1½ lbs (625 to 750 g)

•

1 medium bunch curly kale = 1 lb (500 g), including 10 oz (300 g) leaves and 6 oz (175 g) stems

•

1 small bunch black or young curly kale = 12 oz (375 g), including 8 oz (250 g) leaves and 4 oz (125 g) stems

•

2 oz (60 g) coarsely chopped or shredded curly kale = 4 cups (1 L), loosely packed; black or red kale = 3½ cups (875 mL), loosely packed

•

2 oz (60 g) finely chopped leaves = 2 cups (500 mL), loosely packed

•

2 oz (60 g) stems cut into 1-inch (2.5 cm) pieces = ¾ cup (175 mL), loosely packed

•

2 oz (60 g) chopped stems = ½ cup (125 mL), loosely packed

•

2 oz (60 g) baby kale (leaves and stemlets) = 5 cups (1.25 L), loosely packed

Baby kale is sold in plastic clamshells. It has recently begun to claim supermarket real estate among the salad mixes and specialty greens.

Ornamental flowering kale is usually sold potted. It comes in pearly shades of lavender, purple, pale green and variegated, as well as the standard ruffled dark greens. Specialty miniature ornamental kales that have been bred for culinary use rather than decoration are appearing in some supermarkets. I recently bought (and ate) a gorgeous briny, slightly nutty cultivar with mauve leaves on thin, tender stems in a rosette formation.

Store It

Kale is tall. If you have room in your fridge, place a bunch in a vase of water like a bouquet, with a plastic bag draped over the foliage; then refrigerate. A less awkward method is to trim kale and store it, washed or unwashed, in resealable bags with the addition of damp paper towels.

Kale is hardy. It will keep in the refrigerator for up to one week or, in a pinch, even longer. For the best results, however, don't keep it longer than two days. Older kale takes longer to cook and the texture quickly transitions from tender-crisp to leathery.

Prep It

Kale leaves grow as frills along the stems. Use a slashing technique to separate leaves from stems: holding the end of a stem with the top of the leaf pointing slightly downward, use a sharp knife to slash and scrape along the stem into the center rib of the leaf, letting the leafy pieces fall onto the cutting board. Alternatively, fold each leaf in half before cutting out the stem and center rib at an angle (this works best on the flatter leaves of black kale).

Kale stems and center ribs are fibrous and most cooks discard them. However, they may be sautéed or pickled. If you want to eat the stems, cut off and discard any that are wider than ¼ inch (0.5 cm). For a decent result, slice the stems into small pieces or, preferably, chop them.

Rinse kale leaves well in several changes of cold water, as the frills provide a fine hiding place for insects and dirt.

Consume It

Kale is traditionally cooked to tenderize it and reduce bitterness, but it can be eaten raw. Two of today's trendiest dishes are roasted kale chips and raw kale salad or slaw.

Kale salad requires few ingredients. With dressing and a few embellishments, hearty kale holds its own. Black kale is the best choice for salads, but other types will work as well.

Before serving dressed kale salad, set it aside for about 15 minutes to allow the leaves to soften and absorb the dressing.

Making kale salad requires elbow grease and a willingness to get your hands messy, because the tough leaves are best after being massaged into submission.

Here are two ways to massage kale:

- In a large bowl, toss washed, shredded kale leaves with salt — add about 1 tsp (5 mL) kosher or sea salt to the leaves from a small (12 oz/375 g) bunch. Using your hands, vigorously squeeze and massage the damp kale leaves for about 2 minutes, until they feel velvety and wilted and look shiny. Discard any bits of rib that pull off. Pat leaves dry and use them in a salad.
- In a large bowl, use your hands to massage washed and dried kale leaves with salad dressing for about 1 minute, until they are shiny and slightly wilted. Set them aside for 15 to 30 minutes to soften.

Kale salads hold up well, even overnight, if refrigerated in an airtight container.

Baby kale leaves (with tender stemlets) are perfect for sophisticated, nutritious salads. They could be considered entry-level kale for people who are unfamiliar with this green.

When steamed, boiled or braised, kale is ready in 5 to 10 minutes. When sautéing kale, add a bit of liquid, and leave any wash water clinging to the leaves. Kale can be sautéed to tender-crisp in 10 minutes. Cooked red and black kale leaves become less vivid.

Various types of kale can be used interchangeably in cooked dishes, with only small taste and textural differences. Note that red kale will stain food slightly pink.

Ornamental kale in lively colors can be used as a garnish.

SUBSTITUTES

chard, savoy cabbage

Kale Chips

I don't think there are any skeptics left about kale chips, today's trendiest snack. Kale chips seemed to appear overnight en masse in mainstream supermarkets. But homemade ones are finer, with no icky toppings or suspicious additives. They are not the loveliest chips in the world, but they're probably the healthiest. Roasting the leaves creates a deep, briny flavor that snackers find addictive.

Makes 4 servings

Vegan Friendly

Appetizer

Tips

Red kale is best for making kale chips; it has the biggest, thinnest leaves, so the results are ultra-thin and crispy. Black kale is not frilly but the crinkled leaves are slightly thicker, so you may need to increase the roasting time by 1 to 2 minutes. Curly kale roasts unevenly because of the large frills. Make sure you cut out the center ribs; they end up tough and chewy, not crisp.

For every 4 to 6 cups (1 to 1.5 L) torn kale leaves, you'll need about 1 tbsp (15 mL) oil. For efficient coverage, use your hands to toss the kale with the oil.

For dramatic presentation, toss whole leaves on their stems with oil, sprinkle with salt and roast. The roasted stalks may be stacked upright in canisters, vases or jars. This type of roasted kale is crumbly and hard to eat, but presentation is half the battle. Snackers can hold a stalk, eat the leaf and discard the stem.

• Preheat oven to 350°F (180°C)

1	small bunch kale (12 oz/375 g; see Tips, left)	1
3 tbsp	extra virgin olive oil	45 mL
	Kosher or coarse sea salt	

1. Trim kale, separating leaves from stems and center ribs (see page 189). Discard or save stems and ribs for other uses. Tear leaves into potato chip sized pieces.
2. In a large bowl, toss kale with oil to coat thoroughly (see Tips, left). Working in batches, transfer enough leaves to cover a baking sheet in a single layer. Sprinkle with salt to taste.
3. Roast in preheated oven for about 15 minutes, until edges of leaves are dark but not blackened and leaves are shiny and crisp. Transfer to a wire rack to cool. Repeat with remaining kale.

Variations

Use mustard leaves instead of kale leaves.

Experiment with flavorings. When tossing the kale with oil, add 1 tsp (5 mL) lemon juice. Instead of using just salt, sprinkle kale with sesame seeds or a spice blend such as Cajun seasoning.

Tuscan Kale Pesto

This is a tasty and healthful pesto — unless you give in to temptation and eat it by the spoonful, right then and there. Kale better lends itself to pesto once blanched; otherwise, the texture is too grainy.

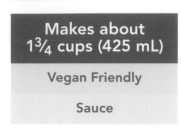

Makes about 1¾ cups (425 mL)

Vegan Friendly

Sauce

Tip

To toast pine nuts, cook them in a dry skillet over medium heat, stirring often, for 2 to 3 minutes, until golden and aromatic. Transfer to a bowl to cool.

• Food processor

1	bunch black kale (12 oz/375 g)	1
2	large cloves garlic	2
½ cup	pine nuts, toasted (see Tip, left)	125 mL
1 tbsp	freshly squeezed lemon juice	15 mL
1 tsp	kosher or coarse sea salt	5 mL
⅛ tsp	freshly ground black pepper	0.5 mL
½ cup	extra virgin olive oil	125 mL

1. Using a sharp knife, trim kale, separating leaves from stems and center ribs (see page 189). Discard stems and ribs or save for other uses. Coarsely chop leaves; you should have 12 to 14 cups (3 to 3.5 L), loosely packed.

2. In a pot of boiling water over medium heat, blanch kale for 5 minutes, until softened but not limp. Drain and immediately rinse with cold water until kale is at room temperature. Drain.

3. Using food processor fitted with the metal blade, chop garlic. Squeeze handfuls of kale to extract excess liquid and transfer to work bowl. Add pine nuts, lemon juice, salt and pepper. Pulse just until chopped and combined. With the motor running, drizzle oil through the feed tube until pesto is puréed and blended but not pasty. Store in an airtight container and refrigerate for up to 1 week.

Variation

If you are not a vegan, add ½ cup (125 mL) freshly grated Parmesan-style cheese, if desired.

Kaleslaw

There's more than one way to make a slaw. I modernize this traditional favorite by using kale and a lime-pepper dressing.

**Makes
4 servings (about
7 cups/1.75 L)**

Vegan Friendly

Salad

Tips

To finely shred the kale and cabbage, use a food processor fitted with a shredding disk.

Use green or black kale. Red kale creates a nice color contrast but will stain the cabbage pink.

Cane sugar is likely to be filtered through bone char, while beet sugar is not. Most labels don't indicate the source of the sugar. If you are following a vegan diet, use unbleached organic sugar that has not been filtered through bone char, or a sweetener such as agave syrup.

Slaw

4 oz	kale leaves, finely shredded (about 6 cups/1.5 L, loosely packed; see Tips, left)	125 g
8 oz	green cabbage, finely shredded (about 2 cups/500 mL, loosely packed; see Tips, left)	250 g
1	carrot, shredded	1
1	cup diced red onion	250 mL

Dressing

6 tbsp	freshly squeezed lime juice	90 mL
1½ tbsp	extra virgin olive oil	22 mL
3 tbsp	granulated sugar (see Tips, left)	45 mL
1½ tsp	kosher or coarse sea salt (see Tips, page 196)	7 mL
¼ tsp	freshly ground black pepper	1 mL

1. *Slaw:* In a large heatproof bowl, toss together kale, cabbage, carrot and onion. Set aside.

2. *Dressing:* In a small saucepan over medium heat, combine lime juice, oil, sugar, salt and pepper and bring to a full boil.

3. Remove dressing from heat and immediately pour over kale mixture. Toss to combine. Transfer to an airtight container and refrigerate for at least 3 hours or preferably overnight before serving.

Variation

Substitute an equal amount of lemon juice for the lime.

I Knead Kale Salad

Lately I can't get enough of kale salad. Preparing it does, however, require effort. You shouldn't just toss kale with dressing as you would lettuce. You've got to work it over. The massage technique in this recipe tenderizes kale like crazy, but the dressed salad holds up well all day and even overnight. The simple lemon dressing makes it bright, bold and shiny.

Makes 4 to 6 servings

Vegan Friendly

Salad

Tips

This recipe makes about ⅓ cup (75 mL) dressing. Use any leftover portion on other salads.

For raw salads, choose black kale, the tenderest kind. You can, however, substitute curly or red kale.

To toast hazelnuts, roast them on a baking sheet in a preheated 400°F (200°C) oven for 5 minutes, or until skins split. Wrap them in a clean kitchen towel and set them aside to cool for 2 minutes. Rub them with the towel to remove the skins (don't worry about getting all the skins off). Set aside to cool to room temperature, about 15 minutes, before chopping.

Substitute pecans or walnuts for the hazelnuts, if desired.

Dressing

2 tbsp	freshly squeezed lemon juice	30 mL
1	clove garlic, minced	1
1 tsp	granulated sugar (see Tips, page 193)	5 mL
¼ cup	extra virgin olive oil	60 mL

Salad

1	bunch black kale (12 oz/375 g)	1
1 tsp	kosher or coarse sea salt	5 mL
1 cup	hazelnuts, toasted and coarsely chopped (see Tips, left)	250 mL
½ cup	dried cherries or cranberries	125 mL

1. *Dressing:* In a small bowl, whisk together lemon juice, garlic and sugar. Whisk in oil.

2. *Salad:* Using a sharp knife, trim kale, separating leaves from stems and center ribs (see page 189). Discard or save stems and ribs for other uses. Slice leaves into thin ribbons; you should have 12 to 14 cups (3 to 3.5 L), loosely packed.

3. In a large serving bowl, toss kale with salt. Using your hands, vigorously squeeze and massage leaves for about 2 minutes, until they feel velvety and wilted and look shiny. Discard any bits of rib that pull off. Add dressing to taste (you will have some left over) and toss to coat well. Set aside for about 15 minutes to absorb dressing. Sprinkle hazelnuts and cherries overtop.

Tuscan Kale Salad

Hearty and healthy, kale salad is popular every which way. This one has lively Italian accents: sun-dried tomato vinaigrette, pine nuts and, if you wish, grated cheese. The kale is massaged into submission with the dressing.

Makes 4 to 6 servings

Vegan Friendly

Salad

Tip

If you don't have a cheese slicer, shave the cheese with a vegetable peeler.

1	bunch black or curly kale (12 oz/375 g)	1
½ cup	Sun-Dried Tomato Vinaigrette (page 450)	125 mL
⅓ cup	pine nuts, toasted (see Tip, page 192)	75 mL
⅔ cup	shaved Parmesan-style cheese, optional	150 mL

1. Using a sharp knife, trim kale, separating leaves from stems and center ribs (see page 189). Discard stems and ribs or save for other uses. Slice leaves into thin ribbons; you should have 12 to 14 cups (3 to 3.5 L), loosely packed.

2. In a large bowl, pour dressing, to taste, over kale (you may have some left over). Using your hands, massage leaves with dressing for about 1 minute, until shiny and slightly wilted. Set aside for 15 to 30 minutes to soften.

3. Add pine nuts and toss. Scatter cheese (if using) overtop and serve.

Baby Kale Salad for Grownups

This salad is vibrant, sophisticated and healthful. The kale craze has escalated with the introduction of baby kale leaves in supermarket produce departments. In this recipe I pair baby kale with avocado, pepitas and grape tomatoes and toss the lot in a bright lemon-lime dressing.

Makes 4 to 6 servings

Vegan Friendly

Salad

Tips

This recipe makes about ⅓ cup (75 mL) dressing. Use any leftover portion on other salads.

Pepitas are shelled pumpkin seeds. To toast them, cook in a dry skillet over medium heat for 2 to 3 minutes, stirring often, until they are turning golden and start to pop.

Dressing

1 tbsp	freshly squeezed lemon juice	15 mL
1 tbsp	freshly squeezed lime juice	15 mL
1	clove garlic, minced	1
1 tsp	granulated sugar	5 mL
¼ cup	extra virgin olive oil	60 mL

Salad

12 cups	loosely packed baby kale leaves (5 oz/150 g)	4 L
1 cup	grape tomatoes, halved	250 mL
1	avocado, diced or sliced	1
¼ cup	pepitas, toasted (see Tips, left)	60 mL

1. *Dressing:* In a small bowl, whisk together lemon and lime juices, garlic and sugar. Whisk in oil.

2. *Salad:* In a large serving bowl, toss kale with dressing to taste (you will have some left over). Arrange tomatoes and avocado on top. Scatter pepitas overtop and serve immediately.

Simple Sautéed Kale

I love the earthy taste and hearty texture of these greens, which are nicely complemented by a splash of balsamic vinegar. This recipe makes use of the nourishing kale stems. Enjoy the dish as is or add it to pasta, rice or other cooked grains. You can mix it with cubes of warm tofu too.

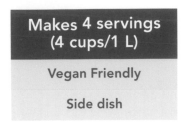

Makes 4 servings (4 cups/1 L)

Vegan Friendly

Side dish

Tips

I prefer kosher salt because it tastes better than iodized table salt and (ideally) contains no additives. Table salts and some sea salts contain additives such as iodine compounds (iodides), anti-clumping agents and even sugar (in the form of dextrose, which is used to stabilize iodine). Although the North American Salt Institute states that kosher salt "contains no additives," some kosher salt brands do contain additives such as anti-clumping agents. If you have concerns, check the label.

Whenever possible, use reduced-sodium vegetable stock. Not only is it healthier, it allows you to better control the saltiness of a dish.

1	bunch kale (1 lb/500 g)	1
2 tbsp	extra virgin olive oil	30 mL
2	cloves garlic, chopped	2
1 tsp	kosher or coarse sea salt (see Tips, left)	5 mL
1/8 tsp	freshly ground black pepper	0.5 mL
1/2 cup	vegetable stock or water (see Tips, left)	125 mL
	Balsamic vinegar	

1. Using a sharp knife, trim kale, separating leaves from stems and center ribs (see page 189). Discard parts of stems wider than 1/4 inch (0.5 cm). Coarsely chop leaves and tender stems (with ribs), placing them in separate piles.

2. In a large saucepan over medium heat, heat oil until shimmery. Add kale stems and garlic. Cook, stirring often, for about 1 minute, until softened. Stir in salt and pepper. Add kale leaves. Cook, stirring often, for 1 to 2 minutes, until coated and slightly wilted. Pour in stock. Cover, reduce heat to medium-low and cook, stirring occasionally, for about 10 minutes, until kale is tender-crisp and stock has evaporated. Drizzle with vinegar to taste. Serve warm.

Variations

Drizzle the kale with lemon juice instead of vinegar.

Scatter toasted nuts, such as pecans or walnuts, overtop.

Add chopped sun-dried tomatoes with the leaves in Step 2.

Kale Soup with Roasted Garlic and Smoked Paprika

This soup is a party for your taste buds and a feast for your eyes. Red and green flecks of kale look lovely in the smoky, creamy yellow base.

Makes 4 to 6 servings (about 7 cups/1.75 L)

Vegan Friendly

Soup

Tips

Yellow-fleshed potatoes are the best choice for this soup; they make it creamy. The most famous variety is Yukon Gold.

Smoked paprika, one of Spain's culinary claims to fame, is sold in fine food shops and some supermarkets. It comes in sweet (mild) and hot (spicy) versions.

I use a mixture of green and red kale leaves because the result looks pretty. You can, however, use only green ones. Note that the colors start to darken as the soup stands.

- Preheat oven to 400°F (200°C)
- Stand or immersion blender

2 tbsp	extra virgin olive oil	30 mL
2	leeks (white and light green parts), sliced	2
1 tsp	kosher or coarse sea salt	5 mL
1/8 tsp	freshly ground white pepper	0.5 mL
2 1/2 cups	vegetable stock	625 mL
2 1/2 cups	water	625 mL
2	small potatoes (6 oz/175 g total), cut into 1-inch (2.5 cm) dice (see Tips, left)	2
1	sprig fresh rosemary	1
1/2 tsp	sweet smoked paprika (see Tips, left)	2 mL
4 cups	finely chopped green and red kale leaves (4 oz/125 g)	1 L
1	head Roasted Garlic (page 454)	1

1. In a saucepan over medium heat, heat oil until shimmery. Add leeks, salt and pepper. Cook, stirring often, for 3 to 5 minutes, until softened and turning golden. Add stock, water, potatoes, rosemary and paprika. Cover, reduce heat to low and simmer for about 20 minutes, until vegetables are very tender.

2. Remove from heat and discard rosemary stalk. Squeeze cloves from prepared roasted garlic into pan, discarding skins. Using blender, purée soup. Return to pan if necessary. Stir in kale and bring to a simmer over medium heat. Cover, reduce heat to low and simmer for 10 to 15 minutes, until kale is tender. Season with additional salt to taste.

3. Ladle into serving bowls. Dust with additional smoked paprika to taste. Serve immediately.

Caldo Verde

I make both refined and rustic versions of Portugal's signature green soup, depending on my mood. This one is refined, with tiny bits of kale swimming in a satiny pastel green base.

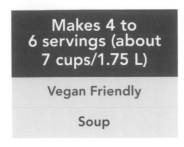

Makes 4 to 6 servings (about 7 cups/1.75 L)

Vegan Friendly

Soup

Tips

To prepare the kale for this recipe: Trim kale, separating leaves from stems and center ribs. Discard any parts of stems wider than ¼ inch (0.5 cm). Chop tender stems and ribs. Chop one-quarter of the leaves finely. Place them in separate piles.

Yellow-fleshed potatoes are best for this recipe. Neither waxy nor dry, they are good all-purpose potatoes. The best-known yellow-fleshed potatoes are Yukon Golds.

Piri piri is Portuguese hot sauce. You can find it in well-stocked supermarkets. If you don't have any, substitute your favorite hot sauce.

- Stand or immersion blender

2 tbsp	extra virgin olive oil, divided	30 mL
8 oz	kale (½ bunch), trimmed and chopped (see Tips, left)	250 g
1	onion, diced	1
½ tsp	kosher or coarse sea salt	2 mL
½ tsp	freshly ground black pepper	2 mL
2	large cloves garlic, chopped	2
4 cups	vegetable stock	1 L
2 cups	water	500 mL
6	small potatoes (1½ lbs/750 g), peeled and cut into 2-inch (5 cm) chunks (see Tips, left)	6
	Piri piri sauce (see Tips, left)	

1. In a large saucepan over medium heat, heat 1 tbsp (15 mL) oil until shimmery. Add kale stems and ribs, onion, salt and pepper. Cook, stirring often, for about 3 minutes, until softened. Stir in garlic for 20 seconds. Add stock, water, potatoes and whole kale leaves. When mixture comes to a simmer, cover, reduce heat to low and cook for 20 minutes, until potatoes are tender.

2. Using blender, purée soup. Return to saucepan if necessary. Stir in chopped kale and bring to a simmer over medium-high heat. Cover, reduce heat to low and simmer for 10 minutes, until kale is tender. Season with salt to taste.

3. Ladle soup into a tureen or individual serving bowls. Drizzle with remaining oil and dash in piri piri sauce to taste. Serve warm.

Variation

Rustic Caldo Verde: Finely chop all the kale leaves so the soup doesn't end up swampy (with unappealing clumps of greens). In Step 2, omit the kale and simmer for 15 minutes, until potatoes are barely tender. Use a masher to coarsely crush the potatoes in the pan. Stir in the kale. Simmer, covered, over low heat for about 15 minutes, until kale is tender. Finish with oil and piri piri sauce as described in Step 3.

Ribollita

Ribollita is a Tuscan vegetable stoup (soup/stew). Peasant food at its best, it was traditionally made with black kale, day-old bread and leftovers. In Italian, ribollita *means "twice cooked" or "re-boiled." So, if you can wait, re-boil it the next day before serving. If you eat it immediately, you can call it* minestra di pane *("bread soup stew").*

	Makes 4 servings (about 10 cups/2.5 L)
	Vegan Friendly
	Main course

Tips

To prepare the kale for this recipe: Trim kale, separating leaves from stems and center ribs. Discard stems thicker than 1/4 inch (0.5 cm). Chop remaining stems, ribs and leaves, placing them in separate piles. Don't leave the kale leaves in large pieces; the result will be swampy (with unappealing clumps of greens).

If desired, splurge on San Marzano tomatoes. These premium plum tomatoes from Italy are sold in well-stocked supermarkets. The easiest way to crush them is to squeeze them with your hands and add them directly to the pot, followed by their juices.

If desired, sprinkle ribollita with finely grated Parmesan-style cheese before serving. Vegetarians should check labels. Traditional cheeses are made with animal-based rennet. However, many companies now use vegetarian rennet instead.

1/4 cup	extra virgin olive oil, divided	60 mL
1	bunch black kale (12 oz/375 g), trimmed and chopped (see Tips, left)	1
2	carrots, cut into 1/2- to 1-inch (1 to 2.5 cm) chunks	2
1	onion, diced	1
1	stalk celery, with leaves, diced	1
4	cloves garlic, chopped	4
1 tsp	kosher or coarse sea salt	5 mL
1/2 tsp	hot pepper flakes	2 mL
4 cups	vegetable stock, divided	1 L
3 cups	water	750 mL
1 cup	canned plum tomatoes, with juices, crushed (see Tips, left)	250 mL
1	potato, cut into 1-inch (2.5 cm) chunks	1
2	sprigs fresh thyme	2
1	bay leaf	1
1	can (15 oz/340 mL) cannellini (white kidney) beans	1
2 cups	cubed (1 inch/2.5 cm) crustless day-old rustic Italian bread	500 mL

1. In a large saucepan over medium heat, heat 2 tbsp (30 mL) oil until shimmery. Add kale stems, carrots, onion, celery, garlic, salt and hot pepper flakes. Cook, stirring often, for 5 minutes, until softened. Add 3 cups (750 mL) stock, water, tomatoes with their juices, kale leaves, potato, thyme and bay leaf. When mixture comes to a simmer, cover, reduce heat to low and cook for about 30 minutes, until vegetables are very tender.

2. Discard thyme stems and bay leaf. Stir in beans and bread. Simmer for 5 minutes.

3. Transfer to an airtight container, cool, cover and refrigerate overnight. If desired, add remaining stock to loosen soup. Reheat in a large saucepan over low heat, stirring often, until it comes to a simmer. Ladle into a tureen or individual serving bowls. Drizzle remaining oil overtop and serve hot.

Variations

Substitute diced celeriac, with leaves, for the celery.

Besides kale, many other kinds of greens can be added to this dish, including cabbage, chard and beet greens.

Kale, Chickpea and Pickled Onion Sandwiches

Here's another one of my serious sandwiches. It's a delicious meal, not a slapdash throw-together. Quick-pickled onions are a great finishing touch. Eating one of these sandwiches is a bit messy, but it's worth the effort.

Makes 4 servings
Vegan Friendly
Sandwich

Tips

Bottled reconstituted lemon and lime juices usually contain additives. To avoid them, use freshly squeezed juice. Squeeze a whole lemon or lime and store the leftover juice in a small container in the fridge, or freeze it in 1 tbsp (15 mL) portions in an ice-cube tray.

If you don't have a food processor, mince the garlic, and mash the chickpea mixture with a fork.

I use triangular buns because I like the shape. You can use any type you prefer.

• Food processor (see Tips, below)

Chickpeas

1	large clove garlic	1
1	can (19 oz/540 mL) chickpeas, rinsed and drained	1
1 tbsp	freshly squeezed lemon juice (see Tips, left)	15 mL
¼ tsp	kosher or coarse sea salt	1 mL
⅛ tsp	freshly ground black pepper	0.5 mL
¼ cup	mayonnaise or vegan alternative	60 mL

Kale

1 tbsp	extra virgin olive oil	15 mL
4 oz	kale leaves, coarsely chopped (about 8 cups/2 L)	125 g
¼ tsp	kosher or coarse sea salt	1 mL
¼ tsp	hot pepper flakes	1 mL
¼ cup	water	60 mL

Sandwiches

4	6-inch (15 cm) crusty triangle buns, split (see Tips, left)	4
	Quick Pickled Onions (page 455)	
	Mayonnaise or vegan alternative	

1. *Chickpeas:* In food processor fitted with the metal blade, chop garlic. Add chickpeas, lemon juice, salt and pepper and pulse a few times, until coarsely chopped. Add mayonnaise. Pulse until puréed, but with some texture. Set aside.

2. *Kale:* In a saucepan over medium heat, heat oil until shimmery. Add kale, salt and hot pepper flakes. Cook, stirring often, for 1 to 2 minutes, until coated and slightly wilted. Pour in water. Cover, reduce heat to medium-low and cook, stirring occasionally, for 10 minutes, until kale is tender-crisp and water has evaporated. Set aside.

3. *Sandwiches:* Spread chickpea mixture on bottom half of each bun. Using tongs, transfer a batch of pickled onions to paper towels, blot quickly to remove excess juices, then scatter them to taste over chickpea mixture (you may have some left over). Top with kale, dividing equally. Spread mayonnaise to taste on cut side of top of each bun. Replace tops of buns, cut each sandwich in half and serve immediately.

Kalesadillas

Here's a simple green vegetarian take on a fast family favorite, the quesadilla. Serve it with a big salad to double up on your greens.

Makes 4 servings

Main course

Tips

I prefer kosher salt because it tastes better than iodized table salt and (ideally) contains no additives. Table salts and some sea salts contain additives such as iodine compounds (iodides), anti-clumping agents and even sugar (in the form of dextrose, which is used to stabilize iodine). Although the North American Salt Institute states that kosher salt "contains no additives," some kosher salt brands do contain additives such as anti-clumping agents. If you have concerns, check the label.

If you are a vegetarian, check cheese labels. Cheeses are traditionally made with animal-based rennet. However, many companies are now using vegetarian rennet instead.

2 tbsp	extra virgin olive oil	30 mL
1	small onion, diced	1
½ tsp	kosher or coarse sea salt (see Tips, left)	2 mL
½ tsp	hot pepper flakes	2 mL
1	large clove garlic, chopped	1
4 oz	kale leaves, trimmed and coarsely chopped (about 8 cups/2 L)	125 g
¼ cup	vegetable stock or water	60 mL
8	medium (7 inches/18 cm) whole wheat tortillas	8
1 cup	shredded Cheddar cheese (4 oz/125 g)	250 mL

1. In a large saucepan over medium heat, heat oil until shimmery. Add onion, salt and hot pepper flakes. Cook, stirring often, for about 3 minutes, until onion is softened and turning golden. Stir in garlic for 20 seconds. Add kale and cook, stirring often, for 1 to 2 minutes, until coated and starting to wilt. Add stock. Cover, reduce heat to medium-low and cook for 10 minutes, until kale is tender-crisp and liquid has evaporated.

2. Place half the tortillas on a work surface. Scatter half the cheese overtop. Top with equal amounts of kale, then remaining cheese. Top with remaining tortillas.

3. In a large, dry skillet (preferably cast iron) over medium heat, cook kalesadillas in batches for 1 to 2 minutes per side, until tortillas are golden brown and slightly crisp and cheese is molten. Cut each in half and serve warm.

Kale, Pear and Gorgonzola Pizza

Here's a pizza for grownups — sophisticated and unusual. You can speed up and simplify the pizza-making process by using store-bought dough.

Makes one 12-inch (30 cm) pizza or 4 to 6 servings

Main course

Tips

The pears should be ripe but firm. You can use Bartlett pears instead of Anjous, but avoid Boscs — they are too coarse in texture when roasted.

Gorgonzola is a traditional designation-of-origin cheese prepared with animal rennet. However, some companies make Gorgonzola-style cheese with vegetarian rennet. If you are a vegetarian, check the label.

Baking the pizza near the bottom of the oven allows the crust to turn golden before the toppings start to overcook.

- Preheat oven to 500°F (260°C), placing rack in the lowest position (see Tips, left)
- Preheated pizza stone or inverted baking sheet

	Flour for dusting	
1 lb	pizza dough, at room temperature	500 mL
1/2 cup	Tuscan Kale Pesto (page 192)	125 mL
2	Anjou pears (1 lb/500 g total), peeled, cored and sliced (see Tips, left)	2
1 1/2 tbsp	extra virgin olive oil	22 mL
4 oz	Gorgonzola-style cheese, crumbled (1 cup/250 g; see Tips, left)	125 g

1. On a lightly floured piece of parchment paper, stretch or roll dough into a 12-inch (30 cm) circle. Brush pesto evenly overtop, leaving a 1/2-inch (1 cm) border. Cover evenly with pear slices (you should have about half a pear left over). Brush pear slices and exposed edges of dough with oil. Scatter cheese evenly overtop.

2. Transfer pizza, with parchment paper, to preheated pizza stone or baking sheet. Bake in preheated oven for 15 to 20 minutes or until bottom is golden brown, pears are tender and cheese is bubbly. Serve hot.

Whole Wheat Pasta with Kale and Chickpeas

I'm a big fan of pasta with greens and beans, particularly this combination. It's bound to become a classic pairing.

Makes 4 servings

Vegan Friendly

Main course

Tips

For the finest minced garlic, push it through a press.

To prepare the kale for this recipe: Using a sharp knife, separate kale leaves from stems and center ribs. Discard or save stems and ribs for other uses. Finely chop leaves.

If you are a vegetarian, check cheese labels. Traditional cheeses, especially artisanal types such as Parmesan, are made with animal-based rennet. However, many cheese companies now use vegetarian rennet instead.

12 oz	whole wheat fusilli	375 g
1/4 cup	extra virgin olive oil	60 mL
1	large onion, diced	1
1 tsp	kosher or coarse sea salt	5 mL
1 tsp	hot pepper flakes	5 mL
1/8 tsp	freshly ground black pepper	0.5 mL
2	large cloves garlic, minced (see Tips, left)	2
1/2 cup	oil-packed sun-dried tomatoes, drained (oil reserved) and chopped	125 mL
1	bunch kale (1 lb/500 g), leaves separated from center ribs and chopped (see Tips, left)	1
1/2 cup	water	125 mL
1	can (19 oz/540 mL) chickpeas, drained and rinsed	1
	Grated Parmesan-style cheese, optional (see Tips, left)	

1. In a large pot of boiling salted water, cook fusilli for 12 minutes or until al dente. Drain, reserving 1 cup (250 mL) cooking water.

2. In a large saucepan over medium heat, heat oil until shimmery. Add onion, salt, hot pepper flakes and pepper. Cook, stirring often, for about 3 minutes, until onion is softened. Stir in garlic, sun-dried tomatoes and their oil for 30 seconds. Add kale and cook, stirring often, for 1 to 2 minutes, until coated. Add water. Cover, reduce heat to low and simmer for 10 to 15 minutes, stirring occasionally, until kale is tender-crisp.

3. Stir in cooked fusilli and chickpeas. Add some or all of the pasta cooking liquid to moisten as needed. Sprinkle with grated cheese to taste (if using). Serve immediately.

Red, Green and Black Portuguese Rice

I became smitten with Portuguese rice while attending a wedding hosted by my neighbors. Later the lady of the house kindly taught me how to make it. As an added attraction, I've embellished this version with kale.

Makes 4 servings (about 5 cups/ 1.25 L)

Vegan Friendly

Side dish

Tips

Cook the rice until firm, not sticky. Converted, or parboiled, rice holds its shape and is less likely to get mushy. Do not confuse it with precooked rice, an inferior option. If you don't have converted rice, use long-grain white rice.

Be sure to mince the vegetables very finely. The red pepper should be almost puréed.

The olives are traditionally tossed in whole, but it's wiser to pit them. You don't want a diner to inadvertently crack a tooth.

Piri piri is Portuguese hot sauce. You can find it in well-stocked supermarkets. If you don't have any, substitute your favorite hot sauce.

2 cups	water	500 mL
	Kosher or coarse sea salt	
1 cup	converted rice (see Tips, left)	250 mL
3 to 4 tbsp	extra virgin olive oil, divided	45 to 60 mL
½ cup	minced red bell pepper (see Tips, left)	125 mL
1	shallot, minced	1
½ tsp	kosher or coarse sea salt	2 mL
2	cloves garlic, minced (see Tips, page 203)	2
1 oz	kale leaves, finely chopped (about 1 cup/250 mL)	30 g
2 tbsp	tomato paste	30 mL
	Piri piri sauce (see Tips, left)	
	Freshly ground black pepper	
2 tbsp	chopped fresh parsley	30 mL
16	black olives (see Tips, left)	16

1. In a saucepan over high heat, salt water to taste and bring to a boil. Stir in rice, cover, reduce heat to low and simmer for about 18 minutes, until rice is just tender and water is absorbed. Remove from heat. Uncover and set aside for 5 minutes.

2. Meanwhile, in another saucepan over medium-low heat, heat 2 tbsp (30 mL) oil until shimmery. Add red pepper, shallot and salt. Cook, stirring often, for about 10 minutes, until very soft (do not brown — the mixture should not fry vigorously; lower heat if necessary). Stir in garlic for 30 seconds. Stir in kale for about 1 minute, until coated. Cover and cook, stirring occasionally, for 5 to 10 minutes, until kale is tender-crisp. Stir in tomato paste.

3. Fluff rice with a fork. Add kale mixture and mix gently with fork. Add piri piri sauce and pepper to taste. Season with salt to taste.

4. Transfer to a shallow serving bowl or individual dishes. Drizzle with remaining oil to taste. Scatter parsley and olives overtop and serve immediately.

Kohlrabi Tops

Brassica oleracea gongylodes

Other names: **German turnip greens, stem cabbage greens, turnip cabbage greens.**

Depending on where you are shopping, you may find kohlrabi identified as *ganth gobi, nookal* **or** *monji.*

Tasting Notes

The raw leaves and stems are tough, succulent, sharp, mustardy and slightly bittersweet. When cooked, they become milder and slightly sweet, with a hint of broccoli, especially in the stems.

Health Notes

Although no official government analysis is available, kohlrabi tops are similar to but likely more nutritious than the bulbs. This would suggest that kohlrabi tops contain vitamins B_6 and C, copper, folate, magnesium, manganese, phosphorus and potassium.

In folk medicine, boiled kohlrabi leaves have been applied as poultices for gout, rheumatism, arthritis and sciatica. The juice has been used to treat ulcers, eliminate worms and encourage hair growth. Kohlrabi has also been said to improve circulation and prevent gallstones and used to treat edema, asthma, bronchitis and liver conditions.

Kohlrabi, a form of cabbage, was artificially bred in northern Europe. It is a popular vegetable in Germany and eastern and central Europe, as well as southern India and Kashmir.

Kohlrabi is one of the coolest-looking vegetables, inviting comparisons with space satellites and hot-air balloons. Technically the entire kohlrabi is a leafy green — the bulb is a swollen stem that grows above ground, not a root vegetable. You rarely find the bottoms without the tops, and never the tops without the bottoms. However, the perfectly edible leaves are usually discarded.

Varieties

Kohlrabi may be green or purple. Both types have edible green leaves; the latter has purple veins.

Buy It

Kohlrabi is a supermarket staple. The stalks sprout from small, light green bulbs and the stems are topped by firm, deep green leaves. Choose kohlrabi that seems heavy for its size. Avoid specimens with soft spots on the bulbs or yellowing leaf tips.

Kohlrabi can grow as big as 40 pounds (18 kg), but small bulbs (with correspondingly small leaves) are best. The bulbs become woody as they grow larger and their greens toughen and dry up.

The kohlrabi bulb is sweeter after the first frost, but by then the leaves are past their prime.

Store It

Kohlrabi tops don't last long and don't travel well: they will wilt and discolor right in the store. As soon as you get a bunch home, remove the stalks from the bulbs and store them separately. Use the greens as soon as possible. Trim the stalks, wrap in paper towels, place in resealable bags and refrigerate.

Equivalents

1 bunch kohlrabi =
1¾ to 2 lbs (825 g
to 1 kg), comprising
1 lb (500 g) bulbs
(5 small) and 12 to 16 oz
(375 to 500 g) tops

•

12 to 16 oz (375 to
500 g) tops = 8 to
10 oz (250 to 300 g)
leaves and 4 to 6 oz
(125 to 175 g) stems

•

1 bunch, trimmed
(leaves and tender
stems) = 8 oz (250 g)

•

2 oz (60 g) coarsely
chopped or
shredded leaves
and tender stems =
2½ cups (625 mL),
loosely packed

•

2 oz (60 g) chopped
leaves and
tender stems =
1¼ cups (300 mL),
loosely packed

•

2 oz (60 g) coarsely
chopped or
shredded leaves =
3¾ cups (900 mL),
loosely packed

•

2 oz (60 g) chopped
leaves = 1½ cups
(375 mL)

SUBSTITUTES

collards, turnip
greens, kale

Kohlrabi tops will keep in the refrigerator for up to two days.

Prep It

The main stems are edible but stringy, so I prefer to ignore them. If you are very frugal you can peel the stems, chop or cut them into pieces and cook them like broccoli. To separate the leaves, cut out the stems and thick center ribs at an angle. You can use stems and ribs no wider than ¼ inch (0.5 cm) and no farther than 4 inches (10 cm) from the bottom of the leaf. Discard the remaining thick stems — they are too woody to eat.

The stemlets attached to the leaves and thin center ribs may be cooked with the leaves.

Wash leaves in cold water, then spin-dry and cut.

Consume It

Kohlrabi leaves are almost never eaten raw, as the texture is too grainy. However, the tiniest, tenderest leaves may be added sparingly to mixed salads. Curiously, they are more pungent but taste better than mature leaves.

Wet heat works best for kohlrabi greens. When boiled or steamed, mature leaves take about 15 minutes to tenderize, while tiny leaves are done in 5 minutes. Undercooked leaves have an unpleasant papery texture.

Avoid sautéing kohlrabi leaves. It can take 45 to 60 minutes to tenderize them (with some water added), but they don't lose their coarse texture.

Total Kohlrabi Salad with Apple and Walnuts

Give this unusual salad a chance and you will fall in love with its crunchy, savory, naturally sweet, nourishing goodness. Raw kohlrabi bulb has a texture similar to jicama and a mild, slightly sweet turnip taste. Tossing in the cooked greens adds dimension, not to mention nutrients.

Makes 2 to 4 servings (about 4 cups/1 L)		
Vegan Friendly		
Salad		

Tips

Cane sugar is likely to be filtered through bone char, while beet sugar is not. Most labels don't indicate the source of the sugar. If you are following a vegan diet, use unbleached organic sugar that has not been filtered through bone char, or a sweetener such as agave syrup.

Choose a bunch of kohlrabi with small bulbs. They are the tenderest.

I like to use a tart Granny Smith or crunchy Honeycrisp apple in this salad.

To toast walnuts, cook in a dry skillet over medium heat, stirring often, for about 3 minutes, until beginning to turn golden and aromatic.

Dressing

1 tbsp	freshly squeezed lemon juice	15 mL
1 tsp	granulated sugar (see Tips, left)	5 mL
1/4 tsp	Dijon mustard	1 mL
1/2 tsp	kosher or coarse sea salt	2 mL
1/8 tsp	freshly ground white pepper	0.5 mL
1 tbsp	walnut oil	15 mL
1 tbsp	extra virgin olive oil	15 mL

Salad

1	bunch kohlrabi (1¾ to 2 lbs/825 g to 1 kg; see Tips, left)	1
1	large tart apple, cut into ½-inch (1 cm) cubes (see Tips, left)	1
½ cup	walnuts, toasted and coarsely chopped (see Tips, left)	125 mL

1. *Dressing:* In a small bowl, whisk together lemon juice, sugar, mustard, salt and pepper. Whisk in walnut and olive oils. Set aside.

2. *Salad:* Using a sharp knife, separate kohlrabi stalks from bulbs. Trim stalks, discarding stems and center ribs. Coarsely chop 4 oz (125 g) leaves; you should have about 7 cups (1.75 L). Set aside the remaining leaves for other uses. Trim bulbs, peel (see Tips, page 208) and cut into batons about ¼ inch (0.5 cm) thick. Set aside.

3. In a saucepan of boiling salted water, cook chopped leaves over medium heat, partly covered, for about 15 minutes, until very tender. Drain and immediately rinse with cold water to stop the cooking. Drain. Gently squeeze handfuls to extract excess liquid and transfer to a cutting board. Using a sharp knife, chop leaves finely. Set aside.

4. In a serving bowl, toss kohlrabi batons, cooked leaves and apple with dressing. Scatter walnuts overtop and serve immediately.

Kohlrabi Oven Fries
with Green Aïoli

Who needs french fries? Roasting kohlrabi brings out its gentle natural sweetness, but it is far from bland. Accompanying these fries is a dipping sauce that makes use of kohlrabi's nutritious greens. As a bonus, this addictive green mayonnaise is also great in sandwiches or alongside steamed vegetables. It can be prepared with any leaves you like.

Makes 4 servings

Vegan Friendly

Side dish

Tips

This recipe makes about ⅔ cup (150 mL) aïoli.

Trim center ribs and stemlets from kohlrabi leaves.

Peel kohlrabi bulbs thoroughly, using a sharp knife and vegetable peeler. Beneath the tough green skin is a fibrous layer, particularly at the base, that won't soften when cooked. So keep peeling until you reach the crisp lighter green flesh.

Multitask — while the greens cook, start the kohlrabi fries.

- Preheat oven to 400°F (200°C)
- Mini blender or food processor
- Rimmed baking sheet

Green Aïoli

2 oz	kohlrabi leaves, coarsely chopped (about 3¾ cups/900 mL, loosely packed; see Tips, left)	60 g
1	small clove garlic	1
½ cup	mayonnaise or vegan alternative	125 mL
1 tbsp	freshly squeezed lemon juice	15 mL
½ tsp	kosher or coarse sea salt	2 mL
⅛ tsp	freshly ground black pepper	0.5 mL

Kohlrabi Fries

2 lbs	kohlrabi bulbs (8 to 10), peeled and cut into ½-inch (1 cm) thick batons	1 kg
4 tsp	extra virgin olive oil	20 mL
	Kosher or coarse sea salt	
	Freshly ground black pepper	

1. *Green Aïoli:* In a saucepan of boiling salted water, cook kohlrabi leaves over medium heat, partly covered, for about 15 minutes, until tender (see Tips, left). Drain and immediately rinse with cold water to stop the cooking. Drain.

2. In blender or food processor fitted with the metal blade, chop garlic. Gently squeeze handfuls of cooked kohlrabi leaves to get rid of excess liquid and transfer to blender or food processor. Add mayonnaise, lemon juice, salt and pepper. Pulse a few times, until puréed.

3. *Kohlrabi Fries:* In a large bowl, toss kohlrabi batons, oil and salt and pepper to taste. Arrange in a single layer on baking sheet. Roast in preheated oven for 20 to 25 minutes, until browned and tender, turning with a spatula halfway through. Drain on a plate lined with paper towels. Serve fries with prepared aïoli in dipping bowls alongside.

Komatsuna

Brassica rapa perviridis, B. rapa komatsuna

Other names: **Japanese mustard, Korean greens, mustard spinach, tendergreen.**

Depending on where you are shopping, you may also find komatsuna identified as *mo cha* or *moutarde épinarde*.

Komatsuna is an heirloom vegetable that until recently was cultivated almost exclusively in Japan, Taiwan and Korea. Now North American growers are beginning to plant it. Although it is still relatively obscure in the West, this up-and-coming leafy green receives rave reviews for its tastiness and tenderness.

In modern Japan komatsuna is commonly eaten during New Year festivities. It is identified as one of the *dento yasai* (traditional vegetables) of Edo (now Tokyo). Some references say that *komatsuna* means simply "small pine-tree greens," while others say that its name derives from the Komatsugawa district. A more colorful story involves a shogun (military commander) visiting a temple in Edo centuries ago. During a meal there, the shogun asked a monk for the name of the vegetable he was eating. The monk said it had no name, although they grew it regularly. The shogun decided to call it *komatsuna*, naming it after the nearby Komatsu River and adding *-na*, which means "leaf."

Varieties

Komatsuna is reminiscent of mustard greens in a milder guise, but it is more closely related to bok choy. Despite the common name "mustard spinach" it has no botanical relationship with spinach (page 359).

Komatsuna comes in green and red varieties; the latter has purple leaves and green stems. Chijimi komatsu is a new, smaller variety with crinkled leaves like spinach. Baby komatsu is also cultivated.

Sensopai is a new hybrid of komatsuna and cabbage. Its leaves resemble those of collards.

Buy It

Komatsuna is occasionally sold in Asian grocery stores. It may be found tied in small bunches, unlabeled, and set next to the

Tasting Notes

Komatsuna has a mild but distinct mustard flavor. It is slightly sharp, slightly sour, yet slightly sweet. The stems are succulent.

Health Notes

Komatsuna contains vitamins A, B$_6$ and C, calcium, copper, folate, iron, manganese, niacin, potassium, riboflavin and thiamin. It is particularly high in fiber.

In herbal medicine, komatsuna has been used to stimulate the gallbladder and liver, lower cholesterol, control blood sugar and regulate thyroid functions.

Equivalents

1 bunch = 1¼ lbs
(625 g)

•

2 oz (60 g) coarsely
chopped or
shredded leaves =
2¾ cups (700 mL),
loosely packed

•

2 oz (60 g)
chopped leaves =
1½ cups (375 mL),
loosely packed

•

2 oz (60 g) stems
sliced into ½-inch
(1 cm) pieces =
½ cup (125 mL),
loosely packed

SUBSTITUTES

mustard greens,
yu choy sum

mustard greens and mustard cabbages. However, it is presently more accessible to gardeners than shoppers.

Komatsuna has large, rounded dark green leaves on rounded succulent stems that are joined in clusters. Avoid any with yellowed leaves or cracked stems and check the leaves for insect damage.

Store It

Wrap komatsuna loosely in paper towels, place in a resealable bag and refrigerate it.

It will keep in the refrigerator for up to three days.

Prep It

Before cooking komatsuna, trim the base to release the clusters. Cut the leaves from the stems and discard tough stem ends. Chop or slice tender stems, ribs and leaves.

Rinse the komatsuna in cold water and spin-dry.

Consume It

Although young leaves may be used in salads, komatsuna is usually cooked. It may be simmered as a vegetable, pickled or added to soups, stir-fries or curries. Both stems and leaves are tender. As the plant matures, it tastes more potent. When young, the leaves may be prepared like spinach. The leaves from mature plants are cooked like kale and the stems like Asian cabbage such as bok choy.

Komatsuna will cook to tender-crisp in 5 to 10 minutes. If desired, stems and leaves may be cooked separately or in stages. In the latter case, give the stems a 3- to 5-minute head start.

Soba, Greens, Mushrooms and Tofu in Miso Broth

This dish, with buckwheat noodles, komatsuna and mushrooms in a dark, rich broth, is typical of Japanese soups — wholesome and full of the savory deliciousness known as umami. Although technically a soup, it's really a meal in itself. Eat the noodles and vegetables with chopsticks, then drink the broth.

Makes 6 servings		
Vegan Friendly		
Main course		

Tips

Soba noodles are Japanese buckwheat noodles that look like whole wheat spaghetti. You can find them in well-stocked supermarkets.

There are many types of miso, or soybean paste. Here I use mild white miso so as not to overpower the other ingredients.

Mirin is sweet Japanese cooking wine. You can find it in well-stocked supermarkets.

Shimejis are cute little brown or white mushrooms that grow in clumps; they are also known as beech mushrooms. I prefer brown shimejis because they taste earthier. Separate clumps at the base and use the mushrooms whole. If you can't find them, substitute sliced shiitake caps.

Japanese chile blends are called *togarashi*. Shichimi togarashi includes red pepper, orange peel, sesame seeds, seaweed and ginger.

8 oz	soba noodles (see Tips, left)	250 g
2 tbsp	white miso (see Tips, left)	30 mL
3 cups	vegetable stock, divided	750 mL
1 cup	water	250 mL
3 tbsp	mirin (see Tips, left)	45 mL
2 tbsp	soy sauce	30 mL
3 to 4 cups	chopped komatsuna, loosely packed (4 to 6 oz/125 to 175 g)	750 mL to 1 L
6 oz	whole shimeji mushrooms (see Tips, left)	175 g
8 oz	medium-firm tofu, drained and cut into ½-inch (1 cm) cubes	250 g
6	small green onions (white and light green parts), slivered (see Tips, page 268)	6
	Shichimi togarashi chile blend (see Tips, left)	

1. In a large pan of boiling salted water, cook noodles over medium heat for 7 to 8 minutes, until tender but firm. Drain.

2. Meanwhile, in a saucepan, whisk together miso and 1 cup (250 mL) stock, until combined. Add remaining stock, water, mirin and soy sauce. Place over medium-high heat and bring to a simmer. Add komatsuna to taste and mushrooms; cover, reduce heat to medium-low and simmer for about 5 minutes, until greens are tender-crisp. Add tofu, cover and heat for about 1 minute, until warmed through.

3. Divide prepared noodles evenly among six large, shallow serving bowls. Using a slotted spoon, scoop out komatsuna, mushroom and tofu mixture and place in bowls. Ladle equal quantities of broth over noodles. Scatter green onions overtop. Sprinkle with togarashi to taste, and serve warm.

Variations

If you can't find komatsuna, don't worry — this dish will work with any kind of tender green you prefer, from chard to bok choy.

La Lot Leaf

Piper lolot

Other names: **barbecue/pepper leaf, lolot pepper.**
Depending on where you are shopping, you may also find la lot leaf identified as *lolo de Tonkin* **or** *ye-thoei*.

It may be called "pepper leaf," but la lot should not be confused with chile pepper leaf (page 287), which comes from *Capsicum* plants.

The use of pepper plants dates back 9,000 years. Pepper was an integral part of the spice trade that fueled exploration and commerce around the globe.

Wrapping meat or other food in vine leaves originated in the Middle East, then caught on in India and Southeast Asia (dolmades, or stuffed grape leaves, are the most famous). However, grapevines don't flourish in tropical climates, so the Vietnamese started substituting la lot leaves, which are native to Indochina.

Varieties

Piper is the family name of hundreds of species of pepper plants and vines. They are beloved as the source of peppercorns, from which black and white pepper are ground. However, their leaves may also be eaten. La lot leaf (*P. lolot*) is one member of the family. Unknown to most North Americans, it is a niche leafy green even in Asia.

Buy It

La lot leaf is sold in Asian grocery stores specializing in Vietnamese ingredients. Except for betel pepper leaf (page 214), the likelihood of stumbling upon other species of pepper leaves is low.

Haphazard labeling is likely to leave you in the dark unless you shop with a picture in your mind. Knowing la lot's various names may not help. The last package I bought in Chinatown was mysteriously labeled "fragrant leaf."

Thick, inedible notched stems hold leaves ranging in size from a human palm to a small hand. The heart-shaped dark green leaves are glossy on top and matte on the bottom. Avoid leaves that look faded or dry.

Tasting Notes

La lot leaf has hints of basil or anise, peppery and lemon accents and a bitter finish. When grilled as a wrapper, it is reminiscent of nori, although it is more pliable and papery. It is pleasantly chewy and nutty.

Health Notes

Although no official government analysis is available, la lot leaf is thought to contain calcium, iron and phosphorus.

In folk medicine, various pepper plants have been used to rejuvenate, detoxify and stimulate; to kill bacteria, worms and fungal conditions such as ringworm; to alleviate inflammations, mastitis and sore throats; to banish boils, abscesses and itchy rashes; to treat snakebites; and to relieve constipation.

SUBSTITUTES

perilla, grape leaves

Store It

Snip the leaves from their stems and discard the stems. Stack the leaves to eliminate creases, wrap them in paper towels, place in a resealable bag and refrigerate.

La lot will keep in the refrigerator for up to three days.

Prep It

Before consuming la lot leaves, rinse them in cold water and place on paper towels to air-dry.

Consume It

La lot leaf's only claim to fame is its role as a wrapper for one specific dish: Vietnamese barbecued beef rolls. The rolls are essential in the "beef seven ways" feast, a special-occasion meal featuring seven iconic Vietnamese beef dishes. However, you can make vegetarian alternatives.

La lot leaf may also be shredded and stir-fried or fried until crispy, which takes about 1 minute. Fried leaves, which taste similar to fried parsley, make an interesting garnish.

You can substitute la lot leaves in recipes that call for wild betel (and vice versa), and few people will be the wiser. Wild betel is used raw as wrappers for Thai snacks and in Malaysian and Laotian salads. It is the signature ingredient in a traditional Thai curry known as *kaeng khae*, which includes vegetables such as acacia leaves (page 293) and eggplant, as well as frog, water buffalo, chicken or pork.

La Lot More Where That Came From

Noteworthy relatives in the *Piper* family include the following:

- The Vietnamese also use the name "la lot" for its cousin **wild betel** (*P. sarmentosum*), also known as *khae, bakik, kado-kado, cha-plu, jia ju* or *pokok kadok*. Wild betel is found in a wider geographic area, has smaller leaves, tastes less intense and has a greater variety of culinary uses (for instance, in salads and curries).
- **Wild betel** should not be confused with either the **betel pepper leaf** (*P. betle*), also known as betel vine, or the **betel nut** (*Areca catechu*), the seed of the betel palm. The nut is wrapped in a betel pepper leaf, then chewed as an invigorating stimulant. The concoction, called *paan* or *pupulu*, is popular across Asia and India. It increases the heart rate, creates a sense of euphoria and dyes the mouth and teeth orangey brown. This unhealthy habit dates from ancient times.
- **Mexican pepperleaf** (*P. auritum*) is also known as sacred leaf/pepper, Vera Cruz pepper, *hoja/hierba/yerba santa, acuyo, tlanepa, anisillo* or root beer plant. It is native to South America and cultivated in Mexico. Its complex flavor is variously described as including accents of eucalyptus, anise, nutmeg, tarragon, pepper or sassafras (which is used to make root beer). The big heart-shaped, velvety leaves are used as tamale wrappers and added to green mole sauces.
- **West African black pepper** (*P. guineense*), also known as Ashanti pepper, Benin pepper or Guinea cubeb, has large climbing vines. In Africa the leaves are known as *uziza* and used in stews.
- A distant relative is **salad peperomia** (*Peperomia pellucida*), also known as Vietnamese crab claw herb, pepper elder, silverbush, rat-ear, man-to-man, clearweed, *coracaozinho, derva-de-vidro, rau cang cua, pak krasang, suna kosho* or *ulasimang-bato*. It is a salad green with heart-shaped succulent leaves and stems. Peperomia is valued as a food and medicinal plant in places as far-flung as Brazil, Oceania, Vietnam, the Philippines and Nigeria.

La Lot Rolls

In this vegan riff on the grilled Vietnamese tidbits served at banquets, marinated tofu replaces the usual ground beef. Grilled la lot leaf looks a bit like the grape leaves in Greek dolmades (page 162).

Makes 20 rolls

Vegan Friendly

Appetizer

Tips

Toasted sesame oil, also known as Asian sesame oil, is made from toasted or roasted sesame seeds. Dark and aromatic, it is sold in small bottles as a flavoring agent. Do not confuse toasted sesame oil with golden sesame oil, which is pressed from raw seeds.

Use only the tender heart of the lemongrass bulb and chop it as finely as possible. To save time and effort, you may buy frozen minced lemongrass in some Asian grocery stores.

To grate or purée gingerroot, use a kitchen rasp such as the kind made by Microplane.

The tofu should be drained but doesn't need to be pressed. Before using, drain it in a fine-mesh sieve for 20 to 30 minutes, then pat dry.

If desired, you can broil the rolls in the oven, on a rack set over a baking sheet, for 2 to 3 minutes per side.

- 20 wooden toothpicks, soaked for at least 1 hour
- Grilling tray, lightly greased

Filling

1 tbsp	toasted sesame oil (see Tips, left)	15 mL
1	green onion (white and green parts), minced	1
1	clove garlic, minced	1
1 tsp	minced lemongrass (see Tips, left)	5 mL
1 tsp	puréed gingerroot (see Tips, left)	5 mL
8 oz	medium-firm tofu, drained (see Tips, left)	250 g
1 tbsp	soy sauce	15 mL
1 tsp	granulated sugar	5 mL
½ tsp	kosher or coarse sea salt	2 mL
⅛ tsp	freshly ground black pepper	0.5 mL
1 tsp	cornstarch	5 mL

Rolls

20	medium-large la lot leaves, stemmed	20
20	very thin slices shiitake mushroom (about 2 caps)	20
½	carrot, cut into matchsticks	½
1 tbsp	oil	15 mL

1. *Filling:* In a small pan over medium-low heat, warm oil. Add onion, garlic, lemongrass and ginger and cook, stirring often, for 1 minute. Remove from heat. Add tofu in chunks, then soy sauce, sugar, salt and pepper. Using a fork, mash together coarsely. Sprinkle cornstarch overtop and briefly mash until mixture resembles ground beef. Set aside.

2. Place grilling tray on barbecue grate. Preheat barbecue to medium.

3. *Rolls:* Lay leaves, shiny side down, on work surface. Place about 1 tbsp (15 mL) filling at stem end of each leaf. Top each with 1 slice shiitake and 3 carrot matchsticks (you will have some left over). Working with one leaf at a time, roll up bottom over filling, fold in sides, finish rolling and insert a toothpick through the center to secure. Lightly brush each roll with oil.

4. Transfer rolls to grilling tray. Cover and grill for 2 to 3 minutes per side, until leaves look slightly shriveled and start to char. Serve immediately.

Leaf Lettuce

Lactuca sativa crispa

> *Other names:* **bunching/cutting lettuce, loose-leaf lettuce, salad bowl lettuce.**
>
> **Depending on where you are shopping, you may find leaf lettuce identified as** *lechuga* **or** *lechuga sangría.*

Tasting Notes

Leaf lettuce is mild and slightly nutty. It is crisp yet tender, with crunchy ribs and soft, pliable leaves.

Health Notes

Green leaf lettuce contains vitamins A, B_6, C and K, calcium, folate, iron, magnesium, manganese, phosphorus, potassium, riboflavin and thiamin. Red leaf lettuce also contains selenium.

The greener or more colorful the lettuce, the more healthful it is. Red leaf lettuce gets its color from anthocyanins, the beneficial compounds also found in red wine and red cabbage, which appear to be anti-inflammatory, among other health benefits.

Historically, lettuce was used to calm the nerves and induce sleep. The ancient Egyptians, however, believed that lettuce increased sexual prowess; they considered it sacred to the fertility god Min.

In herbal medicine, lettuce has been used for maintaining good vision and healthy skin, preventing osteoporosis and anemia, cleansing the liver and alleviating acid indigestion, colitis, constipation and gout.

In North America leaf lettuce traditionally played second fiddle to hardy iceberg, but it has gained a lot of ground in the past two decades as a versatile choice for salads.

Varieties

Leaf lettuce (*Lactuca sativa crispa*) comes in many green and red varieties. The most common supermarket types are frilled green leaf lettuce and red lettuce, which has green leaves tipped and tinted purplish red. Less commonly available ruby lettuce leaves are almost all red.

Famous cultivars include lollo rosso, tango and oak leaf. Tango has green or red frilly leaves that resemble curly endive at the tips. Lollo rosso has dramatic purple and green leaves. Oak leaf, named for the familiar shape of its leaves, comes in red, green and bronze types; the heads are squatter and the leaves softer than those of common green leaf lettuce. Black-seeded Simpson lettuce is an heirloom variety introduced in the mid-1800s; it has crinkled light green leaves.

Buy It

Leaf lettuce is a supermarket staple. It has crisp, moist-looking, loosely gathered leaves with perky frills or tips. Avoid any with yellowed, wilted or broken leaves or ribs tainted with rusty-looking patches.

Commercially grown green leaf lettuces tend to have firmer, thicker, coarser leaves than red varieties. For either type, choose lettuce with a rich color.

Equivalents

1 head leaf lettuce =
12 to 16 oz
(375 to 500 g)

•

2 oz (60 g) torn or
coarsely cut leaves
= 3½ cups (875 mL),
loosely packed

•

2 oz (60 g)
chopped leaves =
2 cups (500 mL),
loosely packed

SUBSTITUTES

butter lettuce, romaine
hearts, mesclun

Store It

Leaf lettuce is more perishable than head lettuce. Store it in a perforated resealable bag. Or clean and dry the leaves well, roll them loosely in paper towels and store in resealable bags.

Leaf lettuce will keep in the refrigerator for up to four days.

Prep It

Before consuming leaf lettuce, pull off and discard any wilted, discolored or damaged outer leaves.

Wash leaf lettuce well, as the curled leaves provide a hiding place for dirt and insects. Gently swish the leaves, whole or torn, in cold water. Drain, then spin-dry. Allow lettuce to dry completely; otherwise, salad dressings won't cling properly.

Leaf lettuce is generally torn, because cut edges turn brown. However, lightning won't strike if you chop or shred it, as long as you use it immediately.

Consume It

Leaf lettuce is most often used raw, in salads and sandwiches, as a decorative bed for dishes or as low-calorie, gluten-free wrappers.

If dressing leaves with oil and vinegar, add the vinegar first. It won't adhere properly to oiled leaves.

Leaf lettuce may be added to cooked dishes to supply crunch or moisture. If cooking it, be brief — the cooking time is about 5 minutes.

Lettuce, Cress and Hearts of Palm

The ghosts of chefs past haunt restaurants with visions of hearts of palm. They were so trendy in the eighties. This salad reminds me how much I still like them.

Makes 2 to 4 servings

Vegan Friendly

Salad

Tips

I prefer kosher salt because it tastes better than iodized table salt and (ideally) contains no additives. Table salts and some sea salts contain additives such as iodine compounds (iodides), anti-clumping agents and even sugar (in the form of dextrose, which is used to stabilize iodine). Although the North American Salt Institute states that kosher salt "contains no additives," some kosher salt brands do contain additives such as anti-clumping agents. If you have concerns, check the label.

Many supermarkets sell canned hearts of palm. If you can't find whole ones, buy sliced hearts of palm.

Cocktail tomatoes are sold in supermarkets. They are also known as Camparis.

Some supermarkets are now selling red watercress (page 406). If you can't find any, use green watercress.

2 tbsp	extra virgin olive oil	30 mL
1 tbsp	freshly squeezed lemon juice	15 mL
½ tsp	kosher or coarse sea salt (see Tips, left)	2 mL
½ tsp	granulated sugar (see Tips, page 207)	2 mL
⅛ tsp	freshly ground white pepper	0.5 mL
1	can (14 oz/398 mL) whole hearts of palm, drained and rinsed (see Tips, left)	1
4	leaf lettuce leaves	4
2	cocktail tomatoes, quartered (see Tips, left)	2
1 cup	red watercress sprigs (see Tips, left)	250 mL

1. In a medium bowl, whisk together oil, lemon juice, salt, sugar and pepper. Add hearts of palm and toss gently to combine. Set aside for 15 minutes to marinate.

2. Line a serving platter or individual plates with lettuce. Using tongs, remove hearts of palm from oil mixture and arrange in rows over lettuce. Drizzle oil mixture overtop. Arrange tomatoes at edge of platter or plates. Mound watercress on hearts of palm. Serve immediately.

Tomato Salad on Leaf Lettuce with Crispy Shallots

Tender lettuce, luscious ripe tomatoes, sweet-and-sour basil dressing and crunchy shallots make this salad a taste sensation. Once you start eating it, you may not be able to stop!

Makes 2 to 4 servings

Vegan Friendly

Salad

Tips

It's best to tear leaf lettuce, because cut edges turn brown. However, you can chop the lettuce if you are using it immediately.

For best results, use sweet vine ripened tomatoes.

3 oz	leaf lettuce (see Tips, left)	90 g
4	small tomatoes (1 lb/500 g total; see Tips, left)	4
	Kosher or coarse sea salt	
1/3 cup	Basil Balsamic Vinaigrette (page 450)	75 mL
1 1/3 cups	Crispy Shallots (page 455)	325 mL

1. Tear or chop leaf lettuce into bite-sized pieces; you should have about 5 cups (1.25 L). Arrange lettuce on a serving platter and set aside.

2. Using a sharp knife, cut tomatoes into thin slices. Lay them, overlapping in two rows, over the lettuce. Lightly sprinkle with salt to taste. Drizzle with dressing (you may have some left over) and scatter shallots overtop. Serve immediately.

Multi-Bean Salad on Leaf Lettuce

The stereotypical bed of lettuce is not simply decorative. In this bonanza for bean lovers it provides crunchy contrast to the creamy, garlicky legumes. Set out a platter during a cookout or patio party, or simply make this dish a meal, adding soup as a starter.

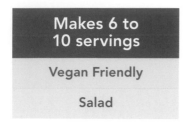

Makes 6 to 10 servings

Vegan Friendly

Salad

Tips

Cannellinis are also known as white kidney beans.

The Roasted Garlic Sage Dressing recipe yields about ½ cup (125 mL), which makes for a very lightly dressed bean salad. I usually double the dressing recipe, add it to taste and use the remainder for other salads.

6 oz	green beans, cut into 2-inch (5 cm) pieces (about 2 cups/500 mL)	175 g
1	can (14 oz/398 mL) cannellini beans, rinsed and drained (see Tips, left)	1
1	can (14 oz/398 mL) red kidney beans, rinsed and drained	1
1	can (14 oz/398 mL) black beans, rinsed and drained	1
¾ cup	coarsely diced red onion	175 mL
	Roasted Garlic Sage Dressing (Variation, page 454; see Tips, left)	
	Kosher or coarse sea salt	
8	very large leaf lettuce leaves (6 oz/175 g)	8
12	grape tomatoes, halved	12
2 tbsp	chopped fresh parsley leaves	30 mL
1⅓ cups	Crispy Shallots (page 455)	325 mL

1. In a covered steamer basket over 1 inch (2.5 cm) of boiling water, cook green beans for about 5 minutes, until tender-crisp. Immediately rinse with cold water to stop the cooking, then drain.

2. In a large bowl, gently toss green beans, cannellinis, kidney beans, black beans and onion with dressing to taste. Add salt to taste. Set aside for 15 to 30 minutes to allow beans to absorb the dressing.

3. Line a serving platter with lettuce. Top with bean mixture. Scatter tomatoes over beans. Sprinkle with parsley and shallots and serve immediately.

Thai Noodle Salad

I love this cross-cultural salad. It's light and refreshing yet qualifies as a satisfying hot-weather meal. The lettuce adds plenty of lively crunch to slippery rice noodles doused in a tangy honey-lime dressing.

> **Makes 4 to 6 servings**
>
> **Vegan Friendly**
>
> **Salad**

Tips

This recipe makes about 1 cup (250 mL) dressing.

Bottled reconstituted lemon and lime juices usually contain additives. To avoid them, use freshly squeezed juice. Squeeze a whole lemon or lime and store the leftover juice in a small container in the fridge, or freeze it in 1 tbsp (15 mL) portions in an ice-cube tray.

For the finest minced garlic, push it through a press.

To maintain more control over the saltiness of dishes, use reduced-sodium soy sauce. Depending on the type, 1 tbsp (15 mL) regular soy sauce can contain 1,000 mg or more sodium. Reduced-sodium soy sauce contains about half that amount.

You can use salted or unsalted roasted peanuts, as desired.

Dressing

1/3 cup	freshly squeezed lime juice (see Tips, left)	75 mL
2	cloves garlic, minced (see Tips, left)	2
1 tbsp	soy sauce (see Tips, left)	15 mL
2 tbsp	liquid honey or vegan alternative	30 mL
1 tsp	kosher or coarse sea salt	5 mL
1/2 tsp	hot pepper flakes	2 mL
1/2 cup	oil	125 mL

Salad

2	mini cucumbers, peeled and thinly sliced into semicircles	2
1/2 tsp	kosher or coarse sea salt, divided	2 mL
8 oz	rice vermicelli noodles	250 g
3 1/2 cups	loosely packed chopped leaf lettuce (4 oz/125 g)	875 mL
1	large carrot, shredded	1
1/4	red bell pepper, cut into slivers	1/4
1/2 cup	diced red onion	125 mL
1/3 cup	roasted peanuts, coarsely chopped (see Tips, left)	75 mL
2 tbsp	chopped fresh cilantro leaves	30 mL

1. *Dressing:* In a bowl, whisk together lime juice, garlic, soy sauce, honey, salt and hot pepper flakes. Whisk in oil. Set aside.

2. *Salad:* In a fine-mesh sieve, toss cucumbers with 1/4 tsp (1 mL) salt. Set aside for 15 to 30 minutes to drain.

3. In a large saucepan of boiling salted water, cook vermicelli for 2 to 3 minutes, until just tender. Drain and immediately rinse with cold water to cool just to room temperature. Drain.

4. Arrange lettuce on a large serving platter or individual plates. Arrange vermicelli over lettuce. Scatter cucumbers, carrot, red pepper and onion over vermicelli. Drizzle dressing overtop and sprinkle with remaining salt. Garnish with peanuts and cilantro. Serve immediately.

Red Greens Salad

I was seeing red in the produce section while gathering greens and this colorful salad is the result. The recipe is very freeform. You can use any greens you favor, as long as they are red (or reddish — most so-called red greens are actually purple).

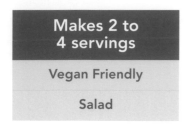

Makes 2 to 4 servings
Vegan Friendly
Salad

Tip

For a smoother dressing, dissolve the honey and salt by whisking them with the vinegar before adding the oil.

Dressing

1 tbsp	red wine vinegar	15 mL
1 tsp	liquid honey or vegan alternative	5 mL
¾ tsp	kosher or coarse sea salt	3 mL
3 tbsp	extra virgin olive oil	45 mL

Salad

2 oz	red leaf lettuce, torn into bite-size pieces (about 3 cups/750 mL, loosely packed)	60 g
2 oz	radicchio, coarsely chopped (about 1½ cups/375 mL, loosely packed)	60 g
1 oz	red chard or beet leaves, coarsely chopped (about 1½ cups/375 mL, loosely packed)	30 g
1 oz	red catalogna, coarsely chopped (about 1¼ cups/300 mL, loosely packed)	30 g
1 oz	red watercress leaves (about 1¼ cups/300 mL, loosely packed)	30 g
1 oz	red mustard leaf, chopped (about ¾ cup/175 mL, loosely packed)	30 g
½ oz	red kale , coarsely chopped (about 1 cup/250 mL, loosely packed)	15 g
1	small red endive, sliced	1
12	grape tomatoes, halved	12
½ cup	sliced red onion	125 mL

1. *Dressing:* In a small bowl, whisk together vinegar, honey and salt. Whisk in oil (see Tip, left).

2. *Salad:* In a large bowl, combine lettuce, radicchio, chard, catalogna, watercress, mustard leaf, kale, endive, tomatoes and onion. Add dressing to taste (you may have some left over), and toss to coat evenly. Serve immediately.

Mâche

Valerianella locusta

Other names: **corn salad, fetticus, field lettuce/ salad, lamb's tongue, loblollie, Mary Magdalene's herb, milkgrass, lamb's nut lettuce, Pawnee lettuce, valeriana, rosette, white pot herb.**

Depending on where you are shopping, you may find mâche identified as *bourse, doucette, feldsalat, koon saruda, kuzu gevregi, lechuga de campo, maashu, maroulaki, moench, neusslisalad, raiponce, veldsla, vogerlsalat* **or** *ye ju.*

Mâche is native to Europe but it also grows wild in Africa, Asia and North America.

Peasants in Europe foraged for mâche, and it was traditionally eaten during Lent. After it appeared in a 1597 plant catalog, the British began to grow it commercially. The royal gardener of King Louis XIV of France cultivated it in the 17th or 18th century. So did former American president Thomas Jefferson, in his Virginia garden in the early 1800s. Today mâche is a particular cultivated specialty of France; it is also popular in Germany, Spain and the United Kingdom. San Francisco chefs are sometimes credited with introducing mâche to North American diners two decades ago.

At one time mâche was botanically classed as a lettuce and dubbed *Lactuca agnina*, the latter derived from the Latin word for lamb. Mâche was a favorite of grazing lambs — hence the name "lamb's lettuce." It is not related to corn but was often found growing wild in fields of corn, wheat and other cultivated crops — hence the name "corn salad."

Tasting Notes

Mâche tastes like a love child of lettuce and baby spinach. It is slightly sweet and nutty, with delicate, moist, light yet crisp leaves.

Equivalents

1 package =
3½ oz (100 g)

•

2 oz (60 g) whole clusters = 6 cups (1.5 L), loosely packed

•

2 oz (60 g) coarsely chopped mâche = 3½ cups (875 mL), loosely packed

Varieties

Mâche (*Valerianella locusta*) is the most prominent member of a group of greens called corn salads. Mâche, or common corn salad, is sometimes divided into curly types (with round leaves) and blond types (with spoon-shaped leaves).

Obscure cousins include Italian corn salad (*V. eriocarpa*), also known as hairy-fruited corn salad; European corn salad (*V. carinata*); and Texas corn salad (*V. florifera*).

Although mâche is sometimes called lamb's lettuce or rapunzel, do not confuse it with lamb's quarters (page 364) or rampion, which is also called rapunzel (page 225).

Buy It

Mâche is cultivated as a specialty green and sold in many supermarkets, sometimes seasonally. It is packaged in clamshells or bags.

This is a gourmet green and relatively expensive, partly because its fragile stems and low-lying growth make mâche difficult to harvest.

Rosettes of small, round dark green leaves are attached to short, tender stems in clusters with roots attached. Avoid specimens with leaves that are crumpled, yellowed or blackened at the edges.

Store It

Handle mâche with care, as the leaves bruise easily.

Store mâche in its original clamshell. Or wrap it loosely in paper towels and place in a resealable bag with some air left in it to act as a cushion, then refrigerate.

Mâche will keep in the refrigerator for up to three days.

Prep It

The leaves and stemlets are tender. Trim the bunch by pinching off the root ends.

Mâche comes prewashed but I rinse it anyway, gently swishing it in cold water. Dirt tends to collect at the base of the root clusters.

To break up clumps, chop mâche coarsely just before using it. However, it may be used intact.

Consume It

Mâche is eaten raw; it is rarely cooked.

This green is ideal for sophisticated salads. It has body and crunch, yet is exceptionally tender. Mâche salad requires little more than a light bath of vinaigrette. Avoid heavy or creamy dressings that will weigh it down.

Stretch mâche by mixing it with other, less expensive salad greens.

Use mâche to add interest to sandwiches or vegetable dishes. It may be steamed briefly and served as a vegetable. However, cooking mâche is not making the best use of it.

SUBSTITUTES

chickweed, purslane, watercress, baby spinach, butter lettuce

A Tale of Two Rapunzels

Scholars studying the Brothers Grimm story "Rapunzel" cite two possibilities for the plant that plays a pivotal role in this fairy tale. One is mâche, the other rampion. Thus both are also called "rapunzel."

The original 1812 story, which is more complicated than the sketchy version most of us recall from our childhoods, begins with a theft of tasty greens. A couple lives next to a garden that belongs to an enchantress. The pregnant wife notices a rapunzel plant in the garden and desperately craves it. The husband steals some for her but is caught. The enchantress lets him go in exchange for the baby at birth. She names the child Rapunzel, then eventually cloisters her in a tower. The tower is accessible only when Rapunzel hangs her long hair out the window. Then a prince comes along . . .

Rampion (*Campanula rapunculus*) is more versatile than mâche. It was widely cultivated in Europe in days of yore, particularly in Shakespearean England, but has since fallen out of favor. The leaves were prepared like spinach, the shoots like asparagus and the roots like radish. An Italian superstition says children will quarrel if they are close to rampion. A rampion relative called harebell (*C. versicolor*) is an ingredient in Greek cuisine.

Beet, Mâche and Egg Salad

This simple French classic is a beautiful thing to behold — and to eat. Add some baguette and you've got a light meal.

Makes 2 to 4 servings

Salad

Tips

To avoid staining your hands, use gloves when handling beets, especially when you peel them.

When cooking beets whole, leave the rattail root (tap root) and about ½ inch (1 cm) of stem attached. This reduces loss of nutrients and leakage of dye.

To toast walnuts, cook them in a dry skillet over medium heat, stirring often, for about 3 minutes, until they are turning golden and aromatic.

2	beets (4 oz/125 g each), scrubbed (see Tips, left)	2
¼ cup	Lime Herb Dressing (page 452)	60 mL
2 oz	mâche (about 6 cups/1.5 L, loosely packed)	60 g
2	hard-cooked eggs	2
	Kosher or coarse sea salt	
¼ cup	walnuts, toasted (see Tips, left)	60 mL

1. In a pot of boiling water, cook whole beets over medium heat for about 30 minutes, until tender but firm and easily pierced with a skewer. Set aside in cooking water to cool to room temperature.

2. Peel beets. Using a sharp knife, cut each beet into 10 to 12 small wedges. Transfer to a small bowl and gently toss with dressing. Set aside for 30 minutes.

3. Arrange mâche on a serving platter or in individual bowls. Spoon beets, with dressing, into center. Cut each egg into 4 wedges and arrange around edges of platter or bowls. Crumble salt, to taste, over eggs. Scatter walnuts over beets and greens. Serve immediately.

Mâche, Corn and Fingerling Potato Salad

Simple flavors come together in this lovely and unusual potato salad. Serve it on the patio for ambience.

Makes 4 servings		
Vegan Friendly		
Salad		

Tips

You can substitute mini potatoes for the fingerlings.

For the finest minced garlic, push it through a press.

Sweet onions include Vidalias and Walla-Wallas. You can find them in most supermarkets.

You can use either fresh corn or thawed frozen corn.

1 lb	fingerling potatoes (see Tips, left)	500 g
¼ cup	extra virgin olive oil	60 mL
1 tbsp	white wine vinegar	15 mL
1	clove garlic, minced (see Tips, left)	1
1 tsp	kosher or coarse sea salt	5 mL
1 cup	diced sweet onion (see Tips, left)	250 mL
1 cup	lightly cooked corn kernels (see Tips, left)	250 mL
1	large roasted red bell pepper, cut into ½-inch (1 cm) dice	1
2 oz	mâche (about 6 cups/1.5 L, loosely packed)	60 g
	Freshly ground black pepper	

1. In a large pot of boiling salted water, cook potatoes over medium heat for about 15 minutes, until tender. Drain, rinse with cold water and set aside to cool to room temperature.

2. Meanwhile, in a small measuring cup, whisk together oil, vinegar, garlic and salt. Set aside.

3. Using a sharp knife, cut any large potatoes in half crosswise. In a large bowl, toss potatoes, onion, corn and red pepper with oil mixture to taste (you may have some left over). Season with salt to taste.

4. Line a serving platter with mâche. Spoon potato mixture overtop. Season generously with pepper and serve immediately.

Malabar Spinach

Basella alba

Other names: Asian/Ceylon/Indian/Philippine/Vietnamese spinach, basella, climbing/vine spinach, flowering water vegetable, Malabar nightshade, phooi leaf, slippery vegetable, thick-leaf callaloo.

Depending on where you are shopping, you may find Malabar spinach identified as *alugbati, bachali, bhaji, gondola, genjerot, jingga, libato, lo kwai, malayu, mong toi, phakkang, poi baagi, pui shaks, saan choy, tembayung* or *tsuru murasa kai.*

Tasting Notes

Slimy or slippery? The adjective you choose depends on how much you like Malabar spinach. It is more correctly described as mucilaginous.

Malabar spinach looks and tastes like spinach but is more mineral in flavor, with hints of citrus and pepper. It has stiff, slightly spongy leaves that are cool and crisp when raw and silky when cooked.

Health Notes

Malabar spinach contains vitamins A, B_6 and C, calcium, copper, folate, iron, magnesium, manganese, niacin, phosphorus, potassium, riboflavin and thiamin. Malabar spinach also contains mucilage, which is considered a detoxification agent as well as a rich source of soluble fiber.

As an herbal remedy, Malabar spinach has been used to combat anemia and fatigue, quell stomachaches, relieve constipation and increase milk production in new mothers. The leaf pulp has been used in poultices to treat sores and rashes.

Although Malabar spinach is sometimes called buffalo spinach, it should not be confused with the water plant known as buffalo spinach (page 420).

Malabar spinach is not related to common spinach. This summer green flourishes in torrid weather. It is native to India and tropical Asia, where it is a staple leafy vegetable (Malabar is a coastal region in India). It is also consumed in Africa and the Caribbean.

In Europe and North America, red basellas are planted as ornamentals. Gardeners fall in love with this plant's good looks, especially the *B. rubra* variety, which has red stems, pink flowers and purple berries (they are not usually eaten).

Varieties

Common Malabar spinach (*Basella alba*) has green stems. Cultivars include red Malabar spinach (*B. alba rubra*), which has purplish red stems.

Buy It

Malabar spinach is sold in Asian and Indian supermarkets.

SUBSTITUTES

spinach, sweet potato
leaves, amaranth,
jute leaf

Round or heart-shaped dark green leaves — some as large as a sandwich plate, some as small as baby spinach — are attached to long stems that are correspondingly thick or thin. Look for glossy leaves with no wilting, browning, crumpling, bruising, weeping or darkening.

Store It

Once purchased, Malabar spinach needs TLC. It bruises easily and rapidly starts to look forlorn. Store in a perforated resealable bag.

Malabar spinach will keep in the refrigerator for up to two days.

Prep It

Handle Malabar spinach with care. While rinsing and drying, avoid vigorous swishing or spinning, which can bruise the leaves and release mucilage. Even the weight of wet leaves can cause the leaves beneath to crumple or tear. Spin-dry leaves in small batches or place them on a clean kitchen towel to air-dry.

Do not soak the leaves, as they can get waterlogged.

Stems may be trimmed or used along with the leaves, if desired. The stems are edible and crunchy, even ones that are as wide as ½ inch (1 cm).

Chop leaves and stems coarsely just before using them.

Consume It

Malabar spinach is rarely eaten raw, although the leaves, big or small, can be used in mixed salads or sandwiches for an interesting change. They hold up well to warm dressings too.

If using raw Malabar spinach, tear rather than chop it, as cutting releases more mucilage.

When cooking, you can substitute Malabar spinach for common spinach in any recipe. It stays crisper than common spinach, and because the stems are largely edible, there's less waste.

Stems and leaves may be separated and sautéed. The leaves cook to tender-crisp in 2 minutes; the stems are ready in 2 to 3 minutes.

Long cooking turns Malabar spinach slimy. Add it to stir-fries at the last minute. Alternatively, you can harness the thickening power of the mucilage for soups, stews and curries.

Malabar Dal

Dal is the Indian name for peas, lentils and beans that have been skinned and split. They don't hold their shape but instead give curries a rib-sticking, creamy consistency. This recipe features a popular combo: Malabar spinach, dal, coconut and chiles. It's a saucy curry, so serve it over basmati rice or mop it up with warm flatbread.

Makes 4 to 6 servings (about 6 cups/1.5 L)
Vegan Friendly
Main course

Tips

Don't confuse cardamom seeds with their pods. The green or beige pods contain the seeds. The seeds are sold separately in Indian stores and spice shops.

I like to use 5-inch (12.5 cm) long cayenne chile peppers for this dish, but you can use any kind you like.

Some supermarkets sell dal, including a "rainbow mixture" of various types. Indian grocery stores have a large selection. The legumes are fairly interchangeable in recipes. In this dish I use toor dal, or yellow pigeon peas (sometimes labeled "yellow split lentils").

Dal may be soaked for 30 minutes before cooking, but this is not vital. If you do soak it, count on a shorter cooking time for the dish and start with 1 cup (250 mL) less water.

I buy tamarind concentrate instead of wrestling with dried blocks of tamarind to create a paste. You can find it in Indian grocery stores or spice shops.

- Mini blender

Spice Paste

¼ cup	unsweetened desiccated coconut	60 mL
1 tsp	cardamom seeds (see Tips, left)	5 mL
1 tsp	coriander seeds	5 mL
1 tsp	kosher or coarse sea salt	5 mL
¼ tsp	freshly ground black pepper	1 mL
¼ tsp	turmeric	1 mL
⅛ tsp	asafoetida (see Tips, page 240)	0.5 mL
½ cup	coconut milk	125 mL

Curry

¼ cup	oil	60 mL
1	onion, diced	1
2	green or red finger chiles, seeded and thinly sliced (see Tips, left)	2
2	large cloves garlic, chopped	2
1 cup	toor dal (split yellow pigeon peas)	250 mL
2 cups	vegetable stock	500 mL
2 cups	water	500 mL
1 tbsp	tamarind paste (see Tips, left)	15 mL
1 tsp	kosher or coarse sea salt	5 mL
1 tsp	granulated sugar (see Tips, page 207)	5 mL
1 lb	Malabar spinach, trimmed and chopped	500 g

1. *Spice Paste:* In a small, dry skillet over medium heat, toast coconut, cardamom, coriander, salt, pepper, turmeric and asafoetida, stirring often, for about 2 minutes, until fragrant. Transfer to blender, add coconut milk and purée. Set aside.

2. *Curry:* In a large saucepan over medium heat, heat oil until shimmery. Add onion and chiles. Cook, stirring often, for about 3 minutes, until softened and turning golden. Stir in garlic for 20 seconds. Stir in prepared spice paste and cook for about 1 minute. Add dal, stock and water. When mixture comes to a simmer, cover, reduce heat to medium-low and cook for 30 to 45 minutes, until dal is soft and mixture has thickened to porridge consistency.

3. Stir in tamarind paste, salt and sugar, then Malabar spinach. Cover and cook for about 5 minutes, until spinach is wilted and stems are tender-crisp. Season with salt to taste and serve immediately.

Sri Lankan Spinach and Lentils

Coconut curry is the base for this fabulous combination of pulses and greens, accentuated by the pop of mustard seeds. I've been preparing this with standard spinach for years, inspired by a recipe lost in the mists of time. It is even better with Malabar spinach. Lentils are a good option when you crave legumes — unlike dried beans, they don't have to be soaked or cooked for a long time.

Makes 2 to 4 servings (about 5 cups/1.25 L)		
Vegan Friendly		
Main course		

Tips

Brown or black mustard seeds are smaller and more pungent than the common yellow mustard seeds used in pickles. You can find them in Indian grocery stores and some supermarkets.

Garam masala is a fragrant blend of warm spices, including cinnamon. You can find it in Indian stores, spice shops and some supermarkets.

Standard "red" lentils look more like orange to me. Of all the types of lentils, they cook the fastest.

Make sure the spinach is dry. Otherwise the thick, rich sauce can become too watery.

Do not double this recipe — it won't work properly.

1 tbsp	oil	15 mL
2 tsp	brown or black mustard seeds (see Tips, left)	10 mL
1	green bell pepper, finely diced	1
1	onion, diced	1
2	cloves garlic, chopped	2
1 tbsp	curry powder	15 mL
1 tbsp	garam masala (see Tips, left)	15 mL
1½ tsp	kosher or coarse sea salt	7 mL
½ to 1 tsp	hot pepper flakes	2 to 5 mL
1	can (14 oz/400 mL) coconut milk	1
1 cup	water	250 mL
⅔ cup	dried red lentils (4 oz/125 g; see Tips, left)	150 mL
1 lb	Malabar spinach, trimmed and chopped	500 g
¼ cup	chopped red bell pepper	60 mL

1. In a large saucepan over medium heat, heat oil until shimmery. Stir in mustard seeds for about 10 seconds, until they start to pop. Add green pepper, onion and garlic. Cook, stirring often, for 3 to 4 minutes, until softened and turning golden. Add curry powder, garam masala, salt and hot pepper flakes. Cook, stirring, for 20 seconds. Stir in coconut milk and water, then lentils. When mixture comes to a simmer, cover, reduce heat to low and cook for 5 to 10 minutes, until lentils are almost tender.

2. Stir in Malabar spinach. Cover and cook for about 5 minutes, until lentils are tender and spinach is tender-crisp. Season with salt to taste.

3. Transfer to a serving dish or individual bowls and garnish with chopped red pepper. Serve immediately.

Malabar Saag

Saag is Indian spinach curry. I adore saags of all types, with their lively color, taste and satiny texture. This one includes substantial cubes of paneer (Indian fresh cheese). Normally I use standard spinach, but Malabar spinach makes a fine stand-in. It creates a chunkier sauce you can sink your teeth into, while regular spinach ends up as a smoother, softer sauce. This is a spicy curry, but you can tone down the heat if desired.

	Makes 2 to 4 servings

Makes 2 to 4 servings

Vegan Friendly

Main course

Tips

A masala is an Indian spice mixture that gives a curry its individuality. Curry powder is the most famous masala. Garam masala is also often used and readily available.

Cayenne varies in heat depending on brand and age. If you are worried the saag will be too spicy, halve the amount of cayenne in Step 1, then add more to taste in Step 5.

Ghee is Indian clarified butter. Indian grocery stores and some supermarkets sell it. If you don't have any, substitute 1½ tbsp (22 mL) each unsalted butter and canola oil.

Some supermarkets now sell paneer, which is a fresh, mild Indian cheese. If yours doesn't have it, look for it in an Indian grocery store. There is no good vegan cheese equivalent of paneer, but tofu may be substituted.

Masala

2 tsp	ground fenugreek	10 mL
1 tsp	kosher or coarse sea salt	5 mL
1 tsp	ground cumin	5 mL
½ tsp	ground coriander	2 mL
½ tsp	cayenne pepper (see Tips, left)	2 mL
¼ tsp	ground turmeric	1 mL
⅛ tsp	ground nutmeg	0.5 mL

Curry

1 lb	Malabar spinach (leaves and tender stems)	500 g
3 tbsp	ghee (see Tips, left)	45 mL
12 oz	paneer or firm tofu, cut into 1-inch (2.5 cm) cubes (see Tips, left)	375 mL
1	large onion, shredded (see Tips, page 233)	1
4	cloves garlic, minced (see Tips, page 227)	4
1 tsp	puréed gingerroot (see Tips, page 250)	5 mL
½ cup	coarsely chopped methi (leaves and tender stems; page 238)	125 mL
2	large plum tomatoes, chopped into small pieces	2
1 cup	full-fat plain yogurt or non-dairy alternative	250 mL
	Kosher or coarse sea salt	

1. *Masala:* In a small bowl, combine fenugreek, salt, cumin, coriander, cayenne, turmeric and nutmeg. Set aside.

2. *Curry:* In a large saucepan over medium-high heat, cook Malabar spinach (with wash water clinging to leaves), stirring occasionally, for about 5 minutes, until just wilted. Drain but do not press to extract more liquid. Set aside until cool enough to handle, then chop. Reserve pan.

3. In a nonstick skillet over medium-high heat, heat ghee until hot. Pat paneer dry with paper towels. Add paneer to skillet and cover with a splatter guard. Fry, turning occasionally with tongs, for about 5 minutes, until golden brown on most sides. Using tongs or a slotted spoon, transfer paneer to a plate. Set aside.

Tip

Shredding onion using the large holes of a box grater is an Indian culinary trick that I learned from the movie *Bend It Like Beckham*. Shredding releases the juices without turning them bitter, a hazard with food processors. Be warned: this technique will make you cry.

4. Measure 2 tbsp (30 mL) ghee from skillet (discarding remainder) and add to reserved pan; heat over medium heat until hot. Add onion and cook, stirring often, for 3 to 4 minutes, until softened. Stir in garlic and ginger, then masala. Stir for 30 seconds. Stir in methi, then tomatoes, then prepared Malabar spinach. Add paneer and stir to coat evenly. Cover, reduce heat to low and simmer for about 5 minutes, until heated through.

5. Remove from heat and stir in yogurt. Season with additional salt to taste. Serve warm.

Variation

Use regular spinach, but chop it finer and cook it longer. In Step 4, cook it for 2 minutes after stirring it into the pan, and for 5 minutes after stirring in the paneer.

Kenyan-Style Spinach and Pumpkin

Simple, colorful, healthful and delicious — what more could one ask of a dish? Serve this on a bed of rice, couscous or quinoa.

Makes 4 to 6 servings
Vegan Friendly
Side dish

Tips

Miniature pie pumpkins are sold seasonally, in the fall and early winter. You can substitute the same quantity of any pumpkin or winter squash.

A grapefruit spoon, with its serrated edges, is a good tool for scraping the seeds and strings from pumpkin.

To test if the pumpkin is done, pierce it with a metal skewer. It should go through the skin and flesh easily but feel somewhat firm. (If you want mashed pumpkin, continue to roast it for another 15 minutes.)

- Preheat oven to 375°F (190°C)
- Rimmed baking sheet

1	pie pumpkin (2 lbs/1 kg; see Tips, left)	1
3 tbsp	oil, divided	45 mL
1	onion, thinly sliced	1
1 lb	Malabar spinach, trimmed and coarsely chopped	500 g
1 tsp	kosher or coarse sea salt	5 mL
1/2 tsp	freshly ground black pepper	2 mL
1/4 cup	toasted pepitas (see Tips, page 195)	60 mL

1. Using a sharp knife, halve pumpkin vertically and scrape out seeds and strings (see Tips, left). Discard or save seeds for roasting and snacking. Brush cut surfaces with 1 tbsp (15 mL) oil. Place halves, cut side down, on baking sheet. Roast in preheated oven for about 30 minutes, until just tender (see Tips, left). Turn cut side up and set aside until cool enough to handle. Use a paring knife, pull off peel and cut flesh into 1-inch (2.5 cm) chunks; you should have about 4 cups (1 L). Set aside.

2. In a large skillet over medium heat, heat remaining oil until shimmery. Add onion and cook, stirring often, for about 3 minutes, until softened and turning golden. Add half the Malabar spinach; stir often for 1 minute or until wilted. Add remaining spinach, salt and pepper. Cook, stirring often, for 1 to 2 minutes, until wilted and tender. Gently stir in roasted pumpkin chunks and cook for about 2 minutes, until hot.

3. Transfer to a serving dish or individual plates. Scatter pepitas overtop and serve immediately.

Mesclun

Other names: **boutique salad, designer/field/ gathered greens, salad/spring mix, spring salad mix, gourmet salad mix.**

Depending on where you are shopping, you may find mesclun identified as *mezclum* or *misticanza*.

The Provence region of France lays claim to the introduction of mesclun. The name is derived from the Provençal dialect word *mescler*, meaning "to mix," or *mesclumo*, meaning "a mixture."

Mesclun has been enjoyed in France for hundreds of years, but it didn't become a staple in North America until the 1980s. Originally French mesclun was an equal mix of baby lettuce, arugula, endive (probably frisée) and chervil. North Americans ran with the concept, experimenting with and expanding the spectrum of leafy greens.

Some mesclun greens used to be wild-harvested, but mescluns are now cultivated in mixed beds. North American mesclun is usually from California and often organic.

Mesclun has elevated some salads to gourmet status but is no longer considered exotic. It has taken over a large swath of real estate in the produce aisles and is partly to blame for the drop in popularity of humble lettuce, particularly iceberg. Mesclun is certainly more nutritious, interesting, tastier and prettier than ordinary lettuce.

Tasting Notes

Mesclun greens are delicate, with the taste varying according to the mix.

Health Notes

Mesclun contains vitamins A and C, calcium and iron.

Varieties

Mesclun is not a specific type of lettuce but rather a potpourri of baby lettuces and leafy greens. Commercial mesclun mixes are a blend of the usual suspects plus a smattering of more exotic greens. Potential additions include specialty lettuces such as oak leaf, lollo rosso, red romaine or tango; leafy greens such as arugula, beet greens, chard, cress, dandelion, frisée, kale, mizuna, mustard greens, mâche, purslane, radicchio, sorrel, spinach and tatsoi; herbs such as chervil, parsley or fennel; and edible flowers.

Every company makes its own custom mixes that include some but not all of the greens listed above. Mixes depend on brand and vary by season. Some so-called salad lines are mild and some are pungent; some are exotic, some familiar, depending on the balance of greens. For eye appeal, producers like to include various shapes, from frilly to serrated to flat, and a spectrum of colors from pastel to kale green, mixed with some reds and/or purples.

SUBSTITUTES

butter lettuce, red
leaf lettuce, frisée,
baby arugula, baby
kale, mizuna, mâche,
chickweed, watercress

Buy It

Mesclun is sold in supermarkets. It is usually packed in medium to large clamshells but is sometimes sold in bags or even loose in bulk. Check expiry dates and use mesclun as soon as possible.

The leaves should be crisp, with no moist dark spots, which are signs of rot. Check the bottom of the package as well as the top.

Instead of buying premixed greens, you can select and buy separate greens and create your own custom mesclun mix. Gardeners are fond of growing their own mesclun and snipping greens as needed.

Store It

Store mesclun in the sealed clamshell it came in. If bagged or loose, transfer to a resealable bag with some air left in it to act as a cushion, then refrigerate.

Loosen clumps and do not cram mesclun into boxes or bags. Rot will begin in the center of the pile.

Mesclun will keep in the refrigerator for up to four days.

Prep It

Mesclun often comes double- or triple-washed. For food safety reasons a producer may first wash mesclun in water spiked with chlorine to kill microbes, then rinse the greens well. I wash mesclun anyway, not just as insurance but also to perk up these greens, which dehydrate quickly. Don't wash mesclun until you are ready to use it.

For the prettiest presentation, never chop or tear mesclun. Use whole leaves.

Consume It

Mesclun is never cooked. It is tossed raw in salads, stuffed into sandwiches or wraps, and used as a decorative green bed for other ingredients or dishes.

Keep your mesclun salad light. Avoid heavy or creamy dressings and hearty ingredients such as chickpeas, shredded cheese or croutons. They weigh down, mangle and overpower the delicate greens.

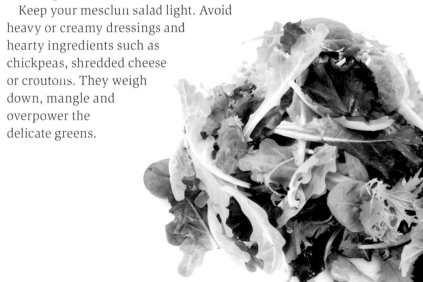

Mandarin Salad

Mandarin salad is so popular you can get it at drive-throughs. Don't. This Asian-inspired classic is easy to prepare at home.

Makes 2 to 4 servings

Vegan Friendly

Salad

Tips

The mandarin is a type of easy-peel orange; clementines and tangerines are the most famous cultivars. I use small seedless clementines for this salad. For an even quicker salad, you can substitute a 10-oz (284 mL) can of mandarin orange segments, drained, for the fresh fruit; scatter them over the salad in Step 2.

You can find roasted cashews (salted or unsalted, as desired) and crunchy chow mein noodles at most supermarkets.

4 oz	mesclun (about 6 cups/1.5 L, loosely packed)	125 g
2	small seedless mandarin oranges, peeled, segmented and stripped of pith (see Tips, left)	2
1 cup	diced (½ inch/1 cm) red onion	250 mL
⅓ cup	Sesame Dressing (page 453)	75 mL
½ cup	roasted cashew nuts, coarsely chopped (see Tips, left)	125 mL
1 cup	crunchy chow mein noodles	250 mL

1. In a large bowl, toss mesclun, mandarins and onion with dressing to taste.
2. Transfer mixture to individual plates. Scatter cashews and crunchy noodles overtop. Serve immediately.

Variation

Instead of mesclun, use a mixture of chopped tender Asian greens such as tatsoi, mizuna, napa cabbage and/or baby bok choy.

Strawberry Mesclun Salad

I feasted on a gorgeous strawberry salad at a luncheon at Springridge Farm in Milton, Ontario, during picking season. This is my take on it.

Makes 2 to 4 servings

Vegan Friendly

Salad

Tips

Sweet onions include Vidalias and Walla-Wallas. You can find them in most supermarkets.

To toast almonds, cook them in a dry skillet over medium heat, stirring often, for 2 to 3 minutes, until they are turning golden and aromatic.

Vinaigrette

1 tbsp	balsamic vinegar	15 mL
1 tbsp	strawberry jam	15 mL
½ tsp	kosher or coarse sea salt	2 mL
3 tbsp	extra virgin olive oil	45 mL

Salad

4 oz	mesclun (about 6 cups/1.5 L, loosely packed)	125 g
1 lb	strawberries, hulled and quartered (about 3 cups/750 mL)	500 g
1 cup	diced sweet onion (see Tips, left)	250 mL
	Kosher or coarse sea salt	
	Freshly ground black pepper	
⅓ cup	slivered almonds, toasted (see Tips, left)	75 mL

1. *Vinaigrette:* In a small bowl, whisk together vinegar, jam and salt. Whisk in oil. Set aside.

2. *Salad:* In a large bowl, toss mesclun, strawberries and onion with prepared dressing to taste (you may have some left over).

3. Transfer mixture to a serving platter or individual plates. Crumble salt overtop and season with pepper to taste. Scatter almonds overtop. Serve immediately.

Variation

Balsamic vinegar goes exceedingly well with strawberries. However, it does make the dressing dark. For a lighter vinaigrette, substitute white wine vinegar.

Methi

Trigonella foenum-graecum

> *Other names:* fenugreek leaves.
>   **Depending on where you are shopping, you may find methi identified as *abesh, helba, hibeh, menthya, menthulu, shanbalile, venthayam* or *uluwa*.**

Methi, or fenugreek, is a clover-like plant native to southeastern Europe and western Asia. It may have first been cultivated from wild plants in the Middle East. Some historians speculate that fenugreek seeds found in Iraq date to 4000 BCE. Seeds were also recovered from King Tut's tomb (besides consuming fenugreek, the ancient Egyptians used it in the embalming process). The ancient Greeks grew methi as fodder — hence the species name *foenum-graecum*, which is Latin for "Greek hay."

Fenugreek is best known as an ingredient in the cuisine of India, where it is both foraged and cultivated. India is the world's largest fenugreek producer. It is also cultivated in Iran, Nepal, Bangladesh, Pakistan, Argentina, Egypt, France, Spain, Turkey, Morocco and China. Fenugreek is an ingredient in Persian, Ethiopian and Yemeni cuisines as well.

Varieties

The fenugreek plant (*Trigonella foenum-gracecum*) is cultivated for its greens as well as its seeds. The leaves are more commonly known as methi and the seeds as fenugreek. Fresh leaves are cooked like greens or used like herbs. Dried leaves, differentiated as *kasoori methi*, are used as herbs. The seeds, either whole or ground, are a type of spice.

Fresh methi plants are also harvested as microgreens. In India they are differentiated by the name *samudra methi* (*samudra* means "ocean" or "sea" in Sanskrit). Methi microgreens are grown near seashores and in dry riverbeds in India. Nowadays they are also being cultivated in North America, where they are referred to as fenugreek microgreens.

Buy It

Methi leaves are sold fresh in Indian grocery stores and some supermarkets. They are also marketed as microgreens (page 241),

Tasting Notes

Fresh methi is bitter, astringent and tangy, with lemony, nutty accents. When cooked, it tastes like watercress.

Health Notes

Although no official government analysis is available, methi leaves are thought to contain vitamins C and K, iron, magnesium, phosphorus and potassium.

In folk medicine, methi has been used as a diuretic as well as to lower blood sugar and cholesterol, treat diabetes, increase libido, induce childbirth and stimulate lactation. Methi poultices have been applied to abscesses, boils, burns and eczema, rubbed on skin to get rid of pimples and blackheads, and daubed on the scalp to banish dandruff.

Equivalents

1 large bunch = 12 to
16 oz (375 to 500 g),
including 6 oz (175 g)
leaves and stemlets

•

2 oz (60 g) leaves
and stemlets =
3 cups (750 mL),
loosely packed

SUBSTITUTES

watercress,
celeriac leaves

but not widely. Dried methi leaves are sold in packages in Indian stores and spice shops.

This attractive plant has small, spatulate leaves in clusters, often with tiny white buds in the center. Sometimes it is sold with the roots attached. Avoid any with wilted or discolored leaves.

Store It

Place methi in a glass or vase of water like a bouquet, with a plastic bag draped over the foliage; then refrigerate it. Or wrap a damp paper towel around the base of the stems and store in a resealable bag. You can also pluck the leaves and stemlets from the stalks, wrap them loosely in paper towels and store in a resealable bag.

Methi will keep in the refrigerator for up to three days. Its bitterness increases with age.

Prep It

The stems are too woody and fibrous to eat, except for the stemlets attached to the leaf clusters. To strip stems, pull or pinch off clusters of leaves.

Swish leaves and stemlets in a bowl of cold water. Spin-dry or set them on paper towels to air-dry.

To extract moisture and temper bitterness, the leaves (with the wash water clinging to them) may be tossed with salt and sugar in a fine-mesh sieve. Set aside for 10 minutes to drain, then squeeze out excess moisture before using.

Consume It

Fresh methi leaves straddle the fence between herbs and cooking greens. They are rarely eaten raw.

In India methi leaves are used liberally in soup, dal (pulse porridge) and curry and are also added to paratha and other flatbreads. Do not substitute dried leaves for fresh ones; dried methi is best in smaller quantities.

Aloo Methi (Punjabi Fenugreek Potatoes)

Methi is popular in the Punjab region of northwest India, where this dish is common. It is a dry curry, meaning that it is moist but not saucy. Scoop it up with paratha or another Indian flatbread.

Makes 4 servings

Vegan Friendly

Side dish

Tips

Start with moist methi leaves that have been washed and spun-dry.

I like to use a 5-inch (12.5 cm) serrano chile in this dish, but you can use any chile you prefer.

Asafoetida is a powdered pungent gum. An acquired taste, it is also called hing or devil's dung (for a reason). Besides providing compelling flavor, it is added to legume dishes to prevent flatulence. You can find it in Indian grocery stores and spice shops.

Yellow-fleshed potatoes are best for this recipe; neither waxy nor dry, they are good all-purpose potatoes. The best-known yellow-fleshed potatoes are Yukon Golds.

Garam masala is a fragrant blend of warm spices, including cinnamon. You can find it in Indian stores, spice shops and some supermarkets.

3 oz	methi leaves and stemlets (about 4 cups/1L, loosely packed)	90 g
2 tsp	kosher or coarse sea salt, divided	10 mL
1/2 tsp	granulated sugar	2 mL
2 tbsp	oil	30 mL
1 tsp	cumin seeds	5 mL
1	small onion, diced	1
1	red chile pepper, thinly sliced (see Tips, left)	1
2	large cloves garlic, chopped	2
1	tomato, chopped	1
1/4 tsp	turmeric	1 mL
1/4 tsp	asafoetida (see Tips, left)	1 mL
4	potatoes (1 1/2 lbs/750 g), cut into 1/2-inch (1 cm) chunks (see Tips, left)	4
1/4 cup	water	60 mL
	Garam masala (see Tips, left)	
4	Lemon wedges	4

1. In a fine-mesh sieve, toss methi with 1/2 tsp (2 mL) salt and the sugar (see Tips, left). Set aside.

2. In a saucepan over medium heat, heat oil until shimmery. Add cumin and sauté for about 1 minute, until seeds start to pop. Add onion and chile. Cook, stirring often, for about 2 minutes, until softened. Stir in garlic for 20 seconds. Stir in tomato, turmeric and asafoetida. Add potatoes, water and remaining salt. Stir to coat, cover, reduce heat to low and cook for 20 to 30 minutes, stirring once, until potatoes are almost tender.

3. Gently squeeze methi to remove excess moisture. Using a sharp knife, chop finely. Stir into potato mixture, cover and cook for about 10 minutes, until potatoes are tender. Uncover and cook for about 1 minute to evaporate any excess moisture.

4. Ladle into bowls. Sprinkle with garam masala to taste and place lemon wedges alongside to squeeze overtop. Serve warm.

Microgreens

Other names: mini greens, shoots.

Depending on where you are shopping, you may find microgreens identified as *maikeulo geulin, maikurogurin, mikro horta, mikro gulay, mikro zelen, mikwo vet, si kheiyw khnad lek, sikhiav chunlaphak, suksma saga, vi xanh* or *wei guo ling.*

Microgreens are among the top food trends of the new millennium. Their popularity is a natural offshoot of the sprouts trend of the 1970s and the baby vegetables trend of the 1980s. Microgreens originated in California, the leafy greens capital of North America, where they have been produced since the 1990s.

Microgreens vary in size depending on the species, but all are tiny. Harvested as seedlings, microgreens are newborn greens rather than baby greens or sprouts. They are distinguished from sprouts because they have developed their true leaves. If left to grow, they become baby greens.

Plants start life with a pale immature first set of leaves, called cotyledons, which do not resemble those of the mature plant. They then grow their true leaves.

Consumers still confuse microgreens with sprouts and baby greens. The following are some differences:

- Sprouts are seeds germinated in a moist, dark environment but not in soil. The roots, stems and cotyledons are eaten. (Mung bean sprouts, a Chinese restaurant and supermarket staple, are the best known.) Sprouts are harvested either before the cotyledons open or when they first start to open. In the latter case the sprouts may be differentiated as "shoots." Unfortunately for shoppers, some microgreens are also labeled or referred to as shoots.
- Microgreens are grown in soil, peat moss or fibrous material such as paper pulp, and exposed to sunlight. They are harvested when the roots are established and their true leaves have begun to develop. Generally speaking, they are less than a month old and 1 to 3 inches (2.5 to 7.5 cm) tall, with threadlike shoots and tiny leaves. However, harvesting age and size depend on the species.
- Baby greens develop as microgreens mature. Baby greens are sold as gourmet leaves or blended in mesclun mixes (page 234). Baby arugula, baby kale and baby romaine are examples of popular baby greens.

Tasting Notes

Microgreens are flavorful but never overpowering. Each type has a distinctive taste like the vegetable or herb it will become.

Varieties

"Microgreen" does not refer to a particular species but rather to delicate greens harvested in infancy. Most commonly eaten vegetables and herbs can be grown as microgreens. There are numerous varieties, including alfalfa, amaranth, arugula, basil, beans, beets, bok choy, borage, broccoli, buckwheat, cabbage, carrot, cauliflower, celery, chard, chervil, chia, chrysanthemum, cilantro, clover, collards, corn, cress, cucumber, daikon, fennel, fenugreek, garlic, kale, kohlrabi, komatsuna, lettuce, lavender, lime, mâche, mint, mizuna, mustard, onion, orach, peas, radish, sorrel, spinach, sunflower, tatsoi, tangerine leaf and wasabi.

Health Notes

Microgreen nutrients vary by species. However, the vitamins, minerals and antioxidants are highly concentrated. In a recent study, scientists found that microgreens offer 4 to 40 times more nutrients than their mature counterparts.

SUBSTITUTES

baby greens, butter lettuce, chickweed, watercress, frisée

Buy It

These infants are considered premium greens and are sold at premium prices. Supermarkets carry a small selection. For a better selection, check farmers' markets, gourmet food shops and health food stores.

Microgreens are sold in clamshell boxes, potted or as hydroponic plants with roots intact. They are sometimes mislabeled as "sprouts."

Two commonly marketed microgreens are red kale (nutty tasting, with tiny heart-shaped leaves and pastel purple stems) and mixed radishes (attractive heart-shaped purple or green leaves with a sharp, lively bite). One of the most interesting is "popcorn shoots," from corn plants, which have tiny, sweet leaves that taste like corn.

Some people grow their own windowsill microgreens and snip them as needed. Most seeds can be planted and harvested as microgreens. Microgreen seed mixes are also available.

Store It

Wrap microgreens loosely in paper towels and place them in a resealable bag with some air in it to act as a cushion, then refrigerate.

Microgreens will keep in the refrigerator for up to two days.

If they are potted, keep microgreens on a sunny sill, watering and snipping as needed.

If they are hydroponic, store like a bouquet in water, draped with a plastic bag, and refrigerate.

Prep It

Wash microgreens gently. They are so delicate they will sag from the weight of the water. Swish them gently in cold water and scoop them out with a fine-mesh sieve. Do not use a vigorous spin-dryer. Transfer rinsed microgreens onto paper towels to air-dry. If you're in a hurry, put the damp greens in a bowl and, with a paper towel in each hand, scoop them up and gently toss (the paper towels will capture excess moisture).

Consume It

Microgreens are never cooked. They are best as lovely garnishes or as finishing touches in mixed salads. They may also be stuffed into sandwiches. Add microgreens just before serving, as they wilt quickly.

Add a handful of microgreens to cream soups or other dishes once they have been ladled out.

Microgreens are now also being added to cocktails and green power shakes.

Baby Salad

This baby salad is so cute I just want to eat it up. The "babies" are veggies and microgreens. With its green and purple shoots, yellow flower petals and fairytale-sized vegetables, this salad is a treat for the eyes too.

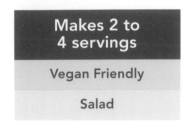

Makes 2 to 4 servings

Vegan Friendly

Salad

Tips

You can find baby vegetables at specialty greengrocers or food boutiques. They range in size. For this recipe the carrots and zucchini were 3 inches (7.5 cm) long, the cauliflowers 2½ inches (6 cm) wide, the pattypan squashes 1½ inches (4 cm) wide and the turnips 1 inch (2.5 cm) wide. You can substitute other baby vegetables as desired. Some come with edible greens, which you can use in other dishes.

Pattypan squash is a small summer squash shaped like a flying saucer with scalloped edges.

For eye appeal, leave on about ¼ inch (0.5 cm) green stem on the carrots and turnip.

Mix your own microgreens or use a prepared blend as I did. Mine included radish, sunflower, popcorn, pea, arugula, chard and amaranth microgreens, along with edible flowers.

- Steamer basket with lid

4	baby pattypan squashes, trimmed (see Tips, left)	4
4	baby turnips, trimmed (see Tips, left)	4
4	baby carrots, trimmed (see Tips, left)	4
2	baby zucchinis, trimmed	2
2	baby cauliflowers, trimmed	2
⅓ cup	Garlic Herb Vinaigrette (page 449)	75 mL
1	bag (3½ oz/100 g) mixed microgreens and flower petals (see Tips, left)	1
	Kosher or coarse sea salt	
4	grape tomatoes, halved	4
1 tbsp	hulled raw sunflower seeds, toasted (see Tips, page 246)	15 mL

1. In covered steamer basket set over 1 inch (2.5 cm) boiling salted water, steam baby vegetables, removing in stages when tender-crisp. It will take about 5 minutes for the zucchini; about 8 minutes for the squashes, turnips and cauliflowers; and about 12 minutes for the carrots. Immediately rinse each with cold water to stop the cooking. Drain and set aside until cooled to room temperature.

2. Place cooked squashes, turnips and carrots in a bowl. Cut zucchini in half lengthwise and cauliflowers in half crosswise; add to bowl. Add dressing to taste (you may have some left over) and toss gently.

3. Pile microgreens on a serving platter or individual plates. Place vegetables with dressing in center. Season with salt to taste. Top with tomatoes and sunflower seeds. Serve immediately.

Creamy Onion Soup with Microgreens

The onion is my favorite vegetable, but it usually gets no respect. There's nothing humdrum about the humble onion in this recipe, a creamy soup crowned with onion microgreens and oniony pumpernickel rye croutons.

Makes 6 to 8 servings (about 8 cups/2 L)

Vegan Friendly

Soup

Tips

Yellow-fleshed potatoes are best for this recipe; neither waxy nor dry, they are good all-purpose potatoes. The best-known yellow-fleshed potatoes are Yukon Golds.

If substituting soy milk for the cream, use full-fat unflavored soy milk for best results. The soup, however, will be thinner.

If you can't obtain onion microgreens, use your favorite kind. Or stir in baby spinach leaves.

To save calories, the croutons are baked instead of fried. Note that baked croutons get soggy faster, so add them to the soup at the last minute.

- Preheat oven to 350°F (180°C)
- Rimmed baking sheet
- Stand or immersion blender

Croutons

2 tsp	onion powder	10 mL
1 tsp	kosher or coarse sea salt	5 mL
3	large slices pumpernickel rye (4 oz/125 g), cut into ½-inch (1 cm) cubes	3
2 tbsp	extra virgin olive oil	30 mL

Soup

2 tbsp	extra virgin olive oil	30 mL
2 lbs	onions (6 to 8), sliced	1 kg
1 tsp	kosher or coarse sea salt	5 mL
1	large potato (8 oz/250 g), cut into chunks (see Tips, left)	1
4 cups	vegetable stock	1 L
¼ tsp	ground nutmeg	1 mL
⅛ tsp	freshly ground white pepper	0.5 mL
1 cup	half-and-half (10%) cream or soy milk (see Tips, left)	250 mL
4 cups	loosely packed onion microgreens (see Tips, left)	1 L

1. *Croutons:* In a small bowl, combine onion powder and salt. Set aside.

2. In another bowl, toss bread cubes with oil. Transfer to baking sheet and spread out in a single layer. Bake in preheated oven for 10 to 15 minutes, until toasted. Immediately sprinkle with onion powder mixture and toss with a spatula. Set aside to cool and crisp.

3. *Soup:* In a large saucepan over medium heat, heat oil until shimmery. Add onions and salt. Cook, stirring often, for about 10 minutes, until softened and turning golden. Stir in potato for 1 minute. Add stock, nutmeg and pepper. When mixture comes to a simmer, cover, reduce heat to low and cook for about 20 minutes, until vegetables are very soft. Purée, using blender, and return to pan if necessary. Stir in cream and heat over medium heat until steaming (do not allow soup to boil). Season with salt to taste.

4. Ladle soup into individual bowls. Mound croutons and microgreens on top and serve immediately (see Tips, left).

Microgreen and Herb Salad

Salads don't get much daintier than this one, thanks to butter lettuce, fine herbs and delicate microgreens. Try this salad as a sophisticated side dish or starter.

Makes 2 to 4 servings		
Vegan Friendly		
Salad		

Tips

Use sesame leaves or shiso perilla (see page 291). If you don't have perilla, substitute 4 mint leaves.

To toast sunflower seeds, cook them in a dry skillet over medium heat, stirring occasionally, for 2 to 3 minutes, until turning golden.

Any type of microgreen will work well in this recipe. I used red kale and radish microgreens. Choose any kind you like.

Assemble and dress this salad right before serving it. These delicate greens and herbs wilt quickly.

1	small head butter lettuce, large leaves torn	1
½ cup	loosely packed fresh basil leaves	125 mL
½ cup	loosely packed fresh flat-leaf (Italian) parsley leaves	125 mL
½ cup	loosely packed fresh chives, cut into 1-inch/2.5 cm pieces	125 mL
¼ cup	loosely packed fresh tarragon leaves	60 mL
2	large perilla leaves, slivered (see Tips, left)	2
⅓ cup	Simple Garlic Vinaigrette (page 448)	75 mL
	Kosher or coarse sea salt	
3 tbsp	unsalted sunflower seeds, toasted (see Tips, left)	45 mL
3 to 4 cups	loosely packed mixed microgreens (2 oz/60 g; see Tips, left)	750 mL to 1 L
4	large grape tomatoes, quartered	4

1. In a large bowl, combine lettuce, basil, parsley, chives, tarragon and perilla. Toss with dressing to taste (you will have some left over).

2. Transfer greens to individual serving plates. Season with salt to taste. Scatter sunflower seeds over greens. Pile microgreens on top. Place equal quantities of tomatoes alongside on each plate. Serve immediately (see Tips, left).

Mock Mashies and Microgreens

A tangled mound of delicate kale microgreens is the perfect finishing touch for mashed cauliflower, a clever and lower-glycemic substitute for mashed potatoes. The creamiest versions include a few spuds, but this hardcore, 100 percent cauliflower rendition is healthier, looks lovely and tastes fabulous.

Tips

You can tweak the recipe measurements if you want to cook a whole head of cauliflower. Use tender florets only, saving the stalks and core for other uses.

To reduce the fat, I use skim milk in this recipe. If you are not counting calories, use whole milk or even cream to create a richer dish.

Extra virgin olive oil makes a good substitute for the butter.

If you can't obtain kale microgreens, use your favorite kind.

Mashing by hand leaves the mixture too chunky, while a ricer (my tool of choice for standard mashed potatoes) requires muscle power. Use a food processor for the creamiest results.

A bit of liquid may separate out as the puréed cauliflower stands. Just stir it back in.

- Food processor

2 lbs	cauliflower florets, coarsely chopped (about 9½ cups/2.25 L; see Tips, left)	1 kg
2	cloves garlic, thinly sliced	2
1 tsp	kosher or coarse sea salt	5 mL
3 tbsp	milk or non-dairy alternative ` (see Tips, left)	45 mL
1 tbsp	unsalted butter or non-dairy alternative, cut into pieces (see Tips, left)	15 mL
⅛ tsp	freshly ground white pepper	0.5 mL
1 oz	kale microgreens (about 2 cups/500 mL, loosely packed; see Tips, left)	30 g

1. In a saucepan, combine cauliflower, garlic and salt. Add enough water to barely cover. Cover pan and bring to a boil over high heat. Reduce heat to medium-low, and simmer for about 15 minutes, until very tender. Drain, then return to pan and cook over low heat for about 1 minute, shaking pan to release excess steam.

2. In food processor fitted with the metal blade, combine cooked cauliflower mixture, milk, butter and pepper. Purée until smooth (see Tips, left). Season with salt to taste.

3. Transfer cauliflower purée to a serving bowl (see Tips, left). Mound microgreens on top and serve warm.

Mizuna and Mibuna

Brassica rapa nipposinica

Other names: **California peppergrass, cut-leaf mustard, Japanese cabbage, Japanese salad greens, japonica, potherb/spider mustard, water vegetable.**

Depending on where you are shopping, you may find mizuna or mibuna identified as *irana, kyona, moutarde des rizières, shui cai* **or** *xue cai.*

Mizuna and mibuna are indigenous to China and Korea but are more closely associated with Japan, where they have been grown for centuries.

Mizuna means "water vegetable." Mibuna was named after the Mibu Temple in Kyoto, where it was grown, and is thus also known as Mibu greens. In modern Japan, mizuna is categorized as one of the *dento yasai* ("traditional vegetables") or, more specifically, *kyo yasai* or *kyona* ("Kyoto vegetables"). Kyoto vegetables are considered superior and particularly significant in Japan's national cuisine. Chefs must be specially trained and pass an exam to be certified as *kyo yasai* masters. *Kyo yasai* were first cultivated in Japan on royal farms and in Buddhist gardens in and around the former capital of Kyoto between the 5th and 12th centuries. Mizuna is an essential ingredient in the New Year's Day soup eaten in Japan for good luck.

Varieties

Mizuna and mibuna (*Brassica rapa nipposinica*) are closely related petite, mild types of mustard greens (page 257), or so-called mustard spinaches. (Do not confuse mizuna or mibuna with komatsuna, page 209, which is also known as mustard spinach.)

Mizuna comes in green and purple cultivars with either colored leaves or green leaves with purple veins and stems. Mibuna is a cultivar with long, spear-shaped leaves that are smooth rather than serrated.

Buy It

Mizuna can be purchased at specialty greengrocers and farmers' markets, as well as Asian supermarkets. You are most likely to find mizuna in mesclun (page 234); it is a typical ingredient in salad blends. Mibuna is sold in some Asian grocery stores and farmers' markets, but it is a rare commodity.

Tasting Notes

Mizuna is peppery and nutty tasting, with tender, feathery leaves and crunchy, juicy stems.

Mibuna is less delicate and stronger tasting, with a slight sweetness and anise accents. It has crisp, peppery, chewy stems and somewhat bitter, nutty, slightly smoky leaves.

Health Notes

Although no official government analysis is available, mizuna and mibuna are thought to contain vitamin C, chromium, folate, iron, potassium, selenium and zinc.

Mizuna and mibuna have not played an extensive role in herbal medicine, but in general mustard greens have been used to improve the function of the liver, gallbladder and thyroid gland, control blood sugar or stimulate appetite.

Despite their close relationship, mizuna and mibuna look different. Mizuna has feathery notched or jagged light green leaves. Mibuna is sturdier, with long, flat, spear-shaped dark green leaves like giant blades of grass, sold in clusters joined at the root end. The leaves are generally 6 to 12 inches (15 to 30 cm) tall but can grow longer (my most recent batch was 18 inches/45 cm tall). The undersides of the leaves are lighter and less shiny than the top surfaces. For both mizuna and mibuna, the stems and veins can be a thin creamy white or pastel green.

Look for crisp leaves, with no wilting, browning or insect damage.

Mibuna blades should be perky, not folded or crumpled. Buy younger, smaller leaves, as their flat, thin stems are less fibrous. Mibuna gets tougher with age.

Store It

Mizuna dehydrates and wilts quickly. Wrap mizuna or mibuna loosely in paper towels and place in a resealable bag with some air in it to act as a cushion, then refrigerate.

Mizuna will keep in the refrigerator for up to two days. Mibuna will keep for up to three days.

Prep It

Mizuna stems are edible. Cut off 1 to 2 inches (2.5 to 5 cm) of the base of the stem, where it is dried or yellowed.

Use mizuna whole for a pretty presentation, or tear or coarsely chop it. If chopping mizuna, discard the stem segments.

You'll love or hate mibuna, depending on the batch you get. The tenderness varies. Stems may be juicy, crisp and sweet or too stringy to eat, either raw or cooked. The stems, however, are too small to be peeled. The best bet is to pinch them off where they meet the leaves.

Insects tend to hide among the leaves, so wash them well and spin-dry.

If mizuna or mibuna leaves look dry, refresh them in a bowl of cold water for a few minutes.

Consume It

Mizuna is a tried-and-true salad green, perfect for delicate mixed salads. Mizuna and mibuna are herblike — in that they may be used in small amounts to flavor a dish — but they are treated like leafy vegetables. In Japan, usually neither is eaten raw. Mibuna is traditionally pickled or salt-fermented.

Mizuna and mibuna cook in less than 2 minutes. Sauté lightly, blanch and dress these greens as a cooked salad, or add them to stir-fries, soups or *nabemono* (Japanese hot pot, or stock fondue). Steaming or stir-frying intensifies their taste. Cook these greens just until they wilt; do not boil them.

When cooked, mibuna may be considered either chewy or toothsome, depending on how tender the particular bunch is.

SUBSTITUTES

baby arugula, frisée, watercress, komatsuna

Citrus Mizuna Salad with Lime Ginger Dressing and Candied Pecans

This salad is beautiful and refreshing. Here I use a shortcut to candy the pecans instead of fussing with oil and boiling sugar, so you can enjoy the dish sooner.

Makes 4 servings

Vegan Friendly

Salad

Tips

Be careful when candying the pecans: the pecans and sugar burn quickly. The sugar will continue to darken off the heat. If you heat it past an amber color, it will taste bitter.

Make sure the sugar you use is fairly fine so that it melts evenly. A vegan alternative is unbleached organic sugar that has not been filtered through bone char; it is only slightly coarser than standard granulated sugar.

To grate or purée gingerroot, use a kitchen rasp such as the kind made by Microplane.

Normally I segment citrus fruit over a bowl to catch the juices. In this case I drained the citrus segments so they wouldn't drown the greens, and then I drank the juice.

Candied Pecans

1 cup	pecan halves	250 mL
2 tbsp	granulated sugar (see Tips, left)	30 mL
	Cayenne pepper	

Dressing

1 tbsp	freshly squeezed lime juice	15 mL
½ tsp	puréed gingerroot (see Tips, left)	2 mL
1 tbsp	granulated sugar	15 mL
1 tsp	kosher or coarse sea salt	5 mL
⅛ tsp	freshly ground black pepper	0.5 mL
3 tbsp	oil	45 mL

Salad

2	oranges	2
1	small pink grapefruit	1
½ cup	diced red onion	125 mL
6 cups	torn mizuna, loosely packed (3 oz/90g)	1.5 L

1. *Candied Pecans:* In a dry skillet over medium heat, toast pecans for 2 to 3 minutes, until turning golden and aromatic. Sprinkle with sugar. Cook, stirring constantly, for 30 to 60 seconds, until sugar melts and turns honey-colored and pecans are lightly browned (see Tips, left). Sprinkle with cayenne to taste, then immediately transfer to a sheet of waxed paper and spread in a single layer. Set aside to cool.

2. *Dressing:* In a small bowl, whisk together lime juice, ginger, sugar, salt and pepper. Whisk in oil. Set aside.

3. *Salad:* Peel oranges and grapefruit. Using a sharp knife, cut them into segments (see Tips, left); seed, if necessary, and discard white pith. Cut grapefruit segments crosswise in half. Transfer oranges and grapefruit to a small bowl and toss with red onion and prepared dressing.

4. Arrange mizuna on a serving platter or divide equally among individual plates. Spoon citrus mixture over mizuna. Scatter pecans overtop and serve immediately.

Smoked Tofu and Mizuna Panini

I'd send my compliments to the inventor of smoked tofu, but my mouth is full! Smoked tofu is a relatively new product, and this cross-cultural recipe takes tasty advantage of it. You can halve or double the recipe. As a bonus, use the addictive sesame spread in other sandwiches or as a vegetable dip.

Makes 2 servings

Vegan Friendly

Sandwich

Tips

This recipe makes about ½ cup (125 mL) sesame spread. Use any leftover portion for other sandwiches.

I use sriracha or sambal oelek chile paste for this. Both are tasty and readily available.

Ciabatta rolls that are about 6½ inches (16 cm) long work well for these sandwiches. They look like miniature ciabatta loaves, and the tofu slices fit neatly and exactly widthwise. However, you can substitute other kinds of crusty rolls with a hearty crumb.

Use whole mizuna, as it's easiest to work with in sandwiches. If desired, pinch off the thicker stems.

If you don't have a toaster oven or panini press, use the ingredients at room temperature and toast the rolls in the oven.

- Toaster oven or panini press, preheated to Medium

Sesame Spread

½ cup	mayonnaise or vegan alternative	125 mL
1 tsp	toasted sesame oil (see Tips, page 256)	5 mL
½ tsp	finely grated lime zest	2 mL
¼ tsp	chile paste (see Tips, left)	1 mL
¼ tsp	soy sauce	1 mL
2 tsp	sesame seeds, toasted (see Tips, page 314)	10 mL

Panini

2	ciabatta rolls, split (see Tips, left)	2
6 oz	smoked tofu, thinly sliced	175 mL
1	small tomato, thinly sliced	1
	Kosher or coarse sea salt	
1 oz	mizuna (about 2 cups/500 mL, loosely packed; see Tips, left)	30 g

1. *Sesame Spread:* In a small bowl, combine mayonnaise, sesame oil, lime zest, chile paste, soy sauce and sesame seeds.

2. *Panini:* Slather prepared sesame spread over cut sides of rolls (you will have some left over). Lay bottoms of rolls on work surface. Top with equal amounts of smoked tofu and tomato. Lightly sprinkle tomato slices with salt to taste. Arrange mizuna on top. Replace tops of rolls.

3. In preheated toaster oven or panini press, heat for about 2 minutes, until bread is slightly golden and tofu is warm (see Tips, left).

Mustard Cabbage

Brassica juncea rugosa

Other names: broad-leaved mustard, cabbage leaf mustard, Chinese mustard greens, heading mustard, heading leaf mustard, heart mustard cabbage, Swatow cabbage/mustard, wrapped heart mustard.

Depending on where you are shopping, you may find mustard cabbage identified as *bao xin jie cai, da xin jie cai, dai gai choy, moutarde chou* or *pahaadi rai.*

Mustard cabbage is native to central Asia. It is widely used in the cuisines of China, Thailand, Laos, the Philippines, Vietnam, Korea, Singapore and Malaysia. Traditionally pickled, mustard cabbage has been eaten for centuries in Asia as a crucial source of vitamins over the cold winter months.

Although introduced to the West wherever Asians have settled, mustard cabbage is largely ignored by North American consumers.

Tasting Notes

Mustard cabbage tastes best as a salty pickle. It is too pungent to eat raw and is bittersweet when cooked. The distinctive sharp mustard flavor gives it a big, bad bite. The core is crunchy, juicy and slightly sweet. The leaves and ribs are fleshy and succulent.

Equivalents

1 head = 1 lb (500 g)

Varieties

Mustard cabbages (*Brassica juncea rugosa*) belong to the family of mustard greens (page 257) but are formed in heads rather than in loose leaves. They have firm, succulent hearts and more closely resemble bok choy than their leafy relatives. Some heads are more compact than others.

Buy It

Mustard cabbage is sold in Asian supermarkets. The cabbage head is generally flattened, with a thick stem and broad-ribbed leaves that curve in toward the top like a baseball glove. The heart is solid. Choose heads that are heavy for their size. Stems should be chunky and succulent, with no breakage or discoloration, and leaves should be crisp.

In addition to fresh heads, a huge selection of pickled mustard cabbage is available in vacuum packs.

Store It

Swathe mustard cabbage in plastic wrap. Or wrap it loosely in paper towels, place in a plastic bag and refrigerate.

Fresh mustard cabbage will keep in the refrigerator for up to five days.

SUBSTITUTES

mustard greens, rapini

To ensure that homemade or leftover commercial pickled mustard cabbage doesn't dry out too much, swathe it in plastic wrap, place in an airtight container and refrigerate for up to two months.

Prep It

Before using mustard cabbage, pull off any damaged or wilted outer leaves. Cut the cabbage in half lengthwise. Trim only a thin slice from the discolored base so the halves don't fall apart.

To wash and crisp mustard cabbage, soak the halves in ice water for 15 to 30 minutes.

Consume It

Mustard cabbage is too ferocious to eat raw. Small heads are occasionally used in soups or stir-fries; they are mellowed somewhat by blanching or slow cooking. Standard large heads are considered indigestible unless preserved.

As a pickle, mustard cabbage is as popular as it is pungent. It is usually salt-pickled and fermented like sauerkraut (page 168). Mustard cabbage is traditionally fermented in clay pots; however, it may also be pickled in a vinegar bath.

Pickled mustard cabbage is served as a side dish with Chinese barbecue or, chopped, as a lively addition to stir-fries or soups.

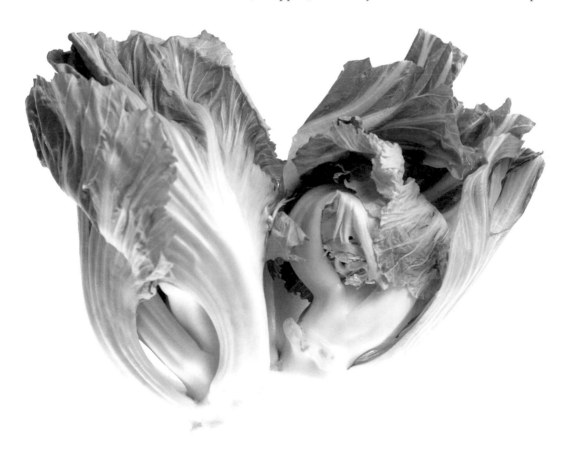

Salt-Pickled Mustard Cabbage

The vast array of pickled mustards in Asian supermarkets attests to the popularity of these preserves. However, they are certainly an acquired taste. Mustard cabbage is not pickled as we think of the term, but rather brined and fermented. Unlike milder-mannered mustard cabbage pickled in a vinegar solution (page 255), this type is very salty and sharp, with a pleasing crunch and a yellow tinge, thanks to turmeric.

Makes 8 servings

Vegan Friendly

Side dish

Tips

You can find pickling salt, a coarse salt without additives, at well-stocked supermarkets.

Taste the brine to make sure you like it. Adjust the seasoning if desired. The brine should be salty, but not overwhelmingly so. Don't forget that the cabbage is salted too.

To discourage unfriendly bacteria or mold, I pour boiling water over the jars, lids and utensils.

The cabbage will bubble up slightly, so leave the lids loose enough to let air escape. Also, it helps to place the jars in a container to catch any brine that bubbles out.

Store cabbage in a spot where the temperature is between 60°F and 70°F (15°C and 20°C) and doesn't fluctuate much.

• Two 32-oz (1 L) preserving jars

Brine

6 cups	water, divided	1.5 L
2 tsp	white or brown rice flour	10 mL
1/4 cup	coarse pickling salt (see Tips, left)	60 mL
2	thin slices gingerroot	2
1/4 tsp	ground turmeric	1 mL
2 tbsp	rice vinegar	30 mL

Cabbage

1	head mustard cabbage (1 lb/500 g)	1
2 tbsp	coarse pickling salt	30 mL

1. *Brine:* In a small saucepan, combine 1/4 cup (60 mL) water and rice flour and stir until smooth. Add remaining water, salt, ginger and turmeric. Bring to a full boil over high heat. Immediately remove from heat and stir in vinegar (see Tips, left). Set aside to cool to room temperature.

2. *Cabbage:* Using a sharp knife, cut mustard cabbage in half lengthwise through the core. Trim only a thin slice from the base (so the halves don't fall apart). Transfer to a large bowl, cover with cold water and soak for 30 minutes. Drain.

3. Rub salt all over cabbage, including between the leaves. Transfer to a sieve and set aside for 4 to 5 hours, until moisture is drawn out and leaves are wilted.

4. Using a sharp knife, cut each cabbage half lengthwise through the core into two equal pieces. Stuff two pieces of cabbage into each jar, core end down. Cover with equal quantities of prepared brine, making sure cabbage is completely submerged by at least 1/2 inch (1 cm). Screw on lid loosely (see Tips, left) and set aside in a cool, dark place for 1 week to ferment. If the cabbage starts to smell fetid or looks slimy, throw it out.

5. Drain cabbage, discarding brine and ginger. Wrap tightly in plastic wrap and transfer to an airtight container. Refrigerate for up to 2 months (see Tips, page 255). To serve, slice, dice or shred as desired.

Sweet-and-Sour Pickled Mustard Cabbage

Blanching and pickling tames and tenderizes mustard cabbage, although it doesn't do much to improve its homely appearance. These pickles are sweet, sour and salty, but not so aggressively as Salt-Pickled Mustard Cabbage (page 254).

Makes 8 servings		
Vegan Friendly		
Side dish		

Tips

To discourage unfriendly bacteria or mold, I pour boiling water over the jars, lids and utensils.

You can find pickling salt, a coarse salt without additives, at well-stocked supermarkets.

Taste the pickling solution to see if it appeals to you, then make adjustments if desired. It should be sweet and salty but not overly so, and tangy but not acrid. Don't forget that the cabbage is already salted.

Store cabbage in a spot where the temperature is between 60°F and 70°F (15°C to 20°C) and doesn't fluctuate much.

The pickled mustard cabbage is wrapped in plastic, then stored in an airtight container to keep it moist and prevent odors from escaping.

- Two 32-oz (1 L) preserving jars

1	head mustard cabbage (1 lb/500 g)	1
1/4 cup	pickling salt, divided (see Tips, left)	60 mL
6 cups	water	1.5 L
6 tbsp	granulated sugar	90 mL
3/4 cup	rice vinegar	175 mL

1. Using a sharp knife, cut mustard cabbage in half lengthwise through the core. Trim only a thin slice from the base (so the halves don't fall apart). Transfer to a large bowl, cover with cold water and soak for 30 minutes. Drain.

2. Rub 2 tbsp (30 mL) salt all over cabbage, including between the leaves. Transfer to a sieve and set aside for 4 to 5 hours, until moisture is drawn out and leaves are wilted.

3. To make the pickling solution, in a small saucepan, bring water, sugar and remaining salt to a full boil over high heat. Immediately remove from heat, stir in vinegar and set aside to cool to room temperature (see Tips, left).

4. In a large saucepan of boiling water, blanch cabbage over medium heat for 1 to 2 minutes, just until water returns to a boil. Drain, then cut each half lengthwise through core into two pieces.

5. Stuff two pieces of cabbage into each jar, core end down. Cover with equal quantities of prepared pickling solution, making sure cabbage is completely submerged by at least 1/2 inch (1 cm). Screw on lid and set aside in a cool, dark place for 3 to 5 days, until cabbage turns a khaki color (see Tips, left). If the cabbage starts to smell fetid or looks slimy, throw it out.

6. Drain, discarding pickling solution. Wrap tightly in plastic wrap and transfer to an airtight container (see Tips, left). Refrigerate for up to 2 months. To serve, slice, dice or shred as desired.

Asian Noodles with Pickled Mustard Cabbage

Pickled mustard cabbage perks up stir-fries and noodle dishes, Asian or otherwise, with its lively taste and pleasing crunch. You can add a small amount to any stir-fry or make it the star of the show, as in this recipe.

Makes 4 servings

Vegan Friendly

Side dish

Tips

Toasted sesame oil, also known as Asian sesame oil, is made from toasted or roasted sesame seeds. Dark and aromatic, it is sold in small bottles as a flavoring agent. Do not confuse toasted sesame oil with yellow sesame oil, which is pressed from raw seeds.

You can find fresh Asian wheat noodles (sold in vacuum packs) in supermarkets, in or near the produce section.

Use salted or unsalted roasted peanuts, as desired.

- Wok

2 tbsp	soy sauce	30 mL
1 tbsp	toasted sesame oil (see Tips, left)	15 mL
1 tsp	granulated sugar	5 mL
1 lb	fresh Asian wheat noodles (see Tips, left)	500 g
2 tbsp	oil	30 mL
4	large green onions (white and green parts), cut diagonally into 1/2-inch (1 cm) pieces	4
1	red bell pepper, diced	1
1	large clove garlic, chopped	1
1/2 tsp	hot pepper flakes	2 mL
1 1/2 cups	coarsely chopped Salt-Pickled Mustard Cabbage (page 254) or Sweet-and-Sour Pickled Mustard Cabbage (page 255)	375 mL
1/4 cup	roasted peanuts, chopped (see Tips, left)	60 mL

1. In a small bowl, combine soy sauce, sesame oil and sugar. Set aside.

2. In a large saucepan of boiling salted water, cook noodles over medium heat for about 5 minutes, until tender but firm. Drain.

3. Meanwhile, heat wok over medium-high heat for about 1 minute. Add oil, swirling to coat bottom of pan. Add green onions, red pepper, garlic and hot pepper flakes. Stir-fry for about 1 minute, until vegetables are softened. Add mustard cabbage and stir-fry for about 1 minute, until heated through. Stir in prepared noodles. Pour soy sauce mixture overtop and toss briefly to coat.

4. Transfer to individual serving bowls. Sprinkle peanuts overtop and serve immediately.

Mustard Greens

Brassica juncea

Other names: **brown/leaf/oriental mustard, Chinese/Indian/Russian mustard, mustard callaloo, sarepta, sow cabbage.**

Depending on where you are shopping, you may see mustard greens identified as *jie cai, gai choy, foglie de mostarda, gorchista, hwerneh, jatilai, kaduga, karashina, moutarde jonciforme, mustasa, phakkat-khieo, sawi, senape* **or** *takana.*

Tasting Notes

Mustard greens bite back. All of them taste like mustard. Some are fiery enough to clear your sinuses, while others are delicate enough to add to salad. Sharp, bright, peppery and pungent flavors with wasabi accents are characteristics of popular large-leaf mustards. The stems are succulent, crunchy and juicy, although often fibrous. Cooking tames the pungency but the stems may remain bitter.

Mustard plants are best known as the source of the condiment mustard, but they also yield tasty greens. However, mustard was first used in herbal medicine. Wild mustard's origins are still debated: it may be indigenous to the Middle East or the foothills of the Himalayas. In any case, the plant spread to Europe, India, China, Japan and North America.

The earliest historical documentation of mustard dates to 3000 BCE. It is cited in Sumerian, Sanskrit, Egyptian and Chinese texts, as well as the Bible. Mustard plants were cultivated in ancient Greece and Rome. The word *mustard* is derived from the Latin *mustum ardens*, meaning "burning wine" or "hot must." This is probably because the ancient Romans mixed unfermented grape juice (must) with mustard seeds to create a condiment.

Eventually the mustard plant garnered appreciation as a vegetable. Mustard greens are used in Asian, Indian, African and European cuisines. Also, along with collards (page 130) and turnip greens (page 399), they are a soul food ingredient in the American South.

Varieties

Mustard plants are divided among the *Brassica* and *Sinapsis* families. They are particularly useful plants: the seeds, stems, leaves and flowers are all edible.

Mustard seeds are pressed for oil as well as being used as a spice and a base for condiment mustard. Black mustard (*Brassica nigra*) and white mustard (*Sinapsis alba*) are grown mainly for their seeds, but their greens are also consumed. Black mustard seeds are actually brown; they are used in Dijon-style mustard. White mustard seeds are actually yellow and are used for mustard powder and American-style mustards — the neon-hued, nostalgia-tinged ballpark mustards.

Leaf mustard (*Brassica juncea*) has yellow or brown seeds but is best known for its cooking greens — considered more lush and flavorful than those of black or white mustards. Leaf mustard is the variety sold in grocery stores as mustard greens.

Mustard greens are delightfully diverse: loose-leafed or in heads; stems thick or thin, fibrous or succulent; leaves red, green, ruffled, crinkled, feathery, serrated, scalloped, lobed or smooth, shiny or matte, giant or petite; colors ranging from jade to burgundy. All do have one thing in common: their bite, which can range from ferocious to merely nippy (see "Cutting the Mustard," page 260).

A wild ancestor of cultivated mustard is charlock (*Sinapis arvensis*), also known as corn or field mustard. The young leaves are eaten in Ireland, the Scottish Hebrides and Sweden.

Unrelated edible mustard-like plants include:

- **garlic mustard** (*Alliaria petiolata, A. officinalis*), also known as hedge garlic, jack-by-the-hedge, jack-in-the-bush, penny hedge, poor man's mustard or sauce-alone. Garlic mustard is an invasive weed that's abundant in wild woodlands, especially along the east coast of North America. The small-leaved foliage is described as having the kick of mustard but with a garlic scent.

- **Mediterranean mustard** (*Hirschfeldia incana*), also known as shortpod mustard, buchanweed or hoary mustard. This variety is a black mustard with edible leaves. It is abundant in the Mediterranean basin, where it is considered a weed.

Health Notes

Mustard greens contain vitamins A, B₆, C, E and K, calcium, copper, folate, iron, magnesium, manganese, niacin, phosphorus, potassium, riboflavin and thiamin.

In folk medicine, mustard greens have been used to stimulate the gallbladder, liver and thyroid; lower blood sugar and cholesterol; clear the respiratory tract; relieve arthritis, rheumatism, lumbago and headaches; treat abscesses, ulcers and scorpion stings; and repel mosquitoes.

SUBSTITUTES

mustard cabbage, komatsuna, arugula, radish greens, escarole, curly endive, turnip greens

Buy It

Mustard greens are sold in Asian and Indian grocery stores, as well as some supermarkets.

The leaves should be crisp and rich green or variegated, not yellowed, flabby or pitted. Choose bunches with smaller, younger leaves. Mustard greens become coarser and spicier with age.

Store It

Wrap a damp paper towel around the bottom of the stems and place the mustard greens in a large plastic bag. Or trim the greens, separating stems, ribs and leaves; then wash, wrap in paper towels, place in resealable bags and refrigerate.

Mustard greens will keep in the refrigerator for up to five days, depending on the type. Larger, coarser greens last longer.

Prep It

Before consuming mustard greens, trim the base where the stalks are joined. Separate leaves from the stems and thick center ribs. Slash the leaves off the stems and ribs, or fold each leaf in half and cut out the stems and ribs at an angle.

The leaves may be chopped or sliced. The stems and thick ribs are often fibrous and thus usually discarded. However, the stems may be pickled or sliced and stir-fried, if desired.

Consume It

Mustard greens vary so much in sharpness that it's a good idea to taste them before you decide how to use them or in what amount.

Mustard greens may be eaten raw but are usually cooked. Baby mustard greens are good in salads and are found in some commercial blends. Also, try tender leaves in sandwiches in place of lettuce and mustard. Curiously, stems that are normally too stringy when cooked may be fine raw for diehards, if sliced thinly for salad.

Mustard greens are famously pickled or eaten as cooked salads in Japanese, Korean and Chinese cuisines. Chopped pickled greens perk up stir-fries.

You can steam, braise or sauté mustard greens or add them to soups or stews. I recommend a cooking time between 10 and 20 minutes, or even longer if you are sensitive to bitter flavors. When boiled, stems are tender-crisp in 5 minutes and leaves are wilted in 2 minutes, but they will still be too bitter and/or pungent for most tastes. The longer the cooking time, the tamer the mustard greens.

To reduce pungency, blanch greens in a pot of boiling salted water for about 1 minute, drain and rinse with cold water before cooking or using as an ingredient.

In the American South, the nutritious liquid saved from cooking greens is called "pot likker" and is used for dunking cornbread or corn pones.

Cutting the Mustard

The tastiest mustard greens come from the large and lively *Brassica juncea* species of plants. This diverse and often confusing family is divided into the following groups:

- **plain-leaved mustards** (*B. juncea foliosa*), which come in green and red varieties and have crinkled rather than curly leaves. Green mustards are favored by the Chinese, red by the Japanese and Koreans. Chinese plain-leaved green mustard is also known as bamboo/common/stickleaf mustard, little leaf mustard, *juk gai choy* or *setsuriko*. It resembles yu choy sum (page 426) with its narrow stems and relatively small, thin leaves. Japanese and Korean red giants (actually purple) are also known as giant-leaved mustard, red mustard or *takana*. They have crisp stems and grainy, spicy, crinkled variegated leaves that can grow to a foot long. Akin to this group are **wedge-shaped leaf mustard** (*B. juncea cuneifolia*) and **lyrate-shaped mustard** (*B. juncea sareptana*), also known as sarepta mustard, *mei cai* or *senape indiana*.
- **curly-leaf mustards** (*B. juncea crispifolia*, *B. juncea integrifolia*), also known as American mustard, southern curled mustard, southern mustard greens, *hagoromo karashina*, *moutarde frisée* or *yang jie cie*. Used in soul food, curly-leaf mustards are the most commonly sold mustard greens in North America. They have ruffled leaves resembling curly kale and a hot mustardy or wasabi flavor. Varieties include Southern Giant and Green Wave; the latter, particularly attractive, has vibrant ruffled leaves and fine white veins.
- **multi-shoots mustards** (*B. juncea multiceps*, *B. juncea multisecta*), also known as chicken mustard, cut-leaved green-in-snow, nine-headed mustard, red-in-snow, serrated-leaved mustard, silverthread mustard, snow cabbage, thousand-headed mustard, thousand-nerved cabbage, *hseuh-li hung*, *moutarde de chine à mille feuilles*, *serifong*, *sher-li-hon* or *tsin kan tsoi*. Multi-shoots mustards are loose-leafed smaller varieties with jagged, deeply lobed dark green leaves on tender stems. They may be related to mizuna (page 248) and resemble dandelion. They are described as having herbal or cabbage flavors with a mild kick. Akin to this group is **Hakka mustard** (*B. juncea longidens*), also known as one thousand leaves, *hyakka*, *manba* or *oona*. This variety is soaked overnight to get rid of bitterness and is mainly served pickled.
- **cut-leaf mustards** (*B. juncea nipposinica*), a group that includes mizuna and mibuna. For information on these greens, see page 248.
- **large-petiole mustards** (*B. juncea strumata*), also known as horned mustard, Szechuan mustard, *amithaba* or *kobu takana*. These rare mustards are distinguished by a thick petiole (botanical talk for a leafstalk) with a swollen "horn," or protuberance, in the center. The frilled leaves are edged with tiny teeth.
- **big-stem mustards** (*B. juncea tatsai*), also known as stem vegetable, swollen-stem mustard, Szechuan pickling mustard, Yangtze mustard, *cha tsoi* or *zha cai*. The relatively sparse leaves of these mustards may be used in cooking or for salads. However, a knobby swollen stem with a broccoli-like texture is this variety's claim to fame. The stem is peeled and pickled in China and India. Thus big-stem mustard is sometimes confused with mustard cabbage (page 252), which is also mainly pickled.
- **head mustards** (*B. juncea rugosa*), a group that includes mustard cabbage. For information on this green, see page 252.
- **root mustards** (*B. juncea napiformis*), also known as Pailleux's large-rooted mustard, turnip-rooted mustard or *chong cai*. These mustards have fleshy roots that resemble turnips. They are sliced and pickled. In shops they are sometimes labeled "pickled turnip." The leaves are smaller and sparser, but they are also eaten.

Black and Green Stew with Curry Oil

Simple curry oil adds oomph to this tasty mélange of beans and mixed vegetables. Serve it over rice or couscous.

Makes 4 servings

Vegan Friendly

Main course

Tips

I use Madras curry paste, which is a good all-purpose curry spice blend. Use any kind you prefer.

Save any remaining curry oil for other dishes or blend it with vinegar to make an unusual salad dressing.

Curry Oil

½ cup	extra virgin olive oil	125 mL
2 tbsp	bottled curry paste (see Tips, left)	30 mL

Stew

3	carrots, cut into ¼-inch (0.5 cm) dice	3
2	stalks celery, cut into ¼-inch (0.5 cm) dice	2
1	onion, diced	1
2	cloves garlic, chopped	2
1 tsp	kosher or coarse sea salt	5 mL
⅛ tsp	freshly ground black pepper	0.5 mL
4 cups	loosely packed coarsely chopped mustard leaves (3 oz/90 g)	1 L
2 tbsp	tomato paste	30 mL
1 tbsp	vegetable stock or water	15 mL
1	can (19 oz/540 mL) black beans, rinsed and drained	1
¼ cup	coarsely chopped fresh cilantro leaves	60 mL

1. *Curry Oil:* In a small jar or airtight container, shake oil and curry paste to combine. Refrigerate overnight, allowing oil to separate from paste. When ready to use, carefully pour infused oil into a small bowl and reserve curry paste for other uses. Set aside oil.

2. *Stew:* In a large skillet over medium-low heat, heat ¼ cup (60 mL) curry oil until hot. Add carrots, celery, onion, garlic, salt and pepper. Cover and cook, stirring occasionally, for 7 to 8 minutes, until barely tender-crisp. Stir in mustard leaves. Cover and cook for about 5 minutes, until leaves are wilted and other vegetables are tender-crisp.

3. In a small bowl, combine tomato paste and stock; stir into vegetable mixture. Add beans to skillet and toss gently to combine. Season with salt to taste.

4. Ladle into individual serving bowls. Drizzle remaining curry oil overtop to taste (you may have some left over). Sprinkle with cilantro and serve immediately.

Napa Cabbage

Brassica rapa pekinensis

Other names: **Chinese leaves, Chinese white cabbage, large white vegetable, mock pak choi, Napa bok choy, Peking cabbage.**

Depending on where you are shopping, you may find napa cabbage identified as *baechu, cai dai, cai xin, cavolo cinese, couve chinesa, da bai cai, hakusai, kapusta kitajskaja, kinakai, kubis cina, pechay, pahit, shu-tso, tsina* **or** *wong bok.*

Tasting Notes

Napa cabbage is milder and more delicate than green or savoy cabbage. It is slightly sweet and faintly bitter, with notes of mustard, celery and nuts. It has a peppery finish. The leaves are fleshy and the ribs are juicy and sweet.

Equivalents

1 large head napa = 2½ lbs (1.1 kg); 1 large head michihli = 2¾ lbs (1.25 kg)

•

2 oz (60 g) napa cut into 1- to 2-inch (2.5 to 5 cm) pieces = 1½ cups (375 mL), loosely packed

•

2 oz (60 g) finely shredded napa = 1 cup (250 mL), loosely packed

Napa cabbage is native to central Asia; the first record of it appeared in the fifth century. Never found in the wild, napa cabbages are thought to be a cross between bok choy and turnips.

Napa is widely used in Chinese, Thai, Filipino, Vietnamese, Korean, Malaysian and other Asian cuisines. It was introduced to the West by Asian immigrants. In the 1970s napa caught on in Europe, then North America. Marketers in the United States named their cultivars after the California valley where they were grown — hence the name "napa cabbage."

Varieties

Napa (*Brassica rapa pekinensis*) has become the generic catch-all name for Asian head cabbages, although it is but one type. Collectively, Asian head cabbages are more correctly known as pe-tsai. There are two categories of pe-tsai:

- **che-foo**, also known as napa, Kasumi, Nerva or Santo. This group is barrel-shaped, with yellow or yellowish-green leaves, and is commonly found in mainstream supermarkets.
- **michihli**, also known as celery cabbage, *chihli*, Jade Pagoda cabbage, Shantung/Tientsin/Tianjin cabbage or *sui choy*. This type is elongated and cylindrical, with pointed dark green tips.

Buy It

Napa cabbage is a supermarket staple. Heads can weigh up to 5 pounds (2.5 kg), but bigger is not better. Choose a smaller, younger head that seems heavy for its size. Look for thick, crunchy white ribs and compact, crinkly, crisp and delicate but thick-veined leaves, transitioning from creamy pastel to light/medium green at the tips. Michihli types are slightly coarser. Tiny brown freckles on some napas are naturally occurring, not a sign of rot.

Health Notes

Napa cabbage contains vitamins A, B_6 and C, calcium, folate, magnesium, manganese, niacin, phosphorus, potassium, riboflavin and thiamin.

In folk medicine, cabbages have been used as an anti-inflammatory. Cabbage paste or leaves were applied to affected areas.

Store It

Swathe whole napa or cut sections tightly in plastic wrap, then refrigerate.

Whole napa cabbage will keep in the refrigerator for up to one month. Cut napa will keep for up to four days.

Because it is so hardy, napa cabbage is favored over bok choy in northern China, where people may stack and store a cache for the whole winter. Napa is also popular in chilly Korea. However, Koreans are more likely to ferment napas into kimchi (page 267).

Prep It

If outer leaves are not perky, discard them.

Using a sharp knife, cut the head lengthwise into quarters. Take a section and, starting at the tip, shred it crosswise thickly or thinly, as desired. Or cut each section lengthwise, then crosswise, to obtain 1- to 2-inch (2.5 to 5 cm) pieces. The core helps hold the section together while you are cutting, so keep it intact until the last minute, then cut it out at an angle. (Don't forget the core is edible and nutritious; eat it out of hand or chop it for soups or other dishes.)

Beware of bugs. Napas were sometimes grown as sacrificial crops because they attracted insects away from other produce. To clean napa most efficiently, cut it, then swish the slices or pieces in cold water. Drain and, if desired, spin-dry.

It's best to use napa immediately after cutting and washing.

Consume It

Napa deserves a fan club. It is tender enough to be eaten raw in salads, yet it remains crunchy when cooked.

Stir-fry, sauté or steam napa, or add it to soups at the last minute. Boiling would be overkill. Napa is done in 1 to 4 minutes, depending on the method.

Try barrel-shaped napa for salads and cooked dishes and the slightly heartier michihli types for cooked dishes, kimchi or other pickling and fermenting jobs. However, for the most part these varieties are interchangeable.

Napa leaves can be used raw as food "cups" or raw, steamed or blanched as wrappers. Full-sized napa leaves are pliable yet crunchy when boiled for 1 to 2 minutes, but use only the top half of the leaf, as the fleshy white rib gets fibrous closer to the base.

Chinese cooks line steamer baskets with cabbage leaves to prevent the contents from sticking.

SUBSTITUTES

savoy cabbage, baby bok choy, tatsoi, iceberg lettuce, Taiwan lettuce

A Relative from Taiwan

Taiwan bok choy (also known as Fengshan bok choy) is similar to napa cabbage. Although it is botanically a bok choy (*Brassica rapa chinensis*), this cultivar is better viewed as an Asian head cabbage because it looks (and cooks) as if it were a mini napa. Taiwan bok choy recently started appearing in supermarkets. Developed in Taiwan, it has a small, romaine-shaped head and frilled, lettuce-like pastel green leaves that are thin and fine yet crisp and firm. The ribs are whiter and thinner than those of bok choy and are considered almost as tender as the leaves. Taiwan bok choy is mild and juicy. The leaves may be dunked in boiling water for 30 seconds and used whole as wrappers for dim sum treats. They turn pliable and transparent, and although thin, remain strong enough to hold their shape.

Napa Slaw

Asian-style coleslaw is great with sandwiches or as a change from green salad. With tender, sweet napa, you don't have to wait hours for your slaw to be ready. The leftovers, moreover, keep well in the fridge. I prefer to prepare slaw in small batches so I don't get tired of it, but this recipe can be doubled.

Makes 4 servings (about 4 cups/1 L)

Vegan Friendly

Salad

Tips

Toasted sesame oil, also known as Asian sesame oil, is made from toasted or roasted sesame seeds. Dark and aromatic, it is sold in small bottles as a flavoring agent. Do not confuse toasted sesame oil with yellow sesame oil, which is pressed from raw seeds.

To grate or purée gingerroot, use a kitchen rasp such as the kind made by Microplane.

Cane sugar is likely to be filtered through bone char, while beet sugar is not. Most labels don't indicate the source of the sugar. If you are following a vegan diet, use unbleached organic sugar that has not been filtered through bone char, or a sweetener such as agave syrup.

Slaw

4 cups	shredded napa cabbage, loosely packed (8 oz/250 g)	1 L
2	carrots, shredded (about 1 cup/250 mL)	2
½ cup	diced red onion	125 mL
¼ cup	finely diced red or green bell pepper	60 mL

Dressing

1 tbsp	oil	15 mL
1 tbsp	toasted sesame oil (see Tips, left)	15 mL
¼ cup	rice vinegar	60 mL
1	clove garlic, minced	1
1 tsp	puréed gingerroot (see Tips, left)	5 mL
2 tsp	granulated sugar (see Tips, left)	10 mL
1 tsp	kosher or coarse sea salt	5 mL
¼ tsp	hot pepper flakes, optional	1 mL
⅛ tsp	freshly ground black pepper	0.5 mL

1. *Slaw:* In a large bowl, toss together napa, carrots, onion and bell pepper.
2. *Dressing:* In a small saucepan, combine oils, vinegar, garlic, ginger, sugar, salt, hot pepper flakes (if using) and pepper. Bring to a full boil over medium-high heat. Immediately pour over napa mixture and toss with a fork until coated.
3. Transfer slaw to an airtight container, cover and refrigerate for at least 1 hour, turning once to redistribute dressing. Serve with a slotted spoon.

Quick Napa Noodles

In less than half an hour, prep included, you can be sitting down to a steaming bowl of luscious hoisin noodles stir-fried with crunchy vegetables. Here's the recipe. Enjoy!

Makes 2 to 4 servings

Vegan Friendly

Main course

Tips

You can find vacuum-packed fresh Chinese noodles in supermarkets, in or near the produce section. For this recipe, use the soft type that resembles spaghetti and requires no boiling. Check the labels: some are vegan, some not. If the size of your package is similar but not exactly the same, this recipe will still work.

Any type of chile paste works well in this dish. Sambal oelek is one of my favorites. The amount in this recipe is meek — if you like spicy food, double or triple it.

- Wok

1	package (14 oz/400 g) fresh Chinese wheat noodles (see Tips, left)	1
¼ cup	vegetarian hoisin sauce	60 mL
2 tbsp	freshly squeezed orange juice	30 mL
1 tsp	toasted sesame oil	5 mL
½ tsp	chile paste (see Tips, left)	2 mL
2 tbsp	oil	30 mL
1	onion, cut into ½-inch (1 cm) chunks	1
½	green bell pepper, cut into ½-inch (1 cm) chunks	½
½ tsp	kosher or coarse sea salt	2 mL
2	cloves garlic, slivered	2
1 tsp	finely chopped gingerroot	5 mL
4 cups	shredded napa cabbage, loosely packed (8 oz/250 g)	1 L
1	carrot, shredded	1
1 tbsp	chopped fresh cilantro leaves	15 mL

1. Place noodles in a colander and rinse under hot running water for 1 to 2 minutes, to soften. Separate gently with fingers, then drain. Set aside.

2. In a small bowl, combine hoisin, orange juice, sesame oil and chile paste.

3. Heat wok over medium-high heat for 1 minute. Add oil and swirl to coat bottom of pan. Stir in onion, green pepper and salt. Cook, stirring often, for 3 to 5 minutes, until softened and turning golden. Stir in garlic and ginger for 30 seconds. Stir in napa and carrot for about 1 minute, until tender-crisp. Stir in noodles and cook, stirring often, for 1 to 2 minutes, until heated through. Pour hoisin mixture overtop and mix well.

4. Transfer to serving plates. Sprinkle cilantro overtop and serve warm.

Napa Kimchi

Koreans prepare kimchi with all kinds of vegetables and eat it with every meal. Kimchis are fermented and very spicy. My favorite kind is napa kimchi, the mother of all kimchis. I prefer the vegan type, prepared with miso, over the ones prepared with fish sauce, anchovy paste or dried shrimp. Since my kimchi consumption is miles behind that of the average Korean, I prepare it in small batches. However, this recipe can be doubled. Kimchi keeps for three to four weeks in the fridge but grows increasingly pungent. When it gets to that point, use it in cooked dishes.

Makes 2 cups (500 mL)

Vegan Friendly

Side dish

Tips

You'll need a quarter of a small head of napa cabbage for this recipe. Koreans often ferment the napa whole, but cut napa is easier to work with and the resulting kimchi is not as unwieldy at the dinner table.

Miso is a fermented paste made with soybeans, rice, barley and/or other grains. I keep white miso on hand for various cooking chores. You can substitute your favorite kind.

Gochugaru is Korean dried chiles; it comes in both powder and flake forms. I prefer the small, shiny, coarse flakes, which are a bit smoky and have a lovely sheen. For a relatively mild kimchi (in Korean terms), halve the amount. For a super-fiery kimchi, double it.

Kimchi is traditionally fermented in clay pots. This small batch, however, fits perfectly in a preserving jar. Pack it tightly.

- One 2-cup (500 mL) preserving jar

8 oz	napa cabbage (see Tips, left)	250 g
1 tbsp	kosher or coarse sea salt	15 mL
2 tbsp	water	30 mL
½ tsp	white rice flour	2 mL
2 tbsp	white miso paste (see Tips, left)	30 mL
2 tbsp	gochugaru chile flakes (see Tips, left)	30 mL
1 tbsp	granulated sugar	15 mL
2	cloves garlic, minced (see Tips, page 278)	2
2 tsp	puréed gingerroot	10 mL
4	large green onions (white and green parts), slivered (see Tips, page 268)	4

1. Using a sharp knife, cut napa into 1- to 2-inch (2.5 to 5 cm) pieces. Transfer to a large bowl and toss with salt. Set aside for 3 to 4 hours, tossing twice, to extract liquid.

2. Meanwhile, in another large bowl, combine water and rice flour. Stir in miso, gochugaru, sugar, garlic and ginger to form a paste. Set aside.

3. Drain napa. Squeeze handfuls to remove excess liquid and add napa to spice paste. Add green onions and toss with a fork to coat evenly.

4. Using tongs and a spatula, pack napa mixture tightly into jar (see Tips, left). Seal tightly and turn jar to distribute liquid evenly. Loosen lid and place jar in a cool, dark place to ferment for 1 to 2 days. Open the lid to release any gases, then re-cover and refrigerate for at least 2 more days before eating.

Variation

Use chopped Asian chives, which look like giant blades of grass, in place of the green onions. You can find Asian chives in Chinese and Korean supermarkets.

Kimchi Tofu in Broth

Custardy tofu and crunchy kimchi in a fiery broth warms bellies in Korea — and here. This comfort food, variously described as a soup or a stew, is usually served over steamed rice.

Makes 2 to 4 servings (about 4 cups/1 L)

Vegan Friendly

Main course

Tips

To drain the tofu, place in a fine-mesh sieve over a bowl and set aside for 15 minutes before cutting.

To sliver green onions, start at the root end and, using a sharp knife, cut thin slices on an extreme diagonal, working your way up the stalk.

2 tbsp	toasted sesame oil (see Tips, page 265)	30 mL
1	small onion, diced	1
1	clove garlic, minced (see Tips, page 278)	1
1 cup	tightly packed Napa Kimchi (page 267), chopped	250 mL
2 cups	vegetable stock	500 mL
1 tbsp	soy sauce	15 mL
	Gochugaru chile flakes (see Tips, page 267)	
1	package (10 oz/300 g) silken (soft) tofu, drained and cut into 1-inch (2.5 cm) cubes (see Tips, left)	1
2	large green onions (white and light green parts), slivered (see Tips, left)	2

1. In a saucepan over medium-low heat, heat oil until hot. Add onion and garlic. Cook, stirring often, for about 2 minutes, until softened. Add kimchi and cook, stirring occasionally, for 2 to 3 minutes, until hot and sizzling. Add stock and soy sauce, then gochugaru liberally to taste, until broth is fiery. When mixture comes to a simmer, gently stir in tofu. Cover and simmer for 5 minutes.
2. Ladle into bowls. Scatter green onions overtop.

Grilled Kimcheese Sandwiches

Everything tastes better with kimchi, including this riff on a diner classic.

Makes 2 servings

Sandwich

Tips

If the kimchi looks too wet, drain it in a fine-mesh sieve for 5 minutes, then press on it with a wooden spoon.

The soft, thick-cut white sandwich bread sold in Asian supermarkets works well for these sandwiches.

4	slices sandwich bread	4
	Unsalted butter, softened	
4	large slices havarti cheese (4 oz/125 g)	4
1/3 cup	tightly packed Napa Kimchi (page 267), finely chopped and drained (see Tips, left)	75 mL

1. Slather butter on one side of each slice of bread. Place 2 slices butter side down and top each with 1 slice of cheese and kimchi to taste. Top each with another slice of cheese. Top with remaining bread, butter side up.
2. In a large, heavy skillet (preferably cast iron) over medium heat, place sandwiches side by side. Top with another skillet to weigh them down. Cook until bottoms are golden brown, for 1 to 1 1/2 minutes. Flip, replace weight and cook for another 1 to 1 1/2 minutes, until, cheese is molten and kimchi is warm.
3. Using a sharp knife, cut each sandwich and serve immediately.

Kimchi and Shiitake Fried Rice

Surely the Chinese invented fried rice as a clever way to use up leftovers. Kimchi gives this iconic dish a fabulous jolt of spice and crunch. When making Chinese food, be prepared: everything happens at once when you start stir-frying, so lay out all the ingredients beforehand. Otherwise the logistics will give you a headache.

Makes 4 servings (about 6 cups/1.5 L)

Vegan Friendly

Side dish

Tips

To get that Chinese takeout texture, refrigerate the cooked rice overnight to dry it out before frying it (otherwise it will turn to mush). If starting from scratch, cook 1½ cups (375 mL) raw rice in 3 cups (750 mL) water. One cup (250 mL) raw rice yields 3 to 4 cups (750 mL to 1 L) cooked rice.

Don't stir the rice too frequently or vigorously — it will get mushy. Spread it out, let it cook until it starts to form a crust on the pan, then flip and scrape.

Don't try to double this recipe, as it won't cook properly in the wok. If you want more, make two batches.

- Wok

1½ tbsp	soy sauce	22 mL
2 tsp	toasted sesame oil (see Tips, page 265)	10 mL
2 tsp	rice vinegar	10 mL
⅛ tsp	freshly ground black pepper	0.5 mL
5 tbsp	oil, divided	75 mL
8 oz	shiitake mushrooms, stemmed and sliced (about 3½ cups/875 mL)	250 g
4	large green onions (white and green parts), cut diagonally into 1-inch (2.5 cm) pieces	4
1	carrot, shredded (about 1 cup/250 mL)	1
2	cloves garlic, minced (see Tips, page 278)	2
1 cup	tightly packed Napa Kimchi (page 267), drained and coarsely chopped	250 mL
4 to 5 cups	cold day-old cooked long-grain white rice (see Tips, left)	1 to 1.25 L
1 tbsp	chopped fresh cilantro leaves	15 mL

1. In a small bowl, combine soy sauce, sesame oil, vinegar and pepper. Set aside.

2. Heat wok over medium heat for 1 minute. Add 2 tbsp (30 mL) oil and swirl to coat bottom of pan. Stir in mushrooms, onions, carrot and garlic. Stir-fry for 2 to 3 minutes, until glossy and softened but not limp. Increase heat to medium-high and stir in kimchi. Cook for about 1 minute, until excess moisture evaporates and kimchi is hot. Scrape mixture into a bowl. Set aside.

3. Add remaining 3 tbsp (45 mL) oil to wok and heat over medium-high heat until shimmery. Add rice and cook for 5 to 7 minutes, until glossy and hot, occasionally stirring and flipping with a small spatula and scraping up crust as it forms on bottom of pan (see Tips, left). Stir in soy sauce mixture, then vegetable mixture.

4. Transfer to a large serving platter. Garnish with cilantro and serve immediately.

Nettles

Urtica dioica

Other names: **common/great/jaggy/hairy nettle, stinging nettle.**

Depending on where you are shopping, you may see nettles identified as *bicchu-booti, hsieh tzu tsao, kandeli, ortie, sisnu, soi* **or** *tsouknida.*

Tasting Notes

Nettles are mild, a bit nutty and lightly herbaceous. When cooked, they are slightly spinachy, with a hint of cucumber.

Dozens of species of nettles are native to North America, Europe, Asia and Africa, mainly in temperate climates. Stinging nettle (*Urtica dioica*) is abundant in moist fields, pastures and woodlands in North America and Europe.

Stinging nettles have a long history as foraged edibles, medicinal herbs and pesky weeds. England is home to the Great Dorset Stinging Nettle Eating Competition. Contestants vie to see how many feet of stalks of oversized nettles they can strip and eat. The contest was launched in the mid-1980s as a corollary to a long-standing stinging nettle competition among local farmers struggling with nettle infestations in their fields, and arguing over who had the tallest ones. The Ortie Folies, an annual nettle celebration in Normandy, France, puts a more positive spin on these weeds — the festival encourages "urticamania."

As well as being the subject of numerous scientific studies, nettles are the intriguing stuff of rhyme and folklore. In the Hans Christian Andersen tale "The Wild Swans," a long-suffering princess has to weave a coat of nettles to break an evil spell.

As a verb, *nettle* means to irritate or vex, but it's not clear whether it's based on the nettle plant or vice versa. The word is derived from the Anglo-Saxon *noedl*, meaning "needle." Nettles are covered with tiny white bristles or hairs with chemical irritants in the shaft, akin to insect venom. The plant's sting comes not from the prick; rather, it is a chemical burn. Formic acid and histamines are widely believed to be the irritants in stinging nettles, but some experts cite oxalic or tartaric acid. The plant's tiny hairs are brittle, so when you touch them, the hairs pierce the skin, break and release the irritants. The result is urticaria, a painful, itchy rash with welts. Inhaling the plant's chemicals can irritate the nasal passages, and eating them can burn the mucous membranes of the mouth. However, there is no lasting harm.

I have never been stung by nettles, but some stings are described as hitting quickly and sharply, then lessening in about a quarter of an hour. However, the rash may remain sore until the next day, especially when it comes in contact with water. Since the sting is caused by an acid, it may be soothed by a baking soda paste, which is alkaline. Poultices of sorrel or dandelion leaves are a folk remedy for nettle stings.

This daunting information makes me wonder about the brave souls who first tried to collect and eat stinging nettles centuries ago. But forage them they did, as a substitute for spinach or kale. Nettles are popular in northern and eastern Europe and cultivated in Germany. They are also cooked in parts of India. Nettles are sometimes used in cheese-making or brewed as beer. Large nettles are cultivated in some parts of the world as a source of coarse fiber that is woven into material akin to burlap.

Varieties

"Nettle" is a name given to diverse plants, not all of which are related. Many nettles are infamous for their sting, as well as being noted for their culinary and medicinal uses.

Stinging nettle (*Urtica dioica*) is the most prominent culinary variety; a subspecies, *U. dioica gracilis*, is found mainly in North America. Common stinging nettle is the kind most North American shoppers are likely to encounter.

The term *stinging nettle* can be confusing, as it is not only the official name of the common stinging nettle (*U. dioica*) but is also used as a descriptive phrase for nettles in general. Here are some other notorious and notable nettles in the *Urtica* family:

- **dwarf nettle** (*U. urens*), also known as annual/burning nettle. This Eurasian native has smaller leaves than the stinging nettle.
- **heartleaf nettle** (*U. chamaedryoides*), also known as fireweed, ortiguilla, slim stinging nettle or weak nettle. The species name roughly means "burning dwarf." Native to Florida and environs, its sting is considered more powerful and painful than that of other North American nettles.
- **Masai stinging nettle** (*U. massaica*), also known as forest nettle. This variety is used as a medicinal food in Africa.
- **biting nettle** (*U. thunbergiana*), also known as biting cat. This species is found in Japan and China.
- **scrub nettle** (*U. incisa*), considered a tasty vegetable by Australian Aborigines, who bake the leaves between hot stones.
- **tree nettle** (*U. ferox*), also known as killer nettle or *ongaonga*. This is a particularly dangerous variety that is common to New Zealand. It can grow 16 feet (5 meters) tall and has unusually large stinging bristles.

Health Notes

Although no official government analysis is available, nettles are thought to contain vitamins A, E and K, iron, magnesium, manganese, niacin, potassium, riboflavin and thiamin. Nettles are particularly high in protein.

In herbal medicine, nettles have been revered for their anti-inflammatory and antimicrobial properties, and they have been used to treat everything from arthritis to acne to hair loss. Consuming nettle tea is thought to alleviate allergies such as hay fever and asthma; it has also been used as mouthwash. Ironically, some people are allergic to stinging nettles. In addition, if eaten after flowering, nettles can irritate the urinary tract.

In the 1600s the English were warned that nettle seeds would whip up lust and promote fertility.

Equivalents

1 bunch = 3 oz (90 g)

•

2 oz (60 g) leaves and stemlets = 8 cups (2 L), loosely packed

Unrelated nettles include Canadian wood nettle (*Laportea canadensis*) and spurge nettle (*Cnidolscolus stimulosus*), also known as tread-softly or finger-rot. The latter's bite is not as powerful or long-lasting as that of the common stinging nettle; it is foraged mainly for its roots and seeds rather than its large trilobed leaves. The leaves of its relative the bull nettle (*C. texanus*) are not eaten either.

Buy It

Specialty greengrocers and farmers' markets sell stinging nettles, thoughtfully stemmed and packed in plastic bags with the warning "Do not touch without gloves!"

Pointed leaves with scalloped edges grow in bushy clusters along the stems. The leaves become variegated with yellow once they are past their prime. Fine hairs grow along the stems and undersides of the leaves, which are lighter green.

A harbinger of spring, the stinging nettle is often foraged. The youngest leaves, also known as "spring tips," are considered the best — and the least prickly. Discerning foragers may pick only the top four leaves on each stalk. If nettles are picked too late, gritty crystals form in the leaves and the stems harden. To reduce the chance of stings, foragers are advised to pick leaves at their base near the stem and avoid touching the stems, leaf tips and veins on the undersides of leaves, where the bristles are located.

Store It

Nettles are fragile, bruising and darkening quickly. Although generally tender, their stems get stringy as they age.

Trim and place nettles in a resealable bag with some air in it to act as a cushion, then refrigerate.

Nettles will keep in the refrigerator for up to two days.

Prep It

According to nettle experts, since the stinging hairs grow upward, nettles should be grasped firmly rather than tentatively, so the hairs are crushed and can't penetrate the skin. There's even an Aesop's fable about preparing nettles, with advice to "grasp it boldly, and it will be soft as silk to your hand." I prefer the insurance of wearing gloves and handling nettles with tongs.

Before consuming nettles, pluck the leaves and stemlets off the stems, which are edible but unappetizingly hairy.

Soaking, cooking, wilting, refrigerating, drying and dehydrating all neutralize the irritants in stinging nettles.

Consume It

Never eat nettles raw or after they have flowered. You can use nettles in soup, pesto or pasta, or even put them on pizza.

Young shoots and leaves are cooked in 5 to 10 minutes. Cooked nettles have visual appeal, as they keep their emerald hue.

Leftover cooking water may be kept for soup or tea.

SUBSTITUTES

spinach, chickweed

Poke Salad Annie, Weeds Got Your Granny

"Poke Salad Annie" must be the only toe-tapping classic pop song about foraging for edible weeds. The lyrics had always puzzled me. Now I know that if the gators hadn't gotten poor old Granny, as the song goes, the poisonous pokeweed might have.

Poke salad or, more correctly, poke sallet or salit, is a name for the boiled greens of pokeweed (*Phytolacca americana*), which is also known as pokeroot, poke bush, Virginia poke, American nightshade, cancer jalap, coakum, garget, inkberry, pigeon berry, pocan, redweed, scoke, red ink plant or *chui xu shang lu*.

If you pick pokeweed too late in its season or don't boil the heck out of it, poke sallet will make you 911 sick. Consuming the mature leaves and stems, roots, berries or seeds can send you to hospital; if they are eaten raw, they induce convulsions and coma. Apparently poke poisonings were common in the 19th century.

Despite its dangerous reputation, pokeweed's spring shoots are a delicacy. The plant is a traditional part of the cuisine and folk medicine of the rural American South, as well as some Native peoples. There are several annual poke sallet festivals, and the weed is occasionally sold regionally via farmers' markets or online. Although it is a common weed, it was even commercially canned once upon a time.

Pokeweed is found throughout the Gulf states. The leaves are picked in spring, then boiled in salted water and drained three times. Cooking times vary from granny to granny but can be an hour or more. Triple-boiling removes some but not all of the three different types of plant toxins believed to be in pokeweed.

The lyrics of "Poke Salad Annie" say that the weed looks like turnip greens, and singer Tony Joe White, musing about his famous hit, once described the leaves as tasting a bit like spinach. I won't be testing that anytime soon.

Nettle Soup

When I get my hands on a bagful of nettles, my thoughts turn to soup. Puréed nettles make a gorgeous emerald spring tonic, with a clean, green flavor.

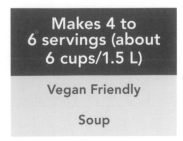

Makes 4 to 6 servings (about 6 cups/1.5 L)

Vegan Friendly

Soup

Tips

To wash the leek: Using a sharp knife, halve it lengthwise and slice it thinly crosswise. Transfer to a large bowl of cold water and swish the pieces around. The dirt will fall to the bottom and you can scoop out the leek pieces floating on top.

The uncooked rice is added to thicken the soup. If desired, substitute a yellow-fleshed potato (such as Yukon Gold), peeled and cut into chunks.

About ½ cup (125 mL) uncooked white rice makes 1½ to 2 cups (375 to 500 mL) cooked rice.

• Stand or immersion blender

2 tbsp	extra virgin olive oil	30 mL
1	small onion, diced	1
1	leek (white and green parts), sliced (see Tips, left)	1
1	stalk celery, diced	1
2	large cloves garlic, chopped	2
1 tsp	kosher or coarse sea salt	5 mL
¼ tsp	freshly ground black pepper	1 mL
3 cups	vegetable stock	750 mL
1 cup	water	250 mL
2 tbsp	uncooked white rice	30 mL
2 oz	nettle leaves and stemlets (about 8 cups/2 L, loosely packed)	60 g
1 tbsp	freshly squeezed lemon juice	15 mL
1 to 1½ cups	cooked white or brown rice (see Tips, left)	250 to 375 mL
	Sour cream or non-dairy alternative	
¼ cup	chopped fresh chives	60 mL

1. In a saucepan over medium-low heat, heat oil until hot. Add onion, leek, celery, garlic, salt and pepper. Cook, stirring often, for about 5 minutes, until softened and golden. Add stock, water and uncooked rice. When mixture comes to a simmer, cover, reduce heat to low and cook for about 15 minutes, until rice is tender. Stir in nettles, cover and cook for about 5 minutes, until wilted.

2. Purée, using blender, and return to pan if necessary. Stir in lemon juice and cooked rice to taste.

3. Ladle into serving bowls. Top each with a dollop of sour cream, to taste, and a sprinkling of chives. Serve warm.

Variations

In Step 2, substitute cooked quinoa or tiny pasta for the cooked rice.

For a double dose of nettle goodness, finish the soup with a dollop of Pesto d'Urtica (page 275).

Gnocchi with Pesto d'Urtica

*In springtime Italians make nettle pesto, which they call **pesto d'urtica** and often toss with gnocchi. It's a delicious combination. You can make pesto using almost any type of leaf, raw or blanched, depending on the type of green.*

Tips

To toast pine nuts, cook them in a dry skillet over medium heat, stirring often, for 2 to 3 minutes, until golden and aromatic.

Like many cheeses, Parmesan is made with animal-based rennet and is unsuitable for vegetarians. However, some brands of Parmesan-style cheese are made with vegetarian rennet as a suitable substitute. Check labels to be sure.

For a vegan version, use gnocchi made without eggs (check the labels). Gnocchi are sold in vacuum packs in supermarkets.

Be careful not to overprocess the pesto into a paste. Traditionally the ingredients for pesto are ground together, so some texture is desired.

Use leftover pesto in sandwiches or add a dollop to soups.

- Food processor

Pesto

2 oz	nettle leaves and stemlets (8 cups/2L, loosely packed)	60 g
3	cloves garlic	3
¼ cup	pine nuts, toasted (see Tips, left)	60 mL
2 tbsp	freshly grated Parmesan-style cheese, optional (see Tips, left)	30 mL
1 tbsp	freshly squeezed lemon juice	15 mL
1 tsp	kosher or coarse sea salt	5 mL
⅛ tsp	freshly ground black pepper	0.5 mL
¼ cup	extra virgin olive oil	60 mL

Gnocchi

1 lb	prepared gnocchi (see Tips, left)	500 g
¼ cup	oil-packed sun-dried tomatoes, drained and chopped	60 mL
	Kosher or coarse sea salt	

1. *Pesto:* In a large pot of salted boiling water over medium heat, blanch nettles, stirring often, for about 1 minute, until wilted. Drain and immediately rinse with cold water to stop the cooking. Drain and set aside.

2. In food processor fitted with the metal blade, chop garlic. Squeeze handfuls of nettles to extract excess moisture and transfer to work bowl. Add pine nuts, cheese (if using), lemon juice, salt and pepper. With the motor running, add oil through the feed tube and process until ingredients are puréed, with some texture (see Tips, left). Set aside.

3. *Gnocchi:* In a saucepan of boiling salted water, cook gnocchi according to package directions or for 3 to 4 minutes, until they rise to the top and are tender. Drain well and return to pan. Gently stir in sun-dried tomatoes and about ½ cup (125 mL) pesto to taste (you will have some left over). Serve warm.

Parsley Root Tops

Petroselinum crispum radicosum

> *Other names:* **Dutch/Hamburg parsley, parsnip-rooted parsley, rock parsley, turnip-rooted parsley tops.**
>
> **Depending on where you are shopping, you may find parsley root identified as *heimischer, knoldpersille, padrushka, persil à grosse racine, persil tubéreux, prezzemolo da radici, persillerot, rotpersilja* or *salsa tuberosa*.**

Tasting Notes

Parsley root tops taste like common parsley but are coarser and nuttier.

Health Notes

Parsley root tops contain vitamins A, B$_6$, C, E and K, calcium, copper, folate, iron, magnesium, manganese, niacin, pantothenic acid, phosphorus, potassium, riboflavin, thiamin and zinc. They are strongly anti-inflammatory.

In herbal medicine, parsley has been used to freshen breath; to treat bronchitis, stomachaches and menstrual problems; and to alleviate urinary tract ailments and kidney stones.

Native to rocky hillsides in the Mediterranean, parsley plants are widely cultivated as both herb and vegetable. Although it is now the world's most common herb, parsley did not have an auspicious start in culinary history, because of its ancient association with death and ill fortune. There are many myths surrounding this plant, including the amusing one that parsley will grow only in households where the wife is the boss.

Parsley was cultivated before recorded history. The ancients didn't eat parsley, however. They used it as a medicine, for animal fodder and as a garden ornamental. It was also employed in burial rituals. The Greeks took parsley as an antidote to poison, wove it into funeral wreaths and planted it near graves. The saying "in need of parsley" was a euphemism for being close to death. The ancient Romans wore parsley garlands to ward off drunkenness — not very effectively, judging by their decadent history.

It was not until the Middle Ages that parsley was commonly eaten. This turnaround is credited to either Charlemagne or Catherine de' Medici, who both grew it in their gardens as a culinary green. Still, in the Christian world, parsley was associated with the devil, and virgins were not allowed to plant it.

In Britain, parsley sauce was a favorite of Henry VIII. However, the herb was also associated with death, "Welsh parsley" being a nickname for the gallows rope.

Parsley's dire reputation may have been due to its resemblance to fool's parsley (*Aethusa cynapium*), a poisonous relative of hemlock. However, the herb is now ubiquitous and humdrum. "Just like parsley" is the Greek description of a person who seems to be everywhere but is insignificant.

Varieties

There are dozens of varieties of parsley. They are classified as either as leaf parsley or root parsley. Leaf parsley is also known as common parsley or garden parsley. This variety includes curly parsley (*Petroselinum crispum*) and flat-leaf or Italian parsley (*P. crispum neapolitanum*). True to its name, root parsley (*P. crispum radicosum*) is grown for its root rather than its foliage. However, its greens are also edible.

Do not confuse parsley root with lookalike parsnips, which are creamy, sweet and usually sold topless.

Buy It

Parsley roots (with their tops) are sold at greengrocers and some supermarkets.

This is a popular vegetable with Eastern European soupmakers. Large, lush heads of foliage are attached to the roots, and it's a shame to let them go to waste. Look for bunches with feathery bright green leaves. Avoid any with yellowing or moist black patches.

Store It

Separate parsley tops from the roots before storing them. They are awkward to store in bunches, and the tops rob the roots of moisture. Leave about 1 inch (2.5 cm) of stem attached to the root.

Place the tops in a glass or vase of water like a bouquet, with a plastic bag draped over the foliage, then refrigerate. Or trim, wash, spin-dry and roll in paper towels, then place in a resealable bag. Unlike common parsley, hardier parsley root tops may be washed and dried well before storing, if desired. They are usually very gritty, and the dirt damages the leaves and promotes deterioration.

Prep It

Before consuming parsley root tops, strip the leaves from the main stems, which are thin but tough and inedible. You can keep the tender stemlets attached to the leaves, if desired.

Wash the greens in several changes of cold water until the water looks clear.

To soften parsley root tops and extract any bitterness, toss damp leaves with a spoonful of salt in a sieve and set aside for 30 minutes to drain. Grab handfuls, squeeze out excess liquid, transfer to a cutting board and chop.

Consume It

Parsley root tops are coarser than common parsley. They can be used raw, like parsley, if you chop them finely and stick to small amounts. However, you can make better use of these greens in larger quantities as a cooking ingredient. You can add them to soups, stews, pastas, and rice and grain dishes.

SUBSTITUTES
celeriac tops, carrot tops, mizuna

Brown Rice Tabbouleh

This is a tasty variation on a Middle Eastern favorite, parsley salad. I make use of parsley root tops and replace the usual bulgur with brown rice. The dish should be nice and tangy, so don't skimp on the lemon juice.

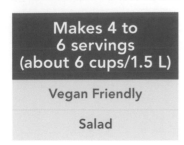

Makes 4 to 6 servings (about 6 cups/1.5 L)
Vegan Friendly
Salad

Tips

Bottled reconstituted lemon and lime juices usually contain additives. To avoid them, use freshly squeezed juice. Squeeze a whole lemon or lime and store the leftover juice in a small container in the fridge, or freeze it in 1 tbsp (15 mL) portions in an ice-cube tray.

For the finest minced garlic, push it through a press.

Leftover rice stiffens in the fridge. This salad is best when eaten the same day it is made.

• Rimmed baking sheet

Dressing

¼ cup	extra virgin olive oil	60 mL
3 tbsp	freshly squeezed lemon juice (see Tips, left)	45 mL
1	large clove garlic, minced (see Tips, left)	1
1 tsp	kosher or coarse sea salt	5 mL
¼ tsp	freshly ground black pepper	1 mL

Tabbouleh

1 cup	short-grain brown rice	250 mL
2 oz	parsley root leaves (about 5 cups/ 1.25 L, loosely packed)	60 g
1 tsp	kosher or coarse sea salt	5 mL
4	green onions (white and green parts), thinly sliced	4
1 cup	grape tomatoes, halved	250 mL
3	mini cucumbers, peeled, quartered lengthwise and sliced	3
½	red bell pepper, cut into ⅛-inch (3 mm) dice	½

1. *Dressing:* In a small measuring cup, whisk together oil, lemon juice, garlic, salt and pepper. Set aside.

2. *Tabbouleh:* In a saucepan of boiling salted water, cook rice over medium-low heat for 30 to 40 minutes, until tender but chewy. Drain, then spread out on baking sheet to cool to room temperature.

3. Meanwhile, in a fine-mesh sieve, toss parsley root leaves (with wash water clinging to them) with salt. Set aside for 30 minutes to drain. Grab handfuls and squeeze out excess liquid, transfer to a cutting board and chop. Set aside.

4. Transfer cooled rice to a large serving bowl. Add green onions, tomatoes, cucumbers, red pepper and parsley root leaves. Pour dressing overtop and, using a fork, toss to coat evenly. Serve at room temperature (see Tips, left).

Pea Shoots

Pisum sativum macrocarpon

> ***Other names:*** **pea leaves/tendrils/tips/tops/vines, pea pod leaves.**
>
> **Depending on where you are shopping, you may find pea shoots identified as *arveja cometodo, dau miu, mange-tout, saya endou, tohbyo* or *wandusaan*.**

It is probably better to refer to these greens as "pea vines," to differentiate them from pea sprouts or pea microgreens, which are sometimes labeled "pea shoots" too, causing confusion.

Wild peas are native to the Mediterranean basin and the Middle East. Cultivation dates back to the dawn of agriculture, during the Neolithic era.

Pea shoots are a traditional ingredient in the cuisine of southern China, as well as parts of Africa. They are growing in popularity in North America and are particularly cultivated in the Pacific Northwest.

Varieties

The greens of diverse field and garden peas, as well as beans and other pulses, are consumed around the world. However, commercially "pea shoots" refers specifically to the leaves, vines and tendrils of snow peas (*Pisum sativum macrocarpon*). Sugar snap peas are their botanical twins and yield similar greens.

Buy It

Long prominent in Asian cuisine, pea shoots are now attracting a wider audience. They can be found at farmers' markets, some supermarkets and even big-box stores. Availability is usually seasonal, from spring to fall.

Pea shoots are sold bagged, in tangled masses of bright green leaves, stems, tendrils and, occasionally, lovely white flower buds. The young top sets of leaves, known as the tips, are marketed commercially, as they are the choice parts of the pea plant. Avoid greens with browned, yellowed or damaged leaves, or stems with mushy ends. Check in the center of the batch for signs of rot.

Store It

Place pea shoots in a resealable bag with some air left in to act as a cushion, then refrigerate. Do not squash shoots together, as rot sets in at the center of the bunch.

Tasting Notes

Pea shoots are reminiscent of peas and spinach, tasting slightly sweet and grassy. Their leaves are delicate and their stems crunchy.

Health Notes

Although no official government analysis is available, pea shoots are thought to contain vitamins A, B_6, C, E and K, folate, thiamin and riboflavin.

Pea shoots are rarely mentioned in herbal medicine but have been used to relieve constipation, maintain digestive health and control blood sugar.

Equivalents

2 oz (60 g) whole pea shoots = 3 cups (750 mL), loosely packed

•

2 oz (60 g) coarsely chopped pea shoots = 2¾ cups (700 mL), loosely packed

SUBSTITUTES

baby spinach, sweet potato leaves

Pea shoots spoil quickly. Ideally they are best within a day or two of picking. However, they will keep in the refrigerator for up to three days.

Prep It

The leaves, stems, tendrils and buds are all edible. For salads, however, I am fastidious about trimming and discarding thicker stems, which can be coarse and chewy. Also, the tendrils are wiry; pinch them off or save them for garnishing.

Pluck any coarse or yellowed stems off the vines. Snap off any tough ends of vines. Discard faded or wilted leaves.

Do not wash the shoots until you are ready to use them. Swish them in cold water and spin-dry.

Chop the greens or use whole leaves.

Consume It

Pea shoots may be eaten raw or cooked, in salads, soups, stir-fries and pasta dishes. The leaves hold up well to salad dressing without wilting.

Steam, blanch or sauté the greens. Leaves wilt and stems soften in 1 minute. Don't be afraid to start with a large quantity — these greens wilt down a lot, like spinach.

Peas and Beans with Greens

Edible greens of other peas, beans and pulses include the following:

- black-eyed peas (*Vigna unguiculata*), also known as cowpeas. The young shoots are a staple leafy green in tropical and subtropical regions. Relatives include **catjang** (*V. unguiculata cylindrica*), which is native to Africa, and **yard-long beans** (*V. unguiculata sesquipedalis*), also known as snake, bodi or borah beans. Yard-long beans are widely cultivated in Asia.
- chickpeas (*Cicer arietinum*), also known as Bengal gram leaves or *channa bhaji*. In India chickpea greens are cooked as a vegetable or eaten in salads.
- **common green beans** (*Phaseolus vulgaris*), **runner beans** (*P. coccineus*) and **lima beans** (*P. lunatus*), also known as butter beans.
- **fava beans** (*Vicia faba*), also known as broad beans.

Pea Bonanza with Mint Vinaigrette

Thankfully you can't overdose on peas and their greens. This salad, featuring the fragrant combination of peas and mint, is delicious proof.

	Makes 4 servings
	Vegan Friendly
	Salad

Tips

To trim and string snap and snow peas: Use a paring knife to nip off the tip at one end of the pod, then pull until a thin string peels off the seam. Repeat, starting at the other end.

If desired, substitute thawed frozen green peas for the fresh ones. Halve their cooking time.

3 oz	pea shoots	90 g
4 oz	sugar snap peas (about 1 cup/250 g, loosely packed), trimmed (see Tips, left)	125 g
4 oz	snow peas (about 2 cups/500 mL, loosely packed), trimmed	125 g
4 oz	shelled fresh green peas (about ¾ cup/175 mL; see Tips, left)	125 g
⅓ cup	Mint Vinaigrette (page 449)	75 mL
	Kosher or coarse sea salt	
½	small red bell pepper, cut into matchsticks	½

1. Using a sharp knife, trim pea shoots, discarding tough stems and setting aside curly tendrils and flower buds. Coarsely chop tender greens; you should have about 4 cups (1 L). Set aside in separate piles.

2. In a saucepan of boiling salted water, cook snap peas over medium heat for about 1 minute. Add snow peas and green peas. Cook for about 4 minutes, until all the peas are tender-crisp. Drain and immediately rinse with cold water to bring to room temperature. Drain.

3. In a bowl, toss mixed peas with mint vinaigrette to taste (you may have some left over). Add salt to taste. Set aside.

4. Arrange chopped pea greens on a serving platter. Spoon mixed peas over bed of greens. Scatter red pepper overtop. Garnish with reserved tendrils and flower buds.

Thai-Style Pea Soup

Slightly spicy and coconutty, with hints of garlic and lemongrass, this is a hot soup for the green soul. It's good for what ails you, tastes great and has a gorgeous emerald hue.

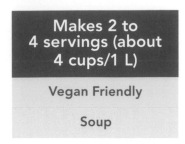

Makes 2 to 4 servings (about 4 cups/1 L)

Vegan Friendly

Soup

Tips

For the finest minced garlic, push it through a press.

To reduce the fat content in this dish, use light coconut milk.

You can find Thai curry pastes, both green and red, at most supermarkets.

If desired, substitute thawed frozen green peas, drained, for the fresh ones.

• Blender

6 oz	pea shoots	175 g
1 tbsp	oil	15 mL
1	small onion, diced	1
1	clove garlic, minced (see Tips, left)	1
1	can (14 oz/400 mL) coconut milk (see Tips, left)	1
1 tbsp	Thai green curry paste (see Tips, left)	15 mL
2 cups	vegetable stock	500 mL
1 tsp	kosher or coarse sea salt	5 mL
⅛ tsp	freshly ground black pepper	0.5 mL
1 cup	shelled fresh green peas (6 oz/175 g; see Tips, left)	250 mL

1. Trim pea shoots, discarding tough stems and setting aside curly tendrils and flower buds; you should have about 9 cups (2.25 L). Set aside in separate piles.

2. In a saucepan over medium heat, heat oil until shimmery. Add onion and cook, stirring often, for about 2 minutes, until softened and turning golden. Stir in garlic for 20 seconds. Stir in coconut milk and curry paste, then stock, salt and pepper. When mixture comes to a simmer, add pea shoots, reduce heat to medium-low and cook for about 15 minutes, until very tender.

3. Transfer mixture to blender and purée until smooth. Return to pan over medium heat. When mixture comes to a simmer, add green peas, reduce heat to medium-low and cook for 4 to 5 minutes, until peas are tender.

4. Ladle into serving bowls. Garnish with reserved tendrils and buds and serve warm.

Give Peas a Chance

Quadruple your peas and quadruple your pleasure. In this tasty green dish, snow peas, snap peas, garden peas and shoots are embellished with caramelized pearl onions and mint.

<table>
<tr><td>3 oz</td><td>pea shoots</td><td>90 g</td></tr>
<tr><td>2 tbsp</td><td>extra virgin olive oil</td><td>30 mL</td></tr>
<tr><td>12</td><td>small pearl onions, peeled (see Tips, left)</td><td>12</td></tr>
<tr><td>6 oz</td><td>sugar snap peas (about 1½ cups/375 mL, loosely packed), trimmed (see Tips, left)</td><td>175 g</td></tr>
<tr><td>6 oz</td><td>shelled fresh green peas (about 1 cup/ 250 mL; see Tips, left)</td><td>175 g</td></tr>
<tr><td>4 oz</td><td>snow peas (about 2 cups/500 mL, loosely packed), trimmed (see Tips, left)</td><td>125 g</td></tr>
<tr><td>1 tsp</td><td>kosher or coarse sea salt</td><td>5 mL</td></tr>
<tr><td>⅛ tsp</td><td>freshly ground black pepper</td><td>0.5 mL</td></tr>
<tr><td>3 tbsp</td><td>vegetable stock</td><td>45 mL</td></tr>
<tr><td>¼ cup</td><td>shredded or chopped fresh mint leaves (see Tips, left)</td><td>60 mL</td></tr>
</table>

Makes 2 to 4 servings (about 4 cups/1 L)

Vegan Friendly

Side dish

Tips

To peel pearl onions: Blanch onions in a saucepan of boiling water for 30 seconds, then drain and rinse with cold water until cool enough to handle. Using a small knife, trim the root ends and pull off the skins.

To trim and string snap and snow peas: Use a paring knife to nip off the tip at one end of the pod, then pull until a thin string peels off the seam. Repeat, starting at the other end.

Shelled fresh green peas are sweet and tender. Before using, rinse them under cold water until the water no longer looks foamy. Warning: They don't keep long. After a day or two in the crisper, they are apt to turn olive green and sour.

If desired, substitute thawed frozen green peas for the fresh ones. Make sure they are well drained and add them along with the pea greens in Step 2.

To shred mint leaves: Stack leaves, roll them up like a cigar and, using a sharp knife, cut the roll crosswise.

1. Using a sharp knife, trim pea shoots, discarding tough stems and wiry tendrils. Coarsely chop tender greens; you should have about 4 cups (1 L). Set aside.

2. In a large sauté pan over medium-low heat, heat oil until hot. Stir in onions and cook, shaking pan occasionally, for about 5 minutes, until golden brown and softened. Reduce heat to medium. Stir in snap peas for about 1 minute, until softened slightly. Add shelled peas, snow peas, salt and pepper. Cook, stirring often, for 30 seconds. Add stock, cover and steam for 2 to 3 minutes, until peas are tender-crisp and most of the liquid has evaporated. Add pea greens and stir for about 1 minute, until leaves wilt and stems soften.

3. Remove pan from heat. Season with salt to taste and stir in mint. Serve warm.

Pennywort

Centella asiatica

Other names: **Asiatic/Vietnamese pennywort, Asian coinwort, centella, kula bud, mother vegetable, spadeleaf, water pennywort, thunder god's root.**

Depending on where you are shopping, you may find pennywort identified as *bopop, brahmi, erba della tigri, gotu-kola, jie xuo cao, kodakan, ondelaga, pak nork, perook, rau ma, sombrerillo de agua, thankuni pata, tsubo kusa* **or** *vallaari.*

Native to India, Asia and the South Pacific, pennywort grows in swampy areas. It is both foraged wild and cultivated. As a leafy green it is popular in Vietnam, Thailand and Sri Lanka.

Pennywort has a long history as a medicinal green. It is mentioned in Ayurvedic and Chinese medical texts dating as far back as 3,000 years ago. In the 1800s pennywort was used to treat leprosy.

Varieties

"Pennywort" is a name applied to a diverse group of aquatic or moisture-loving low-lying or creeping plants with rounded leaves. Of the edible pennyworts, North American shoppers are most likely to encounter centella (*Centella asiatica*).

Unrelated stand-ins include water pennyworts such as Java pennywort (*Hydrocotyle javanica*) and dollarweed (*H. umbellata*). The latter is native to the Americas, where it is used in salads or as an herb. Water pennyworts are also known as marsh penny, Indian pennywort, rot grass or white rot.

Buy It

Pennywort is sold in Asian grocery stores, particularly those specializing in Vietnamese greens.

The leaves are small and circular and the stems are round and hollow, with some tinted purple. Look for firm leaves with no browning at the edges.

Store It

Wrap a damp paper towel around the stems and store the bunch in a resealable bag. Or pluck the leaves and discard the stems, wrap in paper towels, place in a resealable bag and refrigerate.

Tasting Notes

Pennywort is astringent and celery-like. Its flavor is grassy, with hints of cucumber and mint.

Health Notes

Although no official government analysis is available, pennywort is thought to contain vitamins A, B_6 and C, calcium, iron, niacin, phosphorus, riboflavin and thiamin.

Pennywort has been the subject of several scientific studies, some of which verified its efficacy in treating wounds and leg edemas. Pennywort has also been used in traditional Chinese, African and Indian (Ayurvedic) medicine to alleviate anxiety and nervous disorders, enhance memory and attention span, reduce blood pressure, improve eyesight, quell arthritis and boost sexual stamina. A practical Asian folk remedy for maintaining youthful vigor is to eat two pennywort leaves a day and spend an hour in the sun.

SUBSTITUTES

Chinese celery leaves

Pennywort will keep in the refrigerator for up to two days.

Prep It

For salads, use the leaves only. If making juice (see page 286), pinch off the leaves and tender stemlets. The stems look delicate but are too fibrous to consume.

To shred leaves, stack them, roll them up like a cigar and, using a sharp knife, slice the roll crosswise.

To clean it, rinse pennywort in cold water and spin-dry or pat dry with paper towels.

Consume It

Pennywort leaves may be shredded and eaten, raw or blanched, as a salad. Onion, citrus juice, chile and fresh coconut are sometimes added. The leaves are also added to cold summer rolls (rice-paper rolls) or used to make sambal, a kind of relish.

Pennywort's main claim to fame is as the base for a cold green beverage that the Vietnamese were drinking long before wheatgrass became the darling of juice bars. Pennywort juice is a staple in Vietnamese restaurants and is even sold canned. An optional preparation before juicing: soften the greens for up to 30 minutes by soaking them in cold water with a pinch of baking soda.

Pennywort leaves may also be steeped to prepare a light broth or tea.

Vietnamese Pennywort Juice

Icy refreshment comes with a side order of nutrition in this delightful beverage. I like to add lime as an accent, although it is neither necessary nor traditional. I add salt too, because it actually brings out the sweetness of the sugar, so you can use less.

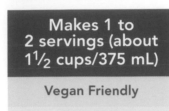

Makes 1 to 2 servings (about 1½ cups/375 mL)

Vegan Friendly

Beverage

Tips

Baking soda helps to soften the greens, making it easier to purée them and extract the juice. If you are in a hurry, you can skip soaking them.

If desired, you can use honey to taste instead of sugar. If you are a vegan, agave syrup is another option.

The juice will separate if it sits. Just stir it back together.

- Blender

1	bunch pennywort (2½ oz/75 g)	1
Pinch	baking soda (see Tips, left)	Pinch
1¼ to 1½ cups	water, divided	300 to 375 mL
2 tbsp	granulated sugar (see Tips, left)	30 mL
⅛ tsp	kosher or coarse sea salt	0.5 mL
1 tbsp	freshly squeezed lime juice	15 mL
	Ice cubes	

1. Pluck pennywort leaves and tender stemlets from stems; discard stems. Transfer greens to a bowl and add enough cold water to just cover. Add baking soda, swish to mix and set aside for 15 to 30 minutes.

2. Meanwhile, in a heatproof measuring cup, combine ¼ cup (60 mL) boiling water, sugar and salt; stir until dissolved. Stir in 1 cup (250 mL) cold water. Set aside.

3. Drain pennywort, rinsing and reserving bowl. In blender, combine pennywort and prepared sugar water. Pulse a few times to break down greens, then purée until smooth.

4. Using a fine-mesh sieve, strain mixture into reserved bowl. Press down with a spatula to extract as much juice as possible, then discard solids. Add lime juice. Taste and add remaining ¼ cup (60 mL) water, if desired.

5. Fill glasses with ice cubes. Pour in juice and serve immediately (see Tips, left).

Pepper Leaf

Capsicum frutescens

> *Other names:* **chile/sili leaves, bird's-eye chile leaves, chile bird pepper leaves, hot pepper leaves.**
>
> **Depending on where you are shopping, you may find pepper leaf identified as** *dahon ng sili, feuilles de piment* **or** *sili labuyo.*

Pepper leaf is not to be confused with la lot leaf (page 212), which is also called pepper leaf.

Chile pepper plants are cultivated as well as foraged worldwide, mainly for their fruit but also for their edible leaves. Peppers are a vital ingredient in cuisines around the globe. Pepper leaf, however, is an obscure commodity except in Southeast Asia.

Pepper plants originated in South America and were first cultivated more than 6,000 years ago. Chile peppers spread to Europe after Christopher Columbus and his crew encountered them in the Caribbean. They were named "peppers" because they invited comparisons to spicy black peppercorns. Portuguese and Arab traders traveling the spice routes introduced them to India, Asia and Africa.

Tasting Notes

Thawed frozen leaves have an herbal, spinachy scent and a distinct black pepper flavor, though capsicums are unrelated to peppercorn plants.

Health Notes

Although no official government analysis is available, pepper leaf is thought to contain vitamin A and calcium.

Pepper leaf is regarded as a potent herbal medicine. It has been used to alleviate respiratory conditions from colds to asthma and sinusitis. It has also been used to treat headaches, arthritis, varicose veins, menstrual cramps, muscle spasms and ulcer pains, as well as to strengthen the immune system, purge cholesterol and toxins, stimulate circulation and digestion, fight fatigue, lower blood sugar and blood pressure, and boost sex drive.

Varieties

There are many species of *Capsicum*. In recipes, pepper leaf is most often cited as the greenery from *C. frustescens*, a species that includes small, hot chiles such as bird's-eye, tabasco and cherry peppers. However, the leaves of other chiles are also edible.

Botanists are still arguing over the *C. frustescens* species. Some consider it to be part of the species *C. annuum*, so pepper leaf may be identified as such. *C. annuum* is the most extensively cultivated pepper species. Cultivars come in all shapes and sizes, from mild to hot, including bell peppers, jalapeños and cayennes.

Buy It

Pepper leaf is sold in Asian supermarkets, particularly those specializing in Filipino, Korean and Vietnamese ingredients. I have seen only packages of frozen leaves, which may be labeled "sili leaves."

SUBSTITUTES

spinach, la lot leaf,
watercress

Pepper leaves grow on notched stems. They are harvested when young, with the size depending on the cultivar. Chile pepper plants may be grown in home gardens. However, gardeners beware: the leaves of many cultivars must be cooked to neutralize plant toxins.

Store It

Store fresh leaves in resealable bags and refrigerate for up to two days.

Keep frozen packages in the freezer until you are ready to use them. Defrost overnight in the fridge.

Prep It

More than half of a frozen package of pepper leaf may be water. If desired, use that herbal, peppery liquid in your recipes in place of some stock.

Before using thawed pepper leaf, discard any tough stems you find among the leaves, then chop the leaves coarsely.

Consume It

Pepper leaf is never eaten fresh, and some cultivars are considered toxic unless cooked.

Add pepper leaf to stir-fries, eat it as a vegetable, or use it in Korean *banchan* (side dishes) or kimchi. It is also the star of a Filipino soup/stew called tinola (page 290).

When simmered, thawed frozen leaves are tender in about 10 minutes.

D Is for Drumstick

The **drumstick tree** (*Moringa oleifera*), also known as *malunggay, zogale* or *saragvani sing*, is famous for its long, thin seed pods as well as its nutritious leaves.

The pods and leaves are best known as Indian vegetables but are cultivated in the Philippines, Southeast Asia, Africa and Central and South America. Cultivation has also begun in Hawaii for distribution to the United States.

The leaves are eaten like spinach, fresh or cooked, in anything from curries to omelets. In North America the pods are widely sold in Asian grocery stores, but the fresh leaves are rare greens.

However, frozen drumstick leaves are available. Once thawed, they taste similar to but milder than pepper leaf. They are confusingly labeled "horseradish leaves" because the drumstick tree is also known as the horseradish tree — not because it is related to real horseradish, but because the roots resemble horseradish.

Rich in vitamins A, C and K, calcium and iron, these leafy greens have been used in folk medicine for a long list of ailments.

Relatives include southwest **African moringa** (*M. ovalifolia*) and **Ethiopian moringa** (*M. stenopetala*).

New Tinola

Tinola is classic comfort food from the Filipino kitchen. This simple vegetarian version omits the usual chicken, but pepper leaf, green papaya and garlicky, gingery stock ensure that it hits the spot. I'm not sure whether tinola is a thick soup or a thin stew. It is traditionally served with rice, but you don't need it.

Makes 4 servings (about 5½ cups/1.3 L)

Vegan Friendly

Soup

Tips

For the finest minced garlic, push it through a press.

To grate or purée gingerroot, use a kitchen rasp such as the kind made by Microplane.

To maintain more control over the saltiness of dishes, use reduced-sodium soy sauce. Depending on the type, 1 tbsp (15 mL) regular soy sauce can contain 1,000 mg or more of sodium. Reduced-sodium soy sauce contains about half that amount.

Be sure to use green papaya, which has cream-colored flesh and is not sweet. Do not substitute ripe papaya. When cooked, green papaya plays the role of a vegetable; it is mild and firm. A large green papaya weighs about 2 pounds (1 kg).

2	packages (8 oz/250 g each) frozen pepper leaf, thawed	2
2 cups	vegetable stock (approx.)	500 mL
¼ cup	extra virgin olive oil	60 mL
2	small onions, halved and thinly sliced	2
4	large cloves garlic, minced (see Tips, left)	4
1 tbsp	puréed gingerroot (see Tips, left)	15 mL
2 tbsp	soy sauce (see Tips, left)	30 mL
½	large green papaya, peeled, seeded and cut into ¼-inch (0.5 cm) pieces (see Tips, left)	½
	Kosher or coarse sea salt	
	Hot sauce	

1. Using a sieve, strain thawed pepper leaf, reserving liquid in a large measuring cup. Add enough stock to liquid to measure 4 cups (1 L). Set aside. Remove and discard any tough stems from leaves (thin stems are okay). Using a sharp knife, chop leaves coarsely. Set aside.

2. In a large saucepan over medium heat, heat oil until shimmery. Add onions and cook, stirring often, for about 3 minutes, until softened and golden. Stir in garlic and ginger for 30 seconds. Stir in stock mixture, soy sauce and papaya. When mixture comes to a simmer, cover, reduce heat to medium-low and cook for about 10 minutes, until papaya is barely tender. Stir in pepper leaves. Simmer, uncovered, for about 10 minutes, until papaya and leaves are tender. Season with salt to taste.

3. Ladle into bowls and dash in hot sauce to taste. Serve warm.

Variations

Filipinos substitute chayote when they don't have green papaya, and drumstick leaves (page 288) — which they call *malunggay* — when they don't have pepper leaf.

Perilla

Perilla frutescens

Other names: **beefsteak leaf/plant, Chinese/ Japanese basil, purple mint, rattlesnake weed, sesame leaf, shiso, tia-to, wild coleus.**

Depending on where you are shopping, you may find perilla identified as *ban tulsi, bai sui, bhangira, bladmynte, gee so, jen, kemangi, perillablad, nga khi mon, qing sui, silam, zi su* **or** *veripeippi.*

Perilla originated in East Asia and eventually spread to North America, where it may grow wild.

Wild perilla is considered an inedible weed, particularly the red types. The leaves and seeds contain abundant perilla ketone, an oil that causes fluid to accumulate in the lungs of grazing animals; this condition is called perilla mint toxicosis. Over the centuries perilla ketone has been bred out of cultivated perilla.

Perilla is now widely enjoyed as a leafy green and herb. It was bred in China and transplanted to Japan, Korea, Vietnam and Laos. It is also cultivated in India, Iran, Russia, Ukraine, parts of Europe and North America.

Varieties

Perilla is a member of the mint family. There are green and red (purple) types. Different cultivars are linked to different cultures: Korea's perilla is known as sesame leaf, Japan's as shiso and Vietnam's as tia-to.

Sesame leaf (sometimes differentiated as *Perilla frustescens japonica*) is not related to the sesame plant (*Sesamum indicum*). It is sometimes called "oil perilla" because it was originally grown for the oil pressed from its seeds, which was used in lamps in Asia during the Middle Ages. Today sesame leaf is the common form of culinary perilla in Korea.

Sesame leaf is also known as plain green perilla, red leaf perilla, wild sesame, *dulketip, kkaennip* or *tulkkae*. In Japan this variety may be called *daun shiso, egoma* or *junen* — the last translated as "ten years" because it supposedly adds that much to one's lifespan. However, sesame leaf is rarely used in Japan. The perilla of choice there is known as shiso.

Shiso (*P. frutescens crispa*), also known as ooba or big leaf, has softer, smaller leaves and is more potent than sesame leaf

Tasting Notes

Complex flavors and intriguing fragrances make perilla leaves delightful, but they are an acquired taste.

Perilla is fragrant and pleasantly peppery, with subtle mint and anise accents. Sesame leaf perilla offers hints of basil and lemon, while shiso and tia-to both have vanilla and horseradish accents.

Sesame leaf perilla is milder than shiso because of the absence of an essential oil called perillaldehyde, which is used by perfume makers. Shiso and tia-to have a potent, pronounced flavor with perfume-like accents — enough, perhaps, to be off-putting.

perilla. Shiso is a mainstay of Japanese cuisine. There is a green type (*ao-shiso*) and a red type (*aka-shiso*), plus cultivars of both with ruffled leaves (*chirimen-shiso*). Purple shiso (sometimes differentiated as *P. frustescens acuta*), also known as purple mint, is mainly used to prepare pickled *ume* (Japanese plums) or a sweet shiso beverage, and its flowers (ear shiso) are used as edible garnishes.

Tia-to (*P. frustescens tia-to*), the perilla variety that is widely used in Vietnam, is similar to shiso.

Besides the three main varieties, there is a lesser-known cultivar called lemon-scented perilla (sometimes differentiated as *P. frustescens citriodora*). It is more common in India.

Buy It

Various types of perilla are sold in Asian supermarkets, particularly those specializing in Japanese, Korean or Vietnamese ingredients. Perilla stalks are sold either *au naturel* or the leaves are plucked and packaged.

Korean shops sell perfect large sesame leaves, neatly stacked in packets, for customers who crave seasoned sesame leaves (page 294), a fermented side dish. Sesame leaves also come spiced and canned. Shiso leaves are sold stacked in small plastic bags. Tia-to leaves are sold on the stem.

Perilla leaves are serrated. Sesame leaves are larger, broader and flatter than shiso leaves, which are in turn larger than tia-to. Sesame leaves are saw-toothed; they are dark green on top and lighter green with a purple tinge on the underside. Shiso leaves are deeply jagged and more evenly colored. Tia-to is purple on the underside, with some edible green, bulrush-shaped shoots at the tops of the leaf clusters.

Store It

Perilla leaves wilt and dry out easily. Pluck the leaves from the stems and discard the stems. Stack the leaves and, if desired, wrap a barely damp paper towel around them; place in a resealable bag, then refrigerate.

Sesame and tia-to leaves will keep in the refrigerator for up to two days. Shiso leaves will keep for one day.

Prep It

Perilla stems are stringy; discard them. If leaves are purchased trimmed and stacked, cut off the stem stubs and any center veins that look too thick. However, if cooked, the tender stemlets attached to the leaves are edible.

Rinse leaves in cold water just before using, then pat dry or air-dry.

Consume It

Perilla is extremely versatile. It may be used as an herb or a leafy green, raw or blanched, in savory or sweet dishes.

The leaves are found in everything from soup to beverages. They are served with sushi or sashimi as a garnish or an ingredient, tossed in raw mixed salads and chopped and stirred into cold dishes such as summer rolls (rice-paper wraps with fresh fillings). They can also be used as wrappers; fried as tempura; added to rice noodles, stir-fries and stews; pickled or marinated as a Korean *banchan* (side dish) or kimchi; used to prepare granita or a simple syrup for desserts; or dried and mixed with salt to sprinkle over food. In Japan they are even added to commercial cola.

Sesame leaves are the least like herbs and the most likely to be served on their own. Shiso and tia-to are more herblike.

SUBSTITUTES

mizuna, la lot leaf, methi

Timber! Tree Greens

Trees large and small are a source of edible greens around the world. Here are some examples not covered in other parts of this book:

- The leaves, buds and shoots of **Chinese toon** (*Toona sinensis*), also known as Chinese mahogany cedar, *hsiang tsun* or *telekucha*, are used as vegetables in China. The leaves are said to be aromatic, with an onion flavor. Red leaves are considered superior to green leaves.
- Also used as vegetables in various parts of the world are **tree lettuce leaves** (*Pisonia grandis*). In Australia they are "bush tucker" — wild leaves eaten as salad greens or cooked vegetables.
- The leaves of **climbing wattle** (*Acacia pennata*) and **cassod tree** (*Senna siamea*) play a role in Burmese and Thai cuisine. Cassod leaves are preboiled and the water is discarded before they are added to curries.
- The young leaves and shoots of **teakwood** (*Tectona grandis*) are used in curries and jackfruit dumplings in its native India, Indonesia and parts of Thailand.
- Leaves, flowers and pods of the **hummingbird tree** (*Sesbania grandiflora*), also known as scarlet wisteria or agati, are eaten in parts of Southeast Asia. The leaves are also used medicinally, to disinfect the mouth and throat.
- The leaves of **ujuju** (*Myrianthus arboreus*) are a popular indigenous vegetable in Nigeria, where they are usually eaten in soup.
- **Olive leaves** (*Oleo europaea*) have been used medicinally in Mediterranean countries for thousands of years. The leaves may be brewed as tea, and olive leaf tea is now sold in North America.

Seasoned Sesame Leaves

Marinated and fermented sesame leaves are an iconic Korean **banchan** *(side dish).*
Although **banchan** *are small, some Koreans confess to the guilty pleasure of scarfing down*
these intensely spicy, salty and fragrant leaves with just hot rice. The dish is an acquired
taste but, after trying it, I appreciate its addictive qualities.

	Makes 2 servings
	Vegan Friendly
	Appetizer

Tips

If desired, you can double this recipe.

Gochugaru is Korean chile powder. It comes in fine, medium and coarse versions. I prefer the medium grain, which comes as shiny flakes.

Cane sugar is likely to be filtered through bone char, while beet sugar is not. Most labels don't indicate the source of the sugar. If you are following a vegan diet, use unbleached organic sugar that has not been filtered through bone char, or a sweetener such as agave syrup.

For the finest minced garlic, push it through a press.

Use large Korean sesame leaf perilla, not shiso or tia-to, for this recipe. Make sure you pat dry the washed leaves before starting the recipe.

This dish tastes best after a week. Leftovers will last a couple of weeks in the fridge.

1 tbsp	soy sauce	15 mL
1 tbsp	vegetable stock	15 mL
½ tsp	rice vinegar	2 mL
2 tsp	gochugaru chile flakes (see Tips, left)	10 mL
1 tsp	granulated sugar (see Tips, left)	5 mL
¼ tsp	kosher or coarse sea salt	1 mL
1	clove garlic, minced (see Tips, left)	1
1 tbsp	finely chopped fresh chives	15 mL
12	trimmed sesame leaves (see Tips, left)	12

1. In a small bowl, prepare a marinade by combining soy sauce, stock, vinegar, gochugaru, sugar, salt, garlic and chives.

2. In an airtight container just big enough to hold sesame leaves in a stack, spread a small spoonful of marinade over the bottom. Top with a leaf facing up (the darker green side). Using the back of a small spoon, smear some marinade thinly over leaf. Top with another leaf, apply marinade and repeat, to create a stack of 12 leaves. Spoon any leftover marinade overtop.

3. Cover and refrigerate for at least 2 days and up to a week before eating (see Tips, left).

Purslane

Portulaca oleracea

Other names: **common/garden/green purslane, little hogweed, Mexican parsley, pusley, verdolaga.**

Depending on where you are shopping, you may find purslane identified as *antrakla, bakleh, buglosa, ghol, glystida, hierba grasa, koorsa, lonica, ma chi xian, perpehen, phak bia yai, postelein, pourpier, punarva, semitozu, tarfela* **or** *yerba aurato.*

Purslane is sometimes called pigweed, but it should not be confused with amaranth (page 28), which is also called pigweed. In some translated Middle Eastern recipes, purslane is mistakenly called mâche (page 223).

Purslane is both a weed and a leafy green, both foraged and cultivated worldwide. It is thought to be native to Eurasia, perhaps to India or Iran.

Purslane spread through the ancient world 4,000 years ago. Evidence of it has been found at archeological sites in the Mediterranean. The ancients valued purslane for its supposed healing powers. Pliny suggested that purslane amulets be worn to repel evil. In China the earliest recorded use dates to 500 CE. Purslane reached Europe, then was naturalized in the Americas during colonization. It is also found in North Africa and Australasia.

Purslane is particularly valued as a salad green or vegetable in France and other European countries, the Middle East and Mexico. It is also used in the cuisines of the Caribbean, Asia, India (where it is sometimes cited as Gandhi's favorite food) and Japan (where it is one of the symbolic greens traditionally served for the New Year).

In North America purslane is often dismissed as a weed. Pesky and persistent, it grows as groundcover even in the most arid sandy or rocky soils, as well as the proverbial crack in the sidewalk. Recently some non-mainstream farmers — notably in California — recognized its potential and began cultivating it.

Tasting Notes

Purslane is mildly sweet and sour, with hints of lemon and rhubarb. It has crunchy, slightly mucilaginous paddle-shaped leaves with succulent stems. When cooked, it has a spinach-like taste.

Varieties

Many varieties of purslane, both wild and cultivated, have spread across the globe. Common purslane (*Portulaca oleracea*) is the best known. Although it is also known as wild purslane, it may be cultivated. Its sibling, kitchen garden purslane (*P. oleracea sativa*), also known as large-leaf purslane, is a domesticated form that is considered tenderer. Garden purslane comes in the cultivars red purslane (with reddish stems and green leaves) and milder golden purslane (smaller and tinged with yellow). Common purslane spreads in mats, while garden purslane is more upright.

Close relatives include pink purslane (*P. pilosa*), also known as kiss-me-quick, which is used as a medicinal herb in South America, and chicken weed (*P. quadrifida*), also known as Formosa purslane. Moss rose purslane (*P. grandiflora*), also known as time flower, ten-o'clock/eleven-o'clock flower, Mexican rose or sunplant, is an ornamental admired for its blooms rather than eaten.

Edible plants that are dubbed purslane but are unrelated include:

- **winter purslane** (*Claytonia perfoliata*), also known as Cuban spinach, Indian lettuce, verdolaga de Cuba and miner's lettuce (so called because California gold rush miners ate it to ward off scurvy). This is a hardy winter salad green that reportedly tastes like spinach, watercress or mâche and looks like miniature lily pads. Winter purslane is cultivated in Europe.
- **Siberian miner's lettuce** (*C. sibirica*), also known as pink purslane, Siberian spring beauty or candy flower, has beet-flavored leaves and is widespread in the United Kingdom.
- **sea purslane** (*Halimione portulacoides*) and **sea/shoreline purslane** (*Sesuvium portulacastrum*), found in tidal basins and salt marshes. Both are considered succulent, crunchy, salty specimens.

SUBSTITUTES

sorrel, watercress,
mâche, jute leaf,
Malabar spinach

Buy It

Although it grows willy-nilly in North America (a boon for foragers), purslane is rarely found in mainstream supermarkets. It makes brief appearances from spring to fall at specialty greengrocers, farmers' markets and Middle Eastern and Hispanic shops.

Purslane is often likened to a miniature jade plant. Small rounded or spatulate crisp green leaves, about 1 to 2 inches (2.5 to 5 cm) long, grow in clusters on smooth stems. Look for purslane that appears perky, not wilted or browned. Stems and leaves should be juicy.

Store It

Purslane doesn't keep long. Wrap a damp paper towel around the base of the stems and place in a resealable bag, then refrigerate.

Purslane will keep in the refrigerator for up to two days.

Prep It

Purslane wilts and bruises easily, so handle it gently. Golden purslane is considered particularly delicate.

If desired, pluck the leaves from the stems for separate cooking. Leaves may be used whole and the stems sliced or chopped. Late in the growing season, however, the stems are too fibrous to eat. Cut off and discard parts of stems more than ⅛ inch (3 mm) thick or the tough reddish parts of the stems. Rinse purslane gently in cold water and place on paper towels to air-dry.

Consume It

The young stems, leaves and flower buds are all edible. If desired, cook the stems like spinach and use the leaves like watercress. The leaves are best raw.

The leaves and stemlets make a tangy addition to salads or sandwiches. The tips — the upper inch or two (2.5 to 5 cm) of leaves and stems on the plant — are the tenderest and thus best for raw dishes. Purslane is famously tossed in Middle Eastern salads such as fattoush (page 300) and may be used in Greek salads in place of lettuce. Purslane pesto is another popular option. The stems and larger leaves are often pickled.

Purslane may be sautéed as a vegetable or added to soups or pastas. The leaves may be breaded or fried.

This green is mucilaginous, so it has the power to slightly thicken dishes but winds up slimy and limp if overcooked. Cook stems and leaves separately. Purslane stems will cook to tender-crisp in 1 to 3 minutes when boiled, steamed or sautéed. Leaves wilt in 10 to 20 seconds; they may simply be stirred into a hot dish.

Don't be alarmed if black specks appear in your purslane dish — they're the seeds. Tiny and edible, though tasteless, the seeds appear after the plant flowers.

Verdolaga Tortilla Soup

*In Mexico, cooks use a variety of wild and cultivated greens, including purslane, which they call **verdolaga**. Whatever you call it, you will enjoy it in this delicious south-of-the-border soup.*

**Makes 4 servings
(about 6 cups/1.5 L)**

Vegan Friendly

Soup

Tips

Vegans should check the label on tortillas to make sure they do not contain lard.

For the finest minced garlic, push it through a press.

Canned chipotle chiles in adobo sauce are sold in supermarkets.

Mexican crema is sold in Hispanic grocery stores and well-stocked supermarkets. Crema is Mexico's version of crème fraîche. It is a type of soured cream, but not as tangy as standard sour cream.

To prepare the purslane for this recipe: Trim, discarding tough parts of stems. Pluck leaves from stems. Coarsely chop stems. Place leaves and stems in separate piles.

- Baking sheet lined with paper towels

6 tbsp	extra virgin olive oil, divided	90 mL
4	corn tortillas (6 inches/15 cm in diameter), each cut into 8 wedges (see Tips, left)	4
1	small white onion, diced	1
1 tsp	kosher or coarse sea salt	5 mL
2	large cloves garlic, minced (see Tips, left)	2
2 tsp	mashed chipotle chile in adobo sauce (see Tips, left)	10 mL
4 cups	vegetable stock	1 L
1 cup	fresh or thawed frozen corn kernels	250 mL
1	ripe plum tomato, peeled and diced	1
1	bunch purslane (4 oz/125 g), trimmed and stems chopped (see Tips, left)	1
2 tbsp	chopped fresh cilantro leaves	30 mL
1 to 2 tbsp	freshly squeezed lime juice	15 to 30 mL
	Freshly ground black pepper	
1	large ripe but firm avocado	1
	Sour cream, non-dairy alternative or Mexican crema (see Tips, left)	

1. In a large skillet over medium heat, heat $1/4$ cup (60 mL) oil until shimmery. In batches, fry tortilla wedges for about 2 minutes, turning once, until golden brown. Drain on prepared baking sheet. Set aside.

2. In a saucepan over medium-low heat, heat remaining oil until hot. Add onion and salt. Cook, stirring occasionally, for about 10 minutes, until soft and golden. Stir in garlic and chipotle for about 1 minute. Add stock, corn and tomato. When mixture comes to a simmer, cook for 3 to 5 minutes, until corn is tender-crisp. Stir in purslane stems, and cook for about 1 minute, until tender-crisp.

3. Remove from heat. Stir in purslane leaves, cilantro and lime juice and season with salt and pepper to taste.

4. Cut avocado into $1/2$-inch (1 cm) chunks or thin slices. Ladle soup into wide, shallow serving bowls. Top with avocado pieces, prepared tortilla wedges and a dollop of sour cream. Serve immediately.

Fattoush

Fattoush is Lebanon's most famous salad and a staple in other regions of the Middle East. Also known as peasant salad, it is fabulously tangy and crunchy. Fattoush is often served at meze tables (meze being the Mediterranean equivalent of tapas).

	Makes 6 to 10 servings (about 12 cups/3 L)	
	Vegan Friendly	
	Salad	

Tips

Pomegranate molasses is sometimes labeled pomegranate concentrate. It is not very sweet. You can find it in Middle Eastern grocery stores.

For the finest minced garlic, push it through a press.

I prefer kosher salt because it tastes better than iodized table salt and (ideally) contains no additives. Table salts and some sea salts contain additives such as iodine compounds (iodides), anti-clumping agents and even sugar (in the form of dextrose, which is used to stabilize iodine). Although the North American Salt Institute states that kosher salt "contains no additives," some kosher salt brands do contain additives such as anti-clumping agents. If you have concerns, check the label.

A romaine heart is the tender inner part of a head of romaine.

- Preheat oven or toaster oven to 400°F (200°C)
- Baking sheet with rack on top

Dressing

1½ to 2 tbsp	freshly squeezed lemon juice	22 to 30 mL
1 tsp	pomegranate molasses (see Tips, left)	5 mL
2	cloves garlic, minced (see Tips, left)	2
1 tsp	kosher or coarse sea salt (see Tips, left)	5 mL
⅛ tsp	freshly ground black pepper	0.5 mL
¼ cup	extra virgin olive oil	60 mL

Salad

2	pocket pitas (8-inch/20 cm diameter)	2
4 tsp	extra virgin olive oil	20 mL
	Kosher or coarse sea salt	
1	romaine heart, sliced crosswise into ½-inch (1 cm) strips (see Tips, left)	1
2 oz	purslane leaves (about 1¾ cups/425 mL, loosely packed)	60 g
1 cup	fresh flat-leaf (Italian) parsley leaves	250 mL
¼ cup	fresh mint leaves, slivered	60 mL
12	cherry tomatoes, halved	12
4	mini cucumbers (12 oz/375 g), quartered lengthwise and sliced into ½-inch (1 cm) pieces	4
4	radishes, sliced	4
½	green bell pepper, cut into ½-inch (1 cm) pieces	½
1 cup	coarsely diced red onion	250 mL
1 tbsp	ground sumac (see Tips, page 301)	15 mL
12	oil-cured black olives, pitted	12

1. *Dressing:* In a small bowl, whisk together 1½ tbsp (22 mL) lemon juice, pomegranate molasses, garlic, salt and pepper. Whisk in oil. Whisk in remaining lemon juice, if desired. Set aside.

2. *Salad:* Brush pitas with oil on both sides and place on prepared baking sheet. Sprinkle lightly with salt to taste. Transfer to oven and toast for 10 minutes or until golden brown (see Tips, page 301). Set aside to cool completely. Break into bite-size pieces.

Sumac is a tangy spice made from the ground red berries of a decorative shrub. It is a signature ingredient in Middle Eastern cuisine. Ground sumac can be found in spice shops and Middle Eastern grocery stores.

For fattoush, the pitas are traditionally fried, but I prefer to bake them instead, to cut fat and calories.

3. In a large bowl, toss romaine, purslane, parsley, mint, tomatoes, cucumbers, radishes, green pepper and onion with dressing until evenly coated. Add pita pieces and toss briefly. Season with salt to taste.
4. Transfer salad to a serving platter. Sprinkle with sumac and scatter olives overtop. Serve immediately.

Variations

If you don't have purslane, use mâche, watercress or sorrel.

If you enjoy radish greens (see page 310), chop and add some to the salad along with the radishes.

If you are not a vegan, try adding crumbled feta to taste.

Purslane Succotash

There'll be no shouts of "sufferin' succotash!" when you serve this savory mélange of lima beans and vegetables.

	Makes 2 to 4 servings (about 4 cups/1 L)	
	Vegan Friendly	
	Side dish	

Tip

Slightly sweet white wine balances the flavors in this dish and complements the tangy purslane. I used leftover champagne that had gone flat. However, if you only have dry white wine, it's fine to use that.

To prepare the purslane for this recipe: Trim, discarding tough part of stems. Pluck leaves from stems. Coarsely chop stems. Place leaves and stems in separate piles.

1 tbsp	unsalted butter or non-dairy alternative	15 mL
1 tbsp	extra virgin olive oil	15 mL
2	shallots, chopped	2
1	red bell pepper, finely chopped	1
2	cloves garlic, finely chopped	2
1 cup	fresh or thawed frozen corn kernels	250 mL
1 cup	thawed frozen lima beans	250 mL
1	bunch purslane (4 oz/125 g), trimmed and stems chopped (see Tips, left)	1
1 tsp	kosher or coarse sea salt	5 mL
½ cup	slightly sweet white wine (see Tip, left)	125 mL
2	small plum tomatoes, peeled, seeded and diced	2

1. In a large skillet over medium heat, melt butter with oil. Add shallots, red pepper and garlic. Cook, stirring often, for about 1 minute, until softened. Add corn, lima beans and salt. Cook, stirring often, for 3 to 4 minutes, until softened. Add purslane stems and wine, increase heat to high and cook for about 2 minutes, until almost evaporated.
2. Remove from heat. Stir in tomatoes and purslane leaves. Season with salt to taste and serve warm.

Fiesta Salad

Tortillas, greens, beans and cheese turn this Tex-Mex dinner salad into a fiesta. You won't walk away from the table hungry.

Makes 4 large servings

Salad

Tips

I prefer kosher salt because it tastes better than iodized table salt and (ideally) contains no additives. Table salts and some sea salts contain additives such as iodine compounds (iodides), anti-clumping agents and even sugar (in the form of dextrose, which is used to stabilize iodine). Although the North American Salt Institute states that kosher salt "contains no additives," some kosher salt brands do contain additives such as anti-clumping agents. If you have concerns, check the label.

Slice the avocado just before adding it to the salad; otherwise, it will discolor.

- Baking sheet lined with paper towels

3 tbsp	extra virgin olive oil	45 mL
4	corn tortillas (6 inches/15 cm in diameter), each cut into 8 wedges	4
	Kosher or coarse sea salt (see Tips, left)	
4 oz	leaf lettuce, torn into bite-size pieces (about 6 cups/1.5 L, loosely packed)	125 g
1 cup	loosely packed purslane leaves	250 mL
2	small tomatoes, diced	2
1 cup	diced red onion	250 mL
½ cup	diced red bell pepper	125 mL
½ cup	diced yellow bell pepper	125 mL
½ cup	diced green bell pepper	125 mL
½ cup	Lime Herb Dressing (page 452)	125 mL
1	can (14 oz/398 mL) black beans, rinsed and drained	1
4 oz	Monterey Jack cheese, shredded (1 cup/250 mL)	125 g
1	avocado, sliced (see Tips, left)	1

1. In a large skillet over medium heat, heat oil until shimmery. In two batches, fry tortilla wedges for 3 minutes or until golden brown, turning once. Transfer to prepared baking sheet to drain. Salt lightly. Set aside.

2. In a large bowl, combine lettuce, purslane, tomatoes, onion and bell peppers. Add dressing to taste (you will have some left over) and toss to coat evenly. Season with salt to taste.

3. Transfer to a serving platter or individual plates. Top salad with beans, cheese and avocado. Pile tortilla wedges on top. Serve immediately.

Variation

If you don't have purslane, use watercress, mâche or sorrel.

Radicchio

Cichorium intybus rubifolium

Other names: **Italian chicory, leaf/red chicory, red endive.**

Depending on where you are shopping, you may find radicchio identified as *chicorée sauvage rouge* **or** *hong ju ju.*

Radicchio is descended from the cultivated chicory eaten since ancient times. Modern cultivars were first bred in 15th-century Italy. Dark red radicchio is a relative latecomer, however; it appeared after 1860. Varieties of radicchio are named after the Italian towns or regions where they originated, such as Treviso. Italians consider radicchio a culinary treasure, and they began exporting it to North America in the 1970s. It caught on slowly, first gaining acceptance as a colorful ingredient in mixed salads.

Red radicchio is the most common type in North America. Shoppers who are familiar with only red radicchio may be puzzled to find this vegetable classified as a leafy *green*. However, radicchio comes in colors ranging from white to purple, and these relatively unusual varieties have started to appear in mainstream supermarkets.

Varieties

Radicchio is a cultivated chicory that comes in a spherical or football shape and varying colors. Red radicchio (*Cichorium intybus rubifolium*) has purplish red leaves with white ribs and veins. Three common types of red radicchio are Chioggia (round, grapefruit-sized, sturdy), Verona (small, loose, oval head) and Treviso (tapered head with narrow, pointed leaves ranging from pink to dark red). Other radicchios have variegated or speckled leaves in shades of pink, red and green. There is also an all-white cultivar.

My favorite is radicchio di Castelfranco (*C. intybus variegatum*), also known as edible rose or rose of winter, because it unfolds like a flower. It is a psychedelic delight, with freckles and swirls of purple on pastel lime leaves in a small, round head. An heirloom variety from the Veneto area near Venice, it is protected by Italian designation-of-origin rules (which aim to prevent the

Tasting Notes

Red radicchio is juicy, with a bittersweet finish and a hint of beet. The leaves are tender but firm. Various types of radicchio taste similar, although some are milder than others.

Health Notes

Radicchio contains vitamins B_6, C, E and K, copper, folate, iron, magnesium, manganese, pantothenic acid, phosphorus, potassium and zinc.

In herbal medicine, chicories have been used to treat gallstones, sinus problems, internal parasites and cuts or bruises, as well as used as a liver stimulant. The ancients gave it to insomniacs. They were on to something — radicchio contains intybin, a sedative and painkiller found in the *C. intybus* species of plants.

1 round radicchio = 6 to 10 oz (175 to 300 g); 1 football-shaped = 4 to 6 oz (125 to 175 g)

•

8 oz (250 g) head, cored, leaves torn, coarsely chopped or shredded = 6½ cups (1.5 L), loosely packed

•

2 oz (60 g) torn, coarsely chopped or shredded radicchio = 1½ cups (375 mL), loosely packed

SUBSTITUTES

Belgian endive, escarole

marketing of copycat varieties originating elsewhere). The leaves are delicate and relatively mild.

Sugarloaf radicchio (*C. intybus pan de zucchero*) is green, romaine-shaped and sometimes classified as a separate chicory. It is not usually seen in North American supermarkets.

Buy It

Radicchio is a supermarket staple. Look for crisp, vibrant leaves with marble-white veins. Avoid specimens with leaves that are withered or browned at the edges. Check the stem end for reddish mold.

Store It

Swathe radicchio tightly in plastic wrap. Or wrap it in paper towels, place in a resealable bag and refrigerate.

Radicchio will keep in the refrigerator for up to one week.

Prep It

Before consuming radicchio, pull off any outer leaves that are wilted or cracked. If eating it raw, cut out the firm core.

Tear the leaves into bite-sized pieces. Or halve the head lengthwise and core, then slice the pieces crosswise.

To wash, rinse cut radicchio in cold water and spin-dry.

Consume It

In Europe radicchio is often cooked, but in North America it is usually served raw. Although it is famous as a salad "green," it can be sautéed, roasted or grilled. It can also be used as a topping for pizza.

People who are sensitive to bitter flavors should try cooking radicchio. When cooked, it turns brown and sweet and the bitterness is tamed.

B Is for Blanching

Although they look different, red radicchio and white Belgian endive are both engineered by the same technique: blanching. The young shoots are pulled from the earth and transferred to darkened conditions to grow. The lack of sunlight prevents chlorophyll, the green pigment in plants, from becoming active. Thus the background colors dominate — red in the case of radicchio, white in the case of Belgian endive. Other vegetables such as celery are blanched too. Because chlorophyll is bitter, blanching also makes plants sweeter and more delicate.

There are various ways to accomplish blanching: covering growing plants completely with soil (white asparagus is an example), shading them with boards or pots, or transferring them to dark sheds. Some vegetables, such as lettuce and cabbage, are naturally somewhat blanched, as the outer leaves protect the inner ones from sunlight.

Radicchio and Cauliflower Salad with Crumb Topping

I enjoy substantial winter salads like this one. For a full vegetarian meal, add a soup course. This recipe makes a big salad; you can halve the amount, if desired.

Makes 4 to 8 servings

Vegan Friendly

Salad

Tip

You'll need most of a tiny head of cauliflower. The florets should be about 2 inches (5 cm) wide. Cut larger ones into chunks.

1 lb	cauliflower florets (see Tip, left)	500 g
1	head radicchio, leaves torn or sliced	1
1 cup	pitted, sliced oil-cured black olives	250 mL
⅓ cup	Garlic Herb Vinaigrette (page 449)	75 mL
1 cup	Garlic Herb Crumb Topping (page 456)	250 mL

1. In a covered steamer basket set over 1 inch (2.5 cm) of boiling water, cook cauliflower over medium heat for about 10 minutes, until tender but firm. Uncover and set aside to release steam and cool to room temperature.

2. In a large bowl, toss cooked cauliflower, radicchio and olives with vinaigrette. Transfer to a serving platter or individual plates. Sprinkle with crumb topping and serve immediately.

Which Chicory Is Which?

If ever there was a confusing group of greens, chicory is it. Chicory comes in many varieties: wild, cultivated and even so-called cultivated wild chicory. Chicories may be loose-leafed or formed into heads, with thin stems or thick leaves. They may be green, red, purple, yellow or white. Some resemble dandelion greens, some look like lettuces. Distinguishing between them is confusing, and so is talking about them. Judging by appearances, it's hard to believe these greens are relatives. To top it all off, the names *chicory* and *endive* are all over the map, their usage often depending on which side of the pond you are on.

To sort them out, think of the chicory clan as two related families (or species). Endives (*Cichorium endivia*) include escarole, curly endive and frisée. Common chicories (*Cichorium intybus*) include Belgian endive, radicchio and catalogna.

Then there are the wild ones. Wild chicory (*C. intybus*), also known as coffee weed, blue sailors or wild cornflower, is a common roadside plant with edible leaves and flowers. Some varieties have been cultivated as greens or animal fodder. Root chicory (*C. intybus sativum*) is also known as Magdeburg chicory or large-rooted wild chicory. It is most famously grown as a coffee substitute: the roots are roasted and ground to create chicory coffee, nostalgically known by the brand name Camp Coffee. Medieval monks grew this variety.

Italian wild chicory (*C. intybus foliosum*), small-leaved chicory (*C. intybus parvifolium*) and bitter wild chicory (*C. intybus sylvaticum*) are other close relatives. Meanwhile, endive's ancestors include wild annual endive (*C. endivia pumilum*) and wild endive (*C. endivia divericatum*), also known as cultivated annual endive.

Big Bold Salad

This one's a beauty. Bitter greens, herbs, smoked cheese, pickled onions and roasted garlic dressing make it a taste sensation. Serve this as a dinner salad, following a soup course.

Makes 2 to 4 servings

Vegan Friendly

Salad

Tips

To shave fennel, use a sharp knife to slice it very thinly crosswise.

I prefer kosher salt because it tastes better than iodized table salt and (ideally) contains no additives. Table salts and some sea salts contain additives such as iodine compounds (iodides), anti-clumping agents and even sugar (in the form of dextrose, which is used to stabilize iodine). Although the North American Salt Institute states that kosher salt "contains no additives," some kosher salt brands do contain additives such as anti-clumping agents. If you have concerns, check the label.

3 oz	radicchio, torn into pieces (about 2 cups/500 mL, loosely packed)	90 g
2 oz	baby arugula (about 5 cups/1.25 L, loosely packed)	60 g
1 cup	shaved fennel (see Tips, left)	250 mL
1 cup	coarsely chopped fresh parsley leaves	250 mL
½ cup	fresh basil leaves, slivered	125 mL
½ cup	Roasted Garlic Dressing (page 454)	125 mL
4 oz	smoked gouda cheese, shredded (about 1½ cups/375 mL), or smoked tofu, cubed	125 g
½ cup	Quick Pickled Onions (page 455)	125 mL
2	tomatoes, cut into wedges	2
	Kosher or coarse sea salt (see Tips, left)	
	Freshly ground black pepper	

1. In a large bowl, combine radicchio, arugula, fennel, parsley and basil. Add dressing, to taste (you will have some left over), and toss to coat. Transfer to a serving platter.

2. Scatter cheese over center of greens. Scatter pickled onions around cheese. Arrange tomato wedges around perimeter. Season tomatoes with salt and pepper, to taste. Serve immediately.

Salad Sicilia

Sicilian salad is traditionally prepared with wild chicory, but you don't have to stumble through the woods to enjoy this fabulously assertive dish. I have substituted some cultivated close relatives: radicchio and escarole.

Makes 4 servings

Vegan Friendly

Salad

Tips

If you can't find blood oranges, which are sold seasonally in supermarkets, use navel oranges.

Cane sugar is likely to be filtered through bone char, while beet sugar is not. Most labels don't indicate the source of the sugar. If you are following a vegan diet, use unbleached organic sugar that has not been filtered through bone char, or a sweetener such as agave syrup.

To toast almonds, cook them in a dry skillet over medium heat for about 3 minutes, stirring often, or until golden and aromatic.

You can pit the olives or leave them intact. If opting for the latter, warn diners.

• Cutting board with trough

2	blood oranges (see Tips, left)	2
1 tbsp	white wine vinegar	15 mL
2 tsp	granulated sugar (see Tips, left)	10 mL
1 tsp	kosher or coarse sea salt (see Tips, page 306)	5 mL
1/8 tsp	freshly ground black pepper	0.5 mL
1/4 cup	extra virgin olive oil	60 mL
1	small head radicchio, halved, cored and thinly sliced	1
3 oz	escarole, torn (about 1 1/2 cups/1 L, loosely packed)	90 g
1 cup	shaved fennel	250 mL
1/4 cup	whole unsalted raw almonds, toasted (see Tips, left)	60 mL
1/2 cup	oil-cured black olives (see Tips, left)	125 mL

1. On cutting board with trough (to catch juice), peel oranges, slice into thin rounds and remove seeds. Set orange slices aside.

2. Pour orange juice into a small bowl. Whisk in vinegar, sugar, salt and pepper. Whisk in oil. Set aside.

3. In a large bowl, combine radicchio, escarole and fennel. Add dressing mixture to taste (you will have some left over), and toss to coat evenly.

4. Transfer to a serving platter. Arrange orange slices overlapping on greens. Top with almonds and olives. Serve immediately.

Red Leaf and Sweet Potato Salad

Roasted sweet potatoes add hearty nourishment to this dinner salad, and Lime Herb Dressing adds liveliness.

Makes 2 to 4 servings

Vegan Friendly

Salad

Tips

I prefer kosher salt because it tastes better than iodized table salt and (ideally) contains no additives. Table salts and some sea salts contain additives such as iodine compounds (iodides), anti-clumping agents and even sugar (in the form of dextrose, which is used to stabilize iodine). Although the North American Salt Institute states that kosher salt "contains no additives," some kosher salt brands do contain additives such as anti-clumping agents. If you have concerns, check the label.

To toast pecans, cook them in a dry skillet over medium heat for 2 to 3 minutes, stirring often, until golden brown and aromatic.

- Preheat oven to 450°F (230°C)
- 8-inch (20 cm) square baking dish

1	sweet potato (about 12 oz/375 g), peeled and cut into 1-inch (2.5 cm) chunks	1
½	small red onion, cut into 1-inch (2.5 cm) chunks	½
1 tbsp	extra virgin olive oil	15 mL
½ tsp	kosher or coarse sea salt (see Tips, left)	2 mL
⅛ tsp	freshly ground black pepper	0.5 mL
½	red bell pepper, cut into matchsticks	½
½ cup	Lime Herb Dressing (page 452)	125 mL
3 oz	radicchio, torn into bite-size pieces (about 2¼ cups/600 mL, loosely packed)	90 g
2 oz	red leaf lettuce, torn into bite-size pieces (about 3 cups/750 mL, loosely packed)	60 g
¼ cup	pecan halves, toasted and coarsely chopped (see Tips, left)	60 mL

1. In baking dish, combine sweet potato, onion, oil, salt and pepper and toss to coat evenly. Roast for 30 minutes or until sweet potato is tender but firm. Remove from oven and cool for 30 minutes or until at room temperature. Add red pepper and dressing to taste (you may have some dressing left over). Toss gently to combine.

2. On a serving platter or in individual bowls, arrange a bed of radicchio and lettuce. Top with sweet potato mixture. Sprinkle with pecans and serve immediately.

Truffled Radicchio, Mushroom and Roasted Garlic Pizza

With not a speck of cheese but plenty of sophistication, this vegan pizza is bound to please omnivores too. The heady scent of truffles is irresistible.

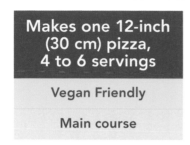

Makes one 12-inch (30 cm) pizza, 4 to 6 servings

Vegan Friendly

Main course

Tips

You can find truffle oil in gourmet food shops and some supermarkets. It is the least expensive option if you crave a hit of truffle.

It's best to halve any large garlic cloves lengthwise, but you can use the rest whole.

Transferring and baking the dough right on the parchment paper simplifies the pizza-making process.

Baking the pizza on the bottom rack allows the crust to turn golden before the toppings start to overcook.

This is a messy pizza, piled with "greens." The radicchio will settle and less will fall off if you let it stand before cutting.

- Preheat oven to 400°F (200°C), placing rack in the lowest position
- Preheated pizza stone or inverted baking sheet

3 tbsp	truffle oil, divided (see Tips, left)	45 mL
8 oz	cremini mushrooms, thinly sliced (4 cups/1 L)	250 g
	Kosher or coarse sea salt	
1	head radicchio (6 to 8 oz/175 to 250 g), cored and shredded	1
	Flour for dusting	
1	head Roasted Garlic (page 454)	1
1 lb	pizza dough, at room temperature	500 g
	Freshly ground black pepper	

1. In a large skillet over medium heat, heat 1 tbsp (15 mL) truffle oil until shimmery. Add mushrooms and season with salt to taste. Cook, stirring often, for 4 to 5 minutes, until mushrooms turn golden and start to sound squeaky. Set aside.

2. In a large bowl, toss radicchio with 1 tbsp (15 mL) truffle oil and salt and pepper to taste. Set aside.

3. On a lightly floured piece of parchment paper, stretch or roll dough into a 12-inch (30 cm) circle. Brush remaining 1 tbsp (15 mL) truffle oil overtop.

4. Transfer dough, on parchment paper, to preheated pizza stone or baking sheet (see Tips, left). Bake in preheated oven for 7 to 8 minutes, until edges are golden. (Check after 2 minutes to see if dough is bubbling up; if so, pierce bubbles with a knife.) Remove from oven. Scatter cooked mushrooms, then peeled roasted garlic cloves overtop (see Tips, left). Mound radicchio on top and bake for about 5 minutes more, until radicchio is slightly wilted.

5. Remove from oven and set aside to cool for 2 to 5 minutes before cutting and serving (see Tips, left).

Variation

If you are not a vegan, in Step 3, mix 4 oz (125 g) chèvre with remaining truffle oil and smear it over the pizza dough, if desired.

Radish Greens

Raphanus sativus, R. sativus longipinnatus

> *Other names:* **Chinese/Japanese radish, cultivated radish, daikon, European radish, green oriental radish, lo bok, oriental/white radish, red radish, spring radish, summer radish.**
>
> **Depending on where you are shopping, you may also find radish identified as** *alibanos, cu cai trang, fejil, hua piah, lobak putih, lobanos, mooli, rabanos, rabao, raeddike, rafano, ramenas, red'ka* **or** *rettich.*

Tasting Notes

The leaves of the common small red radish are peppery, herbaceous, juicy and sharp, with a bitter finish. Daikon leaves are milder, pleasantly peppery and pungent rather than bitter. In general, radish leaves are firm but tender, while the stems are tender-crisp or juicy but stringy. The leaves of both types mellow when cooked.

The origins of the radish have been traced to western Asia. Cultivated by the pharaohs, the plant eventually spread through the Mediterranean and eastward. The ancient Greeks made gold replicas of radishes as offerings to the god Apollo. China gave radishes to Japan in 700 BCE. They were introduced to England in 1500 and then transplanted to the New World. Radishes are now commercial crops around the globe, as well as being common home-grown garden vegetables.

Radish festivals are held in countries ranging from England to Mexico. During Christmas celebrations in Oaxaca, religious and famous figures are carved out of radishes and displayed in the town square.

Varieties

Radishes and their greens taste similar but look different. They range from three-bite red radishes that the French genteelly dip in butter to $1\frac{1}{2}$-foot (0.5 m) Japanese giants with full heads of coarse foliage. Radishes may be red, pink, purple, yellow, black or white. They may be round, oval or icicle-shaped and weigh from 1 ounce (30 g) to 20 pounds (9 kg). Specialty cultivars include round black Spanish radishes and watermelon radishes, which are white with pink flesh.

Small red radishes (*Raphanus sativus*) are the standard Western type; they are also called European radishes. The best-known varieties are cherry radishes (round) and breakfast radishes (elongated and mainly red, with white ends). Daikons (*R. sativus longipinnatus*) are favored in Asia; they are big, oval or tapered white radishes, some like fat parsnips on steroids.

Radishes are grown mainly for their pungent, crunchy, juicy roots, but their lively greens are edible. Some are grown as popular microgreens (page 241).

Ancestors include the wild radish (*R. raphanistrum*), also known as jointed charlock. This variety can upset the stomach when raw, so it must be boiled.

Health Notes

Although no official government analysis is available, radish greens are thought to contain vitamins A, C and K, calcium, iron and magnesium.

In folk medicine, radish leaves have been used to stimulate the gallbladder and liver, alleviate jaundice, and flush the bladder and kidneys.

The French, who dare to serve an appetizer of radishes with baguette and butter, may be on the right track. For thousands of years radishes were considered appetite stimulants or, as the Roman poet Horace put it, a vegetable to "excite the languid stomach." However, he didn't have anything to say specifically about the greens.

SUBSTITUTES

mustard greens,
arugula

Buy It

Red radishes and daikons are sold topless as well as in fresh bunches with their tops. The quantity of greens per bunch can vary a great deal; foliage is skimpier during the winter. As far as the greens go, daikons are superior to common red radishes. Their foliage is milder and more plentiful.

Red radishes have small, oval, crinkled leaves with a slight ruffle. They are attached to thin, crunchy stems with a pale red blush at the bottom. Daikons have lush foliage, with large, soft, matte green leaves frilled along stems that can be more than a foot (30 cm) tall.

Choose vibrant radishes that feel firm when squeezed, with crisp, green leaves. Avoid bunches with withered or yellowed leaves. Cracks in the roots are a sign of old age and dehydration.

Store It

Radish leaves yellow and wilt quickly at room temperature, so refrigerate them promptly. Separate radishes from their tops (which steal moisture from the roots). Wash, rinse and dry the greens, wrap them in paper towels and place in a resealable bag, then refrigerate. Do not squash the greens together; rot will develop in the center of the mass.

Radish greens will keep in the refrigerator for up to two days.

Prep It

If you are eating them raw, pinch off the stems of common red radish greens. If you are cooking them, you can use the leaves and the crunchy stems — nothing goes to waste.

For daikon greens, use a sharp knife to carefully slash the leaves from the stems. Portions of stems wider than about ⅛ inch (3 mm) are tough and should be discarded.

Radish greens are filthy. Wash them in several changes of cold water, drain, then spin-dry.

Consume It

You can use radish greens raw in mixed salads or sandwiches, but remember — a little goes a long way.

Radish greens may be sautéed, stir-fried or added to soups, stews or omelets. They just need to be wilted, which takes 1 to 2 minutes.

W Is for Wasabi

Wasabi (*Wasabia japonica*) is neither radish nor horseradish. Its spicy leaves, however, are considered edible. True wasabi is a rare find in North America because it is difficult to cultivate.

Radish Tea Sandwiches

Tea sandwiches are dainty, but these come with a one-two kick: sliced radishes and garlicky butter with radish greens. I based this recipe on a concept from the French, who serve crunchy radishes with bread and butter as an appetizer, even in restaurants.

Makes 20 triangles

Vegan Friendly

Sandwich

Tips

For this recipe you'll need 10 medium to large radishes. Save any extra radishes and greens for other recipes.

If you have one, use a mandoline — carefully! — to shave the radishes into the thinnest possible slices. You'll be left with stubs that can be saved, chopped and tossed into a salad later.

For tea sandwiches, use old-fashioned sandwich bread. If you can find it, purchase a Pullman loaf, which is baked in a pan with a lid to create even, square edges; you'll end up with larger, neater slices and won't have to cut off as much crust. Curiously, Asian supermarkets often sell Pullman bread.

For healthier and prettier bites, use a combination of white and whole wheat bread.

Weighing down the sandwiches makes them easier to cut and neater. The goal is to compress, not flatten. The softer and fresher the bread, the less time this will take. Firm whole wheat bread takes a bit longer.

1	bunch red radishes (see Tips, left)	1
½ cup	unsalted butter or non-dairy alternative, softened	125 mL
1 tbsp	finely chopped fresh chives	15 mL
1	clove garlic, minced	1
1 tsp	finely grated lemon zest	5 mL
½ tsp	kosher or coarse sea salt	2 mL
15	slices white and/or whole wheat sandwich bread (see Tips, left)	15

1. Using a sharp knife, separate greens from radishes. Trim and slice 10 radishes paper-thin (see Tips, left), arranging each in an individual pile. Pinch off and discard stems from leaves. Finely chop ½ oz (15 g) leaves; you should have ⅔ cup (150 mL). Set aside.

2. In a bowl, using a fork, mash together butter, radish leaves, chives, garlic, lemon zest and salt. Set aside.

3. Arrange bread slices on work surface in sets of three. Working with one set at a time, lightly smear two slices with butter mixture on one side only, right to the edges. Smear the third slice on both sides, right to the edges. Arrange one sliced radish, overlapping the slices, on buttered side of bottom piece of bread, leaving a narrow border. Cover with double-buttered piece of bread. Top with another sliced radish, overlapping the slices and leaving a narrow border. Top with remaining slice of bread, butter side down. Transfer to a baking sheet. Repeat with remaining sets of bread slices and other ingredients.

4. Place a second baking sheet over sandwiches and put light weights (such as cans) on top (see Tips, left). Set aside for about 5 minutes, depending on the texture of the bread, until slightly compressed. Using a serrated knife, cut off the crusts. Cut each sandwich into four triangles. Serve immediately or store in fridge (wrapped in plastic, then stacked in an airtight container) for several hours or overnight.

Variations

Instead of butter, vegans can use dairy-free cream cheese, loosened with dairy-free sour cream.

Inexperienced or in a hurry? Make regular double-decker sandwiches rather than triple-deckers, then quarter them.

If desired, you can use a round cookie cutter to make circular sandwiches, or try other shapes. Alternatively, cut each sandwich into three or four fingers.

Roasted Radishes and Sesame Greens

This unusual and delicious dish takes full advantage of a bunch of radishes. Roasting mellows the peppery bite of radishes so they taste like turnips. The vegetables are surrounded by their sautéed greens.

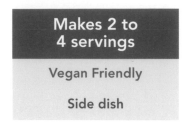

Makes 2 to 4 servings

Vegan Friendly

Side dish

Tips

Toasted sesame oil, also known as Asian sesame oil, is made from toasted or roasted sesame seeds. Dark and aromatic, it is sold in small bottles as a flavoring agent. Do not confuse toasted sesame oil with yellow sesame oil, which is pressed from raw seeds.

Toasted sesame seeds are available in most supermarkets. To toast your own, cook them in a dry skillet over medium heat for about 2 minutes, stirring occasionally, until seeds start to clump and turn golden and aromatic. For an attractive presentation, use toasted mixed white and black sesame seeds.

Roasting time will depend on the size and shape of the radishes. Check partway through the cooking time, and don't let them get too soft.

- Preheat oven to 500°F (260°C)

1	bunch red radishes	1
1 tbsp	extra virgin olive oil	15 mL
	Kosher or coarse sea salt	
1 tsp	toasted sesame oil (see Tips, left)	5 mL
1 tsp	toasted sesame seeds (see Tips, left)	5 mL
1 tsp	freshly squeezed lemon juice	5 mL

1. Using a sharp knife, separate greens from radishes. Trim radishes. Coarsely chop leaves and stems. Set aside in separate piles.

2. In a small baking pan, toss radishes with oil and salt to taste. Roast in preheated oven for about 20 minutes, shaking the pan once, until radishes are tender-crisp and skin is rosy with golden patches and starting to wrinkle (see Tips, left).

3. Meanwhile, in a large skillet over medium heat, heat sesame oil until hot. Add radish greens and salt to taste. Cook, stirring, for about 1 minute, until wilted.

4. Arrange greens around the perimeter of a shallow serving bowl. Sprinkle sesame seeds over greens. Spoon radishes and their juices into center of bowl. Drizzle lemon juice over radishes. Serve warm.

Ramps

Allium tricoccum

Other names: **Eastern onion, ramson, spring onion, spring/wood leek, Tennessee truffle, wild garlic, wild leek.**

Depending on where you are shopping, you may find ramps identified as *ail des bois* or *ail sauvage*.

Ramps are foraged wild. They can be cultivated, but they are slow to grow.

Ramps are native to mountainous regions of the eastern seaboard of North America, from Quebec to the Carolinas, but they also grow in some areas of the American Midwest and other parts of Canada. They spread over vast patches in the Catskills and the Appalachians, where they are proudly heralded as traditional "hillbilly" food. Because of overpicking in the 1970s and '80s, Quebec banned the commercial sale of ramps as a protective measure.

The word *ramp* is derived from *ramson*, meaning "wild garlic" in an Elizabethan dialect. It was first mentioned in English print in 1530. *Ramson* commonly referred to European bear onions (see below), but immigrants to the southern Appalachians adopted the name.

One theory (still debated) is that Chicago was named after a carpet of ramps near Lake Michigan; the local Native Americans called them skunk plants and dubbed the site *shikako* or *chickagou*, meaning "skunk place."

These expensive vegetables have become the darlings of modern chefs and locavores. Their arrival every spring has long been a cause for celebration, inspiring numerous festivals that feature ramp-eating contests and Appalachian music. One, in Bradford, Pennsylvania, is colorfully called Stinkfest.

Tasting Notes

Although they look delicate, ramps are more robust and fragrant than leeks. When raw, ramps have an onion-garlic flavor with a whiff of forest musk. The leaves taste fiercer than the stems; they are sharp, spicy, juicy and slightly sweet. When cooked, ramps retain a persistent garlicky flavor but their harshness is tempered. Because of their lingering odor, ramps have been dubbed "leek with a reek" and "garlic with attitude." The garlic scent of ramps becomes increasingly fainter after harvesting. However, the flavor can linger on the palate for an hour — or longer.

Varieties

Ramps (*Allium tricoccum*) are the most coveted of the diverse wild alliums around the world. Relatives include the following:

- **Eurasian bear onion** (*A. ursinum*), also known as bear leek, bear's garlic, buckram, broad-leaved garlic or wood garlic. Appreciative bears (and wild boars) dig these up — hence the name. The leaves are used in salads or cooked like vegetables;

the stems are often pickled. These greens are cultivated in Hungary, where they are called *medvehagyma*. The 19th-century Swiss were fond of garlicky butter, the product of garlic-flavored milk from cows that grazed on bear onions.

- **broadleaf wild leek** (*A. ampeloprasum*), a variety that has grown in rocky soils in Britain since prehistoric times. It has traveled as far east as Asia, as well as across the pond to Virginia, where it is called Yorktown onion. It is a wild ancestor of leeks, elephant garlic and pearl onions, as well as the Middle Eastern *kurrat*, or Egyptian leek, which is grown for its leaves.
- **victory onion** (*A. victorialis*), also known as alpine leek, caucus, *gecong* or *shancong*. This is another broad-leaved wild onion, with a garlicky odor described as more intense than that of garlic itself. It is found across Europe and Asia all the way to Japan, where it is a traditional food of the indigenous Ainu people. The species name is derived from its German moniker, *siegwurz*, or "root of victory." Bohemian miners wore amulets of this onion in order to be victorious against evil spirits.

Buy It

Ramps are foraged wild or sold at specialty greengrocers, gourmet food shops and well-stocked supermarkets. They are seasonal and expensive. Chefs and gourmands stampede to acquire them, so when you see them, don't hesitate.

Ramps are the first leafy green vegetables of spring. They appear from March to May or June, depending on the location. Ramp season lasts just two to three weeks, as the plants become inedible once they put out seed pods.

Foragers are warned that ramps and other leafy wild alliums resemble several poisonous plants, including lily of the valley. A distinctive garlicky odor in the leaves sets them apart.

Ramps look like green onions, but each stalk consists of a spindly stem topped by a head of large, broad, smooth spear-shaped leaves (the stems may be referred to as bulbs but are not rounded). Ramps vary a great deal in thickness and size. Generally speaking, commercially sold ramps are 10 to 12 inches (25 to 30 cm) tall, with three leaves and stems about as thick as a pencil: from $1/4$ to $1/2$ inch (0.5 to 1 cm) wide at the root end.

These greens should be firm and bright, with no wilting. The leaves should stand up when you hold the root end. Stems usually transition from white to a purple or reddish tinge. Orange or yellow hues are signs of old age.

Store It

Ramps wilt quickly at room temperature, so refrigerate them promptly. Swathe each ramp tightly in plastic wrap. Or wrap a slightly damp paper towel around the root ends, place ramps in a resealable bag and refrigerate. If the ramps are particularly smelly, double up on the bags.

Ramps will keep in the refrigerator for up to three days.

Prep It

Ramps are edible from top to bottom. First, cut off the roots. The stems may be covered by a loose, thin coating that is slimy or dirty; slip it off and discard it. For easier handling, halve the ramps, separating them where the leafy tops meet the tinted white stems. The tops are very dirty. Swish the leaves quickly in several changes of cold water, spin-dry and place on paper towels. The leaves are very absorbent, so do not allow them to soak or they will become limp. Rinse stems under cold running water and pat dry with paper towels.

Slice or chop the whole ramp or leave the stems intact.

Consume It

Raw ramps are tender but taste harsh, so they are best cooked.

In Appalachia, chopped ramps are traditionally fried with potatoes or scrambled with eggs and served with bacon, beans and cornbread alongside. Pickling is another traditional treatment.

Cooked ramps retain a pleasant springiness; they don't get mushy like green onions. They are cooked to tender in 5 to 8 minutes.

Be careful when sautéing ramps. Stems quickly toughen, turn bitter and even burn. Sauté whole stems or cut them into large pieces, as chopped ramps are more likely to toughen. Leaves wilt in 30 to 60 seconds. However, to help keep stems moist, they may be sautéed with the leaves. Adding stock (up to $1/4$ cup/60 mL per bunch) once the stems turn golden also helps.

Ramps may be blanched before cooking. Blanch for 1 to 3 minutes before sautéing them, adding them to cooked dishes, using them as pizza toppings or turning them into pesto.

A substitute for expensive ramps is an equal weight of sliced green onions and minced garlic cloves — use 1 clove garlic for every 2 green onions. Another substitute is green garlic (immature garlic that resembles green onions).

SUBSTITUTES
scapes

French Lentils, Ramps and Glazed Carrots

Ramps are a harbinger of spring. When the time comes, pair them elegantly with glazed carrots and lentilles du Puy. *These small dark green French legumes are known as "the caviar of lentils" because they stay firmer than common green lentils, taste richer and cost more. For a meatless meal, serve this tempting dish with a crusty baguette, hot rice or quinoa.*

Makes 4 servings		
Vegan Friendly		
Main course		

Tips

To cook lentils: In a saucepan over medium-high heat, combine lentils, 3 cups (750 mL) water, 2 sprigs thyme, 1 bay leaf, 1 tsp (5 mL) salt and ¼ tsp (1 mL) freshly ground black pepper. Bring to a boil, then cover, reduce heat to low and simmer for about 25 minutes, until lentils are tender. Drain and discard thyme stalks and bay leaf. Cover and set aside.

Cut each ramp where the leaves meet the stem. Slice leaves crosswise into ½-inch (1 cm) pieces. Put leaves and intact stems in separate piles.

Whenever possible, use reduced-sodium vegetable stock. Not only is it healthier, it allows you to better control the saltiness of a dish.

¾ cup	French (Puy) lentils, cooked and drained (see Tips, left)	175 mL
1 tbsp	extra virgin olive oil	15 mL
2	bunches ramps (4 to 5 oz/125 to 150 g total), trimmed and cut (see Tips, left)	2
	Kosher or coarse sea salt	
¼ cup	vegetable stock (see Tips, left)	60 mL
1 tbsp	unsalted butter or non-dairy alternative	15 mL
4	carrots (8 oz/250 g), cut diagonally into ¼-inch (0.5 cm) slices	4
½ tsp	granulated sugar	2 mL
½ tsp	finely grated orange zest	2 mL
¼ cup	freshly squeezed orange juice	60 mL
4	small lemon wedges	4

1. In a skillet over medium-low heat, heat oil until hot. Add ramp stems and lightly sprinkle with salt to taste. Cook, turning once, for 2 to 3 minutes, until golden. Pour in stock, cover and cook for 3 to 5 minutes, until stems are tender but firm and most of the liquid has evaporated. Using tongs, transfer stems to a plate and set aside. Add leaves to skillet and sauté for 30 to 60 seconds, until wilted. Scrape into a bowl and set aside.

2. In same skillet over medium heat, melt butter. Stir in carrots, sugar, orange zest and juice and ¼ tsp (1 mL) salt. Cover, reduce heat to low and cook, shaking skillet occasionally, for about 15 minutes, until carrots are tender. Uncover, increase heat to medium and cook for about 2 minutes, shaking pan, until carrots are glazed and most of the liquid has evaporated. Set aside.

3. Transfer cooked lentils to a serving dish or individual bowls. Top with ramp leaves. Scrape carrots and glaze overtop. Lay ramp stems on top. Place lemon wedges alongside to squeeze overtop. Serve immediately.

Ramp Noodles

These simple but addictively tasty Asian noodles are inspired by the trendy Momofuku Noodle Bar's menu. They are less oily than the kind served there. The tender-crisp ramps, briefly cooked, provide a surprising contrast to the soft noodles.

Tips

For this recipe, unrefined sesame oil is a tasty choice. It is sold in gourmet food shops and well-stocked supermarkets. Do not confuse this golden oil with standard dark toasted sesame oil.

Cut each ramp where the leaves meet the stem. Cut the stems into 1-inch (2.5 cm) lengths. Coarsely chop the leaves.

To grate or purée gingerroot, use a kitchen rasp such as the kind made by Microplane.

You can find thick Asian wheat noodles in vacuum packs in or near the produce department in supermarkets.

To maintain more control over the saltiness of dishes, use reduced-sodium soy sauce. Depending on the type, 1 tbsp (15 mL) regular soy sauce can contain 1,000 mg or more of sodium. Reduced-sodium soy sauce contains about half that amount.

2 tbsp	oil (see Tips, left)	30 mL
2	bunches ramps (4 to 6 oz/125 to 175 g total), trimmed and cut (see Tips, left)	2
½ tsp	kosher or coarse sea salt	2 mL
1 tbsp	puréed gingerroot (see Tips, left)	15 mL
1 lb	fresh thick Asian wheat noodles (see Tips, left)	500 g
2 tbsp	soy sauce (see Tips, left)	30 mL
1 tsp	rice vinegar	5 mL
	Hot sauce	

1. In a saucepan over medium-low heat, heat oil until hot. Add ramps and salt. Cook, stirring often, for about 1 minute, until tender-crisp. Stir in ginger for about 1 minute, until fragrant. Remove from heat and set aside.

2. In a large saucepan of boiling salted water, cook noodles for 3 to 5 minutes or according to package directions, stirring occasionally to break up clumps, until heated through. Drain.

3. Stir soy sauce and vinegar into cooked ramps. Add hot noodles and toss. Season with salt to taste. Dash in hot sauce to taste, or serve it alongside.

Forage Gastronomy

The pursuit of obscure wild greens to titillate gourmands has been dubbed "forest gastronomy." However, gourmet greens further afield are ripe for the picking too. They are foraged in forests and fields, marshlands and meadows, seashores and tidal basins.

Top chefs have been whetting their creative juices with wild greens. Among the trendiest are succulent, salty samphires and other seaside plants, such as oyster leaf. Some are cultivated as well as foraged.

Samphire

Samphire may be a corruption of the French name *herbe de Saint-Pierre*. Several species are identified as samphires:

- **marsh samphire** (*Salicornia europaea*), also known as Norfolk samphire, glasswort, sea asparagus, sea beans, sea pickle, pickleweed or *salicorne de mer*. The edible tips are not leafy but rather fleshy and succulent; they resemble slim green beans with knobby joints. Marsh samphire is found in coastal salt marshes and estuaries, particularly in Nova Scotia and eastern and central North America.
- **rock samphire** (*Crithmum maritimum*), also known as crest marine or sea fennel. It was mentioned by Shakespeare and became a popular garden plant in 19th-century England. The leaves are described as aromatic and spicy by fans, or as unpleasant tasting and smelly, by detractors. They are considered best pickled. True to its name, rock samphire grows on rocky shores.
- **golden samphire** (*Inula crithmoides*) and **elecampane** (*I. helenium*), species with edible leaves that are cooked. The latter, however, is better known for its root, which is used to make absinthe.

Of these wild greens, only marsh samphire is widely available; specialty greengrocers sell it seasonally. Neither seaweed nor land plant, marsh samphire offers lovers of greens the best of both land and sea. It is distinctively crisp and salty. When eaten raw, it yields a burst of briny juice followed by a nutty finish. When cooked, it tastes of the sea, with a smoky accent that lingers pleasantly on the palate. It is used raw in salads, cooked or pickled. Only the succulent tips of this plant are eaten. They are generally tender but, rarely and unpredictably, a fibrous string may be found in the center of one. A piece plucked from close to the main stem or wider than ⅛ inch (3 mm) is more likely to include this unpleasant surprise.

Oyster Leaf

Trending in North America is **oyster leaf** (*Mertensia maritima*), also known as vegetarian oyster or sea bluebell. The smooth gray-green leaves are said to taste surprisingly like oysters. "Anchovies," "mushrooms" and "ocean brine" are other descriptors. This plant rose to prominence at elBulli restaurant in Spain, where fooling the senses was part of the chef's culinary artistry.

Until recently, oyster leaf was a foraged rarity. The arctic Inuit boiled and ate it, and the plant also grows wild in some isolated coastal areas of the British Isles. However, farmers specializing in niche crops have started cultivating it, and its prices are on par with the high level of enthusiasm for these greens.

Salsify

Do not confuse oyster leaf with **common salsify** (*Tragopogon porrifolius*), also known as oyster plant, vegetable oyster or purple salsify. It is grown mainly for its roots, which also supposedly taste like oysters. The plant is found wild as well as cultivated. It is sometimes sold with its leek-like tops (called "chard" but unrelated to the real thing; page 104). Relatives include **western salsify** (*T. dubius*) and **goat's beard** (*T. pratensis*). Salsify was popular in 18th-century England, but interest in it has generally waned. It does, however, have fans, particularly in France, Germany and Italy.

More popular in modern times, at least in Europe, is **Spanish salsify** (*Scorzonera hispanica*), also known as black salsify or viper grass. It is grown mainly as a root crop but has edible lettuce-like leaves. It developed a reputation as an anti-venin in the Middle Ages in Spain, where it was used to treat snakebites.

French scorzonera (*Reichardia picroides*), also known as galatsida or brighteyes, is better known as a flowering daisy-like plant. However, it has tender edible leaves and shoots and may be foraged. On Crete the greens are boiled and eaten.

Plantains

Several plantains are a source of wild greenery:

- **minutina** (*Plantago coronopus*), also known as erba stella or buck's horn plantain. It is sometimes cultivated as a leaf vegetable.
- **broadleaf plantain** (*P. major*), a nutritious wild plant.
- **long-leafed plantain** (*P. lanceolata*), an invasive weed steeped to make tea.
- **sea plantain** (*P. maritima*), also known as goose tongue. It has been compared to samphire.

Burnet

Burnet is another once popular but now unusual wild green. **Salad burnet** (*Sanguisorba minor*) was brought to North America by English colonists. It is said to have a cucumber flavor and is used in salads and dressings. One notable relative is **great burnet** (*S. officinalis*), also known as medicinal burnet. Another is **Canadian burnet** (*S. canadensis*); its edible leaves must be cooked to eliminate bitterness.

Rapini

Brassica rapa broccoletto, B. rapa ruvo

> *Other names:* broccoli raab/rabe/rape, Italian broccoli, rape kale/mustard, ruvo kale, turnip broccoli.
>
> Depending on where you are shopping, you may find rapini identified as *brocoletti di rape, brocoletto, cime di rapa/rabe, friarielli, grelos, rappi, ravizzone, shalgam* or *wu ching*.

Rapini is descended from wild turnips that grew in the Mediterranean basin. It was cultivated in southern Italy and brought to North America in the 1920s by immigrants. North Americans, not enamored of its bitter taste, often used it as animal fodder. Although rapini is now cultivated around the world, it is not particularly popular with the average North American cook. Still, many consumers have developed a taste for it and rapini has become a staple in produce departments as well as Italian restaurants.

Tasting Notes

Rapini has crisp, juicy stems with a sweet mustard finish. The leaves are bitter and mustardy.

Health Notes

Rapini contains vitamins A, B_6, C, E and K, calcium, copper, folate, iron, magnesium, manganese, niacin, pantothenic acid, phosphorus, potassium, riboflavin, thiamin and zinc. It is particularly high in fiber.

In herbal medicine, rapini has been used to regulate blood sugar, ensure proper digestion, maintain bone density, alleviate PMS and prevent cataracts and hair loss.

Varieties

The *Brassica* genus that rapini belongs to is cultivated in various incarnations, as oilseed or canola plants, leafy vegetables and animal fodder. Vegetable rapini (*Brassica rapa broccoletto* or *B. rapa ruvo*) differs from canola plants, which are grown on a massive scale for oil production. Canola plants are cultivars of rapeseed (*B. napus*), from which they were originally bred, or field mustard (*B. rapa campestris*). A milder Chinese relative is the vegetable known as yu choy sum (page 426).

Buy It

Rapini is a mainstay in supermarkets, where it is often labeled "broccoli rabe."

Stalks are arranged in clusters, with frilled, spiky dark green leaves and small, broccoli-like bluish-green florets. The bunch may include small edible yellow flowers; the buds should be closed. Yellowing leaves, moist black patches and florets that are no longer compact are signs of old age.

The thinner and firmer the stem, the tenderer the rapini.

Store It

Wrap rapini in paper towels, place in a resealable bag and refrigerate.

Rapini will keep in the refrigerator for up to five days.

SUBSTITUTES

Chinese broccoli, yu
choy sum, mustard
greens, komatsuna

Prep It

Stems, leaves and florets are edible, but they cook unevenly.

Before cooking rapini, trim about 1 inch (2.5 cm) off the base of the stems where they are woody, discolored or dried. Some stalks grow in large clusters; separate them. Chop leaves and florets.

The thick stems are fibrous. Some cooks discard them, but that's a waste; they can be tenderized. Peel any that are wider than ½ inch (1 cm) and halve them lengthwise (or several times if very thick). Better still, prevent stringiness by chopping stems coarsely or cutting them into ½- to 1-inch (1 to 2.5 cm) pieces before cooking.

Here are three ways to tame bitterness before cooking:

- Soak rapini in cold water.
- Place in a bowl, pour boiling water overtop and set aside for 5 minutes.
- Blanch for 1 minute in a pan of boiling salted water, then drain and shock with cold water. If you are sensitive to bitter flavors, blanch rapini for up to 5 minutes. Note, however, that this can leave it limp.

Consume It

Rapini is not eaten raw. It may be steamed, braised, sautéed, grilled, roasted or added to soups, stews and pastas.

If sautéing, it's best to steam-fry rapini. Sauté briefly in oil, cover and cook until tender-crisp, then uncover and finish over high heat to evaporate any excess liquid. Rapini exudes a lot of moisture as it wilts. While sautéing, some cooks add up to ½ cup (125 mL) stock or water per bunch to tenderize and temper its bitterness. The more stock added, the soggier but less bitter the rapini — it's a conundrum. I prefer to cook rapini with just the wash water clinging to its leaves. The result is a vibrant, tender-crisp but classically bitter green.

Rapini stems cook in about 5 minutes, leaves and florets in 1 to 2 minutes. If steaming, double the time.

Cooks sensitive to bitterness may double or triple cooking times. The texture suffers but the rapini ends up milder.

Blanching is okay, but boiling is a bad cooking method for rapini. Thoroughly boiled rapini is less bitter but sadly soggy, rubbery and khaki-colored.

Steamed Rapini with Garlic Confit

Garlicky, lemony oil and braised garlic cloves transform ho-hum steamed rapini into a crave-worthy dish. Serve this with crusty bread to dip into the juices, or lay the rapini on a bed of brown rice.

Makes 2 servings		
Vegan Friendly		
Side dish		

Tips

To trim rapini, separate large clusters and peel stalks thicker than ½ inch (1 cm).

If you are sensitive to bitterness, boil the rapini instead of steaming it. Drain it well and pat dry before drizzling with the oil.

Drizzle any leftover garlic oil over steamed vegetables, stir it into mashed potatoes or scramble eggs in it.

¼ cup	extra virgin olive oil	60 mL
1	head garlic, cloves peeled	1
1	strip lemon zest (1 inch/2.5 cm wide)	1
¼ tsp	hot pepper flakes	1 mL
10 oz	rapini (about ½ bunch), trimmed (see Tips, left)	300 g
½ tsp	finely grated lemon zest	2 mL
¼ tsp	kosher or coarse sea salt	1 mL
⅛ tsp	freshly ground white pepper	0.5 mL

1. In a small saucepan over low heat, combine oil, garlic cloves, lemon zest strip and hot pepper flakes. Bring to a simmer and cook, stirring occasionally, for about 30 minutes, until garlic is very soft and golden.

2. In a covered steamer set over 1 inch (2.5 cm) of boiling water, cook rapini over medium-low heat for about 10 minutes, until tender-crisp. Using a sharp knife, chop coarsely or, if desired, leave stalks whole and transfer to a serving platter.

3. Using a fine-mesh sieve, strain garlic oil into a small bowl, reserving garlic cloves and discarding remaining solids. Add grated lemon zest, salt and pepper to oil. Cut garlic cloves in half lengthwise.

4. Drizzle oil over rapini (you will have some left over; see Tips, left). Scatter garlic cloves overtop and serve warm.

Addictive Rapini

I can't stop eating this rapini embellished with fragrant orange zest and crunchy pecans. Serve it over rice, pasta or grains to capture the scented juices, or mop them up with rustic bread.

Makes 2 to 4 servings (about 4 cups/1 L)

Vegan Friendly

Side dish

Tips

For the finest minced garlic, push it through a press.

If you are sensitive to bitterness, the rapini may be blanched before sautéing.

To toast pecans, cook them in a dry skillet over medium heat, stirring often, for 2 to 3 minutes, until golden and aromatic.

1	bunch rapini (1¼ lbs/625 g)	1
2 tbsp	extra virgin olive oil	30 mL
1	large leek (white and green parts), thinly sliced	1
2	cloves garlic, minced (see Tips, left)	2
1 tsp	finely grated orange zest	5 mL
½ tsp	kosher or coarse sea salt	2 mL
¼ cup	vegetable stock, optional	60 mL
½ cup	pecans, toasted and coarsely chopped (see Tips, left)	125 mL
¼ cup	chopped fresh parsley leaves	60 mL
	Freshly ground black pepper	

1. Using a sharp knife, trim rapini. Peel thick stems and halve lengthwise. Cut rapini into 1-inch (2.5 cm) pieces. Set aside.

2. In a large saucepan over medium heat, heat oil until shimmery. Add leek and cook for 2 to 3 minutes, until softened. Stir in garlic for 20 seconds. Add rapini (with wash water clinging to leaves), orange zest and salt. Cook, tossing with tongs, for about 2 minutes, until slightly wilted. Add stock, if using. Cover and cook for about 2 minutes, until tender-crisp. Uncover, increase heat to medium-high and cook for about 1 minute, until most of the liquid has evaporated. Remove from heat. Stir in pecans and parsley. Season with salt and pepper to taste and serve immediately.

Rapini, Cauliflower and Olive Toss-Up

Caramelized, slightly charred, unevenly cooked vegetables? No, this is not a kitchen nightmare but rather a dreamy, delicious dish that will wake up your taste buds. Serve it over pasta or rice.

Makes 2 to 4 servings

Vegan Friendly

Main course

Tips

To maintain the proper timing and textures, use a 12-inch (30 cm) skillet.

In Step 3 avoid the temptation to stir too much, as this will leave the veggies steamed and cooked too evenly. This dish is supposed to have both soft and crisp bits.

10 oz	rapini (about ½ bunch)	300 g
12 oz	cauliflower	375 g
½ cup	extra virgin olive oil, divided	125 mL
	Kosher or coarse sea salt	
1 tbsp	capers, drained and coarsely chopped	15 mL
4	cloves garlic, chopped	4
½ tsp	fennel seeds, crushed or chopped	2 mL
¼ tsp	hot pepper flakes	1 mL
½ cup	oil-cured black olives, pitted and coarsely chopped	125 mL
2 tbsp	chopped fresh parsley leaves	30 mL

1. Using a sharp knife, trim rapini. Peel thick stems and slice lengthwise. Cut stems into ½-inch (1 cm) pieces. Coarsely chop leaves. Set aside.

2. Slice cauliflower lengthwise no thicker than ⅛ to ¼ inch (3 to 5 mm), creating a variety of pieces plus crumbs. Set aside.

3. In a large skillet over medium heat, heat ¼ cup (60 mL) oil until shimmery. Add cauliflower, then rapini, but leave the smallest crumbs and pieces on the cutting board. Sprinkle with salt to taste. Cook, occasionally swirling oil in skillet but not stirring, for about 5 minutes, until edges start to brown (see Tips, left). Using a spatula, stir and toss gently. Add 2 tbsp (30 mL) oil, capers and remaining cauliflower crumbs and rapini bits. Cook, occasionally swirling oil in pan but not stirring, for about 5 minutes, until edges begin to brown. Using a spatula, stir and toss gently.

4. Reduce heat to low and add remaining oil. Season with salt to taste, garlic, fennel seeds and hot pepper flakes; stir and toss. Cook for about 2 minutes, until vegetables are tender-crisp. Remove from heat. Stir in olives and parsley and serve immediately.

Pasta e Fagiole

What's not to love about pasta, beans and greens? This is one of my absolute favorite Italian dishes. It is a Tuscan peasant dish, although North Americans may recognize it better under the bastardized name "pasta fazool." My vegetarian version has some flourishes that include roasted garlic and fresh wee tomatoes. Any small pasta will work, but farfalle (bows) are the most attractive. The only question remaining: is this a pasta soup or a soupy pasta? I vote for the latter.

Makes 4 to 6 servings (about 8 cups/2 L)

Vegan Friendly

Main course

Tips

Celery hearts are the tender inner stalks of a bunch of celery.

Romano beans are also known as borlotti or cranberry beans. They are commonly used in Italian soups, stews and pasta dishes.

This dish thickens as it sits. If desired, thin leftovers by stirring in some vegetable stock before reheating.

Rapini's bitter edge kicks up the flavor of this iconic dish. You can, however, substitute almost any kind of less bitter, fairly fast-cooking, green, such as escarole (blanched and chopped) or romaine hearts. Avoid using slow-cooking greens such as collards.

• Preheat oven to 400°F (200°C)

6 oz	rapini	175 g
1	head Roasted Garlic (page 454)	1
6 oz	farfalle pasta (bows)	175 g
¼ cup	extra virgin olive oil	60 mL
1	small onion, diced	1
1	small carrot, diced	1
1	stalk celery heart with leaves, diced (see Tips, left)	1
¼ cup	marsala	60 mL
3 cups	vegetable stock	750 mL
1 tsp	kosher or coarse sea salt	5 mL
½ tsp	freshly ground black pepper	2 mL
¼ tsp	hot pepper flakes	1 mL
8 oz	grape tomatoes (1½ cups/375 g), quartered	250 g
½ cup	chopped fresh parsley leaves	125 mL
1 tbsp	chopped fresh oregano leaves	15 mL
1	can (19 oz/340 mL) romano beans, rinsed and drained (see Tips, left)	1
2 oz	freshly grated Parmesan-style cheese (1 cup/250 mL), optional	60 g

1. Using a sharp knife, trim rapini, separating large clusters. Peel thick stems. Chop stems, leaves and florets; you should have about 3 cups (750 mL), loosely packed. Set aside.

2. Squeeze roasted garlic cloves into a small bowl. Mash with a fork. Set aside.

3. In a large saucepan of boiling salted water, cook farfalle over medium heat for about 15 minutes, until al dente. Drain.

4. In the same saucepan over medium heat, heat oil until shimmery. Add onion, carrot and celery. Cook, stirring often, for about 5 minutes, until softened and turning golden. Stir in marsala for 30 seconds. Stir in stock, rapini, roasted garlic, salt, pepper and hot pepper flakes. When mixture comes to a simmer, reduce heat to medium-low and cook for about 10 minutes, until vegetables are tender. Add tomatoes, parsley, oregano, beans and cooked farfalle. Heat for about 5 minutes, until warmed through. Stir in cheese, if using. Serve warm (see Tips, left).

Giant Stromboli with Rapini and Smoked Mozzarella

Here's something to sink your teeth into: stromboli with rapini, smoked mozzarella and homemade tomato-basil pizza sauce. Stromboli are pizza rolls, and this big one makes a hearty meal. Serve it with soup or salad.

Makes 4 to 6 servings

Main course

Tips

This recipe makes about 1½ cups (375 mL) pizza sauce. Use any leftover portion on other pizzas or freeze it for future use.

When the sauce thickens, it will bubble and spit vigorously. Use a splatter screen if you have one.

In a hurry? Use store-bought pizza sauce.

If you find rapini too bitter, temper it by increasing the stock to ½ cup (250 mL) and cooking it for 10 minutes or until softened.

For the finest minced garlic, push it through a press.

- Preheat oven to 425°F (220°C)
- Preheated pizza stone or inverted baking sheet

Pizza Sauce

2 tbsp	extra virgin olive oil	30 mL
1	large clove garlic, minced (see Tips, left)	1
¼ cup	dry white wine	60 mL
2 cups	bottled strained tomatoes (see Tips, page 329)	500 mL
½ tsp	kosher or coarse sea salt	2 mL
⅛ tsp	freshly ground black pepper	0.5 mL
¼ tsp	dried oregano leaves	1 mL
¼ cup	packed slivered fresh basil leaves	60 mL

Stromboli

8 oz	rapini	250 g
2 tbsp	extra virgin olive oil, divided	30 mL
½ tsp	kosher or coarse sea salt	2 mL
¼ cup	vegetable stock	60 mL
	Flour, for dusting	
1 lb	pizza dough, at room temperature (see Tips, page 329)	500 g
8 oz	smoked mozzarella, shredded (about 2 cups/500 mL)	250 g

1. *Pizza Sauce:* In a saucepan over medium heat, heat oil until shimmery. Stir in garlic for 10 seconds. Add wine and cook, stirring occasionally, for about 2 minutes, until partly evaporated. Stir in tomatoes, salt, pepper and oregano. When mixture comes to a simmer, reduce heat to medium-low and cook for 10 to 15 minutes, stirring often, until mixture is reduced to about 1½ cups (375 mL) and spitting (see Tips, left). Remove from heat. Stir in basil and set aside.

2. *Stromboli:* Using a sharp knife, trim rapini, separating large clusters. Peel thick stems. Thinly slice stems and chop leaves and florets; you should have about 4 cups (1 L). Set aside.

You can find bottles of the strained tomatoes known as *passata di pomodori* in supermarkets. They are often labeled "passata."

Cold pizza dough is springy and hard to handle. Always set it aside in advance to warm it to room temperature before stretching it.

3. In a large skillet over medium heat, heat 1 tbsp (15 mL) oil until shimmery. Add rapini and salt. Cook, stirring often, for about 1 minute, until wilted. Add stock, cover and cook for 1 to 2 minutes, until tender-crisp. Uncover and cook for about 1 minute, until tender. Transfer to a fine-mesh sieve and set aside to drain and cool to room temperature.

4. On a lightly floured sheet of parchment paper, roll dough into an 8- by 16-inch (20 by 40 cm) rectangle. Brush to the edges with about $1/3$ cup (75 mL) sauce (you will have some left over; see Tips, page 328). Squeeze handfuls of rapini to extract excess liquid and arrange evenly over sauce, leaving a $1/2$-inch (1 cm) border. Scatter mozzarella evenly overtop, leaving the border clear. Starting at a long side, roll up like a jellyroll. Rub remaining oil over dough. Using a sharp knife, cut four diagonal slashes across the top.

5. Transfer stromboli, still on parchment paper, to preheated pizza stone or baking sheet. Bake in center of preheated oven for 25 to 30 minutes, until dough is golden brown and filling bubbles out of the slashes. Cool for 5 minutes before cutting into pieces. Serve warm.

Polenta with Rapini, Sun-Dried Tomatoes and Pine Nuts

No vigorous or prolonged stirring is required for this fuss-free, lump-free polenta. The bold spiced, tangy rapini topping gives you something to sink your teeth into.

Makes 4 to 6 servings
Vegan Friendly
Main course

Tips

For the finest minced garlic, push it through a press.

If you are sensitive to the bitterness of rapini, temper it by increasing the stock to 1 cup (250 mL) and cooking the rapini for 10 minutes or until softened.

To toast pine nuts, cook them in a dry skillet over medium heat, stirring often, for about 3 minutes, until golden and aromatic. Transfer to a bowl to cool.

If you are not a vegan, stir some of your favorite shredded cheese into the polenta, if desired.

- Double boiler

Polenta

3 cups	vegetable stock	750 mL
3 cups	water	750 mL
1½ cups	medium-grind cornmeal (polenta)	375 mL
1 tsp	kosher or coarse sea salt	5 mL
2 tbsp	extra virgin olive oil	30 mL

Topping

1	bunch rapini (1¼ lbs/625 g)	1
½ cup	oil-packed sun-dried tomatoes, drained (oil reserved) and slivered	125 mL
3 tbsp	extra virgin olive oil (approx.)	45 mL
4	cloves garlic, minced (see Tips, left)	4
½ tsp	hot pepper flakes	2 mL
1 tsp	kosher or coarse sea salt	5 mL
¼ cup	vegetable stock	60 mL
3 tbsp	pine nuts, toasted (see Tips, left)	45 mL

1. *Polenta:* In top pan of double boiler, whisk together stock, water, cornmeal and salt. Bring to a boil directly over medium-high heat, then immediately place over simmering water in bottom pan of the set. Cover, reduce heat to low and simmer, stirring occasionally, for about 1 hour, until soft and thick. Stir in oil. Season to taste with additional salt.

2. *Topping:* Meanwhile, using a sharp knife, trim rapini, separating large clusters. Peel thick stems. Cut stalks into 1-inch (2.5 cm) pieces. Set aside.

3. In a measuring cup, mix oil from sun-dried tomatoes with enough olive oil to measure ¼ cup (60 mL). Transfer to a large skillet and heat over medium heat until shimmery. Stir in sun-dried tomatoes, garlic and hot pepper flakes for 20 seconds. Stir in rapini and salt. Cook, tossing with tongs, for about 2 minutes, until slightly wilted. Add stock, cover and cook for about 2 minutes, until rapini is tender-crisp. Uncover, increase heat to medium-high and cook, stirring often, for about 1 minute, until liquid is almost evaporated.

4. Ladle polenta into wide, shallow bowls. Top with equal quantities of rapini mixture. Sprinkle pine nuts overtop.

Hands-Off Lemon Rapini Risotto

Risotto's endless stirring is a turnoff for busy cooks. I learned this mostly hands-off technique from **Cook's Illustrated** *magazine, a fount of information. It gives me time to multitask, and the technique can be applied to any risotto. My version mates edgy rapini, tart lemon and creamy butter with the rice.*

Makes 4 to 6 servings (about 8 cups/2 L)

Vegan Friendly

Side dish

Tips

Whenever possible, use reduced-sodium vegetable stock. Not only is it healthier, it allows you to better control the saltiness of a dish.

Risotto rice is short-grained, creamy and starchy. Arborio is the most popular type, while Carnaroli and Vialone Nano are pricier.

The speed at which risotto cooks depends on the width of the pan, the level of heat and the temperature of the stock. I use a 10-inch (25 cm) saucepan to cook risotto at a lively pace.

10 oz	rapini (about ½ bunch)	300 g
5 cups	vegetable stock (see Tips, left)	1.25 L
1 cup	water	250 mL
3 tbsp	unsalted butter or non-dairy alternative, divided	45 mL
1 tbsp	extra virgin olive oil	15 mL
4	green onions (white and light green parts), cut into 1-inch (2.5 cm) pieces	4
1½ cups	Arborio rice (see Tips, left)	375 mL
2	cloves garlic, chopped	2
¼ cup	dry white wine	60 mL
1 tsp	kosher or coarse sea salt	5 mL
¼ tsp	hot pepper flakes	1 mL
½ cup	freshly grated Parmesan-style cheese (1 oz/30 g), optional	125 mL
2 tbsp	chopped fresh parsley leaves	30 mL
1 tsp	finely grated lemon zest	5 mL
4 to 6	small lemon wedges	4 to 6

1. Using a sharp knife, trim rapini, separating large clusters. Peel thick stems and halve them lengthwise, then slice stems thinly. Chop leaves and florets into small pieces. In a pot of boiling salted water over medium heat, cook rapini for 3 to 5 minutes, until tender. Drain well and set aside.

2. In a small saucepan on a back burner, bring stock and water to a boil over medium-high heat. Reduce heat to low.

3. In a wide saucepan (see Tips, left) over medium heat, melt 1 tbsp (15 mL) butter with oil. Add green onions and cook, stirring often, for 2 to 3 minutes, until softened and turning golden. Add rice and cook, stirring often, for about 1 minute, until coated. Stir in garlic for 10 seconds. Stir in wine for about 1 minute, until absorbed. Add 5 cups (1.25 L) hot stock mixture, salt and hot pepper flakes. When mixture comes to a simmer, reduce heat to medium-low, cover and cook for about 20 minutes, until most of the liquid is absorbed and rice is almost tender. Stir in remaining stock. Cook, stirring constantly, for about 3 minutes, until rice is creamy and tender.

4. Remove pan from heat, cover and set aside for 5 minutes to absorb steam. Stir in remaining butter, cheese (if using), parsley and lemon zest, then prepared rapini. Serve immediately, with lemon wedges alongside.

Romaine

Lactuca sativa longifolia

> **Other names: cos.**
>   Depending on where you are shopping, you may find romaine identified as *bindsalat, kosu retasu, lattuga romana, lechuga orejona, letsugas, marouli, romin* or *zi li wo ju.*

Tasting Notes

Romaine is balanced between crispness and tenderness. It is juicy and crunchy (especially the center rib) and more flavorful than iceberg. The older outer leaves and green tips are herbaceous and somewhat bitter.

Health Notes

Romaine contains vitamins A, B_6, C and K, calcium, copper, folate, iron, magnesium, manganese, phosphorus, potassium, riboflavin and thiamin.

In folk medicine, lettuce has been used to treat insomnia, acid indigestion, colitis, constipation, gout and stress; to cleanse the liver; and to build bone density. The ancient Egyptians believed that lettuce increased sexual prowess.

Romaine is the second most common lettuce in North America, after iceberg. It is the sturdiest, stiffest form of leaf lettuce.

Ancient Romans ate a similar lettuce, known as Roman or Cappadocian lettuce. One emperor erected a lettuce statue to honor the supposed healing powers of its milky sap. In Syria, romaines were bred with stiff ribs so they could be used to scoop up food.

There are various explanations for the name *romaine* — take your pick. The ancient Romans were believed to be the first to use romaine-type lettuce in salads. *Romaine* is a French name for the lettuce grown in the papal gardens when the popes temporarily relocated from Rome to Avignon. In 17th-century England they called it "Roman lettuce." Romaine reached North America via Rome.

Meanwhile, the name *cos* may be derived from the Greek island of Kos, where this type of lettuce was widely cultivated during the Byzantine period, or from the word *khus,* which is Arabic for "lettuce."

Romaine's fortunes skyrocketed thanks to the popularization of Caesar salad. It was once virtually unknown in North America, living in the shadow of its sibling, iceberg lettuce. Until the 1970s, only one out of every ten heads of lettuce sold in North America was a romaine. Then trendy chefs and casual eateries alike discovered Caesar salad, previously a regional specialty, and diners started flocking to salad bars, which were hip and happening. Romaine cultivation and sales have since exploded. A bar graph would show sales of romaine rising and those of iceberg dropping, while butter and leaf lettuces remain fairly constant.

Varieties

Green romaine (*Lactuca sativa longifolia*) is the most common. Specialty romaines include a red variety that is tenderer and bruisable, and freckles lettuce, a type with green leaves and maroon spots.

Romaine hearts are the tender inner leaves of whole heads of lettuce.

Baby romaine leaves, picked when young, are added to salad mixes or sold on their own.

Buy It

Romaine is a supermarket mainstay. You can buy loose heads, bagged romaine hearts and baby romaine in plastic clamshells. Baby romaine is a relatively new addition to produce sections.

Elongated heads of romaine have light green leaves and large, crunchy ribs. The heads should be compact, the leaves crisp and the ribs free of rusty discolorations or cracks. Avoid romaine with dried or wilted tips or a browned stem end.

Store It

Swathe a head of romaine tightly in plastic wrap. Or separate the leaves, rinse and dry thoroughly, roll in paper towels, place in resealable bags and refrigerate.

Romaine will keep in the refrigerator for up to one week.

Prep It

Before consuming romaine, pull off and discard any withered or damaged outer leaves.

Swish torn romaine or whole leaves gently in cold water. Drain, then spin-dry or blot and allow to dry completely (otherwise salad dressing won't cling properly to the leaves).

To clean a head of romaine, cut it in half lengthwise and soak in cold salted water for 5 to 15 minutes. To dry, lay the halves, cut side down, on paper towels or a clean kitchen towel, or dry them on a rack.

Because cut edges tend to brown quickly, tearing is better than slicing, but romaine may be chopped or shredded if using immediately.

To shred romaine, quarter the head lengthwise, keeping the base intact. If smaller pieces are desired, cut each quarter lengthwise again. Then slice crosswise, starting at the top. Discard the base.

Consume It

Romaine is a good all-purpose lettuce for salads and sandwiches. It holds up well to heavy, creamy dressings. You can use the small, firm inner leaves as scoops for dips or salads such as tabbouleh.

If you are dressing romaine with oil and vinegar, add the latter first. Vinegar won't adhere properly to oiled leaves.

Romaine (particularly the hearts) is the lettuce of choice for Caesar salad. The leaves may be left whole or chopped before being bathed in the garlicky dressing.

You can add romaine to cooked dishes to supply crunch or moisture. In that case, be brief — about 5 minutes of cooking time is enough.

SUBSTITUTES

leaf lettuce, butter lettuce, iceberg lettuce, Taiwan lettuce

Grilled Romaine Caesar

The Caesar has got to be the most popular salad in North America. Chefs have been playing with it for decades. The latest fad: grilled Caesars. In my version, romaine halves are lightly charred on the barbecue until warm, juicy and a bit smoky, then drizzled with dressing and embellished with cheese, chapons (giant croutons) and tomatoes (for color).

Makes 4 servings

Salad

Tips

I prefer Caesar vinaigrette rather than a creamy dressing for grilled salad. To keep it vegetarian, I replaced the standard anchovies with white miso.

This recipe makes about ⅔ cup (150 mL) dressing. Use any leftover portion on other salads.

Fine, dry grated cheese gives this dressing a better texture than the freshly grated kind.

Cut each romaine heart lengthwise through the core (to hold leaves together). The romaine halves must be washed and left to dry completely before grilling. Soak them in cold salted water for 5 to 15 minutes, then air-dry on a rack.

Grilling brings out the juiciness of the lettuce, but don't overdo it or the greens will be tough.

To shave the cheese into ultra-thin slices, use a cheese slicer or vegetable peeler.

- Preheat barbecue to medium

Caesar Vinaigrette

2	cloves garlic, minced	2
1 tbsp	minced shallot	15 mL
1 tbsp	white wine vinegar	15 mL
1 tsp	vegetarian Worcestershire sauce	5 mL
1 tsp	white miso (see Tips, left)	5 mL
½ tsp	kosher or coarse sea salt	2 mL
½ tsp	freshly ground black pepper	2 mL
Dash	hot sauce	Dash
½ cup	extra virgin olive oil	125 mL
2 tbsp	dry grated Parmesan-style cheese (see Tips, left)	30 mL

Salad

2	romaine hearts, trimmed and halved lengthwise (see Tips, left)	2
4 tsp	extra virgin olive oil	20 mL
	Kosher or coarse sea salt	
4	cocktail tomatoes, quartered (see Tips, page 182)	4
	Freshly ground black pepper	
	Chapons (page 456)	
1 cup	shaved Parmesan-style cheese (1 oz /30 g; see Tips, left)	250 mL

1. *Caesar Vinaigrette:* In a large bowl, using a fork, mash together garlic, shallot, vinegar, Worcestershire, miso, salt, pepper and hot sauce. Whisk in oil, then cheese.
2. *Salad:* Brush cut sides of romaine hearts with oil and sprinkle with salt to taste. Place, cut sides down, on preheated barbecue grate. Cover and grill for about 2 minutes, until cut sides are lightly charred and tops feel warm. Do not turn.

3. Using a large spatula, carefully transfer each romaine heart to a serving plate. Drizzle with vinaigrette to taste (you may have some left over). Arrange tomato wedges alongside. Season generously with pepper. Arrange chapons, to taste, alongside romaine. Scatter cheese over romaine and serve immediately.

Variation

Instead of barbecuing, use a grill pan (preferably cast iron). Heat it over medium heat for 3 to 5 minutes, add the romaine halves (in batches) and sear for about 5 minutes, pressing down occasionally with a spatula, until bottoms are lightly charred and tops no longer feel cool.

Greco-Roman Salad

Who can resist classic Mediterranean ingredients? In this recipe, a garlic-basil-balsamic dressing provides the perfect finishing touch for a sunny salad.

Makes 2 to 4 servings

Vegan Friendly

Salad

Tips

There are many kinds of feta — made with sheep's, goat's or cow's milk — and they range in texture from creamy to crumbly. For this recipe, choose a fairly soft, moist feta.

To toast pine nuts, cook them in a dry skillet over medium heat, stirring often, for about 3 minutes, until golden and aromatic. Transfer to a bowl to cool.

4 oz	romaine lettuce, trimmed and torn into bite-size pieces (about 3½ cups/875 mL, loosely packed)	125 g
⅓ cup	Basil Balsamic Vinaigrette (page 450)	75 mL
2 oz	feta cheese or extra-firm tofu, crumbled (½ cup/125 mL; see Tips, left)	60 g
¼ cup	sliced red onion	60 mL
4	cherry tomatoes, halved	4
1	small roasted red pepper, sliced into strips	1
8	oil-cured black olives, pitted	8
1 tbsp	pine nuts, toasted (see Tips, left)	15 mL

1. In a large bowl, toss romaine with dressing to taste (you will have some left over).

2. Transfer romaine to a serving platter or individual plates. Top with feta, onion, tomatoes, roasted red pepper, olives and pine nuts. Serve immediately.

Savoy Cabbage

Brassica oleracea capitata sabauda

> *Other names:* **cole, colewort, curly cabbage, Lombardy/Milan cabbage.**
>
> **Depending on where you are shopping, you may find savoy cabbage identified as *band gobhi, cavolo di Milano, cavolo verza, chirimen kanran, chou fries, couve crespa* or *krambolahano*.**

Savoys are latecomers to the cabbage patch. Cabbages were domesticated in Europe before 1000 BCE and widely consumed by the Middle Ages. However, savoys were not developed until the 16th century.

The savoy was cultivated from loose-head cabbages called romanos, then renamed *chou d'Italie* and *chou de Savoie*. German gardeners are credited with developing the savoy, although culinary historians say it originated in the former Duchy of Savoy, which bordered on Italy, France and Switzerland.

Tasting Notes

Savoy tastes milder than green cabbage. It is mellow, nutty and slightly sweet.

Health Notes

Savoy cabbage contains vitamins A, B$_6$ and C, calcium, copper, magnesium, phosphorus, potassium and thiamin. It is high in fiber.

In European folk medicine, cabbage was used to treat inflammations and engorged breasts in new mothers. A paste of raw cabbage was put in a cabbage leaf and wrapped over the affected area.

Varieties

There are various cultivars of savoy cabbages. They range in size, but all have ruffled leaves. In fact, when cabbage leaves are ruffled, they are described as "savoyed."

One rare variety is the baby green cabbage that originated in the Middle East. It has an elongated head and, of course, savoyed leaves.

Buy It

Savoy cabbages are sold in supermarkets. Like other cabbages, the savoy is a winter vegetable, but it is available almost year-round.

Heads range from 1 to 5 pounds (500 g to 2.5 kg). Smaller savoys (less than 2 lbs/1 kg) are tenderer and taste better.

The savoy is a kinder, gentler head cabbage. The leaves are looser, greener and softer than those of green cabbages. The crinkled, deeply veined leaves range from pastel to dark green. Choose a head that feels heavy for its size. Avoid savoys with leaves that are limp, yellowed or dry at the edges. If the leaves have begun to separate from the stem end, the cabbage is past its prime.

Store It

Head cabbages last a long time. Swathe the savoy tightly in plastic wrap.

Savoy cabbage will keep in the refrigerator for up to two weeks or longer. Older cabbage may be salvaged by pulling off the wilted outer leaves, but it will be less sweet.

Use cut cabbage within three days, as the edges turn gray and dry. You can cut off discolored parts before using them.

Prep It

Before cooking with savoy cabbage, peel off and discard dry or damaged outer leaves.

To preserve the vitamin C content, don't cut or wash cabbage until you are ready to use it.

SUBSTITUTES

green cabbage, napa

Carbon-steel knives are rare in home kitchens, but if you have one, don't use it on cabbage. It can react with chemical compounds in the leaves and darken them. Use a stainless steel knife instead.

To core savoy cabbage, turn the head upside down. Cut it through the core into quarters, evenly from base to top. Lay each quarter on its side. Using a large knife, slice out the core at an angle. Don't forget that the core is edible and nutritious; it can be chopped or sliced and eaten raw.

To cut the cabbage, after coring, slice it crosswise into shreds or ribbons. If desired, chop into large or small pieces.

Generally head cabbages aren't washed. However, quartered cabbage may be rinsed under cold running water. Better still, I prefer to cut and wash cabbage, then spin-dry if necessary, as each recipe requires.

To make cabbage crisper for salad, soak chunks in ice water before chopping.

To make cabbage sweeter and milder, shred and soak it in salted water for an hour before cooking. (However, I prefer unsoaked cabbage; it has more character and tastes nuttier.)

To make cooked cabbage sweeter and nuttier, simmer shredded cabbage in skim (nonfat) milk for 5 minutes before using it in a recipe.

If you are steaming, grilling or roasting, you can prevent cabbage from falling apart by shoving a metal skewer lengthwise through a wedge, by leaving the core intact, or both.

For wrappers and cabbage rolls, blanch the leaves in batches of 4 to 6 in a large pot of boiling water for 1 to 3 minutes. The time will depend on the coarseness of the leaf and how soft you need it to be. If your recipe calls for a long baking time or a sauce will be added to coat the rolls, blanch the leaves for a shorter period. Pat dry each leaf before filling.

Lightning won't strike if you don't use whole leaves for cabbage rolls. For tender rolls, make a triangle cut to remove the thick center rib, or cut off the coarser bottom part of the leaf straight across. While rolling stuffed cabbage, cut off any excess flaps and trim thick ribs.

Consume It

Savoy cabbage can be eaten raw but is usually cooked. Steam, boil, braise, grill or roast it. Cooks consider savoy cabbage tastier, tenderer and easier to work with than green cabbage, and thus superior. It is better for cooking and not as odorous. Its softer leaves are perfect for cabbage rolls.

Cabbage and Chestnut Minestrone

I admit it — combining savoy cabbage with chestnuts does seem odd. The result, however, is magically delectable. This Italian soup is excellent comfort food.

Makes 4 to 6 servings
Vegan Friendly
Soup

Tips

You can find peeled roasted chestnuts in foil bags in the produce section of well-stocked supermarkets.

Whenever possible, use reduced-sodium vegetable stock. Not only is it healthier, it allows you to better control the saltiness of a dish.

- Blender

2 tbsp	extra virgin olive oil	30 mL
1	onion, diced	1
1	carrot, diced	1
½ tsp	kosher or coarse sea salt	2 mL
4	cloves garlic, chopped	4
1 tsp	chopped fresh rosemary leaves	5 mL
¼ tsp	hot pepper flakes	1 mL
½ cup	dry white wine	125 mL
6 oz	savoy cabbage, chopped (about 3 cups/750 mL, loosely packed)	175 g
2	bags (3½ oz/100 g each) peeled roasted chestnuts, coarsely chopped (see Tips, left)	2
4 cups	vegetable stock (see Tips, left)	1 L
	Freshly ground black pepper	
2 tbsp	chopped fresh parsley leaves	30 mL

1. In a saucepan over medium heat, heat oil until shimmery. Add onion, carrot and salt. Cook, stirring often, for about 3 minutes, until softened. Stir in garlic, rosemary and hot pepper flakes for 20 seconds. Add wine and cook, stirring and scraping up brown bits from bottom of pan, for 1 to 2 minutes. Stir in cabbage and chestnuts until coated. Add stock. When mixture comes to a simmer, cover, reduce heat to low and cook for about 30 minutes, until cabbage is very tender.

2. Transfer about three-quarters of the mixture to blender and purée until smooth. Return to pan and stir into remaining soup. Season with salt and pepper to taste.

3. Ladle into a tureen or individual bowls. Sprinkle with parsley and serve hot.

Double Savoy Cabbage Rolls

Cabbage lovers can double their pleasure with these rolls. The savoy cabbage leaves are filled with more peppery cabbage, carrots and kasha. Cabbage and kasha taste so good together!

Makes 12 rolls

Side dish

Tips

Use the big outer leaves of the cabbage for wrappers and chop the tender pastel heart. Cabbages vary quite a bit in size. You may need 2 smaller ones.

Kasha is roasted buckwheat groats. In this dish I use whole kasha, not ground, which can get too mushy.

Stirring an egg into the kasha keeps the grains separated and helps prevent mushiness.

I prefer kosher salt because it tastes better than iodized table salt and (ideally) contains no additives. Table salts and some sea salts contain additives such as iodine compounds (iodides), anti-clumping agents and even sugar (in the form of dextrose, which is used to stabilize iodine). Although the North American Salt Institute states that kosher salt "contains no additives," some kosher salt brands do contain additives such as anti-clumping agents. If you have concerns, check the label.

- Preheat oven to 350°F (180°C)
- 13- by 9-inch (33 by 23 cm) baking dish, brushed with oil

12	outer leaves of savoy cabbage (see Tips, left)	12
5 tbsp	extra virgin olive oil, divided	75 mL
1 cup	whole kasha (see Tips, left)	250 mL
1	large egg, beaten (see Tips, left)	1
2 cups	water	500 mL
2 tsp	kosher or coarse sea salt, divided (see Tips, left)	10 mL
3	carrots (6 oz/175 g total), chopped	3
1	large onion, diced	1
12 oz	savoy cabbage, chopped (see Tips, left)	375 g
	Freshly ground black pepper	
1½ cups	freshly grated Parmesan-style cheese (see Tips, page 341)	375 mL

1. In a large pan of boiling water, blanch half the cabbage leaves over medium-high heat for 2 to 3 minutes, until softened. Using a mesh scoop, transfer leaves to a clean kitchen cloth and arrange in a single layer to dry. Repeat with remaining leaves.

2. In a medium saucepan over medium heat, heat 1 tsp (5 mL) oil until shimmery. Stir in kasha briefly, to coat. Still stirring, pour in egg. Cook, stirring, for about 1 minute, until kasha no longer looks wet and grains are separated. Add water and 1 tsp (5 mL) salt. When mixture comes to a simmer, cover, reduce heat to low and cook for about 15 minutes, until water is absorbed and kasha is tender. Remove from heat, uncover and set aside for 5 minutes. Fluff with a fork.

3. Meanwhile, in a large skillet over medium heat, heat ¼ cup (60 mL) oil until shimmery. Add carrots and onion. Cook, stirring often, for 3 minutes, until softened. Add chopped cabbage and remaining salt. Season generously with pepper to taste. Cook, stirring often, for about 5 minutes, until cabbage is wilted and tender-crisp. Remove from heat. Gently stir in prepared kasha. Season with salt to taste. Set aside to cool for 15 minutes.

4. Lay dry cabbage leaves on work surface, veined side down. Using a sharp knife, cut a small triangle out of the center rib of each leaf and discard. Scoop $1/2$ to $3/4$ cup (125 to 175 mL) kasha mixture onto each leaf, according to size of leaf. (You may have some filling left over — it is delicious on its own.) Sprinkle about 2 tbsp (30 mL) cheese over each. Roll up each leaf: pull bottom of leaf over filling, fold both sides over the middle, roll tightly and place seam side down in prepared baking dish. Lightly brush remaining oil over rolls. Cover baking dish with foil. Bake for about 30 minutes, until cabbage leaves are tender. Remove foil and bake for 5 minutes more, to allow excess steam to evaporate. Serve hot.

Variations

Kasha and Cabbage: Instead of making cabbage rolls, serve the delicious cabbage and kasha filling on its own. In that case, increase the amount of chopped cabbage to 1 lb (500 g).

Drizzle some of your favorite tomato sauce over the rolls before serving them.

Savoy Smashies

Never mind mashed potatoes — smashed potatoes are all the rage. In this satisfying version, they are combined with cabbage, basil and garlic. Serve the smashies with a big salad or soup to make a vegetarian meal.

Makes 4 servings
Vegan Friendly
Side dish

Tips

For colorful smashies, use mixed yellow and red potatoes.

For the finest minced garlic, push it through a press.

Don't crush the potatoes too enthusiastically. They should be smashed, not mashed.

- Preheat oven to 400°F (200°C)
- 8-inch (20 cm) square baking dish

1 lb	mini potatoes (see Tips, left)	500 g
5 tbsp	extra virgin olive oil, divided	75 mL
1 tsp	kosher or coarse sea salt, divided	5 mL
3 oz	savoy cabbage, shredded (about $2^1/2$ cups/625 mL, loosely packed)	90 g
$1/4$ cup	chopped fresh basil leaves	60 mL
4	cloves garlic, minced (see Tips, left)	4
	Freshly ground black pepper	

1. In baking dish, toss potatoes with 1 tbsp (15 mL) oil and $1/2$ tsp (2 mL) salt. Roast in preheated oven, shaking pan once, for about 45 minutes, until browned and soft.

2. Meanwhile, in a medium pan of boiling salted water, cook cabbage over medium heat for about 5 minutes, until tender-crisp. Drain and pat dry.

3. In a large serving bowl, using a fork, toss together cabbage, basil and garlic until well combined. Add hot potatoes, pepper and remaining oil. Using a fork, push on each potato until the flesh pops out of the skin (see Tips, left). Stir roughly to combine. Season with salt to taste and serve warm.

Minestrone Soup

I love thick vegetable minestrone with romaine stirred in at the end to add an appealing crunch. This recipe is yet more proof that lettuces can be cooked. Savoy cabbage, meanwhile, deliciously ups the green content. This makes a big batch of soup — feed your friends or freeze the leftovers.

<table>
<tr><td colspan="2">Makes 8 to 12 servings (about 17 cups/4.25 L)</td></tr>
<tr><td colspan="2">Vegan Friendly</td></tr>
<tr><td colspan="2">Soup</td></tr>
</table>

Tips

The tender inner stalks of celery are called the celery heart.

Whenever possible, use reduced-sodium vegetable stock. Not only is it healthier, it allows you to better control the saltiness of a dish.

Fire-roasted canned tomatoes are sold in well-stocked supermarkets and gourmet food shops. They add a delicious smoky flavor to the minestrone. If you can't find any, use regular canned diced tomatoes and, if desired, a dash of liquid smoke.

If you are a vegetarian, check cheese labels. Traditional cheeses, especially artisanal types such as Parmesan, are made with animal-based rennet. However, many cheese companies now use vegetarian rennet instead.

If you prefer a thinner soup, add extra stock, to taste, at the end.

¼ cup	extra virgin olive oil	60 mL
1	large onion, diced	1
2	large cloves garlic, chopped	2
4	carrots (8 oz/250 g total), sliced	4
2	stalks celery heart with leaves (see Tips, left)	2
2 oz	savoy cabbage, finely shredded (about 2 cups/500 mL, loosely packed)	60 g
4 oz	green beans, halved (about 1¼ cups/300 mL)	125 g
3 oz	small cauliflower florets (about 1 cup/250 mL)	90 g
½ cup	thinly sliced fennel	125 mL
2 tsp	kosher or coarse sea salt	10 mL
6 cups	vegetable stock (see Tips, left)	1.5 L
4 cups	water	1 L
1	can (14 oz/398 mL) diced fire-roasted tomatoes (see Tips, left)	1
1	can (19 oz/540 mL) romano beans, rinsed and drained	1
1 cup	elbow pasta	250 mL
1	zucchini (6 oz/175 g), halved lengthwise and sliced	1
¼ cup	chopped fresh parsley leaves	60 mL
1 tbsp	chopped fresh oregano leaves	15 mL
1 tbsp	chopped fresh basil leaves	15 mL
¼ tsp	freshly ground black pepper	1 mL
3	leaves romaine, finely chopped (about 2 cups/500 mL, loosely packed)	3
	Freshly grated Parmesan-style cheese, optional (see Tips, left)	

1. In a large pot over medium heat, heat oil until shimmery. Add onion and garlic, and cook, stirring often, for about 3 minutes, until softened. Add carrots, celery, cabbage, green beans, cauliflower, fennel and salt. Cook, stirring often, for about 5 minutes, until softened. Add stock, water and tomatoes. When mixture comes to a simmer, cover, reduce heat to low and simmer for 15 to 20 minutes, until vegetables are tender-crisp.

2. Stir in beans, pasta, zucchini, parsley, oregano, basil and pepper. Increase heat to medium and return to a simmer. Cover, reduce heat to low and cook for about 15 minutes or until pasta is al dente. Stir in romaine. Season with salt to taste. Ladle into serving bowls. Sprinkle cheese overtop, to taste, if using. Serve hot.

Belgian Stoemp

Belgian stoemp takes smashed potatoes up a notch by combining them with tasty vegetables. In keeping with the Belgian theme, you can serve the stoemp in endive boats.

Makes about 6½ cups (1.6 L)		
Vegan Friendly		
Side dish		

Tips

I prefer kosher salt because it tastes better than iodized table salt and (ideally) contains no additives. Table salts and some sea salts contain additives such as iodine compounds (iodides), anti-clumping agents and even sugar (in the form of dextrose, which is used to stabilize iodine). Although the North American Salt Institute states that kosher salt "contains no additives," some kosher salt brands do contain additives such as anti-clumping agents. If you have concerns, check the label.

For best results, use russet potatoes, which are fluffy when mashed. Waxy red or white potatoes tend to become gluey when mashed.

For a boost of greens, in Step 1, add up to ¼ cup (60 mL) each chopped leaves from the carrot and turnip.

You can use green cabbage instead of savoy.

¼ cup	unsalted butter or non-dairy alternative	60 mL
1	large leek (white and light green parts), thinly sliced	1
1	large carrot (4 oz/125 g), diced (½ inch/1 cm)	1
1	turnip (6 oz/175 g), diced (½ inch/1 cm)	1
3 oz	savoy cabbage, chopped (about 2 cups/500 mL, loosely packed)	90 g
2 tsp	kosher or coarse sea salt, divided (see Tips, left)	10 mL
½ cup	vegetable stock (see Tips, page 342)	125 mL
1 tbsp	cider vinegar	15 mL
3	potatoes (2 lbs/1 kg total), peeled and cut into 2-inch (5 cm) chunks	3
½ cup	whole milk or unflavored soy milk	125 mL
¼ tsp	freshly ground white pepper	1 mL
5	Belgian endives, leaves separated, optional	5

1. In a large skillet over medium heat, melt butter. Add leek, carrot, turnip, cabbage and 1 tsp (5 mL) salt. Cook, stirring often, for about 5 minutes, until softened. Add stock. Cover, reduce heat to medium-low and cook for about 10 minutes, until carrot and turnip are tender-crisp. Stir in vinegar, cover and set aside.

2. Meanwhile, in a large saucepan of boiling salted water, cook potatoes for about 15 minutes, until tender. Drain, then return to pan over low heat for 1 minute, shaking once or twice, to release steam. Set aside.

3. In a microwave-safe measuring cup, scald milk for 1 minute, but do not boil. Add milk, remaining salt, and pepper to potatoes. Using a potato masher, mash until chunky. Transfer to vegetable mixture in skillet and stir to combine.

4. If desired, serve in endive boats: Scoop about 2 tbsp (30 mL) stoemp onto each endive leaf.

Scapes

Allium sativum ophioscorodon

Other names: **garlic curls/greens/shoots/spears/sprouts/stems/tops/whips.**

Depending on where you are shopping, you may find scapes identified as *bawang, knoflook, lahsan, ninniku, skordo, saum, suan* **or** *tum.*

Scapes are garlic shoots — the young, rounded green flower stems that grow directly from underground garlic bulbs. Garlic is one of the most important, ubiquitous and compelling ingredients in cuisines around the world. Garlic scapes, however, are still considered exotic produce.

Garlic is native to Asia, with more than 7,000 years of history behind it. Although grown in England by the mid-1500s, in North America garlic was considered a smelly Mediterranean specialty until relatively recently. Now it is a kitchen staple. In fact, North American food lovers are proudly garlic-crazy.

Scapes eaten as vegetables are a fortunate byproduct of garlic farming. In the past few years a growing contingent of curious shoppers has been discovering these garlicky greens. They are still relegated mainly to Asian grocery stores and farmers' markets, but it seems only a matter of time before scapes find their way into mainstream supermarkets.

Tasting Notes

Scapes are garlicky but milder than garlic, with accents of chive and green onion. After cooking, they lose their bite and develop asparagus accents.

Varieties

Botanically, scapes are the long flowering stems that grow directly from underground bulbs. In culinary terms, scapes are the immature round flower stalks of hard-neck garlic (*Allium sativum ophioscorodon*), also known as stiff-neck garlic, serpent garlic, top-setting garlic, Spanish garlic, *hua san* or *rocambole*. The other main type of garlic, soft-neck or braidable garlic, which is overwhelmingly abundant in supermarkets, does not produce scapes.

Less commonly, *scapes* also refers to the stalks of elephant garlic (*A. ampeloprasum*), also known as great-headed garlic or Levant/Russian garlic. It is botanically a leek, starting as a single white bulb that develops into giant cloves. In its wild form it is foraged like ramps.

Farmers chop off scapes in the spring before flower heads (bulbils) form, to prevent them from sapping nutrients from the bulb. Lucky for us — then we get to buy them.

Besides scapes, the leaves of garlic plants are also eaten as vegetables, particularly in Asia. In stores, however, the label "garlic leaves" may refer to the foliage of garlic plants; to garlic chives, also known as Chinese/Korean chives, which resemble tall blades of grass; or to ramps (page 315).

Shoots and greens from wild garlic plants are edible, though considered inferior or even upsetting if ingested in excess. Wild garlic (*A. ongicuspis*), which grows in central and southwestern Asia, is considered the ancestor of common garlic. Field garlic (*A. oleraceum*) grows wild in northern Europe, while Canada garlic (*A. canadense*), also known as meadow garlic or Canada onion, grows in North America. Crow garlic (*A. vineale*), like some other types of wild garlic, is considered an invasive weed.

Do not confuse scapes with green garlic. Before a baby garlic plant forms cloves, it is called green garlic. It looks like a green onion, but sometimes the stem is tinged with purple and the leaves are flat, not tubular. Green garlic is sold seasonally at farmers' markets; it's now quite trendy.

Health Notes

Although no official government analysis is available, scapes are thought to contain vitamins A, B_6 and C, folate, iron, manganese, phosphorus and selenium. Scapes are strongly anti-inflammatory.

Garlic has been studied by scientists, particularly regarding its reputed ability to lower cholesterol. In folk medicine, garlic has been used to treat stomach ulcers, parasites, coughs and congestion, and toothache. It was believed to stimulate sex drive and aggression, and thus ancient yogis and meditating Buddhists shunned it.

Buy It

Garlic scapes are sometimes described as gourmet food — if so, they must be the least expensive gourmet food in town. Asian supermarkets sell huge bags for a pittance.

SUBSTITUTES

ramps

Scapes look like chives on steroids. As they grow, they curl and coil into loops, with tight conical buds topped by long tips, like lightning rods. The name "garlic whips" refers to their whip-like appearance. Tangled masses of scapes are attractive. Sometimes, later in the season, scapes are cut into straight, straw-like segments and bagged tightly.

Because they have been growing in popularity, scapes are now sold into the fall, when they are firmer, tougher and turning fibrous.

Store It

Scapes lose their garlicky flavor and their bite mellows as they stand. Place scapes, cutting them if necessary, in resealable bags, then refrigerate.

Garlic scapes will keep in the refrigerator for up to one week.

Prep It

Scapes vary a great deal in tenderness. Cut off and discard 1 inch (2.5 cm) or more of the lighter green or beige base, which may be woody.

Like garlic proper, the more finely scapes are chopped, the more intense their flavor.

Consume It

Scapes are never eaten raw. You can stir-fry, sauté or braise them, add them to soups or omelets, pickle them or turn them into pesto.

Cook scapes until tender-crisp or tender. This takes 5 to 10 minutes if sautéing or simmering.

To prevent chewiness, cook over medium-low heat and do not allow scapes to brown when stir-frying or sautéing.

After simmering scapes in stock for a creamy soup, purée and push the mixture through a sieve to get rid of any short, wiry inedible fibers, particularly in older scapes.

Garlic Power

Through the millennia, garlic's magical powers were considered as important as its culinary clout. In popular culture, garlic is best known as a vampire repellent, although it has also been used to fend off witches, demons and other evildoers. In Greece and Turkey, new houses and boats were once draped with garlic to repel the envious. In India, garlic, lemons and red chiles were hung in doorways to ward off unspecified "evil."

The ancients ate garlic for strength and energy. It was fed to the slaves building the pyramids. Roman soldiers consumed garlic to develop brawn in battle (if that didn't work, they could perhaps repel the enemy with their breath).

Festivals around the world are devoted to this stinky plant. An annual event in Gilroy, California, is one of world's largest food festivals. Gilroy is the self-styled garlic capital of the world, although it doesn't grow the most garlic. China is by far the world's largest producer, followed by India.

Double Garlic Soup

Alliums are king in this creamy soup packed with garlic and scapes as well as onion. Slow simmering mellows the garlic, but still, I wouldn't advise preparing it on date night. This is my take on garlic soup, which is enjoyed around the world, including in Hungary. Like many Hungarian immigrants, my family had lodgers when I was a teenager. One lodger often cooked garlic soup, proclaiming that it strengthened his "sword of love." I just rolled my eyes, figuring that either his vanity or his breath would repel the ladies. Mind you, garlic soup is tasty enough to suffer bad breath for.

Makes 4 to 6 servings (about 7 cups/1.75 L)

Vegan Friendly

Soup

Tips

Whenever possible, use reduced-sodium vegetable stock. Not only is it healthier, it allows you to better control the saltiness of a dish.

Yellow-fleshed potatoes are best for this recipe; they help make the soup creamy but not gluey. The best-known yellow-fleshed potatoes are Yukon Golds.

If substituting soy milk for the cream, use full-fat unflavored soy milk for best results. The soup, however, will be thinner.

Cajun seasoning is a spice and vegetable blend that you can find in most supermarkets. If desired, substitute your favorite spice blend.

Note that refrigerating garlic soup overnight may cause the flavor to intensify and even become too pungent.

- Stand or immersion blender

2 tbsp	extra virgin olive oil	30 mL
1	Spanish onion (1 lb/500 g), diced	1
2	heads garlic, cloves separated and peeled	2
½ cup	dry white wine	125 mL
4 cups	vegetable stock (see Tips, left)	1 L
1	large potato (8 oz/250 g), diced (see Tips, left)	1
1 tsp	kosher or coarse sea salt	5 mL
⅛ tsp	freshly ground white pepper	0.5 mL
8 oz	scapes, thinly sliced (about 1⅓ cups/325 mL, loosely packed)	250 g
½ cup	heavy or whipping (35%) cream or soy milk (see Tips, left)	125 mL
	Cajun seasoning (see Tips, left)	

1. In a large saucepan over medium heat, heat oil until shimmery. Add onion and garlic. Cook, stirring often, for about 5 minutes, until softened and turning golden. Stir in wine, scraping up brown bits from bottom of pan. Add stock, potato, salt and pepper. When mixture comes to a simmer, cover, reduce heat to low and cook for about 30 minutes, until vegetables are soft.

2. Using blender, purée soup. Return to pan, if necessary. Add scapes and bring to a simmer over medium heat. Cover, reduce heat to low and cook for about 10 minutes, until scapes are tender. Stir in cream. Season with salt to taste.

3. Ladle into serving bowls. Sprinkle Cajun seasoning overtop and serve hot.

Scape Vichyssoise

I love to play with vichyssoise, an American take on France's classic leek and potato soup, because the recipe lends itself to endless experimentation. In this version, garlicky green scapes boost the flavor while potatoes add creaminess without cream. By the way, this vichyssoise tastes good warm too.

Makes 4 to 6 servings (about 6 cups/1.5 L)		
Vegan Friendly		
Soup		

Tips

In soups I often use yellow-fleshed potatoes, which are starchy without being gluey. They help add creaminess without cream. The best-known yellow-fleshed potatoes are Yukon Golds.

Whenever possible, use reduced-sodium vegetable stock. Not only is it healthier, it allows you to better control the saltiness of a dish.

- Blender

¼ cup	extra virgin olive oil	60 mL
1 lb	scapes, cut into 1-inch (2.5 cm) pieces (about 4 cups/1 L, loosely packed)	500 g
4	potatoes (1½ lbs/750 g), cut into ½-inch (1 cm) dice (see Tips, left)	4
1 tsp	kosher or coarse sea salt	5 mL
2	cloves garlic, chopped	2
6 cups	vegetable stock (see Tips, left)	1.5 L
1 cup	whole milk or full-fat soy milk	250 mL
¼ tsp	freshly ground white pepper	1 mL
2 tbsp	chopped chives	30 mL

1. In a large saucepan over medium heat, heat oil until shimmery. Add scapes and cook, stirring often, for 3 to 5 minutes, until softened but not browned. Stir in potatoes and salt. Cook, stirring often, for 2 minutes. Stir in garlic for 30 seconds. Stir in stock, scraping up brown bits from bottom of pan. When mixture comes to a simmer, reduce heat to low, cover and cook for about 15 minutes, until vegetables are very tender. Set aside to cool for 5 minutes.
2. Transfer soup to blender and purée. Push purée through a fine-mesh sieve set over a large bowl. Discard solids. Pour soup into an airtight container. Cool briefly, cover and refrigerate until chilled, for at least 4 hours or preferably overnight.
3. Before serving, stir in milk and pepper and season with salt to taste. Ladle into serving bowls and garnish with chives.

Variation

You can serve this soup warm. In Step 2, instead of refrigerating it, add the milk and pepper and reheat over low heat (do not allow the soup to boil). Adjust the salt and garnish with chives.

Savory Peach and Scape Soup

I first tried peach soup in the 1980s at Trappers, a Toronto restaurant dedicated to Canadian cuisine. The soup was a revelation — imagine, peach dishes could move beyond the dessert menu! Tangy fruit, garlicky scapes and a hint of curry make this soup a taste sensation.

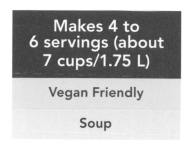

Makes 4 to 6 servings (about 7 cups/1.75 L)

Vegan Friendly

Soup

Tips

Whenever possible, use reduced-sodium vegetable stock. Not only is it healthier, it allows you to better control the saltiness of a dish.

Choose peaches that are firm and just barely ripe. Soft, very ripe peaches are too sweet for this dish.

Do yourself a favor and use freestone peaches for this dish. They are much easier to work with because the pits release easily. Freestone peaches appear later in the summer than semi-freestones.

Using a serrated peeler is the easiest, quickest way to peel peaches.

- Stand or immersion blender

4 oz	scapes, thinly sliced (about ⅔ cup/150 mL, loosely packed)	125 g
2 cups	vegetable stock (see Tips, left)	500 mL
1 cup	water	250 mL
2 tbsp	extra virgin olive oil	30 mL
1	small onion, diced	1
1	stalk celery with leaves, coarsely chopped	1
¼	small red bell pepper, coarsely chopped	¼
¼ cup	all-purpose flour	60 mL
1 tsp	curry powder	5 mL
1 tsp	kosher or coarse sea salt	5 mL
4	ripe but firm peaches (1½ lbs/750 g), peeled, pitted and cut into large chunks (see Tips, left)	4
1 to 1½ cups	whole milk, rice milk or unflavored soy milk	250 to 375 mL
1 tbsp	chopped fresh chives	15 mL

1. In a saucepan over medium heat, bring scapes, stock and water to a simmer. Cover, reduce heat to medium-low and simmer for 5 to 8 minutes, until scapes are tender. Using a fine-mesh sieve set over a medium bowl, drain. Set aside scapes and stock.

2. In same saucepan over medium heat, heat oil until shimmery. Add onion, celery and red pepper. Cook, stirring often, for 4 to 5 minutes, until softened. Sprinkle in flour, curry powder and salt. Cook, stirring constantly, for about 30 seconds, until golden brown. Stir in reserved stock and peaches. When mixture comes to a simmer, reduce heat to low, cover and cook for about 30 minutes, until vegetables are very tender.

3. Purée, using blender. Return to pan if necessary. Stir in reserved scapes and add milk to desired consistency. Season with salt to taste. Garnish with chives and serve warm or at room temperature.

Variations

Instead of the celery, use chopped celeriac tops or Chinese celery.

Almond Cauliflower Scape Soup

Cauliflower and garlicky scapes in a creamy almond base make this fragrant soup a comfort food fit for both family and guests.

Makes 4 to 8 servings (about 9 cups/2.25 L)		
Vegan Friendly		
Soup		

Tips

In soups I often use yellow-fleshed potatoes, which are starchy without being gluey. They help add creaminess without cream. The best-known yellow-fleshed potatoes are Yukon Golds.

You can substitute black pepper for the white pepper. White pepper is used mainly for aesthetic reasons, to avoid black specks in finished dishes. It is ground from white peppercorns, which are riper than black peppercorns and have had the skins stripped off. Also unlike black peppercorns, they are not dried and left to darken and shrivel.

To toast almonds, cook them in a dry skillet over medium heat, stirring often, for 2 to 3 minutes, until golden and aromatic.

- Stand or immersion blender

6 oz	scapes, thinly sliced (about 1 cup/250 mL)	175 g
3 cups	vegetable stock	750 mL
2 cups	water	500 mL
2 tbsp	extra virgin olive oil	30 mL
1	small onion, diced	1
1	cauliflower (3 to 3½ lbs/1.5 kg), cored and coarsely chopped	1
1	potato (6 oz/175 g), cut into chunks (see Tips, left)	1
1 tsp	kosher or coarse sea salt	5 mL
¼ tsp	freshly ground white pepper (see Tips, left)	1 mL
2 cups	plain almond milk	500 mL
1 tbsp	finely chopped fresh chives	15 mL
½ cup	slivered almonds, toasted (see Tips, left)	125 mL

1. In a large saucepan over medium heat, bring scapes, stock and water to a simmer. Cover, reduce heat to medium-low and simmer for 5 to 8 minutes, until tender. Using a fine-mesh sieve, drain over a medium bowl. Set aside scapes and stock.

2. In same saucepan over medium heat, heat oil until shimmery. Add onion and cook, stirring often, for about 3 minutes, until softened and turning golden. Stir in cauliflower and potato. Cook, stirring occasionally, for about 3 minutes, until turning golden. Add reserved stock, salt and pepper. When mixture comes to a simmer, cover, reduce heat to low and cook for about 30 minutes, until vegetables are very tender.

3. Purée, using blender. Return to pan if necessary. Stir in scapes and almond milk. Season with salt to taste. Reheat over low heat if necessary, but do not allow soup to boil.

4. Ladle into serving bowls. Garnish with chives and almonds. Serve warm.

Sweet Potato Mash with Olive Oil and Scapes

These casually mashed sweet potatoes have a rustic appeal. Top-quality olive oil and garlicky scapes make them sing.

3	sweet potatoes (2½ lbs/1.25 kg), peeled and cut into 2-inch (5 cm) chunks	3
6 tbsp	extra virgin olive oil, divided (see Tip, left)	90 mL
6 oz	scapes, sliced (about 1⅓ cups/325 mL, loosely packed)	175 g
2 tsp	kosher or coarse sea salt	10 mL
½ tsp	coarsely ground black pepper, divided	2 mL

Makes 4 to 6 servings

Vegan Friendly

Side dish

Tip

To make the most of this dish, reach for a bottle of fragrant premium extra virgin olive oil and don't be afraid to use a good quantity. Besides its health appeal, quality olive oil adds flavor and satiny texture to the sweet potatoes.

1. In a saucepan of boiling salted water, cook sweet potatoes over medium heat for about 15 minutes, until tender.

2. Meanwhile, in a skillet over medium-low heat, heat 2 tbsp (30 mL) oil until hot. Add scapes and lightly sprinkle with salt to taste. Cook, stirring often, for about 5 minutes, until tender-crisp but not browned. Set aside.

3. Drain sweet potatoes. Return them to pan and heat over low heat for 1 minute, shaking pan occasionally, to evaporate excess moisture. Remove from heat and, using a hand masher, mash until crushed but not pasty. Stir in salt, ¼ tsp (1 mL) pepper and 3 tbsp (45 mL) oil.

4. Transfer potatoes to a large serving bowl and make a well in the center. Scrape prepared scapes into well. Drizzle remaining oil over sweet potatoes. Season with remaining pepper. Serve warm.

Sorrel

Rumex species

> *Other names:* acid/cock/cow/horse/gentleman's sorrel, bread-and-cheese, brown sugar, dock, donkey's oats, green snob, ranty-tanty, redshanks, red-top sorrel, sharp/sorrel/sour dock, sour grass/leaf/leek/weed, sower-grass, sure, toad's sorrel, Tom Thumb's thousand fingers, vinegar leaf.
>
> Depending on where you are shopping, you may find sorrel identified as *acedera, azeda, chukapalam, cizaña, erba brusca, hime suiba, kuzu kulagi, oseille, shchavel, soska, suan mo, surette, vinagrillo, vinette* or *yakuwa*.

Tasting Notes

Sorrel has pucker power. Its leaves and stems are astringent, very sour and lemony, with hints of gooseberry and rhubarb. Sorrel takes some getting used to, but it is delightful.

Sorrel is a name given to a group of plants famous for their acidic bite. Two common species names, *Rumex acetosa* and *R. acetosella*, are derived from the Latin *acetum*, meaning "vinegar."

Sorrels grow wild across the Americas, Europe and Asia, invading lawns, gardens, meadows and fields. Sorrels have also been cultivated for centuries by folks enamored of their tangy flavor. They are popular in Europe and parts of Asia and Africa. Most North Americans, however, have yet to discover their deliciousness.

Varieties

Sorrels are members of the large *Rumex* genus. All have exceptionally sour edible leaves; there are green, purple and pretty red-veined varieties. Sorrels are called a host of wacky names, often inspired by their tartness.

The three most notable varieties are common sorrel (*Rumex acetosa*), also known as garden sorrel, spinach dock or Belleville sorrel; sheep sorrel (*R. acetosella*), also known as field/red/sour sorrel; and French sorrel (*R. scutatus*), also known as buckler sorrel, shield-leaf sorrel or green-sauce (for one of its culinary uses).

Common sorrel and French sorrel are cultivated and sold commercially. North American shoppers are most likely to encounter common sorrel. True to its name, French sorrel is grown particularly in (but not limited to) France. Sheep sorrel is better known as a foraged plant. Its popularity peaked in 16th-century England, when young shoots were used in sauces, jams, jellies and even ale. Other Rumex relatives include:

- **patience dock** (*R. patientia*), also known as spinach dock, garden patience or monk's rhubarb. This variety is considered the mildest sorrel. It is a seasonal spring leaf vegetable in Eastern Europe, especially Bulgaria, Macedonia, Serbia and Romania.
- **butter dock** (*R. obtusifolius*), also known as bluntleaf or broad-leaved dock. Its large leaves were once used to wrap butter. It is considered an invasive weed in the Great Lakes area.
- **curly dock** (*R. crispus*), also known as yellow or sour dock. This plant grows around the world as a pesky weed, but its young leaves are also cooked as a leaf vegetable.
- **canaigre** (*R. hymenosepalus*), also known as rhubarb dock, Arizona dock or tanner's dock. This variety is native to the United States and Mexico. It has been cooked by Native Americans as both food and medicine, but canaigre's main claim to fame is its cultivation for tannins used in leather tanning.

Buy It

Sorrel is usually sold in small bunches, as it is one of the more expensive leafy greens. Specialty greengrocers and some supermarkets sell sorrel, but it may be purchased more economically at farmers' markets. It is seasonal from spring through early fall, depending on the area.

Common and French sorrels have thin stems topped by leaves from 2 to 12 inches (5 to 30 cm) long. The leaves are spinach-like but more tapered and a lighter green. Sheep sorrel has smaller leaves with a distinctive arrowhead shape. Avoid sorrels with yellowed or wilted leaves or woody stems.

Health Notes

Sorrel contains vitamins A, B_6 and C, calcium, copper, iron, magnesium, manganese, niacin, phosphorus, riboflavin and thiamin.

In folk medicine, sorrel leaves have been chewed, brewed as teas or ground to make poultices to treat inflammation, fever, excessive menstrual bleeding, scurvy, tuberculosis, kidney and urinary disorders, mouth ulcers, sore throat, upset stomach, cramps and nausea. They have also been considered an aphrodisiac.

The sour flavor of *Rumex* and *Oxalis* sorrels is due to oxalic acid (see "O Is for Oxalates," page 355), which is common in many foods but can upset the stomach in large doses.

Store It

Wrap sorrel in paper towels and store in a perforated resealable bag. Or place the bunch in a glass or vase of water like a bouquet, with a plastic bag draped over the foliage, then refrigerate.

Sorrel will keep in the refrigerator for up to two days.

Prep It

Stems wider than $1/8$ inch (3 mm) are too stringy; pinch them off and discard unless you are making a puréed soup and pressing the solids through a sieve.

Sorrel leaves can be chopped or torn.

To wash, rinse sorrel in cold water, drain and spin-dry.

Those Other Sorrels

In addition to the plants belonging to the *Rumex* family, there's a second group of tart, lemony greens that are called sorrels. More specifically, they are wood sorrels from the Oxalis genus that resemble shamrocks. They include:

- **common wood sorrel** (*Oxalis acetosella*), also known as cuckoo bread or cuckoo's nest/sorrow. This is the best known *Oxalis* sorrel. However, in North America, "common wood sorrel" also refers to **mountain wood sorrel** (*O. montana*) and **redwood sorrel** (*O. oregano*).
- **white oxalis** (*O. albicans*), also known as hairy wood sorrel or radish-root yellow sorrel. This variety is native to the west coast of North America and is particularly plentiful in California.
- **creeping wood sorrel** (*O. corniculata*), known in India as *chichoda bhaji*.
- **scurvy-grass sorrel** (*O. enneaphylla*), once consumed by sailors to prevent scurvy, notably those who accompanied Charles Darwin on HMS *Beagle*.
- **iron cross sorrel** (*O. tetraphylla*), also known as four-leaf sorrel or lucky leaf. This Mexican plant is popular for its lemony edible leaves and flowers, but it is also grown as an ornamental.
- **pickle plant** (*O. stricta*), also known as lemon clover or common yellow wood sorrel. It is used in salads and brewed as drinks.
- **soursob** (*O. pes-caprae*), also known as African wood sorrel, Bermuda buttercup/sorrel, cape sorrel, goat's-foot or English weed. This plant is a traditional ingredient in a South African dish, water flower stew. It has exceptionally high acidity.

Yet another sorrel — unrelated to either the *Rumex* or *Oxalis* family — is **mountain sorrel** (*Oxyria digyna*), also known as Alpine sorrel or *qunguliq*. Native to mountainous areas and the arctic tundra, it was eaten by the Inuit to prevent scurvy.

Don't confuse sorrels with the Caribbean beverage sorrel, which is made from edible red hibiscus flowers (*Hibiscus sabdariffa*) also known as roselle or red sorrel.

Consume It

Treat sorrel as a salad green, herb or leafy vegetable. Serve it raw or cooked. Sorrel is most famously the star of a classic French cream soup and an Italian raw *verde* (green) sauce.

Sorrel leaves are tender and may be eaten raw in salads, but only with mixed greens, as they are too sour on their own. You can add sorrel to sandwiches instead of lettuce and mustard, and it also makes a tangy pesto. Sorrel becomes more acidic as it matures. Use smaller, younger leaves in salads or as sautéed vegetables, and older sorrel in cooked dishes such as sauces and soups.

Don't cook sorrel in an aluminum or cast-iron pan; the acid in it will react with the metal.

Sorrel may be puréed and ladled over dishes as a sauce. Puréeing releases acids and other chemical compounds, so the sauce may become slightly bitter.

Sorrel turns olive green when cooked. Boiled stems and leaves are ready in less than a minute.

SUBSTITUTES
purslane, arugula

O Is for Oxalates

Oxalates in your food? That sounds alarming. Oxalates include oxalic acid and calcium oxalate. In large doses these naturally occurring chemical compounds can cause ailments ranging from stomach upsets to kidney damage.

But don't panic. We don't normally eat huge doses of these compounds, and the risk of poisoning is minuscule. A wide variety of foods that we commonly consume contain oxalates. In fact they are often found in superfoods such as nuts, berries, leafy greens, tofu, tea and cocoa.

Edible greens rich in oxalic acid include spinach, chard, beet greens, parsley, sorrel, lamb's quarters, amaranth, purslane and cassava leaves. These greens are enjoyed worldwide and are not considered dangerous when properly prepared and eaten in reasonable quantities.

However, oxalic acid can reduce the nutritional assets of some greens. It bonds to minerals such as calcium and iron, forming insoluble compounds. This reduces the so-called bioavailability of these important nutrients, meaning that the body can't take full advantage of them. For example, because spinach is famously high in both iron and oxalates, not all the iron it contains can be absorbed by the body.

High levels of oxalic acid are dispersed in cooking water. Note: Do not use an aluminum or cast-iron pan to cook foods that are high in oxalic acid. The acid will react with the metal in the pans.

Many plants also contain calcium oxalates, which form tiny, needlelike crystals called raphides. Botanists speculate that raphides evolved to stop predators from eating the plants. That didn't stop humans, though.

Calcium oxalates are the irritants found in the popular taro culinary family (page 389). They can cause an itchy sensation in the mouth and throat and a stinging, burning rash on the hands. Some people are more sensitive than others to these substances. The remedy is thorough cooking, which neutralizes (but doesn't destroy) the calcium oxalate crystals.

Sorrel Pesto

Sorrel is the perfect candidate for pesto because its lemony accents are a foil for the rich oil and nuts. Slather sorrel pesto in sandwiches and wraps, dollop it into soups or toss it with pasta. Once the sorrel pesto bowl is empty, I am always tempted to lick it.

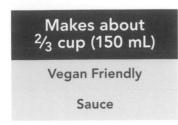

Makes about ⅔ cup (150 mL)

Vegan Friendly

Sauce

Tips

Before preparing pesto, make sure the washed sorrel is completely dry, to ensure that it mixes properly.

Be careful not to overprocess the pesto into a paste. Traditionally the ingredients for pesto are ground together, so some texture is desired.

• Mini food processor

1	large clove garlic	1
1	large bunch sorrel (3 oz/90 g), stemmed and coarsely chopped (about 4 cups/1 L, loosely packed; see Tips, left)	1
¼ cup	chopped flat-leaf (Italian) parsley leaves	60 mL
3 tbsp	pine nuts	45 mL
½ tsp	kosher or coarse sea salt	2 mL
⅛ tsp	freshly ground black pepper	0.5 mL
¼ cup	extra virgin olive oil	60 mL

1. In food processor fitted with the metal blade, chop garlic. Add sorrel, parsley, pine nuts, salt and pepper. Pulse a few times to chop. With motor running, drizzle oil through the feed tube and process until pesto is puréed but with some texture (see Tips, left).

Variation

If desired, add 2 tbsp (30 mL) freshly grated Parmesan-style cheese, made without animal rennet if you are a vegetarian.

Creamy Sorrel Soup

Delightfully lemony sorrel counterbalances the creamy base of this luscious soup. Sorrel soups of all kinds are popular in Europe.

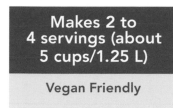

Makes 2 to 4 servings (about 5 cups/1.25 L)

Vegan Friendly

Soup

Tips

In soups I often use yellow-fleshed potatoes, which are starchy without being gluey. They can add creaminess without cream. The best-known yellow-fleshed potatoes are Yukon Golds.

If you don't have small sorrel leaves, garnish with some slivered sorrel.

- Stand or immersion blender

2 tbsp	extra virgin olive oil	30 mL
1	small onion, diced	1
1	leek (white and light green parts), sliced	1
2	cloves garlic, chopped	2
2	potatoes (12 oz/375 g), cut into 1-inch (2.5 cm) chunks (see Tips, left)	2
2 cups	vegetable stock	500 mL
1 cup	water	250 mL
2	sprigs fresh thyme	2
1 tsp	kosher or coarse sea salt	5 mL
1/8 tsp	freshly ground white pepper	0.5 mL
2	small bunches sorrel (2 oz/60 g each), leaves and stems chopped (about 6 cups/1.5 L, loosely packed)	2
1 cup	whole milk or unflavored soy milk	250 mL
	Sour cream or non-dairy alternative	
2 to 4	small sorrel leaves (see Tips, left)	2 to 4

1. In a saucepan over medium heat, heat oil until shimmery. Add onion and leek. Cook, stirring often, for about 3 minutes, until softened. Stir in garlic for 20 seconds. Add potatoes and cook, stirring, for 1 minute. Add stock, water, thyme, salt and pepper. When mixture comes to a simmer, cover, reduce heat to low and cook for about 30 minutes, until vegetables are very tender.

2. Stir in sorrel for about 1 minute, until wilted. Discard thyme stalks. Using blender, purée soup. Return to pan, if necessary, and stir in milk. Season with salt to taste. Reheat over medium-low heat, if necessary, but do not allow soup to boil.

3. Ladle into serving bowls. Garnish each with a dollop of sour cream and a small sorrel leaf. Serve warm.

Garlic Lover's Beans and Greens Soup

Sorrel adds a nice lemony finish to this garlic-laden soup. However, almost any quick-cooking leafy green (along with a squeeze of lemon juice) would work in this recipe. Beans and greens are a match made in heaven. As for the garlic, don't be afraid of using a whack of it — caramelizing in oil makes it mellow.

Makes 4 to 6 servings (about 6 cups/1.5 L)
Vegan Friendly
Soup

Tips

Be careful not to brown the garlic or it will taste bitter. Reduce the heat if necessary.

Cannellinis are also known as white kidney beans.

To avoid a swampy effect — unappealing clumps of greens in the soup — chop the sorrel leaves into small pieces.

- Stand or immersion blender

4	heads garlic, broken into cloves	4
2 tbsp	extra virgin olive oil	30 mL
2 tsp	kosher or coarse sea salt, divided	30 mL
3 cups	vegetable stock	750 mL
1 cup	water	250 mL
2	cans (19 oz/540 mL each) cannellini beans, rinsed and drained (see Tips, left)	2
6	sprigs fresh thyme	6
½ tsp	freshly ground white pepper	2 mL
2	large bunches sorrel (3 oz/90 g each), stemmed and chopped (about 8 cups/2 L, loosely packed)	2
	Sour cream or non-dairy alternative	
¼ cup	chopped fresh parsley leaves	60 mL

1. In a small pan of boiling water, blanch unpeeled garlic cloves for about 1 minute. Drain and immediately rinse under cold running water until cool enough to handle. Pull off the skins. Using a sharp knife, trim hard root ends and cut large cloves in half lengthwise. Set aside.

2. In a large skillet over low heat, heat oil for 1 to 2 minutes. Add garlic, cover and cook, stirring occasionally, for about 20 minutes, until turning golden. Stir in 1 tsp (5 mL) salt. Cover and cook, stirring occasionally, for 5 to 10 minutes, until very tender and lightly browned (see Tips, left). Remove from heat and set aside.

3. In a saucepan over medium-high heat, combine stock, water, beans, thyme and remaining salt. Bring to a simmer, then cover, reduce heat to low and simmer for 15 minutes. Remove from heat and discard thyme sprigs. Add garlic and pepper. Using blender, purée. Return to pan, if necessary, and stir in sorrel. Simmer over medium-low heat for about 2 minutes, until sorrel is wilted and tender.

4. Ladle into serving bowls. Add a dollop of sour cream to each serving and sprinkle with parsley. Serve warm.

Spinach

Spinacia oleracea

Other names: **common/cultivated spinach, prickly-seeded/round-seeded spinach.**

Depending on where you are shopping, you may find spinach identified as *bayuam, bo cai, épinard, espinaca, hourensou, ispany, palaak, pinni, spinacio* **or** *spinat.*

The origins of spinach have been traced to ancient Persia (now Iran), where it was called *aspanakh*, or "green hand." Traders introduced it to India, then China, where they called it "Persian greens."

Arabs lauded spinach as the "captain of leafy greens" and wrote medicinal and agricultural treatises on it. They introduced it to Sicily in the 9th century, then to Spain. Via Spain, spinach spread to France and England in the 14th century. It became a popular food for Lent and was cultivated by religious communities. The British called it *spinnedge* or "the Spanish vegetable." In the 1500s Catherine de' Medici, Queen of France, demanded that spinach be served at every meal. Catherine was from Florence, and her culinary obsession may be behind the fact that, even today, many dishes prepared with spinach are dubbed "Florentine."

In North America, spinach wasn't cultivated until after the turn of the 19th century. In 1929 spinach entered popular culture with the introduction of the Popeye cartoons. The sailorman's obsession with spinach captured the imagination of the public. Suddenly kids everywhere started to believe in the power of spinach — and their moms had an excuse to nag them about eating their greens.

Tasting Notes

Spinach is astringent, herbaceous, nutty and slightly juicy. The stems are succulent and slightly fibrous.

Equivalents

1 small bunch spinach
= 8 oz (250 g)

•

1 medium bunch =
10 oz (300 g), including
5 to 6 oz (150 to 175 g)
stemmed leaves

•

1 large bunch = 12 oz
(375 g), including 8 to
10 oz (250 to 300 g)
stemmed leaves

Varieties

There are two main categories of cultivated spinach (*Spinacia oleracea*):

- **savoy spinach**, also known as curly-leaf spinach. This variety has frilly, crinkled leaves. It is the sturdiest, coarsest type.
- **smooth-leaf spinach**, also known as flat-leaf spinach or salad spinach. This type has broad, flat leaves. It is easier to clean than savoy spinach.

Hybrid semi-savoy spinach has slightly crinkled leaves.

2 oz (60 g) baby
spinach leaves =
2¾ cups (700 mL),
loosely packed

•

2 oz (60 g) stemmed
whole leaves = 4 cups
(1 L), loosely packed

•

2 oz (60 g) coarsely
chopped leaves
= 2 cups (500 g),
loosely packed

•

12 oz (375 g) leaves
and tender stems,
cooked and drained =
2 cups (500 mL)

•

12 oz (375 mL) leaves
and tender stems,
cooked, drained,
squeezed and
finely chopped =
1½ cups (375 mL)

•

12 oz (375 g) cooked
(wilted) leaves =
1¾ cups (425 mL)

•

12 oz (375 g)
cooked (wilted)
leaves, squeezed =
1½ cups (375 mL)

Spinach is available in both mature and baby sizes. The rise in spinach sales in the past decade was partly due to the introduction of baby spinach in the wider marketplace.

The ancestors of cultivated spinach are wild spinach (*S. turkestanica*) and Armenian wild spinach (*S. tetranda*). With habitats in West Asia and parts of India, they are regional and not widely distributed.

Buy It

Spinach is a supermarket staple, available in fresh bunches and bags. Bagged spinach is usually savoy, semi-savoy or mature spinach. Fresh bunches tend to be the more appealing smooth-leaf spinach. Baby spinach comes in bags or clamshell packages.

Spinach has crisp dark green leaves and a pleasant scent. It is prone to rot, so check the center of the bunch. Limpness, tears, yellow spots, moist dark patches, weepy bruises and dry, curled-up stem ends are signs of old age. Pinch a stem to check whether spinach is fresh and moist. Spinach with narrow stems is tenderer.

Store It

Place spinach in a glass or vase of water like a bouquet, with a plastic bag draped over the foliage, then refrigerate it. Or roll it in paper towels and store in a perforated resealable bag. Do not cram spinach into the bag; rot will develop in the center, where moisture collects.

Spinach will keep in the refrigerator for up to three days.

Prep It

Stems are usually pinched off and discarded; only leaves are used in dishes such as creamed spinach. However, the stems are edible, particularly in the case of bunched fresh spinach and baby spinach. The stems on mature savoy spinach are thicker and tougher. If using the stems, chop them before adding to cooked dishes. To keep salads delicate, do not use raw stems in them.

Wash spinach just before using it, swishing it in cold water. If using it in a salad, spin-dry. If cooking it, you may leave the water clinging to its leaves.

Consume It

Spinach is the world's go-to cooking green. It's good raw in salads and sandwiches and cooked in dishes of every sort.

For salads, smooth-leaf spinach is superior to savoy spinach. Baby spinach is tender yet firm and holds up well in salads.

Once you apply heat, spinach becomes the incredible shrinking vegetable. In smaller amounts, raw spinach may be added to dishes such as soups. However, for recipes such as creamed spinach and curries, wilting and draining the greens beforehand is a good strategy. This prevents the dish from becoming too watery.

Health Notes

Spinach contains vitamins A, B$_6$, C, E and K, calcium, copper, folate, iron, magnesium, manganese, phosphorus, potassium, riboflavin, thiamin and zinc. It is high in fiber, high in sodium and strongly anti-inflammatory. Although spinach is touted as being rich in iron, the body can't absorb all of it (see "O Is for Oxalates," page 355).

The *"Spinach, Popeye, Iron, Decimal Error" Story:* As the story goes, 19th-century scientists misplaced a decimal point and thus misrepresented the amount of iron in spinach as being 10 times greater than it is — a mistake that supposedly wasn't corrected until the 1930s. This story still circulates, but it has been debunked as a myth. Interestingly, Popeye was originally shown scarfing spinach for its vitamin A content, not its iron.

In herbal medicine, spinach has been used to treat anemia, urinary tract disorders, skin problems, bleeding gums and congestion in the throat and lungs. It was also considered a laxative and bowel cleanser, as well as an aid to restful sleep.

SUBSTITUTES

Malabar spinach, chard, kale, amaranth, jute leaf, sweet potato leaves

To wilt spinach, cook it in a large saucepan over medium heat — with just the water clinging to its leaves — for about 5 minutes, until wilted and dark green. You can also use the microwave. Place spinach in a large, microwave-safe bowl with $1/4$ cup (60 mL) water per pound (500 g), cover and microwave on High (cooking time depends on the amount of spinach). Drain, cool, squeeze out excess moisture and chop.

You can effectively squeeze out excess liquid by hand. Other alternatives include using a potato ricer or wide tongs, or press the wilted spinach between two plates. Squeeze until most of the liquid runs out — there's no need to apply herculean force.

Spinach Wannabes

"Tastes like spinach" is the vegetarian equivalent of "tastes like chicken." Spinach has become a catch-all designation for tender, fairly mild, fast-cooking leafy greens used around the world — a testament to the virtues of kitchen-friendly *Spinacia oleracea*.

The following pseudo-spinaches may be close enough for cooks, but they do not make the cut with botanists; they are not related to the one true spinach.

- **New Zealand spinach** (*Tetragonia tetragonioides*), also known as Botany Bay greens, Warrigal greens or Cook's cabbage. Indigenous to Australasia and grown in the tropical Americas, these greens spread on vines rather than forming bunches. The triangular, medium green "arrowhead" leaves are best cooked. New Zealand spinach was eaten by Captain Cook's crew to prevent scurvy. A relative is **bower spinach** (*T. implexicoma*), which has smaller thick, spade-shaped leaves.
- **Lagos spinach** (*Celosia argentea*), also known as quail grass, wild/plumed coxcomb, soko *yokoto* or *farar alayyafo*. This brightly colored plant is grown as an ornamental, but it is edible. Fresh young leaves, stems and flower spikes are used to make a nutritious soup that is daily fare in parts of West Africa.
- **chaya** (*Cnidoscolus aconitifolius*), also known as leaf/tree spinach or Maya spinach. Native to Yucatán, it is a traditional cooking green in parts of Central and South America. Chaya is always cooked to neutralize toxins in the raw leaves.
- **orach** (*Atriplex hortensis*), also known as garden/red orach, butter leaves, mountain spinach or French spinach. Described as salty but not astringent, orach has been eaten as a leafy green since prehistoric times. It was cultivated by the ancients in southern Europe but eventually fell out of favor and was supplanted by true spinach.
- **waterleaf** (*Talinum fructicosum*), also known as Florida/Philippine/Ceylon spinach, Surinam purslane, Lagos bologi, *cariru*, potherb fameflower or sweetheart. This green was introduced to the world via Central and South America and is now cultivated throughout the tropics. It is high in oxalic acid (see "O Is for Oxalates," page 355) and described as slightly sour, with a bitter finish. **Jewels-of-Opar** (*T. paniculatum*), a succulent shrub with edible leaves, is a relative. Edible *Talinum* species are considered similar to both spinach and purslane.
- **Okinawan spinach** (*Gynura bicolor, G. crepidioides*), also known as *hongfeng cai* or *kin-jiso*. This Asian medicinal vegetable is grown commercially. It comes in green and bicolor (green/purple) cultivars. **Cholesterol spinach** (*G. nepalensis*), also known as leaves of the gods, scrambling gynura, Moluccan spinach or googoolipid, is a relative. Its name is derived from its supposed ability to lower cholesterol.
- **sissoo spinach** (*Alternathera sissoo*), also known as samba lettuce or Brazil spinach. Described as crunchier than spinach, this tropical vegetable is cooked to neutralize oxalates (see "O Is for Oxalates," page 355). In Saigon it is planted citywide as an ornamental.

Q Is for Quelites

A spinach-like vegetable with a hazy reputation is **lamb's quarters** (*Chenopodium album*), also known as wild spinach, white goosefoot, *bathua* or *quelites*. Across North America and Europe, this plant may be foraged as an herb or leafy green, but it is more often dismissed as a common weed. In contrast, it is appreciated and even cultivated for its greens, shoots and seeds in Africa, India and Mexico.

North of the border, *restos* with their tacos, enchiladas, refried beans and cheesy casseroles have given us the impression that leafy greens are ignored in Mexico. Not so. Mexicans enjoy both wild and cultivated greens, which they have been eating since antiquity. Before the conquistadors arrived, their diets were heavily vegetarian.

Quelites is a catch-all term for "wild greens" in Mexico. It also specifically refers to lamb's quarters (*C. album*), part of the so-called goosefoot family of edible greens. Relatives include:

- **epazote** (*C. ambroisiodes*), also known as Mexican/Jesuit's tea, Indian goosefoot, Jerusalem oak, stinkweed or wormwood. Native to Central and South America, it is used as a bitter herb and a leaf vegetable. It is added to bean dishes because it is believed to counter flatulence. In North America, dried epazote is more accessible than fresh.
- **huauzontle** (*C. berlandieri nuttaliae*), also known as Aztec/Mexican spinach or Nuttall's goosefoot. Mexicans batter and deep-fry this green, which looks like a long stick of broccoli. Also dubbed spinaches are **tree spinach** (*C. giganteum*) and **wild spinach** (*C. bonus-henricus*), better known as Good King Henry or fat hen.
- **quinoa** (*C. quinoa*) — yes, this is the grain, and yes, the leaves are edible.

Mexicans and Central Americans enjoy the foliage of various types of produce. The leaves of the **Mexican avocado** (*Persea americana drymifolia*), also known as *hoja de aguacate*, are used both fresh and dried, in soups and stews or as wrappers. The Mexican avocado specifically is used; other varieties are reportedly toxic.

Romerito (*Suaeda mexicana*), also known as seepweed, is a cooking green traditionally eaten during Christmas and Lent. Its succulent leaves hang on the stems like fringes. It may be sautéed with garlic, fried in batter, coated with mole or pepita sauce, or added to soup. The name means "little rosemary."

Chipilin (*Crotalaria longirostrata*), also known as *chepil, empanadilla* or *vaca*, is a leguminous plant native to Central America. It is used as a cooked leaf vegetable, not a legume, in soups and *pupusas*. Chipilin is cultivated on a small scale and foraged wild in Mexico, but it is classified as a noxious weed in the United States.

Spinach Dip

My collection of delectable dips would not be complete without this classic. I don't bother baking spinach dip. I just zap it in the microwave, then keep it warm in a mini slow cooker. It tastes good at room temperature too, and — bonus! — the refrigerated leftovers make a tasty spread.

Makes 6 servings (about 1½ cups/ 375 mL)

Appetizer

Tips

If desired, use 4 oz (125 g) frozen spinach instead of fresh spinach. Thaw, cook, drain and then mince it.

For this recipe, buy firm cream cheese, sold in blocks, not the soft deli cream cheese that's scooped into tubs.

If desired, use light mayonnaise. The dip will be a bit looser.

Like many cheeses, Parmesan is made with animal-based rennet and is unsuitable for vegetarians. However, some brands offer Parmesan-style cheese made with vegetarian rennet as a suitable substitute. Check the label to be sure.

You can prepare this dip in advance. Finish Step 2, then transfer to an airtight container and refrigerate for up to 2 days. To serve, microwave until bubbly and stir.

3 cups	stemmed, coarsely chopped spinach leaves (3 oz/90 g; see Tips, left)	750 mL
6 oz	cream cheese, cut into chunks (see Tips, left)	175 g
⅓ cup	mayonnaise (see Tips, left)	75 mL
2 tbsp	freshly grated Parmesan-style cheese (see Tips, left)	30 mL
1 tsp	vegetarian Worcestershire sauce	5 mL
1 tsp	freshly squeezed lime juice	5 mL
1 tsp	garlic powder	5 mL
¼ tsp	kosher or coarse sea salt	1 mL
⅛ tsp	ground nutmeg	0.5 mL
2 tbsp	finely chopped red onion	30 mL
2 tbsp	pimiento, chopped	30 mL

1. In a large saucepan over medium heat, cook spinach with just the wash water clinging to it, stirring often, for 4 to 5 minutes, until wilted and tender. Drain and set aside until cool enough to handle, then squeeze to extract as much liquid as possible. Transfer to a cutting board and chop finely. Set aside.

2. In a microwave-safe serving bowl, combine cream cheese and mayonnaise. Heat on High for about 45 seconds, until hot. Stir until smooth. Stir in grated cheese, Worcestershire, lime juice, garlic powder, salt and nutmeg. Stir in onion and pimiento. Add reserved spinach and stir with a fork until combined. Season with salt to taste.

3. Return to microwave and heat on High for about 1 minute, until bubbly. Serve warm.

Variation

For a looser dip, stir in ¼ cup (60 mL) sour cream before serving.

Spinach Pesto

All kinds of greens lend themselves to pesto. Spinach pesto is a people-pleaser. Dollop this versatile condiment into stews or soups or toss it with pasta, rice or steamed vegetables.

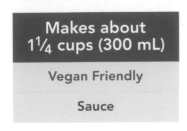

Makes about 1¼ cups (300 mL)

Vegan Friendly

Sauce

Tips

To toast pine nuts, cook them in a dry skillet over medium heat, stirring often, for about 3 minutes, until golden and aromatic. Transfer to a bowl to cool.

For a vegan version, omit the cheese and increase the spinach to 3 cups (750 mL) or 3 oz (90 g).

Be careful not to overprocess the pesto into a paste. Traditionally the ingredients for pesto are ground together, so some texture is desired.

Like many cheeses, Parmesan is made with animal-based rennet and is unsuitable for vegetarians. However, some brands offer Parmesan-style cheese made with vegetarian rennet as a suitable substitute. Check the label to be sure.

- Food processor

2	large cloves garlic	2
2 cups	stemmed, coarsely chopped spinach leaves (2 oz/60 g)	500 mL
¼ cup	fresh basil leaves, loosely packed	60 mL
½ cup	pine nuts, toasted (see Tips, left)	125 mL
¾ cup	freshly grated Parmesan-style cheese (1½ oz/45 g; see Tips, left)	175 mL
⅛ tsp	freshly ground black pepper	0.5 mL
½ cup	extra virgin olive oil	125 mL
1 tsp	freshly squeezed lime juice	5 mL

1. In food processor fitted with the metal blade, chop garlic. Add spinach and basil and pulse until finely chopped. Add pine nuts, cheese and pepper; pulse to chop. With motor running, drizzle oil in a steady stream through the feed tube and process until puréed but with some texture (see Tips, left). Add lime juice; pulse once to mix.
2. Serve immediately or transfer to an airtight container and refrigerate for up to 1 week.

Spinach Salad with Poppyseed Dressing

Who doesn't love spinach salad? This vegetarian dinner salad is finished with an old-school dressing. Although I'm not crazy about sweet dressings, my poppyseed vinaigrette hits the spot.

Makes 4 to 6 servings

Vegan Friendly

Salad

Tips

This recipe makes about 1 cup (250 mL) dressing. Use any leftover portion on other hearty greens or fruit salads. Poppyseed dressing is often paired with salads that include apples, pears or strawberries.

I use canola oil to give the dressing a classic flavor. You can substitute any neutral vegetable or seed oil. Extra virgin olive oil, however, is too bold for this.

Smoked tofu cubes are a delicious vegan alternative to the hard-cooked eggs. Add about 4 ounces (125 g), if desired.

To toast almonds, cook them in a dry skillet over medium heat, stirring often, for 2 to 3 minutes, until turning golden and aromatic.

- Blender

Poppyseed Vinaigrette

2 tbsp	liquid honey or vegan alternative	30 mL
2 tbsp	cider vinegar	30 mL
2 tbsp	diced onion	30 mL
½ tsp	Dijon mustard	2 mL
½ tsp	kosher or coarse sea salt	2 mL
½ cup	oil (see Tips, left)	125 mL
2 tsp	poppy seeds	10 mL

Salad

4 oz	baby spinach leaves (about 5 cups/1.25 L)	125 g
½ cup	thinly sliced red onion circles	125 mL
1 cup	thinly sliced button mushrooms (2 oz/60 g)	250 mL
1 cup	bean sprouts	250 mL
2	hard-cooked large eggs, quartered, or vegan alternative (see Tips, left)	2
2 tbsp	dried cranberries	30 mL
2 tbsp	slivered almonds, toasted (see Tips, left)	30 mL

1. *Poppyseed Vinaigrette:* Using blender, combine honey, vinegar, onion, mustard and salt. With motor running, drizzle in oil, blending until smooth and creamy-looking. Transfer to a small cup with a spout. Stir in poppy seeds and set aside.

2. *Salad:* Divide spinach among serving plates. Drizzle with dressing to taste. Scatter onion circles and mushrooms evenly overtop. Arrange a small mound of bean sprouts in the center of each serving. Place egg wedges at edges. Scatter cranberries and almonds over greens. Serve immediately, with remaining dressing alongside.

Spinach Chickpea Salad with Lemon Cumin Dressing

This irresistible salad has a Tunisian vibe. Spinach and chickpeas go so well together, and the cumin dressing is just the right accent. Serve this as a dinner salad or a side dish.

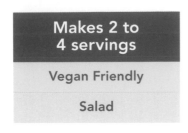

Makes 2 to 4 servings

Vegan Friendly

Salad

Tip

Harissa is a Tunisian spiced chile paste. If you don't have any, substitute your favorite chile paste.

1	can (19 oz/540 mL) chickpeas, drained and rinsed	1
½ cup	diced red onion	125 mL
½ cup	coarsely chopped fresh parsley leaves	125 mL
⅓ cup	Lemon Cumin Dressing (page 453)	75 mL
3 oz	baby spinach leaves (about 4 cups/1 L)	90 g
	Unflavored yogurt or vegan alternative	
	Harissa (see Tip, left)	

1. In a bowl, toss chickpeas, onion and parsley with dressing.
2. Divide spinach among serving plates. Spoon chickpea mixture overtop. Finish with a dollop of yogurt topped by dab of harissa, to taste. Serve immediately.

Pretty Sautéed Spinach

This quick, appealing sauté is versatile as well as good-looking. Serve it over rice, noodles or grains, as a side dish or even in sandwiches.

Makes 2 to 4 servings (about 1¾ cups/425 mL)

Vegan Friendly

Side dish

2 tbsp	extra virgin olive oil	30 mL
2	shallots, chopped	2
1	small red bell pepper, chopped	1
2	cloves garlic, minced	2
1	bunch spinach (12 oz/375 g), trimmed and chopped	1
½ tsp	kosher or coarse sea salt	2 mL
⅛ tsp	freshly ground black pepper	0.5 mL

1. In a large saucepan over medium heat, heat oil until shimmery. Add shallots and red pepper. Cook, stirring often, for about 5 minutes, until softened and golden. Stir in garlic for 20 seconds. Add spinach, salt and pepper. Cook, stirring often, for about 2 minutes, until spinach is wilted and tender. Season with salt to taste. Serve warm.

Bento Box Spinach

Gomae, or sesame spinach salad, is a fine example of the Japanese less-is-more aesthetic. A bonus recipe here is the gomashio, or toasted sesame salt. Everything tastes better with gomashio, so I double the amount when I make it to have some on hand for sprinkling over other greens or steamed veggies.

**Makes
4 small servings**

Vegan Friendly

Side dish

Tips

If you don't have a mortar and pestle, use a mini food processor or spice grinder.

To toast sesame seeds, cook them in a dry skillet over medium heat, shaking the skillet frequently, for about 2 minutes, until turning golden and starting to pop.

To maintain more control over the saltiness of dishes, use reduced-sodium soy sauce. Depending on the type, 1 tbsp (15 mL) regular soy sauce can contain 1,000 mg or more of sodium. Reduced-sodium soy sauce contains about half that amount.

Mirin is sweet Japanese cooking wine. You can find it in most supermarkets. It may or may not be considered vegan, depending on the type of sugar used (and the opinion of the individual vegan).

Be careful not to overcook the spinach. It should be wilted but still substantial, with a tender/chewy balance.

• Mortar and pestle (see Tips, left)

Gomashio

2 tbsp	sesame seeds, toasted (see Tips, left)	30 mL
½ tsp	kosher or coarse sea salt	2 mL

Spinach

1 tbsp	soy sauce (see Tips, left)	15 mL
1 tbsp	mirin (see Tips, left)	15 mL
¼ tsp	granulated sugar	1 mL
1	bunch spinach (12 oz/375 g), trimmed	1

1. *Gomashio:* Using mortar and pestle, lightly crush together sesame seeds and salt (do not create too fine a powder). Set aside.

2. *Spinach:* In a large bowl, combine soy sauce, mirin and sugar. Set aside.

3. In a large saucepan of boiling salted water over medium heat, blanch spinach for 30 seconds (see Tips, left). Drain and immediately rinse with cold water to stop the cooking. Drain and set aside until cool enough to handle. Using your hands, gently squeeze excess liquid from spinach. Add to bowl with soy sauce mixture and toss until coated.

4. Pile prepared spinach evenly in a stack on a cutting board. Using a sharp knife, cut into stacks 2 inches (5 cm) wide. Place each stack in a serving dish (dipping bowls are the right size). Drizzle soy mixture left in bowl over spinach. Sprinkle gomashio, to taste, over spinach (you may have some left over). Serve at room temperature.

Creamed Spinach

Spinach has a decadent side, and creamed spinach is proof of this. My version is rich, but I do show a shred of restraint by replacing some of the cream with milk. Ladle creamed spinach over hot rice and top it with a poached egg — now that's memorable comfort food.

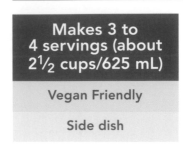

Makes 3 to 4 servings (about 2½ cups/625 mL)

Vegan Friendly

Side dish

Tips

You'll need 2 bunches of spinach for this dish. Save the remainder for other dishes.

A ball whisk, which has separate tines with little balls attached, works best for mixing this dish, rather than a standard whisk with loops that the spinach can get tangled in.

For the creamiest spinach, it's important to start with a very thick white sauce as a base, then tweak it with the remaining cream. The spinach adds moisture that can loosen the sauce, so make sure you squeeze it well.

Note that results will be different if you opt to use soy milk instead of cream: the dish will be much thinner and looser.

12 oz	stemmed spinach leaves (see Tips, left)	275 g
2 tbsp	unsalted butter or non-dairy alternative	30 mL
1	small onion, finely chopped	1
1	large clove garlic, chopped	1
¼ cup	all-purpose flour	60 mL
1½ cups	2% milk or unflavored soy milk	375 mL
½ cup	heavy or whipping (35%) cream or unflavored soy milk (see Tips, left), divided	125 mL
2 tsp	finely grated lemon zest	10 mL
1½ tsp	kosher or coarse sea salt	7 mL
¼ tsp	freshly ground white pepper	1 mL
¼ tsp	ground nutmeg	1 mL

1. In a large pot, cook spinach — with just the wash water clinging to its leaves — for 4 to 5 minutes, stirring often, until wilted and dark green. Drain and set aside until cool enough to handle. Using your hands, squeeze out excess liquid and transfer to a cutting board; you should have about 1½ cups (375 mL). Using a sharp knife, chop coarsely. Set aside.

2. In a medium saucepan over medium-low heat, melt butter. Add onion and cook, stirring often, for about 3 minutes, until softened and golden. Stir in garlic for 30 seconds. Add flour and cook, stirring, for 1 minute. Gradually whisk in milk and ¼ cup (60 mL) cream (see Tips, left). Add lemon zest, salt, pepper and nutmeg. Cook, stirring, for about 2 minutes, until thickened. Stir in spinach and cook for about 1 minute, until bubbly. Stir in some or all of the remaining cream, to desired consistency (see Tips, left). Season with salt to taste and serve immediately.

Variations

If desired, stir in some drained, chopped pimientos in Step 2, or substitute finely chopped red pepper, to taste, for the onion.

This recipe can be used to cream any type of green. However, in Step 1 some greens require blanching or boiling rather than wilting. Check the cooking instructions under "Consume It" for individual greens.

Spring Tonic Soup

When I spy the first signs of spring, I come out of hibernation, grab a mess of greens and prepare this intensely dark, delicious green soup. It's a great way to detox and refuel.

Makes 6 to 8 servings (about 8 cups/2 L)		
Vegan Friendly		
Soup		

Tips

Yellow-fleshed potatoes are best for this recipe. Neither waxy nor dry, they are good all-purpose potatoes. The best-known yellow-fleshed potatoes are Yukon Golds.

Whenever possible, use reduced-sodium vegetable stock. Not only is it healthier, it also allows you to better control the saltiness of a dish.

If you prefer a thinner soup, add ½ cup (125 mL) stock after puréeing the soup (Step 2).

You'll have a lot of leftover greens from the bunches you purchase. Use them as ingredients in other recipes in this book.

When reheating leftovers, do not allow the soup to boil or it may curdle.

- Blender

2 tbsp	extra virgin olive oil	30 mL
2	leeks, sliced	2
2	carrots, sliced	2
4	large cloves garlic, chopped	4
1 tsp	kosher or coarse sea salt (see Tips, page 402)	5 mL
2	large potatoes (1 lb/500 g total), peeled and cut into chunks (see Tips, left)	2
2 cups	loosely packed coarsely chopped spinach leaves (2 oz/60 g)	500 mL
2 cups	loosely packed coarsely chopped Swiss chard leaves (1½ oz/45 g)	500 mL
2 cups	loosely packed coarsely chopped escarole (1½ oz/45 g)	500 mL
2 cups	loosely packed coarsely chopped black kale leaves (1 oz/30 g)	500 mL
1 cup	loosely packed coarsely chopped arugula leaves (¾ oz/25 g)	250 mL
1 cup	loosely packed coarsely chopped dandelion leaves (¾ oz/25 g)	250 mL
1 cup	loosely packed watercress leaves and tender stems (1 oz/30 g)	250 mL
1 cup	trimmed and coarsely chopped fresh parsley leaves and tender stems	250 mL
4 cups	vegetable stock (approx; see Tips, left)	1 L
1 cup	half-and-half (10%) cream or unflavored soy milk	250 mL
2 tbsp	freshly squeezed lemon juice	30 mL
	Plain yogurt or non-dairy alternative	
	Freshly ground black pepper	

1. In a large pot over medium heat, heat oil until shimmery. Add leeks, carrots, garlic and salt. Cook, stirring often, for about 4 minutes, until turning golden. Add potatoes and cook, stirring constantly, for 1 minute. Add spinach, chard, escarole, kale, arugula, dandelion, watercress and parsley. Cook, stirring often, for about 2 minutes, until slightly wilted. Add 4 cups (1 L) stock. When mixture comes to a simmer, cover, reduce heat to low and cook for about 30 minutes, until greens are very tender.

2. Purée in batches, using blender. Return to pan. Stir in cream and lemon juice. Season with salt to taste.

3. Serve warm or at room temperature. Ladle into bowls, add a dollop of yogurt to each serving and season with pepper.

Florentine Winter Tomato and Spinach Soup

I named this tomato soup, with its greens and tiny pasta, as an homage to Florence, where they appreciate spinach intensely. Serve this thick, creamy soup steaming hot on a cold day. The recipe calls for canned tomatoes, so you can make it year-round.

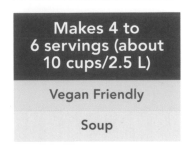

Makes 4 to 6 servings (about 10 cups/2.5 L)

Vegan Friendly

Soup

Tips

If desired, splurge on San Marzano tomatoes. These premium plum tomatoes from Italy are sold in well-stocked supermarkets.

Cane sugar is likely to be filtered through bone char, while beet sugar is not. Most labels don't indicate the source of the sugar. If you are following a vegan diet, use unbleached organic sugar that has not been filtered through bone char, or a sweetener such as agave syrup.

Acini de pepe are tiny pasta that resemble peppercorns in size and shape. You can substitute any petite pasta, including stars and pastina ("beads"), or add nostalgia by using alphabet pasta.

Don't be tempted to cook the pasta in the soup. It creates an unpleasant starchiness.

- Blender

2 tbsp	extra virgin olive oil	30 mL
1	onion, diced	1
1	carrot, coarsely chopped	1
2	cloves garlic, chopped	2
1	can (28 oz/796 mL) plum tomatoes (see Tips, left)	1
4 cups	vegetable stock (see Tips, page 373)	1 L
2 tbsp	coarsely chopped fresh basil	30 mL
1 tbsp	granulated sugar (see Tips, left)	15 mL
1 tsp	kosher or coarse sea salt	5 mL
1/8 tsp	freshly ground black pepper	0.5 mL
1/2 cup	acini de pepe pasta (4 oz/125 g; see Tips, left)	125 mL
6 cups	stemmed, coarsely chopped spinach leaves (6 oz/175 g), loosely packed	1.5 L
1 cup	whole milk, light (5%) cream or unflavored soy milk	250 mL

1. In a saucepan over medium heat, heat oil until shimmery. Add onion, carrot and garlic. Cook, stirring often, for 3 to 4 minutes, until softened and turning golden. Stir in tomatoes, stock, basil, sugar, salt and pepper. When mixture comes to a simmer, cover, reduce heat to low and cook for about 20 minutes, until vegetables are very tender.

2. Meanwhile, in a saucepan over medium heat, cook pasta in boiling salted water for about 8 minutes, until al dente (see Tips, left). Drain and set aside.

3. Using blender, purée tomato mixture. Return to pan, if necessary, and add spinach. Cook over medium heat, stirring often, for 2 to 3 minutes, until wilted. Stir in cooked pasta. Remove from heat and stir in milk. Season with salt to taste. Serve hot.

Variations

You can replace the pasta with cooked bulgur or quinoa.

Mushroom, Barley and Spinach Soup

This Jewish comfort food nourishes both body and soul. I adore the chewy, creamy texture of barley. Don't omit the dill — it gives this hearty soup a lift. Like many soups, this one tastes better the next day, so cherish those leftovers.

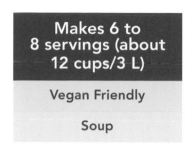

Makes 6 to 8 servings (about 12 cups/3 L)

Vegan Friendly

Soup

Tips

Whenever possible, use reduced-sodium vegetable stock. Not only is it healthier, it allows you to better control the saltiness of a dish.

I use pearl barley in this dish because it cooks faster. If desired, substitute pot barley and simmer the soup for about 90 minutes, until the barley is tender. Consumers are most familiar with pearl barley, which is husked and polished. Pot barley, or Scotch barley, is husked but not as heavily refined. It takes longer to cook but contains more healthy fiber.

This soup thickens as it sits. Before reheating leftovers, add more stock to reach the desired consistency.

1 cup	boiling water	250 mL
1	package (½ oz/15 g) dried porcini mushrooms	1
2 tbsp	extra virgin olive oil	30 mL
3	carrots (6 oz/175 g total), cut into ¼-inch (0.5 cm) dice	3
3	stalks celery, cut into ¼-inch (0.5 cm) dice	3
2	onions, diced	2
2	cloves garlic, chopped	2
1 tsp	kosher or coarse sea salt, divided	5 mL
1 lb	button mushrooms, thinly sliced	500 g
5 cups	vegetable stock (see Tips, left)	1.25 L
3 cups	water	750 mL
½ cup	dry sherry	125 mL
2 tbsp	tomato paste	30 mL
½ cup	pearl barley (4 oz/125 g; see Tips, left)	125 mL
¼ cup	chopped fresh dill fronds	60 mL
¼ cup	chopped fresh parsley leaves, divided	60 mL
½ tsp	freshly ground white pepper	2 mL
4 oz	baby spinach leaves (about 5 cups/ 1.25 L, loosely packed)	125 g

1. Pour boiling water into a large, heatproof measuring cup. Stir in porcinis and set aside for about 15 minutes, until softened. Using a fine-mesh sieve set over a bowl, strain, reserving liquid. Using a sharp knife, coarsely chop porcinis. Set aside.

2. In a large saucepan over medium heat, heat oil until shimmery. Add carrots, celery, onions, garlic and ½ tsp (2 mL) salt. Cook, stirring often, for about 10 minutes, until softened and golden. Add button mushrooms and cook, stirring often, for about 5 minutes, until their liquid is released. Stir in stock, water, sherry, porcinis and their soaking liquid, tomato paste, barley, dill, 3 tbsp (45 mL) parsley, pepper and remaining salt. When mixture comes to a simmer, cover, reduce heat to low and cook for about 45 minutes, until barley is tender.

3. Stir in spinach and cook for about 1 minute, until wilted. Season with salt to taste.

4. Ladle soup into a tureen or individual bowls. Sprinkle remaining parsley overtop and serve hot (see Tips, left).

Turkish Bride's Soup

Legend has it that an unhappy bride created this lentil and bulgur soup for her impossible-to-please mother-in-law. Eventually it became a Turkish tradition to serve the soup to brides before their wedding night. The spinach adds a pop of color to this satisfying dish.

	Makes 6 to 8 servings (about 11 cups/2.75 L)
	Vegan Friendly
	Soup

Tips

Bulgur is steamed wheat berries that have been cracked. You can find it in health food or bulk stores and most supermarkets.

Harissa is a Tunisian spiced chile paste. It is not fiery. Look for it in spice shops, specialty stores or well-stocked supermarkets.

¼ cup	unsalted butter or non-dairy alternative	60 mL
2	onions, diced	2
2 tsp	paprika	10 mL
1 cup	red lentils, rinsed	250 mL
½ cup	coarse bulgur, rinsed (see Tips, left)	125 mL
8 cups	vegetable stock	2 L
2 cups	water	500 mL
2 tbsp	tomato paste	30 mL
1 tbsp	harissa (see Tips, left)	15 mL
1 tsp	kosher or coarse sea salt	5 mL
4 oz	baby spinach leaves (about 5 cups/1.25 L, loosely packed), coarsely chopped	125 g
¼ cup	chopped fresh mint leaves	60 mL
	Unflavored yogurt or non-dairy alternative	
	Thin lemon slices	
	Tiny fresh mint leaves	

1. In a large saucepan over medium-low heat, melt butter. Add onions and cook, stirring occasionally, for about 15 minutes, until soft and golden. Stir in paprika, then lentils and bulgur, until coated. Stir in stock, water, tomato paste, harissa and salt. Increase heat to medium-high and bring to a simmer. Cover, reduce heat to low and cook for about 45 minutes, until bulgur is very soft. Stir in spinach and mint for about 1 minute, until spinach is wilted. Season with salt to taste.

2. Ladle soup into serving bowls. Garnish each with a dollop of yogurt, a lemon slice and a mint leaf. Serve immediately.

Spinach and Black Olive Grilled Cheese Sandwiches

Gourmet grilled cheese sandwiches are all the rage. These are monster specimens, with cheese, sautéed spinach and olives crammed between thick sourdough slices. The recipe was inspired by a combo I tasted in Toronto's Kensington Market.

4	large, thick slices sourdough bread (see Tips, left)	4
	Unsalted butter, softened	
6 oz	Cheddar, Havarti or mozzarella cheese, sliced	175 g
½ cup	black olives, pitted and finely chopped (see Tips, left)	125 mL
½ cup	Pretty Sautéed Spinach (page 368)	125 mL

Makes 2 sandwiches

Sandwich

Tips

Cut from the center of a round sourdough loaf to obtain large slices. For example, my slices were ¾ inch (2 cm) thick and 8 inches (20 cm) long. If the sandwiches don't fit side by side in your skillet, cook them individually.

For intense flavor, buy crinkly ripe black olives. To pit olives, rap each one with the flat side of a knife blade. The olives will split and the pits will pop out.

1. Slather butter on one side of each slice of bread. Place 2 slices buttered side down and top with half the cheese slices. Scatter olives over cheese. Arrange spinach on top of olives. Top with remaining cheese and remaining bread, buttered side up.

2. Place sandwiches in a large, heavy skillet (preferably cast iron). Top with another skillet to weigh them down. Cook over medium heat for about 3 minutes, until golden brown on the bottom. Flip, replace weight and cook for about 3 minutes more, until golden brown and cheese is molten, reducing heat if necessary. Cut each sandwich in half and serve immediately.

Variation

Instead of sourdough bread, use slices cut from a large, round pumpernickel loaf.

Thai Curry Noodle Bowl

Asian noodle bowls are so appealing, and the variations seem infinite. Spinach and accents of curry and coconut define this pretty one.

6 oz	snow peas (3 cups/750 mL, loosely packed), trimmed and halved lengthwise (see Tips, left)	175 g
12 oz	dried chow mein noodles (see Tips, left)	375 g
2 tbsp	oil	30 mL
2	large cloves garlic, minced	2
1 tbsp	Thai red curry paste	15 mL
4 cups	vegetable stock	1 L
1	can (14 oz/400 mL) coconut milk	1
1 tbsp	granulated sugar (see Tips, page 383)	15 mL
4 oz	baby spinach leaves (about 5 cups/ 1.25 L, loosely packed)	125 g
1/4 cup	chopped fresh cilantro leaves	60 mL
2	large green onions (white and green parts), slivered (see Tips, left)	2
	Kosher or coarse sea salt	
1/2 cup	Crispy Shallots (page 455)	125 mL
1	red finger chile, thinly sliced (see Tips, left)	1
6	small lime wedges	6

Makes 6 servings

Vegan Friendly

Main course

Tips

To trim and string snow peas, nip off the ends with a paring knife and pull off the tough strings along both sides.

You can find dried chow mein noodles and Thai red curry paste at most supermarkets. Dried chow mein noodles are like dried pasta; do not confuse them with the crunchy fried chow mein noodles eaten as snacks.

To sliver green onions, use a sharp knife to cut thin slices on an extreme diagonal, from the root end to the stalk.

As a shortcut, instead of preparing Crispy Shallots, you can buy packaged crispy onions. Asian and Indian grocery stores sell them in bags.

Finger chiles are also known as cayenne peppers. They are slender, with pointed tips. You can substitute any kind of red chile you prefer.

1. In a large saucepan of boiling salted water over medium heat, blanch snow peas for about 1 minute, until tender-crisp. Using a mesh scoop, transfer to a colander (leave cooking water in pan) and immediately rinse with cold water to stop the cooking. Drain peas and set aside.

2. Return pan of cooking water to a boil over medium heat. Add noodles and cook for about 10 minutes or according to package directions, until tender but firm. Drain.

3. Meanwhile, in a saucepan over medium heat, heat oil until warm. Stir in garlic and curry paste for 30 seconds. Stir in stock, coconut milk and sugar until smooth. When mixture comes to a simmer, reduce heat to low and add spinach, cilantro and green onions. Cook for about 1 minute, until heated through.

4. Divide prepared noodles among 6 wide, shallow serving bowls. Top with equal quantities of snow peas. Ladle hot broth with spinach over noodles. Pile crispy shallots in center of each bowl. Scatter chile slices over each serving. Place a lime wedge at the edge of each bowl, to squeeze over the noodles. Serve immediately.

Spinach and Black Pepper Tofu

Think tofu is boring? This vibrant, peppery treat will change your mind. Serve it over brown rice to max out on nutrients.

Tips

To prepare the tofu for this recipe: Drain the block of tofu in a fine-mesh sieve for 15 to 30 minutes, then pat dry. Using a sharp knife, cut the block in half horizontally to make 2 rectangles, each about 1 inch (2.5 cm) thick. Cut each rectangle lengthwise into 3 sticks, each about 1 inch (2.5 cm) wide. Cut each stick into ½-inch (1 cm) cubes.

To grate or purée gingerroot, use a kitchen rasp such as the kind made by Microplane.

Ponzu is a citrusy soy sauce. You can find it in most supermarkets.

Mirin is sweet Japanese cooking wine. You can find it in most supermarkets. It may or may not be considered vegan, depending on the type of sugar used (and the opinion of the individual vegan).

Finely ground pepper is not the right type for this recipe. Use a pepper mill to grind peppercorns to a medium consistency.

1	bunch spinach (12 oz/375 g), trimmed	1
1 lb	block medium or firm tofu, cubed (see Tips, left)	500 g
1 tbsp	cornstarch	15 mL
2 tbsp	soy sauce	30 mL
2 tbsp	ponzu (see Tips, left)	30 mL
2 tbsp	mirin (see Tips, left)	30 mL
¼ cup	oil	60 mL
2 tbsp	unsalted butter or non-dairy alternative	30 mL
2	shallots, chopped	2
2	large cloves garlic, chopped	2
1 tsp	puréed gingerroot (see Tips, left)	5 mL
1 tbsp	freshly ground black pepper (see Tips, left)	15 mL
2	large green onions (white and green parts), chopped	2

1. In a large saucepan over medium heat, cook spinach — with just the wash water clinging to its leaves — for 4 to 5 minutes, stirring often, until wilted. Drain and set aside until cool enough to handle. Squeeze handfuls to extract excess liquid and transfer to a cutting board. Using a sharp knife, chop finely and set aside.

2. In a large bowl, toss tofu cubes gently with cornstarch. Set aside for 5 to 10 minutes.

3. In a small bowl, combine soy sauce, ponzu and mirin. Set aside.

4. In a large skillet over medium-high heat, heat oil until shimmery. Add prepared tofu and cook, turning occasionally with a spatula, for about 5 minutes, until golden and crisp in spots. Transfer to a large plate.

5. Using tongs and a paper towel, gently wipe oil from skillet, leaving any golden brown bits stuck to the bottom. Add butter and melt over medium-low heat. Add shallots, garlic and ginger. Cook, stirring often, for about 3 minutes, until softened and golden brown. Stir in spinach for 1 minute. Stir in soy sauce mixture for 20 seconds, scraping up brown bits from bottom of pan. Add fried tofu and sprinkle with pepper. Toss with spatula to coat well. Heat through for 1 minute.

6. Transfer to a serving platter or individual plates. Scatter green onions overtop and serve immediately.

Provençal Bean and Spinach Casserole

This bean casserole is fortified with spinach and topped with a garlic-parsley crumb crust. It's a hearty, good-looking meal. Serve it with rice and salad.

	Makes 4 to 6 servings
Vegan Friendly	
Main course	

Tips

You don't need to squeeze the spinach in this recipe. It adds moisture to the bean mixture.

This recipe makes about 1 cup (250 mL) crumb topping.

Cannellinis are also known as white kidney beans. You can find them in most supermarkets.

- Preheat oven to 350°F (180°C)
- 8-inch (20 cm) square baking dish
- Food processor

Beans

1	bunch spinach (12 oz/375 g), trimmed	1
2 tbsp	extra virgin olive oil	30 mL
1	onion, diced	1
½	red bell pepper, cut into ½-inch (1 cm) dice	½
½	yellow bell pepper, cut into ½-inch (1 cm) dice	½
2	large cloves garlic, chopped	2
1 tbsp	balsamic vinegar	15 mL
1 cup	canned tomatoes, crushed, with juices	250 mL
1 tbsp	chopped fresh sage leaves	15 mL
1	bay leaf	1
1 tsp	kosher or coarse sea salt	5 mL
⅛ tsp	freshly ground black pepper	0.5 mL
1	can (19 oz/540 mL) cannellini beans (see Tips, left)	1

Topping

1	large clove garlic	1
½ cup	coarsely chopped fresh parsley leaves	125 mL
1	slice whole wheat or rustic white bread, torn	1
1 tbsp	extra virgin olive oil	15 mL

1. *Beans:* In a large saucepan over medium heat, cook spinach — with just the wash water clinging to its leaves — for 4 to 5 minutes, until wilted and dark green. Drain and set aside until cool enough to handle (see Tips, left). Using a sharp knife, chop finely.

2. In same saucepan (dry it with a paper towel) over medium heat, heat oil until shimmery. Add onion and bell peppers. Cook, stirring often, for about 3 minutes, until softened. Stir in garlic for 30 seconds. Stir in vinegar for about 10 seconds, until almost evaporated. Add tomatoes, sage, bay leaf, salt and pepper. When mixture comes to a simmer, reduce heat to low, cover and cook for about 5 minutes, until peppers are tender-crisp. Discard bay leaf. Stir in wilted spinach, then beans. Season with salt to taste. Spoon into baking dish and set aside.

3. *Topping:* In food processor fitted with the metal blade, chop garlic. Add parsley and pulse a few times, until finely chopped Add bread and pulse a few times, until bread is chopped into medium crumbs. Drizzle oil through the feed tube and pulse once or twice to combine. Sprinkle evenly over bean mixture.

4. Bake casserole in preheated oven for about 30 minutes, until beans are bubbly and topping is golden. Serve warm.

Spinach and Grilled Zucchini Subs

I love a spinach-ricotta filling in pasta, so why not in sandwiches? In this recipe the mixture is slathered on buns and mated with grilled zucchini. These subs are sandwiches worth working for and are mighty fine for dinner or as a hearty lunch. They are messy too, so set out plenty of napkins.

Makes 2 to 4 servings

Sandwich

Tips

To drain ricotta, place in a fine-mesh sieve and set aside for 30 minutes. It will still be somewhat wet and will soak into the bread, so don't leave these sandwiches sitting around.

If you have one, use a mandoline to slice the zucchini evenly. Discard the first and last slices, which will be uneven and include large portions of peel.

Toast the buns for about 5 minutes in a toaster oven or an oven preheated to 400°F (200°C).

- Grill pan

2 tbsp	extra virgin olive oil, divided	30 mL
1	clove garlic, minced	1
4 cups	trimmed, chopped spinach leaves (4 oz/125 g), loosely packed	1 L
1 cup	ricotta cheese, drained (see Tips, left)	250 mL
1 tsp	kosher or coarse sea salt	5 mL
1/8 tsp	freshly ground white pepper	0.5 mL
1	zucchini (6 oz/175 g), sliced lengthwise 1/4 inch (0.5 cm) thick (see Tips, left)	1
2	sub-shaped crusty buns, split	2

1. In a large saucepan over medium heat, heat 1 tbsp (15 mL) oil until warm. Stir in garlic for 20 seconds. Add spinach and cook, stirring often, for 3 to 4 minutes, until tender and fairly dry. Set aside to cool to room temperature.

2. In a bowl, stir together spinach, ricotta, salt and pepper. Set aside.

3. Brush zucchini slices generously on both sides with remaining oil (you will have some left over). Lightly sprinkle with salt to taste.

4. Heat grill pan over medium-high heat for 1 minute. In batches, sear zucchini slices for 2 to 3 minutes per side, until tender but firm and with grill marks. Transfer to a plate and set aside.

5. Toast buns until golden but not too crisp (see Tips, left). Spread equal quantities of ricotta mixture over all four cut surfaces. Arrange zucchini slices on bottom halves of buns. Replace tops, cut each sub in half and serve immediately.

Variation

If you don't have a grill pan, barbecue the zucchini or simply sear the slices in a skillet.

Spanish Chickpea and Spinach Stew

This smoky tapas dish is too tasty to just nibble. It makes a fine main course too. Serve it with crusty bread.

Makes 4 to 6 servings (about 6 cups/1.5 L)		
Vegan Friendly		
Main course		

Tips

Smoked paprika, one of Spain's culinary claims to fame, is sold in fine food shops and well-stocked supermarkets. It comes in sweet (mild) and hot (spicy) versions.

Saffron is the world's most expensive spice by weight. Luckily it is light and used only in tiny quantities. Actually the stigmas of crocus flowers, saffron comes in "threads." It is orange-yellow and is used as a pleasing food dye as well as a flavoring agent.

Using a serrated vegetable peeler is the easiest way to peel tomatoes.

2 tsp	sweet smoked Spanish paprika (see Tips, left)	10 mL
¼ tsp	ground cumin	1 mL
1 tsp	kosher or coarse sea salt	5 mL
⅛ tsp	freshly ground black pepper	0.5 mL
¾ cup	vegetable stock	175 mL
⅛ tsp	saffron (see Tips, left)	0.5 mL
1	bunch spinach (12 oz/375 g), trimmed	1
3 tbsp	extra virgin olive oil, divided	45 mL
1	small Spanish onion (12 oz/375 g), diced	1
2	large cloves garlic, chopped	2
2	tomatoes (12 oz/375 g total), peeled and coarsely chopped (see Tips, left)	2
1	can (19 oz/540 mL) chickpeas, rinsed and drained	1
½ cup	golden raisins	125 mL

1. In a small bowl, combine paprika, cumin, salt and pepper. Set aside.
2. Place stock in a small measuring cup. Crumble saffron into stock. Set aside.
3. In a large saucepan over medium heat, cook spinach — with just the wash water clinging to its leaves — for 4 to 5 minutes, until wilted and dark green. Drain and set aside until cool enough to handle. Squeeze handfuls to extract excess liquid and transfer to a cutting board. Using a sharp knife, chop and set aside.
4. In same saucepan (dry it with a paper towel) over medium heat, heat 2 tbsp (30 mL) oil until shimmery. Add onion and cook, stirring often, for about 5 minutes, until softened and golden. Stir in garlic for 30 seconds. Stir in paprika mixture. Add wilted spinach and tomatoes and stir for 1 minute. Add stock mixture, chickpeas and raisins. When mixture comes to a simmer, reduce heat to low, cover and cook for about 15 minutes, stirring occasionally, until spinach is very soft.
5. Transfer to individual serving bowls. Drizzle remaining oil overtop and serve warm.

Sweet Potato Leaves

Ipomoea batatas

Other names: **boniato leaves, camote tops, sweet potato tips, tuberous morning glory leaves.**

Depending on where you are shopping, you may find sweet potato leaves identified as *la khoai lang* or *talbos ng camote*.

Sweet potatoes originated in Central or South America, where archeological remnants date back 8,000 years. They were domesticated at least 5,000 years ago in Central America and spread from there to Polynesia. The sweet potato is one of the so-called canoe plants carried across the ocean by ancient Polynesian explorers and transplanted throughout the South Pacific and Australasia.

Sweet potato leaves are staples in the cuisines of Africa, Asia and the Philippines. The young leaves are even used as baby food. However, some Africans consider sweet potato leaves a poor man's vegetable and toss them to the animals.

Varieties

There are hundreds of relatives in the *Ipomoea* genus, but few of those plants are edible. Sweet potatoes and their leaves are one exception. Another is water spinach (page 419). Many *Ipomoea* are cultivated as ornamental morning glories. However, the wild ones are often toxic, and some are used as psychedelics in tribal rituals.

Buy It

Sweet potato leaves are sold in Asian, Africentric and Filipino grocery stores. They are sometimes mislabeled "yam leaves" (true yams are also tubers, but they are not related to sweet potatoes).

The tender new leaves at the tips of the shoots are plucked from vines before the sweet potatoes mature in the fall. The older leaves are coarse.

Clusters of delicate, heart-shaped deep green leaves grow on long, thin stems. Leaves that are discolored, blemished, folded or crumpled are past their prime.

Tasting Notes

Sweet potato leaves are mild, grassy and creamy, with hints of Szechuan peppercorn. When cooked, they are slippery, with a pleasant potato scent and a somewhat spinachy taste and texture.

Health Notes

Sweet potato leaves contain vitamins A, B_6, E and K, folate, magnesium, manganese, niacin, phosphorus, potassium and riboflavin.

In folk remedies, sweet potato leaves have been used to treat dengue fever, asthma, nausea and diarrhea, to boost blood cell production and to lower blood sugar in diabetics. Crushed leaves are applied to boils, burns, bug bites and acne.

SUBSTITUTES

spinach, Malabar spinach, jute leaves

Store It

Sweet potato leaves dry out easily. Wrap them in barely damp paper towels, place in a perforated resealable bag and refrigerate.

Sweet potato leaves will keep in the refrigerator for up to four days.

Prep It

The thin stems are deceptively tender-looking; they are actually fibrous. Pluck leaves and tender stemlets off the main stems. Pinch or cut off stems wider than ⅛ inch (3 mm) and discard.

To wash, swish the greens vigorously in cold water. Spin-dry if necessary for use in your recipe.

Consume It

Despite their delicate appearance, sweet potato leaves are too grassy to eat raw. However, the tiniest leaves could be added to mixed salads or sandwiches.

Sweet potato leaves may be blanched and used in Filipino-style cooked salads. To blanch lightly, place in a large bowl and add boiling water. Set aside for 2 minutes, drain, then rinse with cold water.

Chop the greens before adding them to cooked dishes. Pieces that are too large tend to make soups or stews swampy, with unappealing clumps of greens. Alternatively, purée leaves simmered in stock for creamy soups.

Sweet potato leaves cook in 3 to 5 minutes and tender stem pieces in 5 to 10 minutes. Leaves and sliced stems may be cooked separately, but why fuss? Go to the 5-minute mark for nicely wilted leaves and tender-crisp stems. Africans simply toss the greens into a pot and cook until the stems are tender, letting the leaves take care of themselves. If the leaves look ready to dissolve and the stems are pale green, they are overcooked.

To preserve nutrients, steam or stir-fry the greens instead of boiling them. If sautéing sweet potato leaves, adding a bit of water or stock yields the best result. Sauté to wilt them slightly, add the liquid, cover and steam briefly. Remove the lid and turn up the heat to evaporate excess moisture.

Sweet potato leaves are similar to spinach when cooked, but they don't exude as much liquid.

Filipino Sweet Potato Leaf Salad

Like many Asian salads, this one is prepared with greens that are cooked, then doused in a tart sauce. Filipinos call sweet potatoes **camotes,** *and camote top salad is a traditional favorite. It is customarily served with hot rice but is refreshing and delicious on its own.*

Makes 2 servings

Vegan Friendly

Salad

Tips

This recipe makes about ¼ cup (60 mL) dressing.

To maintain more control over the saltiness of dishes, use reduced-sodium soy sauce. Depending on the type, 1 tbsp (15 mL) regular soy sauce can contain 1,000 mg or more of sodium. Reduced-sodium soy sauce contains about half that amount.

For the finest minced garlic, push it through a press.

Cane sugar is likely to be filtered through bone char, while beet sugar is not. Most labels don't indicate the source of the sugar. If you are following a vegan diet, use unbleached organic sugar that has not been filtered through bone char, or a sweetener such as agave syrup.

Dressing

1 tbsp	freshly squeezed lemon juice	15 mL
1 tbsp	soy sauce (see Tips, left)	15 mL
1	small clove garlic, minced (see Tips, left)	1
1 tsp	granulated sugar (see Tips, left)	5 mL
1 tsp	kosher or coarse sea salt	5 mL
¼ tsp	freshly ground black pepper	1 mL
2 tbsp	oil	30 mL

Salad

8 oz	sweet potato leaves and tender stems	250 g
2	small ripe tomatoes, sliced into semicircles	2
	Kosher or coarse sea salt	
	Freshly ground black pepper	
½ cup	diced sweet onion	125 mL
1	small avocado, sliced or diced	1

1. *Dressing:* In a medium bowl, whisk together lemon juice, soy sauce, garlic, sugar, salt and pepper. Whisk in oil. Set aside.

2. *Salad:* In a large pot of boiling salted water, cook sweet potato greens for 5 to 10 minutes, until stems are tender and leaves are wilted. Drain and immediately rinse with cold water to stop the cooking. Drain. Squeeze handfuls to extract excess liquid and transfer to bowl with dressing. Using a fork, toss to coat.

3. Spread greens, with dressing, over a serving platter or individual plates. Arrange tomatoes over greens in overlapping layers. Sprinkle salt and pepper over tomatoes, then scatter onion overtop. Arrange avocado on top or alongside, to taste. Serve immediately.

African Sweet Potato Leaf Stew

Sweet potatoes cooked with veggies, nuts and dried fruit make a wholesome meal. This African standby is spicy but not too exotic, so expand your culinary horizons. Serve the stew over rice or grains.

Makes 2 to 4 servings		
Vegan Friendly		
Main course		

Tips

I like to use a 5-inch (12.5 cm) cayenne pepper in this recipe. Use any kind you prefer or substitute hot pepper flakes to taste.

Yellow-fleshed potatoes are best for this recipe; neither waxy nor dry, they are good all-purpose potatoes. The best-known yellow-fleshed potatoes are Yukon Golds.

The easiest way to peel a tomato is to use a serrated vegetable peeler.

Use salted or unsalted roasted peanuts, as desired.

2 tbsp	extra virgin olive oil	30 mL
1	onion, halved and thinly sliced	1
1	red or green finger chile, halved, seeded and thinly sliced (see Tips, left)	1
2	potatoes, cut into ½-inch (1 cm) chunks (see Tips, left)	2
1	clove garlic, chopped	1
2	tomatoes, peeled and cut into 1-inch (2.5 cm) chunks (see Tips, left)	2
2 tsp	kosher or coarse sea salt	10 mL
¼ tsp	freshly ground black pepper	1 mL
1 cup	water	250 mL
8	dried apricots, cut into thin strips (about ¼ cup/60 mL)	8
1 cup	fresh or thawed frozen peas	250 mL
12 cups	coarsely chopped sweet potato leaves and tender stems (8 oz/250 g), loosely packed	3 L
½ cup	roasted peanuts, coarsely chopped (see Tips, left)	125 mL

1. In a large saucepan over medium heat, heat oil until shimmery. Add onion and chile. Cook, stirring often, for about 3 minutes, until softened and turning golden. Add potatoes and cook, stirring often, for 1 minute. Stir in garlic, then tomatoes, salt and pepper. Add water. When mixture comes to a simmer, cover, reduce heat to medium-low and cook for about 10 minutes, stirring occasionally, until potatoes are tender. Stir in apricots, peas and sweet potato greens. Cover and cook for about 5 minutes, until leaves are wilted and stems are tender-crisp.

2. Transfer to a serving bowl or individual plates. Scatter peanuts overtop and serve immediately.

Variations

Use a large sweet potato instead of regular potatoes.

Substitute any dried tropical fruit you like in place of the apricots.

Taiwan Lettuce

Lactuca sativa angustana

Other names: **Chinese/Vietnamese lettuce, Chinese pointed lettuce, curled lettuce, long-leaf lettuce, Orient sword leaf, sword lettuce.**

Depending on where you are shopping, you may find Taiwan lettuce identified as *a choy, Chinesischer salat, phak salat, sang choy, selada, shengcai, xa lach* or *yu mai tsai*.

Native to Taiwan, this is the only commonly used leaf lettuce in Chinese cuisine.

Lettuce was first cultivated in ancient Egypt. We know the Egyptians grew stalk lettuces (page 15) because they painted pictures of this variety on tombs. Sword-leaf lettuces, the ancestors of Taiwan lettuce, were likely bred from stalk lettuces. Lettuce was first recorded in China in the fifth century.

Tasting Notes

Taiwan lettuce is more robust and complex than Western lettuces. It is bitter, especially at the tips of its leaves, and has peppery and nutty accents. The texture is tender and crisp and the core is juicy.

Varieties

Asian lettuces are divided into two types: stalk (see celtuce, page 15) and leaf (Taiwan lettuce). Although the two are botanical siblings, they don't resemble each other except for their sword- or spear-shaped leaves. Stalk lettuces are grown for their thick, fleshy stems. Taiwan lettuce appears to have more in common with leaf lettuce or romaine.

Buy It

Taiwan lettuce is sold in Asian supermarkets.

Very tall and slender, it has spear-shaped mint-green leaves formed in a loose head. Old leaves coarsen and grow bitter. Taiwan lettuce is past its peak if it has a browned stem end, rusty discolorations or cracks in the stalks, or yellowed leaves.

Health Notes

No official government analysis is available, but Taiwan lettuce is related to celtuce. That suggests that it contains vitamins A, B_6 and C, calcium, folate, iron, magnesium, manganese, niacin, phosphorus, potassium, riboflavin and thiamin.

In folk medicine, lettuce has been considered a sedative. It has been used to tame anxiety, hyperactivity and sex drive, as well as to soothe coughs and rheumatic pain.

Store It

Taiwan lettuce wilts quickly. Swathe it in plastic wrap or wrap in paper towels and place in a plastic bag, then refrigerate.

Taiwan lettuce will keep in the refrigerator for up to two days.

Equivalents

1 small head Taiwan
lettuce = 6 to 8 oz
(175 to 250 g);
1 medium head =
10 to 12 oz (300 to
375 g); 1 large head =
1 lb (500 g)

•

2 oz (60 g) shredded
or coarsely chopped
Taiwan lettuce =
2½ cups (625 mL),
loosely packed

SUBSTITUTES

romaine lettuce, iceberg
lettuce, Taiwan bok
choy, napa cabbage

Prep It

Before consuming Taiwan lettuce, remove and discard any
withered or damaged outer leaves.

Do not cut Taiwan lettuce until you are ready to use it, as cut
edges discolor. Halve or quarter it lengthwise, keeping the base
intact. Then slice or shred crosswise, starting at the top, until
you reach the core. Slice the core thinly. Cut off and discard the
stem end.

To wash, swish cut leaves gently in cold water, then drain.
Spin-dry if necessary for the recipe.

Consume It

Don't be fooled by the moniker "lettuce." This Asian vegetable
is traditionally cooked, as it is generally not considered mild
enough to add to green salads. If you want to eat it raw, stick to
the sweeter sections near the stem end.

Taiwan lettuce is typically stir-fried, but it may be added to
soups or simply blanched and drizzled with sauce. It cooks in 2 to
3 minutes in a hot wok.

Garlic Chile Taiwan Lettuce Stir-Fry

Taiwan lettuce is the star of this stir-fry with Asian accents. It's simple, so you can get it on the dinner table fast. Serve it over hot rice. As is the case with all stir-fries, it's best to have the ingredients set out and ready, because everything happens super-fast.

Makes 1 to 2 servings

Vegan Friendly

Side dish

Tips

Shaoxing is Chinese rice cooking wine, sold in Asian supermarkets. If you don't have any, substitute dry sherry.

To grate or purée gingerroot, use a kitchen rasp such as the kind made by Microplane.

Toasted sesame oil, also known as Asian sesame oil, is dark and fragrant. It is sold in small bottles in supermarkets. It is usually a seasoning oil, but the Taiwan lettuce cooks so quickly that it is fine to use it for stir-frying in this recipe. Most supermarkets sell toasted sesame oil.

To prepare the Taiwan lettuce for this recipe: Using a sharp knife, quarter lettuce lengthwise. Slice crosswise into 2-inch (5 cm) pieces until you reach the core. Slice core thinly. Cut off and discard stem end.

- Wok

1 tbsp	soy sauce	15 mL
1 tsp	Shaoxing cooking wine (see Tips, left)	5 mL
1 tsp	granulated sugar	5 mL
1	large clove garlic, minced	1
1 tsp	puréed gingerroot (see Tips, left)	5 mL
¼ tsp	hot pepper flakes	1 mL
1 tbsp	toasted sesame oil (see Tips, left)	15 mL
1	head Taiwan lettuce (12 oz/375 g), quartered and sliced (see Tips, left)	1
	Kosher or coarse sea salt	

1. In a small bowl, combine soy sauce, Shaoxing wine and sugar. Set aside.
2. In another small bowl, combine garlic, ginger and hot pepper flakes. Set aside.
3. Heat wok over medium-high heat for 1 minute. Add oil, swirling to coat bottom of pan. Stir in garlic mixture for 10 seconds. Add Taiwan lettuce and stir-fry for about 1 minute, until slightly wilted. Add soy sauce mixture and stir-fry for 1 to 2 minutes, until lettuce is tender-crisp.
4. Remove from heat. Add salt to taste and serve immediately.

Taiwan Lettuce Mei Fun

When you crave Chinese takeout-style food, try this basic noodle stir-fry. Mei fun are thin rice noodles (also known as vermicelli or angel hair) that are either boiled or fried until crispy, then doused in sauce. This dish is not much to look at, but it hits the spot.

Makes 4 servings
Vegan Friendly
Main course

Tips

Asian grocery stores and some supermarkets sell garlic chile paste. It is delightfully pungent.

To sliver green onions, use a sharp knife to cut thin slices on an extreme diagonal from the root end to the stalk.

Shred the carrot using the large holes of a box grater.

To prepare the Taiwan lettuce for this recipe: Using a sharp knife, quarter lettuce lengthwise, then slice it thinly crosswise. Slice core thinly. Cut off and discard stem end.

To prevent this dish from turning mushy, do not overcook the noodles. Keep the heat high when stir-frying and toss the ingredients as little as possible — do not overmix.

* Wok

Sauce

¼ cup	vegetable stock	60 mL
1 tbsp	cornstarch	15 mL
¼ cup	soy sauce	60 mL
1 tbsp	garlic chile paste (see Tips, left)	15 mL
1 tsp	toasted sesame oil	5 mL
1 tsp	granulated sugar	5 mL

Stir-Fry

6 oz	rice vermicelli noodles	175 g
¼ cup	oil	60 mL
6 oz	shiitake mushrooms, stemmed and thinly sliced	175 g
2	large green onions (white and light green parts), slivered (see Tips, left)	2
1	carrot, shredded (see Tips, left)	1
1	green or red finger chile, seeded and thinly sliced (see Tips, page 384)	1
1	medium head Taiwan lettuce (10 oz/300 g), quartered and sliced (see Tips, left)	1
	Kosher or coarse sea salt	
1½ cups	bean sprouts	375 mL

1. *Sauce:* In a small bowl, combine stock and cornstarch. Stir in soy sauce, chile paste, sesame oil and sugar. Set aside.

2. *Stir-Fry:* In a pot of boiling salted water, cook vermicelli over medium heat for about 2 minutes, until softened but not mushy. Rinse briefly with cold water. Drain and set aside.

3. Meanwhile, heat wok over medium-high heat for 1 minute. Add oil and swirl to coat bottom of pan. Add shiitakes, onions, carrot and chile. Stir-fry for about 1 minute, until softened. Add Taiwan lettuce and stir-fry for about 1 minute, until softened. Add prepared noodles and cook, shaking pan rather than stirring, for about 2 minutes, until very hot (see Tips, left). Stir prepared sauce and pour it in. Toss briefly with tongs to combine. Remove from heat and add salt to taste.

4. Transfer to individual serving dishes. Scatter bean sprouts overtop and serve immediately.

Taro Leaves

Colocasia esculenta, Xanthosoma sagittifolium, Alocasia macrorrhizos, Cyrtosperma merkusii

> *Other names:* **African spinach, callaloo, coco, cocoyam, Chinese/Japanese potato, elephant's ear.**
>
> **Depending on where you are shopping, you may find taro leaves identified as** *bhaji, kochu, kontomire* **or** *qian nian yu.*

Do not confuse the taro name *callaloo* with Jamaican callaloo, a dish that actually calls for amaranth leaves (see "Callaloo Confusion," page 30).

Taro-like plants are widely cultivated, mainly for their tubers, but their leaves and stems are also a staple food in the tropical world. Taros are particularly important in the cuisines of Hawaii and other Polynesian islands, the Philippines, Africa, the Caribbean and India.

There are hundreds of edible species of taro-like plants, the most prominent being true taro and malanga.

True taro (*Colocasia esculenta*) is believed to be one of the earliest cultivated plants in the world, having been domesticated in Asia 10,000 years ago. From its origins in Southeast Asia it spread in all directions, to China, Oceania, the Mediterranean basin and the Middle East, Africa, the Caribbean and the Americas. In Europe it was popular only until the fall of the Roman Empire.

Taro cultivation is ingrained in Hawaiian culture and cuisine. It is one of the "canoe crops" that Polynesian explorers transported from island to island. In contrast, malanga (*Xanthosoma sagittifolium*, sometimes called "new taro" is considered inferior in Polynesia.

Malanga does have its fans and is particularly popular in Cuban and Puerto Rican cuisine. Native to South America, it spread to the Caribbean, Central America and the South Pacific. It is also grown in West Africa and the Philippines.

Tasting Notes

Taro leaves taste like spinach when boiled, but with a peppery, bitter aftertaste. They have accents of cabbage, zucchini and asparagus, with a scent that is slightly nutty but subtle. If not cooked long enough to neutralize plant toxins (see page 392), they create a scratchy, tingling sensation at the back of the throat.

Varieties

Taros are a culinary family, not a botanical one. Although unrelated, all the edible taro-like species have big leaves and starchy tubers and require proper handling and cooking to neutralize plant toxins.

Because there are so many types that share diverse names and because they are often interchangeable in the kitchen, taros are a confusing group of greens. Sorting them into the following varieties is the simplest approach:

- **taro** (*Colocasia esculenta*), also known as true taro, old cocoyam, *chembu, karkalo, keladi, khoai mon, kolokass, nduma, ocumo chino, pheuak, rukau, sato-imo* or *yu tou*. The so-called elephant-ear leaves are usually heart-shaped and the stems are green or purple. The brown-skinned, white-fleshed tubers come in different sizes. Taro with tubers that can grow to a foot (30 cm) long is called dasheen or, more colorfully when referring to the greens, dasheen bush. Taro with potato-sized tubers is called eddoe, also known as malanga, a name that is used for other species as well (see page 391).

  These plants are descendants of **wild taro** (*C. antiquorum*). Relatives include **giant elephant's ear** (*C. gigantea*), also known as green taro or *hasu imo*, and **black-leaved taro** (*C. affinis*).

- **malanga** (*Xanthosoma sagittifolium*), also known as new cocoyam/taro, arrowleaf elephant ear, *tannia, yautia*, Fiji/Singapore taro, *bore, chou caraibe, kimpool, macabo, mora, nampi, ocumo criollo, otoy* or *taioba*. The leaves are arrowhead-shaped rather than heart-shaped; the tubers are described as the size of potatoes but more pear-shaped.

  Several of this species' relatives have also been domesticated, including **Indian kale** (*X. atrovirens*), **giant golden taro** (*X. mafaffa*) and **black malanga** (*X. violaceum*), also known as blue taro, *birah hitam* or *batata-de-taxola*. **Celery-stemmed taro** (*X. brasiliense*), also known as tanier spinach, Tahitian taro/spinach or *belembe*, is native to the Amazon and grown only for its leaves and stems.

- **giant taro** (*Alocasia macrorrhizos*), also known as *ta'amu, kape* or *ape*. Originally domesticated in the Philippines, this taro is not as widespread as the species mentioned above. It is valued mostly for its thick, starchy stem. Its giant leaves also serve as umbrellas during tropical downpours.

  A relative, **cunjevoi** (*A. brisbanensis*), also known as native lily, can be lethally toxic if eaten uncooked. Other taro-like relatives are **baibing** (*A. fornicata*) and giant upright **elephant ear** (*A. odora*), also known as night-scented lily, *bac ha* or *toon*.

- **swamp taro** (*Cyrtosperma merkusii*), also known as *babai, pulaka, simiden* or *geli-geli*. This plant, originally domesticated on atolls in Oceania, is another less prominent taro. It is taller than true taro, with bigger leaves and coarser roots.

Taro leaves are sold in grocery stores catering to African, Filipino and Asian populations.

The attractive fine, soft dark green leaves live up to the name "elephant ears." They can grow to more than a foot (30 cm) long. However, smaller, tender leaves are more prized.

Taro leaves should be fresh, green and perky, not folded or crumpled. Check leaves for insect damage and stems for cracks.

Store It

Taro leaves wilt and dehydrate quickly. To make these large greens manageable, separate the leaves from the stems. Wrap the leaves in barely damp paper towels and store in perforated resealable bags. Wrap the stems tightly in plastic or place in resealable bags, then refrigerate.

Taro leaves will keep in the refrigerator for up to four days.

Prep It

Taro is not a friendly food. Calcium oxalate crystals in the tubers and greens can be irritating and even toxic. The remedy is careful handling, proper preparation and thorough cooking.

Health Notes

Taro leaves contain vitamins A, B_6 and C, calcium, copper, folate, iron, magnesium, manganese, niacin, phosphorus, potassium, riboflavin and thiamin.

Looks can be deceiving. This attractive plant hides a toxic secret: calcium oxalate crystals that must be neutralized by proper cooking. Otherwise they can cause itching in the mouth and throat, as well as skin rashes (see "O Is for Oxalates," page 355). Remedies include rinsing the mouth with a mixture of cold water, baking soda and salt or using the same mixture to bathe a rash before applying anti-itch cream.

Cooks around the world employ various strategies while working with taro roots and greens:

- Wear gloves.
- Scrub the root and stems before peeling.
- Peel under cold running water.
- Soak vegetables in cold water overnight.
- Boil with baking soda. (I sensed a vague peppery itch in my throat after trying taro leaves boiled for 15 minutes, but that was not the case when I added a pinch of baking soda to the water for a new batch.)
- Change the water in which the greens are boiled a couple of times.
- Rinse with cold water after cooking.

Some cooks suggest coating the vegetables with oil, which I disagree with wholeheartedly. It's dangerous to work with slippery hands and a slippery knife.

In most cases only the leaves are eaten, but the long, spongy stems, which can range in width from ⅛ inch (3 mm) to ½ inch (1 cm), are mostly edible. The stems are always used in poor countries where food is not taken for granted.

To cut taro greens, fold each leaf in half. At an angle, cut out the stem and thick midrib where it is attached near the center of the leaf, leaving a small hole. Stack the leaves, roll them into giant cigars and cut them crosswise into ribbons, strips or shreds. A good all-purpose size is ½ inch (1 cm) wide.

To prepare the stems, slice off the bases where the stems are dried and discolored. Use a small, sharp knife to pull off the outer layer of skin in strips, grabbing the pieces and starting to pull at the thick end. Don't worry: the skins pull off easily in thin, curly strips. As you work, squeeze each stem to help release sap, then place the stem in a large bowl of cold salted water. When all the stems are peeled, drain and slice them into pieces.

Consume It

Never eat raw taro greens — the toxins must be neutralized by cooking. Before using in a recipe, parboil the greens for 15 minutes or according to recipe instructions, then drain and discard the cooking water. (If desired, add a pinch of baking soda to the water.)

After parboiling for 15 minutes, taro greens cook in 5 minutes. They are tender and light green, with a texture and flavor reminiscent of zucchini. Note, however, that these greens are often cooked longer. Some people are more sensitive to the effects of calcium oxalate crystals and may increase the total cooking time to as long as 45 minutes. This does, however, leave the greens extremely limp and brown.

Parboiled taro leaves and stems may be cooked separately as vegetables or added to soups, stews or curries. The stems may be pickled or battered and fried. The leaves are sometimes used like banana leaves, as wraps for cooked food.

SUBSTITUTES

collards, kale

Trini Callaloo with Okra and Pumpkin

This riff on callaloo soup from Trinidad is very spicy, vivid green and incredibly delicious. Okra and pumpkin accompany the taro in a coconut broth. Serve this as a thick soup or ladle it over rice or dumplings. (For more about this soup, see "Callaloo Confusion," page 30.)

Makes 4 to 8 servings (about 9 cups/2.25 L)	
Vegan Friendly	
Soup	

Tips

Scotch bonnet and habañero chilies are scorching hot. For less spice, devein the pepper or use less.

A winter squash such as calabaza pumpkin or kabocha, buttercup or hubbard works well in this recipe. The rind is hard to peel. To soften it, cut the squash into large chunks and place pieces skin side up in the microwave. Cook on High for 1 minute, then use a sharp knife to shave off the rind. A grapefruit spoon, with its serrated edges, is a handy tool for scraping out seeds and pulp.

This soup is very thick, so I used light coconut milk.

Pepitas are shelled pumpkin seeds. Look for them in most well-stocked supermarkets. To toast pepitas, cook in a dry skillet over medium heat, stirring often, for about 2 minutes, until aromatic.

- Stand or immersion blender

6 oz	taro leaves, shredded (about 12 cups/3 L, loosely packed)	175 g
Pinch	baking soda	Pinch
1 tbsp	extra virgin olive oil	15 mL
1	onion, diced	1
1	Scotch bonnet or habañero chile pepper, seeded and sliced (see Tips, left)	1
2 cups	vegetable stock	500 mL
2 cups	water	500 mL
2 tsp	kosher or coarse sea salt	10 mL
1 tsp	fresh thyme leaves	5 mL
12 oz	pumpkin or squash, cut into ½-inch (1 cm) chunks (about 3 cups/ 750 mL; see Tips, left)	375 g
8 oz	okra pods, trimmed and sliced ½ inch (1 cm) thick (about 2 cups/500 mL)	250 g
1	can (14 oz/400 mL) coconut milk (see Tips, left)	1
4	green onions (white and light green parts), thinly sliced	4
¼ cup	toasted pepitas (see Tips, left)	60 mL

1. In a pot of boiling salted water over medium heat, cook taro leaves with baking soda for about 15 minutes, until soft. Drain and immediately rinse with cold water to stop the cooking. Drain and set aside.

2. In a large saucepan over medium heat, heat oil until shimmery. Add onion and chile. Cook for about 3 minutes, until softened. Stir in stock, water, prepared taro, salt and thyme. When mixture comes to a simmer, reduce heat to medium-low and cook, stirring often, for about 10 minutes, until onion is very tender.

3. Using blender, purée. Return to pan, if necessary, and add pumpkin. When mixture returns to a simmer, cover, reduce heat to low and cook for 5 to 10 minutes, until pumpkin is almost tender. Add okra and cook for 5 to 10 minutes, until tender-crisp. Stir in coconut milk. Season with salt to taste.

4. Ladle into bowls. Garnish with green onions and pepitas and serve hot.

West Indies Pepper Pot Soup

Caribbean folks have been preparing all kinds of delicious dishes with taro roots, leaves and stems for centuries. In this vegetarian version of a classic soup, I have used all three. Pepper pot soup was an import from the Caribbean to colonial Philadelphia. George Washington famously warmed his troops at Valley Forge with a version of this soup.

Makes 3 to 4 servings (about 7 cups/1.75 L)

Vegan Friendly

Soup

Tips

To prepare the taro root for this recipe: Wear gloves as you work, to protect your hands. Wash the root thoroughly, then peel and cut into chunks. It oxidizes, so toss the chunks into a large bowl of cold salted water as you work. The water will get cloudy, so swish the chunks, drain and repeat with fresh water a few times. When boiling the taro root, you may replace the cooking water at half-time to get rid of toxins.

Be careful not to cook taro root to mush (it starts to turn pinkish purple at the 30-minute mark, meaning it is overcooked).

To avoid the soup becoming swampy, with unappealing clumps of greens, chop the cooked taro leaves very fine.

4 oz	taro stems, cut into 1-inch (2.5 cm) pieces (about 3 cups/750 mL, loosely packed)	125 g
4 oz	sliced taro leaves (about 8 cups/2 L, loosely packed; see Tips, left)	125 g
1 lb	taro root, peeled and cut into ½-inch (1 cm) chunks (about 1½ cups/ 375 mL; see Tips, left)	500 g
2 tbsp	extra virgin olive oil	30 mL
1	onion, diced	1
1	small red bell pepper, cut into small dice	1
4	cloves garlic, chopped	4
3 cups	vegetable stock (see Tips, page 403)	750 mL
2 cups	water	500 mL
2 to 3 tsp	freshly ground black pepper	10 to 15 mL
2 tsp	kosher or coarse sea salt	10 mL
1 tsp	chopped fresh thyme leaves	5 mL
¼ tsp	ground allspice	1 mL
	Sour cream or non-dairy alternative	
½ cup	thinly sliced green onions (white and light green parts)	125 mL

1. In a large saucepan of boiling salted water, cook taro stems for about 15 minutes, until soft. Drain and immediately rinse with cold water to stop the cooking. Drain and set aside.

2. In same saucepan with fresh boiling salted water over medium heat, cook taro leaves for about 15 minutes, until soft. Drain and immediately rinse with cold water to stop the cooking. Drain. Using a sharp knife, finely chop leaves and set aside.

3. In same saucepan with fresh boiling salted water over medium heat, cook taro root for about 20 minutes, until center is soft (see Tips, left). Drain and immediately rinse with cold water to stop the cooking. Drain and set aside.

4. In same saucepan, heat oil over medium heat until shimmery. Add onion and red pepper. Cook, stirring, for 3 minutes, until softened and turning golden. Stir in garlic. Add stock, water, 2 tsp (10 mL) pepper, salt, thyme and allspice. Bring to a simmer, reduce heat to medium-low and cook for 10 minutes, until onion is very tender. Add prepared taro root, leaves and stems. Cook until heated through. Season with salt to taste. Add remaining pepper to taste.

5. Ladle into serving bowls. Garnish each with a dollop of sour cream to taste. Scatter green onions overtop and serve hot.

Tatsoi

Brassica rapa narinosa

Other names: broad-beak mustard, Chinese flat cabbage, couch vegetable, rosette bok choy, rosette/spoon cabbage, spoon leaf mustard.

Depending on where you are shopping, you may find tatsoi identified as *chou à plat de Chine, kisaragina, taisai, ta ke tsai, tak choy* or *wu ta cai.*

Tatsoi is sometimes called flat-headed cabbage, but it should not be confused with flathead cabbage, a type of green cabbage (page 164). It is also sometimes called spinach mustard — not to be confused with mustard spinach, another name for komatsuna (page 209).

This little-known cultivar is a hidden gem of the Asian vegetable field. It's gorgeous enough to earn its reputation as an ornamental plant, but so tender and tasty it deserves to become a kitchen staple.

Tatsoi is native to China, where it has been cultivated since the sixth century. It was eventually adopted by Japan, where it is revered as an heirloom vegetable.

Varieties

Tatsoi (*Brassica rapa narinosa*) is a bok choy hybrid. This rosette-shaped Chinese cabbage usually has dark green leaves but also comes in a red cultivar, with leaves that are purple on top and green on the bottom.

New tatsoi hybrids include misome (*B. rapa narinosa*, also known as *choho*), a cross between tatsoi and komatsuna, and mispoona (*B. rapa nipposinica*), a cross between tatsoi and mizuna that has serrated dark green leaves that grow in rosettes.

Buy It

Tatsoi is sold seasonally in Asian grocery stores and at farmers' markets.

It resembles a blooming flower or a giant corsage (the last one I bought was 18 inches/45 cm in diameter). The stems are light green and the leaves are dark green. The spoon-shaped leaves range from 1 to 6 inches (2.5 to 15 cm) wide. They are arranged in concentric circles in a large rosette.

Tasting Notes

Tatsoi takes like a cross of bok choy, spinach and mustard greens. It is astringent and peppery, yet mild enough to eat raw. The wee leaves in the center of the head are slightly nutty. The stems are crunchy, juicy, slightly sweet and milder than the leaves. Cooking mellows tatsoi.

Health Notes

No official government analysis is available, but tatsoi is similar to bok choy, which suggests that it contains vitamins A, B_6, C and K, calcium, folate, iron, magnesium, manganese, niacin, phosphorus, potassium, riboflavin and thiamin.

Tatsoi is not often mentioned in herbal medicine, but it has been considered good for detoxifying the liver and stimulating appetite.

Equivalents

1 head tatsoi = 12 oz (375 g), including 8 oz (250 g) leaves and 3 oz (90 g) trimmed stems

•

2 oz (60 g) coarsely chopped or shredded leaves = 3 cups (750 mL), loosely packed

•

2 oz (60 g) sliced stems = ¾ cup (175 mL), loosely packed

SUBSTITUTES

bok choy, Shanghai bok choy, komatsuna

In stores, tatsoi greens are sometimes bundled up; the heads lose their rosette shape and may be mistaken for Shanghai bok choy. You may have to visit a farmers' market to see an open rosette in all its glory. The shape also depends on the climate: according to gardening annals, tatsoi grows more erectly in warm weather but flattens out if it's colder.

Baby tatsoi greens are sold loose or in salad mixes.

Store It

To store tatsoi, pull up the sides of the rosette, bundle the head in paper towels, place in a plastic bag and refrigerate. Or separate the stalk clusters before storing them in resealable bags.

Tatsoi will keep in the refrigerator for up to four days.

Prep It

It's a shame to deconstruct this pretty plant, but you gotta eat, right? Take a moment to admire your tatsoi before trimming it. Slice off the base to separate the stalk clusters. Cut off the leaves with about ¼ inch (0.5 cm) stem attached. Stack them, roll up like a cigar and slice crosswise. Trim, slice and chop the stems separately.

Wash the greens in cold water before or after cutting them, then drain and spin-dry.

Consume It

Tatsoi is good raw in mixed salads or cooked in soups, stir-fries and braises. Usually only the leaves are added to salads, but the thinly sliced stems are also good raw.

The leaves cook in 1 to 2 minutes and the stems in 2 to 4 minutes, depending on their size. Stems and leaves can be stir-fried in stages or cooked in separate dishes.

Don't let anyone discourage you from eating the stems — they are mild and delightfully crunchy. However, they tend to get stringy when cooked, unless thinly sliced or chopped.

Crunchy Tatsoi Salad

Crunch meets munch in your salad bowl when you pile it full of Asian greens and crispy chow mein noodles. This addictive creation is pretty enough for company, but you will be tempted to keep it for yourself.

Makes 2 to 4 servings

Vegan Friendly

Salad

Tip

Supermarkets sell crispy chow mein noodles in bags, ready to eat as garnishes or snacks. Some brands are egg-free; check labels to be sure.

3 oz	tatsoi leaves and stems, sliced (about 4 cups/1 L, loosely packed)	90 g
3 cups	loosely packed torn leaf lettuce leaves	750 mL
⅓ cup	Sesame Dressing (page 453)	75 mL
2	green onions (white and light green parts), cut diagonally into ½-inch (1 cm) pieces	2
½	yellow bell pepper, cut into matchsticks	½
12	grape tomatoes (about ½ cup/125 mL), halved	12
1 cup	crispy chow mein noodles (see Tip, left)	250 mL

1. In a serving bowl, combine tatsoi and lettuce. Toss with dressing to taste (you will have some left over). Scatter onions, yellow pepper, tomatoes and chow mein noodles overtop. Serve immediately.

Variation

Nutty Tatsoi Salad: Substitute ½ cup (125 mL) coarsely chopped roasted peanuts or cashews for the crispy chow mein noodles.

Tatsoi and Mushroom Noodle Bowl with Lime Broth

Asian noodle soups are total comfort food, just made for slurping. I like the contrasts in this one, with its spicy and mellow flavors and crunchy and slippery textures.

	Makes 6 servings	
	Vegan Friendly	
	Soup	

Tips

Dried chow mein noodles are sold in the ethnic food sections of supermarkets. They are cooked like pasta. Do not confuse them with fried crispy chow mein noodles, which are eaten as snacks.

To prepare the tatsoi for this recipe: Using a sharp knife, trim tatsoi and cut stems from leaves. Thinly slice stems. Coarsely chop leaves.

To sliver green onions, use a sharp knife to cut thin slices on an extreme diagonal from the root end to the stalk.

Straw mushrooms are most often found canned. If you prefer fresh mushrooms, substitute thinly sliced oyster mushrooms.

You can find chile oil in well-stocked supermarkets. If desired, substitute a chile paste such as sriracha or sambal oelek, or dash in some hot sauce.

12 oz	dried Chinese chow mein noodles (see Tips, left)	375 g
1 tbsp	oil	15 mL
6	green onions (white and green parts), slivered (see Tips, left)	6
1	head tatsoi (12 oz/375 g), trimmed and cut (see Tips, left)	1
1 tsp	kosher or coarse sea salt	5 mL
1	large clove garlic, minced	1
2	cans (14 oz/398 mL each) straw mushrooms, rinsed, drained and halved (see Tips, left)	2
4 cups	vegetable stock	1 L
2 cups	water	500 mL
2 tbsp	freshly squeezed lime juice	30 mL
1 tbsp	soy sauce	15 mL
	Chile oil (see Tips, left)	

1. In a large saucepan of boiling salted water, cook noodles over medium heat for about 10 minutes, until tender but firm. Drain.

2. Meanwhile, in a saucepan over medium heat, heat oil until shimmery. Add green onions, tatsoi stems and salt. Cook, stirring often, for about 1 minute, until softened. Stir in garlic for about 1 minute. Stir in mushrooms, then add stock, water and tatsoi leaves. When mixture comes to a simmer, cover, reduce heat to medium-low and cook for 2 to 3 minutes, until tatsoi is tender. Remove from heat. Stir in lime juice and soy sauce. Season with salt to taste.

3. Divide noodles among six large, shallow bowls. Ladle soup overtop. Drizzle with chile oil to taste and serve immediately.

Variations

Instead of chow mein noodles, substitute dried Japanese soba or udon noodles or two vacuum packs of fresh Chinese noodles. Cook according to package directions.

In place of either of the oils called for in this recipe, use leftover curry oil from Black and Green Stew with Curry Oil (page 261).

Turnip Greens

Brassica rapa

> *Other names:* **inflorescence neeps, neep greens, turnip tops, turnip salad.**
>
> **Depending on where you are shopping, you may find turnip greens identified as *goggui agrio, grelos, kabu, nabo, rabano, salgam, suzuna, reuben gruen* or *wo jing*.**

Tasting Notes

Turnip leaves are pungent and bitter, like a cross between rapini and radish. They are milder when cooked.

Health Notes

Turnip greens contain vitamins A, B$_6$, C, E and K, calcium, copper, folate, iron, magnesium, manganese, niacin, pantothenic acid, phosphorus, potassium, riboflavin and thiamin. They are particularly high in fiber and rich in omega-3 fatty acids, as well as strongly anti-inflammatory.

In folk medicine, turnip greens have been used to treat anemia, arthritis and gout, hemorrhoids, cataracts, indigestion, constipation and bladder ailments, jaundice and liver disorders, insomnia, asthma, bronchitis and congestion.

Turnip greens are sometimes called Hanover greens. However, they shouldn't be confused with Hanover salad (page 188).

Native to Eurasia, turnips have been cultivated since prehistoric times. They were grown in India as far back as the 15th century BCE for their seeds, from which oil was pressed. Today turnips are cultivated mainly for their roots. They have been an essential winter vegetable in northern Europe for centuries but are also eaten around the world.

For much of their history, turnips didn't get much respect. They were mainly used as fodder, and ancient peoples regarded eating turnips as demeaning. Ironically, the healthiest parts, the greens, were considered way too bitter and got tossed to the slaves.

Nowadays the leaves remain a regional craving, notably in the American South and Japan. In Japan, turnip greens are among the "herbs" added to rice porridge during the Festival of Seven Herbs, held every January 7. The porridge is eaten to promote good luck and longevity.

Varieties

The greens from various cultivars of turnips (*Brassica rapa*) may be eaten. Some varieties, called foliage turnips, are grown specifically for their leaves and have tiny roots; they are similar to mustard greens (page 257).

Sour turnips (*B. rapa neosuguki*), also known as *sugukina* or Kyoto turnips, are closely related. In Japan their leaves are traditionally pickled to make a dish called *sugukizuke*.

The roots and greens of ancestral wild turnips (*B. rapa campestris*) were consumed by Native Americans on the Great Plains.

SUBSTITUTES

dandelion greens,
mustard greens, kale,
bitter melon vines,
radish greens

Buy It

Turnip greens are sold in farmers' markets, specialty greengrocers and occasionally supermarkets. Although the greens are sold separately in some regions of North America, most of us find them attached to turnips.

The smaller the turnip, the sweeter the leaf. As the plants mature, the leaves grow tough and bitter. Young greens sold before the roots (the turnips) fully develop are preferable. Better still are foliage turnips, the cultivars grown just for their greens.

Turnip leaves are green and ruffled. Choose evenly colored, crisp-looking leaves with no wilting or insect damage.

Store It

Turnips sold in supermarkets do not usually come with the tops attached, probably because the greens don't hold up well. They wilt quickly at room temperature. Also, the crisp stems are prone to snapping and the leaves easily become mangled.

When you get a bunch home, separate the turnips from the greens, leaving about ½ inch (1 cm) stem attached to the roots. Trim the stalks, separating leaves from stems. Wrap the leaves and stems separately in paper towels, place them in resealable bags and refrigerate. If the leaves are badly wilted, soak them in cold water for 30 minutes, drain and spin-dry before storing.

Turnip greens will keep in the refrigerator for up to two days.

Prep It

Before consuming turnip greens, separate the leaves from the stems and center ribs. Hold the bottom of a stem and slash upwards with a sharp knife, releasing the leaves. Discard stem pieces wider than ⅜ inch (0.75 cm); they are too fibrous.

Wash greens thoroughly in cold water, then drain and spin-dry.

Consume It

Both the trimmed stems and leaves may be eaten. The leaves are tender but pungent; small ones may be shredded to add punch (sparingly) to a mixed salad. However, turnip greens are rarely eaten raw.

Steaming or simmering is the simplest preparation method. The greens may also be sautéed or braised.

Simmer greens in water or stock until they are tender enough to cut with the side of a fork. Cook leaves to the consistency of spinach. Don't use a lot of liquid, as the greens will shrink down.

When turnip greens are boiled, nutrients seep into the cooking liquid — don't throw it away. In the American South, this delicious broth, called "pot likker," is used for dunking.

Turnip greens are very bitter. To mellow, cook them slowly. Sauté for at least 10 minutes or simmer for at least 30 minutes; bitter compounds will disperse into the oil or liquid. Salt when cooking; this helps prevents mushiness (and makes them taste good).

Turnip greens are traditionally tossed with vinegar after cooking.

Turnip Greens with Pot Likker

Simmered turnip greens are iconic in the American South, where cooks have a knack for transforming frugal food into delicious dishes. The simmering broth is called pot likker, and it is surprisingly flavorful. Carry on the tradition and serve cornbread or crunchy little fried corn pones alongside to dip into the "likker."

1	bunch turnip greens	1
1 tbsp	extra virgin olive oil	15 mL
1	small onion, diced	1
1	clove garlic, chopped	1
1	turnip, cut into 1/2-inch (1 cm) chunks, optional	1
3 cups	water	750 mL
1 tsp	kosher or coarse sea salt (see Tips, left)	5 mL
1 tsp	granulated sugar (see Tips, left)	5 mL
	Cider vinegar	
1/4 cup	chopped red bell pepper	60 mL

Makes 2 to 4 servings (about 5 cups/1.25 L)

Vegan Friendly

Side dish

Tips

I prefer kosher salt because it tastes better than iodized table salt and (ideally) contains no additives. Table salts and some sea salts contain additives such as iodine compounds (iodides), anti-clumping agents and even sugar (in the form of dextrose, which is used to stabilize iodine). Although the North American Salt Institute states that kosher salt "contains no additives," some kosher salt brands do contain additives such as anti-clumping agents. If you have concerns, check the label.

Cane sugar is likely to be filtered through bone char, while beet sugar is not. Most labels don't indicate the source of the sugar. If you are following a vegan diet, use unbleached organic sugar that has not been filtered through bone char, or a sweetener such as agave syrup.

1. Using a sharp knife, trim turnip greens, separating leaves from stems. Discard tough ends of stems. Cut tender stems into 1/2-inch (1 cm) pieces. Coarsely chop leaves; you should have about 2 cups (500 mL) stems and 8 cups (2 L) leaves. Set aside.

2. In a large saucepan over medium heat, heat oil until shimmery. Add onion and cook, stirring often, for about 3 minutes, until softened and turning golden. Stir in garlic for 20 seconds. Add turnip (if using), stems and leaves, water, salt and sugar. When mixture comes to a simmer, cover, reduce heat to low and cook for about 30 minutes, until very tender. Season with salt to taste. Dash in vinegar to taste or serve it alongside (use sparingly).

3. Spoon greens and their broth into bowls. Garnish with red pepper and serve immediately.

Vegan Scotch Broth

Barley and turnip greens put the Scotch in this thick broth. Rib-sticking and full of fiber and nutrients, it should give you enough energy to toss a caber.

<table>
<tr><td>2 tbsp</td><td>extra virgin olive oil</td><td>30 mL</td></tr>
<tr><td>3</td><td>medium carrots, sliced ¼ inch (0.5 cm) thick (see Tips, left)</td><td>3</td></tr>
<tr><td>2</td><td>medium leeks (white and light green parts), sliced</td><td>2</td></tr>
<tr><td>2</td><td>stalks celery with leaves, sliced diagonally ¼ inch (0.5 cm) thick</td><td>2</td></tr>
<tr><td>1</td><td>medium turnip, cut into ½-inch (1 cm) chunks</td><td>1</td></tr>
<tr><td>2 cups</td><td>coarsely chopped turnip leaves and tender stems (2 oz/60 g), loosely packed</td><td>500 mL</td></tr>
<tr><td>1 tsp</td><td>kosher or coarse sea salt</td><td>5 mL</td></tr>
<tr><td>½ cup</td><td>pearl barley (see Tips, left)</td><td>125 mL</td></tr>
<tr><td>4 cups</td><td>vegetable stock (see Tips, left)</td><td>1 L</td></tr>
<tr><td>2 cups</td><td>water</td><td>500 mL</td></tr>
<tr><td>½ tsp</td><td>freshly ground black pepper</td><td>2 mL</td></tr>
<tr><td>¼ tsp</td><td>ground allspice</td><td>1 mL</td></tr>
<tr><td>¼ cup</td><td>chopped fresh parsley leaves</td><td>60 mL</td></tr>
</table>

Makes 4 to 6 servings (about 9 cups/2.25 L)

Vegan Friendly

Soup

Tips

Be careful not to use large carrots, because they might sweeten the soup too much. Medium carrots weigh about 2 oz (60 g) each.

Pearl barley cooks faster than other types of barley. If desired, substitute pot or whole barley and add 15 to 30 minutes to the cooking time, until barley is tender.

Whenever possible, use reduced-sodium vegetable stock. Not only is it healthier, it allows you to better control the saltiness of a dish.

This soup thickens as it sits and cools — so much so that it can morph from soup to stew. Loosen leftovers by adding more stock to desired consistency.

1. In a large saucepan over medium heat, heat oil until shimmery. Add carrots, leeks, celery, turnip, turnip greens and salt. Cook, stirring often, for about 5 minutes, until vegetables soften. Stir in barley, cover pan and let ingredients sweat for about 1 minute. Stir in stock, water, pepper and allspice. When mixture comes to a simmer, cover, reduce heat to low and cook for about 30 minutes, until barley is tender. Season with salt to taste.

2. Ladle into serving bowls and sprinkle with parsley (see Tips, left).

Glazed Turnips and Greens with Sunflower Seeds

The sweetness of the turnips is a delicious foil for the bitter bite of their greens in this lovely dish. You can serve it to company or keep it all for yourself.

Makes 2 to 4 servings

Vegan Friendly

Side dish

Tips

Cane sugar is likely to be filtered through bone char, while beet sugar is not. Most labels don't indicate the source of the sugar. If you are following a vegan diet, use unbleached organic sugar that has not been filtered through bone char, or a sweetener such as agave syrup.

To toast sunflower seeds, cook in a dry skillet over medium heat, stirring often, for 2 to 3 minutes, until golden and aromatic.

1	large bunch turnips (with greens and roots)	1
2 tbsp	extra virgin olive oil	30 mL
1	onion, diced	1
2	cloves garlic, chopped	2
1½ tsp	kosher or coarse sea salt, divided	7 mL
¼ tsp	freshly ground black pepper, divided	1 mL
2 tbsp	water	30 mL
1 tsp	freshly squeezed lemon juice	5 mL
2 tbsp	unsalted butter or non-dairy alternative	30 mL
2 tbsp	granulated sugar (see Tips, left)	30 mL
¼ cup	raw sunflower seeds, toasted (see Tips, left)	60 mL

1. Using a sharp knife, separate turnips from stalks; you should have 3 turnips, weighing about 1 lb (500 g) total. Peel and cut turnips into ½-inch (1 cm) chunks. Trim stalks, separating leaves from stems. Discard tough ends of stems. Coarsely chop tender stems and leaves; you should have about 2 cups (500 mL) stems and 8 cups (2 L) leaves. Arrange in separate piles.

2. In a large saucepan over medium heat, heat oil until shimmery. Add onion and cook, stirring often, for about 3 minutes, until softened and turning golden. Stir in garlic for 20 seconds. Add turnip stems. Cook, stirring often, for 1 minute. Add leaves, 1 tsp (5 mL) salt and ⅛ tsp (0.5 mL) pepper. Cook, stirring often, for about 1 minute, until wilted. Add water and cook, stirring often, for about 15 minutes, until greens are tender and liquid has evaporated. Stir in lemon juice and remove from heat.

3. Meanwhile, in a saucepan of boiling salted water, cook turnips over medium heat for 3 to 4 minutes, until barely tender. Drain and set aside.

4. In a large skillet over medium heat, melt butter. Stir in sugar for 30 seconds. Add turnips and stir to coat well. Cook, stirring occasionally, for 8 to 10 minutes, until tender, with a golden brown coating.

5. Transfer greens to a serving platter. Spoon turnips over greens. Sprinkle sunflower seeds overtop and serve warm.

Watercress

Nasturtium officinale

> *Other names:* **berros, cressida, cresson.**
> **Depending on where you are shopping, you may find watercress identified as** *agnao, crescione, cresson d'eau, garashi, jembrak, lampaka, mustapa, pakthoy, phakkat-nam, selada air, simsaag, uotakuresu, wasserkresse* **or** *xi yang choy.*

Tasting Notes

Green watercress tastes mustardy, sharp and astringent. It has succulent leaves and thick, juicy stems. Red watercress is less sharp, more mineral tasting and nutty. It has thinner stems.

Health Notes

Watercress contains vitamins A, B_6, C, E and K, calcium, copper, folate, magnesium, manganese, pantothenic acid, phosphorus, potassium, riboflavin and thiamin.

As a folk remedy, watercress has a long list of uses. It is considered a diuretic, an expectorant and a digestive aid. It has been consumed to strengthen the kidneys, cleanse the blood, stimulate the gallbladder and even prevent baldness. In Mexico, watercress *licuados* (smoothies) were blended to relieve renal and pulmonary ailments. Watercress is rich in iodine, so it was used to treat hypothyroidism. It was also mixed with vinegar and used to stop bleeding.

Watercress is native to Eurasia but was transplanted to the wilds of the Americas. It grows in and near cool, shallow, gently running water such as brooks, ponds, lakes and even ditches.

Watercress has been foraged since prehistoric times. Culinary historians believe it was one of the first plants consumed and cultivated by humans. Initially it was used as a medicinal vegetable. The ancient Greeks ate watercress to cleanse the liver and blood and considered it a cure for mental illnesses. The ancient Romans ate it with oil and vinegar as a salad.

Watercress was first commercially cultivated in 1808 in England. Today the United States is the world's biggest watercress grower.

The glory days of watercress were in the Victorian era, when it was held in the highest esteem. The Queen's chefs as well as street laborers prepared watercress, and both the upper classes and the working poor savored its bite. It was sold from street carts and workers ate it with black bread. If they couldn't afford bread, they ate watercress on its own — thus it was known as "poor man's bread." Children took watercress sandwiches to school and adults brewed watercress tea, sipped with lemon and sugar.

During the World Wars, watercress was a British staple in salads and sandwiches. England remains the watercress appreciation capital of the world. The watercress festival and eating contest in Alresford attracts 15,000 visitors annually.

Although watercress always brings to mind Brits nibbling on dainty tea sandwiches, this crisp little green has been adopted by many cultures, from the French to the Chinese.

Varieties

Cress is a culinary category, not a botanical one. Cresses are unrelated but united in the kitchen as small, succulent, peppery, salad-friendly greens. There are hundreds of species of cresses.

Common green watercress (*Nasturtium officinale*) is the most famous — and hailed as the tastiest — member of the cress clan. New on the supermarket scene is red watercress, an attractive wild hybrid cultivated by a Florida company that is said to be the largest watercress grower in the world. The company discovered this so-called mutant heritage variety in the Everglades a few years ago. Maroon with green veins, it has more eye appeal and more antioxidants than green watercress. It also tastes milder and keeps longer.

Buy It

Watercress is a supermarket staple. It is sold in small bunches.

The leaves are small, rounded and dark green, the stems hollow. Watercress must be harvested before the tiny white flower buds appear in the summer. Afterwards the leaves supposedly taste foul (I have never put this to the test).

Look for thick, crisp, shiny bright green leaves with no yellowing and not too much breakage.

Foraging watercress is not recommended, for fear that the water nearby may be tainted with bacteria or liver fluke, a parasitic flatworm carried by snails, sheep, deer, pigs, wild boar and cattle.

Store It

Watercress leaves bruise easily, wilt quickly and become bitter with age. Wrap a damp paper towel around the base of the stems and store watercress in a perforated resealable bag. Or store it in a glass or vase of water like a bouquet, with a plastic bag draped over the foliage, then refrigerate it.

Watercress will keep in the refrigerator for up to two days.

Prep It

Plucking watercress leaves is one kitchen job that drives me crazy — it is too fiddly. If you are impatient like me, strip the leaves by running your fingers up the stems. You'll end up with tender stemlets as well as the leaves.

Do not wash watercress until you are ready to use it. Swish it gently in cold water, then spin-dry or place on paper towels to air dry.

Consume It

You can enjoy watercress raw or cooked. All the parts are edible. The stems are traditionally discarded, but they may be used: tender stemlets in salads and thicker stems in soups.

In salads, temper these astringent greens with sweet ingredients such as berries. Use watercress to add crunch and oomph to sandwiches. Cooking tames its pungency. Watercress is a favorite in soups, particular creamy ones.

In Asian cuisine, watercress is stir-fried or blanched, squeezed, chopped and tossed with dressing as a cooked salad.

Watercress cooks to tender-crisp in less than 5 minutes, but for soup it is simmered longer. For even cooking, stems and leaves may be sautéed separately, in stages.

SUBSTITUTES

purslane, dandelion greens, Belgian endive, baby spinach, mâche

N Is for Nasturtium

Oddly, watercress belongs to the genus *Nasturtium* but **garden nasturtium** (*Tropaeolum majus*) does not.

Garden nasturtium is also known as Indian/Peruvian cress or monk's cress. It originated in South America and was taken to Europe in the late 17th century. It is a North American garden favorite, but also an invasive species in some regions. The name *nasturtium* is translated as "nose-tweaker," because the plant produces an oil similar to that of watercress.

Both the leaves and flowers are eaten, mainly in salads. The leaves, shaped like lily pads, are considered peppery. The yellow, orange and red flowers are milder and decorative. Caper-like nasturtium buds are sometimes pickled.

Relatives include **dwarf nasturtium** (*T. minus*) and **mashua** (*T. tuberosum*). The latter produces an edible tuber.

A World of Cress

It may be cress, but it's not necessarily watercress. Diverse members of the cress clan have leaves ranging from round to frilled, stems from succulent to delicate, and reputations from exemplary to inferior. Among the hundreds of species of so-called cresses, the most popular are watercress, upland cress and garden cress.

Watercress

Watercress (*Nasturtium officinale*) is the standard by which all cresses are measured (page 405). Watercress relatives include **one-row watercress** (*N. microphyllum*), also known as one-row yellow watercress or narrow-fruited watercress, and **Tibetan watercress** (*N. tibeticum*). **Yellow cress** (*N. sterile*), thought to be a cross between *N. officinale* and *N. microphyllum*, has brownish purple leaves and is commonly found in Britain and France.

Upland Cress

Upland cress (*Barbarea verna*) is also known as land cress, American/Bermuda cress, American watercress, bank/blackwood/dryland cress, Belle Isle cress, cassabully, early yellow rocket, scurvy grass, cresson or early winter cress. Some supermarkets sell this cress. It tastes more peppery than watercress but is not as sharp and has mineral accents. The leaves are larger and not as shiny as watercress, and the long, thin stems are delicate. This cress also comes in curly cultivars.

Upland cress likes damp soil but, as per its name, it grows on dryer land than watercress. In England, upland cress has been grown for salads since the beginning of the 17th century. Its genus, **Barbarea**, is named after Saint Barbara, the patron saint of miners and gunners, because upland cress was applied to wounds caused by explosions.

An edible wild relative is **winter cress** (*B. vulgaris*), also known as rocket cress, bittercress or yellow/winter/wound rocket.

Garden Cress

Garden cress (*Lepidum sativum*) is also known as peppergrass, pepper wort, mustard cress, garden pepper cress, *chandrashoor*, *cressonette* or *berro de tierra*. It comes in common, curly and broadleaf cultivars. **Persian cress** (*taratezak*) is a variety with oval leaves and tiny serrations. **Australian cress** is a gold-leafed cultivar.

A World of Cress (continued)

Garden cress is not considered as sharp or crunchy as watercress. It may be grown indoors or hydroponically. If left to flower, it produces fruit described as similar to caperberries. The bright, flat leaves can grow to 4 inches (10 cm) long.

Garden cress belongs to a family of plants called peppergrasses, so named because they are appreciated for their peppery flavor. These include:

- **bastard cress** (*L. campestre*), also known as field cress or pepperweed. It is an invasive but edible weed in North America.
- **broad-leaved peppergrass** (*L. latifolium*), also known as dittander, dittany, poor man's pepper or tall whitetop. It is eaten in salads and cooked like spinach. Growing wild from Europe to the Himalayas, it is believed to have invaded the United States via seeds hiding in a shipment of beets.
- Virginia cress (*L. virginicum*), also known as Virginia pepperweed. It is eaten in salads, sautéed or used as an herb.
- Cook's scurvy grass (*L. oleraceum*), also known as *ngau* or *heketara*. This variety is native to New Zealand and is eaten by the Maoris. It was one of the plants collected by Captain James Cook's crew to ward off scurvy.
- maca (*L. meyenii*), also known as Peruvian ginseng. It is used mainly in the Andes as a root vegetable, medicinal plant and aphrodisiac. However, the leaves are also edible; in addition they may be brewed as tea.

Other Cress Wannabes

Pennycress (*Thlaspi arvense*) is used in salads and sandwich spreads. It may be blanched to mellow its bitterness.

Paracress (*Acmella oleracea*) is also known as toothache plant or *jambu*. It is eaten as a sharp-tasting leafy green in its native Brazil and is used in curries in Thailand. Its biggest claim to fame is its flower buds, which are perfectly named — buzz buttons, electric buttons or Szechuan buttons. These buds shock the tongue, leaving it tingling, then numb.

Two so-called spring cresses are **bulbous cress** (*Cardamine bulbosa*), also known as bittercress, and **hairy bittercress** (*C. hirsuta*), also known as lamb's cress or flick/shot weed. Both these species can be used as bitter herbs.

Classic Watercress Soup

I can't get enough of the complex, nutty deliciousness of this traditional favorite. The astringent watercress is bolstered by leek and celery and balanced by creamy potato. Serve this soup warm or cold. Frugal folks will like the fact that the recipe uses both leaves and stems.

Makes 4 to 8 servings (about 8 cups/2 L)
Vegan Friendly
Soup

Tips

Whenever possible, use reduced-sodium vegetable stock. Not only is it healthier, it allows you to better control the saltiness of a dish.

Yellow-fleshed potatoes are best for this recipe. Neither waxy nor dry, they give soup a creamy but not gluey consistency. The best-known yellow-fleshed potatoes are Yukon Golds.

Crème fraîche is sold in well-stocked supermarkets. You can substitute sour cream, but crème fraîche is more subtle. For a vegan version, substitute a mixture of non-dairy sour cream and unflavored soy milk for the crème fraîche.

- Stand or immersion blender

2 tbsp	unsalted butter or non-dairy alternative	30 mL
2	bunches watercress, trimmed, leaves and stems separated, stems chopped	2
1	leek (white and light green parts), sliced	1
1	stalk celery, diced	1
4 cups	vegetable stock (see Tips, left)	1 L
2 cups	water	500 mL
1	potato (8 oz/250 g), cut into 1-inch (2.5 cm) chunks (see Tips, left)	1
1 tsp	kosher or coarse sea salt	5 mL
½ cup	crème fraîche or non-dairy alternative (see Tips, left)	125 mL
4 to 8	tiny sprigs watercress	4 to 8

1. In a large saucepan over medium heat, melt butter. Add watercress stems, leek and celery. Cook, stirring often, for about 5 minutes, until softened. Add stock, water, potato, watercress leaves and salt. When mixture comes to a simmer, cover, reduce heat to low and cook for 15 to 20 minutes, until stems and potato are very tender.
2. Using blender, purée soup until satiny and smooth.
3. Serve warm or transfer to an airtight container, cover and refrigerate for several hours or overnight, until chilled. To serve, ladle soup into bowls. Top each with a dollop of crème fraîche and a sprig of watercress.

Variation

For a light meal, follow the lead of the French, who sometimes float a poached egg in watercress soup.

Canarian Watercress Soup

Perky watercress is the star of this soup, known as **potaje de berros** *in the Canary Islands, a Spanish archipelago off the coast of Africa. This recipe takes full advantage of watercress, stems and all, and the canned beans speed up the soup-making process. Serve this soup with a hunk of crusty bread and you've got a hearty hot meal.*

Makes 6 to 8 servings (about 12 cups/3 L)

Vegan Friendly

Soup

Tips

Whenever possible, use reduced-sodium vegetable stock. Not only is it healthier, it allows you to better control the saltiness of a dish.

Yellow-fleshed potatoes are best for this recipe. Neither waxy nor dry, they give soup a creamy but not gluey consistency. The best-known yellow-fleshed potatoes are Yukon Golds.

Navy beans are also known as pea beans. You can substitute any kind of beans you like.

Fresh corn is best in this soup. After stripping the ears, you will end up with about 2 cups (500 mL) of kernels. If you don't have fresh corn, substitute thawed frozen corn.

1/3 cup	extra virgin olive oil	75 mL
1	bunch watercress, trimmed, leaves and stems separated, chopped	1
1/2	Spanish onion, diced	1/2
1	small green bell pepper, cut into small dice	1
4	cloves garlic, minced (see Tips, page 412)	4
3 cups	vegetable stock (see Tips, left)	750 mL
3 cups	water	750 mL
2	large potatoes (about 1 lb/500 g total), cut into 1-inch (2.5 cm) chunks (see Tips, left)	2
1	small sweet potato (about 8 oz/250 g), cut into 1-inch (2.5 cm) chunks	1
1 tsp	kosher or coarse sea salt	5 mL
1/8 tsp	saffron	0.5 mL
1	can (19 oz/540 mL) navy beans (see Tips, left)	1
2	ears fresh corn, kernels cut off (see Tips, left)	2
	Sour cream or non-dairy alternative	
	Minced red onion	
	Chopped fresh cilantro leaves	

1. In a saucepan over medium heat, heat oil until shimmery. Add watercress stems, onion and green pepper. Cook, stirring often, for about 3 minutes, until softened. Stir in garlic for 20 seconds. Add stock, water, potatoes, sweet potato and salt. Crumble in saffron. When mixture comes to a simmer, cover, reduce heat to low and cook for about 15 minutes, until potatoes are tender. Stir in watercress leaves, beans and corn. When mixture returns to a simmer, cover and cook for about 5 minutes, until heated through. Season with salt to taste.

2. Ladle into serving bowls. Garnish with a dollop of sour cream and a sprinkling of red onion and cilantro.

East Meets Cress Soup

The British may be famous for their love of watercress, but Asians enjoy it immensely too. This fusion soup has elements of both East and West. The ginger, orange and hint of coconut complement the watercress.

<table>
<tr><td colspan="3">• Stand or immersion blender</td></tr>
<tr><td>2 tbsp</td><td>extra virgin olive oil</td><td>30 mL</td></tr>
<tr><td>1</td><td>onion, diced</td><td>1</td></tr>
<tr><td>2</td><td>bunches watercress, trimmed, leaves and stems separated, stems chopped</td><td>2</td></tr>
<tr><td>2</td><td>cloves garlic, minced (see Tips, left)</td><td>2</td></tr>
<tr><td>1 tsp</td><td>puréed gingerroot (see Tips, left)</td><td>5 mL</td></tr>
<tr><td>4 cups</td><td>vegetable stock</td><td>1 L</td></tr>
<tr><td>1 cup</td><td>water</td><td>250 mL</td></tr>
<tr><td>1 tsp</td><td>finely grated orange zest</td><td>5 mL</td></tr>
<tr><td>¼ cup</td><td>freshly squeezed orange juice (about 1 orange)</td><td>60 mL</td></tr>
<tr><td>1 tsp</td><td>kosher or coarse sea salt</td><td>5 mL</td></tr>
<tr><td>1 tsp</td><td>chile paste (see Tips, left)</td><td>5 mL</td></tr>
<tr><td>1 cup</td><td>unsweetened coconut milk beverage (see Tips, left)</td><td>250 mL</td></tr>
</table>

Makes 4 to 8 servings (about 8 cups/2 L)

Vegan Friendly

Soup

Tips

For the finest minced garlic, push it through a press.

To grate or purée gingerroot, use a kitchen rasp such as the kind made by Microplane.

Sambal oelek, an Indonesian chile paste, is one of my favorites. Use any kind you prefer.

You can find coconut beverage in cartons in the supermarket dairy aisle. If you don't have any, use an equal mixture of coconut milk and vegetable stock.

1. In a saucepan over medium heat, heat oil until shimmery. Add onion and watercress stems. Cook, stirring often, for about 3 minutes, until softened. Stir in garlic and ginger for 20 seconds. Add stock, water, orange zest and juice, watercress leaves, salt and chile paste. When mixture comes to a simmer, cover, reduce heat to low and cook for about 30 minutes, until watercress is very soft.

2. Using blender, purée soup until smooth. Return to pan, if necessary, and stir in coconut beverage. Season with salt to taste. Serve warm.

Watercress and Roasted Pepper Spirals

I've been enjoying these cute cocktail nibbles for years. Set some out on a party tray, but be careful — they go down so easily you could end up scarfing ten at a time.

Makes 40 spirals

Vegan Friendly

Appetizer

Tips

For a vegan version, use dairy-free cream cheese, loosening it with enough unflavored soy milk to make it just spreadable.

If desired, use whole wheat or flavored tortillas instead of plain ones.

Speed up production by buying roasted peppers in the supermarket deli section. These tend to be smaller peppers, so you may need 2 extra. Drain before chopping.

To avoid a soggy filling, make sure the watercress leaves are completely dried after washing.

- 4 large paper towels, dampened, wrung out and flattened

8 oz	cream cheese or non-dairy alternative, softened (see Tips, left)	250 g
1 tbsp	chopped fresh basil leaves	15 mL
2 tsp	chopped fresh oregano leaves	10 mL
	Kosher or coarse sea salt	
4	flour tortillas (10 inches/25 cm in diameter; see Tips, left)	4
4	roasted red peppers, chopped (see Tips, left)	4
1	bunch watercress, trimmed, stems removed and leaves chopped (see Tips, left)	1

1. In a bowl, combine cream cheese, basil and oregano, using a fork to mix well. Season with salt to taste.

2. Spread cream cheese mixture evenly over tortillas, right to edges. Scatter peppers overtop to within $1/2$ inch (1 cm) of edges. Arrange watercress on top. Tightly roll up each tortilla, wrap in a damp paper towel and place in a large resealable bag. Seal and refrigerate for 2 hours.

3. Using a serrated knife and occasionally wiping the blade clean, trim and discard uneven ends of each tortilla roll, then slice each roll crosswise into 10 spirals about $3/4$ inch (2 cm) thick. Transfer spirals to a platter and serve.

Variation

Watercress and Roasted Pepper Wraps: Make sandwich wraps instead of spirals. In Step 2, roll up the bottom edge of the tortilla partway, fold in the right and left edges to make them straight, then finish rolling. Serve immediately.

Watercress Tea Sandwiches

Who doesn't love tea sandwiches? These traditional little yummies are filled with cress and a cream cheese spread. They are triple-decker triangles, but you could make rounds instead (using a cookie cutter) or slice the sandwiches into fingers.

Makes 16 triangles

Vegan Friendly

Sandwich

Tips

For this recipe, use the soft cream cheese sold in tubs in the supermarket deli department, not the firm blocks. You can use lower-fat cream cheese.

To avoid a soggy filling, make sure the watercress is completely dry before using it.

For healthier and more attractive little bites, I like to use a combination of white and whole wheat bread for each sandwich.

Weighting the sandwiches makes them easier to cut and neater looking. The goal is to compress, not flatten. The softer and fresher the bread, the less time this will take. Whole wheat bread, which is firmer, takes a bit longer.

- 2 rimmed baking sheets

8 oz	cream cheese or non-dairy alternative (about 1 cup/250 mL; see Tips, left)	250 g
¼ cup	finely chopped fresh parsley leaves	60 mL
1 tsp	finely grated orange zest	5 mL
½ tsp	kosher or coarse sea salt	2 mL
⅛ tsp	freshly ground black pepper	0.5 mL
1	bunch watercress, stemmed (see Tips, left)	1
6	slices white sandwich bread	6
6	slices whole wheat sandwich bread	6

1. In a bowl, combine cream cheese, parsley, orange zest, salt and pepper.

2. Separate watercress leaves into 8 piles. Arrange bread slices on work surface in four sets of three (see Tips, left). Working with one set at a time, spread about ¼ cup (60 mL) cream cheese mixture on one side of bottom and top slices and on both sides of middle slice, leaving a narrow border. Arrange one pile of watercress on bottom slice. Top with middle slice and another pile of watercress. Add top slice. Transfer to baking sheet. Repeat with remaining sets of bread, cream cheese mixture and watercress.

3. Place second baking sheet on top of sandwiches and put light weights (such as cans) on top. Set aside for about 5 minutes, until slightly compressed (timing depends on the texture of the bread; see Tips, left).

4. Using a serrated knife, cut off the crusts. Cut each sandwich into 4 triangles and serve immediately. Alternatively, leave the sandwiches whole, wrap in plastic and place in an airtight container for several hours or overnight. Trim crusts and cut into triangles just before serving.

Watercress and Mock Egg Salad Sandwiches

Watercress and egg salad are soulmates. I make a good facsimile of egg salad by using tofu. Here it is stuffed into heart-healthy vegan sandwiches with watercress.

Makes 8 sandwiches

Vegan Friendly

Sandwich

Tips

This recipe makes about 2 cups (500 mL) mock egg salad. If you don't want to make sandwiches, it is also excellent served on a bed of salad greens.

If desired, you can scale down this recipe. Per sandwich, use ¼ cup (60 mL) mock egg salad, ½ oz (15 g) watercress leaves (about ½ cup/ 125 mL, loosely packed) and 3 slices of tomato. Transfer the remaining mock egg salad to an airtight container, cover and refrigerate for later use. It will keep for up to 4 days.

Celery hearts are the tender inner stalks of a bunch of celery.

Hearty stone-ground flax multigrain bread works well for these sandwiches, but use any type of bread you prefer.

- Mini food processor

Mock Egg Salad

2	green onions (white and light green parts), sliced	2
1	stalk celery heart, with leaves, sliced (see Tips, left)	1
1 tbsp	chopped fresh parsley leaves	15 mL
8 oz	extra-firm tofu, drained and patted dry	250 g
2 tbsp	vegan mayonnaise	30 mL
¼ tsp	Dijon mustard	1 mL
1 tsp	kosher or coarse sea salt	5 mL
½ tsp	garlic powder	2 mL
⅛ tsp	freshly ground white pepper	0.5 mL
⅛ tsp	turmeric	0.5 mL

Sandwiches

16	small slices crusty multigrain bread (see Tips, left)	16
	Vegan mayonnaise	
2	bunches watercress, stemmed	2
24	very thin slices tomato	24
	Kosher or coarse sea salt	
	Freshly ground black pepper	

1. *Mock Egg Salad:* In food processor fitted with the metal blade, combine green onions, celery and parsley and pulse until finely chopped. Transfer to a bowl. Using fingers, crumble in tofu.

2. In a small bowl, combine mayonnaise, mustard, salt, garlic powder and pepper. Add to tofu mixture. Using a fork, mix until well combined but still in pieces. Mix in turmeric roughly, so the color looks slightly uneven.

3. *Sandwiches:* Arrange bread in sets on work surface. Spread mayonnaise, to taste, over each slice. On 8 slices, spread equal quantities of mock egg salad. Press equal quantities of watercress leaves on top. Top with tomato slices. Season with salt and pepper to taste. Cover with remaining bread slices. Using a serrated knife, cut each sandwich in half and serve immediately.

Variation

Curried Mock Egg Salad: In Step 2, add curry powder or paste to taste. Omit the turmeric.

Quinoa with Cress, Pom and Pistachios

Lively pomegranate dressing is the perfect finishing touch for this healthy Middle East–inspired salad. The watercress stands in for the bitter wild greens used in Middle Eastern cuisine. Purslane would be another good choice.

<table>
<tr><td colspan="3">**Makes 3 to 4 servings (about 5½ cups/1.3 L)**</td></tr>
<tr><td colspan="3">**Vegan Friendly**</td></tr>
<tr><td colspan="3">**Salad**</td></tr>
</table>

Tips

This recipe makes about ⅓ cup (75 mL) dressing. Use any leftover portion on other salads.

Pomegranate molasses may be labeled "pomegranate concentrate." It is sweet-and-sour and very bold. Look for it in Middle Eastern grocery stores and some supermarkets.

Pomegranate arils are the fruit's ruby-red seeds. One pomegranate should yield more than enough for this recipe. You can find fresh arils in containers in specialty stores and some supermarkets. Avoid the frozen ones in this dish — they are too soggy when thawed.

Look for shelled pistachios in bulk stores and Middle Eastern supermarkets. To toast, cook pistachios in a dry skillet over medium heat, stirring often, for 2 to 3 minutes, until turning golden and aromatic.

- Mini food processor

Pomegranate Dressing

1 tbsp	pomegranate molasses (see Tips, left)	15 mL
1 tbsp	freshly squeezed lemon juice	15 mL
1	clove garlic, minced	1
1 tsp	liquid honey or vegan alternative	5 mL
1 tsp	kosher or coarse sea salt	5 mL
½ tsp	ground cumin	2 mL
⅛ tsp	freshly ground white pepper	0.5 mL
¼ cup	extra virgin olive oil	60 mL

Salad

1 cup	quinoa, rinsed	250 mL
1 cup	vegetable stock	250 mL
1 cup	water	250 mL
1	bunch watercress, stemmed, leaves coarsely chopped	1
½ cup	pomegranate arils (see Tips, left)	125 mL
½ cup	shelled pistachios, toasted (see Tips, left)	125 mL

1. *Pomegranate Dressing:* In a bowl, whisk together pomegranate molasses, lemon juice, garlic, honey, salt, cumin and pepper. Whisk in oil. Set aside.

2. *Salad:* In a dry saucepan over medium heat, toast quinoa, stirring often, for about 5 minutes, until it smells nutty and no longer steams. Carefully add stock and water (mixture will spatter). Once mixture comes to a full boil, cover, reduce heat to medium-low and simmer for about 15 minutes, until quinoa is tender-firm and liquid is absorbed. Remove from heat, fluff with a fork and set aside, uncovered, for 5 minutes. Transfer to a large serving bowl and set aside to cool to room temperature.

3. Add watercress, pomegranate arils and pistachios. Toss gently with dressing to taste (you will have some left over). Serve at room temperature.

Variation

If you can't find pomegranate molasses, substitute Lemon Cumin Dressing (page 453) for the pomegranate dressing.

Coconut Cress Channa

Chickpea curry is fabulous, filling comfort food. I have been preparing mine with watercress and coconut for many years and enjoy it immensely over rice, with chutney on the side.

Tips

Ghee is Indian clarified butter. It is sold in bottles in well-stocked supermarkets and Indian grocery stores.

Diced canned tomatoes hold their shape better than canned plum tomatoes that have been crushed or chopped. Make sure you drain the tomatoes very well, to avoid a channa that is too watery or tomato-y.

You can find various types of bottled curry pastes in supermarkets. Avoid the tomato-y tandoori kind. I use Madras curry paste in this recipe, which is a good all-purpose curry spice blend.

1 tbsp	oil or ghee (see Tips, left)	15 mL
1	onion, diced	1
1	large clove garlic, minced	1
2	cans (19 oz/540 mL) chickpeas, drained and rinsed	2
1	can (28 oz/796 mL) diced tomatoes, drained and chopped (see Tips, left)	1
1	can (14 oz/400 mL) coconut milk	1
¼ cup	bottled Indian curry paste (see Tips, left)	60 mL
1 tsp	kosher or coarse sea salt	5 mL
½ cup	water (approx.)	125 mL
1	bunch watercress, stemmed, leaves coarsely chopped	1
	Hot sauce	

1. In a saucepan over medium heat, heat oil until shimmery. Add onion and cook, stirring often, for about 3 minutes, until softened and turning golden. Stir in garlic for 20 seconds. Add chickpeas, tomatoes, coconut milk, curry paste and salt. When mixture comes to a simmer, cover, reduce heat to low and cook for 15 minutes. Add some or all of the water to adjust thickness to desired consistency. Stir in watercress leaves. Cook until wilted but still bright green, about 1 minute. Season with salt to taste. Dash in hot sauce to taste. Serve warm.

Watercress Curry Sauce

Add a pinch of France and a dash of India and you've got a lip-smacking all-purpose sauce. Watercress sauce is delicious doled out over steamed veggies, rice or pasta, or you can simmer cubes of tofu or paneer (Indian fresh cheese) in it.

	Makes about 1½ cups (375 mL)	
	Sauce	

Tips

For this recipe, chop the watercress stems and chop the leaves finely. Put them in separate piles.

Celery hearts are the tender inner stalks of a bunch of celery.

Whenever possible, use reduced-sodium vegetable stock. Not only is it healthier, it allows you to better control the saltiness of a dish.

You can find various types of bottled curry pastes in most supermarkets. Avoid the tomato-y tandoori kind for this recipe. I used Madras curry paste, which is a good all-purpose curry spice blend.

- Stand or immersion blender

2 tbsp	unsalted butter	30 mL
1	bunch watercress, trimmed, stems and leaves separated, chopped (see Tips, left)	1
2	shallots, diced	2
1	stalk celery heart, with leaves, diced (see Tips, left)	1
½ cup	dry white wine	125 mL
½ cup	vegetable stock (see Tips, left)	125 mL
1 tsp	kosher or coarse sea salt	5 mL
½ cup	heavy or whipping (35%) cream	125 mL
1 tsp	curry paste (see Tips, left)	5 mL

1. In a saucepan over medium heat, melt butter. Add watercress stems, shallots and celery. Cook, stirring often, for about 5 minutes, until softened and golden. Add wine, stock and salt. When mixture comes to a simmer, reduce heat to medium-low and cook for about 5 minutes, until vegetables are tender.

2. Using blender, purée mixture until smooth. Return to pan, if necessary. Add cream, curry paste and watercress leaves and return to a simmer over medium-high heat. Reduce heat to low and simmer for about 10 minutes, until watercress is very tender and sauce is thick. Season with salt to taste.

3. Use immediately or transfer to an airtight container, cool briefly, cover and refrigerate until ready to use, for up to 3 days.

Variation

Watercress Wine Sauce: Omit the curry paste in Step 2.

Water Spinach

Ipomoea aquatica

Other names: **Chinese morning glory, Chinese spinach, empty heart vegetable, hollow/pitcher vegetable, hollow stalks, long green, morning glory leaf vegetable, river/tropical spinach, swamp morning glory, swamp spinach,** *kangkong*, **water convolvulus, water sweet potato.**

Depending on where you are shopping, you may find water spinach identified as *bai phai, batata acquatica, boniato de agua, camotillo, cancon, furen gadu, kalmi sag, ku-shin-sai, phak bung, rau muong, sisu lumi, ong choy, weng cai* or *you-sai.*

Tasting Notes

Water spinach tastes like a combination of spinach, celery and watercress. When cooked, the flavor becomes more spinachy. It has slightly slippery leaves and crisp stems.

Water spinach is sometimes called swamp cabbage, but it should not be confused with a fleshy palm heart called swamp cabbage (*Symplocarpus foetidus*), which is also known as skunk/clumpfoot/meadow cabbage, fetid pothos or polecat weed. The large, foul-smelling leaves of the latter can burn the mouth if eaten raw. They are used medicinally or dried and stirred into soups and stews.

The origins of water spinach are debated, but it may be native to China or India. It is most anciently known as *kalamba*, in Sanskrit. The oldest Chinese document referring to water spinach was written in 304 CE. The widely used name *kangkong* is sometimes translated as "restless" in Malay, referring to how easily this plant spreads.

Water spinach grows both wild and cultivated as a leaf vegetable in tropical and subtropical regions, having spread to Africa, Oceania and the Americas. It is an important ingredient in the cuisines of China, Thailand, Cambodia, Vietnam, the Philippines, Korea and Malaysia, where it is found everywhere from street carts to five-star restaurants.

Water spinach has secured a place in history as a source of wartime sustenance. During the Vietnam War, bomb craters along the Ho Chi Minh Trail filled with rainwater. To create a ready food supply, Vietnamese soldiers tossed in fish and fast-growing water spinach. A similar strategy was undertaken in the Philippines during the war in 1899, when water spinach was grown in canals dug by the Americans.

Water spinach was introduced to the West wherever Asians settled. It is now cultivated in California. In the hot American South, including Florida, it clogs waterways and is considered an invasive weed.

Health Notes

Although no official government analysis is available, water spinach is thought to contain vitamins C, B_6 and K, calcium, copper, folate, magnesium, pantothenic acid, phosphorus, riboflavin, thiamin and zinc.

Scientists have studied water spinach for its potential to keep blood sugar levels under control. In herbal medicine, it has been used to treat high blood pressure, diabetes, eye ailments, memory loss, stomach disorders, insomnia, constipation, boils and hemorrhoids.

Varieties

Water spinach is a trailing or floating plant with hollow stems. It is related to sweet potato leaves (page 381).

There are two major cultivars:

- **ching quat** (green-stem or upland water spinach), which has spear-shaped leaves and grows in irrigated or moist soil.
- **pak quat** (white-stem or lowland water spinach), which has thicker pastel green stems with arrow-shaped leaves and grows in water, like rice. It is considered superior to ching quat.

Water spinach also comes in a "red" variety, which actually has purple stems.

Wild water spinach, a ubiquitous forage plant, is plucked in freshwater ditches, bogs, marshes and rice paddies worldwide.

Water spinach is sometimes confused with buffalo spinach (*Enydra fluctuans*), a similar but unrelated water plant. Buffalo spinach is also known as *hingcha, chengkuru, kangkong kerbau, phak bung ruem* or *rau ngo*. It grows wild in the Asian and African tropics.

Buy It

Water spinach is sold in grocery stores that carry Chinese, Vietnamese, Malaysian and Filipino ingredients.

Water spinach doesn't look anything like spinach. It has round, hollow stems that are topped by long, narrow leaves. Check for crisp, moist-looking stems and perky green leaves.

Store It

Water spinach doesn't keep well. To make it manageable, remove the stems, wrap the stems and leaves separately in paper towels and store in resealable bags. Or put it in a glass or vase of water like a bouquet, with a plastic bag draped over the foliage, then refrigerate it. Or wrap a damp paper towel around the bottom of the stems and place in a plastic bag.

Water spinach will keep in the refrigerator for up to two days.

Prep It

All parts are edible, but the tender leaves and young shoots are best.

Before consuming water spinach, cut off the leaves and chop them. The coarse, yellowed ends of the stems are fibrous; trim ½ to 1 inch (1 to 2.5 cm), or more if necessary, off the bottoms. Slice or chop the stems.

Do not wash water spinach until you are ready to use it, as the hollow stems hold water. Swish it in cold water, drain and spin-dry.

Consume It

The leaves could be used raw in mixed salads or sandwiches. However, both the leaves and stems are usually cooked. When raw, the stems have strings, like celery.

Water spinach is popular in Asian cuisine because it stays crunchy and the straw-like stems hold sauces. The greens may be stir-fried, added to soups or pickled. The stems are sometimes cooked on their own.

Cook water spinach until the leaves are wilted and dark green and the stems are light green. Do not overcook — these greens are meant to be crisp. Stems cook in 3 to 5 minutes, leaves in about 1 minute. Before stir-frying, stems may be tenderized by blanching for about 1 minute.

SUBSTITUTES

spinach, watercress

Water Spinach Stir-Fry with Coconut, Lime and Garlic Chips

Put the lime in the coconut and eat it all up — because these complementary flavors make water spinach extra tasty. This stir-fry is ready lickety-split.

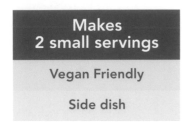

**Makes
2 small servings**

Vegan Friendly

Side dish

Tips

Finger chiles are also known as cayenne peppers. They are slender, with pointed tips. You can substitute any kind of red chile you prefer.

Be careful not to brown the garlic or it will taste bitter. Reduce the heat if necessary.

• Wok

12 oz	water spinach	375 g
2 tbsp	oil	30 mL
6	cloves garlic, thinly sliced	6
1	red finger chile, thinly sliced (see Tips, left)	1
2 tbsp	unsweetened desiccated coconut	30 mL
1 tsp	kosher or coarse sea salt	5 mL
1 tsp	granulated sugar	5 mL
2 tbsp	coconut milk	30 mL
1 tbsp	lime juice	15 mL

1. Using a sharp knife, trim water spinach, separating leaves and stems. Slice stems into 1-inch (2.5 cm) pieces. Coarsely chop leaves. Arrange in separate piles.

2. In wok, heat oil over medium-low heat until warm. Add garlic and fry for about 1 minute, just until golden (see Tips, left). Using a slotted spoon, transfer to a plate lined with paper towels and set aside to firm up.

3. Return wok to medium-high heat. Add chile and water spinach stems. Stir-fry for about 2 minutes, until softened. Stir in coconut, salt and sugar. Stir-fry for 1 to 2 minutes, until softened. Add water spinach leaves and stir-fry for about 1 minute, until leaves are just wilted and stems are tender-crisp. Remove from heat. Stir in coconut milk and lime juice. Season with salt to taste.

4. Transfer to a serving dish. Scatter garlic chips overtop and serve warm.

Wheatgrass

Triticum aestivum

> *Other names:* bread/common wheat, cereal grass.
> Depending on where you are shopping, you may find wheatgrass identified as *gehun*, *komugi* or *xiao mai*.

It is thought that wheatgrass was first consumed in Mesopotamia and that is was used by pharaohs and priests in ancient Egypt. Nowadays it is surrounded by hyperbole as one of the first so-called superfoods. Wheatgrass claims no shortage of true believers, or detractors. It is both mocked for its disgusting taste (untrue) and lauded for its miraculous health benefits (unproven).

Agricultural chemist Charles Schnabel, "the father of wheatgrass," turned the ignition on the wheatgrass bandwagon in the 1930s. Holistic health practitioner Ann Wigmore, "the mother of living foods," started promoting a wheatgrass diet after founding a health institute in Boston in 1968; she followed up with a wheatgrass book in 1985.

Tasting Notes

Wheatgrass is mild and grassy, with lemon accents and hints of broccoli, cucumber and hay. It is slightly sweet and slightly briny. It is also juicy, but the texture is fibrous. It is not fully digestible.

Equivalents

1 package =
4 oz (125 g)

•

2 oz (60 g) blades
= 6 cups (1.5 L),
loosely packed

•

2 oz (60 g) coarsely
chopped blades
= 4 cups (1 L),
loosely packed

Varieties

Chewing on wheatgrass is like chewing on grass — because it is grass. Wheatgrass is the first shoots of the same species of wheat that is grown for flour. Instead of being allowed to mature, the shoots are harvested when green and just a few inches high.

Buy It

Wheatgrass is sold in health food stores and some supermarkets. It is packed in clamshells and bags and is sometimes sold potted as a windowsill plant that can be grown and clipped as needed.

It is sweeter when young. If cut too mature, wheatgrass will be bitter.

Wheatgrass resembles oversized blades of grass about 5 inches (12.5 cm) tall, transitioning from lime to forest green. Choose vibrantly colored grass with moist-looking root ends.

Store It

Store wheatgrass in its original clamshell package. Or roll it loosely in paper towels, place in a resealable bag and refrigerate.

Wheatgrass will keep in the refrigerator for up to one week. Although it is hardy, use it as fresh as possible to get the full benefit of the nutrients.

Health Notes

Wheatgrass contains vitamins A, B₆, C, E and K, copper, iron, manganese, niacin, pantothenic acid, potassium, riboflavin, selenium, thiamin and zinc. Whole wheatgrass (not juiced) is rich in fiber and protein.

Wheatgrass is gluten-free, but experts warn that it may be cross-contaminated with seeds that contain gluten.

Its potency is attributed to the high chlorophyll content. Some people say they experience a brief "wheatgrass high" after consuming it.

In herbal medicine, wheatgrass has been used to boost energy, quell appetite and stabilize blood sugar, create healthier skin and nails, prevent coughs and infections, combat allergies and treat insomnia, impotence and hangovers.

Because of the indigestible fiber in wheatgrass, a little goes a long way. People are advised to juice wheatgrass and increase their consumption in stages, as it has a laxative effect. Negative reactions to wheatgrass may include a mild headache, gastrointestinal distress and increased heart rate.

Prep It

Before consuming wheatgrass, rinse under cold running water and dab dry with paper towels.

Use whole or chop coarsely.

Consume It

Wheatgrass is normally juiced and downed in shots. However, people without juicers can blend it into smoothies and other green drinks. The pulp may be consumed, but is better pressed through a fine-mesh sieve — people react differently to the indigestible fibers.

Some proponents say you don't have to juice wheatgrass to get its benefits. People have been known to chew it raw, then spit out the roughage.

SUBSTITUTES

watercress, parsley root tops, spinach

Wheatgrass Creamsicle-Style Smoothie

The popular kiddie treat of orange ice and vanilla ice cream on a stick is translated into this green smoothie. It brings back delicious memories.

Makes 2 to 4 servings (about 2 cups/500 mL)

Vegan Friendly

Beverage

Tips

Although wheatgrass is hardy, use it as fresh as possible to get the full benefit of its nutrients.

Because of the indigestible fiber in wheatgrass, a little goes a long way. People are advised to increase their consumption in stages.

- Blender

⅔ cup	freshly squeezed orange juice	150 mL
2 cups	coarsely chopped wheatgrass (1 oz/30 g)	500 mL
½ cup	vanilla soy milk	125 mL
1½ cups	ice cubes	375 mL

1. Using blender, purée orange juice and wheatgrass. Pour through a fine-mesh sieve into a bowl. Using a sturdy wire whisk, press and stir mixture in sieve to extract as much liquid as possible. Discard solids.
2. Return liquid to blender. Add soy milk and ice cubes. Blend until slushy and serve immediately.

Variations

Whole Wheatgrass Creamsicle-Style Smoothie: If consuming whole wheatgrass doesn't bother you, you can prepare a thicker drink. Purée 1 cup (250 mL) coarsely chopped wheatgrass (½ oz/15 g) with ½ cup (125 mL) each vanilla soy milk and orange juice with pulp. Add 1 cup (250 mL) ice cubes and blend. (Makes about 1½ cups/375 mL.)

Some people experience an upset stomach after consuming whole wheatgrass or even wheatgrass juice. If you are concerned, substitute milder greens such as spinach in wheatgrass blender drinks.

If desired, substitute 2 seedless oranges, peeled and trimmed of pith, for the orange juice. Note: Some blenders may have trouble completely breaking down the oranges.

For a sweeter drink, add granulated sugar, agave syrup or, if you are not a vegan, liquid honey, to taste.

Yu Choy Sum

Brassica rapa campestris, B. rapa oleifera

Other names: **Cantonese** *pak choy*, **Chinese oil vegetable, Chinese spinach, choy sum, field mustard, edible/turnip rape, flowering edible rape, rape mustard, yellow flowering Chinese cabbage, yu choy.**

Depending on where you are shopping, you may find yu choy sum identified as *abura-na, cai ngot, cai xin, man ching, navette de chine, raapzaad, saishin, sawi bunga, sawi manis, tsoi sim, yai tsoi, you cai* **or** *yuchaeip.*

Tasting Notes

Yu choy sum has cabbage, mustard and spinach accents. The raw stems and flowers are pleasantly nutty. The leaves are sharper, astringent and slightly bitter. When cooked, the leaves are more assertive but not bitter, and the stems are tender, sweet and meaty.

This green is often simply called choy sum and thus gets confused with the generic Chinese "vegetable hearts" that are also known as choy sum (page 428).

Yu choy sum is descended from wild ancestors native to China and the Mediterranean. It was grown for centuries to obtain a seed oil used in lamps and for cooking. It is now cultivated in North America.

Yu choy sum belongs to the large family of rape or rapeseed plants. Worldwide, most are used to produce oil and animal feed (a related cultivar yields canola oil). In contrast, varieties grown for eating, including yu choy sum and rapini, are fine vegetables.

Yu choy sum is used across Asia, especially in Cantonese cuisine. It has been called the most popular vegetable in Hong Kong.

Varieties

Yu choy sum is the Chinese equivalent of rapini (page 322). Two varieties, *Brassica rapa campestris* and *B. rapa oleifera*, are so similar that some botanists consider them synonymous. One is an annual plant, the other biennial.

Three rare cultivars are Mongolian yu choy, which has rounder, slightly curled leaves and more prominent flowers; humong yu choy, which is considered sweeter; and wa wa choy, which has fewer leaves.

Buy It

As one of the tenderest of Chinese vegetables, yu choy sum is now being discovered by mainstream supermarkets. However, it is generally sold in Asian grocery stores.

It is easy to confuse yu choy sum with Chinese broccoli (page 116). Yu choy sum is more slender and leafy. It has yellow flowers, while Chinese broccoli has white ones.

The stalks of yu choy sum can be 1 foot (30 cm) tall. Dense, fleshy light green stems are topped with long, oval leaves with white veins, as well as tiny yellow flowers and green buds. Thick and thin stalks grow in clusters. The thinner the stem, the tenderer it is. Also, look for vibrant leaves, with no yellowing or insect damage.

Health Notes

Although no official government analysis is available, yu choy sum is likely to have a nutritional profile similar to rapini. That would suggest that it contains vitamins A, B_6, C, E and K, calcium, copper, folate, iron, magnesium, manganese, niacin, pantothenic acid, phosphorus, potassium, riboflavin, thiamin and zinc. It is high in fiber.

In herbal medicine, yu choy sum has been used to maintain bone density, regulate blood sugar, alleviate PMS, ensure proper digestion, and prevent cataracts and hair loss.

Store It

To store, wrap a paper towel around the bunch, place it in a plastic bag and refrigerate.

Yu choy sum will keep in the refrigerator for up to three days.

Prep It

Before consuming yu choy sum, trim the base to separate the clusters. The thickest portions of the stems at the bottom are fibrous, whether raw or cooked, so peel them before cooking.

Equivalents

1 large bunch = 1½ to 2 lbs (750 g to 1 kg)

•

2 oz (60 g) stems cut into 1-inch (2.5 cm) pieces = ½ cup (125 mL), loosely packed

•

2 oz (60 g) shredded or coarsely chopped leaves = 2 cups (500 mL), loosely packed

•

2 oz (60 g) coarsely chopped leaves and stems = 1½ cups (500 mL), loosely packed

SUBSTITUTES

rapini, Chinese broccoli, Shanghai bok choy

Cut yu choy sum into manageable pieces before swishing it in cold water, then drain and spin-dry.

If you want to cook the stalks whole, soak them in cold salted water for 15 minutes. Swish upside down in the water, holding the base. Then air-dry on paper towels or a rack set over a clean kitchen towel.

Consume It

All the parts are edible, including the stems, leaves, flowers and buds.

Yu choy sum is rarely eaten raw. The tender stems can be sliced and used in mixed salads, but the leaves need to be cooked.

Stir-frying is the method of choice, but some recipes call for blanching beforehand. For a tender-crisp stem and a wilted but toothsome leaf, blanch no longer than 1 minute.

Generally the leaves are cooked in 1 to 2 minutes and the stems in 2 to 3 minutes. If steaming, the greens are ready in 3 to 5 minutes. Note that steaming brings out bitterness in these greens.

What Is Choy Sum, Anyway?

While maneuvering around the produce aisles of an Asian supermarket, it is helpful to know that the Chinese word for "vegetable" is *cai* or *choy*. It is also helpful to know that *choy sum* means "vegetable heart." "Choy sum," however, can refer to different greens.

"Choy sum" may refer to generic vegetable hearts, which are similar to romaine or celery hearts, in that they are stripped down to the inner stalks at the core. These are the tenderest portions of Chinese greens and are sold at premium prices. Various Chinese greens are sold as choy sum. For example, I have seen bok choy sum, the tender hearts of both bok choy and Shanghai bok choy.

On the other hand, "choy sum" may specifically refer to yu choy sum, China's equivalent of rapini. In southern China, particularly Hong Kong, Cantonese speakers may shorten the name of this green to *choy sum*, while in northern China, Mandarin speakers may shorten it to *you cai* (*yu choy*).

Sizzling Yu Choy Sum

In Chinatown the sound of sizzling hot plates as servers hasten past the tables makes one's mouth water. Sizzling dishes are a Cantonese specialty. You can duplicate the drama by using a cast-iron pan, a heavy skillet or even a small metal baking pan. Make sure you have all ingredients ready to go, as everything happens quickly with Chinese cooking. And stand back — there will be spatter. Serve this dish with hot rice.

Makes 4 servings

Vegan Friendly

Side dish

Tips

To sliver green onions, use a sharp knife to cut thin slices on an extreme diagonal from the root end to the stalk.

To shred the ginger, use the large holes of a box grater.

For this recipe, whole stalks of yu choy sum look best. Be careful not to overcook the greens — they should still be crunchy.

You can find chile oil in Asian grocery stores and some supermarkets. If you don't have any, substitute 2 tbsp (30 mL) oil and ½ tsp (2 mL) hot pepper flakes.

If you don't have a cast-iron pan, use a heavy skillet (it won't smoke) or leave a small rimmed metal baking sheet in a preheated 400°F (200°C) oven for 15 minutes or until very hot.

- Steamer

4	green onions (white and light green parts), slivered (see Tips, left)	4
½	red bell pepper, cut into matchsticks	½
2 tbsp	shredded gingerroot (see Tips, left)	30 mL
1 lb	yu choy sum (see Tips, left)	500 g
¼ cup	oil	60 mL
2 tbsp	chile oil (see Tips, left)	30 mL
¼ cup	soy sauce	60 mL

1. In a bowl, toss together green onions, red pepper and ginger. Set aside.
2. Using a sharp knife, trim yu choy sum, separating it into clusters of stalks. Peel the thickest parts of stems that look fibrous. Transfer to covered steamer basket set over 1 inch (2.5 cm) of boiling salted water and cook for 3 to 4 minutes, until stems are just tender-crisp. Using tongs, arrange greens in a single layer on a clean kitchen towel or paper towels, then pat dry.
3. Heat a large cast-iron pan over medium-high heat for about 3 minutes, until it is searing hot and wisps of smoke are rising from the surface (see Tips, left).
4. Meanwhile, in a small pan over medium-high heat, combine both oils and heat until shimmery. Reduce heat to low.
5. Remove cast-iron pan from heat. Using tongs, quickly place yu choy sum in pan. Scatter onion mixture overtop. Carefully drizzle hot oil mixture, then soy sauce, over greens. Serve immediately.

Variations

You can try this technique with a variety of quick-cooking Asian greens, including Chinese broccoli, Shanghai bok choy and Taiwan lettuce.

Quick Lime Sesame Yu Choy Sum

Tossed with lip-smacking lime sauce, these Asian greens are simply delicious, hot or at room temperature.

Makes 4 servings

Vegan Friendly

Side dish

Tips

To shred the leaves, stack them, roll them like a cigar and then slice the roll crosswise.

Bottled reconstituted lemon and lime juices usually contain additives. To avoid them, use freshly squeezed juice. Squeeze a whole lemon or lime and store the leftover juice in a small container in the fridge, or freeze it in 1 tbsp (15 mL) portions in an ice-cube tray.

To grate or purée gingerroot, use a kitchen rasp such as the kind made by Microplane.

Toasted sesame seeds are available in most supermarkets. To toast your own, cook sesame seeds in a dry skillet over medium heat for about 2 minutes, stirring occasionally, until seeds start to clump and turn golden and aromatic. For an attractive presentation, use toasted mixed white and black sesame seeds.

12 oz	yu choy sum	375 g
2 tbsp	freshly squeezed lime juice (see Tips, left)	30 mL
2 tbsp	soy sauce	30 mL
1 tsp	granulated sugar	5 mL
½ tsp	puréed gingerroot (see Tips, left)	2 mL
1 tbsp	oil	15 mL
¼ cup	toasted sesame seeds (see Tips, left)	60 mL

1. Using a sharp knife, trim yu choy sum, separating leaves and stems. Coarsely shred leaves (see Tips, left). Peel the thickest parts of stems that look fibrous. Cut stems on the diagonal into 3-inch (7.5 cm) pieces. Place in separate piles.

2. In a small bowl, combine lime juice, soy sauce, sugar and ginger. Set aside.

3. In a large skillet over medium heat, heat oil until shimmery. Add yu choy sum stems and sauté for 1 to 2 minutes, until tender-crisp. Add leaves and sauté for 30 to 60 seconds, until tender.

4. Transfer to a serving platter. Drizzle lime mixture overtop. Scatter with sesame seeds and serve immediately.

Yu Choy Sum with Saucy Shiitakes and Baby Corn

This substantial and attractive meal reminds me of Chinatown menus. The stalks of yu choy sum are topped with braised mushrooms and corn. Serve this dish over brown rice or Asian wheat noodles. When cooking Chinese-style, it pays to be prepared, with all your ingredients set out beforehand.

Makes 2 to 4 servings

Vegan Friendly

Main course

Tips

Vegetarian oyster sauce contains mushrooms, not oyster extract. Although it does include sugar, with the type usually unspecified on the label, many vegans eat it.

Toasted sesame oil, also known as Asian sesame oil, is made from toasted or roasted sesame seeds. Dark and aromatic, it is sold in small bottles as a flavoring agent. Do not confuse toasted sesame oil with yellow sesame oil, which is pressed from raw seeds.

In this dish, the yu choy sum is cooked only to tender-crisp. If you prefer softer greens, boil the stems for about 3 minutes or to taste. Add the leaves during the last minute of cooking time.

For the finest minced garlic, push it through a press.

Pull out and discard the stems of shiitake mushrooms. They are too tough to eat.

- Wok

2/3 cup	water, divided	150 mL
1 tsp	cornstarch	5 mL
3 tbsp	vegetarian oyster sauce (see Tips, left)	45 mL
1 tbsp	toasted sesame oil (see Tips, left)	15 mL
12 oz	yu choy sum	375 g
2 tbsp	oil	30 mL
1	clove garlic, minced (see Tips, left)	1
1 tsp	puréed ginger (see Tips, page 430)	5 mL
6 oz	shiitake mushrooms, stemmed, caps quartered or halved (see Tips, left)	175 g
1	can (14 oz/398 mL) baby corn, rinsed, drained and cut into 1-inch (2.5 cm) pieces	1
1 tsp	kosher or coarse sea salt	5 mL

1. In a small bowl, combine 1 tbsp (15 mL) water and cornstarch. Set aside.

2. In a small measuring cup, combine remaining water, oyster sauce and sesame oil. Set aside.

3. Using a sharp knife, trim yu choy sum, separating it into clusters of stalks. Peel the thickest parts of stems that look fibrous. Transfer to a large saucepan of boiling salted water and blanch over medium heat for about 1 minute, until tender-crisp. Drain and immediately rinse with cold water to stop the cooking. Drain and pat dry. Arrange stalks on a serving platter. Set aside.

4. In wok, heat oil over medium heat until hot. Remove from heat. Stir in garlic and ginger for 20 seconds. Stir in shiitakes, corn and salt. Return to heat and stir-fry for 1 to 2 minutes, until mushrooms are softened. Stir in oyster sauce mixture. Reduce heat to medium-low and simmer for 5 minutes. Stir cornstarch mixture well and add to wok. Cook, stirring, for 30 to 60 seconds, until sauce thickens. Pour over prepared yu choy sum. Serve immediately.

Green Beverages

Smooth Operator

To prepare the smoothest smoothies and shakes, keep these five tips in mind.

1. Put the liquid into the blender first, then the solid ingredients. This makes it easier for the blender to get started.
2. Start at the lowest speed and work up to High. If you start at too high a setting, an air bubble may form around the blades and decrease their efficiency. Increase the speed when big pieces of ingredients have broken up and a vortex forms at the center of the mixture.
3. If you are adding ice cubes, in most cases it is wise to prevent overprocessing and melting by blending in stages. First purée fruit and/or vegetables with liquid ingredients, then add the ice and blend until slushy.
4. When adding greens, use only the tender leaves. Trim and discard all stems and center ribs.
5. Avoid using an immersion blender for beverages. Even top-of-the-line models fail to create a super-smooth emulsion.

Avocado and Perilla Shake

Who needs ice cream? This sublime shake is cold and thick enough to eat with a spoon. It may surprise you to discover that avocado shakes are a specialty in Vietnam (where they are called butter-fruit shakes), as well as in Indonesia, the Philippines and Latin America. It's about time we discovered them. In my concoction, fragrant perilla and lime are the perfect finishing touches.

Makes 2 servings (about 1¾ cups/ 425 mL)

Tips

Bottled reconstituted lemon and lime juices usually contain additives. To avoid them, use freshly squeezed juice. Squeeze a whole lemon or lime and store the leftover juice in a small container in the fridge, or freeze it in 1 tbsp (15 mL) portions in an ice-cube tray.

Use Vietnamese tia-to perilla or sesame leaves (see Perilla, page 291).

- Blender

½ cup	skim (nonfat) milk	125 mL
¼ cup	sweetened condensed milk	60 mL
1 tbsp	freshly squeezed lime juice (see Tips, left)	15 mL
1 cup	ice cubes	250 mL
2	large perilla leaves, stemmed and torn (see Tips, left)	2
1	ripe avocado (about 8 oz/250 g)	1

1. In blender, combine skim milk, condensed milk, lime juice, ice cubes, perilla and avocado (see "Smooth Operator," page 433). Blend until smooth. Serve immediately.

Variation

If you don't have perilla, substitute an equal quantity of large mint leaves.

Pineapple Cress Crush

Who needs sherbet when you can have this piquant slushie, bursting with green goodness? Relax and enjoy.

Makes 1 serving (about 1⅓ cups/ 325 mL)

Vegan Friendly

- Blender

¼ cup	Lemonade Syrup (page 445)	60 mL
1 cup	watercress leaves, loosely packed	250 mL
2	fresh mint leaves	2
1 cup	pineapple chunks	250 mL
1 cup	ice cubes	250 mL

1. In blender, combine lemonade syrup, watercress, mint and pineapple. Blend until puréed (see "Smooth Operator," page 433). Add ice cubes and blend until slushy. Serve immediately.

Kale Cider Cooler

The easiest way to eat your apple a day is to drink it — preferably with kale. The bright taste of this healthy beverage matches its bright green color.

Makes 2 servings (about 1¾ cups/ 425 mL)

Vegan Friendly

Tip

The sweetness of this drink will depend on the apple and cider you use. Sweet-tart red apples such as the commonly sold McIntosh, Ida Red and Cortland varieties are good choices. Avoid sweet, mellow Red Delicious apples. If your drink is too sweet, add lime juice.

- Blender

½ cup	apple cider	125 mL
1	small red apple, peeled, cored and cut into wedges (see Tip, left)	1
1 cup	chopped kale leaves, loosely packed (see Tip, below left)	250 mL
Pinch	ground cinnamon	Pinch
1 cup	ice cubes	250 mL
1 tbsp	freshly squeezed lime juice, optional (see Tips, page 434)	15 mL

1. In blender, combine cider, apple, kale and cinnamon. Blend until puréed (see "Smooth Operator," page 433). Add ice cubes and blend until slushy. Add lime juice, if using, and pulse once to blend. Serve immediately.

Berry Good Kale Smoothie

Kale goes down smoothly when blended with berries and yogurt. This is a breakfast that you can drink.

Makes 1 serving (about 1¼ cups/ 300 mL)

Vegan Friendly

Tip

Use whatever kind of kale you have on hand. Curly kale imparts the brightest color; black kale, however, is the tenderest. Use only the top parts of the leaves; cut out and discard the ribs.

- Blender

½ cup	2% vanilla yogurt or non-dairy alternative	125 mL
2 tsp	liquid honey or vegan alternative	10 mL
1 cup	chopped kale leaves, loosely packed (see Tip, left)	250 mL
1 cup	sliced strawberries (4 to 6)	250 mL
½ cup	blueberries	125 mL

1. In blender, combine yogurt, honey, kale, strawberries and blueberries (see "Smooth Operator," page 433). Purée until smooth. Serve immediately.

Green Green Tea

Here's the love child of green tea and dandelion tea, their romance sweetened with honey and spiced up with ginger.

Makes 1 serving (about 1⅓ cups/ 325 mL)

Vegan Friendly

Tips

Make sure the green tea is cooled to room temperature, or the ice will melt too much.

To purée gingerroot, grate it using a kitchen rasp such as the kind made by Microplane.

- Blender

¾ cup	green tea, cooled (see Tips, left)	175 mL
2 tsp	liquid honey or vegan alternative	10 mL
¼ tsp	puréed gingerroot (see Tips, left)	1 mL
1 cup	chopped dandelion leaves, loosely packed	250 mL
1 cup	ice cubes	250 mL

1. In blender, combine green tea, honey, ginger and dandelion. Blend until puréed (see "Smooth Operator," page 433). Add ice cubes and blend until slushy. Serve immediately.

Tropical Storm

Tropical ingredients are whipped into a vortex of deliciousness in these thick, fruity green shakes.

Makes 4 servings (about 3½ cups/ 875 mL)

Vegan Friendly

Tip

Bottled reconstituted lemon and lime juices usually contain additives. To avoid them, use freshly squeezed juice. Squeeze a whole lemon or lime and store the leftover juice in a small container in the fridge, or freeze it in 1 tbsp (15 mL) portions in an ice-cube tray.

- Blender

1 cup	vanilla soy milk	250 mL
½ cup	coconut milk	125 mL
1 tbsp	freshly squeezed lime juice (see Tip, left)	15 mL
1 tsp	puréed gingerroot (see Tips, above left)	5 mL
2 cups	chopped spinach leaves, loosely packed	500 mL
1	mango, cubed	1
1	small banana, broken into chunks	1
1 cup	pineapple chunks	250 mL

1. In blender, combine soy milk, coconut milk, lime juice, ginger, spinach, mango, banana and pineapple. Blend until smooth (see "Smooth Operator," page 433). Serve immediately.

Honeydew, Cucumber and Kale Cooler

These perky mint-green icy drinks are ultra-refreshing on a hot summer's day.

Tip

You can use any type of kale. For beverages, use the top parts of the leaves and cut out and discard the ribs.

- Blender

¼ cup	Lemonade Syrup (page 445)	60 mL
2 cups	honeydew melon chunks	500 mL
2	mini cucumbers, peeled and cut into chunks	2
1 cup	chopped kale leaves, loosely packed (see Tip, left)	250 mL
1 cup	ice cubes	250 mL

1. In blender, combine lemonade syrup, melon, cucumbers and kale. Blend until puréed (see "Smooth Operator," page 433). Add ice cubes and blend until slushy. Serve immediately.

Pear Dandelion Fizzy Lemonade

This green dandelion drink has a delightfully fizzy finale.

Tip

You can substitute a Bartlett pear for the Anjou.

- Blender

⅓ cup	Lemonade Syrup (page 445)	75 mL
1 cup	chopped dandelion leaves, loosely packed	250 mL
1	ripe Anjou pear, quartered and cored	1
1 cup	ice cubes	250 ml
1 cup	soda water	250 mL

1. In blender, combine lemonade syrup, dandelion and pear. Blend until puréed.
2. Divide ice cubes between two large glasses. Pour dandelion mixture over ice. Pour equal quantities of soda water into each glass and stir to accentuate the fizz. Serve immediately.

Spinach Mint Lemonade

The fizzy, creamy layer that develops on top of this healthy cooler looks and tastes luscious.

Makes 2 servings (about 2½ cups/ 625 mL)

Vegan Friendly

- Blender

¼ cup	Lemonade Syrup (page 445)	60 mL
1 cup	ice cubes	250 mL
1 cup	chopped spinach leaves, loosely packed	250 mL
2	fresh mint leaves	2
1 cup	soda water	250 mL

1. In blender, combine lemonade syrup, ice cubes, spinach and mint. Blend until slushy. Add soda water and pulse once to combine. Serve immediately.

Ginger Chard Limeade

From the slightly briny chard to the lingering spicy heat of the ginger, this green drink is bursting with flavor. I like the way the soda water creates a creamy green froth on top.

Makes 2 servings (about 2¼ cups/ 550 mL)

Vegan Friendly

- Blender

1 cup	soda water	250 mL
¼ cup	Limeade Syrup (page 445)	60 mL
½ tsp	puréed gingerroot (see Tip, page 436)	2 mL
1 cup	ice cubes	250 mL
1 cup	chopped chard leaves, loosely packed	250 mL

1. In blender, combine soda, limeade syrup, ginger, ice cubes and chard. Blend until slushy. Serve immediately.

Papaya Power Shake

This shake is thick and rich without all the calories of ice cream, so treat yourself.

Makes 1 to 2 servings (about 1½ cups/375 mL)

Vegan Friendly

Tip

The papaya flesh can be scooped out in chunks with a spoon. A small papaya yields about 1 cup (250 mL).

- Blender

½ cup	unflavored soy milk	125 mL
1 tsp	freshly squeezed lemon juice (see Tips, page 436)	5 mL
1 cup	chopped kale leaves, loosely packed	250 mL
1	small ripe papaya, seeded (see Tip, left)	1
½ cup	ice cubes	125 mL

1. In blender, combine soy milk, lemon juice, kale and papaya. Blend until puréed (see "Smooth Operator," page 433). Add ice cubes and blend until slushy. Serve immediately.

Bananarama Smoothie

Orange, banana and strawberry together are a match made in heaven. The spinach, meanwhile, adds serious substance to this yogurt smoothie.

- Blender

½ cup	freshly squeezed orange juice	125 mL
2 tsp	liquid honey or vegan alternative, optional	10 mL
½ cup	plain 2% yogurt or non-dairy alternative	125 mL
1 cup	chopped spinach leaves, loosely packed	250 mL
1 cup	sliced strawberries (4 to 6)	250 mL
1	banana	1
1 cup	ice cubes	250 mL

1. In blender, combine orange juice, honey (if using), yogurt, spinach, strawberries and banana. Blend until puréed (see "Smooth Operator," page 433). Add ice cubes and blend until slushy. Serve immediately.

Plum Good Dandelion Aperitif

Sparkling wine is the secret ingredient in this refreshing brunch and patio beverage. If you prefer something non-alcoholic, substitute ginger ale.

Tips

Black plums are best in this recipe, but golden plums will work.

Use any kind of sparkling white or rosé wine that's not too sweet.

- Blender

¼ cup	Lemonade Syrup (page 445)	60 mL
1 cup	chopped dandelion leaves, loosely packed	250 mL
4	small plums (about 10 oz/300 g), peeled, pitted and cut into chunks (see Tips, left)	4
1 cup	ice cubes	250 mL
½ cup	sparkling wine (see Tips, left)	125 mL

1. In blender, combine lemonade syrup, dandelion and plums. Blend until puréed (see "Smooth Operator," page 433). Add ice cubes and sparkling wine. Blend until slushy. Serve immediately.

Peach Basil Spinach Cooler

It may surprise you to discover that peaches and basil work brilliantly together. Add spinach and orange juice and you've got a lovely summer beverage.

Tip

I leave the skin on the peach, but you can peel it, if desired.

- Blender

½ cup	freshly squeezed orange juice	125 mL
1 cup	chopped spinach leaves, loosely packed	250 mL
4	fresh basil leaves	4
1	small peach, cut into chunks (see Tip, left)	1
1 cup	ice cubes	250 mL

1. In blender, combine orange juice, spinach, basil and peach. Blend until puréed. Add ice cubes and blend until slushy. Serve immediately.

Perilla Mojito

The mojito traces its lineage back to 1586, when Sir Francis Drake attacked Cuba. A subordinate mixed him a drink of crude rum, sugar, lime and mint. Bartenders have been playing with the theme ever since. Mojito is derived from the African word mojo, which means "to place a spell." In this modern mojito I replace mint with its fragrant, complex cousin the perilla leaf.

Tips

Use sesame leaf perilla or, for a stronger flavor, shiso leaves (see Perilla, page 291).

Use a shot glass to measure the rum: 1 oz = 2 tbsp (30 mL).

Bartenders use a muddler, or wooden paddle, to crush and bruise herbs and other ingredients to release their essential oils. If you don't have one, use a spoon.

4	large perilla leaves, stemmed and torn (see Tips, left)	4
¼ cup	Limeade Syrup (page 445)	60 mL
¾ cup	crushed ice	175 mL
1¼ oz	light or dark rum (see Tips, left)	40 mL
¼ cup	soda water	60 mL

1. In a slim glass, combine perilla leaves and limeade syrup. Stir or muddle, lightly crushing the leaves (see Tips, left). Add crushed ice. Pour rum over ice and stir. Splash in soda water. Serve immediately.

Variation

To make a virgin mojito, omit the rum.

Green Chai Shake

I keep homemade chai base — basically spiced brewed tea — on hand for hot and cold beverages that smell alluring and taste great. In this recipe I use chai base and chard to prepare a pretty mint-green treat with flavors that dance on your tongue.

Makes 2 servings (about 2 cups/ 500 mL)

Vegan Friendly

Tips

This recipe makes about 1½ cups (375 mL) chai base. Use the leftover portion for other beverages.

Star anise is a spice with a lovely star-shaped pod. You can find it in spice shops and Asian grocery stores.

- Blender

Chai Base

2 tsp	loose black tea leaves	10 mL
8	cardamom pods, lightly crushed	8
4	whole cloves	4
1	3½-inch (8.5 cm) cinnamon stick, broken	1
1	star anise (see Tips, left)	1
1	allspice berry	1
2 cups	boiling water	250 mL

Shake

1 cup	vanilla soy milk	250 mL
1 cup	chopped chard leaves, loosely packed	250 mL
1	banana, broken into chunks	1

1. *Chai Base:* In a small pan, combine tea, cardamom, cloves, cinnamon, star anise and allspice. Pour boiling water overtop. Bring to a simmer over medium-high heat. Reduce heat to medium-low or low to maintain a gentle simmer for 5 minutes. Remove from heat and set aside for 10 to 15 minutes to steep.

2. Using a fine-mesh sieve, strain tea into an airtight container, pushing on the solids with a spoon to extract as much liquid as possible. Discard solids. Set tea aside to cool to room temperature. Cover and refrigerate until cold or for up to 1 week.

3. *Shake:* In blender, combine soy milk, chard and banana. Blend until puréed (see "Smooth Operator," page 433). Add ¼ cup (60 mL) chai base, reserving remainder for other beverages. Blend until smooth. Serve immediately.

Variation

If desired, substitute 2 regular tea bags or 3 decaffeinated tea bags for the loose tea.

S'Pina Colada

A beloved cocktail gets a green makeover in the blender. Put on some sunglasses and add some rum if you're in an island mood.

Tip

Cane sugar is likely to be filtered through bone char, while beet sugar is not. Most labels don't indicate the source of the sugar. If you are following a vegan diet, use unbleached organic sugar that has not been filtered through bone char, or a sweetener such as agave syrup.

- Blender

½ cup	coconut milk	125 mL
1 tbsp	granulated sugar (see Tip, left)	15 mL
1 cup	chopped spinach leaves, loosely packed	250 mL
1 cup	pineapple chunks	250 mL
1 cup	ice cubes	250 mL

1. In blender, combine coconut milk, sugar, spinach and pineapple. Blend until puréed (see "Smooth Operator," page 433). Add ice cubes and blend until slushy. Serve immediately.

Tropical Garden Smoothie

Three classic tropical ingredients are combined with greens for a rich, nourishing taste of the Caribbean.

- Blender

1 cup	vanilla soy milk	250 mL
½ cup	coconut milk	125 mL
1 cup	chopped spinach leaves, loosely packed	250 mL
1½ cups	pineapple chunks	375 mL
1	banana, broken into chunks	1

1. In blender, combine soy milk, coconut milk, spinach, pineapple and banana. Blend until smooth (see "Smooth Operator," page 433). Serve immediately.

Cocoa Nut Kale Smoothie

Kale is kissed with cocoa powder and blended with almond milk for a green drink that thinks it's a dessert.

Makes 1 to 2 servings (about 1¼ cups/300 mL)

Vegan Friendly

- Blender

1 cup	unsweetened almond milk	250 mL
2 tsp	liquid honey or vegan alternative	10 mL
1 tbsp	unsweetened cocoa powder	15 mL
1 cup	chopped black kale leaves, loosely packed	250 mL
	Ice cubes	

1. In blender, combine almond milk, honey, cocoa powder and kale. Blend until smooth (see "Smooth Operator," page 433).
2. Fill glasses with ice cubes to taste. Pour smoothie over ice and serve immediately.

Kale Mary

You don't need a sweet tooth to enjoy healthy blender drinks. This one's savory and spicy, like the cocktail it mimics. But it's a thick green Mary rather than a bloody red one.

Makes 2 to 4 servings (about 1½ cups/375 mL)

Vegan Friendly

Tips

If you don't have wasabi powder, add a pinch of horseradish.

Chinese celery leaves are more potent than common celery leaves, so it's worth using them in this drink if you can.

- Blender

1 cup	tomato juice	250 mL
1 tsp	freshly squeezed lemon juice	5 mL
Pinch	wasabi powder (see Tips, left)	Pinch
Dash	hot sauce	Dash
1	small tomato (4 oz/125 g), cored and seeded	1
2 tbsp	diced sweet onion	30 mL
¼ cup	chopped Chinese celery leaves, loosely packed (see Tips, left)	60 mL
½ cup	chopped kale leaves, loosely packed	125 mL
	Kosher or coarse sea salt	
	Ice cubes	

1. In blender, combine tomato juice, lemon juice, wasabi, hot sauce, tomato, onion, celery leaves and kale. Blend until smooth. Season with salt to taste.
2. Place ice cubes in glasses. Pour mixture over ice and serve immediately.

Variations

Bloody Green Mary: You can substitute arugula, watercress, chard or spinach leaves for the kale.

Salad Slushie

This tastes like a salad and a cold fruity drink all at once. You can look virtuous when drinking it. It will taste different each time, depending on the mesclun mixture.

<table>
<tr><td colspan="2">• Blender</td><td></td></tr>
<tr><td>¼ cup</td><td>Lemonade Syrup (page 445)</td><td>60 mL</td></tr>
<tr><td>1 cup</td><td>mesclun, loosely packed</td><td>250 mL</td></tr>
<tr><td>1 cup</td><td>cubed honeydew melon</td><td>250 mL</td></tr>
<tr><td>1</td><td>mini cucumber, peeled and cut into pieces</td><td>1</td></tr>
<tr><td>1 cup</td><td>ice cubes</td><td>250 mL</td></tr>
</table>

Makes 1 to 2 servings (about 1½ cups/375 mL)	
Vegan Friendly	

1. In blender, combine lemonade syrup, mesclun, honeydew and cucumber. Blend until puréed (see "Smooth Operator," page 433). Add ice cubes and blend until slushy. Serve immediately.

Chinese Celery Soda

Fringe pop companies make all kinds of quirky flavors, including celery. Here's a surprisingly good celery soda you can make yourself. I use Chinese celery because it's more potent, and I continue the Asian theme with star anise, a pretty star-shaped spice.

Makes 6 servings (about 1½ cups/ 375 mL each)	
Vegan Friendly	

Tips

Corn syrup prevents crystallization of the sugar during boiling and storage.

If you want to be precise or consistent, you'll need 2 oz (60 g) Chinese celery for this recipe. Use both the leaves and the stems.

Celery Syrup

1 cup	water	250 mL
1 cup	granulated sugar	250 mL
1 tsp	corn syrup (see Tips, left)	5 mL
¾ cup	finely chopped Chinese celery (3 large stalks; see Tips, left)	175 mL
2	star anise	2
2 tbsp	freshly squeezed lemon juice	30 mL

Soda

6 cups	soda water	1.5 L
	Ice cubes	

1. *Celery Syrup:* In a small saucepan over medium-high heat, combine water, sugar and corn syrup. Bring to a boil, stirring at first to dissolve sugar. Add Chinese celery and star anise. When mixture returns to a boil, cover, reduce heat to low and simmer for 10 minutes.

2. Using a fine-mesh sieve, strain into an airtight container, using the back of a spoon to press the solids and extract as much liquid as possible. Discard solids. Stir in lemon juice. Set aside until cooled to room temperature. Cover and refrigerate until needed or up to 1 month.

3. *Soda:* For each drink, combine ¼ cup (60 mL) celery syrup and 1 cup (250 mL) soda water in a glass. Fill glass with ice cubes and serve immediately.

The Beets Go On

This is a nicely spicy drink, with citrus and ginger adding the zing factor.

Makes 2 servings (about 2 cups/ 500 mL)

Vegan Friendly

Tips

To grate or purée gingerroot, use a kitchen rasp such as the kind made by Microplane.

Trim and discard the center ribs from the beet leaves before chopping them.

- Blender

1 cup	freshly squeezed orange juice, with pulp	250 mL
2 tbsp	Limeade Syrup (below)	30 mL
1/4 tsp	puréed gingerroot (see Tips, left)	1 mL
1 cup	chopped beet leaves, loosely packed (see Tips, left)	250 mL
1 cup	ice cubes	250 mL

1. In blender, combine orange juice, limeade syrup, ginger and beet leaves. Blend until puréed (see "Smooth Operator," page 433). Add ice cubes and blend until slushy. Serve immediately.

Lemonade/Limeade Syrup

The best "ades" start with a boiled syrup concentrate. Boiling extracts the essential oils from citrus zest so your drinks taste more intense. And you don't have to worry about sugar granules settling at the bottom of your glass.

Makes about 2 1/4 cups (550 mL)

Vegan Friendly

Tips

Corn syrup prevents crystallization of the sugar during boiling and storage. White corn syrup is colorless.

Strain the mixture while it's hot. It will thicken as it cools.

1 cup	water	250 mL
1 cup	granulated sugar (see Tip, page 442)	250 mL
1 tsp	white corn syrup (see Tips, left)	5 mL
2 tbsp	finely grated lemon or lime zest (about 2 lemons or 3 limes)	30 mL
1 cup	freshly squeezed lemon or lime juice (about 4 lemons or 5 limes)	250 mL

1. In a small saucepan over medium-high heat, combine water, sugar, corn syrup and citrus zest. Bring to a boil, stirring at first to dissolve sugar. Reduce heat to low and simmer for 3 minutes.

2. Remove from heat and immediately strain through a fine-mesh sieve into a heatproof airtight container (see Tips, left). Discard zest. Stir in citrus juice. Set aside to cool to room temperature. Cover and refrigerate for up to 1 month.

Variation

If you prefer a sweeter syrup, increase the sugar to 1 1/2 cups (375 mL).

Dressings and Other Handy Recipes

Simple Dijon Vinaigrette

In the mood for a fuss-free vinaigrette? Look no further.

Makes ⅓ cup (75 mL)

Vegan Friendly

Tip

Cane sugar is likely to be filtered through bone char, while beet sugar is not. Most labels don't indicate the source of the sugar. If you are following a vegan diet, use unbleached organic sugar that has not been filtered through bone char, or a sweetener such as agave syrup.

2 tbsp	white wine vinegar, divided	30 mL
½ tsp	Dijon mustard	2 mL
¼ tsp	granulated sugar (see Tip, left)	1 mL
¼ tsp	kosher or coarse sea salt (see Tips, page 452)	1 mL
¼ tsp	freshly ground black pepper	1 mL
¼ cup	extra virgin olive oil	60 mL

1. In a bowl, whisk together 1 tbsp (15 mL) vinegar, mustard, sugar, salt and pepper. Gradually whisk in oil. Add some or all of the remaining vinegar, to taste. Transfer to an airtight container and refrigerate for up to 1 month.

Simple Garlic Vinaigrette

Simple pleasures are sometimes the best — like this classic salad dressing.

Makes ⅓ cup (75 mL)

Vegan Friendly

Tips

For the finest minced garlic, push it through a press.

You can whisk vinaigrette in a small bowl, but a medium bowl is a better choice. It gives you more room to whisk vigorously without accidental spatter.

2 tbsp	white wine vinegar, divided	30 mL
1	clove garlic, minced (see Tips, left)	1
½ tsp	granulated sugar (see Tip, above left)	2 mL
¼ tsp	kosher or coarse sea salt (see Tips, page 452)	1 mL
⅛ tsp	freshly ground black pepper	0.5 mL
¼ cup	extra virgin olive oil	60 mL

1. In a bowl, whisk together 1½ tbsp (22 mL) vinegar, garlic, sugar, salt and pepper (see Tips, left). Gradually whisk in oil. Add some or all of the remaining vinegar, if desired. Transfer to an airtight container and refrigerate for up to 2 weeks.

Garlic Herb Vinaigrette

This is a perfectly balanced and versatile French vinaigrette. My master recipe includes parsley but I often switch to other herbs, depending on the salad ingredients and my mood.

Makes ⅓ cup (75 mL)

Vegan Friendly

Tip

For the finest minced garlic, push it through a press.

2 tbsp	white wine vinegar, divided	30 mL
1	clove garlic, minced (see Tip, left)	1
1 tbsp	finely chopped fresh parsley	15 mL
½ tsp	Dijon mustard	2 mL
½ tsp	granulated sugar (see Tip, page 448)	2 mL
¼ tsp	kosher or coarse sea salt (see Tips, page 452)	1 mL
⅛ tsp	freshly ground black pepper	0.5 mL
¼ cup	extra virgin olive oil	60 mL

1. In a bowl, whisk together 1½ tbsp (22 mL) vinegar, garlic, parsley, mustard, sugar, salt and pepper. Gradually whisk in oil. Add some or all of the remaining vinegar, if desired. Transfer to an airtight container and refrigerate for up to 1 week.

Variation

Garlic Basil Vinaigrette: Substitute an equal amount of basil for the parsley.

Mint Vinaigrette

This peppery mint dressing is particularly good with peas and pea shoots.

Makes ⅓ cup (75 mL)

Vegan Friendly

Tip

You can whisk vinaigrettes in a small bowl, but a medium bowl is a better choice. It gives you more room to whisk vigorously without accidental spatter.

2 tbsp	white wine vinegar, divided	30 mL
1	small shallot, minced	1
2 tsp	finely chopped fresh mint	10 mL
½ tsp	Dijon mustard	2 mL
¼ tsp	granulated sugar (see Tip, page 448)	1 mL
¼ tsp	kosher or coarse sea salt (see Tips, page 452)	1 mL
¼ tsp	freshly ground black pepper	1 mL
¼ cup	extra virgin olive oil	60 mL

1. In a bowl, whisk together 1½ tbsp (22 mL) vinegar, shallot, mint, mustard, sugar, salt and pepper (see Tip, left). Gradually whisk in oil. Add some or all of the remaining vinegar, if desired. Transfer to an airtight container and refrigerate for up to 2 weeks.

Basil Balsamic Vinaigrette

This fabulous balsamic vinaigrette is adapted from a dressing passed on by my friend Amy Pataki, a Toronto restaurant reviewer.

Makes ⅓ cup (75 mL)

Vegan Friendly

Tip

Cane sugar is likely to be filtered through bone char, while beet sugar is not. Most labels don't indicate the source of the sugar. If you are following a vegan diet, use unbleached organic sugar that has not been filtered through bone char, or a sweetener such as agave syrup.

- Mini blender

1	clove garlic	1
¼ cup	coarsely chopped fresh basil leaves	60 mL
¼ cup	extra virgin olive oil	60 mL
1 tbsp	balsamic vinegar	15 mL
1 tsp	granulated sugar (see Tip, left)	5 mL
¼ tsp	kosher or coarse sea salt (see Tips, page 452)	1 mL
⅛ tsp	freshly ground black pepper	0.5 mL

1. Using blender, mince garlic. Add basil, oil, vinegar, sugar, salt and pepper. Pulse a few times until blended. Transfer to an airtight container and refrigerate for up to 2 weeks.

Sun-Dried Tomato Vinaigrette

Sun-dried tomatoes give this dressing added oomph. It's great with assertive greens.

Makes ½ cup (125 mL)

Vegan Friendly

Tips

For the finest minced garlic, push it through a press.

You can whisk vinaigrettes in a small bowl, but a medium bowl is a better choice. It gives you more room to whisk vigorously without accidental spatter.

2 tbsp	white wine vinegar, divided	30 mL
2	oil-packed sun-dried tomatoes, drained and finely chopped	2
1	large clove garlic, minced (see Tips, left)	1
½ tsp	granulated sugar (see Tip, above left)	2 mL
1 tsp	kosher or coarse sea salt (see Tips, page 452)	5 mL
⅛ tsp	freshly ground black pepper	0.5 mL
¼ cup	extra virgin olive oil	60 mL

1. In a bowl, whisk together 1½ tbsp (22 mL) vinegar, tomatoes, garlic, sugar, salt and pepper (see Tips, left). Gradually whisk in oil. Add some or all of the remaining vinegar, if desired. Transfer to an airtight container and refrigerate for up to 2 weeks.

Variation

Replace some of the olive oil with the oil from the sun-dried tomatoes.

Orange Nut Oil Vinaigrette

I love the sublime fragrance of this dressing, which gives bittersweet greens a real lift. I use walnut oil in the master recipe but often switch to other unrefined nut oils, depending on the dish.

Makes ½ cup (125 mL)

Vegan Friendly

Tips

You'll need 1 orange for this recipe. The zest is the thin, waxy outer layer of the rind, which contains the essential oils. Use a kitchen rasp to grate the zest.

You can find unrefined first-pressed or artisanal walnut oil in fine food shops and some supermarkets.

½ tsp	finely grated orange zest (see Tips, left)	2 mL
1 tbsp	freshly squeezed orange juice	15 mL
1 tbsp	sherry vinegar	15 mL
1 tbsp	liquid honey or vegan alternative	15 mL
½ tsp	kosher or coarse sea salt	2 mL
⅛ tsp	freshly ground black pepper	0.5 mL
¼ cup	unrefined walnut oil (see Tips, left)	60 mL

1. In a bowl, whisk together orange zest and juice, vinegar, honey, salt and pepper (see Tips, below left). Gradually whisk in oil. Transfer to an airtight container and refrigerate for up to 2 weeks.

Variation

Orange Pecan Oil Vinaigrette: Substitute unrefined pecan oil for the walnut oil.

Tangerine Vinaigrette

Tangerine juice gives this dressing its sunny disposition.

Makes ½ cup (125 mL)

Vegan Friendly

Tips

You can also find tangerine juice in small bottles or cartons, refrigerated or shelf-stable, at many supermarkets.

You can whisk vinaigrettes in a small bowl, but a medium bowl is a better choice. It gives you more room to whisk vigorously without accidental spatter.

3 tbsp	freshly squeezed tangerine juice (see Tips, left)	45 mL
½ tsp	Dijon mustard	2 mL
¼ tsp	granulated sugar (see Tip, page 450)	1 mL
½ tsp	kosher or coarse sea salt (see Tips, page 452)	2 mL
⅛ tsp	freshly ground black pepper	0.5 mL
¼ cup	extra virgin olive oil	60 mL

1. In a bowl, whisk together tangerine juice, mustard, sugar, salt and pepper (see Tips, left). Gradually whisk in oil. Transfer to an airtight container and refrigerate for up to 2 weeks.

Lime Herb Dressing

Bursting with tart lime and fresh herbs, this dressing gives all kinds of salads a wonderful lift. Sometimes I whisk the ingredients and sometimes I prepare it as a neon-green blender dressing. Parsley, tarragon and chives are a versatile combo, but you can also play with the herbs that you prefer.

Makes ½ cup (125 mL)

Vegan Friendly

Tips

Cane sugar is likely to be filtered through bone char, while beet sugar is not. Most labels don't indicate the source of the sugar. If you are following a vegan diet, use unbleached organic sugar that has not been filtered through bone char, or a sweetener such as agave syrup.

I prefer kosher salt because it tastes better than iodized table salt and (ideally) contains no additives. Table salts and some sea salts contain additives such as iodine compounds (iodides), anti-clumping agents and even sugar (in the form of dextrose, which is used to stabilize iodine). Although the North American Salt Institute states that kosher salt "contains no additives," some kosher salt brands do contain additives such as anti-clumping agents. If you have concerns, check the label.

2 tbsp	freshly squeezed lime juice	30 mL
2 tsp	finely chopped fresh parsley leaves	10 mL
2 tsp	finely chopped fresh tarragon leaves	10 mL
2 tsp	finely chopped fresh chives	10 mL
1 tbsp	granulated sugar (see Tips, left)	15 mL
¼ tsp	Dijon mustard	1 mL
¼ tsp	kosher or coarse sea salt (see Tips, left)	1 mL
⅛ tsp	freshly ground black pepper	0.5 mL
⅓ cup	extra virgin olive oil	75 mL

1. In a bowl, whisk together lime juice, parsley, tarragon, chives, sugar, mustard, salt and pepper. Gradually whisk in oil. Transfer to an airtight container and refrigerate for up to 1 week.

Variation

Neon Lime Herb Dressing: Increase the amount of each herb to 1 tbsp (15 mL), chopped coarsely rather than finely. Add the ingredients to a mini blender and purée.

Sesame Dressing

This is my go-to Asian dressing. Toasted sesame oil gives it a truly appetizing scent.

**Makes ⅓ cup
(75 mL)**

Vegan Friendly

Tips

For the finest minced garlic, push it through a press.

Toasted sesame oil, also known as Asian sesame oil, is made from toasted or roasted sesame seeds. Dark and aromatic, it is sold in small bottles as a flavoring agent. Do not confuse toasted sesame oil with yellow sesame oil, which is pressed from raw seeds.

2 tbsp	rice vinegar	30 mL
1	clove garlic, minced (see Tips, left)	1
2 tsp	granulated sugar (see Tips, page 452)	10 mL
1 tsp	kosher or sea salt (see Tips, page 452)	5 mL
⅛ tsp	freshly ground black pepper	0.5 mL
2 tbsp	oil	30 mL
2 tbsp	toasted sesame oil (see Tips, left)	30 mL

1. In a bowl, whisk together vinegar, garlic, sugar, salt and pepper. Gradually whisk in both oils. Transfer to an airtight container and refrigerate for up to 2 weeks.

Lemon Cumin Dressing

A whiff of this and my thoughts turn to the compelling cuisines of the Mediterranean and the Middle East.

**Makes 6 tbsp
(90 mL)**

Vegan Friendly

Tip

You can substitute black pepper for the white pepper. White pepper is used mainly for aesthetic reasons, to avoid black specks in finished dishes.

2 tbsp	freshly squeezed lemon juice	30 mL
1	clove garlic, minced (see Tips, above left)	1
2 tsp	liquid honey or vegan alternative	10 mL
1 tsp	kosher or coarse sea salt	5 mL
1 tsp	ground cumin	5 mL
⅛ tsp	freshly ground white pepper (see Tip, left)	0.5 mL
¼ cup	extra virgin olive oil	60 mL

1. In a bowl, whisk together lemon juice, garlic, honey, salt, cumin and pepper. Gradually whisk in oil. Transfer to an airtight container and refrigerate for up to 2 weeks.

Roasted Garlic Dressing

When you want garlicky flavor without sharpness, roasted garlic is the answer. Don't be afraid of using a whole head of roasted garlic — it is mellow and creamy. This dressing is delicious on steamed or roasted vegetables as well as salads.

Makes ½ cup (125 mL)

Vegan Friendly

Tip

Cane sugar is likely to be filtered through bone char, while beet sugar is not. Most labels don't indicate the source of the sugar. If you are following a vegan diet, use unbleached organic sugar that has not been filtered through bone char, or a sweetener such as agave syrup.

1	head Roasted Garlic (below)	1
2 tbsp	freshly squeezed lemon juice, divided	30 mL
1 tsp	finely chopped fresh chives	5 mL
1 tsp	granulated sugar (see Tip, left)	5 mL
1 tsp	kosher or coarse sea salt (see Tips, page 452)	5 mL
⅛ tsp	freshly ground black pepper	0.5 mL
¼ cup	extra virgin olive oil	60 mL

1. Squeeze garlic cloves into a bowl. Using a fork, mash garlic. Whisk in 1 tbsp (15 mL) lemon juice, chives, sugar, salt and pepper. Gradually whisk in oil. Add some or all of the remaining lemon juice, to taste. Transfer to an airtight container and refrigerate for up to 1 week.

Variations

Roasted Garlic Sage Dressing: Substitute finely chopped sage leaves for the chives.

Roasted Garlic Parsley Dressing: Substitute finely chopped parsley for the chives.

Roasted Garlic

Roasting takes the edge off garlic, making the cloves mellow and sweet. Roasted garlic is great in dressings, dips, spreads, sandwiches, soups and stews.

Makes 1 head roasted garlic

Vegan Friendly

Tip

You can prepare roasted garlic in advance or save it for up to 3 days. Refrigerate the head, the separated cloves or the squeezed-out cloves, as desired. Wrap a whole head in plastic, store cloves in a bag, or save the squeezed-out garlic in a small airtight container.

- Preheat oven to 400°F (200°C)

1	head garlic	1
	Extra virgin olive oil	

1. Discard any loose papery husks from garlic head. Using a sharp knife, cut a thin slice off the top to expose the cloves. Place garlic on a square of foil. Lightly drizzle oil, to taste, over exposed cloves. Pull up sides of foil and wrap garlic tightly. Roast in preheated oven for about 45 minutes, until cloves are soft and golden. Unwrap and set aside until cool enough to handle.
2. Separate garlic head into cloves. Squeeze cloves out of skins into a small bowl (see Tip, left).

Quick Pickled Onions

*These carefree pickles add a fine crunch to sandwiches, quesadillas and hearty salads. They are tasty with cheese too. When it comes to pickles, the word **quick** is relative — these are ready to enjoy in an hour.*

Makes about 2 cups (500 mL), undrained

Vegan Friendly

1	small red onion (about 10 oz/300 g), halved and thinly sliced	1
½ cup	white wine vinegar	125 mL
½ cup	water	125 mL
3 tbsp	granulated sugar (see Tip, page 454)	45 mL
1 tsp	kosher or coarse sea salt (see Tips, page 452)	5 mL

1. Place onion slices in a heatproof bowl.
2. In a small pan over medium-high heat, combine vinegar, water, sugar and salt. Bring to a full boil, stirring at first to dissolve sugar. Immediately pour over onion. Cool briefly, cover and set aside for at least 1 hour, or transfer to an airtight container and refrigerate for up to 3 days. Serve with a slotted spoon.

Crispy Shallots

Crispy fried shallots give all kinds of dishes, from salads to mashed potatoes, extra appeal.

Makes 1⅓ cups (325 mL)

Vegan Friendly

Tips

To peel shallots with ease, slice them before peeling, then pull off the strips of skin.

You don't have to be finicky and separate the shallots into every single ring. Just poke the slices apart with your fingers. They will finish separating while frying.

Be careful not to let the shallots get too dark, or they will taste bitter.

- Rimmed baking sheet, topped with wire rack lined with paper towels

8 to 10	shallots (8 oz/250 g; see Tips, left)	8 to 10
	Oil	
	Kosher or coarse sea salt	

1. Using a sharp knife, cut shallots into slices ⅛ to ¼ inch (3 to 5 mm) thick. Separate roughly into rings (see Tips, left). Set aside.
2. In a saucepan over medium-high heat, heat about 1 inch (2.5 cm) oil until shimmery. Add shallots and fry, stirring often, for 4 to 5 minutes, until golden brown (see Tips, left). Using a mesh scoop, transfer shallots to prepared baking sheet to drain, cool and crisp up.
3. Before using, sprinkle with salt to taste.

Chapons

If you like croutons, you'll love chapons. These are croutons gone wild — big, rustic and crunchy.

Makes 4 cups (1 L)

Vegan Friendly

Tips

A mini baguette is 12 inches (30 cm) long, about three-quarters the length of a standard baguette but the same width. Do not buy a skinny French stick for this recipe.

Use the reserved bread for breadcrumbs or stuffing.

- Preheat oven to 400°F (200°C)
- Rimmed baking sheet

1	mini baguette (see Tips, left)	1
2 tbsp	extra virgin olive oil	30 mL
¾ tsp	kosher or coarse sea salt	3 mL
½ tsp	garlic powder	2 mL

1. Using a serrated knife, cut baguette lengthwise in half. Pull out bread, leaving crusts. Set aside bread for other uses (see Tips, left). Slice crusts about ¾ inch (2 cm) thick to create curved chapons. Transfer chapons to a large bowl. Drizzle with oil and, using your hands, toss to coat evenly. Sprinkle with salt and garlic powder and toss to coat.

2. Arrange in a single layer on baking sheet. Bake in preheated oven for 6 to 8 minutes, turning once, until crisp and golden brown. Set aside to cool before using.

Garlic Herb Crumb Topping

Toasted crumb topping is a great finishing touch for cooked greens. I prefer to start with whole wheat breadcrumbs for a heartier, healthier topping.

Makes about ¾ cup (175 mL)

Vegan Friendly

Tips

To make fresh breadcrumbs, place torn bread in the bowl of a food processor fitted with a metal blade. Pulse about 10 times, until medium crumbs form. One standard slice yields about ¾ cup (175 mL) lightly packed crumbs.

Do not substitute the fine, dry breadcrumbs sold in the supermarket for fresh breadcrumbs. Dry breadcrumbs are too gritty.

- Preheat oven to 400°F (200°C)
- Rimmed baking sheet

1 cup	fresh whole wheat breadcrumbs (see Tips, left)	250 mL
1 tbsp	extra virgin olive oil	15 mL
1	clove garlic, minced (see Tips, page 453)	1
1 tbsp	finely chopped fresh parsley leaves	15 mL
1 tbsp	finely chopped fresh chives	15 mL
1 tsp	thyme leaves, chopped	5 mL
⅛ tsp	kosher or coarse sea salt	0.5 mL

1. In a bowl, using a fork, toss breadcrumbs with oil. Transfer to baking sheet and spread out in a thin, fairly even layer, reserving bowl. Bake in preheated oven for 18 to 20 minutes, stirring once, until golden brown and very crisp. Set aside to cool to room temperature.

2. In reserved bowl, using a fork, gently combine cooled crumbs, garlic, parsley, chives, thyme and salt. Use the same day.

Selected Resources

Botany is a complex subject. There's plenty of information available about leafy greens, particularly the common ones, but not all of it is reliable or accurate. The following are print and online sources of scientific, government and agricultural data, botanical and kitchen glossaries, and handy guides for cooks and gardeners. Also useful are seed catalogues; they often include photos and information on cultivars of leafy greens, including Asian and Indian vegetables.

About Food
www.about.com/food

Agriculture and Agri-Food Canada: "Subjects A–Z"
www.agr.gc.ca/index_e.php

Arctos Multi-Institution, Multi-Collection Museum Database: "Taxonomy"
http://arctos.database.museum/TaxonomySearch.cfm

Better Homes and Gardens: "Plant Encyclopedia"
www.bhg.com/gardening/plant-dictionary

Botany.com: "Encyclopedia of Plants and Flowers"
www.botany.com

British Leafy Salads Association
www.britishleafysalads.co.uk

Catalogue of Life
www.catalogueoflife.org

The Chef's Garden
www.chefs-garden.com

Chen, Hong. "Traditional Chinese Vegetables at the IR-4/USDA Crop Grouping Symposium." *IR-4 Newsletter* 33, no. 2 (July 2002). http://ir4.rutgers.edu/newsletter/vol33-2/chinesevegetables.pdf.

Cherry Farms
www.cherryfarms.co.uk

Chow
www.chow.com

Clemson University Cooperative Extension Service: "Japanese Vegetable Fact Sheet"
http://virtual.clemson.edu/groups/psapublishing/pages/hort/hortlf67.pdf

Clove Garden: "Ingredients"
www.clovegarden.com/ingred/index.html

The Congo Cookbook
www.congocookbook.com

The Cook's Thesaurus
www.foodsubs.com

Cornell University, Herbarium of the L.H. Bailey Hortorium: "Tompkins County Flora Project"
http://tcf.bh.cornell.edu

Dave's Garden: "PlantFiles"
http://davesgarden.com/guides/pf

Drewnowski, Adam, and Carmen Gomez-Carneros. "Bitter Taste, Phytonutrients, and the Consumer: A Review." *American Journal of Clinical Nutrition* 72, no. 6 (December 2000): 1424–35. http://ajcn.nutrition.org/content/72/6/1424.full.

Eat the Invaders
www.eattheinvaders.org

Eat the Weeds
www.eattheweeds.com

Edible Wild Food
www.ediblewildfood.com

eFloras.org
www.efloras.org

Encyclopedia of Life: "Plants"
http://eol.org/info/plants

Epicurious
www.epicurious.com

EvergreenSeeds: "Asian Vegetable Seeds"
www.evergreenseeds.com

Fondation Louis Bonduelle
www.fondation-louisbonduelle.org/france/en

Food and Agriculture Organization of the United Nations (FAO)
http://www.fao.org/index_en.htm

Foodland Ontario
www.foodland.gov.on.ca/english/index.html

Global Biodiversity Information Facility: "Kingdom: Plantae"
http://data.gbif.org/species/browse/resource/1/taxon/6

Global Names Index: "Index of Scientific Names"
http://gni.globalnames.org

Gourmet Seed International
www.gourmetseed.com

Graber, Karen Hursh. "Mexico's Leafy Green." *Mexconnect*. www.mexconnect.com/articles/2144-mexico-s-leafy-green.

Grieve, Maud. *A Modern Herbal* [1931]. http://botanical.com/botanical/mgmh/mgmh.html.

Harvest to Table
www.harvesttotable.com

Innvista Library
www.innvista.com

Integrated Taxonomic Information System (ITIS)
www.itis.gov

International Plant Names Index (IPNI)
www.ipni.org

Johnny's Selected Seeds
www.johnnyseedsonlinecatalog.com

Kafka, Barbara. *Vegetable Love: A Book for Cooks*. Leicester: Artisan Press, 2005.

Kew Royal Botanic Gardens: "Electronic Plant Information Centre (ePIC)"
http://epic.kew.org/index.htm

Kitazawa Seed Company
www.kitazawaseed.com

Livestrong.com
www.livestrong.com

Madison, Deborah. *Vegetable Literacy: Cooking and Gardening with Twelve Families from the Edible Plant Kingdom, with over 300 Deliciously Simple Recipes*. New York: Ten Speed Press, 2013.

Manitoba Agriculture, Food and Rural Initiatives: "Asian Vegetables"
www.gov.mb.ca/agriculture/crops/vegetablecrops/pdf/bmz00s30.pdf.

McGill University Centre for Indigenous Peoples' Nutrition and Environment: "Green Leafy Vegetables"
www.mcgill.ca/files/cine/Bhil_greenleafy_veg_Jn06.pdf
"Vegetables, Leafy Vegetables (Shak) and Tubers"
www.mcgill.ca/cine/sites/mcgill.ca.cine/files/Nayakrishi_Datatables_veg_leafy_veg.pdf

Multilingual Multiscript Plant Name Database
www.plantnames.unimelb.edu.au

National Gardening Association (US)
www.garden.org

Ontario Ministry of Agriculture and Food: "Asian Vegetables Grown in Ontario"
www.omafra.gov.on.ca/english/crops/facts/98-033.htm

The Plant List
www.theplantlist.org

Plantlives.com: "Plant Biographies"
www.plantlives.com/plant_biogs.php

Plant Resources of Tropical Africa (PROTA4U)
www.prota4u.org

Plants for a Future
www.pfaf.org/user/default.aspx

Richters Herb Specialists
www.richters.com

Ryder, Edward J. "The New Salad Crop Revolution." In *Trends in New Crops and New Uses*, edited by J. Janick and A. Whipkey, 408–12. Alexandria, VA: ASHS Press, 2002. www.hort.purdue.edu/newcrop/ncnu02/v5-408.html

Salt, Steve. "Around the World at Farmers' Market: Opportunities in Growing and Marketing of Ethnic and Old-Fashioned Fruits, Vegetables and Herbs." In *A Supermarket of Ideas: Proceedings of Future Farms* 2002, November 15–16, 2002. Poteau, OK: Kerr Center for Sustainable Agriculture, 2002. www.kerrcenter.com/publications/2002_proceedings/ethnic_fruits_veggies_herbs.pdf

Schneider, Elizabeth. *Vegetables from Amaranth to Zucchini*. New York: William Morrow, 2001.

Scott, Sarah. *The Wild Table: Seasonal Foraged Food and Recipes*. Studio Books, 2010.

Seedaholic: "Edibles"
www.seedaholic.com/edibles.html/#Edibles

Seeds of Change
www.seedsofchange.com

Seeds of Diversity
www.seeds.ca/en.php

Serious Eats
www.seriouseats.com

The Silver Torch: "Vegetables, Herbs, Fruits and Seasonings of the Caribbean"
http://silvertorch.com/plants-of-the-caribbean.html

Specialty Produce
www.specialtyproduce.com

Sung, Esther. "A Visual Guide to Salad Greens: Get to Know Your Mesclun Mix." www.epicurious.com/articlesguides/seasonalcooking/farmtotable/visualguidesaladgreens.

Tainong Seeds Inc.
www.tainongseeds.com

Toensmeier, Eric. *Perennial Vegetables from Artichokes to Zuiki Taro: A Gardener's Guide to Over 100 Delicious, Easy-to-Grow Edibles*. White River Junction, VT: Chelsea Green, 2007.

Toivonen, Peter M.A., and D. Mark Hodges. "Leafy Vegetables and Salads." In *Health-Promoting Properties of Fruits and Vegetables* (e-book), edited by Leon A. Terry. Cranfield, UK: Cranfield University, 2011.

Trade Winds Fruit: "Vegetables"
www.tradewindsfruit.com/vegetables

United States Department of Agriculture, Natural Resources Conservation Service: "Plants Database"
https://plants.usda.gov

Universal Biological Indexer and Organizer (uBio)
www.ubio.org

University of California, Los Angeles, Mildred E. Mathias Botanical Garden: "Writeups and Illustrations of Economically Important Plants"
www.botgard.ucla.edu/html/botanytextbooks/economicbotany

University of Florida Institute of Food and Agricultural Sciences (IFAS), Electronic Data Information Source (IDIS): "Vegetable Crops"
http://edis.ifas.ufl.edu/topic_vegetables

Victoria (Australia) Department of Environment and Primary Industries: "Vegetables A to Z"
www.dpi.vic.gov.au/agriculture/horticulture/vegetables/vegetables-a-z

Watercress Recipes
www.watercressrecipes.co.uk

Wikipedia
"List of Leaf Vegetables"
http://en.wikipedia.org/wiki/List_of_leaf_vegetables
"List of Plants by Common Name'
http://en.wikipedia.org/wiki/List_of_plants_by_common_name

William Dam Seeds
www.damseeds.ca

WiseGeek
www.wisegeek.com

World Carrot Museum
www.carrotmuseum.co.uk

WorldCrops
www.worldcrops.org

Library and Archives Canada Cataloguing in Publication

Sampson, Susan, author
  The complete leafy greens cookbook : 67 leafy greens and 250 recipes / Susan Sampson.

Includes index.
ISBN 978-0-7788-0457-4 (pbk.)

1. Cooking (Greens). 2. Edible greens. 3. Cookbook I. Title.

TX803.G74S36 2013   641.6'54   C2013-903358-0

Index of Recipes

Index of Plants

London rocket (*Sisymbrium irio*), 34

long green. *See* water spinach

long-leafed plantain (*Plantago lanceolata*), 321

long-leaf lettuce. *See* Taiwan lettuce

loose-leaf chicory. *See* curly endive

loose-leaf lettuces, 14, 216–22

lovage (*Levisticum officinale*), 126

love-lies-bleeding (*Amaranthus caudatus*), 29

luffa gourd (*Luffa aegyptiaca; L. acutangula*), 63

M

maca (*Lepidium meyenii*), 409

mâche (*Valerianella locusta*), 223–27

Malabar spinach (*Basella alba*), 228–33

malanga (*Xanthosoma sagittifolium*), 389, 391

mallow. *See* jute leaf

manioc greens. *See* cassava leaves

margherita. *See* chrysanthemum greens

marsh mallow (*Althaea officinalis*), 184

marsh samphire (*Salicornia europaea*), 320

Mary Magdalene's herb. *See* mâche

Masai stinging nettle (*Urtica massaica*), 271

mashua (*Tropaeolum tuberosum*), 407

Mediterranean mustard (*Hirschfeldia incana*), 257

Mediterranean rocket. *See* arugula

mesclun, 234–37

methi (*Trigonella foenum-graecum*), 238–40

Mexican avocado (*Persea americana drymifolia*), 364

Mexican parsley. *See* purslane

Mexican pepperleaf (*Piper auritum*), 214

mibuna (*Brassica rapa nipposinica*), 248–49, 260. *See also* mizuna

michihli cabbages, 262

microgreens, 241–47. *See also* methi

Milan cabbage. *See* savoy cabbage

milkgrass. *See* mâche

milk witch. *See* dandelion greens

mini greens. *See* microgreens

minutina (*Plantago coronopus*), 321

misome (*Brassica rapa narinosa*), 395

miu bok choy, 65

mizuna (*Brassica rapa nipposinica*), 248–51, 260, 395

mock pak choi. *See* napa cabbage

monk's head. *See* dandelion greens

moringa (drumstick tree), 288

morning glory leaves. *See* sweet potato leaves; water spinach

mother vegetable. *See* pennywort

mountain sorrel (*Oxyria digyna*), 354

mountain wood sorrel (*Oxalis montana*), 354

mouse-eared chickweed (*Cerastium fontanum*), 113

multi-shoots mustards (*Brassica juncea multiceps; B. juncea multisecta*), 260

mustard cabbage (*Brassica juncea rugosa*), 252–56

mustard greens (*Brassica juncea*), 15, 257–61. *See also* mibuna; mizuna; mustard cabbage varieties, 260

mustard orchid. *See* Chinese broccoli

mustard spinach. *See* komatsuna

N

napa cabbage (*Brassica rapa pekinensis*), 16, 262–69

Nasturtium officinale (watercress), 405–18

nasturtiums (*Tropaeolum majus*), 407

neeps. *See* turnip greens

nettles (*Urtica dioica*), 270–75

New Zealand spinach (*Tetragonia tetragonioides*), 362

njamma-jamma (*Solana scabrum*), 60

nut lettuce. *See* mâche

O

oak leaf lettuce, 216

Okinawan spinach (*Gynura bicolor; G. crepidioides*), 362

okra leaf. *See* jute leaf

olive leaves (*Oleo europaea*), 293

one-row watercress (*Nasturtium microphyllum*), 408

orach (*Atriplex hortensis*), 362

oriental mustard. *See* mustard greens

oriental radish. *See* radish greens

Orient sword leaf. *See* Taiwan lettuce

ostrich fern. *See* fiddleheads

oxalates, 355

Oxalis species (wood sorrels), 354

oyster leaf (*Mertensia maritima*), 320–21

P

pak choi cabbages, 16. *See also* bok choy; napa cabbage

pak quat (white-stem/lowland water spinach), 420

pamphrey. *See* collards

paracress (*Acmella oleracea*), 409

parsley root tops (*Petroselinum crispum radicosum*), 276–78

patience dock (*Rumex patientia*), 353

Pawnee lettuce. *See* mâche

pea shoots (*Pisum sativum macrocarpon*), 279–83

pee-a-bed. *See* dandelion greens

Peking cabbage. *See* napa cabbage

pennycress (*Thlaspi arvense*), 409

pennywort (*Centella asiatica*), 284–86

pepper leaf (*Capsicum frutescens*), 287–90. *See also* la lot leaf

peppers (*Capsicum annuum*), 287

perilla (*Perilla frutescens*), 291–94

perpetual spinach. *See* chard

Persian cress (*Lepidium sativum*), 408

pe-tsai cabbages, 16, 262. *See also* napa cabbage

Philippine spinach. *See* Malabar spinach

phooi leaf. *See* Malabar spinach

pickle plant (*Oxalis stricta*), 354

pigweed (*Amaranthus albus*), 29. *See also* purslane

pink purslane (*Portulaca pilosa*), 296

pissenlit. See dandelion greens

pitcher vegetable. *See* water spinach

plain-leaved mustards (*Brassica juncea foliosa*), 260

plantains (*Plantago* species), 321

pokeweed (*Phytolacca americana*), 273

potherb mustard. *See* mibuna; mizuna

priest's crown. *See* dandelion greens

prince's feather amaranth (*Amaranthus hypochondriachus*), 29

prostrate pigweed (*Amaranthus albus*), 29

puffball. *See* dandelion greens

purple amaranth (*Amaranthus blitum*), 29

purple mint. *See* perilla

purslane (*Portulaca oleracea*), 295–302

Q

Queen Anne's lace (*Daucus carota*), 88

quelites, 364

quinoa (*Chenopodium quinoa*), 364

R

radicchio (*Cichorium intybus rubifolium*), 303–9

radish greens (*Raphanus sativus, R. sativus longipinnatus*), 310–14